Scandinavia
Finland

Ph. Body/HOA-QUI

"Snow-covered hills and a smell of heath and moorland. A fresh breeze blowing towards us over crystal-clear water from fjords which wind their way into the remotest corners. Where in summer the sun never disappears, merely touching the horizon before rising again and pursuing its course across the sky. People who express their feelings spontaneously and speak animatedly in a sing-song tone, as if they cannot restrain their joy at escaping from the eternal darkness of winter."

Liv Ullmann

Changes

Travel Publications

38 Clarendon Road – WATFORD Herts WD1 1SX - U.K.
☎ (01923) 415 000
www.ViaMichelin.com
TheGreenGuide-uk@uk.michelin.com

Manufacture française des pneumatiques Michelin

Société en commandite par actions au capital de 2 000 000 000 de francs
Place des Carmes-Déchaux – 63 Clermont-Ferrand (France)
R.C.S. Clermont-Fd B 855 200 507

Dépôt légal juin 2001 – ISBN 2-06-000140-4 – ISSN 0763-1383
Printed in France 06-2001/2.1

Typesetting/Printing/Binding: AUBIN/EURONUMERIQUE, Ligugé

Cover design: Carré Noir, Paris 17ᵉ arr.

THE GREEN GUIDE:
The Spirit of Discovery

*The exhilaration of new horizons,
the fun of seeing the world,
the excitement of discovery: this is
what we seek to share with you.
To help you make the most of your
travel experience, we offer first-hand
knowledge and turn a discerning eye
on places to visit.
This wealth of information gives
you the expertise to plan your own
enriching adventure. With THE
GREEN GUIDE showing you the way,
you can explore new destinations
with confidence or rediscover old
ones.
Leisure time spent with THE GREEN
GUIDE is also a time for refreshing
your spirit, enjoying yourself, and
taking advantage of our selection
of fine restaurants, hotels and other
places for relaxing.
So turn the page and open a window
on the world. Join THE GREEN
GUIDE in the spirit of discovery.*

Contents

Hans Christian Andersen

Doorway of Heddal stave church (detail)

Sami in traditional costume

Typical Scandinavian house

5

Maps and plans

COMPANION PUBLICATIONS

Michelin map 985 Scandinavia Finland

– on a scale of 1: 1 500 000, it links the main tourist sights and makes getting around easier.

And if you are driving to Scandinavia...

Michelin map 970 Europe

– on a scale of 1: 3 000 000, it enables you to choose your itinerary to and across Scandinavia: motorways, international or national roads, sea links.

Michelin road atlas to Europe

– the whole of Europe on a scale of 1: 1 000 000 (Eastern Europe 1: 3 000 000) in one volume

– more than 40 countries, the main-road network and 73 town plans or local maps.

– chart of distances between the main towns

– main driving regulations for each country

– index of place names followed by the name of the country.

P. Bertrand/HOA QUI

LIST OF MAPS AND PLANS

Town plans

Local maps

Using this guide

This guide is designed to help you make the most of your trip to Scandinavia. It is divided into six main parts and includes a careful selection of maps and plans.

● The summary maps on pages 10-15 are designed to assist you in planning your trip: the **Map of principal sights** identifies major attractions, the **Map of principal resorts and festivals** points out pleasant holiday resorts as well as various festivals.

● We recommend that you read the **Introduction** before setting out on your trip. The background information it contains on history, the arts, traditional culture and gastronomy will make your visit more meaningful.

● The sections entitled **Denmark, Norway, Sweden** and **Finland** list the principal natural and cultural attractions of each of the four countries in alphabetical order. Every chapter, devoted either to a town or a region, contains descriptions of sights.

● All practical information, addresses, travel tips, leisure activities, events, can be found in the **Practical information** section. The clock symbol ⊙, placed after the sights described in the previous sections, refers to the Admission times and charges chapter at the end of the guide.

We greatly appreciate your comments and suggestions. You may, if you wish, write to us at the address shown on page 2, visit our web site or send us an e-mail:
www.ViaMichelin.com
TheGreenGuide-uk@uk.michelin.com

Bon voyage!

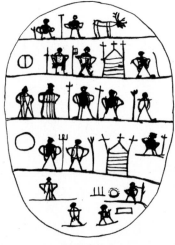

Sami magic drum

Key

★★★ **Worth a journey**

★★ **Worth a detour**

★ **Interesting**

Tourism

⊙	Admission Times and Charges listed at the end of the guide	►►	Visit if time permits
	Sightseeing route with departure point indicated	AZ B	Map co-ordinates locating sights
	Ecclesiastical building		Tourist information
	Synagogue – Mosque		Historic house, castle – Ruins
	Building (with main entrance)		Dam – Factory or power station
■	Statue, small building		Fort – Cave
‡	Wayside cross		Prehistoric site
◎	Fountain		Viewing table – View
	Fortified walls – Tower – Gate	▲	Miscellaneous sight

Recreation

	Racecourse		Waymarked footpath
	Skating rink	♦	Outdoor leisure park/centre
	Outdoor, indoor swimming pool		Theme/Amusement park
	Marina, moorings		Wildlife/Safari park, zoo
	Mountain refuge hut		Gardens, park, arboretum
	Overhead cable-car		Aviary, bird sanctuary
	Tourist or steam railway		

Additional symbols

	Motorway (unclassified)		Post office – Telephone centre
❶ ❶	Junction: complete, limited		Covered market
	Pedestrian street		Barracks
	Unsuitable for traffic, street subject to restrictions		Swing bridge
	Steps – Footpath		Quarry – Mine
	Railway – Coach station	B F	Ferry (river and lake crossings)
	Funicular – Rack-railway		Ferry services: Passengers and cars
	Tram – Metro, Underground		Foot passengers only
Bert (R.)...	Main shopping street	③	Access route number common to MICHELIN maps and town plans

Abbreviations and special symbols

H	Town hall		Youth hostel
J	Law courts		
M	Museum		Rock carving
POL.	Police station		
T	Theatre		Rune stone
U	University		Stave church
A, F, L (DK) (N) (FIN, S)	Local authority offices		National park or reserve

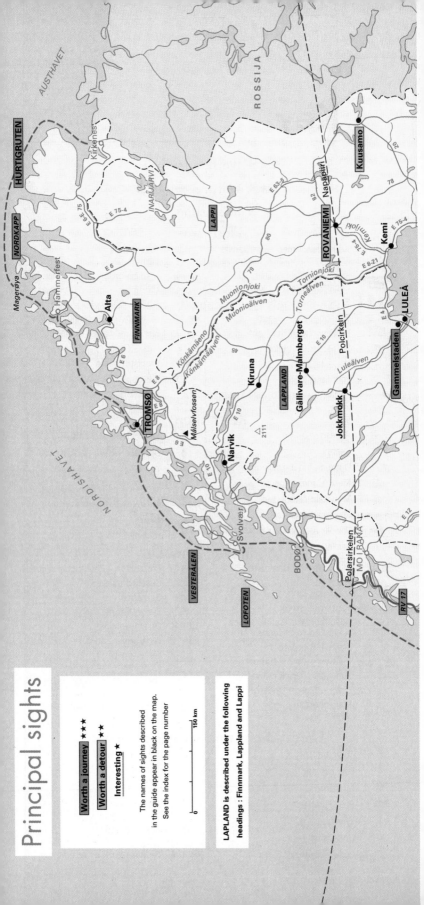

Principal sights

Worth a journey ★★★

Worth a detour ★★

Interesting ★

The names of sights described
in the guide appear in black on the map.
See the index for the page number

0   150 km

**LAPLAND is described under the following
headings : Finnmark, Lappland and Lappi**

NORDISHAVET

AUSTHAVET

ROSSIJA

HURTIGRUTEN

NORDKAPP

Magerøya

VESTERÅLEN

LOFOTEN

Kirkenes

INARIJÄRVI

Hammerfest

Alta

FINNMARK

TROMSØ

Målselvfossen

Narvik

Svolvær

BODØ

Polarsirkelen
MO I RANA

RV 17

LAPPI

Napapiiri

ROVANIEMI

Kemijoki

Kemi

Kuusamo

LULEÅ

Gammelstaden

Jokkmokk

Gällivare-Malmberget

LAPPLAND

Kiruna

Könkämäeno
Könkämäälven

Muonionjoki
Muonioälven

Tornionjoki
Torneälven

Polcirkeln

Luleälven

Napapiiri

E 6

E 8

E 9/E 75

E 75-4

E 63-5

E 6

E 8

E 8

E 10

E 10

E 10

E 6

E 8

E 8-21

E 75-4

E 75-4

E 4

E 12

80

78

82

78

45

79

70

2111

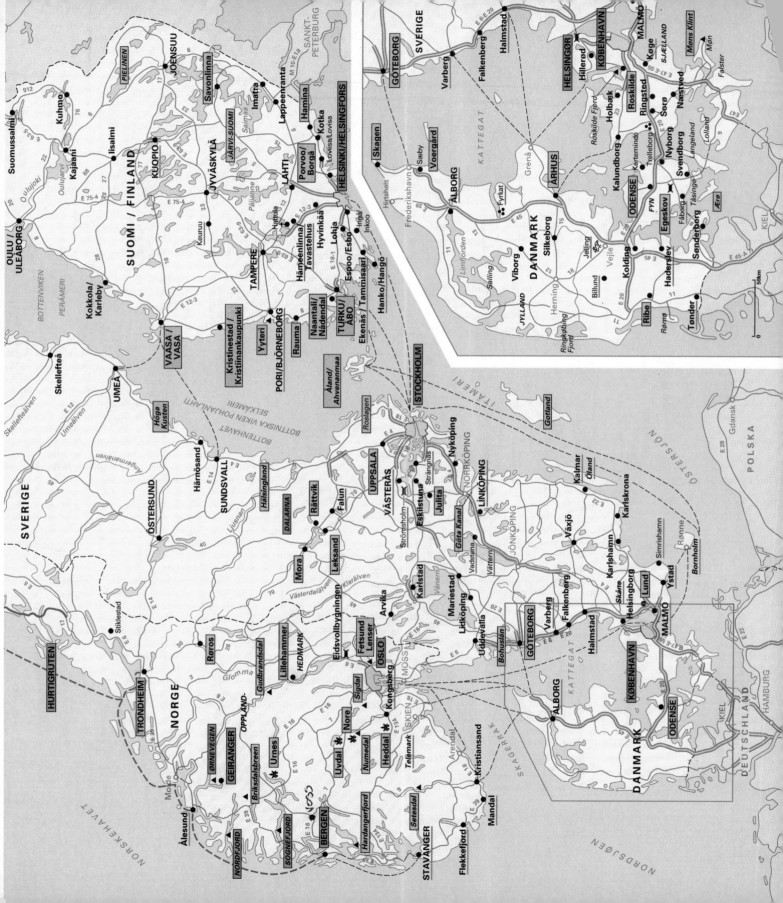

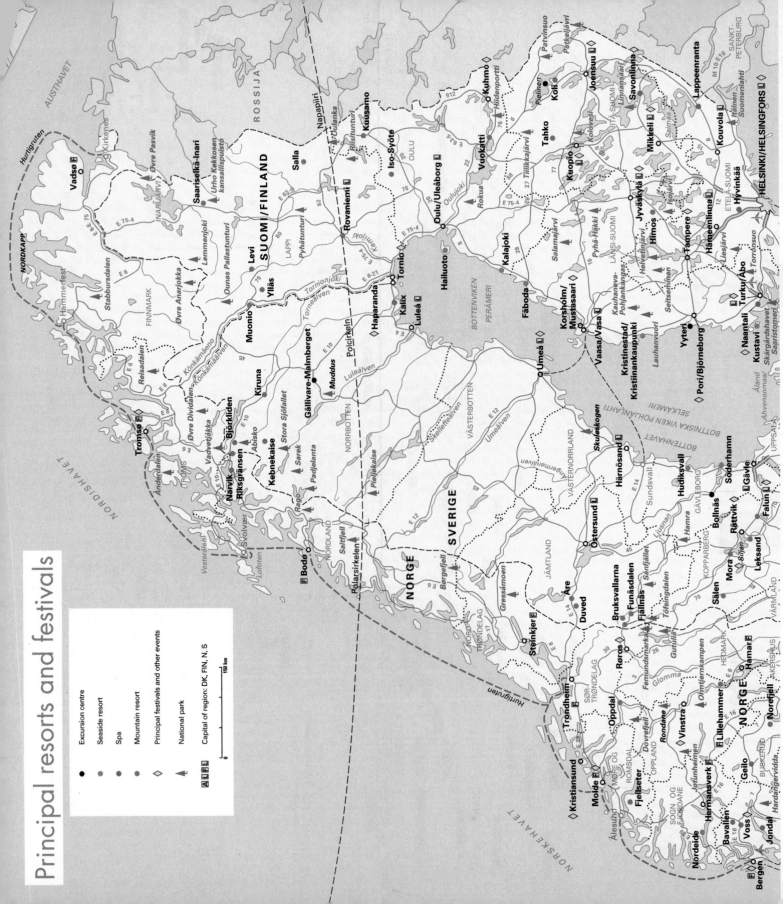

Principal resorts and festivals

Legend:
- ● Excursion centre
- ● Seaside resort
- ● Spa
- ● Mountain resort
- ◇ Principal festivals and other events
- ▲ National park
- Ⓐ Ⓓ Ⓕ Capital of region: DK, FIN, N, S

0 — 150 km

NORGE · **SVERIGE** · **SUOMI/FINLAND** · **ROSSIJA**

AUSTHAVET · NORDISHAVET · NORSKEHAVET · BOTTENVIKEN/PERÄMERI · BOTTENHAVET/SELKÄMERI · BOTTNISKA VIKEN/POHJANLAHTI

Selected places:
Vadsø, Kirkenes, Hammerfest, Tromsø, Anderdalen, Narvik, Riksgränsen, Bjørkliden, Abisko, Vadvetjåkka, Kebnekaise, Stora Sjöfallet, Sarek, Padjelanta, Pieljekaise, Rago, Saltfjell, Bodø, Svolvær, Kiruna, Gällivare-Malmberget, Muddus, Kebnekaise

Saariselkä-Inari, Urho Kekkosen kansallispuisto, Lemmenjoki, Øvre Anarjokka, Ounas Pallastunturi, Levi, Ylläs, Muonio, Salla, Oulanka, Riisitunturi, Iso-Syöte, Kuusamo, Rovaniemi, Tornio, Kemijoki, Haparanda, Kalix, Luleå, Polcirkeln, Muddus, Luleälven

Hailuoto, Oulu/Uleåborg, Oulujoki, Kalajoki, Fäboda, Rokua, Vuokatti, Kuhmo, Hildenportti, Pielinen, Koli, Joensuu, Patvinsuo, Petkeljärvi, Kuopio, Tahko, Koloves, Linnansaari, Savonlinna, Lappeenranta, Kouvola, Itäinen Suomenlahti, HELSINKI/HELSINGFORS, SANKT-PETERBURG

Korsholm/Mustasaari, Vaasa/Vasa, Kristinestad/Kristiinankaupunki, Pori/Björneborg, Yyteri, Lauhanvuori, Seitseminen, Helvetinjärvi, Kauhaneva-Pohjankangas, Jyväskylä, Himos, Pyhä-Häkki, Tampere, Hämeenlinna, Hyvinkää, Naantali, Turku/Åbo, Kustavi, Skärgårdshavet, Ålands hav, Ahvenanmaa/Åland, Torronsuo, Liesjärvi

Umeå, Skuleskogen, Härnösand, Ångermanälven, Hudiksvall, Söderhamn, Gävle, Bollnäs, Rättvik, Siljan, Mora, Leksand, Falun, Orsa, Östersund, Åre, Duved, Bruksvallarna, Funäsdalen, Fjällnäs, Sänfjället, Töfsingdalen, Sälen, Hamra

Steinkjer, Gressåmoen, Børgefjell, Trondheim, Røros, Oppdal, Dovrefjell, Rondane, Vinstra, Jotunheimen, Femundsmarka, Olmtjernkampen, Lillehammer, Hamar, Hermansverk, Fjellseter, Kristiansund, Molde, Ålesund, Nordeide, Bavallen, Voss, Jondal, Bergen, Gello, Hardangervidda, Norefjell

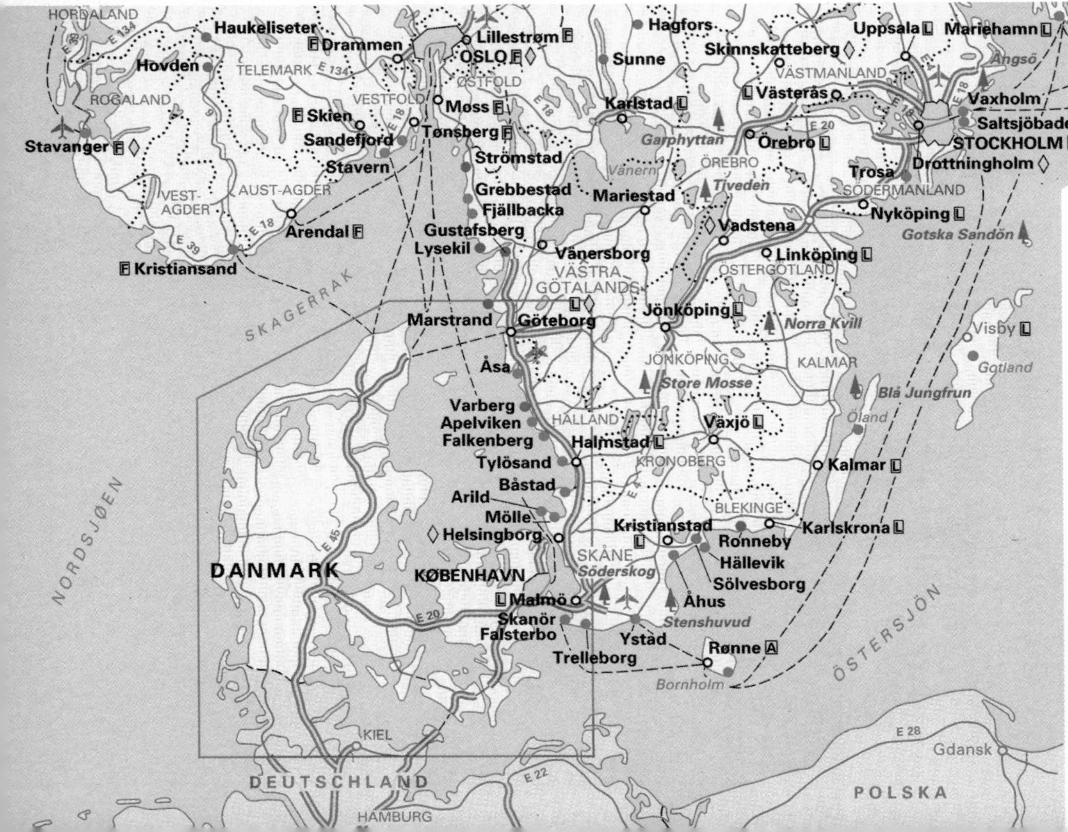

SVERIGE

SKAGERRAK
NORDSJØEN
KATTEGAT
ÖSTERSJÖN

DANMARK
DEUTSCHLAND
POLSKA

Göteborg
Varberg
Halmstad
Frederikshavn
Grenå

Skagen
Hulsig
Skiveren
Blokhus
Saltum
Redhus
Ålborg
Viborg
Ajstrup
Århus

Vederso Klit
Ringkøbing
Hovstrup
Henne
Ribe
Vejle
Kerteminde
Odense
Åbenrå

JYLLAND
Limfjorden
FYN
Ærø
KIEL

Tisvildeleje
Hornbæk
Hillerød
KØBENHAVN
Dragør
Malmö
Liseleje
Rørvig
Roskilde
Vesterlyng
Sorø
Møn
SJÆLLAND

Nykøbing
Marielyst
Maribo
Langeland

50 km
0

E 6 E 20
E 6 E 20
E 20
E 45
E 45 A 7
E 20
E 45
E 20
E 47-E 55

Ekenäs/Tammisaari
Hanko/Hangö
Ingå/Inkoo
Mariehamn
Vaxholm
Saltsjöbaden
STOCKHOLM
Drottningholm

Uppsala
VÄSTMANLAND
Skinnskatteberg
Västerås
Örebro
ÖREBRO
Trosa
Nyköping
SÖDERMANLAND

Hagfors
Sunne
Karlstad
Garphyttan
Tiveden
Vänern
Mariestad
Vänersborg
VÄSTRA
GOTALANDS
Grebbestad
Fjällbacka
Gustafsberg
Lysekil
Marstrand
Göteborg
Åsa

Haukeliseter
Hovden
Stavanger
Kristiansand
Arendal
Stavern
Sandefjord
Skien
Tønsberg
Moss
OSLO
Lillestrøm
Drammen
TELEMARK
VESTFOLD
ØSTFOLD
AUST-AGDER
VEST-AGDER
ROGALAND
HORDALAND

Linköping
Vadstena
ÖSTERGÖTLANDS
Jönköping
JÖNKÖPING
Store Mosse
Norra Kvill
KALMAR
Öland
Kalmar
Karlskrona
Blå Jungfrun
Visby
Gotland
Gotska Sandön

Växjö
KRONOBERG
BLEKINGE
Ronneby
Hällevik
Sölvesborg
Åhus
Ystad
Trelleborg
Skanör
Falsterbo
Helsingborg
Mölle
Arild
Båstad
Tylösand
Falkenberg
Apelviken
Varberg
SKÅNE
Söderåsen
Stenshuvud
Kristianstad
Halmstad
HALLANDS

Skrömstad
Rønne
Bornholm

KØBENHAVN
Malmö
DANMARK
KIEL
HAMBURG
Gdansk

E 134
E 18
E 18
E 39
E 6
E 20
E 20
E 45
E 22
E 28

On the way to Scandinavia

G. Boutin/HOA QUI

Introduction

Facts and Figures

DENMARK
Danmark

Area: 43 069km² excluding the Faroe Islands and Greenland which, with over 2 million km², is the largest island in the world. Denmark consists of 406 islands (97 of them inhabited) and the Jylland peninsula. 70% of the land is cultivated.
Frontier: with Germany in south Jylland.
Latitude: between 54°34' and 57°45' North; Time: GMT + 1
Population: 5 180 640; density per km²: 96
Capital: København (Copenhagen); Main towns: Odense, Ålborg, Århus
Political system: constitutional monarchy with single-chamber parliament (Folketing)
Administrative divisions: 14 *amter* and 2 *kommuner* (København conurbation)
National day: 5 June, Constitution Day.
Language: Danish, a north Germanic language like Swedish and Norwegian.
Religion: Lutheran (over 90%)
Currency: 1 krone (DKR) = 100 øre
Economy: intensive agriculture, dairy farming, fishing, beer, steel, machinery, chemicals, development of solar and wind energy.

NORWAY
Norge

Area: 323 878km² excluding the Svalbard archipelago in the Arctic Ocean. A large proportion of the country is mountainous and only 4% of the land is cultivated.
Frontiers: with Sweden, Finland and Russia
Latitude: between 58° and 71°10' North; Time: GMT + 1
Population: 4 400 000; density per km²: 13
Capital: Oslo; main towns: Bergen, Stavanger, Trondheim; Hammerfest is the northernmost town in the world.
Political system: constitutional monarchy with single-chamber parliament (Storting)
Administrative divisions: 19 *fylker*
National day: 17 May, Constitution Day.
Official languages: Bokmål (influenced by Danish) and Nynorsk (New Norwegian)
Religion: Lutheran (over 90%)
Currency: 1 krone (NOK) = 100 øre
Economy: forestry, fishing, oil related industries (chemicals), service industries (shipping), engineering and electronics; energy: hydro-electric power.

SWEDEN
Sverige

Area: 449 964km², including 40 000km² of lakes and inland waterways; 55% of the country is covered with forests and 10% of the land is cultivated.
Frontiers: with Norway and Finland
Latitude: between 55° and 69° North; Time: GMT + 1
Population: 8 800 000; density per km²: 19, but over three quarters of the population live in the southern half of the country.
Capital: Stockholm; Main towns: Göteborg, Malmö
Political system: constitutional monarchy with single-chamber parliament (Riksdag)
Administrative divisions: 21 *län*
National day: 6 June, Day of the Swedish flag.
Official language: Swedish; Finnish is also spoken by a minority of immigrants.
Religion: Lutheran (over 90%)
Currency: 1 krona (Skr or SEK) = 100 öre
Economy: agriculture, forestry, mining of iron ore and uranium, metal processing, engineering, motor vehicles, chemicals and electrical industries.

FINLAND
Suomi

Area: 338 145km²; 65% of the country is covered with forests, lakes account for 10% of the total area and 8% of the land is cultivated.
Frontiers: with Sweden, Norway and Russia
Latitude: between 60° and 70° North; Time: GMT + 2
Population: 5 147 000; density per km²: 17

Capital: Helsinki (Helsingfors); Main towns: Tampere, Turku
Political system: republic with elected president and single-chamber parliament (Eduskunta or Riksdag)
Administrative divisions: 6 *läänit*
National day: 6 December, Independence Day.
Official languages: Finnish (a Finno-Ugric language related to Estonian) and Swedish
Religions: Lutheran (over 90%); Orthodox (1%)
Currency: 1 markka (FIM) = 100 penniä
Economy: forestry, copper mining, electronics, engineering and service industries.

The land

Scandinavia is the northernmost land mass of the European continent, a vast territory of around 1 155 000km2, almost a third of which is situated above the Arctic Circle (66°33' N). It consists mainly of the Scandinavian peninsula stretching some 1 800km in a north/south direction from 55° to 71° North and separating the North Sea and the Atlantic from the Baltic. It is divided lengthways between Norway and Sweden. In the south, Denmark is the natural bridge between Scandinavia and mainland Europe through Jylland and the main islands of Sjælland and Fyn which act as stepping stones, while in the east, Finland, through its common frontier with Russia, is the geographical link with Eastern Europe.

TOPOGRAPHY

Except for Denmark, Scandinavia is sparsely populated by European standards, with an average of 15 inhabitants per km2, a particularity which is largely explained by the topographical features shared by three of the four Scandinavian countries.
A succession of mountain ranges, extending the whole length of the Swedish/Norwegian border, forms the backbone of the peninsula: an almost uninterrupted chain of high plateaux dominated by peaks culminating at around 2 500m (**Kebnekaise,** west of Kiruna in the north, is Sweden's highest peak, whereas **Glittertind** in the Jotunheimen range of south-western Norway, culminates at 2 470m); these mountainous areas are crowned with mighty glaciers, their relatively low altitude, compared to that of the Alpine range for instance, being compensated by their northern latitude.
West of the mountains, the whole length of the Norwegian coast is deeply indented by fjords which penetrate as far inland as 200km, sometimes to the very foot of the mountains *(see p 23)*. Strings of skerries and islands punctuate the coastline.
The eastern side of the mountains slopes gradually down to form rolling hills alternating with wide river valleys cut in a north-west/south-east direction. The Swedish countryside is dotted from north to south with thousands of lakes glittering among the vast expanses of dark coniferous forests, whereas farmland is mainly to be found in the flat southern part of the country facing Denmark.
Across the Gulf of Bothnia lies Finland with its complex lake systems extending over most of the country from the northern territories of Lapland to the southern **Salpausselka hills** which slope gently down to the Gulf of Finland. The coastal fringe of western and southern Finland, which rises slowly inland, is hemmed by numerous archipelagos, the largest being the **Åland archipelago**.
The northernmost regions of Scandinavia, beyond the Arctic Circle, are areas of barren rock near the coast and meagre vegetation inland: desolate high plateaux stretching uniformly across the county of Finnmark in Norway, birch forests, moorland and bogs in Sweden, unspoilt lakes and high rolling hills called *tunturi* in Finland. These vast expanses, known as **Lapland** in Norway, Finland and Sweden, are inhabited by the Sami, a nomadic indigenous people who traditionally live by reindeer-herding.
Denmark, which consists mainly of islands apart from the Jylland peninsula on the European mainland, is mostly flat land alternating with rolling countryside devoted to intensive agriculture. There are no mountains; low hills barely rise above 170m; the forests have long disappeared, giving way to farming, so that Danish landscapes, dotted with idyllic villages, are mostly tame and untypical of Scandinavian scenery in general, the only unspoilt natural areas being the **heathlands of west Jylland**. However, the deep fjords which punctuate the coastline of **east Jylland and north Sjælland** are a reminder that Denmark belongs to Scandinavia, from a geological as well as from a historical point of view.

GEOLOGY

Scandinavian landscapes bear the strong imprint of the last Ice Age which ended some 10 000 years ago. For thousands of years before that time, northern Europe was completely covered with huge quantities of ice which exerted enormous pressure over the land mass. When the earth's climate became warmer, the ice gradually retreated northwards, the Baltic swelled and linked up with the North Atlantic across central Sweden and with the White Sea in the north, isolating northern Scandinavia; at the same time,

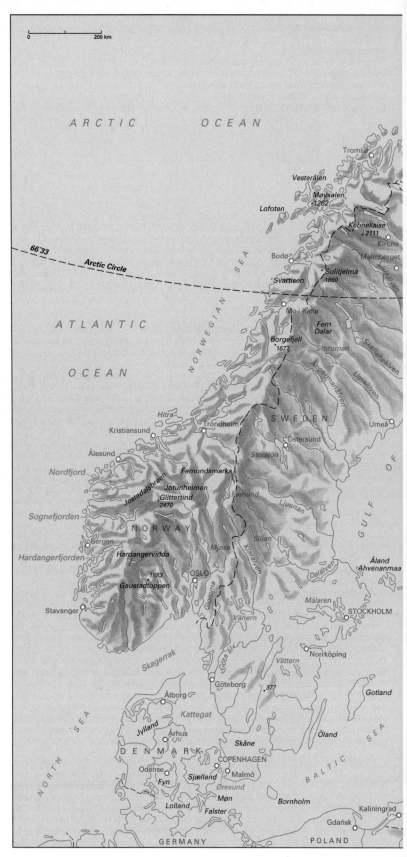

the land, freed from the weight of the ice, rose and the Baltic eventually withdrew leaving behind large lakes such as lake Vänern and Vättern in Sweden as well as the great lake systems of Finland. Only much later, some 7 000 years ago, did the Baltic join up with the North Sea via the Øresund.

Lakes and fjords filled the U-shaped valleys dug out by the mighty glaciers which once covered Scandinavia. Moraines deposited as the ice retreated and formed ridges such as the Salpausselka hills of southern Finland. Other ridges of gravel deposits in river valleys, known as eskers, sometimes enclosed lakes. The ice eroded and smoothed the rocks. But the fjords are no doubt the most characteristic geological feature of Scandinavian scenery.

CLIMATE

Scandinavia enjoys a relatively temperate climate considering that it is situated at the same latitude as Alaska on the North American continent. Mean temperatures are higher, by as much as 25°C on the Scandinavian peninsula, thanks to the Gulf Stream which flows along the west coast of Norway as far north as Svalbard. The effect of this warm current is twofold: first of all, it keeps the north Atlantic and Arctic oceans free of ice throughout the winter, enabling the Coastal Steamer to round the North Cape all year round, whereas the Baltic ports are normally immobilised during the winter months; secondly, it warms the westerly and south-westerly winds blowing in from the sea: this influence is felt in varying degrees over the whole of Scandinavia. Sweden and above all Finland have a more continental type of climate than Norway, with very cold spells blowing over from the east in winter and heat waves making temperatures soar up to 30°C in summer.

As a result of its northern latitude, the Scandinavian peninsula enjoys almost continuous daylight during the summer and is plunged into darkness for several weeks during the winter *(see p 32)*; yet the Arctic regions are inhabited and Hammerfest in Norway is the northernmost

21

town in the world. The seasons are well defined: for instance in Finland, summer ends in a blaze of glorious colours which the Finns call *ruska*. By contrast, winter brings a kind of eerie light due to the moon shining on the snow and enhanced by the unique northern lights illuminating the sky. When the sun returns, nature slowly wakes up and prepares for springtime, staging a well-orchestrated flower festival in May and early June.

Southern Scandinavia enjoys more pleasant climatic conditions. Taking into account variations between eastern and western regions where the oceanic influence is more strongly felt, the average temperature is 18°C in summer and -4°C in winter.

Denmark enjoys a cool oceanic climate with average temperatures ranging from 0°C in winter to 18°C in summer. The weather changes frequently, although there are usually long periods of fair weather between April and July.

Fjords

One of the most characteristic features of the Scandinavian landscape and undoubtedly the most praised and photographed, fjords have become the symbol of breathtakingly beautiful Nordic scenery. And, as any traveller would agree, this reputation is fully justified, particularly in the case of 'Fjordland', an area along the west coast of Norway between Stavanger and Kristiansund, where the most famous fjords are situated. Sognefjord, Geirangerfjord, Hardangerfjord are names which suggest wild, impressive beauty, tranquil grandeur and a harmonious blend of colours against a stunning background of sculptured rocks, snow-capped peaks, still waters and mottled skies.

Discovering the awesome beauty of the fjords

When the word fjord is mentioned certain names automatically spring to mind: Geirangerfjord, Hardangerfjord, Nordfjord and Sognefjord but there are countless other fjords to explore and a variety of ways of doing it. Boat trips or even one of the working ferries, are the ideal way to visit as visitors can relax and enjoy the passing scenic splendour as they are transported to otherwise inaccessible spots. In some cases helicopter or sea-plane trips offer breathtaking bird's-eye views of the rugged beauty of fjord country. Where roads wind up to vantage points drivers are often rewarded with ever widening views or the joy of an enthralling panorama unveiled all of a sudden. Fjord horses are a practical form of transport to some of the more remote beauty spots or the snout of some glacier and its turquoise coloured lake. The more energetic can climb and scramble to some lonely vantage point where the world seems to unfold at their feet. The intrepid looking for a new angle on the fjords can walk over the glaciers and look back down the U-shaped valleys they created.

GEOLOGICAL FORMATION

Fjord is a Norwegian word describing a long and narrow inlet of sea winding its way inland. There are similar topographical features along indented coasts elsewhere in the world, notably in Brittany (western France), but what makes the fjords so specific to Scandinavia in general and Norway in particular is their astonishing size: they can reach up to 200km in length, with numerous arms stretched in all directions forming the complicated network of a gigantic water maze; their amazing depth is comparable to the height of the mountains towering over them; and their width can be in turn moderate and on a grand scale reminiscent of the majestic estuaries of the world's largest rivers. These unique features are the direct result of the formation of Scandinavian fjords during the last Ice Age. The whole of northern Europe was then covered with a great mass of ice, particularly thick over the centre of the Scandinavian peninsula but thinner along the coast. Glaciers occupied ancient river beds and their huge weight cut ever deeper into existing valleys, giving them their distinctive U shape. Along the coast where the weight of the ice mantle was not so great, fjords are more shallow than inland where they can reach depths of up to 1 350m. As the ice gradually melted, the sea filled these deep valleys but the glaciers did not disappear completely, they simply retreated to the mountain tops; however, they still reach down to sea level in places: for instance, an arm of Svartisen, Norway's second largest glacier, carves into Holandsfjord just south of Bodø. Almost everywhere, melt water from the remaining glaciers cascades down abrupt mountainsides, forming picturesque waterfalls and giving the water of the fjords their characteristic pale green colour.

Thanks to their salt sea water, western fjords do not freeze over in wintertime even in mountainous areas, a fact which enables communications from one valley to the next to be maintained by a very efficient ferry system.

Aurlandsfjord, Norway

FJORD SCENERY

The geological process described above took place all along the Scandinavian coasts with varied results which depended on the terrain; in Denmark where the land is flat, fjords like the Isefjord in north Sjælland are wide and dotted with islands, their banks are low, not well-defined, often marshy and lined with reeds; along the Swedish and Finnish coasts of the Gulf of Bothnia, fjords are confined close to the coastline, winding their way through the numerous archipelagos; along the southern coast of Norway and the adjacent Swedish coast, fjords are generally shorter because the pressure of the ice was only moderate; but in western Norway, where the coastal fringe is backed by steep mountains, the process reached exceptional magnitude with magnificent results.

Fjordland offers an amazing variety of scenery not only from one fjord to the next but also within the same fjord, the light often changing very swiftly as well. The narrow Lysefjord, near Stavanger, is lined on both sides with walls of sheer rock up to 600m high. By contrast, Hardangerfjord affords vast open vistas towards high snow-capped peaks beyond its gently sloping banks covered with fields and orchards, offering in springtime a most idyllic sight which inspired Norway's greatest composer, Edvard Grieg. Geirangerfjord, probably the most famous of all the fjords, is an arm of Nordfjord which winds its way to the very heart of the mountains and is surrounded, almost imprisoned it seems, by peaks culminating at 1 500m; there is a breathtaking view of the fjord from the top of Dalsnibba, which can be reached by a steep mountain road. Beautiful waterfalls spray a pure white froth on the dark rockface.

Waterfall near Flam, Norway

Nordic landscapes

The main characteristic of Nordic landscapes is perhaps their infinite variety rich in striking contrasts and subtle nuances. Basic elements vary from one country to the next: for instance Norwegian landscapes seem to be mostly carved out of rock whereas Swedish and Finnish landscapes owe their austere character to the sombre coniferous forests which cover thousands of square kilometres; on the other hand, Danish landscapes draw their peaceful charm from the lush meadows and the gently rolling hills of the islands. Beyond these obvious differences, features common to all Scandinavian landscapes include a wide range of colours and the ever changing light which plays on the omnipresent water, greatly enhancing the dramatic appeal of the scenery and underlining its Scandinavian specificity.

Therefore, the major contrasts, which make Nordic scenery so fascinating, occur essentially between coastal and inland areas, throughout Scandinavia, with marked regional variations.

THE SCANDINAVIAN COASTLINE

In spite of following a reasonably straight line, most of the Scandinavian coastline is deeply indented by fjords and lined with an impressive fringe of islands and skerries, from the south of Sweden to the northernmost regions of Norway, beyond Nordkapp and eastwards to the Russian border. On the North Sea and Atlantic side as well as on the shores of the Baltic, familiar seascapes repeatedly reveal an intricate maze of channels winding in all directions between the islands and the flat rocky coast, often making it difficult to distinguish where the land ends and where the sea begins.

Such scenery is found all along the **west coast of Norway**, particularly between Molde and Kristiansund and between Namsos and Bodø, where roads have been built close to the sea and sometimes partly across it *(see Daring engineering works p 26)* with stunning practical and aesthetic results. The same confusion marks the **east coast of Sweden** in the area around Stockholm where the waters of Lake Mälaren strewn with numerous islands mingle with the Baltic Sea dotted with skerries. Similarly, across the entrance of the Gulf of Bothnia, the **Finnish archipelago** lying offshore all around Turku, offers more typical Scandinavian seascapes. An important feature of these coastal areas is that they are traditionally turned towards the sea from which they derive their main resources through fishing and trading; the skilful skippers who constantly navigate between the islands and skerries, sometimes hardly showing above the water, draw the admiration of most visitors.

North of the Arctic Circle, the coastline changes gradually while remaining extremely rugged.

Less spectacularly indented, the **south coast of Norway** offers a tidier contour with small inlets sheltering picturesque fishing harbours lined with white wooden houses: Risør, Lyngør, Grimstad, Lillesand, Mandal and Flekkefjord are the most typical. One of them, Kragerø, inspired the great Norwegian painter, Edvard Munch. There are some very pleasant beaches along this sunny coastline, in particular at Mandal: backed by dunes covered with dense green bushes, they are sought after by Norwegian holiday makers.

Beaches and dunes are also one of the attractions of **Skåne**, the southernmost province of Sweden with Malmö, the second largest Swedish port, at its centre. Luxury seaside resorts such as Båstad, Ängelholm, Skanör and Falsterbo are crowded in summer.

The **west coast of the Jylland peninsula**, on the North Sea side, offers a complete contrast: vast lagoons imprisoned behind narrow sandbanks and straight white sandy beaches stretching as far as the eye can see *(see Great wilderness areas pp 28-31)*.

THE ISLANDS

The Scandinavian coast is lined with thousands of islands, most of them tiny and barren or lying close to the mainland to which they are usually linked by bridges or tunnels. Even if they are not, they form part of the coastline and offer identical

Coast and islands in the Lofoten area, Norway

features. Wherever the topography lends itself, towns have been built across several islands and the originality of the setting is largely responsible for the fascination these places exert on their visitors; such is the case of **Ålesund**, a picturesque Art Nouveau town of central Norway, and of **Tromsø**, far north of the Arctic Circle *(see p 32)*.

Almost all the large islands lying off the coast of Scandinavia and showing distinct characteristics are situated in the Baltic with the exception of the **Lofoten** and **Vesterålen** islands stretching along the west coast of Norway north of the Arctic Circle.

The Danish islands

Looking like huge stepping stones between the Jylland peninsula and the province of Skåne in southern Sweden, two large islands form the core of Denmark: Fyn and Sjælland. The smaller of the two, **Fyn**, was named the garden of Denmark by its most famous native, Hans Christian Andersen, owing to its lush meadows, its orchards and gently rolling countryside dotted with picturesque villages of thatched timber-framed cottages. **Sjælland** has vast expanses of fertile agricultural land and boasts ancient towns, manor-houses and charming country churches. North Sjælland is the well-looked after recreational ground of the capital Copenhagen situated on the east coast: beautifully tame countryside lying behind a picturesque coastline, often referred to as the Danish Riviera.

The two main islands are linked in the south by a string of smaller islands forming a semicircle; bridges span some of the narrow straits which separate them and a continuous ferry service completes the link. It is on these southern islands that the sunniest beaches are to be found as well as spectacular chalk cliffs, known as **Møns Klint**.

Lofoten and Vesterålen

The austere beauty of the **Lofoten and Vesterålen islands** is legendary and in no way over-rated: steep mountainsides towering over the sea, shallow creeks with just enough space for a few tiny *rorbuer*, the traditional fishermen's cottages made of wood and painted in a distinctive rusty red, picturesque wooden frames covered with stockfish drying in the midnight sun and, above all, an authentic way of life which has been passed on down the centuries; unforgettable impressions left by the awe-inspiring mass of dark rocks which form the backbone of the islands and are among the oldest in the world; seals basking in the sun, whale safaris, bird cliffs, fjords and sounds, colourful wild flowers, white fluffy cotton grass swaying in the wind above peat bogs, layers of seaweed smoothing out the rough contours of a bay and an amazing abundance of fish.

Öland, Gotland and the Åland archipelago

Lying close to the southeast coast of Sweden and linked to it by a bridge, the island of **Öland** consists essentially of wind-blown colourful moorland hemmed by sunny beaches. Further out to sea, the large island of **Gotland** is surrounded with beautiful sandy beaches alternating with strange rock formations known as *raukar*. Roses, lilac and honey-suckle thrive under its sunny climate and rare breeds of sheep and horses still survive. Barring the entrance of the Gulf of Bothnia, the **Åland archipelago** counts several thousand islands, in turn barren or covered with dark forests and wild flowers. It is a fisherman's paradise and yachts find safe moorings among the islands.

STF/SUNSET

Daring engineering works

The topography of the Scandinavian coastline, with its characteristic fringe of innumerable islands and imposing fjords penetrating deeply inland, has rendered communications more difficult and caused road engineers to be particularly imaginative and even daring while observing definite aesthetic principles. Thousands of bridges have been built (17 300 in Norway alone) and tunnels have been cut through solid rock, under the sea as well as under glaciers. The inland road leading from Stavanger to Bergen in Norway skirts the wild Akrafjord; cut through the vertical rockface overlooking the fjord, it goes over 24 bridges and through 12 tunnels over a distance of only 24km! In the same area, the coast road, which links a number of islands, goes 45m under the sea bed, by means of the Byfjord Tunnel, almost 6km long. Still in Norway, the sinuous Atlantic Road between Molde and Kristiansund is an extraordinary piece of engineering running across barren islets, with the ocean on either side, fully exposed to the brunt of Atlantic storms: a total length of 8 274m, including 8 bridges. Denmark, on the other hand, faced the crucial problem of establishing fast links between its main islands and Jylland; the most ambitious project yet undertaken by the Danes is the combined bridge/tunnel across the wide Storebælt, designed to join Sjælland and Fyn. The Swedes have also built one of the longest bridges in the world: its 6 070m span the distance which separates the island of Öland from the mainland.

LAKES AND INLAND WATERWAYS

Finland is famous for its beautiful lakeland, a complex system of lakes and waterways, all linked together, covering over 10% of the total area of the country. The still pale waters of the lakes reflect the dense forests which cover almost all the available land as far as the eye can see, including the numerous islands scattered about. **Lake Päijänne**, north of Helsinki, is the longest lake in Finland whereas **Lake Saimaa** in the east is the largest; between the two lies the most extensive lakeland in Europe, poetically known as the land of a thousand lakes, although there are almost two hundred times that number! Many rivers and streams link the lakes together and rapids are a common sight; however, it is possible to canoe through the maze of waterways over a distance of 360km. Several national parks help visitors to discover and appreciate this unique region.

The atmosphere of Sweden's lakeland is totally different: the country is split in two by two vast lakes, relics of the sea which inundated the central Swedish depression at the end of the last Ice Age. **Lake Vänern** and **Lake Vättern** are linked by the famous **Göta Kanal**, which extends westwards to Göteborg and eastwards to Norrköping, just south of Stockholm. The four-day trip between the east and west coasts offers peaceful views of fields, woodland and ancient villages. Further north, there are untamed rivers flowing down from the Norwegian/Swedish range of mountains to the Gulf of Bothnia, in a north-west/south-east direction. These often widen into peaceful expanses of water, such as **Lake Storuman** along the River Umeälven, before continuing their journey to the sea, halted for a while by the occasional rapids like **Storforsen**, north-west of Piteå. Among the largest lakes in Sweden, **Lake Storsjön** and above all **Lake Siljan** are extremely picturesque, combining unspoilt natural scenery with ancient traditions.

C. Boisvieux

Møns Klint, Denmark

26

Storforsen Sweden

MOUNTAINS AND GLACIERS

There are no mountains in Denmark but there are moderately high isolated peaks in Finnish Lapland; Norway and Sweden share the only real Scandinavian mountain range which stretches between the two countries from Lapland to the south coast of Norway. The comparatively low altitude of these mountains (1 000m lower than the Alps) is off-set by their northerly latitude so that landscapes have an Alpine flavour, particularly on the Norwegian side which has higher peaks and steeper slopes. One of the characteristics of these mountains is their impressive glaciers, left behind at the end of the last Ice Age. **Jostedalsbreen**, at the heart of Norway's highest mountains, is the largest of them, a chaotic mass of bluish ice stretching in all directions and slowly grinding its way down the moun-tainsides. Glacier walking can be a thrilling experience in the company of a local guide! Above 1 000m, where the thick cover of winter snow only partially melts in summer, there are several popular summer ski centres in Norway and Sweden. The mountain lakes often remain trapped beneath a thin layer of ice while lower down in the valleys, cattle graze on the green Alpine slopes. In winter, the whole of central Norway is covered with snow and the high plateaux of the **Jotunheimen** and **Dovrefjell** mountain ranges offer wide open spaces ideal for cross-country skiing, dog-sledging and ice-fishing in the lakes.

The southern mountains of Norway are not so high, the **Gaustadtoppen** culminating at 1 883m, yet the little village of **Morgedal** in the county of Telemark is acknowledged as the birthplace of skiing *(see TELEMARK p 213 and Practical information p 439)*.

Storuman, Sweden

27

Great wilderness areas

Scandinavia has some of the last remaining wilderness areas in Europe and these are not only found north of the Arctic Circle where hard climatic conditions could be put forward as a plausible explanation *(see p 32)*.

One of the reasons is undoubtedly that space is freely available in vast quantities: with a total area of over one million square kilometres and a population of 23 million, the Scandinavian peninsula is very sparsely populated compared to the rest of Europe; moreover, the population is quite unevenly spread so that large areas are uninhabited and have been left in their natural state.

SAFEGUARDING THE ENVIRONMENT

However, space availability would not be sufficient to guarantee that entire regions remain unspoilt to the point of being described as wilderness areas. The land is rich in natural resources such as timber and water and the temptation is no doubt great to over exploit these assets in a world where competitiveness is the key word. Therefore the existence of wilderness areas in Scandinavia today is based on a contradiction in that it stems to a large extent from human determination: the environmental awareness of Scandinavians and their will to preserve what they cherish above everything else, nature, is indeed without equal. They identify quite strongly with their natural environment and their concern for its fragile harmony is deeply anchored in their beliefs; their geographical situation on the northern boundaries of the European continent has not given them a false sense of safety and long before anyone else they faced the growing dangers of pollution with courageous realism. They tackled the problem with typical Nordic singularity, for their environmental protection policy is based on a mixture of strict **conservation laws** and **individual responsibility** *(see Allemansrätten below)*.

Great care is taken to protect **wildlife**, in particular rare species such as the bear, which rapidly declined in Norway because of wide-scale deforestation, the lynx, the wolverine, the musk-ox, the otter, the arctic fox as well as seriously threatened species of birds including the eagle owl and the guillemot. Some victories have been won, for instance in the case of the sea eagle, the elk and the beaver, which have greatly increased in numbers and are even being exported to countries where they were extinct. Although the picking of numerous varieties of wild berries and mushrooms is common practice in Scandinavia, rare plants and trees have long been protected and admiring the flora in its natural surroundings is the only permitted pastime for amateur botanists.

Solitary elk in marshland

Wild west coast of Jylland, Denmark

One of the measures taken to safeguard the natural environment was the creation of **national parks** and **nature reserves**, some 21 in Norway, 20 in Sweden and 30 in Finland; they cover areas of natural beauty where ecosystems are particularly interesting and vulnerable and where no human interference is tolerated, an efficient way to ensure the protection of wilderness areas. Some of these parks have been put on UNESCO's list of protected areas.

Scandinavian countries face roughly the same environmental problems as other industrialised countries and whereas they have learned to recycle their waste, save on energy and halt the despoliation of the land, they have been powerless in controlling air and water pollution for the simple reason that a great proportion of that pollution comes from neighbouring countries. The devastating effects of **acid rain** in particular have made the headlines: smoke from factories mixed with rain and snow forms sulphuric acid which damages forests and kills the flora and fauna living in lakes and rivers. Southern Norway has been affected by acid rain carried by the westerly winds blowing across the Atlantic from the North American continent. Swedish and Finnish lakes on the other hand have been polluted by acid rain from Russia and eastern Europe. Although it is a global concern, the problem is particularly serious in Scandinavia where there is very little limestone in the soil to neutralise the harmful acid and the Swedes have therefore undertaken to add lime to the water of their lakes in order to restore their ecological equilibrium and the Finns have offered their technological know-how in environmental matters to Russia and Poland to try and slow down the acidification process.

Allemansrätten

The public right of way or 'everyman's right' as the Swedes call it, is an old Scandinavian custom which shows great respect for individual freedom and faith in the individual's sense of responsibility. Everyone has the right to wander freely in the countryside and cross any private land so long as no damage or nuisance is caused to the owner. The gathering of berries and mushrooms for one's own consumption is also allowed as is camping for a night or two on uncultivated land, well away from any house.

WILDERNESS AREAS

Even though Denmark shares with the other Scandinavian countries a deep respect for nature, its surface area is only a fraction of that of its neighbours and, therefore, most of the land has been progressively cultivated over the centuries, leaving practically no space for wild unspoilt areas. However, some stretches of the straight weather-beaten **west coast of Jylland**, lined with white sand beaches, still lagoons and shifting sand dunes covered with marram, are the nearest one gets to a wilderness area in Denmark; the weather changes rapidly and the force of nature is clearly felt as the skies put on a threatening display of sombre colours and the biting westerly winds cause the sea to break against the shore with a deafening noise.

Hardangervidda (Norway)

This huge mountain plateau of southern Norway covering an area of approximately 10 000km² is bound on its eastern side by the picturesque green Numedal Valley with its typical traditional wooden farms, while to the south lies the Telemark mountain area. The west side of Hardangervidda is the wildest with narrow mountain stream valleys and numerous waterfalls. Its wildlife is similar to that found in Arctic regions, in spite of the relatively southern latitude. Trekking across the plateau takes several days along marked trails, and one can spend the night in simple log cabins, an occasion to meet the last wild reindeer herds in the world!

Femundsmarka (Norway)

Situated further north, near the Norwegian old mining town of Røros, Femundsmarka extends eastwards from Lake Femund to the Swedish border. An old steamer sailing the whole length of the lake stops at various places along the way, from which hikers must proceed on foot. The **Femundsmarka National Park** covers the whole area to the border. Until recently, a few legendary characters led a solitary life, close to nature, right at the heart of the wilderness area. The land is poor and the ground is covered with reindeer moss, heather and wolf lichen; meagre pine trees make up the forest areas. Musk-ox, wolverine and lynx all live in Femundsmarka as do many bird species including the osprey, Siberian tit and merlin.

Linnaeus

This is the Latin name of the Swedish botanist, Carl von Linné (1707-78), founder of the Swedish Academy of Sciences and a practising physician. He travelled to Lapland and visited several European countries, establishing the principles of classifying plants and giving each one two Latin names, one for genus or group and one for species. This system is still in use today, although modified. Linnaeus described 7 000 plants by this method and became a worldwide authority during his lifetime. In 1734, he visited Norway and went through Femundsmarka on his way to Røros.

Fem Dalar (Sweden)

The term Five Valleys refers to an area of mountains, valleys and lakes situated in the southern part of Swedish Lapland, close to the Norwegian border, between **Ammarnäs** in the north and **Borgafjäll** in the south. The wilderness of Fem Dalar offers contrasting landscapes of marshes, barren mountains, clear, ice-cold lakes, deep ravines and unspoilt rivers descending from the summits in a north-west/south-east direction all the way to the Baltic. The best way to enjoy the exhilarating natural beauty of the area and feel the freedom of untouched wilderness is by taking a dog-sledge or snowscooter ride in winter and by trekking on horseback, canoeing or simply hiking in summer.

Ruska in Finnish Lapland

North Karelia (Finland)

Between Lake Pielinen and the Russian border lies a region of marshland, forests, lakes and tumultuous rivers, with the **Patvinsuo National Park** in its centre. Rafting down the rapids of the River Jongunjoki, northeast of Nurmes, or the River Ruunaa, east of Lieksa, is one of the exciting opportunities this wild area has to offer. Other back to nature activities include hiking along marked trails with enticing names such as Karhunpolku, the **Bear Trail** or Susitaival, the **Wolf Trail**.

Kuusamo (Finland)

Further north along the Russian border the area surrounding Kuusamo is another virgin region: wild rivers rushing through deep canyons, forests and marshland, numerous lakes and the high hills of the Kuusamo plateau offering views over this wilderness. Situated at the heart of the region, the **Oulanka National Park** affords the best scenery.

Oulanka National Park

Wildlife

Animal life thrives better in wild unspoilt areas; thus Scandinavia has managed to retain a great variety of species which are now rare or extinct in other parts of the world. **Bears** and **wolves** still roam the dense forested areas of Finland; **lynx** and **wolverines** cohabit with the more common foxes, deer, badgers and hares. Beside these, there are species specifically found in northern latitudes; among them, the most common are **reindeer** which have increased in numbers, at least the tame variety. **Elks**, which were an endangered species, have been saved by strict conservation regulations and their numbers have grown considerably over the past 40 years. Other inhabitants of polar regions are the **Arctic fox** and the **lemming**, a small rodent preyed upon by the impressive **snowy owl**.

North of the Arctic Circle

The 'real north' lies beyond the latitude 66°33'N, an imaginary line known as the Arctic or Polar Circle which underlines a marked change in landscape, climate and way of life. Travelling through the vast, sparsely populated territories of Finnish, Swedish and Norwegian **Lapland** takes on a new dimension: distances seem greater as the scenery becomes more uniform, except perhaps in the southern areas of Swedish Lapland, and the vegetation of brownish shrubs, lichens and dwarf silver birch, characteristic of the high plateaux of Finnmark, disappears almost completely under the winter snow. Yet for most visitors, the whole region has a fascinating appeal because it has something unique to offer: a chance to return to nature in climatic conditions that few people have experienced before and in a totally unfamiliar environment which produces a host of new sensations.

MIDNIGHT SUN AND NORTHERN LIGHTS

Dog-sledging

H. Donnezan/EXPLORER

One of the great attractions of Lapland is the **midnight sun** and its winter counterpart, the **polar night.** This feature is characteristic of Arctic regions: due to extreme variations in the length of day and night between summer and winter, it can be observed for longer periods in the far north; from the end of May to the end of July, the sun never sets and, around Nordkapp, it seems to hover over the horizon at midnight and start rising again at the beginning of another day. On the other hand, during December and January, the sun never rises above the horizon and the long polar night only gives way briefly at midday to a kind of **blue twilight** enhanced by the whiteness of the snow. From time to time, streamers of light tear through the darkness, underlining the contours of the landscape; this electrical atmospheric phenomenon is known as **aurora borealis** or **northern lights.** The inhabitants of these polar regions have adapted their lifestyle to the long summer days and equally long winter nights; the animal kingdom has developed a sense of urgency and never stops being active and tending to the young throughout the summer, in preparation for the enforced winter hibernation. Human beings do the same, sleeping very little and often feasting through the night.

CONTRASTS

The land lying north of the Arctic Circle covers roughly a quarter of the total area of Scandinavia so that, in spite of common characteristics, there are marked contrasts between coastal and inland areas and between southern Swedish and Finnish Lapland and Norwegian and Finnish northern territories.

The **coastal fringe** is mountainous all the way north, from Bodø to Hammerfest, with summits culminating at almost 2 000m in the **Lyngsalpene** (Lyngen Alps) near Tromsø. The Coastal Steamer steers its way between the numerous islands, passing beneath barren peaks towering above the sea. In winter time, snow scooters can be seen tobogganing across the moonlike landscape in the rugged region stretching between Nordkapp and Kirkenes.

Polar night in Lapland (Finland)

Inland areas of northern Lapland include the desolate open spaces of **Finnmark** and the wild region surrounding **Lake Inari**, both strongholds of Sami culture. The mountain plateau known as **Finnmarksvidda** is the vast grazing ground for thousands of reindeer herded by nomadic Sami. In southern Lapland there are two picturesque mountainous areas: in Finland, between Kittilä and the Swedish border, there is a series of **isolated fells**, rounded and bare-topped, easy to climb, and several rivers abounding in fish; west of Kiruna and Malmberget, are **Sweden's highest mountains**, culminating at over 2 000m; it is great skiing country and nature lovers appreciate the wild lakes and powerful rivers rolling tumultuously towards the Baltic.

Urban landscapes of the far north are equally characteristic. Inland, there are mining towns like **Kiruna** and **Gällivare/Malmberget** in Sweden, built at the end of the last century with the feverish anticipation of economic prosperity but little concern for the environment. There are also Sami settlements like **Karasjok** and **Kautokeino** in Finnmark or **Utsjoki**, **Inari** and **Menesjärvi** in northern Finland, traditional meeting places for nomadic reindeer-herders; they have the feel of frontier towns which would hardly leave any trace behind if they disappeared suddenly. On the Norwegian coast on the other hand, towns such as **Narvik** and above all **Tromsø** have a much wider appeal. The setting of Tromsø among islands and surrounded by snow-capped pointed peaks is particularly attractive under the silvery Arctic light.

Polar exploration

The Polar Museum in Tromsø depicts traditional activities such as trapping, sealing and whaling in Arctic regions; it also illustrates the Polar expeditions of Roald Amundsen, one of Norway's most famous explorers, the first man to reach the South Pole in 1911, just days ahead of Robert Falcon Scott who died on the way back. Fridtjof Nansen was his contemporary and an equally successful explorer; at the age of 26, he crossed the Greenland ice-cap and later undertook several successful expeditions in regions close to the North Pole, collecting invaluable scientific information aboard his polar ship, the *Fram*, now in its own museum in Oslo.

History

In italics: meanwhile... in the rest of Europe and the world.

EARLY SETTLERS

BC	
7000-1800	**The Stone Age:** settlements of hunters and fishermen in southern Sweden, Denmark and along the coast of Norway; the rock carvings in Alta, Norway, date from this period. Farming appears during the Neolithic period. Arrival of the 'boat-axe' people.
1800-500	**Bronze Age:** extensive trade with continental Europe develops alongside farming and metal-working. Archaeological finds: clothing, jewellery, various objects and rock carvings depicting daily life.
500-AD 500	**The Iron Age:** in southern Scandinavia, a farming culture develops as traces of villages surrounded by small fields testify; archaeological finds include well-preserved bog-bodies (Tollund Man and Grauballe Man). *Advance of the Celts across Europe.* Arrival of the Finns from the east.
AD	
1C	*Roman occupation of southern and western Europe.* The Romans build a flourishing trade with Scandinavia.
3C	First runic inscriptions.
6C	The Svear are firmly established in Sweden, which is named after them.

Scandinavia's first inhabitants were hunters and fishermen who lived some 10 000 years ago, at the end of the last Ice Age, when the great ice sheets which covered northern Europe were slowly retreating. They settled in Denmark then migrated along the west coast of Norway which was freed from ice some time before inland areas. These early settlers used tools chiefly made from bone and, later, flint; their way of life is illustrated by the ancient rock carvings discovered in northern Norway.

Rock carvings

Scandinavia is particularly rich in carvings and drawings made by early settlers on smooth rock-surfaces; they provide invaluable information about the life of prehistoric man from the Stone Age to the Bronze Age. The more recent ones, such as those discovered near Tanum in southern Sweden, depict fertility rites but also show work in the fields as well as boats which look very much like the ancestors of the Vikings' Drakkars. The oldest rock carvings were discovered in 1973 along the Altafjord in northern Norway; there are literally thousands spread over a vast area, depicting a variety of animals, reindeer, elks, bears, fish, birds and boats as well as hunting and fishing scenes and even reindeer herding. The carvings have been added to Unesco's World Heritage list of cultural monuments.

Rock carvings from the Tanum area, Sweden

After photographs E. Sevo/MICHELIN

During the latter part of the Stone Age, known as the Neolithic period, agriculture gradually developed in southern Scandinavia and traces of permanent farming settlements have been found; the first pottery dates from that period. At the same time, various immigrants arrived from the south and the east: some of them built dolmens and passage graves in Denmark *(see MØN: Grønjægers Høj)* and southern Sweden. They were followed by the 'boat-axe' people who brought with them more sophisticated tools and weapons and possibly their Indo-European language.

Trade developed during the Bronze Age as amber, furs and slaves were exchanged for copper and tin used to make the precious alloy. Rock carvings again tell us how Bronze-Age Scandinavians worked the land and were already an experienced seafaring people.

From around 500 BC, iron-making became known to the inhabitants of Scandinavia who extracted the ore from bogs and used peat as fuel; and indeed bogs yielded the main archaeological finds from that period: various objects believed to have been placed there as offerings to the peat god but, above all, well-preserved bodies, such as the Tollund Man found near Silkeborg in Jutland, probably the victims of human sacrifices.

During the first 500 years AD, when continental Europe was the scene of important migrations, runic inscriptions began to appear and forts were built for defensive purposes. The Svear dominated Sweden, the Finns began to make their way inland but, on the whole, Scandinavia remained outside the great European turmoil until the Viking era.

VIKING PERIOD 800-1050 *(see Vikings p 44)*

800	*Charlemagne Emperor of the Franks.*
c 875	Harald Fairhair unifies most of Norway.
9C-10C	Danish and Norwegian Vikings raid northern, western and southern Europe while Swedish Vikings plunder the Baltic coasts.
911	*The Viking chieftain Rollon becomes duke of Normandy as Robert I.*
980	Unification and Christianisation of Denmark by Harald Bluetooth.
c 1000	*Discovery of North America by Norwegian Vikings established in Iceland.* King Olof Skötkonung is the first Christian king of Sweden, but the country is only gradually Christianised over the next century.
1000-1013	Conquest of Norway and England by Danish King Sven I. His son Knut the Great (King Canute of England) rules over a large empire.
1015-1030	St Olav of Norway imposes the Christian faith on his country. He is killed at the battle of Stiklestad (1030) and becomes Norway's national hero.
1048	Foundation of Olso by Harald årdråde, St Olav's half brother.

VIKING AGE
(late 8C to early 11C)

▨ Area of Scandinavian settlement

● Scandinavian towns
(866) ● Town founded or transformed by the Vikings
Itil , ● Trading centre
(965) ● Town besieged or plundered

Christianity

The conversion of the Vikings to the Christian faith coincided with the decline of their undisputed supremacy over the seas of north-west Europe and marked the arrival of Scandinavia on the complex European chessboard of nations. There is no doubt that if the widespread Christianisation of the Nordic countries was not the only cause of the Vikings' weakening influence in northern Europe, it accelerated the process. Their spirit of conquest and their undeniable fighting superiority crumbled in a relatively short time; **Knut the Great**, who ruled over England as King Canute, employed himself in the thorough Christianisation of his mighty empire with the help of the English Church. However, this political unity was brief and, after his death, there was renewed internal strife among ambitious lords who nevertheless had to contend with the growing power of the Church. Once Christianity was established in Scandinavia, its sphere of influence widened continually and the Church assumed the rôle it already played on the continent of Europe, that of precious ally or dreaded opponent, depending on the circumstances. In this climate of continuous struggle for power, a **feudal system** was gradually installed and Denmark, Norway and Sweden emerged as rival **Christian kingdoms**; by the end of the 11C, a fragile unity had been achieved in each of the three countries, but this time it had been done under the Christian banner. Bishoprics were founded throughout the land; pagan beliefs, however, lingered on for a long time in the whole of Scandinavia, as the motifs decorating the stave churches of Norway show, but the survival of the Christian faith in Nordic countries was never under serious threat.

Finland had remained outside the Viking turmoil and, by the middle of the 12C, it had not yet become a political entity. It now seems almost certain that the Christian religion was not entirely unknown to the Finns when, in **1157**, the Swedes launched a **crusade** against their 'heathen' neighbours with the support of Bishop Henry of Uppsala and took over the country. This domination of Finland by Sweden was to last until 1809.

The Church acted as a channel through which western European culture and architecture reached the Nordic countries during the 11C and the 12C; this applies particularly well to Denmark where the Church could rely on the support of a powerful dynasty, the Valdemars.

THE VALDEMAR DYNASTY RULES OVER DENMARK 1157-1375

	The country prospers and expands eastwards.
1165	Foundation of Copenhagen.
12C-13C	Building of stave churches in Norway.
	The first stone churches are built in Sweden (at Uppsala and Lund).
	Sweden conquers Finland and spreads Christianity there.
1255	Foundation of Stockholm.
1350	An epidemic of plague kills a third of the Scandinavian population.
1370	The Hanseatic League acquires trading rights in the Øresund.
14C	Finland becomes a Swedish province; Swedish is the official language, Turku the capital. Karelia in eastern Finland is split between Sweden and Russia by the Treaty of Pähkinäsaari (1323).

From Baltic to North Sea

The economic and political influence of the **Hanseatic League** in northern Europe was at its height between the 13C and the 15C. Headed by the city of **Lübeck**, a group of German towns formed an economic alliance with the aim of controlling the Baltic trade; the Hanseatic League, as this alliance was called, then expanded towards the North Sea and became so powerful that it could dictate its own terms to kings and nations. By the middle of the 14C, Hansa merchants had established a thriving *kontore* (commercial base) in **Bergen** on the west coast of Norway and by the beginning of the 15C the League numbered some **70 cities**. However, when Valdemar became king of Denmark in 1340, he set out to curb German influence in the Baltic and restore Danish supremacy; he conquered the island of **Gotland** where the town of **Visby** was an important Hanseatic trading base. In response, a coalition rose against Denmark and Valdemar was forced to sign the **treaty of Stralsund in 1370**: the League secured its trading rights in the Baltic by gaining control of three strongholds along the south-west coast of Sweden; it had reached the height of its power *(see also BERGEN p 143)*.

KALMAR UNION 1389-1523

1389	Margrethe of Denmark becomes regent of Denmark, Norway and Sweden.
1397	Her nephew, Eric of Pomerania, is chosen as king of the three countries united under the Kalmar Union. Norway becomes a Danish province while the country's economy is in the hands of the Hanseatic League.
1433-1523	Swedish resistance to the Union through a series of uprisings.
1477	Foundation of the first Scandinavian university in Uppsala.
1492	*Christopher Columbus discovers America.*
1521-1523	Christian II is driven out of Sweden by Gustav Vasa who becomes king and sets up a hereditary monarchy. Denmark and Norway remain united.

Kalmar Slott, Sweden

ROGER VIOLLET

At the end of the 14C, Denmark was the strongest and most organised of the four or rather three Scandinavian countries, since Finland formed an integral part of Sweden. King **Valdemar IV** had strengthened the Danish monarchy but there was much political uncertainty in the other two kingdoms which, consequently, were harassed by the Hanseatic League and threatened with German economic supremacy. A union between the Nordic countries in order to stand up to the Germans seemed to many the only salvation, but the Swedes feared Danish control of an eventual union and opposed it. In the end, it was the determination of an ambitious woman, **Margrethe of Denmark**, which secured the union of the three countries under a Danish monarch! Margrethe, daughter of King Valdemar, married Håkon king of Norway. On the death of her father, her son **Olav** became king of Denmark, then king of Norway a few years later when his own father died. Since Olav was under age, Margrethe assumed the rôle of **regent of Denmark and Norway**; this marked the beginning of a union between Denmark and Norway which was to last until 1814. Meanwhile Sweden was being ruled by the heir to a powerful German dukedom and Swedish nobles feared for their privileges as the German influence became overwhelming; Margrethe promptly seized the opportunity and in 1388 she made a deal with the nobles: they would recognise her as the **rightful sovereign of Sweden** and in exchange she would guarantee their privileges. The **treaty of union** was signed in the Swedish town of **Kalmar in 1397**. However, Margrethe's son had died and she named her nephew, **Eric of Pomerania** as her rightful heir.

The Union prospered under Margrethe's rule, but Eric was less successful and, during the 15C, the Swedish nobility made several attempts to free themselves from what they saw as a threat to their independence. They finally succeeded in the early 16C.

THE REFORMATION – THE VASA DYNASTY RULES OVER SWEDEN 1523-1654

	Struggle for supremacy in the Baltic.
1523-1536	The Reformation is adopted by Finland, Sweden, Denmark and Norway.
1534-1536	Denmark and Sweden against the Hanseatic League.
1559	Decline of the League in Norway.
1563-1570	Denmark against Sweden over tolls in the Øresund.
1588-1648	Christian IV, the architect king, on the Danish throne. Flourishing of Renaissance architecture, development of silver and copper mining in Norway, expansion of the herring industry.
1611-1660	Series of wars between Denmark and Sweden during the reigns of Gustavus II Adolphus and his daughter Christina. Denmark loses Swedish territories.

The establishment of the Reformation in Scandinavia between 1523 and 1536 was achieved practically without any resistance. German preachers and Hanseatic merchants had been spreading the teachings of Luther for some time before the new religion was officially introduced. Sweden was the first to make the change; the ambitious newly elected **King Gustav Vasa** was looking for a way to redress the State finances and to strengthen his own position at the same time; he very skilfully saw the opportunities offered by the introduction of **Lutheranism** into Sweden and seized them. A decree issued by the Västerås Parliament recognised the Lutheran Church as the State Church and sanctioned the confiscation by the State of all property belonging to the Roman Catholic Church; thus the king's power was greatly increased. The introduction of the new religion into Finland, by now a loyal Swedish province, went almost unnoticed.

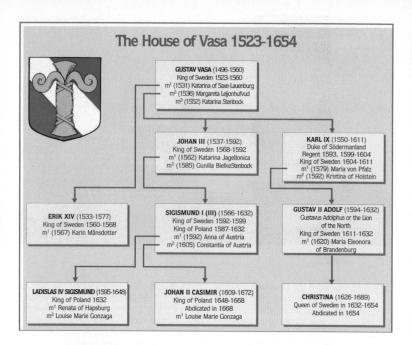

The House of Vasa 1523-1654

GUSTAV VASA (1496-1560)
King of Sweden 1523-1560
m¹ (1531) Katarina of Saxe-Lauenburg
m² (1536) Margareta Leijonhufvud
m³ (1552) Katarina Stenbock

JOHAN III (1537-1592)
King of Sweden 1568-1592
m¹ (1562) Katarina Jagellonica
m² (1585) Gunilla BielkeStenbock

KARL IX (1550-1611)
Duke of Södermanland
Regent 1593, 1599-1604
King of Sweden 1604-1611
m¹ (1579) Maria von Pfalz
m² (1592) Kristina of Holstein

ERIK XIV (1533-1577)
King of Sweden 1560-1568
m¹ (1567) Karin Månsdotter

SIGISMUND I (III) (1566-1632)
King of Sweden 1592-1599
King of Poland 1587-1632
m¹ (1592) Anna of Austria
m² (1605) Constantia of Austria

GUSTAV II ADOLF (1594-1632)
Gustavus Adolphus or the Lion
of the North
King of Sweden 1611-1632
m¹ (1620) Maria Eleonora
of Brandenburg

LADISLAS IV SIGISMUND (1595-1648)
King of Poland 1632
m¹ Renata of Hapsburg
m² Louise Marie Gonzaga

JOHAN II CASIMIR (1609-1672)
King of Poland 1648-1668
Abdicated in 1668
m¹ Louise Marie Gonzaga

CHRISTINA (1626-1689)
Queen of Sweden in 1632-1654
Abdicated in 1654

ROGER VIOLLET

Gustav Vasa

In Denmark, the course of events was totally different but the result was the same and again the will of the monarch prevailed. When **Christian III** succeeded his father after a bitter struggle with his brother, he too needed some money rather urgently to pay his mercenaries, but the Roman Catholic bishops refused; the king then ordered them to be arrested and forced them to recognise Lutheranism as the new official religion. Church property was confiscated and the king sold part of his newly acquired land to the nobility.

A tentative Norwegian resistance was soon crushed and Lutheranism reinforced Danish control of the country because the Bible and all church writings were in Danish.

Thus the Reformation strengthened royal power in all the Scandinavian countries which were soon to become **absolute monarchies**.

17C AND 18C CONFLICTS

1660	Denmark and Norway become an absolute monarchy.
1643-1715	*Reign of Louis XIV, the Sun King.*
1675-1720	Another wave of wars between Denmark and Sweden who gives up her Baltic provinces and ceases to be a great power.
1750	Beginning of a period of neutrality and economic expansion for Denmark and Norway.
1776	*American War of Independence begins.*
1789	*Start of the French Revolution.*
1792	Abolition of slavery in Denmark.
1806	Denmark adheres to Napoleon's Continental Blockade.
1807	Bombing of Copenhagen by the British fleet. Sweden joins the coalition against Napoleon.
1809	**Finland becomes a Russian Grand Duchy.**
1812	Helsinki becomes the capital of Finland.
1814	**Treaty of Kiel:** Denmark cedes Norway to Sweden and acquires the duchies of Slesvig-Holstein as well as Pomerania.

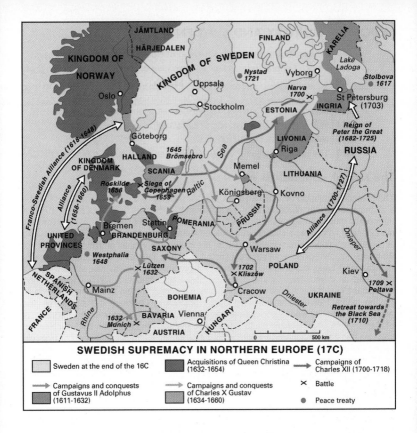

SWEDISH SUPREMACY IN NORTHERN EUROPE (17C)

- ◻ Sweden at the end of the 16C
- ◼ Acquisitions of Queen Christina (1632-1654)
- → Campaigns of Charles XII (1700-1718)
- ◼ Campaigns and conquests of Gustavus II Adolphus (1611-1632)
- ◼ Campaigns and conquests of Charles X Gustav (1634-1660)
- ✕ Battle
- ● Peace treaty

The 17C was marked by the bitter struggle for supremacy of two nations which happened to be powerful at the same time, **Denmark and Sweden**. This long-drawn succession of wars was however highlighted by two strong personalities, King **Christian IV** of Denmark and King Gustav II Adolf, better known as **Gustavus Adolphus.**

The reason for the conflicts was supremacy in the Baltic; this was nothing new, except that this time there was a new balance of power: the decline of the Hanseatic League had left Sweden uncomfortably positioned between a strong Denmark in the west and Poland and Russia in the east, eagerly awaiting their chance.

The southern provinces of Sweden had, for a very long time, been in Danish hands. This became intolerable to a country enjoying a newly acquired national pride; moreover, the Danish occupation blocked Swedish access to the west coast ports, which were vital to the country's growing economic prosperity. Through a series of wars, the Swedes therefore made a determined bid for expansion and for control of the Øresund, the strait separating the Baltic from the North Sea. Between **1611 and 1660**, Sweden regained **Halland, Skåne** and **Blekinge** in the south as well as the island of **Gotland**. Both kings took part in the pan-European **Thirty Years War** but, whereas Denmark gained nothing and was weakened economically, Sweden made substantial territorial gains on the southern shores of the Baltic and on the North Sea. In **1657**, the Swedish king invaded Jutland and took his army across the frozen sea to threaten the Danish capital. Denmark acknowledged defeat and signed the **treaty of Roskilde**. The Swedish Empire was at its zenith. However, the Swedish king broke the treaty and once again marched on Copenhagen; Denmark's allies came to the rescue and the **treaty of Copenhagen** was signed in **1660**, maintaining the status quo. Denmark had thus lost its supremacy in the Baltic straits and could no longer control the Sound trade. Later attempts on the part of Denmark to regain some of the lost territories failed and the Danish nation had to resign itself to sharing control in the Sound and to accept the territorial restrictions of the new frontiers.

In 1700, Russia, Poland and Denmark resumed war against Sweden ruled by Charles XII, who soon crushed the coalition, invaded Poland but was defeated at Poltava (1709) and took refuge in Turkey. He remained there, a virtual prisoner, for 5 years while his enemies, who now included Prussia and Bavaria, occupied his possessions in the Baltic. When he returned to his country in 1715, he had to go to war once more and was killed in 1718, during the siege of Frederikshald, in Norway. After this series of wars, Sweden was reduced to a second-rate nation and was only allowed to retain a few of its possessions.

	Economic progress and awakening of Norway's national awareness.
1818	French General Bernadotte becomes king of Sweden as Karl XIV Johan.
1835	Publication of Finnish epic poem, **Kalevala.**
1849	Denmark becomes a constitutional monarchy.
1857	Abolition of the Øresund toll introduced at the beginning of the 15C.
1864	War between Denmark and Prussia/Austria over Slesvig-Holstein.
1865	New Swedish constitution.
1905	The union between Norway and Sweden is ended by referendum.

The rise of nationalists movements

The French Revolution of 1789 signalled the awakening of nationalism all over Europe and the subsequent revolutions of 1830 and 1848 reinforced the determination of nationalist movements everywhere throughout the 19C. This revival of national awareness sprang from many causes and took different forms but the aim was always to achieve recognition of national identity on the cultural as well as on the political scene. **Denmark's** national pride was severely tested over the fate of the duchies of Slesvig, Holstein and Lauenburg; although these had been under Danish rule since the 13C, they had a mixed Danish and German population and, in 1815, Holstein and Lauenburg joined the confederation of German states and tried to convince Slesvig to do the same. However, enlightened public opinion in Denmark did not agree and wished for Slesvig, whose population was mainly Danish, to become an integral part of Danish territory. Holstein could not accept the separation of the two duchies; an impasse had been reached. In 1848, an uprising of the German population of Holstein gave the Prussians the excuse they were looking for to invade Jylland; Russia, England and Sweden intervened and an armistice was signed in 1850 but the problem had not been solved; the conflict flared up again and after long negotiations, an agreement signed in London granted the duchies full autonomy... under the Danish crown! Dissatisfied with the whole deal, Denmark tried once more to annex Slesvig by revising the constitution.

Prussia declared war in 1864 but none of Denmark's allies wanted to take part; defeat was therefore swift and extremely costly: the three duchies went to Prussia and Denmark's size was thus considerably reduced. Humiliation on the international scene fostered a national romantic movement in the field of art and literature represented by the sculptor Thorvaldsen, the painter Høyen, champion of a form of popular art, and the writers Andersen, Kierkegaard and Grundtvig who all embodied contrasting traits of the Danish people.

There had been a kind of latent nationalism in **Norway** since the end of the 18C, ready to flare up at the first opportunity. This opportunity came in 1814 when the Danes were forced to cede Norway to Sweden as a result of their role in the Napoleonic wars. The Norwegians promptly declared their independence and proclaimed a new constitution on 17 May 1814, asking a Danish prince to be their king. However, fearing a war with Sweden, the European powers did not support Norway's initiative and the original deal was maintained; a union with Sweden was established but Norway retained its new constitution and parliament. In spite of this, nationalism did not die in Norway; on the contrary, it became crystallised in contemporary cultural trends: for instance, love of the Norwegian land was expressed by the painter JC Dahl, the playwright Henrik Ibsen and the composer Edvard Grieg. On the other hand, the politician Johan Sverdrup encouraged the Norwegian parliament to assume its full rôle notwithstanding continual opposition from the king until 1905, when the union with Sweden was dissolved and Norway became an independent constitutional monarchy.

Finland had never been independent but had merely changed from Swedish rule to Russian rule; the capital had also been transferred from Turku to Helsinki, nearer the Russian border. At the beginning of the 19C, the language problem came to a head as the situation was perceived by most Finns as being unfair and ridiculous: Finland, now a Russian Grand Duchy, had retained Swedish as its official language. A Finnish language movement developed round Johan Vilhelm Snellman to demand that Finnish should become the official language. There was strong opposition from the Swedish-speaking minority; it was during that period that the Finnish writer Elias Lönnrot published the *Kalevala*, a national epic based on ancient folktales. Finnish and Swedish were eventually both acknowledged as official languages. Towards the end of the 19C, however, there was a complete reversal and an attempt was made by the then czar of Russia, Nicholas II, to turn Finland into a mere Russian province, causing a general outcry. There was a prompt and spectacular response from Finnish artists and intellectuals like Sibelius, who composed his famous *Finlandia* or Akseli Gallen-Kallela who painted scenes from the *Kalevala*. Nothing swayed the czar's determination and it was only after the October Revolution had overthrown the czar of Russia that Finland gained its independence.

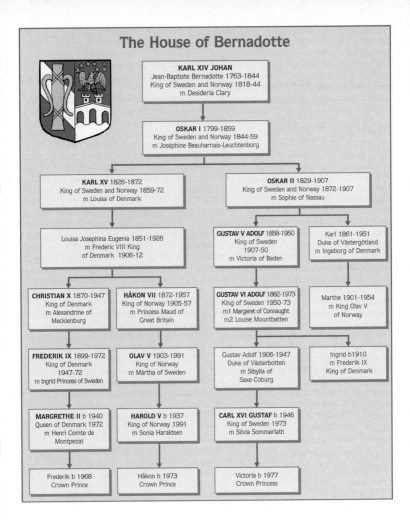

The House of Bernadotte

KARL XIV JOHAN
Jean-Baptiste Bernadotte 1763-1844
King of Sweden and Norway 1818-44
m Desideria Clary

OSKAR I 1799-1859
King of Sweden and Norway 1844-59
m Joséphine Beauharnais-Leuchtenborg

KARL XV 1826-1872
King of Sweden and Norway 1859-72
m Louisa of Denmark

OSKAR II 1829-1907
King of Sweden and Norway 1872-1907
m Sophie of Nassau

Louisa Josephina Eugenia 1851-1926
m Frederic VIII King
of Denmark 1906-12

GUSTAV V ADOLF 1858-1950
King of Sweden
1907-50
m Victoria of Baden

Karl 1861-1951
Duke of Västergötland
m Ingeborg of Denmark

CHRISTIAN X 1870-1947
King of Denmark
m Alexandrine of
Mecklenburg

HÅKON VII 1872-1957
King of Norway 1905-57
m Princess Maud of
Great Britain

GUSTAV VI ADOLF 1882-1973
King of Sweden 1950-73
m1 Margaret of Connaught
m2 Louise Mountbatten

Marthe 1901-1954
m King Olav V
of Norway

FREDERIK IX 1899-1972
King of Denmark
1947-72
m Ingrid Princess of Sweden

OLAV V 1903-1991
King of Norway
m Märtha of Sweden

Gustav Adolf 1906-1947
Duke of Västerbotten
m Sibylla of
Saxe-Coburg

Ingrid b1910
m Frederik IX
King of Denmark

MARGRETHE II b 1940
Queen of Denmark 1972
m Henri Comte de
Montpezat

HAROLD V b 1937
King of Norway 1991
m Sonia Haraldsen

CARL XVI GUSTAF b 1946
King of Sweden 1973
m Silvia Sommerlath

Frederik b 1968
Crown Prince

Håkon b 1973
Crown Prince

Victoria b 1977
Crown Princess

THE 20C

1906	New Finnish constitution; vote granted to Finnish women.
1913	Votes for women in Norway.
1914	*Beginning of the First World War.* Denmark, Norway and Sweden remain neutral.
1915	Votes for women in Denmark.
1917	**Finland declares her independence.**
1918	Finland's War of Liberation.
1919	**Finland becomes a republic.**
1920	**Danish-speaking Slesvig-Holstein is returned to Denmark.** Norway joins the League of Nations.
1925	Svalbard becomes Norwegian.
1939	*Beginning of the Second World War.* Denmark signs a pact of non-aggression with Germany. Finland's Winter War with the Soviet Union. The loss of part of Karelia causes mass exodus.
1940	Germany invades Denmark and Norway (Battle of Narvik). Organisation of resistance movements. The king of Norway and his government flee to Britain. Sweden remains neutral.
1941-1944	Continuation War between Finland and the Soviet Union.

The Second World War tore Scandinavia apart not only because it suffered from the hardships of war but also because the four Scandinavian countries found themselves on different sides.

Even though all of them had expressed the wish to remain neutral before the war had even begun, Scandinavia was too important a pawn on the international chessboard to be ignored either by the Germans or by the Allies.

Sweden alone managed to maintain its neutrality throughout the war although the government had to make concessions to the Germans in order to safeguard it; for instance transit of German troops was allowed as requests from Germany became more and more pressing. These concessions were very unpopular and there was heated controversy over their legitimacy. However a number of courageous humanitarian actions were taken; thousands of refugees from other Scandinavian countries and from the Baltic states, including many Jews from Denmark, found shelter in Sweden.

The position of **Denmark** was no less ambiguous at least until 1943, although the situation was totally different. Feeling in a position of weakness on the eve of the war, the Danes agreed to sign a pact of non-aggression with Hitler in 1939 and, once again, proclaimed their neutrality, but in vain for in April 1940, Denmark was occupied by German forces on their way to Norway. It was all over in a few hours and no resistance was offered. From then on, the Danes tried to steer their way through the war without too much suffering and, in practice, this amounted to collaboration with the Germans. Things changed in 1943 as resistance was organised: underground newspapers flourished, the Danish ambassador in London declared himself openly on the side of the Allies and the Danish Freedom Council, at first an underground movement, was recognised as Denmark's legitimate government. German intimidation and repression followed immediately and continued until the liberation of the country on 5 May 1945.

In April 1940, the Allies and the Germans both turned their attention to the Norwegian port of **Narvik** from which Swedish iron ore was exported. At first the Norwegians resisted fiercely but they were overwhelmed by German superiority and in June 1940 the king fled with his government to London where they remained until the end of the war. Meanwhile civil resistance disrupted the smooth running of the country and the Germans retaliated with massive arrests and deportations. A military resistance movement, acting under orders from London, gathered precious information for the Allies and organised sabotage action all over the country, in particular at Rjukan in Telemark where a heavy water plant was systematically destroyed *(see Telemark p 213)*. Sabotage was intensified after the D-day landings until the Germans surrendered on 7 May 1945.

In the case of **Finland,** aggression came from the east when Russia invaded Karelia in November 1939. The Winter War which followed was valiantly fought by the outnumbered Finns who were eventually forced to sign a treaty with Russia, ceding half of Karelia. After the war, Finland became isolated and turned to Germany for supplies of food and arms, being drawn into another war with Russia which became known as the Continuation War. By then Russia was on the side of the Allies who declared war on Finland at the end of 1941. From then on until August 1944 when a peace treaty ended the war, Finland was torn between Germany and the Soviet Union and therefore doomed to be the loser in the end.

AROUND THE BALTIC TODAY

1945	Norway is a founding member of the United Nations whose first Secretary General is a Norwegian. Denmark joins the United Nations.
1946	Sweden joins the United Nations.
1948	The Faroe Islands become self-governing. Finland and the Soviet Union sign a Treaty of Friendship, Cooperation and Mutual Assistance.
1949	Denmark and Norway join NATO.
1952	**Foundation of the Nordic Council** to promote economic, social and cultural cooperation between Nordic countries.
1953	Dag Hammarskjöld of Sweden is elected Secretary General of the UN. Revision of the Danish constitution to allow women to succeed to the throne; Margrethe becomes heir apparent.
1955	Finland joins the United Nations.
1958	*Signature of the treaty of Rome between the six founding members of the European Economic Community.*
1960	Denmark, Norway and Sweden become members of EFTA.
1961	Finland joins EFTA as an 'associate'.
1962	Signing of the Helsinki Convention intended to promote cooperation between the four Scandinavian countries.
1972	Margrethe II, the present Danish monarch, becomes queen.
1973	Denmark joins the EEC (European Economic Community). Norway and Sweden do not join but sign a free trade agreement. Finland also signs the agreement.

1974	The new Swedish constitution reduces the king's powers still further. Drilling for oil and natural gas begins in the North Sea.
1979	In Sweden, a law is passed to allow the first-born child, male or female, to succeed to the throne.
1989	Finland becomes a member of the Council of Europe. Her status as a neutral country is recognised by the Soviet Union.
1991	Harald V becomes king of Norway.
1992	Norway signs the Agreement on the European Economic Area, due to come into force at the same time as the European single market.
1995	Following a referendum, Finland and Sweden become members of the European Union; Norway refuses.
1996	Copenhagen is Cultural Capital of Europe
1998	Stockholm is the second Nordic capital to become Cultural Capital of Europe

In recent years, the balance of power has changed considerably in the Baltic region: in the east, the break-up of the Soviet Union into several smaller states and the economic breakdown of the former giant have reversed the roles; still pursuing its **policy of strict neutrality**, Finland has retained commercial ties with the new republics and offered them financial assistance to buy food supplies and safeguard the environment. At the same time Finland has become a full member of the European Union while maintaining close cooperation with the other Scandinavian countries.

Sweden's recent foreign policy has been a mixture of involvement in major international issues such as disarmament and peace in the Third World and of **strict non-alliance**, the Swedes thus declining an invitation to join NATO in 1949. On the other hand, their liberal economic policy led the Swedes to become members of the Nordic Council, the European Free Trade Association and, in 1995, the European Union.

Denmark was the first Scandinavian country to join the European Union in 1972, yet failure by the Danes to ratify the Maastricht treaty in the 1992 referendum, albeit by a tiny majority, has left the country in an uncomfortable position, outside the main sphere of influence.

After the war, Norway promptly joined the United Nations and NATO but, for the past thirty years there have been endless arguments for and against becoming a member of the European Union and the 1994 referendum once again rejected the proposed application. This can partly be explained by the wealth Norway derives from its North Sea oil, but the reasons also stem from the highly individualistic Norwegian character.

Vikings

R. Corbel/MICHELIN

The Viking Age, which extends from around AD 800 to 1050, marks the end of Scandinavia's isolation from the rest of Europe. In the space of 250 years, the Vikings changed the course of Scandinavian and European history, although one must speak of 'history' with caution since what is known about this period is based on archaeological finds, on contemporary chronicles written in European monasteries and on 12C and 13C sagas. The archaeological finds provide accurate but incomplete information on the Vikings' lifestyle, while the chronicles and sagas must be considered as less reliable for obvious reasons: the monasteries which relate the Vikings' deeds had either been plundered by the fierce warriors or heard of their fearsome raids and, therefore, could hardly be termed impartial; as for the sagas, they were written down much later and drew on the oral traditions of the *skalds* who, very often, adapted their stories to the requirements of their listeners. However, one thing is certain, the Vikings greatly impressed their contemporaries and their reputation for violence, swiftness and daring seamanship spread like wildfire through Europe and the Arab world.

Weapons

The Vikings' favourite weapon was the axe which they used with great dexterity; next came the long, flat, double-edged iron sword, then the spear, the bow and arrow and the single-edged iron knife; finds excavated from Viking graves indicate that they never used all these weapons together. To protect themselves in battle, Viking warriors wore an iron coat of mail, a round leather or iron helmet and carried a wooden shield. Sagas again tell us that some Vikings were particularly fierce fighters, called *berserks*, who fought without armour, 'like savage beasts'. They must have been greatly responsible for the feeling of terror which spread across Europe at the time!

WHO WERE THE VIKINGS ?

They were simply the descendants of the immigrants who had settled on Scandinavian soil and eventually became farmers and traders in well-organised structured societies. Outside their native land they were known as **Normanni** or Northmen by the Franks and **Dani** or Danes by the Anglo-Saxons; these names referred indiscriminately to Danish and Norwegian Vikings since it seems that there was no distinction made between them at the time. As for the Swedish Vikings who went east to Russia and the Middle East, they were called **Rus**, a name of Finnish origin meaning oars-men. The name **Vikings** on the other hand was used by the Scandinavians themselves: most historians agree that it is a word of Norse origin meaning 'men from creeks or fjords', a name well suited to pirates who hid inside natural inlets, waiting to surprise their prey. At first it must have been used for the raiders only, but later it became synonymous with the whole Scandinavian people whose modern descendants are proud of their Viking origins.

VIKING RAIDS

Even if the Vikings' adventurous, daring temperament goes a long way towards explaining why they set out to raid and plunder most of the then known world, there are also undeniable economic and demographic reasons: at the beginning of the 9C, Scandinavia suffered from what is now called a population explosion and a scarcity of farming land to absorb this sudden increase. Under Viking law, the first born child was sole heir and younger sons therefore had to leave and seek their fortune elsewhere. On the other hand, Scandinavians had become very skilful at extracting iron from bog-ore and at making powerful weapons which gave them boundless confidence. But it was the development of their invincible ships, the famous *drakkars*, which made it possible for them to use their deadly efficient tactic of sudden and swift attack, thereby giving them decisive military superiority.

Viking Ships

The Vikings were great seafarers and, by the 9C, they had developed easily manoeuvrable ships, known as *drakkars*, which were seaworthy even in very rough conditions: they were light and bounced on the waves, they were also fast and needed so little draught that the raiders could land anywhere and easily pull their ships ashore, thus making sure the element of surprise was in their favour. Viking warships had a high curved prow, which has become a symbol of Viking expeditions, and were rigged with a square sail as well as being equipped with oars. They could carry a crew of up to 100 men and sail at a top speed of around 12 knots. Merchant ships of various sizes and shapes, just as seaworthy, were used for trading with distant lands and for carrying emigrants to their chosen country, not to mention bringing back the loot.

The attack on **Lindisfarne Abbey** off the coast of north-east England in 793 marks the beginning of Viking raids which lasted for 200 years. The Vikings killed, plundered and burned, but they also established long-lasting trading agreements with many countries all over Europe and founded new kingdoms; some of these like York and the Danelaw in England did not last, but others such as Kiev and Normandy thrived and became extremely powerful. The Swedish Vikings raided the Baltic coasts and sailed inland along the River Volga and River Dnieper as far as Constantinople, founding Novgorod and Kiev on the way. They traded furs and amber against gold, silver and luxury goods. The Norwegian and Danish Vikings sailed westwards, sometimes separately, sometimes together, to Britain, the Shetlands, the Orkneys, Ireland, France and Spain. They even went through the Strait of Gibraltar into the Mediterranean Sea, joining up with Swedish Vikings in Constantinople. Some Norwegian Vikings settled in Iceland and Greenland and from there sailed west, discovering America 500 years before Christopher Columbus. Their exploits are mentioned in the Icelandic sagas and confirmed by traces of their homes and various artefacts found on the north coast of Newfoundland.

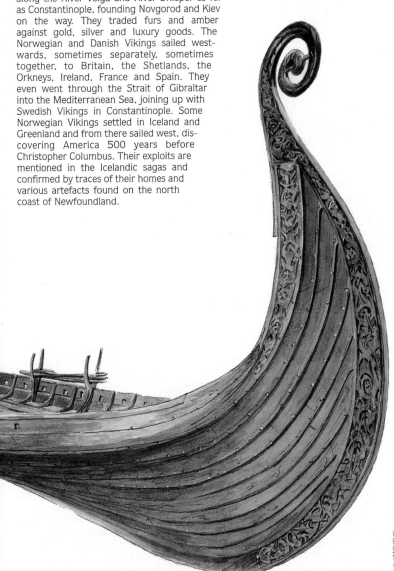

VIKING SOCIETY

Viking society was very well organised; when they were not on long-distance expeditions, the Vikings proved to be competent farmers and craftsmen, particularly gifted in the art of metal-working, as well as hunters and brilliant horsemen; they raised crops of various cereals and kept stock within neat enclosures adjoining their long wooden houses grouped to form villages. Some Vikings lived in towns; their activity was based on craftsmanship and a lively trade with surrounding districts. The main towns were **Birka**, situated on the island of Björkö in Lake Mälaren (near Stockholm), **Kaupang** on the south coast of Norway, **Ribe** in west Jylland and **Hedeby** in south Jylland, the most important Scandinavian town during the Viking period. Of those four towns, only Ribe has survived, but abroad, York and Kiev prospered and developed long after the end of the Viking Age. Men and women wore clothes made from wool, silk or flax. Men carried a sword in their belt and women wore jewellery such as silver and gold bracelets.

The Viking community was divided into three classes: the aristocracy to which the king belonged (at first he was elected by the chieftains but later on the monarchy tended to become hereditary); the peasants who were free men and met in assemblies called *thing* (these enforced the law and discussed local problems); last came the slaves who had no rights whatsoever.

R. Corbel/MICHELIN

Viking burials

Numerous Viking graves have been found all over Scandinavia and their variety is the most striking element of these archaeological finds. Burial and cremation were both practised as it seems that there was great uncertainty and controversy about life after death. Even in the case of burial, customs varied a great deal: some Vikings were buried in wooden chambers, others in full size ships; some graves were covered with huge earth mounds, others were marked by the symbolic shape of a ship outlined by rows of stones. A full array of earthly goods were found in some of the more elaborate ship graves; these revealed invaluable information about the Vikings' concept of life after death: slaves, horses and dogs were often buried with their master, together with weapons, jewellery, leather, clothes, wooden articles decorated with carvings of animals, cooking utensils and food. No doubt life was expected to carry on after death as it had on earth.

PAGANISM AND CHRISTIANITY

R. Corbel/MICHELIN

The Vikings were a polytheistic society with a complex mythology which dealt with the creation of the world and forecast its end; it had its pantheon of gods like Greek and Roman mythology. A profusion of myths and tales, some of them full of poetry, related the adventures of the larger-than-life gods and goddesses, who held precise positions in the well-established hierarchy: **Odin** was the supreme god, the god of war and of warriors who died in battle, but he also inspired man's highest aspirations and feelings. However there was a dark and dangerous side to his personality for he stopped at nothing in order to achieve his aim of acquiring complete wisdom and knowledge. **Thor** was also the god of war, armed with a large hammer, protector of ordinary Vikings; his actions were more positive and beneficial and he was a more popular god than the dreaded Odin. The next most important gods were **Frey** and his sister **Freyja**, who represented love and fertility and seem to have been particularly popular in Sweden. Sacrificial feasts were regularly held in temples which where later replaced by Christian churches, as was the case in Jelling in south Jylland and in Uppsala in southern Sweden.

The Vikings' conversion to Christianity was gradual and more or less complete by the end of the 11C. The raiders were often converted while on their long-distance expeditions and brought back missionaries to help them in their task of imposing the new religion. Raids finally stopped but trade relations were kept alive and Scandinavia became a part of Europe.

Rune stones

Runic inscriptions were the first form of writing used by Scandinavians from the 3C AD; they were carved on wood, stone or metal and have been found not only in Scandinavia but also in the countries visited by the Vikings. Large rune stones weighing several tons seem to have served as memorials commemorating famous deeds and people; they bear the name of the person being remembered and the name of the person who commissioned the memorial. Sometimes they are only concerned with local deeds and sometimes, as in Jelling in south Jylland, they relate important historic events, in this case the unification and Christianisation of Denmark by Harald Bluetooth. Thousands of rune stones were found in Sweden, most of them not far from Stockholm, for instance at Rök and Täby. Towards the end of the Viking Age, rune stones bore Christian signs such as crosses as well as mythological animals like dragons and snakes.

VIKING SITES AND MUSEUMS

Earthworks – Danevirke, a defensive wall built across south Jylland to protect Scandinavia from Saxon invasion.

Major burial places – Birka in Lake Mälaren in south-eastern Sweden – Hedeby and Jelling in south Jylland, Denmark – Lindholm Høje near Ålborg in north Jylland.

Forts – All those discovered up to now are in Denmark: Trelleborg in south Sjælland, Fyrkat and Aggersborg in north Jylland. These circular fortresses surrounded by a strong earth wall could accommodate a garrison of around 1 000 men.

Museums – The Nationalmuseet in Copenhagen, the Museum of National Antiquities in Stockholm, the Viking Ships Museums in Oslo and Roskilde, Denmark.

R. Corbel/MICHELIN

Economy

Scandinavia is often regarded as having achieved a successful blend of capitalism and social progress which has secured the citizens of Denmark, Norway, Sweden and Finland a high standard of living and a high rank among the world nations in the United Nations' annual Human Development Report. This is broadly true; however, high taxes and high salaries, which were the logical consequence of Nordic economic and social policies, undermined the industrial competitiveness of countries relying a great deal on exports.

GENERAL TRENDS

During recent worldwide economic crises, at the end of the 1970s and in 1992, the situation deteriorated, slowing down economic growth to a record low; Scandinavian countries were forced to abandon the fixed exchange rate of their currency; this, in most cases, led to considerable devaluation which, in turn, gave a new lease of life to the export trade. At the same time, public spending was cut, businesses were reorganised along more rational lines, inevitably leading to a rise in unemployment.

The development of high technology, specialised training and research (Sweden's investment in the field of industrial research, which represented 3% of the Gross National Product in 1989, ranks among the highest in the world) also contributed to restoring the competitiveness of Scandinavian manufactured goods on the world market. Moreover, Scandinavian businesses looked for expansion outside their frontiers; some major industrial concerns successfully merged with their counterparts in other countries: such was the case of the Swedish Asea, a specialist in heavy electronics, which joined forces with the Swiss Brown Boveri to become the world's largest group in its field under the name ABB; other companies such as Norske Skog, the Norwegian paper and pulp manufacturer, exported their technology and implanted themselves abroad. Like other industrialised countries, Scandinavia acknowledges a major development of its service industries.

During the past 20 years, the rules of international marketing have been considerably altered by the strengthening of economic alliances such as the European Union and the European Free Trade Association. The four Scandinavian countries, all members of EFTA, applied for membership of the EU at different times; appreciating the invaluable opportunities offered to its agriculture and fisheries, Denmark was the first to join in 1972. Finland and Sweden joined in 1995 while Norway, whose economy was tremendously boosted by North Sea oil and gas exports, eventually declined following a nationwide referendum. However, the Norwegians are keen supporters of the recent European Economic Area agreement between the EU and EFTA.

Danish agriculture

Denmark is the only Scandinavian country where most of the land is cultivated: 70% against less than 10% in each of the other three countries. In spite of this, only 8% of the population is employed in agriculture which is intensive and highly mechanised; farm produce is of high quality, owing to the generalised use of cooperatives. Dairy farming is the main activity, together with the production of pork meat and poultry; Danish butter and Danish bacon are exported all over the world.

Norwegian fishing industry

Fisherman with salmon

O. MARTEL/EXPLORER

Although fishing is important to all Scandinavian countries, which have a long seafaring tradition, Norway quite naturally plays the leading role, since its coastline is 21 000km long and some of the world's richest fishing grounds lie within easy reach! In recent years, **fish farming**, consisting mainly of salmon and trout, has developed along the coast. Well over two million tons of fish are either caught or farmed every year, 90% of which are exported. Moreover the industry is steadily growing with the help of marine research: for instance, **sea ranching**, a combination of fishing and fish farming is under study to ensure regular supplies.

Energy and natural resources

Norway again leads the way in the production of energy. **Hydroelectric power** is vital to the economy of Finland, Sweden and Norway but, whereas Norway produces practically enough hydroelectricity to satisfy its own needs, only 15% of Swedish energy comes from water-power and the percentage is even smaller in Finland.

In addition, Norway has, since the late 60s, been one of the world's major oil-producing countries: the largest **oil fields** lie offshore, west of Bergen and Stavanger. As a result, a thriving petrochemical industry has developed. Denmark, on the other hand, continues to import most of its energy while other types of energy are being experimented with: one of the most successful is **wind-power** which produces electricity by driving modern windmills. Groups of these, known as windmill farms, profile their tall silhouette against the sky of Jylland and south Sjælland. Scandinavia is rich in deposits of various mineral ores which have been extracted since the Middle Ages. Today, the two most important mining centres are **Kiruna** in Swedish Lapland (iron) and **Outokumpu** in west central Finland (copper).

Windmill farm, Denmark

Ch. Bastin-J. Evrard

Forest industry

Finland, Sweden and Norway have an abundance of raw materials from forestry, Finland having the edge on the other two in this case. All three countries produce timber and furniture but also pulp and paper, cellulose and various chemicals; increasing quantities of recycled paper are used in the production process and a large proportion of the end products is exported, as much as 66% of the total output in the case of Finland.

> ### The most forested country in Europe
>
> Over two thirds of Finland is covered by forests: the majority of the trees are conifers (pine and spruce) but deciduous species (birch, oak, maple and ash) grow in the south-west. Tar distillation and exportation were followed by sawmilling in the 1800s. Then in the mid-19C the cellulose and paper industries took over and by the beginning of the 20C forest industry exports amounted to over 85% of Finland's total exports. Although Finland's industrial sector has witnessed a certain diversification, the forestry sector continues to earn more than a third of the country's export income.
> One Finnish family in five owns some forest which means that two thirds of Finnish forests are privately-owned.

Flagships of Scandinavian industry

The leading Scandinavian manufacturers include
ABB (Asea Brown Boveri), Swedish-Swiss power and engineering giant;
Astra, and the recently-merged **Pharmacia & Upjohn**, major Swedish and international pharmaceutical groups;
Bang & Olufsen, Danish hi-fi equipment manufacturer;
Electrolux, the world's largest household appliance manufacturer;
Ericsson, a world leader in telecommunications;
IKEA, the giant furniture and houseware organisation;
Kværner, Europe's largest shipbuilder from Norway;
Nokia, Finland's top manufacturer of telecommunications equipment;
Norske Skogindustrier, Norway's top pulp and paper manufacturer;
Statoil, the world's foremost net exporter of light crude oils outside OPEC;
Tandberg Data, Norwegian manufacturer of high-quality data products;
Tetra-Laval, the world's largest food packaging group based in Lund, Sweden;
UPM-Kymmene, Finland's number one forestry company following a three way merger of Kymmene, Repola and United Paper Mills.

Architecture

The contribution of Scandinavia to world architecture is exceptionally rich and spans eight centuries from the Middle Ages to contemporary times.

All the major European trends were successively represented throughout Scandinavia, but more extensively in Denmark and Sweden. Ribe Cathedral in Denmark, Stavanger Cathedral in Norway and Lund Cathedral in Sweden are fine examples of Romanesque style whereas northern Gothic brick architecture is well illustrated by Roskilde Cathedral in Denmark and Uppsala Cathedral in Sweden; the Dutch Renaissance influence is clearly felt in the imposing Frederiksborg Slot north of Copenhagen or the beautifully proportioned Rosenborg Slot in the Danish capital; as for the flamboyant exuberance of the Baroque style, it was, no doubt, considered most suitable for royal palaces since it was chosen for Christiansborg Palace in Copenhagen and the Royal Palace in Stockholm; on the other hand, the Old Opera House in Stockholm, in pure classical style, offers a marked contrast; the neo-Gothic style, which flourished during the latter part of the 19C, is well represented by the red brick town hall in Copenhagen; however, it was in the 20C that Scandinavian architecture finally played a leading role in the development of international architectural trends.

If one were to single out the most original Scandinavian contributions during the past 800 years, the list would undoubtedly include Danish medieval country churches, the stave churches of Norway (see Wooden Architecture pp 52-55), modern architecture and design.

Danish medieval country churches

Church building flourished in Denmark during the 12C, when hundreds of humble village churches sprang up all over the country; quite a few have been preserved in remarkable condition in south Sjælland, the island of Møn, Jylland and, of course, in Skåne, southern Sweden, which was a Danish province at that time. Their brick-built walls, usually white-washed, make them conspicuous among the green meadows of the Danish countryside and the corbie-stepped gables of their towers form a distinctive outline against the sky. A good many of them are decorated inside with lively frescoes which illustrate the imaginative realism of medieval masters such as the **Elmelunde Master** who decorated several churches in Møn and inspired other artists. The frescoes provide invaluable information on contemporary daily life and on the structure of medieval society, as well as on religious beliefs and taboos.

Where to look for frescoes in Danish medieval churches

Falster-Nørre Aslev: Dance of Death fresco showing members of Danish medieval society;

Hillerød-Skævinge: 16C frescoes depicting biblical scenes and quite surprisingly the national hero, Holger Danske;

Holbæk-Tveje Merløse: wealth of early 13C frescoes showing biblical scenes and soldiers fighting; **Tuse:** 15C frescoes showing scenes from the Bible and everyday life;

Kalundborg-Bregninge: a profusion of frescoes portraying biblical scenes, floral and animal motifs;

Køge-Jungshoved: Dance of Death mural;

Møn-Keldby: outstanding series of frescoes, some by the Elmelunde Master; **Elmelunde:** Last Judgement and Christ in Majesty by the Elmelunde Master; **Fanefjord:** more frescoes by the master;

Ringkøbing fjord-Janderup: 16C frescoes; **Aal:** battle between knights on horseback; **Roskilde fjord-Skibby:** late 12C frescoes including a Christ in Majesty;

Salling-Ejsing: 16C frescoes depicting Adam and Eve and other biblical scenes;

Silkeborg-Grønbæk: early 13C frescoes; **Vinderslev:** interesting set of 13C and late 16C ones;

Sorø-Ørslev: frescoes depicting early medieval village life; **Vester Broby:** variety of frescoes from 12C to 14C; **Fjenneslev:** 12C frescoes;

Sæby: late medieval frescoes;

Sønderborg-Broager: 13C to 16C frescoes showing a Christ in Majesty and scenes from the legend of St George.

Modern Scandinavian architecture

At the turn of the 20C, Finland led the way in making the transition from national romanticism to modern architecture. The architect who made this transition possible and can therefore be considered as the precursor of modern architecture and International Functionalism is **Eliel Saarinen** (1873-1950); he designed the impressive Central Station in Helsinki and later moved to the United States where his work had an impact on modern town planning. His son **Eero** also worked in the States, carrying on in his father's footsteps. At the end of the 1920s, **Alvar Aalto** (1898-1976) became internationally famous as one of the main exponents of Functionalism; he not only worked as an architect, but also as a town planner of cities like Rovaniemi, totally destroyed during the Second World War, which he rebuilt in the shape of a reindeer's antlers.

Meanwhile in Denmark, **Arne Jacobsen** (1902-71) was another Functionalist who made a name for himself by designing the austere concrete-built town hall in Århus in the early 1940s. His Swedish counterpart, **Gunnar Asplund** (1885-1940), was less known internationally.

Among contemporary architects are the Danes **Søren Robert Lund**, who designed Arken, the avant-garde Museum of Modern Art in Ishøj south of Copenhagen, **Jørn Utzon**, designer of the famous Sydney Opera House and **Henning Larsen**, who made a fine job of the Glyptotek's new building in Copenhagen, a perfect " chest " to house the museum's superb collection of French Impressionists; he is also responsible for the new Danish Design Centre across the street from the Glyptotek, which is intended as an international meeting place for designers and innovators. Across the Baltic, the renowned Finnish couple **Reima and Raili Pietilä**, include among their most recent projects the new official residence of the President of Finland. As for the Norwegian architect **Sverre Fehn**, who built the Glacier Museum at the base of the Sognefjord and is currently working on the Royal Theatre in Copenhagen, his aim is not to submit completely to nature but to establish a dialogue between nature and culture and his creations certainly enhance the beauty of his native country's rocky landscapes.

Bregninge Kirke, Denmark

Design

Scandinavian design is renowned all over the world as a symbol of perfect harmony between the functional and the aesthetic. Design has become a universal word which applies to furniture, electronics and various objects of daily life which are both practical and attractive to look at, to the point that they become real works of art. The word industrial, almost always associated with design nowadays, implies that a piece of furniture or an object is factory-produced, which does mean that it is more widely available, without losing any of its aesthetic qualities. Many leading architects, such as Alvar Aalto and Arne Jacobsen, have acquired fame as designers of furniture and furnishings to go with their buildings.

Carrying on a firmly established tradition represented by artists such as **Verner Panton** (d 1998) who, in the 1960s, designed the famous S-shaped Panton chair and a living tower in polyurethane, Danish design has recently enjoyed a come back on the international scene, symbolised by the building in the centre of Copenhagen, close to the very traditional town hall, of a new Danish Design Centre. This new temple of design will stage interactive exhibitions, aimed at encouraging debate, and will deal with research, information and promotion through various activities such as seminars, lectures, audio-visual presentations etc.

Wooden architecture

Long before modern Vikings experimented with glass, steel and concrete in an effort to blend buildings with their natural surroundings, their ancestors remained in total harmony with nature through the extensive use of wood in traditional architecture. Centuries of practical experience enabled craftsmen to acquire a thorough knowledge of the inherent qualities of the material and to develop techniques which made their buildings exceptionally long-lasting. Moreover, the beautiful and intricate carvings and paintings with which they decorated some wooden structures show the confidence these master builders of the past had in their ability to build for posterity with a material they knew intimately and associated with the spiritual elements of their culture. Today, the very existence of **Sylvanum**, a wood museum situated in Gävle north of Stockholm, on the Gulf of Bothnia, which illustrates modern forestry and the by-products of wood, is proof enough that wood is still an essential element of Scandinavian culture.

An obvious choice

The vast forests covering Norway, Finland and Sweden meant that timber was readily available in unlimited quantities and relatively cheap and easy to work; stone, on the other hand, was difficult to extract from the soil which remained frozen for several months of the year; moreover, stone dwellings were more difficult to warm than wooden ones during the long winter months and it was therefore primarily for economic reasons that, in general, the only stone buildings were churches and castles in wealthy communities.

The use of timber became universal throughout Scandinavia (except in Denmark for climatic reasons) well before the Viking period, but the complicated and brilliant techniques which enabled wooden buildings to withstand the test of time were perfected by the Vikings who applied the same innovative spirit to house building as to shipbuilding.

Hopperstad Stavkirke, Norway

Two basic techniques

The diversity of traditional wooden buildings in Scandinavia stems from the use of two very different techniques dating from the 9C. At that time, the roaming Vikings brought back from their eastern travels the art of erecting cog-jointed log cabins: logs, barely stripped of their bark, were stacked on one another without nails or pins and gaps were filled in with mud and moss; the ends of the logs were cogged and joined together; there were no foundations and the roof frame was covered with birch bark held in place by a layer of turf. Log cabins were either square or rectangular and consisted of one room with a hearth in its centre. This simple plan was used with slight variations from Norway right across Scandinavia to Karelia in eastern Finland and there are still many fine examples to be seen. It was used as late as the 19C by emigrants to the New World who proudly built their traditional log cabins in the vast plains of North America.

The technique used to build log cabins is called *laft* in Norwegian, in contrast to another more complex technique called *stav*, which was developed in Scandinavia and reached near perfection during the 12C and 13C with the building of a highly original type of wooden church appropriately known as *stavkirker* or stave churches. The original concept of this technique was to fix rows of vertical logs or planks into a frame of horizontal, grooved beams; the use of a sill thus protected the walls from decay, which explains why buildings erected in this way have been standing for as long as 800 years. Whether the *laft* or *stav* method was used, walls were very often lined externally with vertical or horizontal planks closely assembled and painted in various traditional colours; this served as insulation and protection against driving rain and snow but it also improved the appearance of the buildings and led the way for other refinements such as decorated door and window frames to be introduced.

These basic techniques were used extensively, either separately or together, in traditional architecture, with regional variations, as they could be adapted to suit local climatic conditions and economic requirements.

NORWEGIAN STAVKIRKER

The Norwegian stave churches are the most elaborate wooden buildings ever erected in Scandinavia; the first of them were built during the Viking period, towards the end of the 10C and by the year 1300 there were between 800 and 1 000 of these strange dark structures with pointed steeples and steep gables surmounted with dragon heads. It was as if, when they abandoned their raids across the seas, the Vikings could not resign themselves to giving up the symbol of their might, the fierce-looking dragons, and therefore placed them in a prominent position similar to the one they had occupied at

Hopperstad Stavkirke detail of interior

the prow of their *drakkars*. During the 14C, an epidemic of plague killed a third of the population and, as a result, half the stave churches were left to decay or were destroyed by fire. Later on, a considerable number became too small and were demolished to be replaced by larger churches often built of wood but in a totally different style. The rest decayed slowly through lack of care and by the 19C there were only about 30 of them left in Norway. Public attention was drawn to the eventual disappearance of this unique national heritage by the painter JC Dahl and they were gradually restored.

All of them, dating from the 12C and 13C, are situated in the southern part of Norway and although they vary considerably in size and shape, they are instantly recognisable. This is due to the fact that the same building technique was scrupulously applied in every case and all stave churches have therefore several characteristics in common. Whether they have low lateral aisles or are surrounded by an outer gallery, their stepped roof structure is covered with wood shingles looking like fish scales. The wood tar used to preserve the structures from decay makes them look dark and austere, an impression which is confirmed once one enters through the low doorway, for the original stave churches were designed without windows and daylight only penetrates through a few tiny holes in the walls, high up under the roof. For this reason, there were originally no interior decorations except carvings on the round pillars and capitals; on the other hand, the west doorway was profusely decorated outside with intricate carvings of animals and foliage interwoven to form graceful patterns. Under the Romanesque influence, ground plans evolved into more complex shapes with lateral aisles and semicircular apses but Viking ornamentation remained and the buildings retained their original Christian and pagan appearance. Round arches were introduced to separate the nave from the chancel and, in some cases, windows were set into the walls. At the same time, around the 16C and 17C, frescoes were painted on the walls and the addition of elaborate church furniture tended to offset the original austerity.

The most interesting stave churches include Urnes Stavkirke, the oldest of them all, situated on the Sognefjord; Borgund Stavkirke, not far from Urnes, one of the largest and the most ornate; Heddal Stavkirke, situated in Telemark, the largest and best preserved; Uvdal and Nore Stavkirker, situated in the Numedal Valley, smaller and more intimate but nevertheless decorated with a wealth of interesting and varied ornamentation.

TRADITIONAL RURAL ARCHITECTURE

Over the centuries, the basic *laft* and *stav* techniques were applied to different types of rural buildings, ranging from the simple log cabin to the country manor house, and adapted accordingly. **Farmhouses** have panelled walls and an elegant outside gallery which gives them a comfortable appearance; they are painted in a variety of bright colours : for instance white is the most common colour in southern Norway, but red is popular throughout Scandinavia. On the other hand, **summer farms**, in the mountainous areas of Norway and Sweden, remained very rustic log cabins with turf roofs; called *fäbodar* in Swedish, they can be seen in the Härjedalen area of central Sweden and across the border in Norway, in the region of Røros. Outer farm buildings included granaries which, in Norway, were separate buildings raised on stone or wooden stilts; there are quite a few of these **stabbur** in the Numedal Valley in southern Norway. In Finland, simple log cabins were used as saunas.

In Sweden and western Finland, wealthy landowners traditionally lived in 2-storeyed wooden **manor houses**, large enough to accommodate 30 to 40 people. These overgrown log cabins were laid on stone foundations surmounted a low stone wall.

C. Boisvieux

House in Trondheim open-air museum, Norway

The living room was the only decorated room in the house which was otherwise furnished with extreme simplicity. Those which have been preserved date from the 18C.

Rural churches are not to be disregarded, for, in spite of the fact that they may look insipid compared to stave churches, they possess a certain charm. Such is the case of Olden and Geiranger churches in fjord country, or of the tiny 14C church at Södra Råda in Västergötland in south-west Sweden.

In Sweden where farming settlements were often far removed from the local church, regular church-goers built small houses close by, where they could rest before going back home; whole villages thus sprang up, particularly in the north. They were appropriately called **kyrkstaden** (church villages). Those which remain are situated along the Gulf of Bothnia, between Luleå and Umeå.

Fishermen's cottages are equally typical: traditionally built on the edge of the water, half on rock and half on stilts, and painted in red, they look most picturesque against the austere background of rock and sky. The most charming can be seen in Bohuslän, in south-west Sweden, and in the Lofoten islands off the west coast of Norway.

WOODEN TOWNS

B. Morandi

Røros, Norway

Most of the wooden districts preserved in various Scandinavian towns today date from the 18C, for, even when towns are much older, they have inevitably been destroyed by fire at least once; these old districts can look and feel quite different according to the kind of town and area. The so-called **white towns** of the south coast of Norway are permeated with a cheerful, relaxed, holiday-like atmosphere with elegant little white houses lining the water front. In **Bergen**, on the other hand, the magnificent row of austere wooden warehouses reflected in the water of the old harbour is a truly memorable sight. In **Stavanger**, a busy commercial port, the tastefully restored sailors' and craftsmen's cottages, painted in light colours, quaintly overlook the harbour. **Rauma**, situated on the Gulf of Bothnia, is probably Finland's best preserved wooden town, having not been altered since the last major fire at the end of the 17C; home-made lace curtains enhance the charm of the well-preserved old district. Further north, **Kokkola** offers examples of rich merchant houses as well as more modest craftsmen's houses.

By contrast, mining towns have a more severe appearance; it is obvious to anyone walking through the streets of **Røros** in Norway, that life was hard and totally dependent on the copper works, which even controlled the religious life of the community. Class distinctions were reflected by the size and external appearance of the houses, which ranged from the modest turf-covered log cabin, home to poor factory workers, to the large brightly-painted houses of the mine officials.

Sweden's wooden urban heritage has not been so well preserved. **Göteborg**, on the west coast, has retained the largest number of wooden houses of any town in Sweden.

Literature

International interest in Scandinavian literature and the recognition of its contribution to world culture dates from the 19C. The reasons for this are complex and stem as much from the political and cultural situation in Scandinavia as from the attitude of the rest of the world towards the Nordic countries.

Before the 19C, it was generally considered that Scandinavian culture had been greatly influenced by the main European artistic trends and had drawn its inspiration from Italian, French or German artists and writers but that it had not in return exported any original form of cultural expression. A change occurred in the early 1800s, when the veil on Scandinavian prehistory was partly lifted and it became clear that Scandinavia had been in the vast European melting pot long before it was Christianised in the 11C; the impact of the Vikings on Western civilisation at last began to dawn on historians. It was also around that time that communications became easier and consequently there were numerous accounts from enthusiastic travellers of the beautiful Scandinavian scenery. Then, from about the middle of the 19C, poverty drove millions of Europeans from their homelands across the seas to the New World; among them were one million Norwegians and as many Swedes who took their culture with them and proudly shared it with their fellow Americans.

Children's literature in Sweden

The international renown of Swedish contribution to children's literature is largely due to **Astrid Lindgren** (b 1907) whose *Pippi Långstrump* (Pippi Longstocking), brought to life by the Danish illustrator Ingrid Vang Nyman, became the friend of countless children throughout the world. Until the turn of the century, children's books in Sweden played an essentially didactic role and were largely based on folk tales. **Elsa Beskow**'s output (1874-1953) marked a turning-point in children's literature. Her painting of nature largely contributed to the success of her books abroad. From then on writers were more concerned with the artistic aspect of their work. *The Wonderful Adventures of Nils* by **Selma Lagerlöf**, illustrated by Bertil Lybeck and translated into some thirty languages, is a striking example of this new trend. Another turning-point occurred after the Second World War, when new ideas prevailed in the field of child psychology. At the same time, growing prosperity in Sweden created a considerable increase in demand and children's literature expanded rapidly. This led to a new generation of writers headed by Astrid Lindgren, who depicted the very essence of Swedish society with a great deal of humour through the adventures of Pippi Longstocking, a bundle of energy who was to become the model of liberated children. Combining realism and invention, Astrid Lindgren excels in depicting lonely children in difficult circumstances and in showing how they overcome their difficulties by using their imagination. **Tove Jansson** (b. 1914), a contemporary of Astrid Lindgren, is a Finn who writes in Swedish and illustrates her stories herself. Her fame rests on the many adventures of the Moomin family, written over a period of 25 years and translated into some thirty languages.

A sudden blossoming

However, it was the extraordinary vigour with which Scandinavian literature suddenly blossomed that drew the world's attention. After the upheaval caused by the Napoleonic wars, Denmark and Sweden needed to reassert their national identity, while Norway and Finland were searching for theirs. They did so by turning to their distant past and their common heritage, the **sagas**. It was the custom, in Viking times, for epic tales based on historic events to be recited by *skalds* in front of large audiences during festivities; narrators were usually careful to adapt their tales to please the chieftains who hired them and thus heroic deeds were told time and time again and embellished when necessary. These tales, bordering on legend, were later written down, thus recording for posterity Scandinavia's glorious past.

The themes which run through Scandinavian literature of the 19C and 20C show that writers have drawn their inspiration from these sagas which contained the very essence of the Scandinavian temperament and culture: communion with nature, latent anguish and melancholy, an obsession with solitude from which a kind of strength is derived and a deep love of folklore as the root of Scandinavian identity. Below is a brief account of Scandinavian literature through some of its major writers. It is interesting to note that authors of children's literature were the first to draw international attention to Scandinavian literature, as HC Andersen, Selma Lagerlöf, Astrid Lindgren and Tove Jansson, creator of the Moomins (hippo-like characters), have become household names in their lifetime.

Denmark

The 19C is dominated by three extremely different personalities. **Hans Christian Andersen** (1805-75) was a magical storyteller whose tales reveal a boundless imagination and an incorrigible optimism. The philosopher **Søren Kierkegaard** (1813-55), on the contrary, expressed the anguish of man faced with the responsibility of his own existence. The theologian and teacher, **Nikolaj Grundtvig** (1783-1872), advocated a liberal attitude in religion and in education and was the champion of individual freedom.
Karen Blixen (1885-1962) is probably the most famous 20C Danish writer; several films were made of her novels in particular *Out of Africa*, an autobiographical account of her life on a plantation in Kenya. **Peter Høeg** (born in 1957), author of *Miss Smilla's Feeling for Snow*, a thriller of great depth, is one of the new wave of Danish writers.

H. C. Andersen Hus, Odense

Hans Christian Andersen

Finland

The champions of nationalism in Finland naturally turned to ancient folk tales which symbolised the true soul of their country before it became a Swedish province. In 1835, **Elias Lönnrot** (1802-84) became a national hero when he published his *Kalevala*, a collection of folk tales and legends from all over the country in the form of an epic poem which was to inspire future generations. The main themes of the new Finnish literature were nature and the peasant world and the first novel written in Finnish was the *Seven Brothers* by **Aleksis Kivi** (1834-72). This same theme was taken up later by **Frans Emil Sillanpää** (1888-1964) who is the only Finn to have been awarded the Nobel prize. Modern Finnish writers have turned to more universal preoccupations: **Väinö Linna** (born in 1920) depicts in his *Unknown Soldier* the impact of war on the ordinary soldier while **Arto Paasilinna** (born 1942), in *The Year of the Hare*, rejects man's artificial world with a stinging sense of humour.

Norway

Eminent representatives of 19C and early 20C Norwegian literature are led by the dramatists **Henrik Ibsen** (1828-1906), **Bjørnstjerne Bjørnson** (1832-1910) and by the novelist **Knut Hamsun** (1859-1952); their works are pervaded with anguish, doubt and even despair for they do not believe in man's ability to live in harmony with the world. **Sigrid Undset** (1882-1949) won international fame through a historical trilogy set in medieval Norway. **Tarjei Vesaas** (1897-1970) is considered one of the leading 20C Norwegian writers; a sombre vein runs through his novels in which man's solitude is depicted both as his weakness and his strength.

Sami literature

The Sami homeland covers territory in three of the four Scandinavian countries and during colonization of their territory their culture was oppressed and their language repressed and nearly eliminated. Today the Sami language – an important carrier of culture – and unique Sami music *joik* are experiencing a renaissance, together with Sami visual arts and handicrafts. The oral tradition has always been strong among the Sami and storytellers passed on legends and folktales from generation to generation.
In the mid-1800s a Sami minister, Anders Fjellner, recorded a folk epic, about the origin of the Sami people, entitled the *Daughters of the Sun* and the *Sons of the Sun*. These are now considered genuine examples of Sami poetry.
The first book in Sami was written by a reindeer herder, Johan Turi, and published in 1910. *Turi's Book of Lappland (Muittalus Sámiid birra)* recounts life among the Sami and contains much traditional material about Sami folklore, customs and folk medicine but also takes a clear stand on the colonization of Sami territory. Two years later the first novel in the Sami language was published; Anders Larsen entitled his work *Day Break (Beavi– álgo)* and in it he portrays a Sami youth's development from childhood to adult awareness.
The 1970s saw a blossoming of Sami authors, many of whom considered it their duty to create an ethnic awareness to resist external threats to their cultural identity.

Sweden

The dramatist **August Strindberg** (1849-1912) stands out as the leading Swedish writer. His work, influenced by Ibsen, denotes an obsessive search into the psychology of his characters which made him a forerunner of Surrealism with, for instance, *A Dream Play* published in 1901. **Selma Lagerlöf** (1858-1940), on the contrary, became famous with a fairy tale, the *Wonderful Adventures of Nils*, in which she describes the wonders of her native land. In the 20C, **Stig Dagerman** (1923-54) wrote novels of harsh realism before he committed suicide at the age of 31, whereas the contemporary novelist **Per Olov Enquist** (born in 1934) depicts with extreme lucidity the eternal conflict between the individual and the society in which he lives.

Scandinavian Nobel Laureates for Literature

1903 **Bjørnstjerne Bjørnson** (Norway)
1909 **Selma Lagerlöf** (Sweden)
1916 **Verner von Heidenstam** (Sweden)
1920 **Knut Hamsun** (Norway)
1928 **Sigrid Undset** (Norway)
1931 **Erik Axel Karlfeldt** (Sweden)
1939 **Frans Emil Sillanpää** (Finland)
1951 **Pär Lagerkvist** (Sweden)
1974 **Eyvind Johnson** and **Harry Martinson** (both Sweden)

Painting and sculpture

The situation of Scandinavia on the periphery of Europe greatly influenced the development of Scandinavian art since, for a long time, the Nordic countries had little impact on the main trends of European Art which they were content to follow. During the Middle Ages, foreign artists, mainly Dutch and German, were called upon to decorate Romanesque and Gothic churches and were often imitated by local artists. This was the case of **Bernt Notke** and **Claus Berg** who, in the 15C and early 16C, established a German style of religious sculpture and inspired many Scandinavian disciples.

The practice of importing foreign artists continued through to the 17C which marked the arrival of the Renaissance style in Scandinavia, a century later than in the rest of Europe. Many foreign painters and sculptors, as well as architects, were invited to Denmark and Sweden by the enlightened Danish monarch Christian IV and by the cultured Swedish king Gustavus-Adolphus and his daughter Christina; these patrons of the arts drew on the rich supply of European artists to embellish their palaces and furnish their art galleries.

It was only during the 18C that **national schools of art** began to emerge in Denmark and Sweden; in Denmark, the foundation of the **Royal Academy of Arts** meant that Danish artists could be trained in their own country before going on a tour of Europe; in Sweden, the first truly original artistic style, known as the **Gustavian style**, was best represented by the sculptor **Johan Tobias Sergel** (1740-1814), who carved Gustav III's statue in Stockholm. Then, the national romantic aspirations of the 19C brought on an unprecedented flourishing of Scandinavian art.

The Danish golden age

After the disastrous political consequences of Danish involvement in the Napoleonic wars, the Danes turned their creative energy to art and the 19C became known as Denmark's artistic golden age. **Bertel Thorvaldsen** (1770-1844), who is generally considered as the greatest Danish sculptor, dominated the first half of the century. He spent many years in Rome where he acquired international fame as a brilliant exponent of neo-classicism; he returned to his native country as a hero and left his entire artistic output to the city of Copenhagen where a museum was built in his honour. His contemporary, the painter **Christoffer W Eckersberg** (1783-1853), is essentially known as the father of Danish painting for the influence he had on later generations of painters during the 35 years he taught at the Royal Academy of Arts.

From 1850 onwards, Danish artists turned to realism and nature as a source of inspiration. The **'Skagen painters'**, so-called because they settled in a fishing village in north Jylland, focused their attention on light and depicted scenes of daily life as it unfolded around them. Their example was followed by others such as the **'Fyn painters'** headed by **Johannes Larsen** (1867-1961) or **Peter Hansen** (1868-1928). **JF Willumsen** (1863-1958), acknowledged as one of the greatest Scandinavian painters and a representative of Symbolism and Expressionism, belonged to the Pont-Aven group of painters who worked with Paul Gauguin in Brittany at the end of the 19C.

Famous names of Scandinavian painting

The Norwegian artist **Edvard Munch** (1863-1944), who was a pioneer of Expressionism, was undoubtedly the greatest Scandinavian painter *(see OSLO)* of all time. In Finland, **Akseli Gallen-Kallela** (1865-1931) marked the emergence of a Finnish national style, while **Tyko Sallinen** (1879-1955) led the school of Finnish Expressionism.

In Denmark, the name of **Asger Jorn** (1914-73), founder of the international CoBrA group of painters, stands out together with that of the sculptor and painter **Per Kirkeby** (born in 1938), whose aim is to transpose his own experience onto canvas. In Sweden, **Carl Larsson** (1853-1919) became extremely popular with his detailed rendering of scenes of daily life and his illustrations for children's books whereas **Anders Zorn** (1860-1920), often considered as the greatest Swedish painter of modern times, was a late Impressionist who

Edvard Munch, Self-portrait in Copenhagen, 1909

painted landscapes of his native Dalarna and recorded on canvas the peasant culture he loved. One of his recently rediscovered contemporaries, **Eugene Jansson** (1862-1915), whose favourite subject was Stockholm, never hit the limelight outside Sweden during his lifetime.

Scandinavian sculpture

The leading figure is the Norwegian **Gustav Vigeland** (1869-1943), who was the best exponent of a typically Scandinavian style of monumental sculpture with which he decorated the Frogner Park in Oslo. Sweden too had a famous sculptor, **Carl Milles** (1875-1955), whose monumental works can be seen not only in Millesgården in Stockholm but also in the USA where he spent the latter part of his life creating impressive fountains. In Finland, two artists stand above a wealth of fine sculptors: **Wäinö Aaltonen** (1894-1966) carved quite a few of his works in granite and, beside many fine statues, including those of Paavo Nurmi and Aleksis Kivi in Helsinki, he also produced monumental compositions in true Scandinavian tradition; more recently, **Eila Hiltunen** (born in 1922) gained public recognition with her Sibelius monument in Helsinki. Among several fine Danish sculptors one could certainly single out **Kai Nielsen** (1882-1924), who perfected a truly personal monumental style and **Robert Jacobsen** (1912-93), who worked essentially with metal in an abstract style all of his own.

Music

NORWAY AND FINLAND: THE FOLK INFLUENCE

Two composers share the privilege of embodying the very soul of Scandinavia, the Norwegian **Edvard Grieg** (1843-1907) and the Finn **Jean Sibelius** (1865-1957).
Born at a time of great political upheaval and uncertainty, they took up their country's quest for national identity with all the power of their artistic genius, both receiving an annual grant from their respective countries to pursue their task without the restraint imposed by financial preoccupations.
Both men studied in Germany and were influenced by the powerful German Romantic movement which proved a considerable driving force at the onset of their artistic life. Although their personalities were totally different and their styles truly original, they both drew their inspiration from two typically Scandinavian sources: nature and Nordic folk music. They described the serene and sometimes overwhelming beauty of Norwegian and Finnish nature with a great deal of lyricism and their imagination was

stirred by ancient Scandinavian myths and sagas. But they were also fully immersed in the artistic trends of their time, never setting themselves aside from the mainstreams of European music; on the contrary, they were able to express their deeply emotional concern about national recognition through the musical language of their day.

Grieg lifted Norwegian music onto the European cultural scene and Sibelius was the founder of Finnish music, opening the way for others at a time when Finland was searching for its own unique form of artistic expression.

Grieg and Sibelius both won international recognition from their peers as well as public acclaim during their lifetime. Grieg's most famous works are his piano concerto in A minor, his *Norwegian Dances* and his *Peer Gynt Suites*, incidental music written for Ibsen's play. Sibelius composed no fewer than seven symphonies, a violin concerto in D minor and several tone poems, including the world famous *Finlandia* which has given its name to Helsinki's concert hall.

Edvard Grieg

SWEDEN: A LONG-STANDING MUSICAL TRADITION

Official interest in classical music dates back to the year 1526 when King Gustav Vasa decided to encourage that form of cultural enlightenment in his country by founding the Royal Orchestra which still exists today as the Orchestra of the Royal Opera House in Stockholm. From then on, musicians were systematically imported, mainly from Italy and Germany, in order to stimulate musical life in Sweden. These foreign musicians brought with them continental musical styles and ideas which were readily absorbed and adopted but there was no great genius like Grieg or Sibelius to give Swedish music an identity of its own. However there were world famous performers such as the opera singers **Kristina Nilsson** and **Jenny Lind** who made their career outside Sweden and became legends in their lifetime.

Swedish pop music

The Swedish pop group **ABBA** – **A**gnetha, **B**jörn, **B**enny and **A**nnifrid (Frida) – became a household name when they won the Eurovision Song Contest with *Waterloo* and then went on to top the charts in the 1970s and 1980s with such favourites as *Mamma Mia, Fernando, Knowing Me Knowing You, Voulez Vous and Super Trouper*. They were the most successful pop group to hit Europe since the Beatles and several groups followed in their footsteps attracting the world's attention to pop music " made in Sweden ". Among them, there was the hard rock group **Europe** who reached the top of the hit parades in 1986 with *The Final Countdown*. Next came **Roxette**, formed in 1986 whose members Per Gessle and Marie Fredriksson are still going strong today. The up-and-coming generation includes **Dr Alban** (hip hop), **Erik Gadd** (soul) and groups such as **Ace of Base** and **The Cardigans**. To the point that pop music has become one of Sweden's thriving export businesses as, since the early 1990s, the music business has expanded its export earnings more than twice as fast as the rest of the Swedish economy. However, one must bear in mind that this trend reflects a worldwide increase of around 10% per annum. The Swedes themselves reckon that one of the main factors of this success is the presence of music schools in almost every municipality as many of the current stars had their first musical training from these schools. Another important aspect of Swedish pop music is that it is written and played in English, which makes it readily available on the world's most important markets.

DENMARK: CARL NIELSEN (1865-1931)

The Danish composer Carl Nielsen was, like his contemporaries Grieg and Sibelius, steeped in German Romanticism at the beginning of his career. As a performer (he was a violinist and a conductor), and as a teacher (he was a distinguished director of the Copenhagen Music Conservatory) he played a leading role in the musical life of his country and gained international recognition with his new concept of tonality and his clear, highly personal style. The most famous works of this prolific composer include operas such as *Saül and David*, and *Mascarade*, six symphonies, three concertos and a variety of chamber music.

The cultural scene

In spite of its relative geographical and linguistic isolation, Scandinavia is very much present on the international cultural scene, having repeatedly shown its innovative powers in various aspects of contemporary culture such as modern dance and theatre, music and the cinema, with, of course, the inevitable controversy. As a result, many Scandinavians have come into the limelight and acquired international fame; such as the Swedish film director Ingmar Bergman, his younger Finnish counterpart, Aki Kaurismäki and the young Finnish conductor Esa-Pekka Salonen.

Festivals

Popular everywhere, festivals nevertheless are undoubtedly a Finnish speciality. Most of them take place in summer during the long hours of daylight which encourage a festive mood. One of them stands far above the rest as an international event of great quality: the **Savonlinna International Opera Festival** which takes place in July; beside the great international operatic repertoire, the festival stages the recent works of Finnish composers, Aulis Sallinen and Joonas Kokkonen (1921-96).

Other major festivals in Finland include the **Naantali Music Festival** in June, the **Sodankylä Cinema Festival** also in June, founded in Lapland by the Kaurismäki brothers, the **Tampere Theatre Festival** and the **Helsinki multi-cultural Festival** in August.

Denmark is the land of Jazz and Rock with the **Roskilde Rock Festival** in June and the **Copenhagen Jazz Festival** in July, the annual climax of the Danish capital's extremely active jazz life. The major event in Norway is the **Bergen International Festival** which offers a varied programme of classical music as well as theatre and ballet performances during the first two weeks of June. In Sweden, on the other hand, folk dancing and music is a national hobby and fans and players meet with great enthusiasm at the annual **Lake Siljan Festival** in July.

The theatre is inevitably a less attractive cultural medium for non-Scandinavians because of the language barrier. However, it is interesting to note that the Swedes are great theatre-goers and that there are more theatres in Stockholm than in any other European capital. Performances are of high quality and tickets are relatively cheap.

Music, opera and ballet

In the field of **classical music**, although all the major Scandinavian cities have fine orchestras and concert venues, Finland has undoubtedly made spectacular efforts to achieve world recognition and many performers are now well known in their field and are the regular guests of such prestigious houses as the New York Metropolitan or Covent Garden in London. The recent opening of the new opera house in Helsinki is a sure sign of the confidence the Finns place in their rising stars; among these, the young soprano **Karita Mattila** is well on her way to a fine international career, while the conductor **Esa-Pekka Salonen** has already exported his talent to the United States.

Bergman, Liv Ullman and Bibi Andersson in *Bergman on Bergman*

If opera has been a long-standing tradition in Sweden, the closely related **Music Theatre** has had growing success in recent years; the genre is a mixture of theatre and cabaret in which music is visually incorporated into the performance and musicians play, sing and act on stage; based just outside Stockholm, **Oktober** is one of the most successful music theatre groups, which are constantly growing in number.

Copenhagen has been the **jazz capital** of Scandinavia for the past 30 years, a title which it is keen to retain as the recent opening of the new **Jazz house** clearly shows; it will add another dimension to an already rich jazz life in which, up to now, a score of excellent **jazz clubs** played the leading role.

The **Royal Danish Ballet**, housed in the Royal Theatre in Copenhagen, is one of the finest companies in the world and Danish choreographers have influenced the development of modern ballet for many years. Among the younger generation are **Kim Brandstrup**, who works in London and has his own company and **Peter Martins**, the current director of the New York City Ballet. However, the most prominent choreographer at the moment is undoubtedly the Swede **Mats Ex** whose totally free creations and iconoclastic interpretations of the great classical ballets are unanimously acclaimed.

Ingmar Bergman – Figurehead of the Seventh Art

Bergman the film maker is world famous for his trademark of anguished appraisal of the human situation; but he is also a theatre, television and opera director. His films portray his personal vision of marriage, or as he described it " hell together ", in *Smiles of a Summer Night* (1955) and *Summer with Monika* (1953); the worlds of good and evil in the trilogy of films, *Through a Glass Darkly* (1961), *Winter Light* (1962) and *The Silence* (1963) as well as the *Seventh Seal* (1956); the artist and his world in *The Naked Light* (1953), *Persona* (1966) and *Fanny and Alexander* (1982). His classics include:

1953 The Naked Light	1963 *The Silence*
1957 The Seventh Seal	1966 *Persona*
1957 Wild Strawberries	1982 *Fanny and Alexander*

The photograph above shows Bergman, Liv Ullman and Bibi Andersson in Björkman's documentary *Bergman on Bergman*.

Cinema

In the past, Scandinavian cinema has had international successes with such master-pieces as the Danish film *Babette's Feast*, based on Karen Blixen's novel, and the *Unknown Soldier*, based on the novel by Finnish author Väinö Linna. Several Scandinavian actors and actresses have also acquired international fame and some even rank among the greatest: the legendary **Greta Garbo** and **Ingrid Bergman** are certainly among them; more recently, the Swedish **Max von Sydow** and **Liv Ullman**, Ingmar Bergman's wife, have made brilliant international careers. The situation today shows a firmly established Swedish cinema under the steady and masterful influence of **Ingmar Bergman** with such films as *Persona* and *Fanny and Alexander*, and a revival of the Finnish cinema under the eccentric artistic impulse of **Aki Kaurismäki**. Following a series of highly original films reflecting his personal pessimism and disillusion with his own country (*Ariel*, 1988), he went abroad to catch his breath. He made his comeback with *Drifting Clouds*, 1997.

Scandinavian society

To the outside world, Scandinavian society appears stable, highly organised and, on the whole, confident in its pursuit of success and happiness; the Scandinavian example is often quoted as a model of civilised living and its well-oiled mechanisms are observed with interest by some and with curiosity or scepticism by others.

WHO ARE TODAY'S SCANDINAVIANS?

Owing to its geographical position off the beaten track of Europe, Scandinavia has been able to retain almost intact the homogeneity of its population. The Scandinavian peninsula did not find itself on the path of the great invasions which repeatedly swept across Europe after the fall of the Roman Empire and transformed it into a melting-pot in which numerous tribes from the east mixed with the indigenous inhabitants of Western Europe and with earlier invaders; instead, Scandinavia's population remained virtually unaltered and still does to a great extent, **three major ethnic groups** having cohabited more or less peacefully since the beginning of the Christian era. The great majority of the inhabitants of Denmark, Norway and Sweden are descendants of the **Vikings,** a powerful people who shaped the destiny of Scandinavia and to some extent of western Europe from AD 800 to 1050. Quite distinct from the modern Vikings, the **Sami,** a nomadic people of east European origin, live in the northern part of the Scandinavian peninsula known as Lapland. Having kept quite apart from the rest of society for centuries, many of them have now adopted the Scandinavian lifestyle while showing a real determination to retain their language and traditions. The **Finns** are the third ethnic group to have shared 2 000 years of history with the other two after having migrated from central Russia.

In spite of marked regional differences, the Danish, Norwegian and Swedish languages, of north Germanic origin, are closely related, a fact which has contributed to maintain a special bond between the three nations. The Finnish language is a Finno-Ugric language, totally unrelated to Danish, Norwegian or Swedish but vaguely related to the Sami language, which has several dialects, and to Estonian.

Until recently, immigration was virtually non-existent in Scandinavia; it is still minimal and concerns mainly people from other Scandinavian countries although refugees from the Third World have been admitted in small numbers. The presence of these immigrants is slowly making an impact on the Scandinavian way of life.

THE SCANDINAVIAN TEMPERAMENT

An attempt to depict the portrait of a nation, let alone four distinct even if closely related nations, must be regarded as purely subjective if it is not to arouse controversy. The complexity of the Scandinavian temperament stems from obvious contradictions and a variable blend of certain broad characteristics which account for similarities between the four countries as well as for notable differences.

One trait all Scandinavians have in common is their national pride which is deeply rooted in their mentality through education and traditions; it is based on their ancestral love of their land coupled with a rock-solid confidence in the political and social stability of their country and boundless optimism, best revealed perhaps by the demonstrative Danish character. However, this pride is tempered with an ability to avoid the temptation of taking oneself too seriously; this is expressed with total frankness and a Nordic sense of humour, devoid of cynicism. At the same time Scandinavians are keen individualists, brought up not only to be self-sufficient and independent but to respect the right of others to be independent and act as they please so long as it does not go against the general interest, for their highly developed civic sense quite naturally curbs their individual aspirations for total freedom; this is particularly evident in their extremely positive attitude when it comes to safeguarding the environment.

Emigration

During the second half of the 19C, at the beginning of the industrial revolution, one million Norwegians and one million Swedes, essentially poor farmers in search of a better life for themselves and their families, left their country bound for North America. A smaller number of Danes also emigrated to the New World. This exodus culminated during the 1880s when there were daily departures of ships loaded with emigrants from ports such as Göteborg in Sweden. Most of them found in their new country the prosperity they had dreamt of and sent financial help to the members of their families whom they had left behind; a few emigrants came back to their native country. The **House of Emigrants** was set up in Växjö (southern Sweden) in memory of these pioneers; it is the most complete source of information about emigration available in Europe. Another place, known as **Lincoln's Cabin,** founded by Danish Americans in memory of their ancestors, can be visited in Rold Skov forest in central Jylland (Denmark).

Another characteristic common to all Scandinavians is their legendary efficiency: their organising ability is well known and they are conscientious and thorough in their work. Ambition drives them to excel in their endeavours but it is kept in check by their shrewd sense of pragmatism and passion for equality.

One trait of character which is often a subject of controversy is the Scandinavians' alleged shyness, lack of warmth, indifference, or formalism depending on how one interprets a certain reserve on first acquaintance particularly from the Norwegians and the Swedes, the Finns and above all the Danes being generally more spontaneous and expansive. In any case this restraint is largely compensated by the Scandinavians' faultless sense of hospitality.

THE SCANDINAVIAN WAY OF LIFE

Their passion for equality has been the driving force of the Scandinavian people during the past 50 years: they have built for themselves a kind of classless society, where living standards are high, with relatively little difference between high and low salaries, a high level of taxes and one of the most comprehensive welfare systems in western Europe. But what is amazing is that all this was achieved gradually and peacefully by a kind of consensus.

The modern Vikings have long lost their fighting instincts and nothing makes them happier than spending the weekend in a lonely log cabin, on the edge of a lake, in the mountains or by the fjords, depending on whether they are Swedes, Finns or Norwegians; as for the Danes they have a choice of delightful old cottages in the rolling countryside or among the dunes of west Jylland.

This 'return to nature' is a family affair, for a deep love of nature is common to Scandinavians of all ages and city dwellers are happy to go to the country as soon as they have some free time. Housing is of a high standard with plenty of space, ultramodern comfort and beautifully designed furniture.

Most couples don't have more than two children who, until they are of school age, are looked after in day-care centres while their parents are at work; there, they learn to become independent from a very early age.

An overwhelming majority of women are in full-time employment while bringing up their children, but parental leave has been considerably extended and made more flexible following the demands of the women's movement in the late 1960s and early 1970s.

If it is true to say that Scandinavians are conscientious workers, one must add that they have learned to enjoy their leisure time, essentially at weekends, when they entertain at home, are entertained by their families and friends or pursue outdoor activities such as fishing, cycling or sailing; moreover, the growing tendency is to want more free time and a debate on the question is already engaged.

The Sauna

The habit of taking a sauna regularly with family or friends is deeply rooted in the Scandinavian way of life, particularly in Finland. It is the custom to take a weekly sauna, preferably at weekends when its relaxing effect is most welcome, but this is not always possible for town-dwellers who have to wait for their turn to use the communal sauna. Private houses in town and country all have their own sauna; when a summer house is near a lake, the sauna usually stands close to the edge of the water so that one can plunge into the cold water on coming out

of the dry heated room. Another custom is to roll oneself in the snow in winter or to plunge into the icy water of the frozen lake.

It is an honour to be invited by Scandinavians to share their sauna and to refuse is considered impolite. A substantial meal accompanied by steaming hot coffee usually follows.

N. Martin/VLOO

Relaxing in a sauna

TRADITIONS AND FOLKLORE

Sparsely populated and still deeply rural at heart, Scandinavia has kept alive many of its old traditions which bind people together and strengthen national identity.

Festive celebrations

They are held all over Scandinavia and their origins go back to ancient pagan or Christian or simply rural traditions but they are always nurtured by the Scandinavians' unfailing love of their country. The seasons which offer a marked contrast take on a particular meaning in Nordic countries and, quite naturally the summer solstice on 21 June is celebrated by popular rejoicing in the heart of the beautiful Scandinavian countryside. **Midsummer** is a time for wearing the colourful traditional dress, eating, drinking and dancing under maypoles, covered in wild flowers, to the sounds of folk music. This celebration stems from an ancient pagan tradition and even today some of the old beliefs still impress some Scandinavians. A profusion of colourful decorations with a predominance of reds and greens brightens the **Christmas season** when most of the land is covered with snow; fish, pork and fruit cakes are on the Christmas menu and, of course presents are distributed... by the Christmas gnome! Christmas celebrations, known as Yule, have remained more traditional in the country than in towns; for instance, a special Yuletime beer is brewed on farms all over Norway and people lift their glass on Christmas night with the famous *skål*, as their Viking forefathers did 1 000 years ago. **National day** celebrations are also significant in Scandinavia, especially in Norway where the 17 May marks a turning point in Norwegian history (Independence and Constitution day) and is therefore celebrated with a good deal of national fervour; it is also a kind of spring festival in which children play the leading role.

Folklore and folk art

Steeped in folklore, Scandinavian country culture has produced a varied and colourful range of folk art going back several centuries and still thriving today.

Tales of the supernatural, passed on from generation to generation in a great number of folk tales, stirred the imagination of the Scandinavian people who even today speak with affection of legendary characters such as the **trolls**, strange inhabitants of the mountains, extremely ugly and old, with huge noses, who can only be seen at night and have the power to change their appearance in order to deceive humans; it is wise not to provoke their anger which can be terrible. Totally different are the **vettar**, mischievous little beings who live underground or inside mountains. **Gnomes** on the other hand are friendly beings who look after the farm and fight other gnomes.

Arts and crafts also have deep roots in Scandinavian folklore. **Folk art** flourished in many different forms including wood carving and painting. During the 18C and 19C, peasants in Sweden and Norway decorated the interiors of their houses and storehouses by painting pictures on the walls and on the furniture as well as on utensils used in daily life. They mostly opted for vine and flower designs but sometimes attempted to depict landscapes and religious scenes. This kind of painting was most popular in the Dalarna region of Sweden where it is referred to as **Dalarna kurbits** and in the Telemark region of Norway where it is known as **rose painting**. There are many examples of fine wood-carving created by modest farmers in their spare time; however, the small **wooden horses from Dalarna** are undoubtedly the most famous form of folk art today; they were first carved by 18C lumberjacks during the long periods they spent in the forest, away from home; on their return they made presents of them to their children and over the years they became very popular. From the 19C onwards, these familiar figures were decorated with flower patterns similar to those used on the walls and furniture and the tradition still continues today.

SPORT

A logical consequence of the Scandinavians' love of nature is their addiction to sport. It is fair to say that all the ingredients are there: plenty of space often just outside people's front doors, water for sailing, water-skiing, canoeing and rafting, an abundance of fish for all types of fishing, more than enough snow and ice for winter sports to be practised all year round and vast expanses of flat countryside (except in Norway) for cycling which is more of a way of life than a sport in Nordic countries!

Sport is everybody's business in Scandinavia as the thousands, who take part in cross-country skiing races such as the Vasaloppet in Sweden, the Birkebeiner in Norway or the Finlandia in southern Finland, show quite clearly; it is not surprising then that Scandinavia fares well on the international scene with Olympic and world champions in cross-country skiing, ski jumping and long-distance running; it is, after all to be expected! What is more surprising, however, is that Scandinavia made its most famous contribution to international sport with Swedish tennis and Finnish rally driving; names like Borg, Wilander or Edberg have inspired budding tennis champions all over the world and the toughness of rally drivers Ari Vatanen, Juha Kankkunen and Hannu Mikkola has won the admiration of thousands.

FAMOUS SCANDINAVIANS

Famous Scandinavians connected with the arts are mentioned in the appropriate chapters and the explorers are mentioned on p 34.

Kings

A handful stand out as having considerably influenced the development of their country. **Olav Haraldsson** of Norway was a descendant of Harald Fairhair who had unified the country at the end of the 9C. The authority of the king continued to be challenged by local chieftains supported by the Danes and, in 1015, Olav set out to take full control of his kingdom and Christianise the country once and for all, if need be by force. His mission came to a victorious end at the battle of Stiklestad in 1030. The king lost the battle and his life but he was soon declared a saint and became Norway's national hero. Sweden became a great European power under the Vasa dynasty named after **Gustav Vasa**, who drove the Danes out of Sweden in 1523, thus ending the Kalmar Union. The Vasas ruled until the abdication in 1654 of the popular **Queen Christina** whose father **Gustavus II Adolphus** (1611-32) had stimulated the Swedish economy and expanded Swedish territories in the Baltic. **Christian IV** of Denmark and Norway (1588-1648) was rightly known as the architect king for, although he boosted trade and brought prosperity to his country, he spent most of his long reign building towns and beautiful monuments and collecting works of art. Several towns were named after him including Christianshavn (now a district of Copenhagen), Kristiansand in southern Norway and even the Norwegian capital which he entirely rebuilt in 1624 calling it Christiana, a name it retained until 1925.

Politicians and diplomats

Once the kings had lost most of their powers, the rôle of politicians became prominent. Several names come to the forefront in the 20C: Finland's outstanding figures are Mannerheim and Kekkonen, two post-war presidents with very different backgrounds. **President Marshal Mannerheim** (1867-1951) was a brilliant soldier, trained in the Russian army, who commanded Finnish forces during the Second World War, whereas **Urho Kaleva Kekkonen** (1900-86) came from a modest family of eastern Finland and studied law before becoming a politician. But both men strove to convince the world of their country's wish for neutrality and, as a result, the Conference on Security and Cooperation in Europe was signed in Helsinki in 1975. Several Swedish personalities devoted their life to peace and humanitarian causes: among them, **Count Folke Bernadotte**, a nephew of the king, obtained the release of countless prisoners from the Nazi concentration camps, and **Raoul Wallenberg** saved the lives of thousands of Hungarian Jews but sadly disappeared without a trace after the war. During the cold war years, **Dag Hammarskjöld** became Secretary General of the United Nations, founded the UN peacekeeping force and was ironically killed in an air crash while on a peace mission in the Congo in 1961. In more recent years, **Olof Palme**, several times prime minister, was strongly opposed to American policy in Vietnam and campaigned incessantly in favour of world disarmament. In 1986, he was shot in the street as he came out of a cinema. The Norwegian polar explorer **Fridtjof Nansen** was also a dedicated peacemaker *(see p 34)*.

Scientists and inventors

The Danish astronomer **Tycho Brahe** (1546-1601) spent his life studying the movements of the planets, first in Copenhagen and later in Prague where he died. Another Dane, the physicist **Niels Bohr** (1885-1962) took part in early atomic research and won the Nobel prize in 1922. In 1943 he fled to America and worked on the atomic bomb project although he was unhappy about the political implications. The Norwegian physician

GH Armauer Hansen isolated the leprosy bacillus in 1874, thus contributing greatly to the eradication of the disease. As for **Alfred Nobel**, the Swedish inventor, he is certainly better known nowadays for the prizes he set up in the fields of science, literature and peace than for his invention of dynamite *(see p 68)*.

Sportsmen and women

Scandinavians, as everyone knows, love the great outdoors and are generally very keen on sport; the choice is wide but winter sports are extremely popular for obvious climatic reasons. Skiing is naturally the king of sports in Scandinavia and an exhaustive list of Scandinavian champions would be too long; one of them, however, has become a legend, the Norwegian **Sondre Norheim** who, in the 1870s, designed the prototype of modern skis known as the Telemark ski. Today, **Bjørn Dæhli**, cross-country skiing Olympic champion, and **Lasse Kjus**, Alpine skiing champion, are household names in their own country. Another Norwegian, the ice skater **Sonja Henie** (1912-69), is remembered not only for the ten world championships and three Olympic gold medals she won but also for the centre for modern art which she and her husband founded just outside Oslo. Finland is particularly proud of its long-distance runner, **Paavo Nurmi** (1897-1973) whose brilliant career was marked by nine gold and three silver Olympic medals as well as numerous world records. However, in recent years, the focus of attention has been switched from athletics to formula-1 driving and the world champion **Mika Häkkinen**. Sweden's name on the other hand has, over the past 30 years, been closely associated with tennis, since **Björn Borg** won the coveted Wimbledon championship five times in a row and dominated world tennis for almost ten years. He was followed by other Swedish tennis champions including **Mats Wilander** and **Stefan Edberg**.

Finns in the limelight

Worldwide famous Finns can be found in all walks of life.
Jorma Ollila, took charge of Nokia, the telecommunications giant, in 1992, at the age of 41 and in seven years he steered his company towards unprecedented success.
Another hi-tech star is **Linus Torvalds**, the creator of Linus, a computer operating system spread over the internet and therefore rapidly updated, which makes it a great rival of Microsoft Windows.
Jimi Tenor lives in a totally different world. This eccentric pop star, who wears distinctive black-rimmed glasses and lives in the States, has tried his hand at photography, film-making and, lately, clothes designing.
Esa-Pekka Salonen rose to stardom incredibly fast to become Musical Director of the Los Angeles Philharmonic Orchestra at the age of 34. Today, he is one of the most sought-after conductors in the world.
The Formula-one world champion in 1998 and 1999, **Mika Häkkinen**, who is the current star of the McLaren-Mercedes racing team, is one of the most popular sportsmen in the world.

Politics

PARLIAMENTARY DEMOCRACIES

The four Scandinavian countries are all Western-style democracies with a definite Nordic flavour. Three of them, Denmark, Norway and Sweden, are hereditary **constitutional monarchies**: the king or queen has no independent political power but symbolises the spirit of the nation and is highly respected and loved. The real executive power is vested in the government which consists of the prime minister and his cabinet, chosen among the majority (although minority governments function quite efficiently in Sweden), and fully responsible to a single-chamber parliament elected by all citizens over the age of 18. Ombudsmen (the word is Scandinavian) play an active role in safeguarding the rights of the individual against abuse of power by administrative authorities. Beside the central government, there is an extensive system of local government with local councils responsible for schooling, housing, cultural and leisure activities etc. Finland is a **republic** with a single-chamber parliament with full legislative powers. The president, who holds extensive executive powers, is elected for six years. He governs with the help of the cabinet headed by the prime minister and, in practice, he takes decisions in agreement with his ministers. Here, as in the rest of Scandinavia, local government is of prime importance, each *lääni* (province) being administered by a governor.

INTERNATIONAL RELATIONS

Denmark, Norway, Sweden and Finland form a close association which fully justifies the name of Scandinavian or Nordic countries; in spite of major differences in defence policies, Denmark and Norway being active members of NATO while Finland and Sweden remain neutral, the four countries have established close links and cooperation programmes through organisations such as the Nordic Council, which reflect a similar political philosophy: cooperation between the four countries is based on total freedom of opinion, mutual respect and trust as well as a great sense of fairness in international negotiations. Their unfailing commitment to world peace is a long-standing tradition, symbolised by the annual peace prize founded by Alfred Nobel, and concretely supported by hosting international events such as the Helsinki conference on human rights (1975) and the Stockholm conference on European security and cooperation (1986). More recently, in 1999, the President of Finland was one of the two official negotiators who succeeded in ending the Kosovo war. In addition, substantial aid is allocated to developing countries and environmental protection worldwide.

Alfred Nobel

Alfred Nobel (1833-96)

The 19C Swedish chemist, who has become a symbol of universal peace and learning, began his career manufacturing explosives. Following his invention of dynamite in 1867, he became very wealthy and decided to use his fortune for the benefit of mankind. In his will he set up a foundation with the specific task of allocating substantial annual awards to men and women of outstanding merit in the fields of literature, physics, chemistry, medicine and peace. An economics prize was added in 1969. Five of the prizes are presented in Stockholm on 10 December, the anniversary of Alfred Nobel's death, whereas the sixth, the peace prize, is officially presented in Oslo.

ROGER-VIOLLET

Food and drink

Scandinavians like their food and often consume large quantities of alcoholic drinks with their meals. Meal times, however, are far from rigid and vary from one family to the next to fit in with individual timetables. This explains the number of snack bars and take-away food shops one finds on the streets of large towns, as people at work often have a snack at any time during the day.

Christmas buffet

MEALS

Breakfast is to be taken seriously as it is obviously intended to provide enough energy to last well into the afternoon; at least that is the theory but it does not always work like that in practice. It is a well-balanced and varied meal of soft boiled eggs, cold meats, cheese and above all an amazing array of mouth-watering pickled herrings; all this is served with a great variety of bread and rolls; cereals, fruit and jam or marmalade, as well as coffee rather than tea complete the meal.

Lunch is not a must and quite a few people go without or have a light snack; this is the occasion when a great many Scandinavians eat open sandwiches which they buy from special take-away shops with tantalizing windows or from snack bars or which they simply make at home.

Middag is the main meal of the day, taken at any time from mid-afternoon to early evening. It consists of two or three courses, a main dish of meat or fish and vegetables followed by a dessert. The traditional Scandinavian mixed hors d'oeuvre, considered too copious nowadays, has become a meal in itself in the form of an elaborate cold table with an extensive choice of cold meats, seafood, salads and one or two hot dishes as well. It is known in Sweden as *smörgåsbord*, in Norway as *koldtbord* and in Finland as *voileipäpöytä*. Roasts and game served with a cream sauce, as well as reindeer or elk meat make up the main dish. Desserts include soufflés, cream cakes, rice pudding, ice cream and various berries in summer; cloudberries, wild berries looking like pale raspberries and growing in Lapland, have a very delicate taste.

The Scandinavian snack

The Danes call it *smørrebrød*, the Norwegians *smørbrød*, the Swedes *smörgås* and the Finns *voileipä*... this universal snack is the most versatile of open sandwiches: a thin slice of buttered rye bread topped with almost anything savoury, cold meats, smoked salmon, herrings, eggs, sausages, cheese, and garnished with various salads. The secret of success consists in choosing the right mixture of ingredients; in fashionable snack bars, the menu listing the different fillings is often spread over two pages! The choice is inevitably bewildering, but there is always a helpful server to advise you and recommend the speciality of the house. Eaten with a glass of Danish or Norwegian lager, the Scandinavian open sandwich makes a refreshing and sustaining snack, particularly in summer.

Aftens, taken at the end of the day, is usually a light supper of cakes and tea or coffee.

Seafood forms the basis of Scandinavian food. Fresh salmon, trout and cod are in great demand and are often eaten plain boiled with melted butter and parsley or simply grilled. However, fish is also smoked and marinated with great skill to produce delicacies such as smoked eel, *gravad lax*, salmon marinated in dill, pickled herrings (accompanied by a glass of schnapps) and marinated scallops. Shellfish is also of excellent quality and includes lobster, prawns, oysters, crab and the famous crayfish, which is at the centre of elaborate festivities in both Finland and Sweden and, like herrings, accompanied by several glasses of schnapps.

DRINK

In spite of the high price of alcohol, drinking is often done to excess in Scandinavia and that is perhaps why there are so many teetotallers. **Beer** is the national drink, Denmark and Norway producing internationally known lagers. **Akvavit** is a very strong drink served with hors d'oeuvre in formal receptions: Danish *akvavit* from Ålborg in north Jylland is reputed to be one of the best, as is *linie akvavit* from Norway, which is specially shipped across the world to Australia and back again because crossing the equator is supposed to improve it considerably!

Brewery cart

World Heritage List

In 1972, The United Nations Educational, Scientific and Cultural Organization (UNESCO) adopted a Convention for the preservation of cultural and natural sites. To date, more than 150 States Parties have signed this international agreement, which has listed 690 sites of outstanding universal value on the World Heritage list. Each year, a committee of representatives from 21 countries, assisted by technical organizations (ICOMOS – International Council on Monuments and Sites; IUCN – International Union for Conservation of Nature and Natural Resources; ICCROM - International Centre for the Study of the Preservation and Restoration of Cultural Property, the Rome Centre), evaluates the proposals for new sites to be included on the list, which grows longer as new nominations are accepted and more countries sign the Convention. To be considered, a site must be nominated by the country in which it is located.

The protected **cultural heritage** sites may be monuments (buildings, sculptures, archaeological structures etc) with unique historical, artistic or scientific features; groups of buildings (such as religious communities, ancient cities); or sites (human settlements, examples of exceptional landscapes, cultural landscapes) which are the combined works of man and nature of exceptional beauty. **Natural heritage** sites may be a testimony to the stages of the earth's geological history or to the development of human cultures and creative genius or represent significant ongoing ecological processes, contain superlative natural phenomena or provide a habitat for threatened species.

Signatories of the Convention pledge to cooperate to preserve and protect these sites around the world as a common heritage to be shared by all humanity, and contribute to the **World Heritage Fund**. The Fund serves to carry out studies, plan conservation measures, train local specialists, supply equipment for the protection of a park or the restoration of a monument etc.

Some of the most well-known places which the World Heritage Committee has inscribed include: Australia's Great Barrier Reef (1981), the Canadian Rocky Mountain Parks (1984), The Great Wall of China (1987), the Statue of Liberty (1984), the Kremlin (1990), Mont-Saint-Michel and its Bay (France – 1979), Durham Castle and Cathedral (1986).

UNESCO World Heritage Sites included in this guide are:

Denmark:

Helsingør	Kronborg Castle
Jelling	Runestones
Roskilde	Cathedral

Norway:

Alta	Rock carvings
Bergen	Bryggen
Røros	Copper mining town
Urnes	Stave church

Sweden:

Birka	Viking site and Hovgården
Drottningholm	Royal domain
Karlskrona	Naval base
Lappland	Swedish Lapland
Luleå	Gammelstad – church village
Stockholm	Skogskyrkogården – woodland cemetery
Stockholm	Skärgården – Stockholm archipelago
Tanum	Rock carvings
Visby, Gotland	Hanseatic town
Ängelsberg	Engelsberg ironworks
Öland	Southern landscape

Finland:

Helsinki	Fortress of Suomenlinna
Petäjävesi	Old wooden church
Rauma	Wooden architecture of old town
Verla	19C pulp mill

Egeskov Slot

Denmark

ÅLBORG and ÅRHUS
See the end of the Danish section

BILLUND ★
Ribe
Population 8 600
Michelin map 985 Q 6 or Atlas Europe p 122

The small town of Billund is situated on the edge of the county of Vejle, where the picturesque hills of east Jutland meet the flat expanses of west Jutland. The town itself is modern, ordinary and disappointing for nothing apparently distinguishes it from any other Danish provincial town. Yet Billund has one of the top tourist attractions in Denmark, Legoland Park, situated on the outskirts of the town which appeals to visitors of all ages alike.

★★ Legoland Park ⊘

Legoland Park is a perfect example of Danish industrial success and the story of this success sounds like one of Hans Christian Andersen's fairy tales. During the depression which hit the industrialised world in the 1930s, an unemployed joiner native of Billund, Ole Kirk Christiansen, decided to manufacture wooden toys. His unusual flair for success soon enabled him to have his own factory and prompted him to choose the name **Lego** derived from the Danish *Leg godt* which means play well.

Wood gave way to plastic in 1947 and the small building brick, developed soon afterwards, brought worldwide fame to the name of Lego. It was then that Ole's son, Godtfred, conceived the idea of a theme park where everything would be built with Lego bricks, which he quite naturally called Legoland. Millions of these bricks were used to create **Miniland**, a modern version of Jonathan Swift's land of Lilliput, with faithful reproductions on a miniature scale of famous monuments and even whole districts of main European cities such as Amsterdam and Copenhagen. There are ports, canals, lever bridges, airports, stations, ships and trains, all moving parts being efficiently controlled by a computer. A small train takes visitors on a conducted tour of the park and children can drive one of the Lego cars or miniboats. **Duplo land** is specially designed for small children with fun houses to play in, cars to be driven, a train to ride in and planes to control (with parents as passengers!). Meanwhile, older children can try their hand at building with the help of modern computer technology in the **Lego Mindstorms Center**.

Legoland also prides itself in the possession of an extensive collection of toys including dolls and doll's houses, in particular a miniature palace acquired by Legoland in 1978 and called **Titania's Palace**, built by an Englishman for his daughter at the beginning of this century and filled with the most exquisite furniture. From the top of the observation tower, there is a bird's-eye view of this fairyland, and it is possible to have a meal in the park or even stay overnight at Hotel Legoland for a complete immersion. With well over a million visitors a per year, Legoland has proved as big a success as its neighbour, the Lego factory, which it was intended to promote.

C. Boisvieux

Legoland

BORNHOLM ★

Bornholm
Population 47 000
Michelin map 985 Q 11-12 or Atlas Europe p 123

The tiny granite island of Bornholm is the ideal place to stay, to get away from it all. The island offers a variety of scenery, woodland, attractive fishing villages, a rocky coastline with sandy coves and some magnificent beaches. Lying in mid-Baltic 37km from the Swedish coast and 150km from Copenhagen it has always been prey to its powerful neighbours: the first settlers, the Burgundians, were followed by the Archbishop of Lund, who held sway for over 200 years and was replaced by a short period of Danish rule before the town of Lübeck ruled for 50 years in the 16C. There are numerous picturesque fishing villages (Hasle, Tejn, Gudhjem, Melsted) to visit where the visitor can taste smoked herrings, but Bornholm is essentially known for its 12C round churches (Østerlars Kirke, Nylars Kirke, Ols Kirke and Nykirke). These stoutly built churches were fortified as they also served as a place of refuge in times of danger. The Østerlars Kirke with its three storeys, oval chancel and apse is the best-known.

COPENHAGEN ★★★

See KØBENHAVN

EGESKOV SLOT ★★

Fyn
Michelin map 985 Q 7 or Atlas Europe p 122

One of Denmark's most famous castles, Egeskov is also reputed to be one of Europe's best-preserved island castles of the Renaissance period. If, in general, such claims are exaggerated, it is certainly not the case here, for Egeskov is even more attractive in reality *(see photograph p 72)* than on the numerous postcards and posters one can't fail to notice in tourist offices. Situated in the gently undulating southern part of Fyn, between Svendborg and Odense, near the small town of Kværndrup, the castle stands in the middle of a lake, surrounded by woodland, once part of an oak forest which gave its name to the area (*egeskov* means oak forest in Danish).

A typical Renaissance castle – Thousands of oak trees were felled to provide the piles on which the castle was built in 1554. Its architectural characteristics reflect the pre-occupations of the time: a need to defend oneself against warring lords or simply against bands of marauders and a growing aspiration for a gentler and more comfortable way of life. Thus the castle was provided with a drawbridge and machicolations, defensive features of a bygone age, whereas large windows on all four sides let in plenty of light. The main rectangular structure consists of two adjoining buildings; in the centre, between the two walls, chimneys were fitted and two secret staircases concealed. The castle is flanked on the drawbridge side by two round towers with pointed copper roofs. The outside walls, of a lovely faded shade of red, are surmounted by imposing corbie-stepped gables. The overall impression is one of refined elegance.

Egeskov Slot ⊙ – The castle is privately owned and still inhabited by the descendants of its founder, therefore only part of it is open to the public. Most remarkable of all is the Great Hall, completely restored in 1975 and now regularly used for concerts. At one end hangs an impressive painting of Christian IV on horseback. In the late 16C, the granddaughter of the founder of Egeskov was locked up in the Rigborg Room for five years after having fallen in love with one of the heirs of the Rosenkrantz family and having born him a son. The child was however later officially recognised and became the first member of the Norwegian branch of the Rosenkrantz family. Throughout the castle there are hunting trophies brought back by the previous owner from various African countries. The stair tower leads to the loft where there is an exhibition about the restoration work which was done on the timber structure and on the roof and, since no castle is really complete without its legend, there is a mysterious wooden doll lying below one of the tower structures; according to tradition, if *Træmanden* is removed, the castle will collapse!

Park ⊙ – The park dates from the 1730s and had been badly neglected prior to its restoration in 1959. Today it is one of the best-kept parks in Denmark and is divided into several sections hemmed in by hedges, including a fuchsia garden with 75 different varieties, a Renaissance garden adorned with fountains, an English garden, a water garden and a herb garden, not forgetting the maze.

Museum ⊙ – The estate also has a museum covering 3 000m² which houses a collection of veteran cars, aeroplanes, motor cycles and horse-drawn carriages.

ELSINORE ★

See HELSINGØR

FÅBORG ★

Fyn
Population 7 500
Michelin map 985 Q 7 or Atlas Europe p 122

Framed by rolling hills covered with a mantle of thick woods and known as the Fyn Alps, Fåborg is a lively and picturesque old town on the sunny south coast of Fyn. Lovely surroundings, a beautiful stretch of coastline and a well-preserved historical background all combine to make Fåborg one of Denmark's most attractive small towns. Variety comes from a choice of cultural events, such as art exhibitions and concerts, and of outdoor activities such as windsurfing and yachting. The harbour is equipped with high standard facilities and is one of the two main ports of call (the other being Svendborg) for yachts sailing along the south coast and among the numerous islands of the archipelago. There are also regular ferry services to the larger islands.

The first mention of Fåborg in an official document dates from 1229; during the Middle Ages the town was defended by a castle and surrounded by fortified walls which were destroyed in the 16C. However the town slowly grew, developing strong commercial ties with the duchies of Holstein and Schleswig; by the 18C it was an important trading centre for cereals and meat and to this day the town's architecture has retained many signs of this past prosperity.

OLD TOWN

All that remains of Fåborg's fortifications is the western gate in Vestergade. The old town is centred round the main square, Torvet, where there is an impressive modern bronze fountain by Kaj Nielsen. Nearby stands the tall 15C bell-tower which dominates the whole area. The surrounding narrow cobbled streets are lined with colourful old timbered houses displaying great architectural variety with many small craftsmen's cottages standing next to comfortable merchants' houses.

Grønland

Greenland, the world's largest island, lies off North America. A large part of the island's inhospitable environment lies within the Arctic Circle and its most northerly point extends to within 800km of the North Pole. 85% of the total surface area of 2 million km² is covered by an ice cap. The total population of 55 000 – 11 000 in the capital of Nuuk – includes native Inuits and Europeans.

The Norwegian, Erik the Red, founded the first colony on this green land which was to remain Norwegian until the 18C, when a pastor founded a new colony this time linked to Denmark.

Greenland joined the Common Market along with Denmark in 1973 and achieved Home Rule in 1979, but left the Community in 1985 after a referendum.

The settlements and agricultural land are concentrated on the coasts, especially along the milder west coast, and hunting and fishing are the island's main economic activities. An increasing number of visitors and scientific expeditions are being attracted by the grandiose and somewhat mysterious aspect of Greenland's nature.

Den Gamle Gård – One of these, in Holkegade, has been turned into a Culture and History Museum, **Kulturhistoriske Museet** Ⓥ, retracing the town's prosperous past, with reconstructed interiors, shipping exhibits etc.

Fåborg Museum for Fynsk Malerkunst Ⓥ – Founded by a patron of the arts, Mads Rasmussen, who donated it to the town in 1915, this art museum, situated in Grønnegade, is famous throughout Denmark for its particularly fine collection of Fyn painters including Peter Hansen and Johannes Larsen.

FALSTER

DENMARK

Falster is the central island of a group of three main islands linked to the southern tip of Sjælland, the other two being Lolland and Møn. The port of Gedser, just 2hr away by ferry from northern Germany, is Denmark's most southern town; yet Copenhagen is only 150km to the north along the fast International E 55 road. Like Lolland, Falster enjoys a generally milder and sunnier climate than the rest of Denmark and is reputed for its magnificent beaches along the east coast bordering the Baltic Sea.

Storstrøm and Farø bridges – Two highways link south Sjælland to Falster across a narrow strait called Storstrømmen. The Storstrøm bridge to the west dates from before the Second World War and is 3.2km long. With the considerable increase in traffic in recent years, it became inadequate and in 1985 the Farø bridges were inaugurated. The two new bridges carry the E 55 motorway and have a combined length of 3 322m: one links Sjælland to the tiny island of Farø in the middle of Storstrømmen and the other joins Farø to Falster. The longer and more spectacular is the Farø-to-Falster bridge which rises high above the water between two gigantic pillars in order to allow shipping through.

Nykøbing Falster – This is the island's main town, situated on the shores of the narrow sound which separates Falster from Lolland. There are few reminders of the town's medieval heyday: the Late Gothic church which used to be the chapel of the Franciscan monastery and some timbered houses near the centre. One of these has been called the Czar's House, **Czarens Hus**, since Peter the Great of Russia briefly stopped there on his way to Copenhagen at the beginning of the 18C; it now houses a restaurant and the **Falsters Museum** ⊘ which illustrates local history.

On the other side of the sound, there is an interesting Medieval Centre, **Middelaldercentret** ⊘, devoted to the technological achievements of the Middle Ages with demonstrations held in fully operational workshops.

Marielyst and Bøtø – *10km south of Nykøbing Falster.*
The east coast of Falster south of Nykøbing Falster is lined with more than 20km of white-sand beaches, some of the finest in Denmark, reputed for the exceptional cleanliness of the water. The famous seaside resort of Marielyst is ideally situated along this stretch of coastline and, just south of it near Bøtø, **Sommerland Falster** ⊘ is a vast leisure park covering 20ha, a kind of combined aqualand and amusement park. Nature lovers will also appreciate the **bird sanctuary** near Bøtø.

Nørre Alslev – *15km north of Nykøbing Falster.*
Inside the brick-built Gothic church there is an interesting and rare dance of death fresco depicting various members of Danish medieval society being led by Death into a macabre dance. *See KØGE: Excursion, Jungshoved Kirke.*

FYN

With an area of almost 3 500km², Fyn is Denmark's second largest island after Sjælland. It occupies a central position between Jutland to which it is linked by a bridge across the Little Belt (Lillebælt) and Sjælland in the east, across the Great Belt (Storebælt); a bridge and tunnel were recently completed between Korsør and Nyborg to replace the ferry link; this has brought a radical change to the economic prospects of the island. Indeed, Fyn is not as densely populated as other parts of Denmark and its rich land and temperate climate explain that, up to now, its traditions have been mainly agricultural, particularly in the field of horticulture. Fyn thus offers some of the most attractive landscapes in Denmark, with a wealth of old, beautifully maintained farmhouses picturesque villages with colourful thatched cottages and manor houses scattered around the countryside, most of them still privately owned. Fortunately, the pace of daily life is leisurely and distances are relatively short (even for Denmark!) making Fyn an ideal cycling country.

The north of the island, especially the Hindsholm peninsula is on the whole more austere than the south which is sunnier and turned towards the picturesque archipelago nestling round the indented south coast. There are three main islands: Tåsinge, closest to Fyn, and Langeland, both linked to Fyn by bridges, and Ærø which is accessible by ferry, in just over 1hr, from Fåborg, and Svendborg (Fyn), from Rudkøbing (Langeland) as well as from Als, off the coast of Jutland. South Fyn's maritime tradition makes it a paradise for sailing enthusiasts who can take a cruise round the coast in an old sailing ship or hire a boat and explore some of the smaller islands in the archipelago. Sea trout fishing is yet another of the many activities which attract visitors to Fyn.

Odense is the island's main town and the third most important in Denmark after Copenhagen and Århus. It is the birthplace of Hans Christian Andersen whose love of nature prompted him to describe Fyn as the "garden of Denmark".

FYRKAT★

Nordjylland
Michelin map 985 P 6 or Atlas Europe p 122

A mighty Viking fortress once stood on this wind-swept promontory, 3km south-west of the small town of Hobro, one of the two best-preserved fortresses of its kind found in Denmark, the other being Trelleborg in south-west Sjælland. Built c 980, possibly by Harald Bluetooth, Fyrkat probably served as a garrison for Viking warriors preparing to raid some far-away country, although this theory is now questioned and it is likely that women and children also lived in the fort. The site of such forts was always carefully chosen; in this case, the proximity of Mariager Fjord, leading straight into the Kattegat, was undoubtedly the decisive factor.

TOUR

The building plan of Fyrkat follows the usual pattern: protected by a thick circular wall, the area of the encampment was 120m in diameter and divided into quarters by two perpendicular streets leading to the main gates, each one facing one of the points of the compass. Inside each quarter stood four long wooden houses with convex walls, arranged in a square with a smaller one in the centre. Divided into three sections, each long house could accommodate 50 people. A full size model has been built just outside the site, with oak from nearby forests.

Fyrkat has provided invaluable information about military life during the Viking era but this is only part of an ambitious project to find out more about the powerful people whose influence on the destiny of Northern Europe was considerable. Finds from the site can be seen in **Hobro Museum** ⊘, housed in an attractive old building. Meanwhile the **Vikingecenter** ⊘ is reconstructing a farming settlement of nine houses in the valley below and various activities will eventually show how ordinary Viking farmers lived.

C. Boisvieux

Viking long house, Fyrkat

FÆRØERNE

Michelin map 985 or Atlas Europe p 106

For many the name **Faroes** (Føroyar in Faroese) is often associated with fishing and weather reports but their location remains vague. In reality this group of tiny volcanic islands lies in mid-Atlantic almost equidistant from Scotland, Norway and Iceland. With a total area of 14 000km² and a population of 47 000 the 18 islands form a self-governing community under the Danish crown. Irish missionary monks chose the isles as a place of retreat and they were followed by Viking colonisers, whose struggles to survive in the harsh environment were recounted in the *Faroe Saga (Færeyinga Saga)*. In the 11C St Olav, King of Norway, brought Christianity to the isles and from then on they were under Norwegian tutelage until the union of the Danish and Norwegian crowns, which lasted until 1814. The then Danish province became autonomous in 1948. Island life, friendly hospitality, isolation and seabirds in great numbers are the main attractions. Faroese is akin to Norse.

HADERSLEV ★

Sønderjylland
Population 21 000
Michelin map 985 Q 6 or Atlas Europe p 122

Built on the banks of the narrow Haderslev fjord, some 15km inland, Haderslev is a lively commercial town and a pleasant tourist centre.

Trading has been a long-standing tradition in Haderslev; in fact it was most probably the reason for its foundation since the town is situated along Jutland's main north-south route. By 1292 Haderslev already had its own charter and after that its history was marked by isolated events which underline its importance: in 1448, Christian I signed a charter in the city enabling him to become king of Denmark, and in 1597 Christian IV celebrated his wedding to Anne-Catherine of Brandenburg. But the most significant chapter of the town's history lasted from 1864 to 1920 when Haderslev became part of the duchy of Schleswig-Holstein under Prussian rule.

★★ Domkirke ⊘ – The red-brick cathedral is one of the most interesting Gothic buildings in Denmark. Inside it has been entirely whitewashed and this enhances the light coming through the tall windows in the chancel (15C). The transept and the nave, with its remarkably high vaulting, date from the 13C. The bronze font is late 15C and the Baroque pulpit from 1636. But most interesting of all is the restored Sieseby organ, now regularly played, which has the most beautifully clear yet rounded sound.

Old Town – The old town is built on high ground and nestles round the cathedral which dominates it. Many houses, lining the winding cobbled streets, some of them 400 years old, have been tastefully restored; as a result, Haderslev won the title of Town of the Year in 1984.

No 20 Slotsgade is one of the town's oldest houses dating from the late 16C; it now houses the **Ehlers Samlingen** ⊘, an important collection of pottery and ceramics. The Schleswig Carriage Collection, **Slesvigske Vognsamling** ⊘, in Sejlstensgyde, comprises horse-drawn carriages from the 17C to the 19C.

Haderslev Museum ⊘ – This museum in Dalgade, to the east of the town centre, includes a section devoted to local archaeological finds, including objects dug out of nearby bogs. Opposite there is a small open-air museum with various old buildings going back to the 17C, including a windmill.

HELSINGØR ★

Frederiksborg
Population 56 000
Michelin map 985 P 9 or Atlas Europe p 123 – Local map see SJÆLLAND

Helsingør is situated 45km north of Copenhagen and separated from the capital by a long stretch of coastline known as the Danish Riviera. The town is a busy tourist and commercial centre as well as a thriving port with a fleet of ferries linking it to Helsingborg in Sweden across a 4km-wide strait. Its main attraction is its castle which acquired international fame under the name of Elsinore Castle as the dramatic setting of Shakespeare's tragedy *Hamlet*.

Gateway to the Baltic – After he became king of Denmark, Norway and Sweden, Erik of Pomerania soon decided to take advantage of Helsingør's strategic position at the entrance of the Øresund, a narrow strip of water linking the North Sea and the Baltic; therefore, in 1427 he introduced the Sound Toll, a duty imposed on all passing ships, and he built a fortress to enforce it. The town prospered rapidly, attracting many foreign merchants and threatening to supersede Copenhagen as Denmark's largest city. This prosperity lasted for over 400 years until the Sound Toll was abolished in 1857. However, shipbuilding, tourism and a continuous flow of traffic between Denmark and Sweden have enabled Helsingør to remain a lively and interesting town.

Renaissance Observatory for astronomer-royal

The 16C Danish astronomer-royal, **Tycho Brahe** (1546-1601), chose to build his new observatory (1576) on the tiny island of Ven in the middle of the Sound, halfway between Copenhagen and Helsingør. In pre-telescope days his observations and calculations helped the world to accept the Copernican theory that the sun and not the earth was the centre of the universe. When his royal patron died Tycho was forced to look elsewhere for patronage and he ended his life in Prague where the German astronomer, Johannes Kepler carried on his work.

DENMARK

★★★ KRONBORG SLOT (ELSINORE CASTLE) (BX)

Denmark's most famous castle stands on a peninsula jutting out into the Sound. Its very name seems to play on the imagination of most people first and foremost because it was the romantic setting chosen by Shakespeare for his gloomy Elizabethan drama, *Hamlet*, but also because it is the symbol of former Danish sea power. The mythical character **Holger Danske** (Holger the Dane) is said to be sleeping beneath the castle. Its awe-inspiring outline, enhanced by impressive towers and covered with a green-copper roof surmounted by elegant spires tearing through the low grey sky, continues to defy the sea as it has done for centuries.

From Krogen to Kronborg – In 1574, Frederik II commissioned two Dutch architects, Hans van Paeschen and Anthonius van Opberger, to rebuild and extend **Krogen**, Erik of Pomerania's fortress. In 1577 it was renamed **Kronborg**; the influence of the Dutch Renaissance is particularly noticeable in the east wing. After a fire destroyed most of the castle in 1629, Frederik's son, Christian IV, had it restored to its original splendour. Kronværksport was later added by Christian V at the end of the 17C in order to fortify the castle on the landward side.

TOUR ⊙

Exterior – Cornices underline the windows and a richly carved balustrade runs along the top of the sandstone-covered façade. Surrounded by a moat, the castle is approached across three wooden bridges and through **Mørkeport**, a 16C gate leading to the main courtyard. But before entering the castle, it is worth going round the deep moat on to the seafront to admire the panoramic view of the Sound and the Swedish coast. A platform lined with heavy bronze guns is said to be the very place where Hamlet saw his father's ghost shrouded in thick fog. Not surprisingly, it is only laconically referred to in the play as " A platform before the castle ", since it is almost certain that Shakespeare never visited Elsinore and based his plot on the legend of Prince Amled who may have lived in Jutland long before Erik of Pomerania built the first castle.

Interior – The castle contains a vast number of rooms, most of them open to the public. Of particular interest are: the **Castle Chapel** with its magnificent Renaissance decoration, spared by the 1629 fire; the **King's and Queen's Chambers** with lavish ceiling

Elsinore Castle – Kronborg Slot

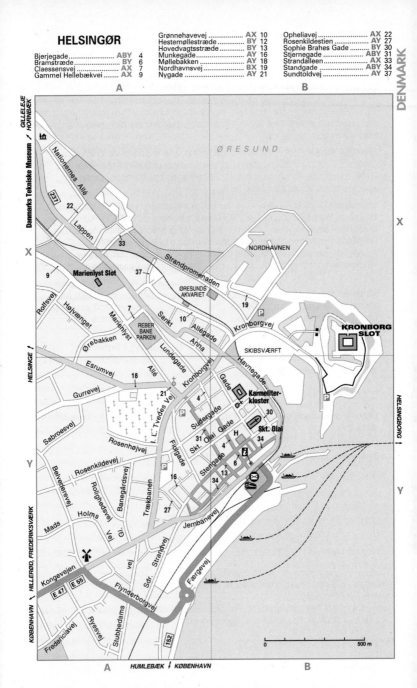

HELSINGØR

Bjerjegade .... ABY 4	Grønnehavevej .... AX 10	Opheliavej .... AX 22
Bramstræde .... BY 6	Hestemøllestræde .... BY 12	Rosenkildestien .... AY 27
Claessensvej .... AX 7	Hovedvagtsstræde .... BY 13	Sophie Brahes Gade .... BY 30
Gammel Hellebækvei .... AX 9	Munkegade .... AY 16	Stjernegade .... ABY 31
	Møllebakken .... AY 18	Strandalleen .... AX 33
	Nordhavnsvej .... BX 19	Standgade .... ABY 34
	Nygade .... AY 21	Sundtoldvej .... AY 37

paintings commissioned by Christian IV and the **Ballroom**, one of the longest in Northern Europe, with its striking chequered marble floor, but unfortunately without its original coffered painted ceiling.

The King's tapestries – Some 40 tapestries portraying 111 Danish kings were hung all round the Ballroom on special occasions. Commissioned by Frederik II, they were woven in Helsingør c 1585, under the supervision of Hans Knieper, a Flemish painter and weaver from Antwerp. Today there are only 14 left; 7 are in the Nationalmuseet in Copenhagen and 7 in Kronborg.

The casemates – Accessible from the kitchens, a statue of Holger Danske who, according to legend, will stand up when his country is in imminent danger and save it by leading an army of young boys and old men, is presented here.

The Danish Maritime Museum (Handels-og Sofartsmuseet) – This museum presents 1 000 years of maritime history and highlights 400 years of Sound Dues, the Danish West India Company and the local shipyard Burmeister & Wain.

OLD TOWN

Helsingør has retained a considerable number of carefully restored timber-framed houses. Rich merchants and shipbuilders clustered round the harbour whereas craftsmen and sailors lived on the outskirts. The old town has been largely pedestrianised and visitors can now take a pleasant stroll along Stengade (the high street) and adjacent streets like Sankt Anna Gade, discovering picturesque alleyways as they go along.

Skt Olai Kirke ⊘ (BY) – Now a cathedral, the medieval St Olaf's Church, built between 1200 and 1560, stands at the junction of Sankt Anna Gade and Skt Olai Gade. Inside, the furniture is mostly Renaissance and Baroque; particularly remarkable are the altarpiece and the font.

Karmeliterklostret ⊘ (BY) – A Carmelite monastery was built close to St Olaf's church at the beginning of the 15C. Dietrich Buxtehude (1657-1707) worked as an organist in **Sct Maria Kirke** ⊘ from 1660 to 1668 before he went on to Lübeck. It is possible to visit the adjoining **cloister** and catch a glimpse of Kronborg Slot from the monastery gardens. The hospital founded by the monks later became a poorhouse (Karmeliterhuset) and now houses the town museum, **Bymuseum**, where a model of the original Elsinore Castle can be seen.

Marienlyst Slot ⊘ (AX) – Along Lappen, the continuation of Sankt Anna Gade, stands King Frederik II's 16C summer residence, modified and extended in the late 18C by the French architect Nicolas Jardin into a Louis XVI style small palace.

Danmarks Tekniske Museum ⊘ – *Leave by Lappen* (AX). Further west on the road to Gilleleje, this national technical museum illustrates scientific and technological development through the ages.

EXCURSION

Ferry trip to Sweden – Crossing the Sound to Helsingborg only takes 25min and, since three ferry lines offer several sailings every hour, it is an experience not to be missed, if only for the splendid views of Helsingør and its castle.

The north coast from Helsingør to Gilleleje – *See SJÆLLAND.*

HILLERØD
Frederiksborg
Population 26 000
Michelin map 985 Q9 or Atlas Europe p 123 – Local map see SJÆLLAND

Situated in the centre of north Sjælland, 35km from Copenhagen and 23km from Helsingør, Hillerød grew in the shadow of the magnificent Frederiksborg Castle which towers over the town.
Today there are few reminders of the past, but Hillerød thrives on tourism as the castle's visitors flock to its excellent shopping centre.

★★★ FREDERIKSBORG SLOT

The castle stands on three small islands in the Castle Lake (Slotssø), north of the town centre.
In 1560, Frederik II bought Hillerød manor which stood on the northern island, extended it and called it Frederiksborg. His son, Christian IV, decided to build an entirely new castle but the project was so vast that work went on for more than 20 years (1599-1622), beginning with the main three-winged building to the north and ending with the tall Barbican Tower on the middle island.
By that time it was decided to keep the structures on the southern island, however, as they were not in alignment with the new castle, an S-shaped bridge was built to link the two.

The symbol of absolute monarchy – For 100 years Frederiksborg was a royal residence and successive monarchs were anointed in the Castle Chapel until the abolition of absolute monarchy. The French gardens were laid in the early part of the 18C.
Later the royal family often used the nearby Fredensborg in preference to the grandiose Frederiksborg which gradually became a kind of royal museum housing a historical portrait collection assembled by Frederik VI.

Frederiksborg Slot

Frederiksborg Museum – Unfortunately, in 1859, a fire destroyed most of the interior and damaged part of the exterior; however, it was quickly restored with contributions from the whole Danish nation and in particular from JC Jacobsen, owner of the Carlsberg Breweries. At his suggestion, Frederiksborg became a museum of Danish national history in 1878 and was to function as an independent department of the Carlsberg Foundation. It was opened to the public in 1882. It houses items of furniture and various objects of historical interest, arranged round the rooms as well as a collection of portraits and paintings expanded from the original one.

TOUR ⏱

Christian IV's castle is built of red brick with sandstone decorations and ornate gables, in the style of the Dutch Renaissance. By contrast, Frederik II's buildings appear almost medieval.
The castle is best approached through the Town Gate on the southern island.

Exterior – At the end of Frederik II's buildings, on either side of the narrow Stable Street (Strædet), stand two low-domed, round towers dating from 1562. The S-shaped bridge leads to the imposing **Barbican Tower**, a very appropriate entrance for Christian IV's grandiose castle. In the centre of the courtyard stands the **Neptune Fountain** deprived of its bronze statues by Adrian de Vries during the Swedish occupation of Frederiksborg in 1659, but reconstructed in 1888. Beyond the fountain, a splendid portal surmounted by a carved frontispiece gives access to the inner courtyard enclosed by the three wings of the main building: to the north the **King's Wing** with its beautiful two-storeyed marble gallery, to the west the **Chapel Wing** flanked with a large tower and to the east the **Princess' Wing**. There are four stair turrets with spiral staircases linking the three floors of the castle. The main entrance to the museum is in the King's Wing.

Interior – On the ground floor, the Princess' Wing is used for temporary exhibitions; the **Rose** or Knights' Room, restored to its original appearance after the 1859 fire, has a vaulted ceiling decorated with intricate stucco work and supported by marble columns. On the first floor, access to the **Chapel** is through an open loggia, level with the gallery running all the way round the richly decorated building, which was practically unharmed by the fire. Painted and gilded stucco decorations cover the entire vaults of the nave; the altarpiece and pulpit in gold, silver and ebony are by Jacob Mores of Hamburg and at the altar end of the gallery stands the original organ built in 1610 by Esajas Compenius, a famous organ-builder from Brunswick. The walls are lined on several rows with coats of arms. A covered bridge, called the **Privy Passage**, leads to the **Audience Chamber** surmounted by a Baroque cupola. Rooms on the first and second floors of the King's Wing and the Princess' Wing display the museum's collections in chronological order. The **Great Hall** above the chapel, with its carved wooden ceiling, black marble fireplace, tapestries and musicians' gallery, was reconstructed from sketches made shortly before the fire.

DENMARK

EXCURSIONS

★**Fredensborg** ⊙ – *9km on road 65 – local map see SJÆLLAND. The palace, the orangery and the vegetable garden are only open in July but the park is open all the year round.*

This Baroque palace was built in the 18C by Frederik IV on the shores of Lake Esrum and named Fredensborg, which means castle of peace, to celebrate the end of the war with Sweden. Inaugurated in 1722, it was only completed some 50 years later; the central part, designed by Johan Cornelius Krieger and surrounding an octagonal courtyard, is the oldest; famous architects, such as Eigtved, Laurids de Thurah and Nicolas Jardin contributed to various other buildings. The whole forms a harmonious white ensemble topped with green copper roofs. The palace is the spring and autumn residence of the royal family.

Most remarkable in the **Palace** are the central hall surmounted by the large cupola, the Rococo Garden Room and the Baroque Chapel.

The **park** spreads from the palace to the shores of Lake Esrum; it was remodelled c 1760 by Nicolas Jardin and the natural surroundings of forest and lake were used to enhance it. Wide shaded avenues lead from the castle to the lake; at the end of one of these, stand two small pavilions built in 1765-66. Throughout the park and in particular the royal family's private garden, Marmorhaven, there is a great variety of statues, including a collection depicting peasants from Norway and the Faroe Islands. The new orangery, inaugurated in September 1995, was designed by the architects' firm Søren D Schmidt after an original plan by Nicolas Jardin.

The forest of **Gribskov** stretches just north of Hillerød, on the western shore of Lake Esrum. There are pleasant drives (and walks) to be had in this vast woodland area where beeches alternate with spruce trees, in particular along road 227 which follows the shore of the lake and goes through the village of Nødebo *(6km from Hillerød)* with an interesting small medieval church.

Skævinge – *10km south-west.* The walls of the village church are covered with 16C frescoes depicting scenes from the Bible but, quite surprisingly, there is also a painting of the Danish national hero, Holger the Dane (Holger Danske) who, according to legend, is sleeping beneath Elsinore Castle.

HOLBÆK

Vestsjælland – Population 22 000
Michelin map 985 Q 8 or Atlas Europe p 122 – Local map see SJÆLLAND

Well situated deep inside the Isefjord, Denmark's second largest fjord, and on the main railway line between Copenhagen and Kalundborg, this ancient market place has developed into an important modern commercial town and has become one of the main tourist centres in the area by preserving its natural and cultural environment: there is a picturesque old harbour linked to the shopping area by small alleyways, there are green open spaces like Strandparken stretching right down to the fjord and in the woodland around the town there are 200-year-old trees as well as deer, wild boar and peacocks. Moreover, at the entrance of Holbæk fjord, there is a modern marina bordering on a vast protected area and a golf course.

Detail of 15C frescoes portraying hell, Tuse Kirke

Holbæk Museum ⊘ – This substantial regional museum in Klosterstræde devoted to local history consists of nine old buildings dating from 1660 to 1867. Various exhibits are on show in the 51 rooms, archaeological finds as well as pottery and ceramics, but there are also reconstructions of the interiors of a farmhouse, a merchant's house and workshops which successfully illustrate the way of life in the past.

EXCURSIONS

★Tveje Merløse Kirke ⊘ – *4km south on road 57.* The stone-built Romanesque church is unique among Danish village churches. Dating from the beginning of the 12C, it has remained virtually unchanged and is now the only medieval church in Denmark to have retained its original massive twin towers surmounting the porch. Inside there is a wealth of frescoes from the early 13C with scenes from the New Testament, particularly in the apse, but also groups of soldiers fighting in full armour on the western wall.

Tuse Kirke – *6km west on road 155.* This is another Romanesque church which also contains an interesting set of well-preserved frescoes *(see previous page).* Dating from c 1450, these are unusual because biblical scenes are depicted next to scenes from medieval daily life involving devils.

JELLING ★

Vejle
Population 2 500
Michelin map 985 Q6 or Atlas Europe p 122

Today Jelling is a peaceful village in a lovely setting of wooded rolling hills and a lake. However, it is not for its idyllic surroundings that Jelling is one of Jutland's main tourist attractions, it is rather for something that happened 1 000 years ago!

The first Danish kings – During the 10C, at the height of the Viking period, Jelling was for sometime the royal seat chosen by two Viking kings, Gorm the Old and his son Harald Bluetooth, who started the Danish royal line. As evidence, they left two large burial mounds and two rune stones, known as the **Jelling stones**, which have given crucial information about early Danish history.

Christian Vikings – From the inscriptions on the rune stones, it appears that the smaller of the two was erected by Gorm: " King Gorm made this monument in memory of Thyra his wife, the pride of Denmark ". The larger stone bears the words " King Harald had this monument made for Gorm his father and Thyra his mother, this Harald who conquered all Denmark and Norway and made the Danes Christians ". It is the first mention of Denmark as a united kingdom and it establishes the date of the Danish people's conversion to Christianity.

Jelling stone

The stones stand just outside the porch of a 12C **church** situated between the two mounds. Excavations revealed a burial chamber underneath the northern mound; however, it contained no human bones although it was probably intended for two persons; there was no burial chamber underneath the southern mound. Later excavations beneath the church showed that there had been three successive wooden churches on that site, the oldest having been built by Harald. Moreover, human bones were found which appeared to have been moved. From this archaeologists have evolved the theory that Harald had his parents removed from the northern mound and placed beneath the church he had built in place of a pagan temple. The reason why he did this is still uncertain, and the argument of a Christian burial is now refuted by some historians. As for the southern mound, it has been suggested that it was built as a memorial.

The church was decorated with some of the oldest murals in Denmark which, unfortunately have been badly restored.

There is a beautiful collection of stuffed birds (more than 300) in the tourist information office, situated at the entrance of the church enclosure.

A 15m-long **Viking ship**, built by volunteers between 1986 and 1990, can be seen sailing on Lake Fårup, just south of Jelling, with its crew dressed in period costume.

The Jelling stones are included on the UNESCO list of World Heritage Sites.

EXCURSION

Givskud: Løveparken ⓥ – *8km north-west on road 442*. In this 160ha safari park, there are lions, elephants, zebras, rhinos, camels, and many other species of wild animals, as well as farm animals and a playground for children.

The runic alphabet

It is generally recognised that the runic alphabet was not a Scandinavian invention, but the runic inscriptions provided the first evidence of literacy in these northern latitudes. The earliest runic alphabet – *futhark* after the first six letters – consisted of 24 letters but around the 9C the number was reduced from 24 to 16. The characteristic angular shapes of the letters, made up of straight strokes, made them ideal for carving on wood and stone. The runic inscriptions were often memorials to raiders and traders, good works, heroic deeds, especially of warriors in far lands, or to life and death. These written fragments by the rune masters give an added dimension to the Viking era.

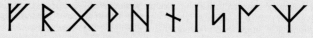

JYLLAND
JUTLAND
Michelin map 985 PQ or Atlas Europe p 122

Jutland is a vast peninsula attached to the mainland of Europe and representing the largest portion of Danish territory. It stretches northwards from the German border for over 300km and is surrounded by the North Sea, the Skagerrak and the Kattegat. Direct exposure to the strong westerly winds blowing across the North Sea, has resulted in impressive wild landscapes that cannot be seen anywhere else in Denmark, and a marked contrast between east and west Jutland. The east is generally greener and its grazing fields alternating with forests of dark fir trees are sometimes reminiscent of Alpine countries. The west is wilder and windswept, with vast expanses of moorland and heath and endless beaches backed by dunes covered with marram grass *(see photograph p 29)*. Along the coast there are enclosed fjords and islands like Rømø and Fanø with preserved natural environments. The west is also traditionally less populated and the east economically more developed, particularly along the main north-south International E 45 road.

Moreover, there are obvious differences between south, central and north Jutland. The south is rather flat, covered with forests, while central Jutland is on the whole undulating and offers a variety of landscapes particularly in the lake district around Silkeborg. As for the north, its extensive barren areas make it look more austere especially north of the Limfjord, in spite of the fine beaches and small fishing villages along the north-west coast.

The differences are not only geographical but cultural as well; the German influence is quite apparent in the south which was occupied by Prussia for over 50 years until 1920 and has kept strong ties with modern Germany. Central Jutland on the other hand is drawn towards the dynamic town of Århus, Denmark's second largest city whereas the north has well-established regular links with Norway and Sweden through the ferry ports of Hirtshals and Frederikshavn.

Jutland has therefore much to offer visitors: beside a variety of stunning landscapes, there are historic cities like Ribe and Viborg, fine castles like Rosenholm and Voergård, important Viking sites such as Fyrkat or Lindholm Høje and a wealth of country churches not forgetting some splendid museums in Silkeborg, Århus and Ålborg.

KALUNDBORG

Vestsjælland
Population 15 500
Michelin map 985 Q 8 or Atlas Europe p 122 – Local map see SJÆLLAND

Situated on the west coast of Sjælland, Kalundborg lies on the northern shore of Kalundborg fjord formed by two peninsulas jutting out into the sea. This busy port owes its development to the important flow of traffic between Sjælland and Jutland; today it is a modern industrial town with a regular ferry service to Århus and a direct railway link to the capital.

Kalundborg was founded by Esbern Snare, Bishop Absalon's brother, who built a church and a castle on the edge of the fjord at the end of the 12C. Another castle was added later by Valdemar IV to reinforce the town's fortifications, and the city grew into an important trading centre and meeting place for the king and the nobility, obtaining its charter in 1485.

The fortifications were destroyed during the Swedish occupation (1658-60) and all that is left of the castles are a few ruins and a lonely tower. A large part of the old town burnt down and the only old houses that remain are to be found in the vicinity of the church, Esbern Snare's original building, and now the town's main tourist attraction.

SIGHTS

★ **Vor Frue Kirke** ⊙ – With its five towers, Our Lady's Church is one of the most unusual Danish churches, rather reminiscent of Byzantine churches. It was founded c 1170 by Esbern Snare, a member of the powerful Hvide family, close to the royal family, who had no doubt travelled abroad and influenced the design of this church. It is built in the shape of a Greek cross with four arms of equal length surmounted by octagonal towers, called St Gertrude, St Catherine, St Anne and St Mary Magdalene, whereas a hefty square tower, higher than the other four, stands over the crossing. Seen from a distance, the building is quite impressive.

Interior – From the inside, the square nave appears relatively small. In each corner, four massive pillars support the central tower. There is an interesting granite font going back to the foundation of the church and a 17C Baroque altarpiece carved in the workshop of Lorenz Jørgensen.

West of the church, in Adelgade, stands a group of old buildings, known as **Lindegård** ⊙, which now houses the interesting museum of local history. In the vicinity of the church, and of the old market square (Torvet), there are other streets worth exploring, such as Præstegade, Lindegade and Kordilgade.

EXCURSION

Ubby, Bregninge and Viskinge churches – *40km – allow about 1hr 30min.* These Romanesque village churches were all built at about the same time as Vor Frue Kirke in Kalundborg.

Drive south on road 22 for 7km and turn left towards Ubby (3km).

Ubby Kirke ⊙ – This church, of exceptionally fine proportions, was built by Esbern Snare in 1179, according to an inscription on the outside wall of the porch, almost at the same time as Kalundborg's five-towered church. Inside there is a remarkable late-17C altarpiece and an earlier pulpit.

Continue on road 219 for 5km and turn left when you reach Lake Tiss. Drive north until you cross road 23, Bregninge is 3km further on.

The imposing **Bregninge Kirke** ★⊙ is built of brick and stone, but painted a vivid red with striking white relief on the corbie-stepped gables. Inside, the nave vaulting is covered with frescoes from different periods showing biblical scenes enhanced by a profusion of floral and animal motifs.

Return to road 23 and turn right to reach Viskinge.

Inside **Viskinge Kirke** ⊙, the beautiful frescoes decorating the nave vaulting and the pillars date from the 15C.

KERTEMINDE

Fyn
Population 5 500
Michelin map 985 Q 7 or Atlas Europe p 122

Kerteminde is a charming small town at the entrance of Kerteminde fjord on the north-east coast of Fyn with fine safe beaches and a modern marina.

Since medieval times fishing has been the town's main activity and the harbour is as colourful and as lively as when Kerteminde's most famous son, the painter Johannes Larsen, described it as the prettiest little town in the world. There are still quite a few old houses lining the narrow streets behind the harbour.

Farvergården, in Landgade, is a large 17C residence housing the **Kerteminde Museum** ⊘ devoted to local history and including the reconstruction of a traditional interior.

Høkeren, in Trollegade, is another renovated old house turned into an old-fashioned grocer's shop.

Johannes Larsen Museet ⊘ – Johannes Larsen, whose favourite subjects were daily life and nature, lived in a small house half way up a hill overlooking the harbour (Møllebakken). It has been turned into a museum devoted to his work and that of other Fyn painters.

The painter's house is dominated by the tall structure of the Swan Mill, **Svanemøllen**, carefully restored.

EXCURSION

Ladby – *3km south-west*. From the village, it is only a short distance to **Ladbyskibet★** *(signposts)*, a Viking ship discovered in 1934, in which a 10C Viking warrior was buried together with his arms, his dogs and his horses. The nails and anchor of the 22m-long ship had been preserved as well as the skeletons and the arms it contained, allowing archaeologists to reconstruct the shape of the *drakkar* and to build a **museum** ⊘ round it.

KOLDING

Vejle
Population 46 000
Michelin map 985 Q 6 or Atlas Europe p 122

Kolding is today an important industrial and commercial town spread on both banks of Kolding Å, which flows into Koldingfjord, and is still dominated by its massive castle standing on a mound overlooking Slotssø (castle lake).

Already a busy trading centre in medieval times, Kolding has, for centuries, played a major role in Danish history both as a royal seat and as a border town when south Jutland was part of the duchy of Schleswig-Holstein. Later, its position at an important east/west-north/south junction became vital for the economic growth of the town which is now the biggest exporter of cattle in Denmark.

Ch. Bastin-J. Evrard

The old and the new, Koldinghus

KOLDINGHUS AND THE OLD TOWN

★ **Koldinghus** ⊙ – In the middle of the 13C, the Danish king Erik Glipping built Kolding Castle to protect the southern border of his kingdom. During the Middle Ages it became one of the most important castles in the country, but today the oldest parts date from the 15C. During the 16C, the castle was redesigned without defences to be used as a royal residence. In the early 18C it was again remodelled by Frederik IV but never used very much after that and in 1808 it was devastated by fire. It stood as a ruin for nearly a century.

Today the restored castle stands as a splendid example of architectural innovation, as modern structures have been unconventionally but successfully blended with the original ruins.

The **Great Hall**, the **chapel** and the **south wing** show in a most striking way the originality of the restoration work. Koldinhus is now a museum containing collections of Danish handicraft and decorative art from the Renaissance onwards.

The **old town** is close to the castle on its south side. There are restored old houses to be seen in cobbled alleyways and along picturesque streets, some of them reserved for pedestrians. One of the most beautiful buildings is a Renaissance gabled house, called **Borchs Gård**, and there are others in Helligkorsgade.

ADDITIONAL SIGHTS

Geografiske Have ⊙ – In Christian IV's Vej, on the outskirts of town, is a botanical garden with more than 2 000 species of plants from all over the world; the rose garden and the bamboo grove, the largest in Northern Europe are most remarkable. With special activities for children, concerts and picnic facilities, it is particularly suitable for family outings.

★ **Kunstmuseet Trapholt** ⊙ – *Æblehaven 23*. The Trapholt Art Museum is beautifully situated in a park overlooking the fjord. It is devoted to 20C Danish art (with works by artists such as Anna Ancher and Richard Mortensen) as well as to Danish craft and design.

The new **Danish Furniture** section, inaugurated in 1996, housed in an original underground structure, illustrates Danish furniture design from 1900 onwards through the work of such famous designers as Arne Jacobsen, Poul Kjærholm and Børge Mogensen, who left their mark on modern international design. The museum also stages special exhibitions where the best in new Danish furniture design is displayed.

EXCURSION

Kolding Fjord – Kolding has one of the largest (1 000-boat capacity) and most modern marinas in Denmark. During the summer there are daily boat trips round the fjord as well as possibilities for hiring boats to explore the variety of landscapes the fjord has to offer.

KØBENHAVN ★★★

COPENHAGEN – København
Population 470 000
Michelin map 985 Q9 or Atlas Europe p 123
Plan of conurbation Michelin map 985 – Local map see SJÆLLAND

A metropolis of moderate size and harmonious proportions, situated on the north-eastern shores of the island of Sjælland, Copenhagen conquers most visitors at first sight and makes them feel at home in no time. This instant appeal is due to a subtle blend of contradictions: there are no grand vistas, yet the large squares, wide avenues, vast green open spaces and lakes create a definite impression of spaciousness; moreover, the contrasting architectural styles, illustrated by the colourful 18C houses crowded on both sides of the old harbour, the austere late-19C town hall or the ultra-modern shopping arcades welcoming the northern light through their huge glass panels, in no way break up the overall unity, emphasised by the numerous red-brick buildings, green-copper roofs and tall spires punctuating the skyline, but the greatest contradiction of all lies in the unique atmosphere of the place, at once conducive to relaxation and arousing a feeling of feverish excitement, which could explain why so many people are fascinated by the lonely figure of the Little Mermaid gazing out to sea at the entrance to one of Northern Europe's busiest harbours. Copenhagen could thus be described in a nutshell as a charming provincial town with the lively atmosphere of a capital city!

The construction of the Øresund fixed link (the last link needed to connect the Scandinavian peninsula to continental Europe) between Malmö in Sweden and the island of Amager close to Copenhagen's international airport has put the Danish capital at the centre of one of Europe's thriving regions with a three-million population, and at the same time creating a wealth of commercial, touristic and cultural openings for decades to come. The city is on the move, doubling the capacity of its international airport, building a fully automatic metro and even planning, over the next 30 years, the construction in the west part of Amager of a new town called Ørestad, which will include a residential district as well as business and shopping areas. Meanwhile, projects are underway for the development of harbour districts such as the dock area behind Langeliniekaj and Holmen (opposite Amalienborg), once the property of the navy, which opened to the public in 1996 and already houses four schools devoted to the arts. The former meat-market district west of the main railway station is also undergoing renovation, starting with Øksnehallen, the covered cattle market, now an exhibition-cum-conference hall!

HISTORICAL NOTES

The merchants' harbour – The name København, meaning merchants' harbour, is a reminder of the town's long-standing commercial tradition which goes back almost to the day of its foundation by Bishop Absalon in 1167. The destiny of Copenhagen was sealed when the ambitious bishop of Roskilde decided to build a castle on the island of Slotsholmen, where Christiansborg Castle now stands; commerce soon flourished under the vigilant control of the bishops of Roskilde until the beginning of the 15C when it became a crown possession and Erik of Pomerania made it the capital of the united kingdom of Denmark, Norway and Sweden. In addition to being the commercial and administrative centre of the kingdom, Copenhagen became a thriving cultural melting pot when the university was founded in 1479. However, in the 16C, the Reformation brought uncertainty and political unrest.

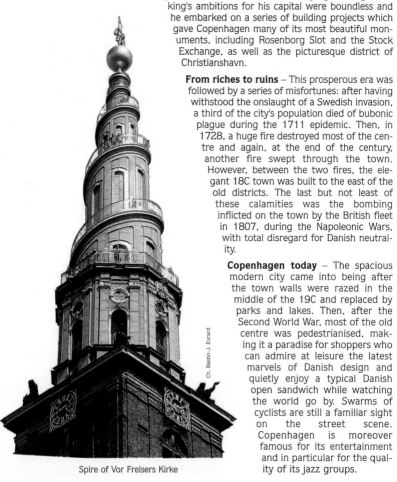

The city's golden age – During the reign of Christian IV (1588-1648), Copenhagen again prospered and developed to such an extent that this period can be described as the city's golden age. The king's ambitions for his capital were boundless and he embarked on a series of building projects which gave Copenhagen many of its most beautiful monuments, including Rosenborg Slot and the Stock Exchange, as well as the picturesque district of Christianshavn.

From riches to ruins – This prosperous era was followed by a series of misfortunes: after having withstood the onslaught of a Swedish invasion, a third of the city's population died of bubonic plague during the 1711 epidemic. Then, in 1728, a huge fire destroyed most of the centre and again, at the end of the century, another fire swept through the town. However, between the two fires, the elegant 18C town was built to the east of the old districts. The last but not least of these calamities was the bombing inflicted on the town by the British fleet in 1807, during the Napoleonic Wars, with total disregard for Danish neutrality.

Copenhagen today – The spacious modern city came into being after the town walls were razed in the middle of the 19C and replaced by parks and lakes. Then, after the Second World War, most of the old centre was pedestrianised, making it a paradise for shoppers who can admire at leisure the latest marvels of Danish design and quietly enjoy a typical Danish open sandwich while watching the world go by. Swarms of cyclists are still a familiar sight on the street scene. Copenhagen is moreover famous for its entertainment and in particular for the quality of its jazz groups.

Ch. Bastin-J. Evrard

Spire of Vor Frelsers Kirke

INSIDER'S COPENHAGEN

Transport – The city has a good bus and train network and special passes are available for tourists.

The **Copenhagen Card** is issued for 24hr (155DKR), 48hr (255DKR) or 72hr (320DKR) (under 12s 75DKR, 125DKR and 160DKR) and must be stamped on the day of purchase. It offers free and unlimited travel in the metropolitan area, free admission to over 60 museums and sights and discounts on ferry sailings to Sweden, car rental and canal tours. A booklet is available from the Tourist Information Centre or from the bus terminal in Rådhuspladsen.

Freewheeling in Copenhagen – Brightly painted bicycles, neatly lined up in racks, are at the disposal of the capital's residents and tourists, absolutely free. These Bycykels (city bikes) work on the same principle as a supermarket trolley. Pop a 20DKR coin into one of the 150 racks throughout the city and off you go. The deposit is retrieved when you return the bike to another stand. The plan is aimed to reduce air pollution and traffic congestion. The thief-proof Bycykel with its multicolour livery is garishly obvious, none of its parts fit standard bicycles and it is equipped with a microchip tracer.

Sightseeing – Comfortable open boats take you on a 50min canal tour of the Danish capital. Starting at 10am boats leave every 30min between mid-April and mid-September. Boats leave from Gammel Strand and Nyhavn. For further information and booking ☎ 33 13 31 05. The Tourist Guide Association organises guided tours of the city in several languages from April to October during weekends and daily during July and August. For further information contact the Tourist Information Centre, 1 Bernstorffsgade, ☎ 33 11 13 25. Bus tours of the city leave from the Lur Blower Column in Rådhuspladsen.The hop-on-hop-off sightseeing tour running all summer until mid-October is very practical and reasonably priced: there are 14 stops and tickets valid for two days are available at hotels or on the bus. For further information ☎ 38 28 01 88.

Disabled – The Danish Tourist Board publishes an inexpensive brochure on wheelchair access to sights, accommodation, public toilets and transportation.

Shopping – Shopping hours have been extended to allow shops to remain open from 6am to 8pm but the majority of shops keep to normal opening hours (9.30am to 5.30 or 7pm, 4pm on Saturdays). The main shopping street Strøget is pedestrianised and has become an open stage where buskers, stalls, musicians and jugglers jostle for space to entertain the passing shoppers, strolling tourists and busy office workers. The two department stores Magasin and ILLUM, are in the same pedestrianised street. The Scala shopping centre right in the heart of the city at 2 Axeltorv has, in addition to a choice of shops and boutiques, a selection of restaurants, cafés, disco and cinemas as does the Shopping Center at Copenhagen Central Station. For souvenirs try the factory shop at Royal Copenhagen (Kongelige Porcelains Fabrik), 47 Smallegade, ☎ 31 86 48 59. Every Sunday from May to September 9am to 2pm there is a giant flea market in Lyngby in northern Copenhagen. On Amagertorv, Danish design comes to the fore with the silverware of Georg Jensen, the delicate porcelain and crystal of Royal Copenhagen, Royal Copenhagen Antiques and the Georg Jensen Museum, and modern design in Illums Bolighus. Continuing along Strøget towards the town hall square, you will soon come to Ravhuset and Ravspecialisten both in Frederiksberggade, which specialise in amber, the Nordic gold as it is sometimes called. Original gifts can also be found in the sweater market a few doors away at 15 Frederiksberggade which has an impressive stock of Scandinavian sweaters.

Little Mermaid

Cafés – For a lunchtime stop choose from one of the many cafés and restaurants on the Nyhavn waterfront or in the Bolten's complex off Store Kongensgade or the bars and restaurants of Gråbrødre Torv (Peder Oxe). Christianshavn also has a selection of restaurants and bars; Café Wilder and Café Luna at the corner of Sankt Annæ Gade where office workers from the nearby ministries mix with inhabitants of the free community of Christiania. In Christiania itself try Den Grå Hal in Prinsessegade or Loppen in

Bådsmandsstræde, both with live music. Try a pastry and beer from the bakery in Christianshavns Torv. Tivoli offers a wide choice of restaurants: the sophisticated Restaurant PH (the initials of the Danish designer Poul Henningsen whose lamps decorate the establishment) or Divan 1 (a mixture of tradition and modernism) and, in striking contrast, Grøften, the haunt of the local showbiz crowd, but many Danes simply eat fresh shrimps on white bread with a glass of beer. Another alternative is one of the family gardens or outdoor restaurants on Pile Allé which usually serve traditional Danish *smørrebrød*. Konditoriet (bakery-cum-café) on Pistolstræde is also worth a visit. The Café Sommersko is a lively place at night in Kronprinsensgade. For Internet surfers here are two addresses in the town centre: Babel at 33 Frederiksborggade and Gamestation at 115 Vesterbrogade.

Entertainment – With the Royal Theatre for ballet, drama and opera and the resident company The Royal Danish Ballet and the more intimate stage Baron Bolten's Gård, the visitor is spoilt for choice. The box office Billetnet sells tickets in post offices or on the web: www.billetnet.dk. The theatre ticket booth at the corner of Fiolstræde and Nørrevoldgade is open Monday to Friday noon to 7pm and Saturday noon to 3pm and sells tickets for same-day performances.

CHRISTIANSBORG AND SLOTSHOLMEN

Surrounded by canals, Slotsholmen is the historic heart of Copenhagen, the original island which Absalon chose to build his fortress on; today, his statue stands on Højbro Plads, over the canal, to the north of the island, as if the famous bishop were still watching over the city.

★**Christiansborg** ⊘ (**CZ**) – The present palace is the fifth built on the site since 1167. The first Christiansborg Palace was erected by Christian VI during the 18C in German Baroque style, but it was almost entirely destroyed by fire in 1794. The second palace, in neo-Classical style, also burned down less than a century later. During the building of the third palace which began in 1907, excavations revealed the ruins of the original fortress and of the medieval castle which can now be visited. Completed in 1928, Christiansborg incorporates the Royal Stables and the Court Theatre (now a museum) of the first palace, the Chapel of the second and imitates the style of the preceding structures with its austere granite façades, green-copper roof and tall square tower. On the palace square stands an equestrian statue of Frederik VII who renounced absolute power in 1849. The palace was never used as a royal residence and now houses the Danish Parliament (Folketing), the Prime Minister's offices, the Supreme Court and the royal reception rooms, which can be visited.

★**Marmorbroen** (**CZ 50**) – This Rococo marble bridge spanning Frederiksholms Kanal gives access to the vast courtyard of Christiansborg Slot; it was designed by the famous 18C architect **Nicolai Eigtved** (1701-54), and built at the same time as the first palace. Seen from a short distance along the shaded canal, its elegant arches offer one of the most attractive views in Copenhagen.

★**Royal Library** ⊘ (**CZ**) – *From the bridge, walk south-east along Frederiksholms Kanal and turn left on Christians Brygge.* The Danes have nicknamed it the Black Diamond. This extension of the Royal Library, founded in 1653 by King Frederik III and first opened to the public in 1793, stands on the waterside as a striking example of contemporary Danish architecture and design; the outside is made of shiny black granite and glass. The Søren K (for Kierkegaard) restaurant and café offers a view of Christianshavn across the water with its row of square modern buildings over which towers the Rococo steeple of Christians Kirke.

On the first level, up a flight of stairs near the information desk, an exhibition room displays manuscripts and first editions of famous Danish authors such as HC Andersen, Søren Kierkegaard and Karen Blixen as well as manuscripts and scores by Carl Nielsen. There is a circular book and record shop on the ground floor.

★★**Thorvaldsens Museum** ⊘ (**CZ M¹**) – The museum stands next to the castle chapel, on the north side of Christiansborg, as a monument to Denmark's most famous sculptor, **Bertel Thorvaldsen** (1770-1844) who spent most of his life in Rome during the early 19C and was greeted like a hero when he came back to his native country; the museum was built in neo-Classical style to house the artist's extensive collection of paintings, antiquities and of his own works.

★ Børsen (CDZ) – *Not open to the public.* Commissioned by Christian IV in 1619, the Stock Exchange is a fine example of Dutch Renaissance style and its slender spire consisting of the entwined tails of four dragons is a distinctive landmark in the city.

Holmens Kirke (CZ B) – Almost opposite, across the bridge, Holmens Bro, stands Holmens Kirke, the Renaissance naval church built by Christian IV and containing a remarkable altarpiece and pulpit. Queen Margrethe II was married in the church in 1967.

THE UNIVERSITY QUARTER AND STRØGET

Copenhagen's lively Latin Quarter is bound to the south by Strøget, the city's main shopping street and to the north by Gothersgade, a large avenue separating Rosenborg and the new town from the old town. Most of the area is pedestrianised and the narrow streets are lined with tiny boutiques often installed in the basement of 18C terraced houses: bookshops, antique shops, fashion boutiques, pizzerias and cafés. A stroll along Købmagergade, Fiolstræde and some of the side streets which link them is a rewarding experience. Løvstræde and Skindergade lead to **Gråbrødretorv★** (CY 28), a quaint and charming little square almost entirely taken over in summertime by the tables and sunshades of its crowded restaurants and cafés.

Vor Frue Kirke ⊙ **(Domkirken)** (BY D) – A short distance from Gråbrødretorv along Skindergade is the square (Vor Frue Plads) on which stands Copenhagen's neo-Classical cathedral designed by CF Hansen in 1829, the third one to be erected on the site as the original Gothic structure was destroyed by the 1728 fire and the second cathedral severely damaged by British bombs in 1807. The interior is decorated with sculptures by Thorvaldsen.

The **University** complex occupies the northern side of Vor Frue Plads: the main building facing onto the square was built at the same time as the cathedral, while the Commons building along Nørregade is a century older. Across Nørregade, at the corner of Skt Pedersstræde, stands the austere St Peter's Church, **Sct Petri Kirke** (BY); although it was burned down and bombed like the cathedral, it has retained its tall dark 16C steeple.

★ Rundetårn ⊙ (CY E) – Across Vor Frue Plads from Sct Petri Kirke, Store Kannikestræde leads to the 35m-high Round Tower, built as an observatory by Christian IV in 1642. A most unusual paved spiral ramp and narrow spiral staircase (31 steps) lead to the platform at the top of the tower. Peter the Great of Russia is said to have ridden to the top when he visited Copenhagen in 1716, followed by the czarina in a carriage. From the platform, there is a wonderful **panoramic view★★** of the city with its forest of tall spires.

The Round Tower is attached to Trinity Church, **Trinitatis Kirke**, intended by Christian IV as a university church with a library on the upper floor; the building was finished by his successor in 1656. Inside there is a beautifully carved Baroque altarpiece and a striking Rococo clock.

North of the church in Åbenrå there is an interesting Museum of Musical Instruments, **Musikhistorisk Museum** ⊙ (CY M²), with exhibits going back to the 16C.

★ Strøget (BCYZ) – This long pedestrian street, which stretches across the old town from Kongens Nytorv (New Royal Square) to Rådhuspladsen (Town Hall Square), is in fact a succession of streets and squares lined with some of Copenhagen's most exciting shops next to the inevitable dazzling Mc Donald's, bustling at all times of the day and offering continuous and varied entertainment: there are street musicians and buskers, pavement cafés, parades by the Queen's Life Guard, picturesque shopping arcades and, of course, reminders of the city's past. Off Østergade on the right, **Pistolstræde** (CY 54) is a delightful street lined with restored 18C houses and interesting shops. Further along on the left, opposite Illum's department store, stands St Nicholas' Church, **Sct Nikolaj Kirke** (CY F), which has retained its massive 16C square tower, supported by six buttresses; the rest of the building is fairly recent and the church is now used as an art exhibition centre.

Strøget crosses Købmagergade and widens into Amagertorv, recently repaved, with the 19C Stork Fountain, **Storkespringvandet**, in its centre; further along on the right is the church of the Holy Ghost, **Helligåndskirken** (CY G) surrounded by a peaceful garden in total contrast with the feverish animation of the street; it used to belong to a monastery which disappeared long ago, but the church was rebuilt after the 1728 fire and has been restored since. The street changes name again and opens out into a wide open square or rather two squares, the Old Square, **Gammeltorv** (BYZ 27) on the right, the oldest market square in Copenhagen and the New Square, **Nytorv** (BZ) on the left. The 17C **Caritas Fountain**, so called because the sculpture mounted on top represents Charity, stands in the centre of Gammeltorv whereas the old Domhuset, now the Court House, is tucked away in one of the corners of Nytorv. Beyond the two squares, Strøget runs into Rådhuspladsen.

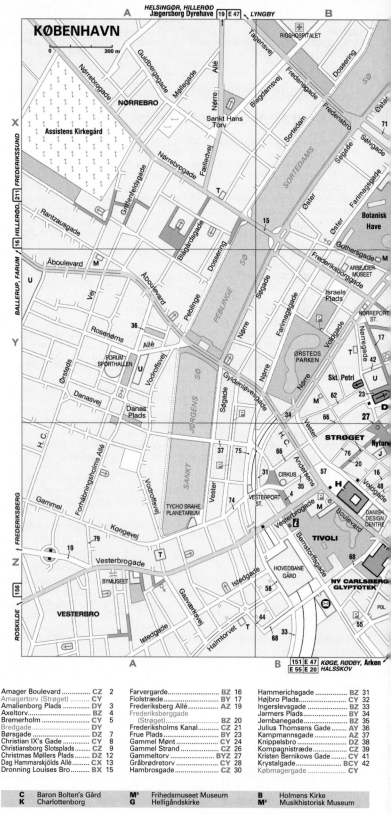

*The diagram on the back cover shows the **Michelin Map** covering the guide; the entry headings specify the map coordinates for the locality*

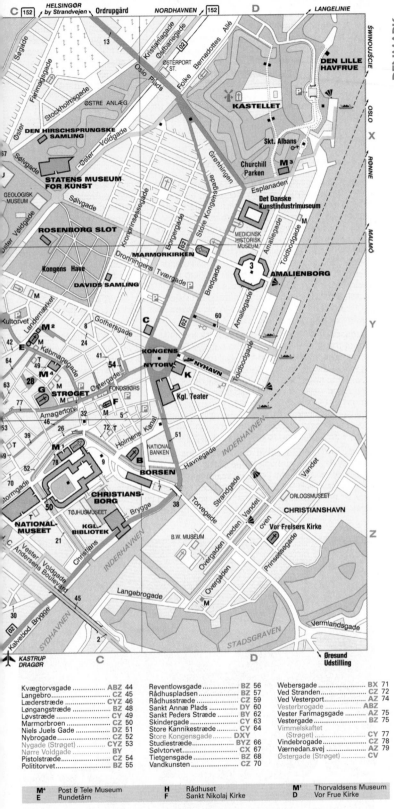

C [152] HELSINGØR by Strandvejen Ordrupgård NORDHAVNEN [152] D LANGELINIE

ØSTERPORT ST.

DEN LILLE HAVFRUE

KASTELLET

Skt. Albans

Churchill Parken M 3

ØSTRE ANLÆG

DEN HIRSCHSPRUNGSKE SAMLING

Det Danske Kunstindustrimuseum

STATENS MUSEUM FOR KUNST

GEOLOGISK MUSEUM

MEDICINSK HISTORISK MUSEUM

ROSENBORG SLOT

MARMORKIRKEN

AMALIENBORG

Kongens Have

3

DAVIDS SAMLING

M 2

KONGENS NYTORV NYHAVN

K

M 4

STRØGET

G

Kgl. Teater

FONDSBORS

F

Amagertorv

NATIONAL BANKEN

M 1

B

BØRSEN

INDERHAVNEN

CHRISTIANS-BORG

TØJHUSMUSEET

CHRISTIANSHAVN

Vor Frelsers Kirke

NATIONAL-MUSEET

KGL. BIBLIOTEK

B.W. MUSEUM

INDERHAVNEN

Langebrogade

SYDHAVNEN

STADSGRAVEN

Vermlandsgade

KASTRUP DRAGØR

Øresund Udstilling

To choose a hotel or restaurant in one of the Scandinavian capitals use the annual **Michelin Red Guide Europe**

Post & Tele Museum ⊙ (**CY M⁴**) – Have a quick look (all explanations are unfortunately in Danish only) at this recent museum's main exhibition on the third floor of no 37 Købmagergade. The attractive displays illustrate the history of Danish communications from Christian IV until today, with Royal Mail coaches, costumes, paintings, seals, stamp-printing blocks, the first telephones and telegraphs, mail bags, telephone booths, postboxes, three-wheeled motorcycles for carrying mail etc.

On the first floor of the building, there is an internet space, the fourth floor houses changing exhibitions and, from the fifth floor, there is a panoramic view of the rooftops of the old town. You can spot the Round Tower and several green-copper spires: Børsen, the town hall and two nearby churches (Helligåndskirke and Sankt Nikolaj Kirke).

RÅDHUSPLADSEN AND TIVOLI

The busy Rådhuspladsen (Town Hall Square) is a vast open space crisscrossed by several main arteries carrying a constant but extremely well-controlled flow of traffic. The central island swarms with strollers who gather round the various stands selling food, apparently oblivious to the animation around them. The no 50 bus terminal is one of several dotted all round the square; a journey on that bus provides an excellent introduction to Copenhagen, as it goes across to the other side of town where the Little Mermaid sits on the waterfront, patiently waiting for her numerous visitors. The imposing red-brick town hall stands on the south side of the square, flanked on the left as one faces the building by the popular bronze statue of **two lur players** erected in 1914 and on the right by the 1923 **Dragon Fountain**, the work of Danish artists Skovgaard and Bindesbøll. A **statue** of Hans Christian Andersen, sitting with a book in his hand and lost in his dreams, has been discreetly placed on the shaded western side of the Rådhuset.

Rådhuset ⊙ (**BZ H**) – The huge red-brick town hall, designed by Martin Nyrop at the turn of the last century, is inspired both by Danish medieval architecture, and by the Renaissance style of northern Italy. From the top of the tower there is a breathtaking **view** of the city and the harbour. Inside the town hall, a couple of rooms have been set aside to house **Jens Olsen's astronomical clock★**. Born in Ribe (south Jutland) in 1872, Jens Olsen never saw the realisation of his life's ambition: as he died before his famous clock was finally installed under its glass domes. This fascinating piece of engineering shows sidereal time as well as solar time anywhere in the world; it indicates the planets' trajectory round the sun and calculates eclipses of the sun and the moon with a precision to the order of half a second every 300 years!

★★ Tivoli ⊙ (**BZ**) – Situated at the heart of the city between Rådhuspladsen and the main railway station, Tivoli is one of the world's oldest leisure parks (its foundation goes back to 1843) and Denmark's number one attraction with over three million visitors a year. It was the brain child of Georg Carstensen, the much travelled son of the Danish Consul General in Algeria, who was inspired by pleasure gardens in Paris and London but whose imagination was stirred by the exotic countries he visited.

A quiet corner in Tivoli

C. Boisvieux

Entertainment, fantasy and charm bring life to these beautiful gardens adorned with a great variety of tall trees lit by Chinese lanterns. The numerous restaurants and cafés decorated with old-fashioned lights create a cosy atmosphere conducive to relaxation while live music can be enjoyed by everyone since concerts are given in the open throughout the day as well as in the concert hall at night with international orchestras and soloists. There are attractive floral arrangements, exotic buildings and thousand-night palaces with arches underlined by hundreds of small white bulbs glittering through the trees. Lying at anchor in Lake Tivoli is the frigate *Skt Georg III* on board which one can have a typical Danish meal. There are colourful parades by the Tivoli Guard dressed in red and white uniforms and wearing shining bearskins, pantomimes staging the traditional characters of the *commedia dell'arte* and sparkling firework displays three times a week, not forgetting the various amusements including bumper cars, the Haunted House and the latest addition, the Flying Trunk, inspired by Andersen's fairy tales. The Christmas Market introduced in 1994 has now become a tradition with three to four hundred thousand visitors a year. Throughout December, people can do their Christmas shopping, kids can meet Father Christmas and families can go ice-skating on Lake Tivoli; many restaurants, open for Christmas dinner, serve traditional Danish fare.

Tivoli's secret seems to lie in the fact that it provides enough variety to satisfy every taste with all the originality and vivacity inherent in the Danish character and temperament. What more could one say except spell it backwards: 'I lov it.'

The secret of success

The gardens cover a total area of 83 000m^2 planted with 875 trees, and 400 000 flowers bloom every year; there are 30 restaurants and 27 different amusements, the roller-coaster being the most popular and covering 48 000km during a single season; 110 000 lamps are lit every night to create the fairy tale atmosphere; the Tivoli Guard consists of 102 young guardsmen and 100 concerts are given in the Concert Hall every season.

Among the many famous artists who have performed there since the inauguration of Tivoli in 1843 are Artur Rubinstein, Benjamino Gigli, Yehudi Menuhin, Isaac Stern, Janet Baker, Mstislav Rostropovich, Anne-Sophie Mutter and many others.

MAIN MUSEUMS

Copenhagen boasts many a fine museum easily visited during the course of a stroll through various parts of town, but three of them possess such rich and extensive collections that they warrant a special visit. The Nationalmuseet and the Glyptotek are close to Rådhuspladsen, whereas the Fine Arts Museum is situated north of the city, near Rosenborg Slot, in a park which was laid out after the town walls were razed to the ground, during the 19C.

★★★ **Nationalmuseet** ⊘ (CZ) – The national Museum has been extended several times since its foundation at the beginning of the 19C, the most recent addition being that of a spacious modern building with an imposing entrance hall. The complex still includes the original **Prince's Palace** (Prinsens Palæ) built in 1744 by Eigtved for the Crown Prince at the same time as the Marble Bridge facing it. The collections are now displayed on three floors with an important amount of space reserved for temporary exhibitions, and an area has been set aside for a children's museum. There are six distinct departments:

Danish Prehistory, which spans the years 13000 BC to AD 1000, is the jewel of the museum with a wealth of bronze and gold exhibits such as the Sun Chariot from Trundholm, found in a bog, dating from c 1200 BC and depicting the sun crossing the firmament on a chariot drawn by a horse. The collection of 10C rune stones from Lolland and Jutland is also remarkable as are the finds from the Viking period.

The Middle Ages and the Renaissance are mainly represented by religious objects, weapons, furniture and tapestries; these include a 12C golden altar from Århus, painted retables, 15C-16C sacred vessels, drinking horns from c 1400 and 16C Dutch tapestries.

The Danish Collections 1660-1830 consist essentially of furniture, glass and china with reconstructions of original interiors.

The collections of **Near Eastern and Classical Antiquities** are less interesting as they mostly comprise Greek pottery and ceramics, Egyptian mummies and burial finds with a very small Roman section.

The Ethnographical Collections on the other hand are among the most important in the world; they concern non-European cultures with a unique section on the Eskimos of Greenland, Canada and Alaska.

The Royal Collection of Coins and Medals contains exhibits from various countries of the world, but is particularly rich in ancient Greek and Roman coins.

DENMARK

★★★**Ny Carlsberg Glyptotek** ⊘ (BZ) – The ambitious art collection founded by the brewer Carl Jacobsen is housed in an imposing building designed by Vilhem Dahlerup and inaugurated in 1897, with a very ornate interior, a most appropriate setting for the collections. Another building by Hack Kampmann was added in 1906 and linked to the original structure by a magnificent winter garden on a grand scale, with huge palm trees, a mosaic floor and a central pond decorated with an allegorical sculpture by Kai Nielsen. There are benches and a pleasant café for visitors who wish to linger on in this haven of peace. In 1996 a new wing was built by Henning Larsen to house the French paintings and Degas bronzes.

Jacobsen's interest lay essentially in Ancient Art but also in 19C French painting and sculpture and, to this day, these constitute the museum's main treasures, which are continually being added to with the help of the Ny Carlsberg Foundation established by Jacobsen.

The **collection of ancient art** from Mesopotamia (the oldest item dating from c 2500 BC), Egypt (including a 5 000-year-old hippopotamus), Greece (marble sculptures, terracottas, bronzes and vases) and Italy (Etruscan sculpture and vases, Roman portrait sculpture) is the largest in Northern Europe.

The rich **collection of French 19C and 20C art** comprises mainly, but not exclusively, a wide selection of Impressionist and Post-Impressionist paintings and an impressive number of sculptures by Degas and Rodin, other sculptors like Carpeaux and Maillol also being represented.

A glazed arcade leads off the winter garden to the new extension whose entrance is guarded by *The Shadow*, a dark bronze statue by Rodin. Beyond the low arch, a white-marble stepped alleyway winds round the new building right to the top, offering an unexpected architectural experience. The French paintings and Degas bronzes are displayed on three floors in chronological order. Five rooms on the ground floor are devoted to painting from David to Manet, including works by Delacroix *(Mirabeau answering the Marquid de Dreux-Brézé)*, several Corots *(The Path, Landscape with Harvesters)*, *Portrait of the Comte de Turenne* by David and some world famous Manets *(The Absinthe Drinker* and a sketch for *The Execution of Emperor Maximilian)*. Two rooms on the first floor house the Impressionist collection: Pissarro *(View of the Seine towards the Louvre from Pont-Neuf)*, Sisley *(Flood)*, Monet *(Pyramides at Port-Coton, Belle-Île-en-Mer, The Artist's son)*, Cézanne *(Women bathing, Self-Portrait with Bowler Hat)*, Degas *(Dancers practising in the Foyer* as well as a lovely set of small bronze statues of dancers, 72 in all), Renoir *(Young Girls, Reclining Odalisque)*. The four remaining rooms on the second floor contain a wonderful collection of Post-Impressionist painting, particularly works by Gauguin (in a room of their own), illustrating all aspects of his art: early carved-wood scenes and ceramics, Brittany period *(Landscape from Pont-Aven, Breton Girl)*, mature Tahitian period *(Tahitian Woman with a Flower)*. Other Post-Impressionist paintings on display include *Portrait of the Painter Suzanne Valadon* by Toulouse-Lautrec, several paintings by Bonnard *(Landscape from the south of France, The Dining Room)*, *Women picking Fruit* by Émile Bernard, *Landscape from St-Rémy* by Van Gogh, *View of Mont-Blanc* by Signac and *Landscape from the River Creuse* by Guillaumin. From the roof terrace there is a fine view of the city's green-copper spires.

French sculpture includes an outstanding selection of works by Rodin *(The Kiss)* and Carpeaux.

The museum also possesses an extensive collection of **Danish sculpture** and a small but significant collection of **19C Danish painting of the Golden Age**.

★★★**Statens Museum for Kunst** ⊘ (CX) – The building housing the National Gallery was also designed by Vilhelm Dahlerup almost at the same time as the Glyptotek; however, the interior was later modernised, the emphasis being given to light and space. However, the original royal collections, which have been considerably extended since 1900 could no longer be satisfactorily exhibited for lack of room and it was decided to build a large new building overlooking the gardens, which was completed in November 1998. At the same time, the old building was renovated and the museum reopened with an entirely new presentation of the collections.

International and Danish art up to 1900 is displayed on the first floor of the original Dahlerup building where the rooms are painted in shades of blue, grey, green and red to suit the works exhibited. There are two sections:

The **European Art section** (1300-1800) includes a wide selection of paintings from the Italian (14C-18C) and the French (17C-18C) schools, but the collection of Flemish and Dutch paintings (15C-18C) is particularly noteworthy with a wealth of works by Bruegel, Rembrandt, Hals, Rubens, Ruisdael and Memling to name but a few. A few rooms, devoted to Danish and European art from 1600 to 1800 illustrate the beginnings of Danish art with Jens Juel's portraits and landscapes and Abildgaard's mythological and historical paintings.

The **Danish and European Art section** (1800-1900) shows the development of Danish painting during the 19C; paintings from the Danish Golden Age are well represented (works by Eckersberg, Købke, Bendz, Lundbye, Sonne, Bissen) but attention is also drawn to the second half of the 19C (the Skagen Painters, Theodor Philipsen and Impressionism, the Funen Painters) and to lesser known periods such as the early 1800s and Symbolism (works by EjnarNielsen, Zahrtmann, Skovgaard, Ring, Edvard Munch, Hammershøi and Willumsen) which leads to the 20C.

A glass-covered arcade, known as the sculpture street because it is lined with large sculptures, makes the transition between the old building and the extension designed by Anna Maria Indrio and Mads Møller, which is the home of the museum's collections of 20C Art displayed on three levels. Gangways link the two buildings above the sculpture street.

On **level 1**, a single room exhibits early-20C Scandinavian paintings including two works by Edvard Munch *(Workers coming Home, 1914-19)*.

It is then advisable to go straight to **level 3** which houses an impressive collection of works by Matisse *(Interior with a Violin, Odalisque, Goldfish)*, Derain, Dufy, Marquet, Modigliani *(Alice)*, Laurens. Organic Surrealist painting follows, represented by R Mortensen *(Vision, Painting for Arthur Rimbaud)*, Max Ernst and Erik Olson *(Aerodynamic landscape)*; then comes the Cobra Group with works by Asger Jorn *(Springtime, Saxnäs)*, Carl-Henning Pedersen *(Red Castle, Reykjavik)*. The remaining rooms contain works by Niels Lergaard, Jens Søndergaard, Harald Giersing *(The Judgement of Paris, Churchyard in Swanninge)*, Georges Rouault *(The Bridge)* and Chaïm Soutine *(The Gipsy)*.

Cubism is well represented on **level 2** with works by Braque, Juan Gris *(The Guitar Player)*, Picasso, Léger, Olaf Rude *(Cubist Composition)*, Edvard Weie *(Romantic Fantasy)*; there is also an important section of post-1950 works by Richard Mortensen *(Double Espace)*, Victor Vasarely, Per Kirkeby *(Romantic picture, a huge five-panelled painting)* and Lockenwitz *(Neon Relief II, Composition)*. The last rooms are devoted to Danish, English and American contemporary art where compositions use photos, light effects, writing and other devices, as well as to Danish, Swedish and German art of the 1980s and 1990s with large paintings such as *Central Park* by Ola Billgren from Sweden; finally, there is a display of American and Danish sculpture of the 1960s and 1990s.

ROSENBORG

Across Gothersgade, a large avenue which marks the northern boundary of the old town, lies an area of parkland with Rosenborg in its centre. When Christian IV decided to build a modest pavilion for himself at the beginning of the 17C, he chose a site outside the city's boundaries, which could offer him a complete contrast to the cramped environment of the old town. In a way this contrast still exists as the whole district surrounding Rosenborg Slot has a definite suburban feel about it.

★★★**Rosenborg Slot** ⊘ **(CX)** –
The exterior aspect of the castle has not changed since 1633, the building having fortunately escaped damage from fire and war. Inspired by the Dutch Renaissance architecture, Rosenborg is built of red brick decorated with sandstone and was originally surrounded by a moat.

From summer house to royal residence – Having acquired land outside the city, Christian IV first designed suitable gardens which were laid out in 1606. Still called **Kongens Have (CXY)**, the King's Garden is a delightful haven of peace, particularly attractive in springtime when the rhododendrons are in bloom. The king then proceeded with the building of a summer house, only two-storeys high, with a modest stair turret. Problems with the foundations were the cause of immediate major changes and by 1615 the

Rosenborg

Prat-Pries/DIAF

house had doubled in size. Then, with the addition during the next decade of the third storey, the Great Tower and the two smaller towers, the summer house became a royal residence. In 1624 Christian IV named it Rosenborg and the castle was finally completed in 1633 by the building of a central stair turret. It ceased to be an official royal residence in 1710 as Frederik IV found it too small!

The collections – The personal treasures of the royal family, comprising paintings, tapestries, rare furniture, silver, and porcelain, have been collected in Rosenborg Slot since the reign of Frederik III, Christian IV's son. In 1833 the collections were arranged in chronological order and the castle opened to the public. Of particular interest are Christian IV's study which has hardly changed and the Winter Room with paintings inlaid in the wall panelling, the Marble Room decorated in Baroque style, with an elaborate stuccoed ceiling, the King's Chamber lined with Dutch tapestries and, on the top floor, the Long Hall with a splendid 18C stuccoed ceiling and three glittering silver lions guarding the throne. The treasury, situated in the basement of the castle, contains the Crown Jewels and the Regalia. Also in the basement is the Green Cabinet where the royal collection of treasures is presented as it was in 1700.

Botanisk Have ⊘ (BX) – Facing Rosenborg Slot, on the other side of Øster Voldgade *(entrance on the corner of Gothersgade)*, are the vast Botanical Gardens laid out in the 1870s on land formerly occupied by the old town walls. The palm house and the greenhouses containing cacti and orchids are particularly remarkable.

★**Den Hirschsprungske Samling** ⊘ (CX) – Bequeathed to the Danish State by Heinrich Hirschsprung, a tobacco manufacturer, the collection is housed in a neo-Classical building inaugurated in 1911, situated just behind the Fine Arts Museum. It consists exclusively of 19C Danish paintings, sculptures, watercolours and drawings. In many of the rooms, the artistic impression is enhanced by furnishings from the homes of the artists.

★**Davids Samling** ⊘ (CY) – Across Kongens Have from Rosenborg, along Kronprinsessegade, stands a harmonious early-19C house, the home of a barrister, CL David, who in 1945 turned it into a public institution and provided the necessary funds for its upkeep. It holds the rich David Collection of Islamic art as well as a collection of 18C European fine and decorative art.

Central Copenhagen has many pedestrian and one-way streets which can make driving difficult for visitors who are not acquainted with the city.
Make life simpler by buying a Copenhagen Card which gives unlimited travel on the well-integrated bus and S-train networks.

KONGENS NYTORV AND THE 18C TOWN *2hr*

This is the elegant and fashionable part of Copenhagen, the new town which developed along the waterfront, to the north-east of the old town, in the late 17C and throughout the 18C. There are wide avenues, luxury hotels and exclusive shops surrounding the royal residence, Amalienborg.

★**Kongens Nytorv** (DY) – The striking contrast between the stately New Royal Square and the picturesque wharves on both sides of Nyhavn is one of Copenhagen's many contradictions which make the discovery of the city so enthralling.
Kongens Nytorv marked the beginning of an ambitious town planning project designed to extend the overcrowded old town and the square was intended to link the two. It was completed in 1688 when the equestrian statue of Christian V was placed in its centre where it can still be seen. Many of the original buildings surrounding the square have now disappeared, but a certain architectural harmony has been preserved; the oldest building is **Charlottenborg** (DY K), situated on the south side of Nyhavn, a palace in Baroque style dating back to 1670, which today houses the Royal Academy of Fine Arts. Walking round the square in a clockwise direction, one next passes in front of the Royal Theatre, **Det Kongelige Teater** (DY), an impressive stone structure built in the 1870s. The 18C mansion across Holmens Kanal has been taken over by a bank. Next comes Copenhagen's most famous department store, **Magasin du Nord** and then the **Hôtel d'Angleterre**, the most fashionable hotel in Copenhagen. The building on the corner of Gothersgade and Store Kongensgade is a new cultural centre called **Baron Bolten's Gård** (DY C), usually referred to simply as Bolten's. At the corner of Bredgade stands the second oldest building on Kongens Nytorv, **Thotts Palæ**, built in c 1685 by one of Denmark's national heroes, Admiral Niels Juel, which now houses the French Embassy. Lined with fashionable antique shops and art galleries, **Bredgade** is the 18C town's main artery, leading north-east to Churchill Parken and beyond to the Little Mermaid.

★★★**Nyhavn** (DY) – This picturesque canal, now one of the most famous sights in Copenhagen, was dug in the late 17C to allow ships to sail right up to Kongens Nytorv at the heart of the city and unload their cargo on the wharves. Commerce soon prospered and merchants built warehouses and rows of tall narrow private dwellings. At the same time, Nyhavn became a popular place as sailors from all over the world came ashore while their ships were loaded or unloaded. Gradually the ground floors of the houses were turned into bars and restaurants and regular brawling gave Nyhavn a bad reputation. However it never ceased to be inhabited by respectable Copenhageners, the most famous of them being undoubtedly Hans Christian Andersen who had rooms in no fewer than three different houses on both sides of the canal, nos 20, 67 and 18 in chronological order. However, the area's notoriety is a thing of the past; the houses have been carefully restored and painted in bright colours, the shabby bars have been turned into quaint little restaurants and cafés overflowing on to the wharf and the only ships to sail up the canal today are picturesque old sailing ships. In summertime, Copenhageners mingle with tourists along the sunny side of the canal (the northern side) which is now a pedestrian area and is at its liveliest late in the afternoon when the pavement cafés are packed and the beer stands can hardly cope with demand.

C. Boisvieux

Nyhavn on a sunny evening

At the Kongens Nytorv end of the canal, the huge ship's anchor, which looks as if it has been washed ashore after a storm, was placed there as a memorial to Danish seamen who died during the Second World War; nearby is the starting point of boat trips along the canals and round the harbour.

★★ **Amalienborg** (DY 3) – The palace, the square and the Marmorkirken beyond were planned in 1749 by Frederik V as the central feature of a magnificent new district which would be called Frederiksstaden. Eigtved designed the four identical mansions round an octagonal piazza and he drew the plans for the church at the same time. According to King Frederik's wishes, four prominent personalities were each granted a plot of land on which to build one of the mansions at their own expense. In 1768, the equestrian statue of Frederik V by the French sculptor Jacques François Joseph Saly (1717-76) was placed in the centre of the square.

★★ **Amalienborg Palace** ⊘ (DY) – The palace became the official royal residence in 1794 when Christiansborg was destroyed by fire. When the Queen is in residence, the colourful changing of the guard ceremony takes place daily at noon. In 1994, Christian VIII's palace, Amalienborg, opened its doors to the public for the first time, revealing regal private and state rooms refurbished as they were during the period 1863 to 1972. Highlights include the study of King Christian IX, the elegant drawing room of his wife, Queen Louise, the study of King Frederik VIII with the original furniture, and King Christian X's and King Frederik IX's studies. The museum also has a costume and jewellery gallery.
A small park, **Amaliehaven**, separates the palace square from the waterfront and its tastefully restored warehouses converted into flats and a hotel.

★**Marmorkirken** ⊘ **(DY)** – The marble church which was planned as part of Frederiksstaden *(see above)* is in fact officially called Frederiks Kirke. Although designed by Eigtved, it was only completed at the end of the 19C. Its huge dome is one of the landmarks of Copenhagen. A short distance from the church along Bredgade stands another building designed by Eigtved, the former Frederik's Hospital, now housing the Museum of Decorative Art, **Det Danske Kunstindustrimuseum** ⊘ **(DX)**, and its collections of Western and Oriental decorative arts from the Middle Ages to the present day.

★KASTELLET AND THE LITTLE MERMAID

North of Amalienborg, beyond Esplanaden, lies an area of parkland with the old citadel, **Kastellet★ (DX)**, in its centre. These former barracks dating from the early 18C consist of rows of red-brick buildings on either side of a paved street, with a gatehouse at each end; the whole is surrounded by still waters lined with reeds and weeping willows and forms an attractive townscape. Keeping to the periphery of the park, called **Churchill Parken**, and walking northwards past the Resistance Museum, **Frihedsmuseet** ⊘ **(DX M³)**, which gives a general picture of Danish society between 1940 and 1945, one comes across the impressive **Gefion Fountain**: the three-tiered fountain is surmounted by a bronze female figure furiously leading two teams of oxen. Immediately on its left is St Alban's Anglican Church, **Skt Albans Kirke**. Behind the fountain, a wrought-iron footbridge leads through the park.

Further along the waterfront, one reaches Copenhagen's most famous symbol, the Little Mermaid, **Den Lille Havfrue★★ (DX)**. The small enigmatic figure sits on a rock on the edge of the water, looking towards the vast entrance of the harbour, and appears so unassuming and so strangely out of place against the hostile background of cranes and chimneys that most people are fascinated and charmed. The bronze statue by Edvard Eriksen was offered to the city of Copenhagen in 1913 by Carl Jacobsen, son of the founder of Carlsberg breweries.

Continuing along the waterfront, one reaches Langeliniekaj, along which cruise liners are moored; a parade of arcaded shops and cafés runs the length of the quay and a walkway along the top offers fine views of the Øresund.

ADDITIONAL SIGHTS

Christianshavn (DZ) – Across Knippelsbro, from Slotsholmen lies Christianshavn, Christian IV's fortified town. When it was built at the beginning of the 17C, a long straight canal was dug through its centre and linked to the harbour for easy access. The district has retained much of its original character and offers pleasant strolls along the canal lined with restored 18C houses. The Baroque Church of Our Saviour, **Vor Frelsers Kirke (DZ)**, in Prinsessegade is famous for its tall slender spire: for a real thrill and a breathtaking view, visitors can climb the flight of stairs which winds its way up to the top on the outside!

Christianshavns Kanal

DENMARK

Frederiksberg – This is a pleasant western suburb of Copenhagen. The main avenue out of the town centre, Vesterbrogade, and then Frederiksberg Allé (**AZ**) lead straight to the park, Frederiksberg Have, with a picturesque canal winding through it. To the north of the park, in Smallegade is the Royal Copenhagen porcelain factory, **Kongelige Porcelænsfabrik** ⊘. South of the park, along Ny Carlsbergvej, stands the imposing building of the **Carlsberg Breweries**; the **Carsberg Visitor's Centre** ⊘ is located at Gamle Carlsberg Vej 11. There is also the **Carlsberg Museum** ⊘ nearby at Valby Landgade 1.

Assistens Kirkegård (**AX**) – This cemetery situated north-west of the town centre contains the graves of Hans Christian Andersen and Søren Kierkegaard.

Christiania, Copenhagen's unique social experiment

Christiania was set up in the 1970s as the world's largest hippie commune and today the squatters, who first occupied the 18C army camp, are middle-aged. Some work as doctors, lawyers and teachers and return to their alternative lifestyle at night whereas others work in the district's workshops. The second generation busy their time with green politics. In 1988 the Ramme Deal gave Christianites civic rights and responsibilities; the freetown was recognised but the 800 or so residents had to pay taxes. Outwardly it has changed little with bright murals, scruffy dogs and stalls selling macrobiotic food.

Experimentarium ⊘ – Housed in Tuborg's old bottling hall in Hellerup, 5km north of the city centre *(Bus no 6 from Rådhuspladsen)*, this interactive science and technology centre has a permanent exhibition offering a wide choice of experiments on seeing, hearing, touching, the environment, health etc with a team of pilots to help visitors. An area set aside for three to six-year-olds is packed with activities designed to encourage children's natural tendency to experiment and explore. In addition, Experimentarium organises one or two temporary exhibitions every year, on a variety of subjects such as sport, the brain, humans at play, future body etc. Although the surrounding area is devoid of any interest, a visit to the centre offers the opportunity of a pleasant family outing.

OUTSKIRTS *Local map see SJÆLLAND*

★ **Dragør** – *13km south of the town centre.* The small seaside town of Dragør lies on the shores of the busy Øresund, at the southern tip of the island of Amager, within a short distance of Kastrup Airport, Copenhagen's international airport. Yet it has miraculously remained a haven of peace in this densely populated corner of Sjælland. Dragør's maritime tradition goes back to the Middle Ages when herring fishing and trading was the main source of wealth. Later on Dragør became one of Denmark's main commercial ports, which explains the exceptional size of its harbour for such a small community. Today its activity is restricted to a ferry service to Sweden and some local fishing.

A restored warehouse dating from 1682 houses the **Dragør Museum** ⊘ with an interesting maritime collection and reconstructions of the interiors of seamen's and fishermen's cottages.

Many of these have been preserved along the quaint narrow cobbled streets around the harbour and are now protected; most of them are painted yellow, some are thatched whereas others are covered with red tiles.

Øresund Broen – *10km south of town centre in Kastrup.* The newly completed Øresund fixed link to Sweden will recreate an integrated Øresund region as was the case in the past. The 16km long fixed link includes a tunnel for the four-lane motorway, two railway tracks and a service tunnel to the artificial island of Pederholm in midstream as well as a two-level, cable-stayed high bridge (cars on the upper deck and trains on the lower one) over to the toll station at Lernacken (south of Malmö) on the Swedish coast.

★★ **Ordrupgaard** ⊘ – *10km north of the town centre.* Ordrupgård stands in a secluded spot, behind a screen of ancient beech trees, and is surrounded by its own landscaped park. The stately home was custom-built in 1918 by the businessman Vilhem Hansen to house his exceptional collection of 19C-20C French and Danish art. Hansen was only 24 when he bought his first picture and, until his death in 1936, he invested all his wealth and boundless energy in the purchase of works of art. When his wife died in 1951, the estate and the collections were bequeathed to the State and the public museum was officially opened in 1953.

The **Danish collection** is displayed on the ground floor of the main house which was the Hansens' private home and still looks very much as it used to when they lived there. Most of the major 19C Danish artists are represented, Christen Købke, Johan Thomas Lundbye, Vilhem Hammershøi who has aroused renewed interest, Johannes Larsen, the famous painter from Fyn, Theodor Philipsen, the Skovgaard family, LA Ring and Peter Hansen, Vilhem Hansen's lifelong friend.

The **French collection** is housed in its own gallery adjoining the main building. The Impressionist section is particularly outstanding but there are also works by all the major French painters of the 19C and early 20C, in particular Corot *(The Bridge at Mantes, Country Road, Memory from the Environs of Amiens)*, Delacroix *(George Sand)*, Manet *(Woman Fastening her Garter)*, Degas *(Woman Seated on a Balcony, Three Dancers)*, Monet *(Waterloo Bridge)*, Pissarro *(Plum Trees in Blossom)*, Renoir *(Moulin de la Galette*, study for the painting in the Musée d'Orsay in Paris), and Gauguin *(Blue Trees, Arles, The Wine Harvest in Arles, Tahitian Woman)*.

Jægersborg Dyrehave – *11km north of the town centre.* This extensive deer park was once a royal hunting ground surrounding the royal hunting pavilion known as the Hermitage, **Eremitagen**, built in 1736. Hunting is a thing of the past but deer still graze on these vast open spaces which have become a favourite haunt of Copenhageners all the year round, whether they like walking, riding, playing golf or even skiing as the hilly terrain is ideal for winter sports. In summertime, visitors who come for the day can either enjoy a picnic in the park, or have a meal in one of several restaurants. As for those who prefer a more sophisticated (and noisier) kind of entertainment, there is of course **Dyrehavsbakken** along Klampenborgvej, Denmark's oldest amusement park, older than Tivoli since its origin is said to go back to a 16C fairground. It has kept up its tradition of popular entertainment to this day with more than 100 attractions, its own choice of restaurants, live music, dancing and cabaret singing.

Lyngby – *10km north of the town centre.* The country town of Lyngby is pleasantly situated in an area of woodland, and lakes and is a convenient starting point for discovering the attractive and varied north Sjælland countryside.

The three lakes closest to the town are connected by the River Mølleåen and there used to be grain mills, copper works and textile factories along its banks. Some of these have been restored like the watermill near Lyngby Hovedgade and the Brede cloth factory complex just north of Lyngby. The **Bredemuseet** ⊙, an annexe of the National Museum, presents a permanent exhibition, Cradle of Industry which depicts the development of early Danish Industry.

Nearby, the open-air museum, **Frilandsmuseet** ★⊙, also part of the National Museum, shows country life as it was in the 18C and 19C: 100 different buildings from Sjælland, Jutland and Fyn, but also from Sweden and the Faroe Islands have been reconstructed on an area covering 35ha and the environment carefully matched to the original one; there are farmhouses, mills and workshops all fitted with the appropriate authentic furniture and tools.

★★**ARKEN Museum of Modern Art** ⊙ – *17km to the west by road 151. In Ishøj turn left to Strandparken.* The angular lines and white form of the museum make an intriguing sight as boat-like it emerges from behind the windswept dunes. In order to get the best view of it, walk to the top of the dunes or to the main road. The museum was inaugurated in 1996, when Copenhagen was European Capital of Culture. The architecture of the building forms part of the overall experience one draws from the museum. The architect Søren Robert Lund has continued the nautical theme in the layout of the interior with steel gangways, riveted doors and a long curved central nave known as the art axis which is the main exhibition space; there are three additional exhibition rooms of varying sizes, a concert hall and a glass-walled café overlooking Ishøj Strand; the view embraces a couple of factory chimneys and groups of three-bladed modern windmills lazily revolving in the distance. The museum is intended to host temporary exhibitions of Danish, Nordic and international contemporary art. Two exhibitions are usually held at the same time. The small permanent collection is constantly growing as the museum acquires the latest in contemporary art, giving priority to recent Danish pictorial art. New acquisitions are displayed in the foyer in the spring.

EXCURSIONS *Local map see SJÆLLAND.*

The north-east coast of Sjælland has a wealth of natural beauty, a great variety of domestic architecture and some of the country's most interesting museums. From Copenhagen, the coast road (Strandvejen) follows the ever changing Øresund, in turn blue, emerald green or a white silvery colour under the blazing sun or even a dark threatening pewter grey when a storm rises on the horizon and the Swedish coast disappears behind the thickening clouds. The road is lined with beautiful villas discreetly dotted among splendid trees of many varieties beside the glorious beech. Now and again a sudden break in the trees allows a glimpse of an idyllic small harbour. This is one of these rare places where man and nature seem to have worked together to produce a beautiful environment.

Karen Blixen (1885-1962)

Karen Blixen was born in the house which her father had bought in 1879, a converted inn dating from the early 16C, surrounded by a large park and bird sanctuary covering 16ha. In 1914, Karen Blixen married Baron Bror von Blixen-Finecke and together they managed a coffee plantation in Kenya. She divorced her husband in 1929 and returned to Denmark in 1931 and settled at Rungstedlund where she remained until her death; she was buried on the estate. *Out of Africa* is an account of her life in Kenya and of the tremendous impact the country had on her. A few years before she died, in complete agreement with her brother and sister, she set up the Rungstedlund Foundation (funded by her royalties) to ensure the preservation of the family home and the protection of its immediate environment.

Rungstedlund, Nivågård and Louisiana are all situated along the coast road so that it is possible to visit one, two or all three without wasting any time. The museums are also easily accessible by S-train from Copenhagen, although the drive is, of course, much more rewarding.

★ **Rungstedlund** – *25km north of Copenhagen.* Situated on the shores of the Øresund, next to a tiny picturesque harbour full of colourful pleasure boats of all sizes, Rungstedlund is the beautiful family home of Denmark's most famous authoress, Karen Blixen, whose autobiographical book *Out of Africa* became known worldwide when a film was made of it in 1985, starring Robert Redford and Meryl Streep.
The house has been turned into the **Karen Blixen Museum** ⊙ but a great part of it has been left as it was when she lived in it. The family furniture is still there as are her drawings, her paintings and the souvenirs of her long stay in Africa. An attic room is devoted to an exhibition about her life and work with photographs and personal objects such as her old Corona typewriter.

Nivågaard ⊙ – *30km north of Copenhagen.* This mansion, situated only 5km north of Rungsted along Strandvejen, houses a collection of paintings by European old masters founded by a landowner, Johannes Hage; the museum was first opened to the public in 1908. The main part of the collection consists of a selection of 17C Dutch paintings by Steen, Ruysdael, Hobbema and Rembrandt *(Portrait of a Lady)*. There are also works by 16C Italian and Flemish masters and only one French painting, a masterpiece by Claude Lorrain from c 1646-47, depicting the *Flight into Egypt* set in a pastoral landscape.

★★★ **Louisiana** ⊙ – *35km north of Copenhagen.* This Museum of Modern Art, **Louisiana Museum for Moderne Kunst**, is one of Denmark's most inspiring museums. Its originality lies in the fact that the beautiful natural surroundings play a leading role in showing the collections to great effect. Thus the sculptures, dotted about the park planted with huge venerable trees, with the vast expanse of the Øresund in the background, create a vivid impression that visitors are unlikely to forget easily.

Louisiana

Louisiana was founded by Knud W Jensen in 1958 to house his personal collection of modern art. Several buildings have been erected since, each one designed to make the most of the terrain and the natural landscape serves as an architectural feature. Glass is naturally and extensively used as an essential link between the buildings and their surroundings.

The collection comprises sculptures by Arp, Calder, Ernst, Dubuffet, Moore, Jacobsen as well as a series of Giacometti's sculptures dramatically displayed in rooms overlooking Lake Humlebæk through floor to ceiling glass panels.

The museum also holds regular temporary exhibitions, mostly devoted to foreign art and featuring either the pioneers of modern art like Matisse, Picasso and Magritte, or contemporary, often controversial artists such as the German expressionist painter Georg Baselitz.

Moreover, other forms of art are represented in Louisiana since films and plays are shown and concerts are given in the concert hall.

Recreation
30min from the capital, Strandparken offers 7km of sandy beaches and a wide range of leisure activities (swimming, riding, golf, tennis, boat and cycle hire as well as windsurfing). For a day at the races choose between trotting races at Charlottenlund Travbane and flat racing at Klampenborg Galopbane. The Copenhagen Action Center at Kalvebod Brygge offers bungy jumping, catapult and a climbing wall for the thrill seeker (☎ 39 27 27 77). There is also the famous Tivoli amusement park.

KØGE ★

Roskilde
Population 32 000
Michelin map 985 Q 9 or Atlas Europe p 123 – Local map see SJÆLLAND

Køge is a lively provincial town, situated on the east coast of Sjælland, 38km south of Copenhagen with an important market on Wednesdays and Saturdays. Local fishermen still unload their daily catch at the main harbour and 2km to the north, yachts of all sizes lie at anchor in the new marina.

Køge is one of the oldest cities in the country with a charter going back to 1288. It grew round the market square and the natural harbour at the mouth of the river. By the 16C, Køge was a prosperous market town with a flourishing Baltic trade.

The battle of Køge Bay – During the 17C, the town suffered considerably from the wars with Sweden, often finding itself in the front line. In 1677, a great naval battle took place in Køge Bay. Watching from the top of St Nicholas' Church tower, King Christian V saw the battle being won by Admiral Niels Juel, Denmark's national hero.

The extension of the S-train (Copenhagen's suburban railway) to Køge has given a new impetus to the town already well provided with modern industries and efficient harbour facilities.

OLD TOWN

Torvet – The focal point of the old town is the market square, Torvet, on which the town hall, **Rådhuset**, stands with its Classical façade from 1803. Several streets, lined with old houses from the 16C to the 19C, radiate from the square. In Nørregade, a splendid half-timbered merchant's store from the early 17C now houses **Køge Museum** ☉ devoted to local history and traditions. There is another interesting half-timbered house in Brogade which leads to the peaceful River Krøge.

Kirkestræde also has retained several fine old houses from the 16C and 17C, including the oldest of them all at no 20, dating from 1527. On the other hand, the houses in Laugshusgade, perpendicular to Kirkestræde, date mostly from the 18C and 19C.

The 14C **Skt Nicolai Kirke** ☉ has a tall gabled tower with a lantern used in former days for guiding ships. Inside, the elaborate 17C furniture includes a carved Renaissance pulpit and a Baroque altarpiece by Lorenz Jørgensen.

LANGELAND

Langeland is a long and narrow island off the south coast of Fyn, often looked upon as a stepping stone between Lolland and Fyn; however, its fine beaches and restful atmosphere are attracting more and more tourists. It is accessible by ferry from Tårs on Lolland and via a long bridge from Tåsinge in the west.

Rudkøbing – Centrally situated on the west coast, Rudkøbing is the island's main town with a friendly marina and a relaxing village atmosphere. Along the narrow, cobbled streets gateways open on to charming courtyards tucked at the back of the brightly painted old houses. The statue of **Hans Christian Ørsted**, the physicist who discovered electromagnetism in 1820, proudly stands in the centre of the square (Torvet). He was born in the **old chemist's shop** in Brogade. There are also imposing merchants' houses in Østergade (Bays Gård) and Nørregade (Bondos Gård).

The Romanesque nave is the oldest part of **Rudkøbing Kirke** ⊙. The discovery of an old bell bearing a runic inscription has confirmed the date of its foundation as 1105. The 18C **mill**, along rue Stræde from Torvet, is the only one remaining of the three Rudkøbing once possessed.

The **Langelands Museum** ⊙ in Jens Winthersvej deals with local prehistory and history.

Tranekær – *10km north of Rudkøbing on road 305.* Tranekær is a picturesque village with colourful tile-covered houses and an interesting inn. The community has been living in close relation to its castle, since one of the owners, known as the General, tried to establish a German-style principality on Langeland in the late 18C, improving the standard of living and creating a certain prosperity.

The bright-red **castle** is a remodelling of the 12C castle, carried out in 1863. It has been lived in by the same family since 1535 and is not open to the public. But there is free access to the wild **park** which is a bird sanctuary and has extensive woodland with many species of trees, rhododendrons, ponds and wooden bridges.

LOLLAND

Lolland is the third largest island after Sjælland and Fyn, directly linked to Sjælland via Falster by several bridges. The port of Rødbyhavn on the south coast has a regular ferry service to Puttgarden in Germany whereas the west coast is linked by ferry to Langeland and Fyn.

Lolland is flat agricultural country with vast expanses of green fields and, on the horizon, the familiar sight of the wind-generators' white spindly wings revolving slowly.

★ **Maribo** – Situated at the heart of Lolland, Maribo is a picturesque provincial town on the edge of a romantic lake, a commercial and cultural centre by tradition. The town developed round a convent and monastery of the Order of Brigettines founded by Erik of Pomerania in 1416. Today, only the church remains; it is now **Maribo Cathedral** ⊙, a massive brick building with buttresses and corbie-steps. Inside, the fairly low-vaulted nave is flanked by double-sided aisles. There are traces of frescoes over the organ on the entrance side. The streets close to the cathedral are lined with 18C houses, built for craftsmen and tradesmen. Apart from the museum of local history, **Kunst-og Stiftsmuseet** ⊙ and the small open-air museum, **Frilandsmuseet** ⊙, Maribo has an extensive art museum, **Lolland-Falsters Kunstmuseum** ⊙, devoted to Danish art from the 18C to the present day.

Knuthenborg Park ⊙ – *8km north of Maribo on roads 9 and 289.*
Set in the park of a privately owned manor house, near the village of Bandholm, this safari park is the largest of its kind in Northern Europe. There are 16km of roads crisscrossing the entire area where more than 800 exotic animals and birds roam freely. At the centre of the park there is an amusement park for children.

★ **Aalholm Automobil Museum** ⊙ – *About 25km south-east of Maribo. It is close to Aalholm Castle which is closed to the public.*
The museum has one of the biggest collections of cars, with over 200 exhibits from 1886 to 1972, displayed in four large halls.

DENMARK

In spite of good communications with Sjælland and Falster and the beauty of its landscapes, Møn has remained slightly off the beaten track and totally unspoilt. The exceptional quality of its natural environment is undoubtedly one more attraction to be added to an already impressive list: white sand beaches sheltered by dunes, beautiful woodland areas, stunning wild cliffs and a fascinating variety of wildlife. It also boasts three of the best fresco churches in Denmark, prehistoric graves and a lively market town.

Stege – The island's main town is an ancient market place, where time seems to have stood still for the delight of visitors and the only Danish town to have preserved in good condition its medieval ramparts and moat as well as one of its three town gates, **Mølleporten**.
Next to the gate, Empiregården houses the **Møn Museum** with interesting prehistoric exhibits. The **Gothic church**, built in the 13C and extended in the 15C, contains some fine frescoes.

★ **Keldby Kirke** ⊙ – *4km east on road 287.* This is the first of three churches on the island, rightly famous for their wealth of outstanding frescoes and in particular for their exceptionally fine examples of 15C narrative painting. Furthermore, Keldby, Elmelunde and Fanefjord churches have in common the fact that the great medieval artist, known as the **Elmelunde Master** *(see below)*, contributed to their decoration.
The Keldby frescoes depict many scenes from the Old and the New Testaments: those in the chancel are 13C, whereas those on the nave vaulting are late 15C, by the Master of Elmelunde.

Detail of 13C frescoes, Keldby Kirke

C. Boisvieux

★ **Elmelunde Kirke** ⊙ – *8km east on road 287.* The medieval master decorated the church of his native village again with biblical scenes, in particular a splendid Last Judgement and Christ in Majesty.

★★ **Møns Klint** ⊙ – *18km east on road 287.* These impressive white chalk cliffs *(see photograph p 26)*, clad with a thick mantle of dark trees, stretch for several kilometres, with a sheer drop of 128m at their highest point. They were formed by glacial deposits combined with the action of the sea. Paths lead through the woods to the edge of the cliffs for a breathtaking view. On the beach below, there are all kinds of fossils to be found.

★ **Fanefjord Kirke** ⊙ – *12km south-west on road 287 as far as Damsholte, then left on a minor road.* This is the third church on Møn to have been decorated by the Elmelunde Master. The frescoes in the chancel date from c 1350, the rest are by the master; the wealth of subjects, the imaginative interpretation and the refinement of colours are just amazing.
Nearby stands **Grønjægers Høj**, an impressive long barrow surrounded by a stone circle.
North of Fanefjord *(8km in the direction of Tostenæs)*, **Kong Asgers Høj** is a large passage grave, consisting of a passage leading to a vast burial chamber.

NYBORG

Fyn
Population 15 500
Michelin map 985 Q 7 or Atlas Europe p 122

DENMARK

Nyborg owes its foundation and its present economic vitality to its position on the east coast of Fyn, along the main line of communications between Sjælland and the rest of Denmark.

The town developed round its castle built in 1170 to defend the channel separating Fyn from Sjælland and for a long time it was a royal residence and the meeting place of the Danehof, the medieval assembly of the nobility and clergy.

Nyborg Slot ⊙ – What remains of the castle stands on a mound surrounded by water; the terrace in front is lined with bronze guns facing the town. The restored west wing contains the Knights' Hall, the Danehof Room, the King's Room and the Royal Children's apartments.

The town gate, **Landporten**, built in 1660, can be seen just north of the castle.

In Slotsgade, a large half-timbered house, dating from 1601 and called **Mads Lerches Gård** after its first owner, has been turned into the **Nyborg Museum** devoted to local history.

Vor Frue Kirke ⊙ – Originally built at the end of the 14C and remodelled in the 19C, the Church of Our Lady contains a wooden Renaissance font, a Baroque pulpit from 1653 and an elegant wrought-iron gate forged by Christian IV's official craftsman, Caspar Fincke, in 1649.

Nearby, the corner of Adelgade and Korsbrødregåde is occupied by **Korsbrødregården**, a large stone-built house dating from 1396.

EXCURSIONS

Storebælt Udstillingscenter ⊙ – *Take the Great Belt Bridge across the Storebælt and leave the motorway at exit 43 for Halsskov. Turn right and drive a further 300m to reach the exhibition centre.*

There are models, plates, videos and full information about the building of a combined tunnel and bridge link between Knudshoved on Fyn and Halsskov on Sjælland.

NÆSTVED

Storstrøm
Population 39 000
Michelin map 985 Q 8 or Atlas Europe p 122 – Local map see SJÆLLAND

Næstved is one of the oldest towns in Denmark; it developed round a monastery founded in the 12C and throughout the Middle Ages it was a prosperous trading centre. The extension of the harbour early this century brought new industries to the town which, however, has remained a traditional market town with a lively market on Akseltorv every Wednesday and Saturday.

Skt Peders Kirke ⊙ – The large Gothic church of St Peter's, remodelled during the 19C, has retained some medieval frescoes, including one depicting King Valdemar IV and Queen Helvig kneeling in prayer dating from c 1375, as well as an interesting bronze font.

Opposite the church stands the oldest purpose-built town hall in Denmark, **Rådhuskirken** c 1450.

Skt Mortens Kirke ⊙ – Similar in style but smaller than St Peter's, it contains a fresco depicting St Martin of Tours, the patron saint of the church, a huge altarpiece carved in 1667 by Abel Schrøder the Younger and a pulpit by his father.

Nearby in Riddergade stands **Apostelhuset**, a half-timbered house from 1510 which derives its name from the carved figures of Jesus Christ and the 12 Apostles framing the windows.

EXCURSION

★ **Gavnø Slot** ⊙ – *6km south-west; drive south on road 22 then turn right towards Gavnø.*

This 18C Rococo castle, standing in the middle of a magnificent park, is still lived in and contains the largest private collection of paintings in Denmark. The collection of paintings includes a great many portraits and a few Old Masters in the Great Gallery. Attached to the main building, the chapel is richly decorated with carved panelling.

The **park★** is particularly enchanting in May when tulips and other bulbs are all out at the same time, as their bright colours sparkle among the tall ancient trees.

ODENSE★★

Fyn
Population 141 000
Michelin map 985 Q 7 or Atlas Europe p 122

Situated at the heart of the greenest of Danish islands, Denmark's third largest city is a modern metropolis looking back more than 1 000 years and at the same time confidently turned towards the future as her position along the main east-west axis is strengthened by the fixed link across Storebælt *(see NYBORG)*. Yet to the thousands of visitors who come flocking in from all over the world, Odense is simply Hans Christian Andersen's home town.

It is no doubt difficult to reconcile the requirements of a rapidly changing modern society with the image of a timeless fairy tale world, which explains why Odense gives the impression of having a kind of split personality and looks in turn disappointingly dull and disarmingly charming; thus the busy pedestrian shopping area in the centre of town is purely functional and quite unaware, it seems, of the poetry of a bygone age which pervades the air of the immaculately preserved old district.

The town centre lies on the north bank of the River Odense (Odense Å) which slowly winds its way towards Odense fjord.

HISTORICAL NOTES

Long before Andersen's time, the town was associated with the powerful world of the imagination since it owes its name to Odin, the supreme god in Scandinavian mythology. Odense was most probably the site of a shrine to Odin in Viking times, but it made its mark in Danish history when King Knud was murdered in St Alban's Church in 1086 and canonised shortly afterwards.

The town then became a famous place of pilgrimage with quite a few monasteries and convents, and its spiritual and economic importance increased throughout the Middle Ages.

After the Reformation, periods of prosperity alternated with destruction by fires and wars until the 19C when the opening of the canal linking Odense to the fjord led to the establishment of a harbour in the city and the development of major industries. At the same time, the worldwide acclaim of HC Andersen gave the town a cultural stature which it has proudly guarded ever since.

★★★HANS CHRISTIAN ANDERSEN QUARTER

The cobbled streets of this old district are lined with tiny low half-timbered houses dating from the end of the 18C and the beginning of the 19C. These have been carefully restored and look quite enchanting with their fresh paint, small square windows and half curtains but, although they are inhabited and form a harmonious ensemble, the whole area conveys the nostalgic impression of a stage-setting forgotten long after the footlights have faded.

Hans Christian Andersens Hus

** **Hans Christian Andersens Hus** ⊘ (BY) – The humble house at the corner of Hans Jensens Stræde and Bangs Boder, where HC Andersen was born in 1805, has been turned into a museum dedicated to the world famous fairy tale writer.

The son of a well-read shoemaker, Andersen learned how to use his imagination from a very early age playing with a home-made theatre. At the age of 14, he left Odense and his hard-working mother for the glittering lights of the capital but he suffered bitter set-backs before his first fairy tales were published in 1835. He travelled all his life and visited many countries, drawing anything that struck his imagination. He would also make picture books for his friends' children and excelled at cut-outs. During his lifetime, he received honours and decorations from all over the world, he was made an honorary citizen of his native town and a statue of him was erected in Kongens Have in Copenhagen. In spite of all this and of his many friends he led a lonely life and died in Copenhagen in 1875.

The museum, which has a large reproduction of one of his cut-outs over the entrance, contains letters, notes, manuscripts and rare editions of his works as well as original illustrations, pictures, personal objects and a reconstruction of his study with the original furniture. In the adjoining library, it is possible to listen to recordings of his fairy tales.

Fyrtøjet ⊘ – The " Tinderbox " located in a garden next to HC Andersen's house is an interactive cultural house for children; fairy tales are told in the Storyteller's Room whilst in the Activity Room, children dress, make-up and are invited to play a role with help from the staff if needed. They can then try their hand at writing a fairy tale or read some in the book corner. There is also a Study for painting and making puppets which can be used for performing fairy tales in the Theatre Room. The visit usually ends in the cafeteria and the shop.

Carl Nielsen Museet ⊘ (BY) – In a totally contrasting setting, in Claus Bergs Gade, this museum is devoted to the composer Carl Nielsen (1865-1931), a native of Funen, and his wife the sculptress Anne Marie Carl-Nielsen. Apart from the usual memorabilia, there is a video presentation and recordings of Nielsen's music.

* **Møntergården** ⊘ (BY) – Just south of the Nielsen Museet, in Overgade, the **Museum of Urban History and Culture** is housed in a remarkable group of merchants' houses from the 16C and 17C.

In an alleyway on the right of the main courtyard, there is a row of workmen's cottages of the same period.

CATHEDRAL AND PRECINCTS

Right in the town centre, just off the main pedestrian street, on a wide square called Flakhaven, stands the massive **Rådhus** (BZ) built at the end of the 19C and, close to it, the cathedral.

* **Skt Knuds Kirke** ⊘ (BZ) – The brick-built Gothic cathedral dedicated to the murdered king replaced an earlier building twice destroyed by fire. Work began in the 13C and was only completed 200 years later. The **crypt** contains the shrines of St Knud and of his brother Benedikt as well as some royal tombs. Behind the altar, the magnificent 5m-high **triptych★★★** by Claus Berg (c 1520) looks strikingly luminous set against the whitewashed walls; it contains more than 300 carved figures, the central panel depicting the Crucifixion. The church also contains some **wrought-iron work** by Caspar Fincke, Christian IV's official craftsman, a 17C bronze **font** and an 18C **pulpit**.

From the cathedral, follow Skt Knuds Kirkestræde and turn left onto Munkemøllestræde.

HC Andersens Barndomshjem ⊘ (AZ) – The house where Andersen spent his childhood until his departure for Copenhagen is now a small museum with mementoes from that period of his life.

Continue down Munkemøllestræde to reach the park on the other side of Klosterbakken.

* **HC Andersen Haven** (BZ) – In this lovely romantic park laid out on an island and on the north bank of the River Odense, stands the statue of the fairy tale writer dating from 1888. Every year on his birthday (2 April), flowers are laid at the foot of the statue.

ODENSE

ADDITIONAL SIGHTS

Skt Hans Kirke ⊙ (AY) – The Gothic St John's Church, once part of St John's Monastery, has an unusual outside pulpit from which priests would preach to lepers who were barred from entering the church. HC Andersen was baptised in this church.

Nearby stands Odense Slot considerably remodelled and now the residence of Fyn's Chief Administrator.

Fyns Kunstmuseum ⊙ (AY) – Situated just north of the pedestrian area, the Fyn Museum of Fine Arts houses one of the best collections of Danish painting in the country, from the 18C to the present day.

Brandts Klædefabrik (AZ) – Housed in a renovated cloth mill, this is Odense's new cultural centre which contains shops, cinemas, restaurants as well as museums including the Danish Printing Museum, **Danmarks Grafiske Museum** ⊙, the Danish Press Museum, **Dansk Pressemuseum** ⊙ and a large exhibition hall.

★ Den Fynske Landsby ⊙ (Fyn Village) – *Leave heading south by Læssøegade* (AZ), *the Svendborg road.*

The open-air museum consists of reconstructed rural buildings from the 18C and 19C arranged to form a typical Fyn village, with its farmhouses, workshops, two mills, school, vicarage etc.

RIBE★★

Ribe is situated on the flat marshy west coast of Jutland and separated from the sea by tidal flats which are one of Europe's most important bird sanctuaries. The River Ribe winds its way through the town before flowing into the sea a few kilometres further on. Ribe is Denmark's most famous medieval town. However, its small size has enabled it to preserve its architectural unity and to retain its old-world atmosphere while remaining a lively town. The main pedestrian shopping street stretching right through the town centre is crowded with people buzzing about and getting on with daily life as they have done for centuries.

HISTORICAL NOTES

The history of Ribe goes right back to the Viking Age when it was already an important centre of the North Sea trade. This importance is confirmed by the fact that one of the first Christian churches was built in Ribe before Denmark officially became a Christian country and the town got its first bishop in 948. During the Middle Ages, Ribe was established as a major port linking Scandinavia and most European cities as well as the Baltic and the North Sea, and at the same time it was one of the first cities to have a printing press. However, towards the end of the Middle Ages, technical progress in shipbuilding caused the trade routes to be changed and the Reformation was a further blow to the town's prosperity when most abbeys and churches were closed. Later on, the increased predominance of Copenhagen due to the establishment of absolute monarchy, competition from other ports and the silting up of the river caused Ribe's steady economic decline. It has never recovered its former glory, however, it has retained an interesting cultural life.

★★RIBE DOMKIRKE ⊘

The Romanesque cathedral which stands on the main square, 1.5m below the present ground level, dates from the second half of the 12C but was remodelled several times. From the top of the 13C massive square-tower bells were sounded to warn the inhabitants of impending danger from attack or from the sea! The climb is well worth it for the remarkable view of the town and surrounding flats. The church bells play various tunes throughout the day. The south portal is a rare example of Danish Romanesque sculpture and is particularly famous for its carved tympanum depicting the Descent from the Cross.

Inside, the wide nave is flanked by two aisles on either side and the crossing is surmounted by a dome. There are traces of medieval frescoes on some of the pillars, but the modern frescoes and mosaics behind the altar are by Carl-Henning Pedersen.

OLD TOWN

The medieval town surrounds the cathedral. On the main square, **Torvet**, across the road from the **Dagmar Hotel**, there is a quaint little inn called **Weis' Stue**, dating from c 1600, with a charming 18C interior including a beamed ceiling, painted panelling and Dutch tiles on the walls and the usual tables and mugs of the time.

Several cobbled streets radiate from the square, all equally picturesque. In Skolegade, on the west side of the cathedral, stands **Hans Tausen's House**, part of the 16C bishop's residence, where Hans Tausen, Denmark's first reformer, spent the last 10 years of his life. The oldest existing town hall in Denmark, **Det Gamle Rådhus** ⊘ (1496) is on the corner of Sønderportsgade and Stenbrogade, still partly used for council meetings.

Walking south along Puggårdsgade, one sees on the left-hand side **Tårnborg**, a stately stone-built canon's residence and further down in Gravsgade, **Puggård** is also a former canon's residence dating from c 1400. To the east of Torvet stands **Skt Catharine Kirke** ⊘ which is, apart from the cathedral, the only remaining church, built before the Reformation. The cloisters of the Dominican abbey are accessible through the church. **Quedens Gaard**, at the corner of Sortebrødregade and Overdammen is an old merchant's house built c 1580 and now a **museum** ⊘ with reconstructed interiors from the early 17C and local exhibits. From Fiskergade, alleyways lead down to the **harbour** (Skibbroen) where a market is held on Wednesdays in summertime.

The **Ribes Vikinger** ⊘ on Odins Plads brings to life the town of Ribe during the Viking period and the Middle Ages.

On the other side of the dikes built to protect the town from flooding, a tractor bus takes passengers across the flats to **Mandø**, a tiny island with a population of 70 and an inn with lodgings.

RINGKØBING FJORD ★

Ringkøbing
Michelin map 985 P 5 or Atlas Europe p 122

North of Esbjerg, the area between Varde and Ringkøbing, offers a variety of land-scapes typical of the west coast of Jutland, including a vast lagoon, heath-covered dunes, long straight beaches, fascinating nature reserves, drifting sands and planta-tions, a word used by the Danes to designate an area deliberately planted with trees in order to stop sands from drifting. There are many walking or cycling paths that go to make the discovery of this unique environment even more enjoyable.

ROUND TRIP FROM VARDE About 150km – allow half a day

From Varde follow road 181 north then turn left to take road 431 west.

★**Janderup Kirke** – The brilliant white shape of this imposing Romanesque church stands out above the clump of dark trees surrounding it as its image is gently reflected in the still waters of the River Varde. Inside, the vaulting of the nave and chancel is covered with frescoes c 1500, with interwoven geometric and fleur-de-lis patterns. A set of painted wooden panels on the organ loft above the entrance illus-trates the 12 Apostles and there are some interesting medieval sculptures including a crucifix from c 1300 and a Virgin and Child from 1503. The intricate altarpiece dates from 1645.

Take road 431 west to Oskbøl.

Aal Kirke ⊙ – Nearby in the village of Oskbøl, another 12C Romanesque church, known as Aal Church, has retained some of its original frescoes; the frieze on the north side of the church is the most famous because of its unusual non-biblical sub-ject: a battle between knights on horseback.

From Oskbøl take a minor road north to join road 465 which leads to the coast.

Blåbjerg – Blåbjerg is the name of an area of sand beaches backed by a row of dunes which were continually drifting until a plantation *(see above)* was established in 1878. The poetic name Blåbjerg, meaning Blue Mountain, originally referred to the highest dune as it appeared, seen from the sea. The area is now protected and there is a network of signposted paths for those who wish to explore it. The beach at **Henne Strand** is particularly attractive.

Follow a minor road north at the back of the plantation, which joins up with road 181.

Tipperne Nature Reserve – The peninsula jutting out into Ringkøbing fjord, the flats and water areas surrounding it constitute an important bird sanctuary. It is a protected area and visiting times are restricted.

Continue along road 181.

Hvide Sande – Situated halfway along Holmsland Klit, the narrow strip of land sep-arating Ringkøbing fjord from the North Sea, the town and fishing harbour of Hvide Sande developed after the canal and the locks were built in 1931 to link the fjord to the sea. Today it is the fifth largest fishing port in Denmark. There is a splendid beach on the seaside and the fjord is the paradise of windsurfers.
A path runs along the dunes between the sea and the fjord with beautiful **views** of both.
From the top of **Nørre Lyngvig Lighthouse**, 5km north of Hvide Sande, there are stun-ning **views** of the whole area, well worth the effort.

Continue until you reach Søndervig then turn right on road 15 which leads to Ringkøbing.

Ringkøbing – The main reminders of Ringkøbing's prosperous past stand on the old cobbled **market square** (Torvet) shaded by ancient lime trees: there is the 15C **Kirke** ⊙ and the former **mayor's residence**, an Empire style building dating from 1807. The **museum** ⊙ in Kongevej is devoted to local history including special exhibits from Mylius Erichsen's Greenland expedition of 1906-08.
Just north of Ringkøbing at Hee, there is an amusement park called **Sommerland West** ⊙ with the usual outdoor activities and a Danish speciality, the Viking Feasts.

Drive along the fjord to Skjern.

The River Skjern is famous in angling circles for trout and salmon fishing from March to October, with an annual contest in August.

Take road 11 back to Varde.

RINGSTED

Vestsjælland
Population 17 500
Michelin map 985 Q 8 or Atlas Europe p 122 – Local map see SJÆLLAND

Today Ringsted is a modern provincial town but it has retained in its centre the symbol of its spiritual influence during the Middle Ages, when it was renowned throughout the kingdom as an important religious centre and seat of justice.

★ **Sankt Bendts Kirke** ⊘ – Standing on the market square, it is one of the oldest brick-built churches in Denmark. It was originally the abbey church of the Benedictine monastery, built during the second half of the 12C. For 200 years monarchs and members of the royal family were buried inside the church which contains paintings of some of them as well as 20 royal tombs including that of Valdemar I who declared the church an official royal burial place.

ROSKILDE★★

Roskilde
Population 41 000
Michelin map 985 Q 9 or Atlas Europe p 123 – Local map see SJÆLLAND

The ancient capital of Denmark, now a peaceful provincial town, lies at the head of a long and narrow fjord, 30km west of Copenhagen. An important commercial town with a lively market held on the main square every Wednesday and Saturday, it is also a fine cultural centre with its own recent university and Europe's biggest rock festival at the beginning of July.

Under the terms of the **Treaty of Roskilde** (1658) Frederik III ceded all three provinces east of the Sound (Skåne, Blekinge and Halland) to Sweden who agreed to guarantee the customary laws and privileges of the Skåne estates.

HISTORICAL NOTES

A Viking Capital – After having united Denmark and Norway, Harald Bluetooth who erected one of the rune stones in Jelling elected Roskilde as the capital of his new kingdom and probably built a wooden church, the first on the site where the cathedral stands today. The importance of Roskilde in Viking times is confirmed by the trouble that was taken to protect it from invasion *(see Viking Ship Museum opposite)*.

The bishops of Roskilde – The town's religious importance grew rapidly and by 1020 it had its first bishop, the first of a long line of powerful clergymen who were to influence the course of Denmark's history for over 300 years. The most famous of the bishops of Roskilde was Absalon who is acknowledged as the founder of Copenhagen.

Royal burial place – Roskilde lost its political significance when, in 1417, Erik of Pomerania chose Copenhagen instead. But by then, Queen Margrethe I had been buried in the cathedral and from then on most Danish monarchs were buried there even after the Reformation (1536) which however, struck a bitter blow to the town's prosperity; all convents and monasteries as well as most churches were demolished and the town went into decline, only regaining a certain stability when it was linked by rail to Copenhagen in the 19C.

★★★ DOMKIRKE ⊘

The twin-towered red-brick cathedral is the symbol of Roskilde's glorious past and is now included on the UNESCO list of World Heritage Sites. It stands on slightly raised ground in the town centre, just north of the main square, Stændertorvet.

Building work started in 1170 when Absalon was bishop of Roskilde and completed during the 13C, therefore the cathedral is both Romanesque and Early Gothic. The **twin towers** were erected in the 14C and later surmounted by slender spires with green copper roofs. The entrance to the cathedral is on the south side.

The Annunciation, detail of 16C altarpiece

C. Boisvieux/EXPLORER

Inside, the whitewashed vaulting increases the impression of spaciousness and height; the plan is straightforward, consisting of a nave flanked by two aisles and ending with a broad apse. The absence of crossing is compensated by an unusual number of side chapels, built at different periods, some of them unusually large and profusely decorated. The Gothic **choir stalls** are richly carved with scenes from the Old and the New Testament and the magnificent golden **altarpiece** was sculpted in Antwerp in the 16C. Behind the main altar lies the white marble **sarcophagus of Queen Margrethe I**, one of the 38 kings and queens buried in Roskilde Cathedral. Most of the other royal tombs are in the chapels; particularly remarkable is **Christian IV's Chapel**, on the north side, closed off by an elegant wrought-iron gate and decorated with murals illustrating the life of the king; there is a bronze statue of him by Thorvaldsen. On the south side, in the 15C **Christian I's Chapel**, equally ornate, there is a column marked with the heights of several kings, a detail which might be more interesting from the psychological than the anatomical point of view! Also on the south side, the late-18C early-19C **Frederik V's Chapel** surmounted by a cupola is larger and much brighter than the others.

***VIKINGESKIBSHALLEN Ⓥ (VIKING SHIP MUSEUM)

This modern museum overlooking Roskilde fjord was created to house the wrecks of five Viking ships found in 1962, at the bottom of the fjord 20km north of Roskilde. They had been sunk in c 1000 to protect the town from marauding pirates, most probably Vikings from Norway. A 15min film explains how the wrecks were salvaged, then preserved by a special lengthy treatment and finally carefully put together piece by piece.

The open-plan museum on several levels affords an excellent view of the recon-structed ships from different angles. There is a 16.5m-long merchant ship used for trading with distant countries, a smaller one used in the Baltic and along rivers, a fishing boat (the shortest of all), a typical warship as well as an impressive one used for long-distance raids along the coast of Western Europe. Throughout the museum, there is an exhibition about life in Viking times, both on land and at sea. Two Viking ships have been built using the same technique as the Vikings more than 1 000 years ago. They are moored just outside the museum in the museum harbour inaugurated in 1997 and it is possible to take a sailing trip in one of them from the beginning of July to mid-August. The boatyard, now housed in a new building, is open to visitors who can watch 1 000-year-old Viking techniques being used to build a replica. Workshops take place in summer opposite the boatyard: visitors are welcome to try their hand at ancient crafts such as rope and sail-making. In addi-tion, there is an archaeological workshop where fragments from more wrecks found in the harbour during the construction of the artificial museum island are being treated and where visitors have access to a wealth of information about the new finds.

Skt Jørgensbjerg Kirke Ⓥ – Close to the museum, the old church of Skt Jørgensbjerg stands on a hill overlooking the fjord, in the centre of what used to be a fishing village in medieval times. The nave and chancel date from the early 12C; the tower and the porch are Late Gothic. During the Middle Ages, Skt Jørgensbjerg also served as the church of a nearby lepers' hospital whose patron saint was Skt Jørgen.

EXCURSIONS

Lejre – *12km south-west – allow from 2hr to half a day. Follow road 14 which passes underneath the dual carriageway, then turn right on road 155 to Holbæk and immediately left on a minor road signposted Lejre and Ledreborg.*

The Lejre Research Centre, **Lejre Forsøgscenter** Ⓥ, at Lejre was established in 1964 on 45ha of undulating parkland with lakes and ponds. Its aim is to explore, reconstruct and explain the craft, buildings and physical conditions of the past and at the same time develop modern man's knowledge about nature. There is a reconstruction of a 2 000-year-old Iron Age village next to an ancient forest and, in different parts of the site, various workshops where experiments are carried out. Farm and semi-wild animals either roam around or are kept in pens as in the case of the wild boar.

All kinds of activities are available such as woodcutting, cooking on prehistoric-type barbecues, rowing in primitive canoes made of hollowed out tree trunks etc.

★ Ledreborg Slot Ⓥ – *Close to the research centre.*

The yellow-painted 17C and 18C castle is a fine example of Danish Baroque archi-tecture. The main building is flanked by two separate identical wings forming a vast courtyard entered as through a gatehouse surmounted by a green copper steeple. Inhabited by the same family since 1739, the castle still contains most of its origi-nal furniture.

The terraced garden sloping down to a pond is surrounded by a wooded park also open to the public.

ROSKILDE FJORD

The region north of Roskilde, known as Fjordland, includes two of the largest fjords in Denmark, Isefjord and Roskilde fjord with a common outlet into Kattegat, as well as the areas bordering them and Hornsherred peninsula separating them. The shores of Roskilde fjord, which is the narrower of the two, are particularly attractive: it is a region of peaceful landscapes, with rolling hills gently sloping down to the fjord's still waters hemmed by reeds swaying in the wind and islets in the distance. There are woods and low-lying meadows, rivers flowing into the fjord and lovely villages on Hornsherred. For a different approach, take a trip on board **M/S Sagafjord**; she sails from Roskilde harbour past picturesque inlets and the bird sanctuary on Ringø Island.

ROSKILDE TO FREDERIKSSUND *50km – allow half a day*

There is an interesting itinerary to follow from Roskilde to Frederikssund on the eastern shore of the fjord along minor roads which zigzag across Hornsherred to Jægerpris Slot just a few kilometres west of Frederikssund; on the way there are many occasions to admire the gentle and discreet beauty of Fjordland.

Drive on road 21-23 west; leave at exit no 15 and turn north towards Lyndby.

★**Sæby and Gershøj**★ – Two picturesque villages, 3km apart, lie on the edge of the fjord. Sæby is slightly more inland, but Gershøj is a fishing village with a tiny harbour, colourful thatched cottages and a bright red church.

Proceed north to Skibby.

Skibby Kirke ⊙ – The exterior of this church is so unattractive that the interior comes as a surprise. It is mostly Romanesque and has retained in the apse a set of beautiful frescoes painted at the end of the 12C, including an impressive Christ in Majesty.

Follow the direction of Selsø to the east.

★**Selsø Slot** ⊙ – The road skirts Selsø Lake before reaching Selsø Church where there is a parking area. The castle stands in an isolated position overlooking the fjord. The present building dates from the 16C but was considerably remodelled during the first half of the 18C to become a fine example of Danish Baroque architecture. The interior has been restored to its 18C splendour with marble panelling, stuccoed ceilings and huge mirrors, as well as paintings by Henrik Krock, the Court Painter at the time. One of the few Renaissance features left is the vaulted cellar with the original kitchens. There is a dungeon beneath the gatehouse and a large medieval well in the courtyard.

Continue northwards through Skuldelev and Gerlev to Jægerpris.

C. Boisvieux

Drakkars on Roskilde fjord

117

Jægerpris Slot ⊘ – The palace has long been associated with royalty, but the most famous occupants were King Frederik VII and his morganatic third wife, Countess Danner. When the king died he left the estate to the countess who donated it to an institution for poor girls, but expressed the wish that the south wing which she and the king had lived in be left unchanged and opened to the public. She is buried in the park. The main entrance to the palace is in the centre of the 17C and 18C south wing; at the back stands the north wing built round the oldest part of the palace dating from the 15C and an imposing stair tower added by Christian IV. A third wing was later built to join the other two.

Drive east on road 207 to Frederikssund.

Frederikssund – Situated on the eastern shore of Roskilde fjord, at its narrowest part spanned by a bridge, the town of Frederikssund is famous for its **Viking Festival** which takes place during the second half of June when a play on a Viking theme is performed in the open. Jens Ferdinand Willumsen (1863-1958), one of the major 20C Danish artists, donated his personal art collection as well as a series of his own works to the town of Frederikssund, which led to the opening of the **JF Willumsen Museum** ⊘ in 1957.

RØMØ
Sønderjylland
Michelin map 985 Q 5 or Atlas Europe p 122

Rømø is the largest of several islands in the Wadden Sea, the name given to the North Sea area close to the coast of south-west Jutland from Esbjerg to the German border and beyond. The low coastline, the shallow waters stretching over vast expanses and the strong influence of the tides have created a unique natural environment with species of flora that can be found nowhere else in the world and an interesting fauna which changes with the tide; large shoals of fish being succeeded by thousands of birds. Seals are also known to come and rest along the west coast which is lined with an amazingly wide beach. It is accessible along a 10km causeway. Channels winding through the shallow waters allow fishing boats and ferries to go in and out of the harbour of Havneby. In the 18C, whaling in the north seas, particularly off the coast of Greenland, brought a certain prosperity to the island and the whaling-masters built fine houses for themselves. One such house, **Kommandørgården** ⊘ in Toftum, has been restored and now houses the local museum. The seamen's church in Kirkeby, **Skt Clemens Kirke** ⊘, with its beautiful models of ancient ships symbolises Rømø's strong ties with its past. The villages are on the east coast, but holidaymakers flock to the magnificent west coast beach where there is excellent windsurfing.

SALLING
Viborg
Michelin map 985 P 5-6 or Atlas Europe p 122

The Salling peninsula and the island of Mors almost completely obstruct the widest section of the tortuous Limfjord, thus creating a complex network of sounds and smaller fjords, a paradise for yachtsmen who have a wide choice of moorings from fishing villages to sheltered marinas such as that of Skive on the east coast of Salling. Overall, this is an area of isolated heathland and woodland with a particularly beautiful nature park round Denmark's largest moorland lake. There are also some very interesting old churches and one of the finest medieval castles in the country. The lively town of Skive is centrally situated and the natural starting point of a tour of the peninsula.

TOUR OF THE PENINSULA *About 75km – allow half a day*

Skive – Before starting on the tour it is well worth looking at the largely Romanesque old church which contains a set of 16C frescoes depicting many saints and holy characters on a floral background.

Leave Skive on road 189 and turn left just outside town on road 34 towards Herning; 7km further on, take the right fork to Sevel.

Sevel – The old **Kirke** ⊘ of this charming village has a carillon which plays a different tune three times a day. From Sevel follow a minor road north to the Hjerl Hede open-air museum.

Hjerl Hede and Flyndersø Lake – Situated in a conservation area covering more than 1 000ha of heath-covered hills and woodland, the open-air museum, **Frilandsmuseum** ⊘, consists of a reconstructed Stone Age settlement and an old village retracing the history of Danish village life from the 16C to the 19C. There are farmhouses, an inn, a school, a church, a water-mill, a smithy and other workshops as well as a grocer's shop. All this comes to life in July when volunteers live and work in the old houses, demonstrating ancient customs for the delight of visitors.

From the old village, follow the sign Udsigten.

There is a splendid view of the long and narrow Flyndersø, which was formed at the end of the Ice Age.

Drive on to Sahl, 3km west.

Sahl Kirke ⊘ – The Romanesque stone-built church dates from c 1150. It contains traces of frescoes from c 1500 and a beautiful set of oak pews (the men's are on the south side and the women's on the north side) from c 1600. Above all it has the most remarkable golden altar made in c 1200 by a craftsman from Ribe: it consists of chased copperplate gilded over and fastened to an oak base. Originally the frontal, the lower part, was placed in front of the altar whereas the predella, the upper part, stood on top.

Drive north for about 4km then turn left towards Ejsing.

Ejsing Kirke ⊘ – This is also a Romanesque church, but with important Gothic additions. Inside there is some lovely painted furniture from 1760 and beautiful 16C frescoes in warm shades of ochre, depicting Adam and Eve and various scenes from the Bible in the apse and in a side chapel accessible through a carved wooden door.

Drive north through Lem to Rødding; Spøttrup Slot is nearby.

Spøttrup Borg ⊘ – This interesting red-brick medieval castle, surrounded by two moats separated by a high earth bank is approached by two successive wooden bridges. Built by the bishops of Viborg to protect their property, it was completed in c 1500 and consisted of three wings with a massive gate tower on the fourth side. After the Reformation, the castle was confiscated by the Crown, but in 1579 it was given to a peer of the realm and became a private manor house; as a result, two stair towers were erected in the courtyard. In 1937 Spøttrup was purchased by the State and gradually restored. It is today the best-preserved late medieval castle in Denmark.

Return to Skive via Sønder Balling.

SILKEBORG

Århus
Population 36 000
Michelin map 985 P 6 or Atlas Europe p 122

Silkeborg is situated at the heart of Jutland's picturesque lake district, a region of relatively high hills, extensive woodland and lakes all connected by the Gudenå, Denmark's longest river. Founded in the middle of the 19C, this pleasant and restful provincial town, lying on the shores of Lake Langsø, possesses two outstanding museums: Silkeborg Museum famous for its Tollund Man, a particularly well-preserved peat body, and Kunstmuseum founded by Asger Jorn, one of Denmark's leading post-war painters.

★★ Kunstmuseum ⊘ – This exciting museum, one of the most interesting modern art museums in Scandinavia, is quite appropriately situated in a lovely park on the south bank of the Gudenå. The museum was built to house **Asger Jorn**'s private collection of some 400 paintings, not only his own but those of other famous artists who were his friends from his early days in Paris before the Second World War until his death in 1973. In 1947, Asger Jorn founded the **CoBrA Group** with artists from Belgium and Holland as well as from Denmark, including Appel, Constant, Alechinsky and Jacobsen. It was a violent reaction not only against the dramatic social disorder brought

Tollund Man

119

about by the war, but also against established artistic trends. Among Jorn's own works, *Stalingrad* stands out as a frightening masterpiece. Other artists represented include Léger, Picasso, Miró, Ernst, Le Corbusier and Dubuffet, and there is an important collection of 20C Danish art.

★ **Silkeborg Museum** ⊘ – Situated near the main square, Torvet, the museum is housed in Hovedgården, a manor house dating from 1767 and the town's oldest building. It deals with regional history and local crafts. An extension has recently been erected in the grounds to house a permanent exhibition devoted to the Iron Age and, more specifically, to the way of life of the Tollund Man's contemporaries, living in c 400 BC. The body of the **Tollund Man★★**, the museum's prize exhibit, was discovered in 1950 in a peat bog near Silkeborg; the man had been offered in sacrifice to the gods, possibly in thanksgiving for successful peat cutting, then carefully laid down in the bog with the rope still round his neck; the expression on his face is uncannily real and very moving.

Men of the Iron Age

The Tollund and Grauballe men and their pastoralist contemporaries lived during the Iron Age (500 BC – AD 500) when Huang-Ti was finishing the Great Wall of China, when Athens was in decline, and the second Punic War was being waged and Hannibal was cajoling his elephants over the Alps. The Scandinavian Iron Age developed a high level of metal craftsmanship in grave goods. The votive sun chariot from Trundholm in Denmark is the most outstanding example. The archaeological research centre at Lejre *(see ROSKILDE: Excursions)* includes a reconstruction of a 2 000 year old Iron Age village.

EXCURSIONS

Ry and Himmelbjerget – *50km tour - allow 3hr.* The whole area is a gem for nature lovers with some of the finest scenery in Denmark and a choice of picturesque old inns.

Drive south-east on a minor road along the north bank of the River Gudenå.

The first stretch of road to Ry follows the river and lakes quite closely through thick forests with, now and again, a lovely view of Himmelbjerget on the other side of lake Julsø.

At Ry, turn right towards Gammel Rye, then right again on road 461.

Himmelbjerget, the sky mountain, only rises to 147m, but it actually looks more impressive than one might presume. From the 25m-high tower which stands on top, there are panoramic **views** of the picturesque, almost Tyrolean, surroundings, with dark alpine forests reflecting in the still waters of the lakes.

Return to the junction with road 445 and turn right towards Silkeborg.

This pleasant **boat trip** is an alternative to the above motor tour. The old steamboat *Hjejlen*, moored by the bridge in the centre of town, has been sailing on the river and lakes since 1861. During the season, the *Hjejlen* sails regularly upstream into Lake Julsø and stops at the foot of Himmelbejrget. From the shores of the lake there is an easy and enjoyable climb to the summit.

Grønbæk, Tange and Vinderslev – *60km. Drive north on road 46 to Grønbæk.* The apse of the small Romanesque Grønbæk Kirke is decorated with magnificent frescoes from the early 13C.

Continue north along a scenic road through Ans to Tange.

Tange reservoir-lake was created when a dam was built across the River Gudenå. The Tange hydroelectric power station founded in 1921 supplies electricity to the whole region and now houses the Electricity Museum, **Elmuseet** ⊘, which illustrates the evolution of the role of electricity in our daily life.

Drive west to Rødkærsbro, then turn south towards Levring and Vinderslev.

Vinderslev Kirke★ is a granite-built Romanesque church with richly carved portals and two sets of frescoes inside, painted at different periods. The nave is extensively covered with biblical scenes dating from the late 13C, whereas the later frescoes in the chancel, probably late 16C are more intricate with interwoven floral patterns.

Road 52 takes you back to Silkeborg.

SJÆLLAND

Close to Sweden in the north and linked to Fyn and the southern islands by several bridges, Sjælland is the largest Danish island and by far the most densely populated with two million inhabitants, 1.5 million living in the conurbation of Copenhagen alone. This concentration of manpower and the political influence of the capital have traditionally given the island an undeniable economic and cultural advantage. It is certainly no coincidence if the most magnificent castles and prestigious museums are to be found in north Sjælland which is the most visited region of Denmark for, apart from its exceptional cultural attraction, it offers a great variety of wonderful scenery, magnificent beech forests, lakes, deep fjords and beautiful beaches, all within a radius of 50km from Copenhagen.

South Sjælland, on the other hand, is also attractive but for different and less obvious reasons. More agricultural than the north, it unfolds a peaceful often idyllic countryside, neat villages with brightly painted half-timbered houses, lively ancient market towns like Køge and Næstved and old village churches containing a wealth of medieval frescoes. The pace of life is less hectic than in the north and the relaxing atmosphere which pervades the southern islands can already be felt here.

EXCURSIONS

The north coast from Helsingør to Gilleleje

25km north-west of Helsingør on road 237

Fine beaches, windswept dunes, colourful fishing villages and fashionable seaside resorts are to be found on this coastline.

Hornbæk – This is one of the oldest fishing villages in north Sjælland and there are still some fishermen's cottages to be seen as well as an interesting 18C church with many votive ships hanging from the ceiling; today, however, Hornbæk is essentially the most popular seaside resort in the area. It has one of the finest beaches in Denmark, a lovely stretch of white sand backed by low grass-covered dunes which provide shelter from the wind. Slightly inland, beautiful and sometimes luxurious summer houses are scattered among the trees that surround Hornbæk.

★ **Gilleleje** – This is also a traditional north Sjælland fishing village but, unlike Hornbæk, Gilleleje has remained very active and is still one of the most important on Sjælland. Fish auctions early in the morning are a sight not to be missed. Nevertheless, some of the picturesque thatched cottages round the harbour, which has retained its authentic simplicity, are now owned by summer residents and the harbour is packed with colourful ships of all sizes, modern yachts and weather-beaten fishing boats moored side by side; a couple of small restaurants tastefully restored and decorated complete this attractive scene.

Søren Kierkegaard (1813-55)

Søren Kierkegaard was born in Copenhagen and studied philosophy and theology at the university there. After having failed in his personal life, he was increasingly influenced by his natural inclination towards pessimism, reflected in most of his works, and the concepts of *existence, subjectivity* and *anguish* became his leitmotif. His philosophy had a significant impact on Heidegger, Sartre and the Existentialists.

West of the village, a path leads to the top of a hill overlooking the sea, known as **Gilbjerg Hoved**; the philosopher Søren Kierkegaard often used to walk up to this spot and admire the breathtaking view of the vast expanse of the Kattegat and the Swedish coastline in the distance.

Isefjord

Situated west of Roskilde fjord and linked to it by a narrow strait, Isefjord widens as it extends far inland and covers a vast area where the environment is protected, offering various possibilities to lovers of nature as well as open-air activities. Sea-trout fishing has become very popular and there are attractive harbours and mooring facilities all round the fjord. On the large inhabited island of Orø there is an unspoilt beach, an animal park and nature trails along the coast.

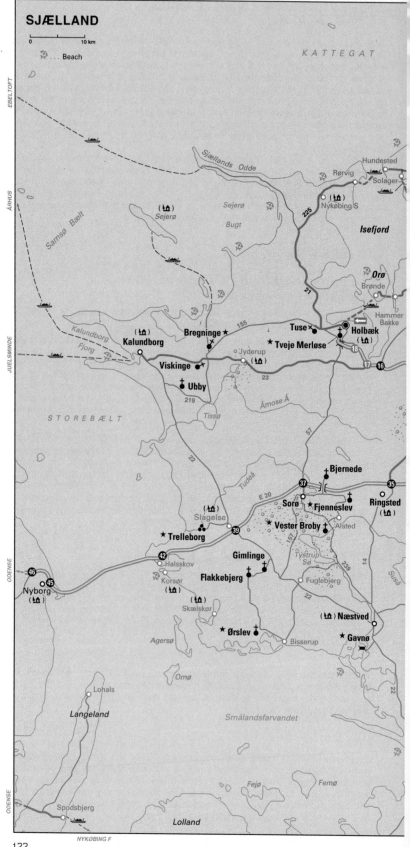

SJÆLLAND

0 _____ 10 km

🏊 ... Beach

KATTEGAT

Sjællands Odde

EBELTOFT

ÅRHUS

Rørvig
Hundested
Solager

225
Nykøbing S

Sejerø

(🏊) *Sejerø*

Sejerø Bugt

Isefjord

21

Orø
Brønde

Hammer Bakke

JUELSMINDE

Kalundborg Fjord

(🏊) **Bregninge** ★
Kalundborg ○

155
↓
Tuse ✕ ┼ **Holbæk** ⊙
Tveje Merløse ★ (🏊)

18

17 16

Jyderup ○
(🏊)

Viskinge ★
23
Ubby ┼

219

Tissø

Åmose Å

STOREBÆLT

22

Tudeå

57

┼ **Bjernede**

35

🄴37
Sorø ○ ★ **Fjenneslev** ┼
Ringsted
(🏊)

(🏊)
Slagelse

E 20
★ **Vester Broby** ┼
Alsted

★ **Trelleborg**

157

🄴42
Halsskov ○

Gimlinge ┼ ┼

Tystrup Sø

239

14

ODENSE

🄴46
🄴45
Nyborg ○
(🏊)

🄴39

Korsør ○
(🏊)

(🏊)
Skælskør ○

Flakkebjerg ┼

Fuglebjerg ○

22

(🏊) **Næstved** ○

Agersø

★ **Ørslev** ┼

Bisserup

★ **Gavnø**

Omø

🏊

22

Langeland

Lohals ○

Smålandsfarvandet

ODENSE

Fejø   *Femø*

Spodsbjerg ○

Lolland

NYKØBING F

122

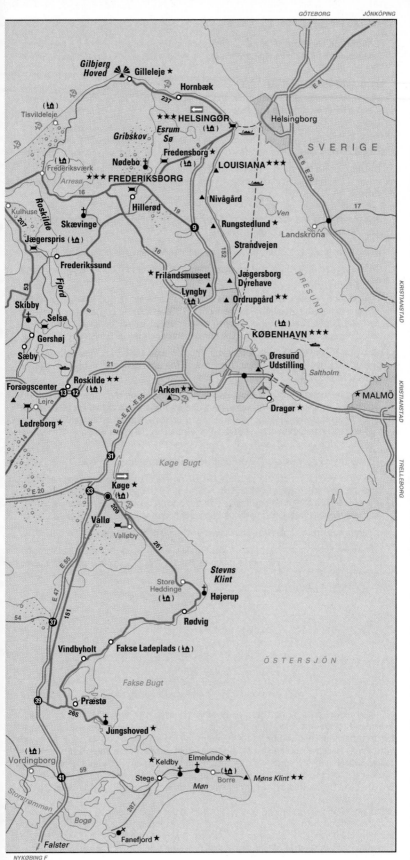

Boating on the fjord – Canoes (some equipped to spend the night in) and motor boats can be hired from Holbæk Marina to explore the shores, creeks and inlets of the fjord.

A round trip of the fjord – Combining driving and ferry crossings, this is an interesting alternative as it makes it possible to visit such sights as Tuse Kirke, Jægerspris Slot and Skibby Kirke on the way.

From Holbæk, drive to Rørvig along the coast road, ferry to Hundersted (25min), drive to Sølager, ferry to Kulhuse (8min), drive to Hammer Bakke, ferry to the island of Orø (6min), drive to Brønde Harbour and ferry back to Holbæk (30min).

Cycling round the fjord – Cycling is a third possibility, using the network of minor roads, lanes and paths clearly indicated on three cycling maps available from tourist offices.

Round trip from Køge: Stevns Klint and the coast road to Præstø *About 120km – allow half a day*

The Stevns peninsula offers some of the most varied scenery in Denmark.

Drive on road 209 south-east for 4km then turn right and follow the signs to Vallø Slot.

Opposite the castle's entrance is **Vallø Slotskro**, a picturesque 200-year-old inn. The elegant Renaissance building dating from c 1580 stands among ancient trees in a secluded **English style park** which is open to the public whereas the castle itself is not, since it is still used as a home for the unmarried daughters of Danish noble families.

Drive on to Valløby then back towards Køge on road 209; turn right on road 261 which leads to Store Heddinge, then follow the direction of Højerup and Stevns Klint (Stevns Cliffs).

The road ends in front of the old **Højerup Kirke** standing on the edge of the cliff. In 1928 the chancel fell into the sea in spite of a tradition which claims that the church moves inland every Christmas night! Several paths lead through the woods to the top of the white cliffs which stretch for 15km along the coast and are 41m above the sea at their highest point.

Follow the coast road south-west until you reach Præstø.

The road goes through the picturesque fishing ports of **Rødvig** and **Fakse Ladeplads**, and the neat little village of **Vindbyholt**, typical of south Sjælland. Lying peacefully on the shores of a sheltered bay, **Præstø** offers the idyllic picture of its colourful fishing harbour, cobbled market square, narrow streets and well-preserved houses.

Continue along the coast to Jungshoved at the tip of the peninsula.

Jungshoved Kirke★ suddenly appears like a lonely white figure against a background of sky, sea, tall trees and grass mounds. Inside, there is an interesting dance of death mural.

Follow road 265 then turn right on road 151 to return to Køge.

SKAGEN★★

Nordjylland
Population 11 500
Michelin map 985 Q 8 or Atlas Europe p 122

Situated at the narrow northern extremity of Jutland, in a barren area of dunes, heathland, bogs and sea, Skagen is one of Denmark's main fishing ports with a modern harbour and an important fishing fleet, as well as a popular seaside town with lovely beaches and a lively shopping centre. Above all it is the place where the **Skagen School** had its roots. Today internationally famous, the name of Skagen evokes the unique story of a simple fishing village which has become one of the best-known Danish holiday resorts since a group of painters settled there at the end of the 19C.

Although it had been a thriving community during the Middle Ages, by the 19C, Skagen had been reduced to a mere village by the overwhelming progress of drifting sands invading the fields and the town. Life was extremely hard for the inhabitants on this narrow inhospitable strip of land and fishing was their only means of survival until the building of the railway line at the end of the 19C. The drifting sands forced them to move their settlement from the Skagerrak coast on the west side, now called Old Skagen (Gammel Skagen), to the Kattegat coast on the east side.

The Skagen painters – In the 1870s, a group of painters discovered Skagen and were fascinated by the windswept desolate landscape and the ever changing light; moreover, they were conquered by the courage of the local people who, in spite of great hardship, continued to defy nature and remained in this forsaken place. Michael and Anna Ancher and their poet-painter friend Holger Drachmann settled there at the end of the 19C and attracted other artists from all over Scandinavia, who visited them regularly and worked with them; among them were Peder Severin Krøyer, Christian Krohg, Oscar Björck, Laurits Tuxen and Carl Locher.

THE PAINTERS' SKAGEN

The interesting part of the town stretches along the sea, between the main street, Skt Laurentiivej, and the harbour. There are many narrow streets lined with old fishermen's cottages, beautifully preserved and painted a deep shade of yellow. **Brøndums Hotel** in Anchersvej, where the artists often met, has retained its quaint 19C charm.

★★**Skagens Museum** ⊘ – Close to the hotel, in Brøndumsvej, the purpose-built museum, founded by Michael Ancher and his friends, opened in 1928 and was extended in 1980 and 1989; it contains some 1 500 paintings, drawings, sculptures and objects by artists who worked in Skagen between 1830 and 1930. Of particular interest is the Brøndum dining room with 81 artists' portraits and other paintings in the panelling. It was transferred to the museum in 1946.

★**Michael & Anna Anchers Hus** ⊘ – Situated a short way from the museum, in Markvej, this is the house where the couple lived from 1884. After the death of their daughter Helga, also a painter, in 1964, the house was carefully restored in order to recreate the special atmosphere of artistic creativity which permeated Michael and Anna Ancher's home; it contains their furniture, books, easels, canvases and, of course, many of their paintings.

Drachmanns Hus ⊘ – The house which the poet and painter Holger Drachmann (1846-1908) bought in 1902 and where he spent the last six years of his life was significantly called Villa Pax. Situated in Hans Baghs Vej, at the other end of the town centre, it contains many paintings by Drachmann himself and by his friends.

ADDITIONAL SIGHTS

Skagen By– og Egnsmuseum ⊘ – The open-air museum provides an interesting insight into the way of life in Skagen in the 19C; it contains the house of a poor fisherman and that of a rich one side by side, as well as a section on shipwrecks and fishing and a lifeboat station.

Skt Laurentii Kirke: Den tilsandede Kirke ⊘ – The 14C St Lawrence's Church dedicated to the patron saint of sailors was buried by drifting sand at the end of the 18C and closed by royal decree in 1795. In 1810, the nave was removed and today the tower alone is visible, rising above the sand. It can be reached through Gammel Kirkesti, just west of the town centre.

EXCURSIONS

Grenen – 3km north-east. Road 40 continues beyond Skagen to Grenen, Denmark's most northern point, and from the car park by the dunes, where Holger Drachmann is buried, it is possible to walk to the very tip of the peninsula which separates Skagerrak from Kattegat and seems to disappear into the waves. The currents here are tremendous and bathing is strictly forbidden.

★**Råbjerg Mile** – 10km south-west. The dunes in the Skagen area form a particularly vulnerable kind of environment since their vegetation is fragile and the sand continually drifting, although the process is now controlled by plantations. However, the vast 41m-high sand dune known as Råbjerg Mile was formed over several centuries and is still drifting east.

Ørnereservatet ⊘ – 15km south-west. Situated roughly half way between Ålbæk and Tversted, this is a rare kind of nature reserve where royal eagles can be observed feeding in a totally natural way. There are also pictures illustrating aspects of the eagle's life.

SORØ

Vestsjælland

Population 6 500

Michelin map 985 Q 8 or Atlas Europe p 122 – Local map see SJÆLLAND

Today Sorø is a peaceful country town picturesquely situated between two lakes and surrounded by woodland, but in medieval times it was an important religious and cultural centre.

A Cistercian monastery was founded here in c 1160, most probably by Bishop Absalon whose family, the Hvide, was connected with the place. At the Reformation in 1536, the monastery was closed and the buildings were turned into a school until, in 1623, Christian IV decided to create an academy for the sons of the aristocracy. This institution, known as the **Sorø Academy**, is still in existence today although it was rebuilt in the 19C following a major fire. In the park, which is open to the public, there is a statue of Ludwig Holberg, the 18C poet and playwright who left his fortune and his library to the Academy.

Klosterkirke ⊙ – It is the old abbey church of the monastery, an imposing Romanesque building restored in the 19C, originally built to the same plan as the Cistercian abbey church of Fontenay. Inside there is an impressive tall 16C crucifix by Claus Berg and Bishop Absalon's tomb behind the altar. The church also had important royal associations and several members of the royal family were buried in other parts of the church during the 14C, including Oluf, Queen Margrethe I's son. When she, in turn, died in 1412, she was at first buried in Sorø according to her wishes, but her body was later removed to Roskilde Domkirke.

EXCURSIONS

Ringsted – Today Ringsted is a modern provincial town but it has retained in its centre the symbol of its spiritual influence during the Middle Ages, when it was renowned throughout the kingdom as an important religious centre and seat of justice. Standing on the market square, **Sankt Bendts Kirke★** is one of the oldest brick-built churches in Denmark. It was originally the abbey church of the Benedictine monastery, built during the second half of the 12C. For 200 years monarchs and members of the royal family were buried inside the church which contains paintings of some of them as well as 20 royal tombs including that of Valdemar I who declared the church an official royal burial place.

Village churches of south Sjælland – *About 85km – allow half a day – local map see SJÆLLAND.*

Most of the churches to be seen on this tour are Romanesque or Early Gothic, brick-built with massive square towers and corbie-stepped gables. Their whitewashed walls and red-tiled roofs, often visible from far away, stand out in the middle of their neat churchyards decorated with colourful flower beds surrounded by tiny boxwood hedges.

Drive south on road 157 through Haldagerlille and turn right on road 22, then left to Gimlinge.

Gimlinge and Flakkebjerg Churches – These two churches are only 3km apart; both have interesting sets of frescoes from the 14C and 15C adorned in Flakkebjerg with floral and geometric motifs.

Follow a minor road south to Ørslev.

★ **Ørslev Kirke** – Its imposing size is unusual for a village church; it contains interesting frescoes depicting medieval village life, including a lively village dance.

Drive east to Bisserup, then north-east through Fuglebjerg along the southern shore of Lake Tystrup until you join road 239; turn left then left again to Vester Broby.

★ **Vester Broby Kirke** ⊙ – This rather small church contains a variety of frescoes from the 12C and the 14C. Painted in a naive style, they are extremely expressive, in particular Adam and Eve eating the forbidden fruit and Cain slaying Abel.

Return to road 239, turn left then right towards Alsted and left again to Fjenneslev.

★ **Fjenneslev Kirke** ⊙ – The twin towers of this Romanesque church built in 1130 by Asser Rig, Absalon's father, were added at the end of the 12C. The frescoes also date from the end of the 12C; one is said to depict Asser Rig and his wife.

Follow the direction of Sorø, then turn right towards Bjernede.

Bjernede Kirke ⊙ – This is the only round church in Sjælland; it was built during the second half of the 12C and, following careful restoration, is the best-preserved round church in Denmark. Inside, the vaulting is supported by four massive round pillars.

SVENDBORG

Fyn
Population 27 000
Michelin map 985 Q 7 or Atlas Europe p 122

Situated on the shores of the narrow sound separating Tåsinge and Fyn, Svendborg is Fyn's second largest town, and an important industrial and commercial centre.

During the Middle Ages, Svendborg was a thriving market town with an already established maritime tradition based in particular on regular trading with the Baltic ports and the Hanseatic League. Today, Svendborg's maritime activities consist mainly in a diversified and essential ferry service to Ærø and other islands of the archipelago lying just off the coast of south Fyn. The town centre is as busy as ever on market days (Wednesdays and Saturdays), an occasion to watch the world go by from one of the picturesque pavement cafés.

OLD TOWN

The old part of the town comprises the market square (Torvet) and the surrounding cobbled streets where, now and then, one can get a glimpse of a charming courtyard.

Vor Frue Kirke ⓥ – The essentially Late Gothic church of Our Lady dominates the market square and its 27-bell carillon can be heard four times a day.

Anne Hvides Gård ⓥ – Situated almost opposite the church in Fruestræde, this is the oldest house in Svendborg, an imposing half-timbered building dating from 1560, now part of the local museum. The rest of the museum is housed in Svendborg's former poorhouse, **Viebæltegård** ⓥ, in Grubbemøllevej, with its original interior, where local archeological finds are exhibited.

Sankt Nicolai Kirke ⓥ – Standing on the corner of Gerritsgade and Skt Nicolai Gade, just south of the market square, St Nicholas is the oldest church in Svendborg, dating from the 13C. It was carefully restored at the end of the 19C and acquired then a large altarpiece by Joachim Skovgaard.

Close by there is a statue by **Kai Nielsen** (1882-1924), a native of Svendborg; this is one of several statues in Svendborg by the famous sculptor.

Near the church in Skt Nicolai Gade, stands Svendborg's latest museum, the Toy Museum **Legetøjsmuseet** ⓥ

EXCURSION

★★**Ærøskøbing and the "fairy-tale" island of Ærø** – A 70min ferry ⓥ journey separates Svendborg from the second largest island in the Fyn archipelago yet, as you step ashore, you will almost certainly feel as if you had journeyed back in time some 200 years! Ærøskøbing is the jewel of this "real" island, as the Danes themselves call it (so many of the others are joined together or to the mainland by bridges!), oriented north-west/south-east and forming a set square with the larger Langeland. The small town shelters inside a natural harbour, at the centre of the island. Its street plan goes back to the Middle Ages but most of the buildings date from the 17C; these brightly painted, flower-decked houses, with their beautiful carved wooden doors, form cheerful rows along the cobblestoned streets, testifying to the islanders' pride in their cultural heritage. Watch out particularly for the old chemist's shop in Vestergade, where the **tourist office** ⓥ is also located; wander along Sluttergyden, Søndergade, Brogade and Nørregade and feast your eyes on the colourful variety of this authentic architectural ensemble.

One of these old buildings houses **Flaskeskibssamlingen** ⓥ, the Bottled-ship Museum at Smedegade 22; it contains the extraordinary collection of Flaske Peter (Peter Bottle as Peter Jacobsen (1873-1960) was nicknamed because of his hobby): more than 700 items are exhibited out of a total of 1 700 which the ship's cook made during his lifetime!

At the western end of the town you will find the beach, **Vesterstrand**, where you can see privately owned beach huts often passed on from one generation to the next.

Ærø being only 30km long and 9km wide, why not rent a bike ⓥ to explore this idyllic island which has two more towns (one at each extremity) and admire the peaceful countryside dotted with windmills; one main road runs the length of the island, past tiny villages and half-timbered farmhouses. It is possible to see quite a lot in one day, but should you wish to stay on, there is a choice of hotels, inns and camp sites as well as a youth hostel *(contact the tourist office)*.

SÆBY

Nordjylland
Population 8 500
Michelin map 985 O 7 or Atlas Europe p 122

The small seaside town of Sæby lies peacefully on the shores of Kattegat, 12km south of Frederikshavn. The town has retained a wealth of domestic architecture, including a few public buildings from the 18C along the main street, Algade, and rows of low brightly painted private dwellings. The whitewashed church towers above the picturesque old town.

★SÆBY KIRKE ⊙

The church belonged to a former Carmelite monastery founded at the end of the 15C and dedicated to the Virgin Mary. There was already a church on the site which the monks extended. At the Reformation in 1536, the monastery was closed and the buildings gradually pulled down.

The church contains some **late medieval frescoes** and some interesting 16C furniture.
The beautiful and rare frescoes were whitewashed at the Reformation and only discovered again in 1905; the oldest ones, dating from the middle of the 15C, are on the north wall of the nave which formed part of the old church. The others, which cover part of the vaulting, were painted after the church was extended. They are extremely expressive and the colours are warm, with a predominance of subtle shades of ochre. Intricate floral and geometric patterns separate the different scenes. There are two sets, the first one depicts a legend about **Joachim and Anna**, Mary's parents, who had a revelation about the impending birth of Mary. The other shows scenes of the **Last Judgement** with some very realistic interpretations, including open graves, a partly wiped-out representation of hell with devils' heads and, among the headgear worn by the damned, the tiara of a pope and the mitre of a bishop! In another place, the Devil takes away the soul of a man lying on his death bed while his wife is being comforted by her lover.

The magnificent **altarpiece**, most probably made in Antwerp c 1520 consists of a carved centre panel, depicting the Virgin and Child surrounded by adoring angels, and painted side panels representing the Adoration of Jesus by the shepherds and the Wise Men.

There is also a beautiful Renaissance **pulpit** with canopy in painted wood, 20 of the original **choir stalls** with some of the misericords still intact and, in the transept, a splendid Late Gothic **woodcarving** of the Virgin and Child, probably from the workshop of Claus Berg.

SØNDERBORG

Sønderjylland
Population 26 000
Michelin map 985 R 6 or Atlas Europe p 122

The modern industrial town of Sønderborg is situated on the island of Als, along the narrow sound separating Als from the east coast of south Jutland and spanned by King Christian X's bridge. All that is left now of the old border town are a few streets lined with tiny colourful old houses covered with red tiles, in the area surrounding the approach to the bridge, and a massive castle overlooking the entrance of the sound.

★SØNDERBORG SLOT ⊙

The castle was built in c 1170, probably by King Valdemar the Great, to defend the coast against attack from the Wends. It was extended several times and by 1500 had become an imposing stronghold. King Christian II, who was deposed by the nobility, was an unwilling guest in the fortress from 1532 to 1549. During the second half of the 16C, it was rebuilt into a Renaissance castle but war and neglect slowly turned it into a ruin. It was saved just in time at the beginning of the 18C and rebuilt once more, this time in Baroque style. However, by 1921, it was again in bad need of repair and the decision was taken to restore it and turn it into a museum.

Interior – The castle houses a historical museum with a special national significance since it contains an extensive section about the 1864 war against Prussia which ended for the Danes with the loss of south Jutland and its subsequent occupation until the end of the First World War.

The museum's collections are arranged on three floors. Particularly interesting is **Queen Dorothea's Renaissance Chapel** on the ground floor with a triptych by Franz Floris of Antwerp as well as a marble and alabaster font by another Dutch artist, Cornelis Floris. The **Great Dancing Hall** occupies the whole of the north wing's second floor. On this floor too are the watchman's gallery and the medieval machicolations.

EXCURSION

Dybbøl Mill, Broager Church and Flensborg Fjord – *25km. If time is short, the drive along the Flensborg fjord can easily be omitted.*

Cross the sound and follow Dybbølgade for about 3km.

Standing in an area where fierce battles took place between Danish and German forces in 1848 and again in 1864, **Dybbøl Mill** ⊘ has become a Danish national symbol and a history centre. **Historisk Center Dybbøl Banke** ⊘, has recently been opened to provide information about the battles in both wars and the reunification in 1920.

Continue on road 481 then turn left on road 8.

Situated on a high hill, **Broager Kirke** can be seen from afar with its attached twin towers surmounted by pointed steeples. The main part of the building is Romanesque and Early Gothic, the towers being added later. The frescoes, discovered in 1923, date from the 13C and the 16C. There is a splendid Christ in Majesty in the apse from c 1250 and scenes from the legend of St George in the north transept from the early 16C. The very ornate altarpiece dates from the 18C.

Continue on road 8 and turn left at Alnor.

A scenic road follows the north bank of **Flensborg fjord**, offering panoramic views of the wide expanse of silvery blue water contrasting with the dark wooded banks of the fjord.

TRELLEBORG ★
Vestsjælland
Michelin map 985 Q 8 or Atlas Europe p 122 – Local map see SJÆLLAND

The landscape has drastically changed since this Viking fortress was established in c 980 and it is difficult today to grasp its strategic position. A thousand years ago, however, it stood surrounded by marshland, some 4km inland, near the confluence of two rivers flowing into Storebælt. This was an ideal place to build a defensive stronghold, which implies that such fortresses *(see FYRKAT)* might not after all have been designed as garrisons for warriors preparing to raid foreign countries and in particular England. One thing is certain though, they were planned on such a vast scale that only the king could gather the materials and the huge workforce necessary to build them. Arguments now put forward seem to indicate that these fortresses served to strengthen royal power towards the end of the 10C, at the time when Harald Bluetooth claimed to have conquered all Denmark and Norway *(see JELLING).*

TOUR

Covering approximately 7ha, the fortress consisted of an inner area surrounded by a circular earth rampart and divided into quadrants by two perpendicular streets which led to four gates pointing precisely north, east, south and west. Inside each quadrant stood four long buildings forming a square. A wide ditch protected the rampart on the east side where there was no marsh and beyond it stood another row of buildings exactly following the curving rampart. This outer area included a cemetery and was in turn protected by an earth bank and a ditch.
The houses were entirely built of oak timber, including the roof, and followed the same plan: there is a reconstruction of one of these houses on the site which gives a good idea of what they looked like apart from one detail: the outer posts were meant to lean against the walls and act as buttresses instead of forming a gallery. The house at Fyrkat, built later, is closer to reality.

TØNDER ★
Sønderjylland
Population 8 500
Michelin map 985 R 5 or Atlas Europe p 122

Situated near the German border, Tønder is a charming old market town on the banks of the River Vidå, with a lively southern atmosphere.
Unbelievable as it may seem now, Tønder was, throughout the Middle Ages, a thriving market town with an important harbour specialising in the export of cattle and horses. Unfortunately, the surrounding area being, in places, below sea level, the town was flooded many times before a series of dykes were built in the 16C, resulting in the loss of the harbour facilities. However, Tønder soon derived new wealth from the lace industry which, by the beginning of the 18C, employed up to 12 000 lacemakers working at home.

OLD TOWN

Most of the old houses, which can be seen in the town today, date from those prosperous times. Along the main street, successively called **Østergade**, **Storegade** and **Vestergade**, stand some stately merchants' houses from the 17C and the 18C, with richly carved portals, whereas the small streets like **Uldgade** and **Spikergade** are lined with more modest bay-windowed houses which once belonged to 17C craftsmen. The richly decorated **Christ Kirke** ⊘ also testifies to Tønder's prosperity in the 17C and the 18C. It was built at the end of the 16C to replace Skt Nicolai Church which had become too small. However the tower was saved as were the font from 1350 and the pulpit from 1586. The splendid rood-loft dates from 1625 and the altarpiece from 1695.

The **Tønder Museum** ⊘ is housed in an old gatehouse which is all that remains of Tønder Castle; extended in the 1920s, it contains a large collection of Dutch wall tiles as well as an important collection of local lace and silver. In the same building, the **South Jutland Art Museum** ⊘ shows different aspects of Danish art, including Surrealist painting and contemporary art.

EXCURSIONS

Møgeltønder and Højer – *12km west*. The charming old-world village of **Møgeltønder**, 5km west of Tønder, looks almost like a fairy-tale setting with its long straight cobbled main street, Slotsgade, lined with low 18C gabled houses, some of them thatched, and its double row of regularly spaced lime trees. At one end of Slotsgade stands the 12C church. Inside there are some interesting frescoes, the older ones being in the chancel (1550) and on the chancel arch (1275). There is also a fine altarpiece from c 1500, as well as a Romanesque font, a Baroque pulpit and an organ made in Hamburg in 1679. Slotsgade leads to Schackenborg, a palace built at the end of the 17C and inhabited by 11 generations of the Schack family until 1978 when it was returned to the Crown. Prince Joachim became the new owner in 1993 and he settled there when he married Princess Alexandra in 1995. Guided tours of the park are organised in summer *(contact the tourist office in Tønder)*.

The picturesque thatched village of **Højer** is situated on a raised sand bank, in an area protected from flooding by dykes and sluices. The restored windmill, **Højer Mølle** ⊘, is now a museum illustrating the flood control system.

TÅSINGE

Michelin map 985 R 7 or Atlas Europe p 122

Squeezed between the south coast of Fyn, and Langeland, and linked to both by bridges, Tåsinge is hardly an island anymore. Most of the traffic goes straight through Tåsinge on its way from Lolland to Odense, but it is well worth making a detour to the east coast of the island to see the seaside village of **Troense**, undoubtedly one of the most picturesque villages in Denmark, with its lovely whitewashed half-timbered cottages, low-cut hedges, white-wooden fences and tiny harbour tucked in the curve of a peaceful cove.

Nearby, in a secluded woodland area, stands Valdemar's Castle, **Valdemars Slot** ★⊘, a stately Baroque building on the edge of a large pond. Originally built between 1639 and 1644 by Christian IV for his son Valdemar, the castle was offered to the national hero Niels Juel who remodelled it into a Baroque mansion at the end of the 17C. His descendants still own it and have opened part of it to the public. The rooms are extensively furnished as if they were in use, from the Great Hall to the servants quarters, recreating the authentic atmosphere of a stately home.

From the tower of **Bregninge** village church, on road 9, there is a breathtaking **view** of the whole south Fyn archipelago.

VIBORG

Viborg
Population 30 000
Michelin map 985 P 6 or Atlas Europe p 122

Situated just south of the Limfjord, at the heart of an area of rolling hills, lakes and forests, Viborg is a peaceful provincial town and one of the oldest Danish cities.

Ancient capital of Jutland – It is probable that it was once a place of pagan worship before it became one of the most important dioceses in the country, with a magnificent cathedral. Throughout the Middle Ages, it was customary for the new king to be elected in Viborg and homage continued to be paid to him there well into the 17C. At the same time, Viborg was an important centre of the lucrative cattle export trade, and what is still called the ancient cattle road went from Viborg to Schleswig across central Jutland. The famous reformer Hans Tausen preached his new creed in the town, thus starting a movement which was to lead to the Reformation in 1536. Several major fires,

the worst being that of 1726, destroyed most of the town and the gradual concentration of power in Copenhagen accelerated Viborg's economic decline. The railway
brought back some prosperity during the 19C and, since then, Viborg has become a
modern commercial and industrial city and a regional administrative centre.

Domkirken ⊘ – Of the vast 12C Romanesque cathedral, only the crypt remains, an
impressive structure dating from 1130, with three naves supported by massive pillars. The present cathedral was built of pink granite in 1876 in a neo-Romanesque
style which tried to be as faithful as possible to the original building. Its most striking feature is the set of **frescoes** painted by **Joachim Skovgaard** at the beginning of the
20C, illustrating scenes from the Bible.

There is little left of the old town, except a few old houses in the streets surrounding the cathedral. In Domkirkestræde, the **Skovgaard Museet** ⊘ houses a collection of
paintings by Joachim Skovgaard and other members of his family.
South of the cathedral, **Søndre Sogn Kirke** ⊘, a former monastery chapel, is now the
oldest church in Viborg: completely remodelled in 1728 after it was partially
destroyed by fire, it contains an ornate 16C Dutch altarpiece.

EXCURSIONS

Hald Sø – *25km tour – allow 1hr. Drive south on road 13 for 3km and turn right
on a minor road.*
The scenic road goes through beautiful wooded countryside and follows the western shore of Lake Hald (Hald Sø), overlooked by Hald Hovedgård mansion.

The road continues south and rejoins road 13. Turn left to return to Viborg.

Danmarks Cykelmuseum ⊘ – *30km north.* Situated in Ålestrup, just west of road
13, the museum illustrates the history of the bicycle from the penny-farthing to the
latest models.

Mariager Fjord – *45km to Mariager.* The narrow Mariager fjord penetrates deeply
inland right through to the town of Hobro, close to the Viking fortress of Fyrkat.

*It is possible to explore both shores of the fjord, following road 555 along the
southern shore, then crossing the bridge at Hadsund and driving along road 541
on the northern shore.*

The road is particularly picturesque between the old town of Mariager and Hadsund
offering a varied landscape of thick woodland sloping down to the water, lush
meadows and winding streams. There are safe moorings along the fjord for sailing
enthusiasts and tiny fishing villages like Stinesminde and it is worthwhile stopping
in **Mariager**. The town jealously preserves its old-world appearance, which makes it
all the more refreshing to stroll along the cobbled streets lined with fine old houses
like Købmandsgården in Kirkegade, now a local museum, and Postgården, an 18C
inn, now a hotel.

VOERGÅRD SLOT★★

Nordjylland

Michelin map 985 O 7 or Atlas Europe p 122

Surrounded by a wide moat and an extensive wooded park, this elegant Renaissance
castle stands in a remote agricultural area of north Jutland between Ålborg and Sæby.
Built at the end of the 16C on the site of a previous stone building now part of the
north wing, the castle changed hands many times, becoming gradually dilapidated until
it was restored at the end of the 19C and again this century by its last owner, Count
Oberbech-Clausen, married to the daughter of the famous French surgeon Jules Péan
and widow of Count Chenu-Lafitte. When his wife died he transferred the large art collection she had left him to Voergård where it is now exhibited. At the same time, he set
up a foundation for the upkeep of the estate and asked that the castle be opened to
the public after his death.

The castle ⊘

The beautiful east wing of the castle appears at the end of a straight cobbled avenue
prolonged by a stone bridge across the moat. The red-brick structure is decorated
with sandstone reliefs and a splendid portal, a gift from Frederik II in 1588 believed
to have originally been designed for Frederiksborg Slot.
The castle contains a magnificent collection of paintings by such masters as Goya,
Rubens, Fragonard and Watteau, antique furniture, porcelain and objets d'art,
mainly French and Chinese, some of which are particularly interesting from a historical point of view; such is the case of a china set used by the French King
Louis XVI and his wife Marie-Antoinette during their imprisonment in the Temple
tower; there is also a dinner set made for Napoleon I during his 100-day-comeback
in 1815.

ÅLBORG ★

Nordjylland
Population 115 000
Michelin map 985 O 6 or Atlas Europe p 122

Ålborg is Denmark's fourth largest city and the main economic and cultural centre of north Jutland, a regional capital which gives the impression of being well organised, enterprising and above all lively, a town where visitors are welcome in a choice of modern hotels, a town with imagination too and a superb modern art museum to prove it. No doubt the spirit of those Vikings who founded Ålborg over 1 000 years ago is still alive in their descendants.

Occupying a convenient position at the narrowest point of Limfjorden, Ålborg was already in the 11C a well-established Viking port with a fishing fleet and regular trade links with Norway.

The Middle Ages were a time of increasing wealth followed by alternating periods of prosperity and decline in the 16C and 17C as fires and wars took their toll. Ironically, the two most splendid old houses in the town centre date from the early 17C *(see opposite)*. Industrialisation and the railways brought new stability to Ålborg in the 19C and the harbour was modernised. Today the town has a solid industrial production based on shipbuilding, cement and railway stock not forgetting Aalborg Akvavit, the other Danish national drink.

Two Danish National Drinks

The city of Ålborg owes a considerable part of its fame to the liqueur aquavit. In the past a single state-owned distillery was responsible for the entire production of this alcoholic drink. Aquavit is made of distilled alcohol spirits, either from rye grain or potatoes, combined with one or more aromatic flavouring substances. Each distillery produces its own distinctive flavour by using caraway seeds, spices, elder flowers, fennel or juniper berries.

Even if Danes are known for drinking considerable quantities of aquavit, they are first and foremost great beer drinkers (second in the world). Their liking for this drink is probably explained by the great care which goes into brewing beer which in turn has produced a quality product with a world-wide reputation. Although Carlsberg and Tuborg have international reputations Thisted, Wiibroe, Albani and Ceres also produce beers which are highly popular in Denmark.

TOWN CENTRE

The 1990 winner of the *Europe's Tidiest City* competition has a compact town centre with neat pedestrian streets surrounded by a wide ring road and green open spaces.

Budolfi Domkirke ⊘ **(BY)** – Dedicated to the English St Botolph, the cathedral was built in c 1400, although there are traces of older parts going back to c 1100. The massive square tower is surmounted by a Baroque spire added in 1779. The carillon plays every hour on the hour from 9am to 10pm. There are lovely late medieval frescoes in the porch but the altarpiece and pulpit were made at the end of the 17C. The rest of the furniture dates from the 18C.

Ålborgs Historiske Museum ⊘ **(ABY M¹)** – Close to the cathedral in Algade, this local history museum houses a collection of exhibits from the Stone Age and from various periods of the town's history. Of particular interest is the Ålborg Room which has a Renaissance interior from 1602 reconstructed from authentic parts.

Helligåndsklostret ⊘ **(BY F)** – The Holy Ghost Monastery stands on CW Obels Plads, behind the museum; it was founded in 1431 as a charitable institution which it has remained to this day, providing a home for 26 senior citizens. There are fine frescoes dating from c 1500.

Jomfru Ane Gade (BY 32) – This pedestrian street north of the monastery is the expression of the Danish sense of humour, a fun street with nothing but cafés, restaurants and discotheques on both sides and a decor looking like a period film set.

Turn right at the end of Jomfru Ane Gade onto Ved Stranden; across Østerågade stands the castle overlooking the fjord.

Ålborghus (BY) – Built between 1539 and 1555, the half-timbered building now houses the county administration.
However, the public is admitted to the courtyard as well as to the dungeon and underground passages.

Østerågade (BY 68) – There are two splendid 17C merchants' houses on the right-hand side of the street, walking away from the fjord. The first one at no 25, **Jørgen Olufsens Gård (BY S)**, is half-timbered; it was built in 1616 by Jørgen Olufsen. The

ÅLBORG

DENMARK

F Helligåndskloster	**S** Jørgen Olufsens Gård	**M¹** Ålborgs Historiske Museum
V Jans Bangs Stenhus	**H** Rådhuset	

second one at no 9, **Jens Bangs Stenhus** (**BY V**), at the corner of Adelgade, is an impressive 5-storey residence built in 1624 by another merchant, Jens Bang. This magnificent red-brick building with stone reliefs and elaborate gables is the finest Renaissance private house in Denmark.

Rådhuset ⊙ (**BY H**) – Standing on Gammeltorv, just off Østerågade, this elegant Late Baroque town hall from 1762, painted a bright yellow colour, cannot pass unnoticed; King Frederik V's motto is written in Latin above the Latin entrance: *Prudentia et Constantia*.

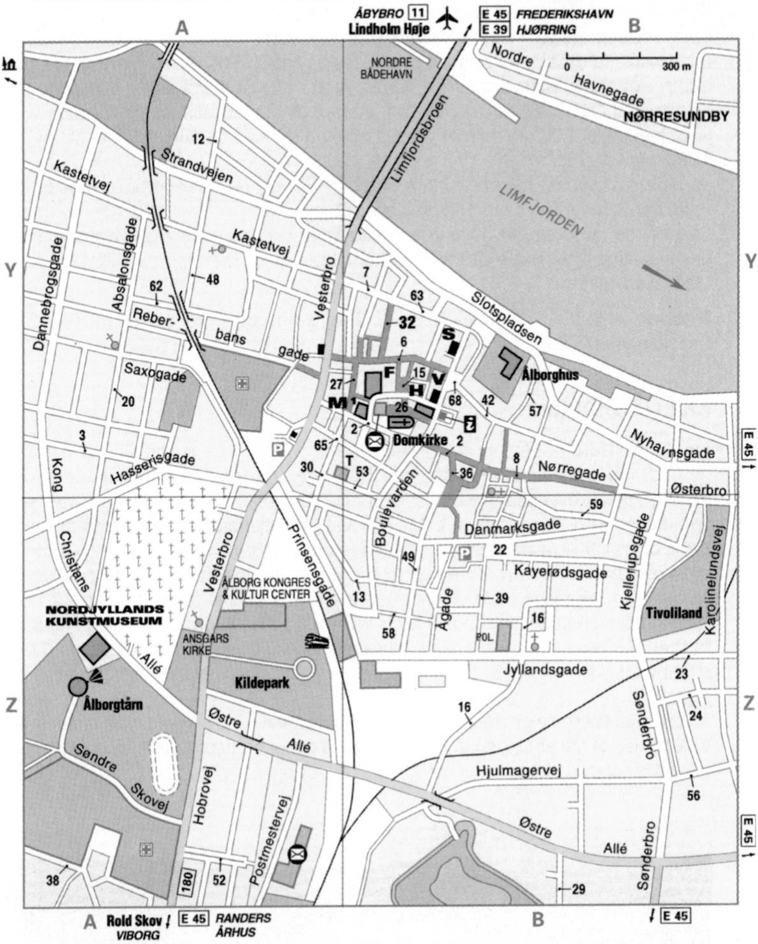

ADDITIONAL SIGHTS

★★ **Nordjyllands Kunstmuseum** ⊙ (**AZ**) – The North Jutland Art Museum is undoubtedly one of the best art museums in Denmark. It is situated in Kong Christians Allé, part of the ring road surrounding the town centre. Inaugurated in 1972, the beautiful modern building, designed by Elissa and Alvar Aalto and Jean-Jacques Baruël, backs onto a wooded park and the contrast between the dark green vegetation and the white Carrara marble is striking. Inside, prominence has been given to space through the use of a mobile partition wall system and to natural light which floods

133

in from above. Apart from exhibition rooms and galleries of varying sizes, there is a chamber music room, lecture rooms, a workshop, a library and a café, as well as a sculpture park and an amphitheatre where music and plays are performed in summer.

The museum houses permanent collections of **Danish and foreign 20C art**, paintings, sculptures, ceramics, textiles and collages, with a majority of Danish works. These collections evolved from two private collections. Firstly, Anna and Kresten Krestensen's collection, acquired in 1967, in which modernism and above all the CoBrA Group are well represented with many works by the founder, Asger Jorn, Ejler Bille and others; foreign art of the 1940s and 1950s is also represented to a lesser extent by such artists as Appel, Alechinsky and Poliakoff. Secondly, the Kirsten and Axel P Nielsen's collection, offered to the museum in 1986, deals with later aspects of 20C art such as Surrealism and the neo-Dadaist movements of the 1960s and 1970s.

Situated just behind the museum, **Ålborgtårnet** ⊘ (**AZ**) offers panoramic **views** of the town and Limfjorden from 105m above sea level.

East of the museum but quite close, **Kildeparken** (**AZ**) contains many classical statues including *The Three Graces* by Thorvaldsen and *The Bacchus Child* by Anne Marie Carl-Nielsen.

Tivoliland ⊘ (**BZ**) – *In Karolinelundsvej.* This is an amusement park modelled on Copenhagen's Tivoli.

EXCURSIONS

★★**Lindholm Høje** – *3km north* (**BY**) *in Nørresundby.* This is the site of a burial ground and settlement from the late Iron Age and the beginning of the Viking period, spread over the wide crest of a hill. The area was covered over with several metres of drifting sand in c AD 700 and this phenomenon helped to preserve it for over 1 000 years. Excavations, ended in 1958, revealed nearly 700 graves most of them marked by stones set in the shape of a triangle (the oldest), a circle, an oval or a ship (the most recent); there is evidence that in most cases the bodies had been cremated. Various objects were found in the graves, some going back to the 5C. Traces of houses, namely hearths, cooking pits and postholes, and of a street were found north of the burial ground, indicating the presence of a large village.

A very interesting small museum, **Lindholm Høje Museet** ⊘, displayed with taste, gives a clear idea of life at Lindholm Høje with the help of archaeological finds and imaginative reconstructions.

Viking cemetery, Lindholm Høje

Rold Skov – *About 25km south on road E 45* (**AZ**). This is the largest forest area in Denmark, offering varied landscapes of heaths, dark coniferous woodland, attractive beech woods and bogs with nature trails for walking or cycling. Rebild, 3km west of Skørping, is a good starting point. In 1912 some Americans of Danish origin bought the hilly area surrounding the village of Rebild and donated it to the Danish State on the condition that it became a national park (Denmark's first) and they were allowed to celebrate American holidays in the hills. Since then, thousands of Americans have come to **Rebild** every year to take part in the 4 July celebrations and visit the Lincoln Log Cabin, **Lincoln Blokhuset** ⊘, a small museum about Danish emigrants who settled in the United States.

ÅRHUS ★★

Århus

Population 205 000

Michelin map 985 P 7 or Atlas Europe p 122

With the eastern part of Denmark firmly under the influence of Copenhagen, Århus has a great role to play as the alternative capital of the west in a country which badly lacks geographical unity.

Ideally situated on the east coast of central Jutland, inside a wide bay protected by the Helgenæs peninsula, Århus is at the centre of a network of communications by land and sea linking it not only to the rest of Jutland, but also to the two main Danish islands, Sjælland and Fyn. This position ensures the town's steady economic growth based on electronics, communications, design, the food industry and the activities of its harbour which is now the second most important in the country. Moreover, Århus has a great cultural vitality, with an important archaeological institute belonging to the university, an expanding art museum, a music complex and a reputed symphony orchestra as well as two major festivals, the **Århus International Jazz Festival** in July and the **Århus Festival** in September with a programme of mixed cultural events.

Viking town – Århus was originally an important Viking settlement probably founded in the early 10C at the mouth of a river, hence its ancient name *Aros* meaning estuary. It grew rapidly, acquired a bishop in 948 and the first episcopal church was established in 1060 on the site of Vor Frue Kirke *(see overleaf)*. This early prosperity was confirmed by the building of the cathedral which began in 1201. However, during the late Middle Ages, wars and epidemics of bubonic plague had a devastating effect on the development of the town which was slowed down further by the Reformation in 1536. Commerce picked up again in the 17C and during the 19C the railways brought industrialisation on a large scale which, in turn, led to an increase in maritime trade.

TOWN CENTRE

The centre of the town has remained close to the harbour, in an area where there is evidence of the ancient Viking city which gave its name to Århus.

Vikingemuseet ⊘ (**BZ**) – The Viking Museum is surprisingly situated in the basement of Unibank in Sankt Clements Torv, in full view of the cathedral. The explanation is simple: the archeological finds on display were discovered while men were digging on the site to lay the foundations of the bank. Part of the ramparts of the old Viking city were unearthed together with traces of houses and some tools. A museum was built around them and a reconstruction of a similar house made.

★★ **Århus Domkirke** ⊘ (**BZ**) – The cathedral was built at the beginning of the 13C in Romanesque style and dedicated to St Clement. During the 15C, it was completely remodelled so that the building we see today is mainly Flamboyant Gothic. The 93m-long nave, flanked with an aisle on either side, is the longest in Denmark, but it is offset by the wide chancel and transept and the overall impression is of pleasing proportions and lofty elegance. The Romanesque chapels in each arm of the transept are reminders of the original building. There are frescoes in different parts of the church, dating from the late 15C: traces are to be found on the walls of the aisles and on the pillars, but they are in a better state of preservation on the transept vaulting.

The splendid triptych over the High Altar was made by Bernt Notke from Lübeck in 1479. The bronze font dates from 1481, but the ornate pulpit is from the late 16C.

★ **Vor Frue Kirke** ⊘ (**BZ**) – From the cathedral, it is only a short distance across Store Torv and along Vestergade to the oldest church in Århus. Our Lady's Church, which was the abbey church of a Dominican monastery, dates from the 13C to the 15C. There are traces of frescoes and a magnificent altarpiece by Claus Berg from c 1520, which depicts a scene from the Passion in a vividly expressive style reminiscent of a painting by Pieter Bruegel the Elder.

ÅRHUS

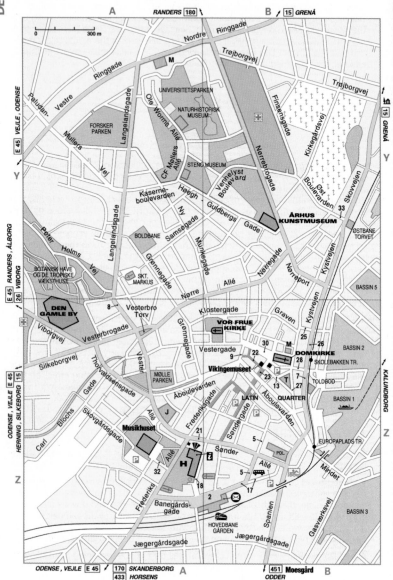

During restoration work undertaken in the 1950s, the crypt of the original Romanesque church built in 1060 was discovered under the chancel; it is the oldest vaulted building in Scandinavia. A flight of steps leads down to it.

The district north of the cathedral is the oldest part of town; it is known as the **Latin Quarter** (BZ) because its narrow streets, cafés, fancy shops and tiny art galleries create a lively youthful atmosphere. South of the cathedral is the busy shopping district and, in its centre, the main pedestrian street, **Sankt Clements Torv** prolonged by **Søndergade** is known as **Strøget**.

Rådhuset ⊘ (AZ H) – This modern town hall, designed by Arne Jacobsen just before the Second World War, looks perhaps too functional to be attractive in spite of the grey marble from Norway which covers the walls. From the top of the tower, there is a good **view** of the town.

Musikhuset ⊘ (AZ) – West of the Rådhuset across Frederiks Allé stands an impressive complex with a glass façade, inaugurated in 1982 and entirely devoted to music. The larger of the two halls can hold 1 600 people. It is the home of the Århus Symphony Orchestra, but ballet and opera are also being performed here.

ADDITIONAL SIGHTS

★★★**Den Gamle By** ⊘ (AZ) – Situated in parkland along Viborgvej, west of the town centre, this is one of the most picturesque and beautiful **open-air museums** in Denmark. It has nothing to do with old Århus, as might be presumed, but is in fact an old town consisting of reconstructed old houses from towns all over the country, dating from the 17C to the 19C.

The museum shows all aspects of urban life during that period including extensively furnished workshops, a school, a chemist's, a baker's, a post office, a customs house and an early 19C theatre. No detail has been overlooked to make it as authentic as possible; moreover it is very successful from an aesthetic point of view and walking through the cobbled streets is a real delight. The splendid half-timbered Mayor's Residence, dating from 1597, comes from Århus, the various rooms showing the evolution of interior decoration through the centuries. The imposing customs house stands on piles on the edge of the river running through the town, as does the tannery. Simonsens Have is an old-fashioned café with a bandstand in the garden for summertime promenade concerts.

Den Gamle By, Århus

★**Århus Kunstmuseum** ⊘ (BY) – The Fine Arts Museum is famous for its extensive collection of Danish art from the mid-18C to the present day. The Danish Golden Age is particularly well represented and, in recent years, the museum has acquired modern art works by Danish artists as well as some works by foreign artists.

★★**Moesgård Museum** – *8km south along the coast road; leave by road 451* (BZ) – *see local map overleaf.*
On the outskirts of town the coast road (Strandvejen) goes through the forest of **Marselisborg skov**, where the royal family has a summer residence, **Marselisborg Slot**, and through the **deer park** (Dyrehaven) where sika deer, fallow deer and wild boar roam freely.
The museum of Danish prehistory, **Moesgård Museum** ⊘, housed in an 18C manor house, illustrates the period from the Stone Age to Viking times. Among the exhibits is the famous Grauballe Man, the 2 000-year-old body of a man found in a peat bog near the village of Grauballe north of Silkeborg. Just like the Tollund Man in Silkeborg, this man had suffered a violent death and probably been the victim of a human sacrifice to some pagan god.
Outside the museum, a prehistoric path leads to reconstructed dwellings from different periods in appropriately recreated landscapes.

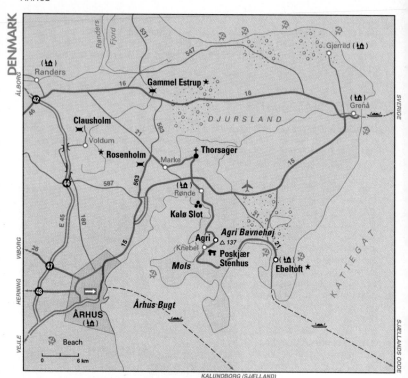

KALUNDBORG (SJÆLLAND)

EXCURSIONS

Round Århus bay – *Round trip of about 120km to the north-east.*
To the north-east of Århus there are varied landscapes of idyllic countryside and sheltered coves dominated by heath-covered hills, lovely villages, a remote castle and the picturesque old town of Ebeltoft.

From Århus, follow the direction of Grenå and turn left on road 563 to Rosenholm Slot then follow the itinerary on the local map above.

★**Rosenholm Slot** ⊘ – This stately Renaissance mansion built in 1559, stands on a small island in the middle of a lake. A bridge guarded by stone lions leads to the main gate with the coat of arms of Jorgen Rosenkrantz and his wife, the first owners of the castle, proudly displayed over the archway. For over four centuries, the castle has belonged to the Rosenkrantz, a noble family whose origins, according to legend, go back to the 7C and a touching love story between an English princess and a Danish prince. The numerous rooms and galleries open to the public are mainly furnished in Rococo or Spanish-Moorish style; in the Winter Room, the ornate gilt leather wallcovering is well preserved, whereas 300-year-old French and Flemish tapestries hang on the walls of the Corner Room and the Tower Room. In the Great Hall, there is a striking portrait of Frederik V by the court painter CG Pilo. The tiny Renaissance pavilion in the grounds is sometimes called Jutland's first university, for it is within its walls that the second owner of Rosenholm, known as Holger the Learned (1574-1642) taught theology, history and Latin.

Thorsager Rundkirke ⊘ – Jutland's only round church, built in the early 13C, stands on a hilltop; the walls are 1m thick and it is thought that it might have played a defensive role.

Kalø Slot – Built in 1313 by King Erik Menved, Kalø was one of several castles erected along the shores of Århus Bay to defend it. King Gustav Vasa of Sweden was imprisoned in the castle in 1519. Today, with its half-crumbled keep, the fortress is no more than a romantic ruin.

Mols peninsula – Its centre is an area of beautiful hills separated by valleys and ravines, covered with heath and woodland, known as Mols Mountain, **Mols Bjerge**. The highest summit, **Agri Bavnehøj**, near the village of **Agri**, rises to 137m only and yet it offers splendid panoramic **views**. The lake at Agri was formed by a depression left in the ground at the end of the last Ice Age; it has no outlet or tributary. **Poskjær Stenhus**, between Agri and Knebel is a burial chamber surrounded by 23 large boulders forming a circle. It is thought to date from c 2000 BC.

★ **Ebeltoft** – This traditional provincial town, whose poetic name means apple orchard, has got a great deal of old-world charm and a stroll along its winding cobbled streets is like a journey into the past. On both sides of the main street, Adelgade, there are some fine half-timbered merchants' houses and on the square (Torvet), stands the world's smallest town hall, **Rådhus**, at least according to local people; today it is a **Ebeltoft Museum** ⊘ but weddings still take place there every Saturday. On either side of the quaint building, Nedergade and Overgade are lined with a wealth of old houses, some of them picturesquely leaning to one side. They lead to the 700-year-old church and the old vicarage nearby housing a dolls' museum, **Missers Dukke– og Legetøjsmuseum** ⊘. Near the ferry harbour, there is an impressive **windmill park** with a great number of wind-operated generators which produce enough electricity to supply 600 houses all year round.

Follow road 21 then road 15 to return to Århus.

★ **Gammel Estrup** – *40km north-east – see local map opposite.*
The elegance of this fine Renaissance manor house is enhanced by the slender octagonal towers, although part of the building dates back to the 15C. It houses the Jutland Manor House Museum, **Jyllands Herregårdsmuseum** ⊘, containing an extensive collection of furniture with a few rare exhibits, which illustrates changing styles through the centuries. The farm buildings have been turned into the Danish Agricultural Museum, **Dansk Landbrugsmuseum** ⊘, which gives an excellent idea of country life with the help of recreated outdoor and indoor scenes.

Clausholm Slot ⊘ – *30km north – see local map opposite.*
This stately Baroque mansion was built in the late 17C by Count Reventlow whose youngest daughter, Anne-Sophie, eloped with King Frederik IV and later became queen of Denmark.
The interior is profusely decorated and in the chapel, where concerts are given in the summer, there is an organ dating from 1601, reputed to be the oldest in Denmark and in perfect working order.

Geirangerfjord

Ph. Body / HOA QUI

Norway

ALTA

Finnmark
Population 10 800
Michelin map 985 C 20 or Atlas Europe p 105

Situated at the head of a deep fjord which bears its name, Alta is one of northern Norway's most important tourist centres, linked to the capital Olso by direct daily flights and within easy reach of the North Cape and the wilderness of the Finnmarksvidda plateau at the heart of Lapland. The Alta region is well known for its superb scenery and its exciting outdoor activities all year round, including deep-sea fishing, salmon fishing, canoeing, skiing, excursions by dog-sledge and snow-scooter safaris. But above all, the name of Alta is internationally famous as the location of the largest site of pre-historic rock carvings in Northern Europe. Alta is included on the UNESCO list of World Heritage Sites.

In spite of its extreme northern latitude (70° north), the same as that of Alaska and Siberia, Alta enjoys a relatively mild climate, thanks to the Gulf Stream and evidence has been found that the coastal area was inhabited by hunters as far back as 8000 BC; by the late Stone Age there were several village type settlements and Alta was a religious centre. From the late Middle Ages, Alta became an important market place for the trading of Sami reindeer products. Today Alta is a thriving new town whose economy is based on agriculture, fishing, mining, slate-quarrying and communications.

★★ALTA MUSEUM ⊘

It is situated on the main E6 road to Tromsø, just south of Alta. Opened in June 1991, the new museum comprises the museum building and the rock carvings park. From the car park, paths lead to the modern spacious building which includes an exhibition area, a café, a shop and a post office. The exhibition area on two floors is divided into five main topics relating to the history and development of the area: **From Rock Art to Christianity** depicts the different phases of rock carving in Alta as well as some aspects of medieval art; **Treasure and Market** shows Alta as a main trading centre; **Alta – River and Fjord – from Ice Age to Hydroelectricity** presents economy and culture through the ages; **War and Peace in Finnmark** illustrates military history with an emphasis on the Second World War; **Northern Lights and Copper Mines** deals with the Northern Lights Observatory on Haldde Mountain nearby and copper mining in the area as well as scientific expeditions and early tourism.

The museum park slopes down from the museum to the shore of the fjord, a silvery stretch of still water framed by snow-capped mountains. A network of elevated wooden paths totalling 5km enables visitors to see part or most of the rock carvings which are spread over a large area; they have been underlined with a reddish brown colour similar to that of contemporary rock paintings. There are guided trips round the park in English and other languages. The carvings were discovered in 1973 and although 3 000 have been listed so far, there are still many more waiting to be uncovered. They were carved during the late Stone Age between 4000 and 500 BC, the oldest being on high land and the most recent along the shore of the fjord as the sea level dropped considerably during the post-glacial period. The variety of subjects depicted is fascinating, there are fishing and hunting scenes, with elks, bears and reindeer clearly recognisable, there are also boats, weapons, tools, birds as well as men, women and children in various situations. It is thought that the carvings may have had a religious significance and been intended for instance as a means of asking for the protection of the gods, but, of course, other interpretations can also reasonably be put forward.

6 000-year-old Stone Age rock carving

EXCURSIONS

There are not many roads in northern Norway, as maintenance problems are very difficult to overcome in an area which is only sparsely populated. However, summer and winter **excursions** are organised by professionals, using various means of transportation such as bus, helicopter, sledge, snowmobile, horse and boat.

Altaelva river – Famous for its salmon, this river offers splendid scenery which can be admired on riverboat trips to the **Savtso Canyon**, the largest canyon in Northern Europe. The canyon can also be reached on foot *(allow 4hr):* drive south from Alta along the old road to Boeskades *(26km)* then follow a marked path to the canyon.

Fjord cruises – Boat trips on the **Altafjord** and round the archipelago can be combined with fishing and eating the day's catch on board.

Haldde Mountain – *Allow 4hr. Drive to Kåfjord, 10km south-west of Alta on the E6 then follow the marked trail.* On top of Haldde (Holy Mountain), about 1 000m above sea level, stands the Northern Lights Observatory, built in 1899, partly destroyed during the Second World War and recently restored. The northern lights *(aurora borealis)* are a natural phenomenon which can be observed during the long polar night, from the end of November to the end of January, when streamers of light illuminate the sky.

ARCTIC CIRCLE
See POLARSIRKELEN

BERGEN★★★
Hordaland
Population 227 202
Michelin map 985 L 2 or Atlas Europe p 110
See plan of the conurbation on Michelin map 985

Often called the wooden city or the gateway to the fjords, Bergen exerts a strange fascination on potential visitors whose enthusiasm is inevitably rewarded by the discovery of a lively cosmopolitan city with a rich past steeped in European history. Built on the spectacular west coast of Norway and within easy reach of some of the most breathtaking scenery in the country, Norway's second largest town occupies a sheltered position between a string of islands on the west side and a ring of seven mountains on the east side. Important harbour activities, shipbuilding and fishing industries have been a long-standing tradition which has brought prosperity to the town for the past centuries, but the rapid development of the North Sea oil industry has set a new challenge to Bergen: how to grow into a modern industrial metropolis and preserve its unique architectural heritage included on UNESCO's World Heritage list. The building of the Bryggens Museum on an important archaeological site right at the heart of the city confirms the strong cultural awareness of this university town which built Norway's first permanent theatre in 1850, acquired a fine new concert hall in 1978 and holds an annual international music and art festival in May and June. Bergen shared with eight other cities the privilege of being declared European City of Culture for the year 2000.

HISTORICAL NOTES

Ancient capital of Norway – Founded in 1070 by King Olav Kyrre, Bergen was one of the first two bishoprics in Norway, the other being Trondheim. Many churches and monasteries were built and the town became a major ecclesiastical centre, a privilege which it held throughout the Middle Ages. Because of its unique harbour setting and its central position along the west coast, the city also developed into an important trading centre exporting dried fish which was in great demand in Europe at that time. Until the end of the 13C Bergen was the capital of Norway and although it was replaced by Oslo in 1299, it continued to prosper and remained the largest city in the kingdom until the 19C.

The Hanseatic League – This association of north German cities gets its name from a medieval guild of merchants known as the Hansa. In 1241, a group of German towns formed a commercial alliance to promote monopolies and develop trade between the eastern and western regions of Northern Europe at a time when Venice controlled Mediterranean and Middle-Eastern trade. Their meetings were held in Lübeck and the Lübeck seal, which featured a ship as a symbol of their activities, gave authority for their decisions to be implemented throughout the Baltic. Their influence soon spread east as far as Russia and west to England and Scotland and the Hansa established commercial bases across the whole of Northern Europe and by the late Middle Ages, the League included no fewer than 100 member towns. The *kontorer* – Bergen, Bruges, London and Novgorod – had their own magistrates, courts and financial systems. Some were the site of important international trade fairs; such was the case of Bruges which, until its harbour silted up at the end of the 15C, was Europe's main commercial centre for the import and export of goods carried by Venetian and Hanseatic ships. Large stocks of spices, silks, wines and fruit from the Mediterranean as well as fish, metals, timber, textiles and furs from Northern Europe were kept in warehouses, ready to be shipped all over the known world and Italian financiers derived huge profits from their banking agencies established there. Apart from Bruges, the Hanseatic League controlled three other main *kontorer*, each specialising in basic products essential to medieval European economy: from Novgorod came the sought-after Russian furs, from London top quality wool and cloth and from Bergen Norwegian timber and dried fish. The Hanseatic League chose Bergen for its convenient position close to the main fishing grounds and to the North Sea and Baltic markets; the town was established as a *kontor* around 1360, importing grain and exporting timber and dried fish mainly from the Lofoten Islands 1 000km away. The town developed rapidly and as the Baltic trade gradually became essential to its prosperity, the League was able to exert greater political influence and to dictate terms to Norwegian kings. The German quarter, situated along Bryggen, on the east side of the harbour, consisted of wooden houses, two or three storeys high, in which workers and merchants lived and worked. After the discovery of America and the opening of new trade routes and markets, the Hanseatic League slowly declined and the *kontor* in Bergen was finally closed in 1754.

TIPS FOR BERGEN

Tourist Information Centre – The new tourist office is housed in Frescohallen, Vågsallmenningen, opposite the Fish Market. The spacious attractive building offers a comprehensive service to visitors of Bergen and the fjord region and holds various exhibitions.

The Bergen Card – This is a must for visitors to the gateway to the fjords. The card costs 130NOK (3 to 16 year olds 60NOK) for a 24hr card and 200NOK (children 90NOK) for a 48hr card and is available from the tourist information centre, some hotels, the railway station and the main post office. The card gives free admittance to most of the city's museums and attractions, free travel on buses and the Fløibanen funicular, discounts for concerts, theatres and cinemas as well as on certain sightseeing tours. A Bus Card and Parking Card are also part of the package. The Bus Card entitles the holder to free travel in central Bergen and to some of the most important attractions (eg Troldhaugen). Airport and night buses are not included. Route leaflets are available from the bus station, Strøngaten 8, ☎ 70 55 32 67 80. The Parking Card entitles the holder to free parking, but parking regulations – including maximum parking time – must be observed. The card gives a 50% reduction for parking in multi-storey car parks. Pay at the manned booth.

Guided tours – Wind back the clock and visit medieval Bergen. Tours leave daily from Bryggens Museum between June and August at 11am and 1pm. Time 1hr 30min. Price 60NOK, children under 10 free (10% reduction for holders of the Bergen Card).

Bus tours – These leave from the Tourist Information Centre and include the central Bergen and Troldhaugen tour (3hr, 200NOK), a tour of medieval and new Bergen (2hr, 125NOK) and an evening tour (2hr, 90NOK). Holders of the Bergen Card are entitled to a 10 to 50% reduction depending on the tour.

Bergens Expressen – The miniature train leaves from the Fish Market daily from May to mid-September (10% reduction for holders of the Bergen Card).

Souvenirs – Take your pick from the delightfully patterned Norwegian sweaters, wood, pewter or glass souvenirs or silver jewellery. The pedestrian streets Gågaten, Torgalmenningen and Marken have a good selection of shops. Shopping centres are to be found at Galleriet, Kløverhuset and Bergen Storsenter.

City centre – All vehicles going into the city centre, Monday to Friday between 6am and 10pm must pay a toll.

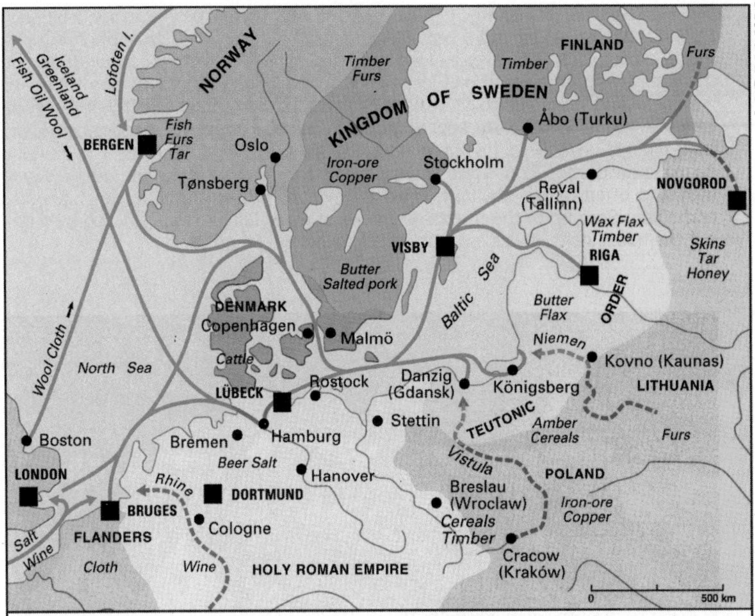

THE HANSEATIC LEAGUE
IN NORTHERN EUROPE (14C-15C)

■ Established commercial enclaves

● Hanseatic towns

—— Main trade routes

★★★BRYGGEN (BV) 2hr

Tyskebryggen (the German wharf), as it used to be known, was the heart of medieval Bergen and is today the only remaining ensemble of wooden buildings illustrating the architecture of the famous *kontorer* set up all over Northern Europe by the Hanseatic League. The densely populated medieval settlement stretched along the eastern shore of Vågen between Bryggen and Øvregaten; the wooden houses, which were used as homes as well as warehouses and workshops, were built in rows with narrow wooden communal passages between them overshadowed by numerous overhangs. Many of these houses were destroyed by fire during the past 600 years and patiently rebuilt each time; there are a number of them left along the waterfront which are now on UNESCO's World Heritage list. They have been carefully restored and most of them are painted a distinctive red-brick or ochre colour; their characteristic pointed gables facing the harbour offer the most picturesque view from the west side of Vågen against the town's mountainous background. Today the houses are occupied by restaurants, cafés and workshops where one can watch craftsmen at work; and a walk through the maze of alleyways leading to the back of the houses gives a fair idea of what it must have been like to live in Bergen during the Middle Ages. From Øvregaten, which runs parallel to Bryggen, there is also an interesting view of the wooden tenements. From the 14C onwards, all imported and exported goods had to transit through Bergen which regulated trade movements for the whole west and north coast of Norway as well as for the islands to the west including Iceland, Greenland, the Faroes, Shetlands and Orkneys. As a result of this monopoly, up to 60 merchant ships called in the harbour every year and, since it was forbidden for anyone to deal directly with these ships, all goods had to be stored in the warehouses occupying the ground floor of the tenements along Bryggen before being sold there or at the market. The whole district of Bryggen was therefore engaged in various activities connected with maritime trade and life was organised accordingly. The wooden buildings on Bryggen were used for specific purposes, those on the seafront comprising the warehouses as well as the living and working quarters, whereas the houses at the back were usually the communal quarters. Many people, mainly workers and servants, lived in these houses apart from the house owners; quite a few of these were Hanseatic merchants who lived in Bergen all the year round and employed young workers and apprentices. Two typical buildings have been turned into museums to show what life was like on Bryggen during the Hanseatic period.

Det Hanseatiske Museum ⊘ (BV) – This is one of the best-preserved wooden buildings along the quayside; rebuilt after the 1702 fire which devastated the city, it is also the oldest. The architecture had hardly changed from medieval times and the 3-storey house gives a vivid idea of the spartan living conditions of a Hanseatic merchant and his household; besides the warehouse, and the merchant's office, where account books were kept together with records of ships' movements and transactions, several rooms were set aside as workshops, whereas the sleeping quarters on the top floor were shared by the merchant's employees, single young men who often came from Germany for a few years to learn the trade or work as craftsmen. Because of the fire hazard, no heating or lighting was allowed throughout the house neither was any cooking done on the premises.

Bryggen

Schøtstuene ⊘ (BV) – This is one of several communal houses situated at the rear of the tenements which were used for several purposes. Food was prepared in the kitchen and served to the merchants and workers in a large refectory; the daily diet consisted essentially of porridge, bread, dairy produce, fish and some meat which were consumed during the two main meals of the day, breakfast and supper complemented by light refreshments during working hours. When it was bitterly cold, men gathered after work in the communal houses to drink beer and keep warm and these were therefore busy centres of social life, which also served as schools for the many apprentices living in the tenements. The communal houses were close to **Øvrestretet** (today's Øvregaten) where the town's main market was held and where many craftsmen displayed their skills, among them shoemakers, comb-makers (using the antlers of reindeer and elks), woodcarvers, goldsmiths, tailors and furriers; each group was assigned a special position along the street.

Bryggens Museum ⊘ (BV) – Several Hanseatic houses were totally destroyed by fire in 1955. Confronted with the irreparable loss of part of Bergen's cultural heritage, archaeologists seized the opportunity to investigate the area situated between Bryggen and Mariakirken, where these houses had stood, in order to find out more about the town's early medieval history. Extensive excavations were undertaken straightaway and went on for 14 years; they revealed remains of the oldest settlement ever discovered in Bergen, dating from the 12C, which provided an insight on various aspects of medieval life in the town. Intended to house the rich archaeological finds brought to light between 1955 and 1969 as well as other archaeological finds discovered on other sites after 1970, the modern museum was actually built around the building remains which form the central part of the collections, shared between two permanent exhibitions.

The Oldest Tenements: building remains from the town's first century – This exhibition comprises the remains of five wooden buildings, most probably warehouses, which have been replaced in the exact spot where they were found, along the original seafront, just below Mariakirken. Four of them were built in the mid-12C and destroyed by fire soon afterwards; the fifth was built immediately after the fire and destroyed at the end of the century by another fire. The buildings were raised on posts so that their floors were kept dry; sections of passageways also found suggest that these 12C tenements were built according to a pattern very similar to that of later tenements: two rows of buildings separated by a common alleyway.

The Medieval Town: Bergen around 1300 – The second exhibition illustrates the main aspects of medieval urban life at a time when Bergen was Norway's capital and an important religious centre with 20 churches and chapels and five monasteries. The guided tour of Bergen as it was nearly 700 years ago starts with the trading area on Bryggen then proceeds to Øvrestretet (now Øvregaten), the main market street and craft centre, and ends at Holmen, marking the entrance to Vågen, where Håkonshallen and Rosenkrantztårnet now stand. It was here that the royal residence stood close to the cathedral and the bishop's residence. Runic inscriptions discovered during excavations provided evidence of the town's active intellectual life particularly in the field of education and of various literary activities mostly connected with religion and the law.

AROUND VÅGEN (BV) *2hr*

Vågen is the old harbour round which the town developed from the early 12C. As Bergen's commercial activities increased, the shoreline was modified and the quay extended out into the deep-water part of the harbour in order to allow large ships to berth directly along the wharf.

Torget (BV) – This open space along the waterfront, right at the heart of the city, is the most lively place in town as the daily fish market attracts a dense crowd of local people as well as visitors who wander with delight through the colourful stands displaying a variety of fresh fish, shellfish, kippers and smoked salmon. Freshly prepared smoked salmon sandwiches, looking most appetizing, are sold in no time. Besides the fish stands, other stands sell fruit, vegetables, flowers and handicraft. Torget is also the starting point of boat trips to various nearby islands.

★★Mariakirken ⊙ (BV) – Of all the town's religious buildings dating from the Middle Ages, only three have survived: St Olav's, the present cathedral, which hardly recalls its medieval origins and is today a blend of various architectural styles, Korskirken, almost entirely rebuilt in the Renaissance style during the 17C and St Mary's Church, the oldest building in Bergen today, a fine and rare example of Romanesque architecture in Norway. Built during the 12C, St Mary's has been in continuous use ever since, being spared destruction from the numerous fires which swept through the town at regular intervals. Thus the building has remained virtually unchanged since the 13C. The nave, flanked with two lower side aisles and surmounted by a triforium, form with the lofty twin square towers an imposing but harmonious ensemble which suggests that St Mary's was probably designed as the town's principal church. From 1408 to 1766, it was used by the Hanseatic merchants as their parish church. The flat beamed ceiling was replaced by ribbed vaulting, possibly at the end of the 12C, in order to minimise the risk of fire. The Gothic choir windows point to the fact that the choir was lengthened during the 13C. The four portals are all medieval but were built at different times, the oldest being the north aisle portal, level with the outer wall and surmounted by a straight lintel. By contrast, the elaborate south portal is of a typical Late Romanesque design. The church is most beautiful inside on account of its charming proportions and the rare furniture it contains. The oldest piece is the fine triptych behind the altar which was probably carved in Lübeck at the end of the 15C. The choir also contains 15 statues of the 12 disciples with Moses, John the Baptist and Paul, dating from 1634. The magnificent pulpit, surmounted by a canopy, was offered to the church by a group of merchants in 1676. This splendid example of Baroque art might have been carved in the Netherlands as the tortoiseshell and lacquer used would suggest. The numerous paintings on the walls of the church are characteristic of the north German style of the 17C and 18C, inspired by the Dutch School. There are also traces of 15C frescoes on the walls of the nave above the triforium and over the chancel arch.

★Rosenkrantztårnet ⊙ (BV) – The tower gets its name from Erik Rosenkrantz who was governor of Bergen Castle, **Bergenhus**, in the 1560s. Designed both as a defensive and residential building, it was erected by Scottish masons who incorporated a massive keep from c 1270 and an outwork from c 1520. On the south side facing the town, the tall 5-storey structure has a Renaissance façade surmounted by a small octagonal tower topped by a cupola. The tower was badly damaged by an explosion in the harbour during the Second World War. King Magnus Lagabøte's (the Law mender) chapel on the second floor of the keep is particularly interesting; above was the king's bedchamber which was altered into an elegant 16C hall. Guns were installed right at the top of the tower, under the roof. There is a good **view** of the town from the battlements.

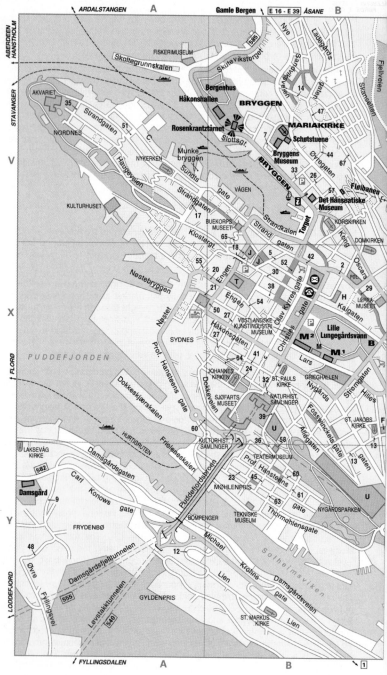

Toll road system - Bompengeringen.

Both Bergen and Oslo make a small charge for cars going into the city centres, Mondays to Fridays between 6am and 10pm. Single tickets and toll
passes can be purchased at the toll booths.
Those with passes should take the lane with a blue sign (abonnement); those
with the correct amount the lane with the yellow sign (Mynt/Coin) and those
with no change the lane with the grey sign (Manuell).
See the plan above for the location of the toll booths.

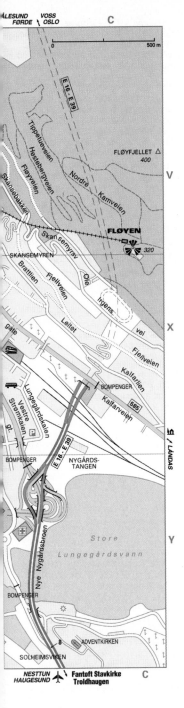

BERGEN

M¹ Rasmus Meyers Samlinger
B Rhododendrarium
M² Stenersens Samling

The Bergens-Express - Bergens-Expressen.

A brightly painted train takes visitors on a round trip of the city which includes the fish market, the Bryggen district with its medieval aspect, one of the most distinctive old districts of the capital and one of the best viewpoints for admiring the « gateway to the fjords ».

The tour lasts an hour and trains leave from opposite the tourist information centre. Tickets are available on the spot or from the tourist office. The trains run daily from May to mid-September.

Håkonshallen ⊙ (BV) – Built between 1247 and 1261 by King Håkon Håkonsson, the father of King Magnus, as a place suitable for royal banquets, it was first used for the wedding and coronation of King Magnus. When the royal residence ceased to be used in the 16C, it fell into disrepair but was eventually restored at the end of the 19C. During the Second World War, it caught fire as a result of the explosion in the harbour, which partly destroyed Rosenkrantz tower, and was damaged to such an extent that only the walls remained. Restored once again after the war, it is now regularly used for ceremonial occasions and for concerts, particularly during the Bergen Festival. A Late Gothic portal set into the south wall during the 15C is today the royal entrance to the Great Hall which is 33m long, 13m wide and 17m high. The woodwork and interior decorations are modern. Below the Great Hall, there are two floors; the middle floor just below was used mainly as a working area; the stone-vaulting was added after the construction of the hall to prevent fire from spreading to the wooden floor of the Great Hall above. The basement, which is the lowest floor, was used for storing provisions.

ADDITIONAL SIGHTS

★★ Fløyen by funicular ⊙ (CV) – *Allow 8min for the ride and 1 to 2hr for the visit.* The funicular (Fløibanen), which has been running since 1918, takes passengers from the city centre (150m from Torget along Vetrlidsalm) to the top of Fløyen, 320m above sea level. It stops three times on the way as it is regularly used by local residents. The **panoramic views★★** of the town and the surrounding islands are really worthwhile and this rewarding experience can be prolonged by a walk through the beautiful woods covering Fløyen.

Rasmus Meyers Samlinger ⊙ (BX M¹) – This fine collection of Norwegian art is housed in a large villa overlooking Lille Lungegårdsvann, a small lake surrounded by lawns and trees. Works by Munch form a large part of the collection which also includes paintings by Swedish and Danish artists, in particular Willumsen who belonged to the Pont-Aven group led by Paul Gauguin.

Stenersens Samling ⊙ (BX M²) – One building down from the Meyers gallery stands the Municipal Museum (Bergen Billedgalleri) devoted to Norwegian painting of the past 150 years. A separate gallery within the museum houses the Stenersen Collection of some 250 works of modern art by internationally acclaimed artists such as Munch, Klee and Picasso.

Rhododendrarium (BX B) – Rhododendrons were first imported to the city around 1850 and it was soon discovered that the quality of the soil and the climate were ideally suited to the growth of these plants. New species were then introduced and it became fashionable to grow rhododendrons until in 1987 Bergen was named The City of Rhododendrons and a Rhododendrarium was officially opened in 1988; it contains 82 different species or hybrids.

Edvard Grieg

Edvard Grieg (1843-1907) is universally acknowledged as Norway's greatest composer and the best exponent of his country's artistic identity. At the age of 15 Grieg left his native town, Bergen, to study music at the Leipzig Conservatory for four years and he was undoubtedly greatly influenced by the German Romantic tradition. After his studies, he settled in Copenhagen and began to compose various works which he later disavowed. In his search for a style of his own he became more and more interested in Norwegian folk music and these early years mark the beginning of a long creative process which eventually enabled him to write mature works combining Norwegian tradition and contemporary European artistic trends. In 1866, Grieg settled in Oslo which was then called Christiana. There he not only composed but taught music and embarked on a performing career both as a pianist and a conductor. In 1868 came his first great masterpiece, the piano concerto in A minor. When he composed, he liked to be surrounded by beautiful scenery and his inspiration stemmed from this contact with Norwegian nature. But he also needed to meet other European artists; he therefore travelled regularly to various European capitals and in 1869 he met Franz Liszt in Rome. During the 1870s, Grieg composed the famous incidental music to Ibsen's *Peer Gynt* and he was awarded an annual grant which enabled him to return to Bergen. There he wrote some of his best works including the Norwegian dances and the Holberg suite. In 1885, he and his wife Nina moved to Troldhaugen where he spent the last 20 years of his life composing when he was not on concert tours in Europe. Not only did his music become extremely popular, but his influence on the development of music was acknowledged by such composers as Ravel and Bartok.

★**Gamle Bergen** ⓥ – *North by road 585* (BV). Situated just north of the city centre along the coast, this open-air museum contains over 40 wooden houses from 18C and 19C Bergen. They have been moved to their present location to preserve them from eventual destruction and are furnished with suitable period furniture in order to give a vivid illustration of life in those days. There is a photographer's studio from 1900, the house of a humble seamstress dating from c 1860, a rich merchant's summer residence built in 1798, a baker's house and shop with the bakery at the back, a barber's shop complete to the last detail and many more.

EXCURSIONS

Fantoft Stavkirke ⓥ – *Paradis, 6km south of the town centre. Leave by road E 39* (CY). Originally built in Fortun in the Sognefjord area in c 1150, the wooden church was moved to its present site in 1883 and was considered such a fine example of a stave church that, when it burnt down in June 1992, it was decided to rebuild it just as it was, using 300-year-old wood from other buildings; the rediscovery of special construction techniques was a unique achievement.

★★**Troldhaugen** ⓥ – *Hop, 8km south of the town centre. Leave by road E 39* (CY). Situated on the outskirts of Bergen, the imposing white wooden house built on high ground overlooking Lake Nordås, acquired international fame as Edvard Grieg's home during the last 22 years of his life. The idyllic setting of the house and the wealth of mementoes it contains have contributed to make Troldhaugen one of the most visited places in Norway. Troldhaugen, meaning Troll Hill, was the name chosen by Grieg's wife for their new house. The dining room and the lounge have hardly changed since the Griegs lived there, with the Steinway piano given to them in 1892 on their silver wedding anniversary occupying a prominent position underneath a large Danish landscape. The hut which he had built in the grounds and where he took refuge in order to compose without being disturbed still contains his writing table and personal objects, his upright piano and rocking chair. After the composer's death, Nina Grieg continued to receive musical friends for a while, but she was eventually forced to sell the house. It was bought by one of Grieg's cousins who offered it to the municipality and it was subsequently turned into a museum.

Ch. Bastin-J. Evrard

Troldhaugen

Since the Bergen International Festival began in 1953, recitals have taken place regularly in Troldhaugen and in 1985, Troldsalen, an auditorium with a capacity of 200, was inaugurated; clever use of the hilly terrain has been made to conceal it so as not to spoil the beautiful surroundings of the house. The new museum, opened in 1995, includes a permanent exhibition, multimedia room and café. Edvard and Nina Grieg's grave, set into the cliff, is accessible by means of stairs and a path through the wooded grounds.

Damsgård ⓥ (AY) – *Laksevåg, 3km west of the town centre*. Built in the 1770s as a country residence, Damsgård is a fine example of a wooden Rococo mansion. Its design was inspired by European architectural trends of the time but remained strongly influenced by Norwegian tradition. Bought in 1797 by a rich merchant, the house was still owned by his descendants when it was sold to the State and the municipality of Bergen in 1983. As a historic monument it was restored to its original state and turned into a museum which provides an authentic illustration of the lifestyle of Bergen's high society in the 18C and 19C. The garden has also been carefully recreated with species of plants which used to be grown in Bergen in the late 18C.

Boat trips – There are many boat trips available from 1 or 2hr cruises among the islands west of Bergen to day excursions round the fjords. The shorter trips are round tours by boat but the longer excursions usually combine several means of transport, namely boat, train and coach. Some of the more interesting ones are listed below.

There are daily afternoon trips round Bergen harbour which last 1hr, or 4hr trips out towards the string of islands protecting the entrance to the harbour. The boats are moored along the quay at Torget (**BV**) in the town centre.

Day trips to the Sognefjord with combined coach and train return journey also start from Torget, whereas the half-day round tours by boat along the coast immediately south of Bergen begin at Strandkaien (**BV**) on the west side of Vågen.

A visit to the picturesque 'inland' island of Osterøya, only 15km north-east of Bergen, can be combined with a boat trip along Osterfjord.

★★ **Norway in a Nutshell** – *Allow a whole day.* This excursion is packed with unforgettable experiences, along beautiful fjords and over steep mountains and it enables visitors to see some of the most spectacular scenery Norway has to offer. The tour starts with a train journey to Voss then up into the mountains to Myrdal where another train takes 40min to descend 900m into the Flåm Valley to the Aurlandsfjord. The building of the line which has one of the steepest gradients in the world was a feat of engineering and the train is fitted with five independent sets of brakes! Apart from an undeniable thrill, the ride offers some breathtaking scenery, including an impressive waterfall. From Flåm the journey continues on board a steamer along Aurlandsfjord and Nærøyfjord, two narrow branches of Sognefjord, to Gudvangen where a coach is waiting to climb up to Stalheim and drive on to Voss. The whole trip is rounded off by a train journey back to Bergen. It is possible to begin and end this excursion in Voss, thus avoiding the return train journey Bergen-Voss.

Voss – *100km east; leave by E16* (**CV**). The E16 from Bergen to Voss follows the beautiful Østerfjord then goes through a picturesque canyon before reaching Voss. The town is an active and bustling holiday resort both summer and winter. It is a very convenient base for excursions to Sognefjord and Hardangerfjord, the two most beautiful of the southern fjords and offers a wide range of activities: whitewater rafting, cycling, hiking, riding, seaplane trips and fishing. Between December and April, the area around Voss is devoted to skiing – alpine, cross-country, telemark – and snowboarding. There are slopes suitable for beginners as well as professionals, with easy access by cable-car or chair-lift. The ski school is open daily during the whole season and it is possible to rent the needed equipment. The interesting Gothic church dates from 1277.

EXPRESS COASTER

See HURTIGRUTEN

FINNMARK ★★★

Norwegian Lapland

Michelin map 985 A-D 18-27 or Atlas Europe pp 104-105

Local map see LAPPLAND in Swedish section

The name Lapland generally has romantic connotations since it evokes the cold wilderness of northern Scandinavia inhabited by nomadic people referred to as the Sami, a kind of primitive enclave in the highly civilized continent of Europe. Reality is both close and totally remote from this simplistic picture.

Lapland covers a vast area stretching across the whole Scandinavian peninsula from the north-west coast of Norway to the White Sea. The county of Finnmark roughly covers the Norwegian part of Lapland although some of the so called Lappish people live further south. With an area of 48 000km2, Finnmark is by far the largest Norwegian county but also the least populated with just over 75 000 inhabitants.

The land – Finnmark is a land of great climatic contrasts between the green coastal areas where a relatively mild climate prevails under the influence of the Gulf Stream and the inland mountain plateaux where the effect of extreme temperatures (+32°C in summer, down to -50°C in winter) has resulted in the wild barren landscapes usually associated with Lapland.

The Arctic light contributes a great deal to the appeal Finnmark has on visitors: in summer, continuous daylight pouring over the vast expanses of moorland emphasise the impression of desolate infinity while in winter the polar night, the timid glowing dawns and the moon reigning unchallenged in the sky create a strangely mysterious and still atmosphere only disturbed from time to time by the northern lights flashing across the night.

The people – Although extremely sparse, the population of Finnmark is quite diversified, since the economic potential of such a large region has attracted waves of immigrants at various times in its history. The native Sami arrived from the east a long time ago and the main waves of immigrants came from southern Norway, Finland and Sweden in the 17C, 18C and 19C. These settlers became farmers and developed the fishing industry and to this day three languages are still spoken in some places: Norwegian, Sami and Finnish. New ventures such as aquaculture, tourism and the search for oil and gas off the coast have recently encouraged more people to settle in Finnmark and the county is now rapidly developing.

The Sami – They are the indigenous population of Finnmark and it is their culture and way of life which continues to attract visitors to Lapland.
This ethnic minority is estimated at around 70 000 people, of which about 40 000 live in Norway.
Some scientists believe that the Sami originally came from the region of Lake Onega in Russia, but it is not known when they moved westwards to northern Scandinavia and whether the Komsa (Kansa) people who lived on the coast of Norway some 10 000 years ago are their direct ancestors. The first written mention of the Sami, although under a different name, is found in a Roman history book; after that they are referred to in the Icelandic sagas and in various medieval chronicles. It would seem that they traded with several border states and were taxed for the privilege. They were christianised in the 18C and, during the 19C and early 20C, the Norwegian State tried to discourage the use of the Sami language; it was only in the 1960s that the rights of the Sami to preserve their own culture was recognised. Today, their language, which is related to Finnish and Estonian, is taught in schools and there is a newly established Sami Parliament sitting in Karasjok. Elected by the Sami, it is empowered to deal with all matters of special importance to the Sami people.

C. Boisvieux

Sami couple in their lavvu

Sami culture and way of life – Until the 16C, the Sami lived by hunting and fishing. From that time they gradually changed their main occupation from hunting wild reindeer to herding and, as a result they became a nomadic people, following their herds across Finnmark, spending the winter on the inland plateaux and moving to pastures along the coast in summer. This ancestral way of life forms the basis of Sami culture, some of its most important elements being:
– the Sami language with a wealth of legends and a recent but rapidly growing literary production;
– Sami music called *Yoik*, which consists of rhythmic poetic songs;
– the Sami costume and the rituals that go with it;
– Sami handicraft or *duodji*;
– the use of reindeer as a means of transport.

Today it has become evident that reindeer herding is essential in keeping Sami culture alive; yet both are threatened by the rapidly changing lifestyle of the Sami. Today only 10% of them are nomads engaged in reindeer herding and even this traditional occupation has been modernised with the aim of increasing the production of meat; families live in houses instead of the traditional *lavvu*, they travel by car or snowmobile and only put on their traditional costume on special occasions.

However, the official recognition of the rights of the Sami to preserve and develop their culture led to renewed interest among the Sami themselves resulting for instance in the establishment of a Sami museum *(see Karasjok below)* and the creation of a Sami theatre group in Kautokeino.

Finnmarksvidda at the heart of Lapland – Finnmarksvidda is a vast and wild high plateau with numerous mountain streams, rivers and lakes. It remains under a thick mantle of snow during the long winter months and the reindeer graze on plants under the snow. At the height of summer the meagre vegetation looks completely desiccated by the scorching sun. Long before that happens, the herds have moved to the coast in search of more suitable grazing land.

Although there are no roads, it is possible to cross Finnmarksvidda using different means of transport and various excursions are organised in winter as well as in summer, either from Karasjok or from Kautokeino. There are Sami riverboat trips, salmon fishing trips in Sami boats, hiking trips with pack dogs and overnight stays at mountain inns and, in winter, when the reindeer herders are back, one or two-day trips by snowmobile to one of their camps, reindeer racing as well as trips by dog sleigh along the old mountain route.

★**Karasjok** – Population 2 700. Karasjok is the most important cultural and administrative centre of Norwegian Lapland. There was a winter settlement nearby from which Karasjok developed in the 18C but it was totally destroyed during the Second World War except for the church dating from 1807 which is the oldest church in Finnmark and can be visited. Today 90% of the population of Karasjok are Sami and local economy rests principally on reindeer herding (which employs 18% of the Sami population), agriculture, industries and services, while tourism and the production of handicraft are becoming more and more important. In addition, several cultural and administrative Sami institutions are now based in Karasjok: the Sami Parliament, Sami radio and television, the Sami Museum, the Sami Library, the Sami Art Centre, the Sami Health Centre and the Sami School of Advanced Studies.

Sápmi ⓥ – This theme park provides an introduction to some aspects of Sami culture, history and daily life in an entertaining way. It comprises four main areas each concerned with one aspect of Sami life: the Magic Theatre which presents the Sami vision of the world and raises the question of the survival of Sami culture in today's conditions; the Sami dwelling site consists in a full scale presentation of Sami tents and turf huts with the possibility for visitors to take part in various activities; the Sami shops offer souvenirs based on Sami handicraft. A Sami café serves snacks based on Sami cooking.

De Samiske Samlinger ⓥ – This national museum of Sami culture illustrates the Sami way of life through objects and clothes used in daily life and on formal occasions.

Kautokeino – Population 3 000. Kautokeino is the only other important Sami centre in Lapland, specialising in the field of education and research. Records mention a settlement in Kautokeino as far back as the 16C, but it only became a permanent one in the 17C when the Sami began herding reindeer. Today this is still the population's main occupation and the Easter Festival, which takes place before the nomadic herders leave for the coast, is now a well-known cultural event. In summer, when the Sami have left, Kautokeino is a much quieter place; it is then time for nature lovers to take part in the numerous hikes organised throughout the area including the famous Nordkalottruta which crosses the border into Sweden *(contact the tourist office)*.

Kautokeino Museum ⓥ – It includes an exhibition illustrating certain aspects of Sami culture and an open-air section containing a series of old buildings, mostly turf huts used for various purposes by farmers in the past. Among several silver workshops selling various handmade objects, Juhl's Silver Gallery is set in a futuristic building designed by the owners and extended as their business prospered.

FLEKKEFJORD ★

Vest-Agder
Population 9 000
Michelin map 985 N 3 or Atlas Europe p 116

NORWAY

This picturesque seaside town is situated on the sunny south-west coast between Kristiansand and Stavanger, known as the green coast because of its tiny green fields, bushy vegetation and hilly woodland.

Until last century, the ports along this stretch of coastline were traditionally turned towards continental Europe as communications were easier across the North Sea than inland across mountainous terrain. Flekkefjord was then one of the busiest ports as it had been trading with Europe since the Middle Ages. The export of timber and herrings to Holland brought prosperity to the town in the early 19C and the importance of this trade is underlined by the fact that the old district is still known as the Dutch Town (Hollenderbyen).

In recent years, Flekkefjord has taken advantage of its splendid setting between Grisefjord and Flekkefjord and of its architectural heritage to become a charming and lively holiday resort, one of the most attractive of the white towns dotted along the coast.

Lots of small shops add a touch of colour to the narrow winding streets lined with whitewashed wooden houses whose entrance is often brightened up by a wrought-iron banister and colourful creepers. Some of the buildings are protected, such as the town hall, **Rådhuset** ⊙, and the oldest house in town dating from 1720, which houses the local museum, **Flekkefjord Museum** ⊙. Another interesting building is the octagonal church from 1833 with its square tower surmounted by a lantern. Close to the water's edge, the wooden houses offer picturesque views with their boat sheds, private moorings and balconies hanging over the water.

EXCURSIONS

Fedafjord – *26km east to Kvinesdal. Leave Flekkefjord by E 39 and drive east for 15km.*

Situated on the western shore of the narrow Fedafjord, a branch of Listafjord, the charming village of **Feda** is one of the best preserved in the area with lots of character and several old buildings, including the post office dating from the 17C and the church from 1802.

Continue on E 39 until you reach Kvinesdal.

After Feda, the road had to be dug out of the rock side in order to follow the edge of the fjord closely, and when it is not going through a tunnel, it reveals an austere landscape of cliffs covered with a wild vegetation of dark green bushes reflected in the pale green water.

Kvinesdal lies at the head of the fjord; more than one out of every 10 of its inhabitants emigrated to the United States and an annual Festival of Emigration celebrates the strong ties which the town maintains with America.

The Sirdal valley – *94km north to Svartevatn. Leave Flekkefjord by E 39 driving north for about 4km then turn right on road 466 towards Sandvatn. Continue north on road 42 to Tonstad.*

The road follows the long and narrow **Sirdalsvatn** which forms the lower part of the Sirdal Valley, a main producer of hydroelectric power in the country; one of the biggest power stations is in the mountain near **Tonstad**. The whole area has numerous signposted trails and is ideal for walking.

Further up the valley, a picturesque annual event takes place in September: more than 40 000 sheep come down from the surrounding mountains where they have been grazing all summer, a festive occasion in the whole valley.

From Svartevatn there are two ways of reaching Stavanger: follow road 45 west towards Sandnes (87km) or continue northwards (road closed in winter).

After about 12km, the road turns east across the mountains, where wild reindeer roam freely, towards the Setesdal Valley, whereas a minor road forks to the left and drops 1 000m to Lysebotn at the head of the **Lysefjord** over a distance of 20km; some 30 hairpin bends have to be negotiated on the way down to the fjord but it is well worth it as the drive affords some spectacular views.

From Lysebotn, a ferry sails along the narrow fjord all the way to Stavanger in summer.

GERANGER ★★★

Møre og Romsdal
Population 300
Michelin map 985 J 4 or Atlas Europe p 110

This modest mountain village bears one of the most famous Norwegian names which, for the majority of people, whether they have already visited Norway or are about to do so, evokes the most beautiful and breathtaking scenery the country has to offer.

THE VILLAGE

Geiranger nestles at the head of Geirangerfjord, surrounded by high mountains towering at almost 1 600m. In spite of its exceptional tourist appeal responsible for a certain amount of crowding at the height of summer, the place has retained its village atmosphere with its camp site on the edge of the water, its powerful mountain stream rushing down the steep banks of the fjord and its small octagonal wooden church, **Geiranger Kyrkje** ⊙, which has not changed for the past 150 years. The hotels and other accommodation are suitably spread around and there is no obvious concentration anywhere that could spoil the wild scenery. Although Geiranger has been a tourist attraction for well over a century and cruise ships have been sailing there from all over the world since 1869, no attempt has been made to create an elaborate harbour so that cruise ships simply lie at anchor 100m or so offshore, their large white shapes looking strangely conspicuous against the deep blues and greens of the fjord and the mountains.

Village near Dalsnibba

There are numerous possibilities for walking in the surrounding countryside along clearly signposted trails with varying levels of difficulty *(contact the Tourist Information Office)*.

GEIRANGERFJORD

A branch of Storfjord which winds its way inland from Ålesund, Geirangerfjord is 16km long, with Geiranger at its head, Hellesylt at its mouth and a regular ferry service linking the two. There are 100km from Geiranger to the sea and it is hard to believe, without knowing something about the formation of fjords, that a huge passenger ship such as the **Queen Elizabeth 2** can safely sail as far inland! During the Ice Age, Norway was completely covered with an ice cap which was relatively thin along the coast but much thicker inland. The weight of these considerable masses of ice widened and deepened existing valleys to such an extent that when the ice melted the sea took its place and the valleys became fjords. Their depth varies considerably: relatively shallow by the coast, they can reach depths of about 1 300m inland. Geirangerfjord is no exception and although it is only 500m wide at its narrowest, it is up to 360m deep in parts and the mountain walls on either side rise to a height of 1 600m.

★★★ **Sightseeing trip along the fjord** – *1hr 30min.* The splendour of Geirangerfjord can only be fully admired from a boat since it is totally enclosed by high steep mountains with snow-capped peaks all year round. The regular ferry between Hellesylt and Geiranger takes 70min each way and sails daily from May to September. However, the sightseeing tour operated several times a day from Geiranger is a better choice as the ship is smaller and therefore able to manoeuvre close to the banks of the fjord whenever necessary to give passengers the best possible view of the different sights. Moreover, it allows plenty of time for taking photographs and filming and there is a running commentary in several languages throughout the trip.

The fjord describes a graceful S between an almost perpendicular wall of dark grey rock partly covered with a thick coat of wild vegetation and as the ship glides on the water, each bend seems to reveal an even more sublime landscape. Everywhere water streams down the rock-face which glitters in the sunlight; there are some splendid waterfalls along the way, some of them, like the famous Seven Sisters, **Sju Søstre** thundering down from an incredible height, others just floating down like a white veil from the mountain top and sparkling in the sunlight which, when the angle is right, is broken up into the different colours of the rainbow. Now and then, impressive overhangs of barren rock, such as the one known as the Pulpit, **Prekestolen**, cast their dramatic shadow on the water. In several places, there are narrow ledges half way up the mountainside with meagre patches of grass and abandoned farm buildings: until 20 years ago these plots of land were farmed and quite often only accessible from the fjord, which required mountaineering skills; consequently, the extremely difficult working conditions and the inevitable isolation drove the farmers away one by one. Some of the farm buildings are now being restored as part of the area's cultural heritage.

There is a choice of interesting hikes in the area, from the easy 1-5hr walks with refreshments available on the way to the more demanding mountain treks lasting from one to several days. There are also geology and botany trips as well as pony treks *(information is available at the various tourist offices in the area).*

EXCURSIONS

Two impressive roads link Geiranger to the outside world across the mountains, one to the north towards Eidsdal and Storfjord, the other to the south towards Langevatn and from there either to Grotli or Stryn; in fact they are one and the same road and it offers such magnificent views that the whole route from Langevatn to Geiranger, Eidsdal and beyond to Andalsnes through Trollstigveien has been named the Golden Route. If travelling by car, one is bound to arrive in Geiranger along either the northern or the southern section of this route, unless of course one takes the Hellesylt-Geiranger ferry. Whatever the case, one must take one's time and savour every minute of both journeys, so powerful are the impressions produced by the breathtaking scenery.

★★★ **Dalsnibba** – *21km south – see local map above.* This section of road 63 was opened in 1889; it winds its way up a steep valley from sea level to 1 500m over a distance of about 15km with many viewpoints on the way, but it is more impressive on the return journey as the fjord, its wild surroundings and the tiny village squeezed between the mountainsides gradually get nearer.

Flydalsjuvet – *4km from Geiranger.* There is a magnificent **view**★★★ over the Flydal gorge and beyond towards the village and the fjord.

Djupvasshytta – Here the road reaches 1 038m above sea level; like many mountain lakes in the area, Djupvatnet is often partly frozen over in summer. Nibbevegen begins, near the café, its climb to the top of Dalsnibba (1 495m). The road is not very wide, the bends are sharp and unguarded but the thrill is guaranteed once the top is reached and a vast **panorama**★★★ unfolds in all directions: lots of snow-capped peaks at eye-level and Geirangerfjord way down in the valley 1500m below, almost unreachable, it seems!

★★★ **Ørnevegen (Eagle's road) and Trollstigveien** – *80km north to Åndalsnes – see local map on the previous page. There is a 15min ferry crossing between Eidsdal and Linge.*

Inaugurated in 1952, the Eagle's road opened the way north from Geiranger towards the towns of Ålesund, which could only be reached via Hellesylt before, and Andalsnes, which could not be reached at all. The road climbs to 620m over a distance of 8km.

From the last hairpin bend known as **Ørnesvingen** (Eagle's Bend – *parking facilities*), there is a fabulous **view**★★★ of Geirangerfjord, which embraces the first of its two broad curves and extends in both directions: towards Geiranger at the head of the fjord and towards Hellesylt.

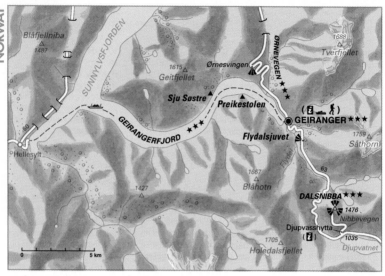

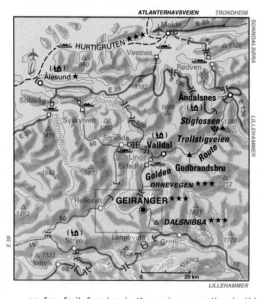

Follow the bridle-path past a wooden gate up to the extremity of the promontory.

From there, the **view★★★** is even more grandiose, with the Seven Sisters, unfolding their white veil along the dark rock face, all the way down to the deep blue-green waters of the fjord.

At Eidsdal, take the ferry across Storfjord to Linge. At Linge there is a road going west towards the coast and Ålesund, whereas road 63 continues north-east towards the mountains and Åndalsnes.

The gentle landscapes of the fertile **Valldal Valley** offer a marked contrast with the wild scenery encountered so far; fruit farming is the main occupation in this sunny valley and the lovely orchards one can see on the way are likely to be the last for a while if one is going up north as more northerly latitudes are unsuitable for fruit growing.

Gudbrandsbru – *13km from Valldal.* From this bridge one can see torrents of foaming water rushing with a thundering noise through a very narrow gorge, **Gudbrandsjuvet**, in a very picturesque setting.

Opened in 1936, **Trollstigveien** crosses one of the most barren areas in Norway. As one reaches the pass, the road goes through a gap between several peaks which culminate at around 1 500m to 1 800m, the highest being the Trolltindene to the east. The steep barren slopes are covered with masses of crumbled rock. Just before the road plunges into the deep valley on the other side, a path on the right leads to a platform built in the rock from which the view is quite exceptional. From this distance the road winding down towards Åndalsnes looks like a mere scratch on the surface of the rock face. On the way down, one comes quite close to two impressive waterfalls; a bridge spans **Stigfossen** which falls from a height of about 180m.

Åndalsnes – This town is situated at the mouth of the River Rauma which flows into Romsdalfjord. Because of its position on the shores of a picturesque fjord and at the start of the Golden Route, which unfolds a wealth of unforgettable scenery, the small friendly town has become a lively tourist centre. From there it is possible to drive west, first along Romsdalfjord through gently undulating countryside dotted with farms and villages, then along Storfjord to the island town of Ålesund.

HARDANGERFJORD ★★
Hordaland
Michelin map 985 M L 2-3 or Atlas Europe p 110

Easily reached from Bergen or Stavanger, Hardangerfjord stretches 179km inland in a north-easterly direction, and divides into several branches. Wide and open near the coast, it has gently sloping banks with orchards, grazing fields and smart villages; then, as it penetrates deep into the mountainous areas, it gets generally narrower and the scenery becomes wilder. However, Hardangerfjord can be full of surprises and it is not unusual to see delightful green pastures, fruit trees and a farm in the middle of an austere mountainous landscape. There are also numerous magnificent waterfalls in the Hardanger area, which just appear suddenly round a bend or can be spotted from afar cascading down the mountainside. This variety of landscapes can be experienced along a succession of scenic roads which follow the fjord closely from Skånevik near the coast, 87km north-east of Haugesund right round to Norheimsund, 81km east of Bergen.

Hardangerfjord

FROM SKÅNEVIK TO NORHEIMSUND

193km along roads 48, 11, 13 and 7

This excursion can easily be done in a day or spread over several days as the area is rich not only in beautiful scenery but in various possibilities of walks, mountain hikes, sightseeing tours, boat trips on the fjord etc. Places to stay, where there is a choice of accommodation: Skånevik, Odda, Lofthus, Kinsarvik, Eidfjord, Ulvik and Norheimsund.

Skånevik – This picturesque ferry port nestles inside a small creek at the head of Skånevikfjord, a branch of Hardangerfjord. The tiny islands planted with a few trees and shrubs and lying just offshore offer the most romantic view against the background of snow-capped mountains when the silvery waters of the fjord glitter in the long summer twilights.

Follow road 48 to Håland (13km) and turn left on road 11; between Tjelmeland (16km) and Fjæra (40km), the road follows Åkrafjord, a branch of Hardangerfjord.

Åkrafjord – Literally burrowed through the mountainside the road is dominated by impressive overhangs projecting from the rock face, when it is not going through tunnels or over bridges. The snow-capped rounded peaks in the distance contrast with the light green colour of the fjord. New scenery unfolds round every bend revealing tiny villages scattered here and there, their brightly painted houses covered with large stone slabs clinging to the rock, a few fishing boats moored along the banks of the fjord and waterfalls sparkling in the sun.

At **Langfoss Bro**, 4km before Fjæra, frothy water bounces off the rock several times all the way down the mountainside from a height of over 600m.

Låtefoss Bro – *5km beyond Jøsendal.* The road now follows the tumultuous course of a mountain stream through varied countryside with a few patches of cultivated land. At one point, the stream and the road enter a deep canyon and suddenly one is confronted with the impressive waterfall at Låtefoss Bro. The amount of water rushing down through two vertical clefts in the mountainside is so great that a transparent sheet of spray partly blurs the view.

Once out of the canyon, the stream becomes a river which meanders through a wider valley and cascades over huge boulders into Sørfjord at Odda.

Odda – Odda is the main town of the Hardanger area and a tourist centre. The principal attraction is an excursion to the Buar glacier, **Buarbreen**, which can be reached by following a minor road starting 2km south of Odda.

6km further on, one comes to the end of the road; from the car park, a marked footpath leads to the edge of the glacier (1hr walk). Tours on the glacier itself are led by local guides.

Buarbreen forms part of **Folgefonna**, Norway's third largest glacier, 37km long and 16km wide with a thickness of up to 170m.

From Buar guided tours are organised to the top of Folgefonna (1 660m) with an overnight stay in a cabin at Holmaskjer.

Sørfjord – From Odda, two scenic roads run along the banks of Sørfjord, another branch of Hardangerfjord. The fjord is long and narrow but the view is more open here than along Akrafjord as the mountainside, covered in turn with wild vegetation and fruit trees, slopes gracefully down to the water whereas the snow-capped peaks above form a continuous white ridge. Road 550, which follows the west bank, goes through **Agatunet**, an ancient farm village consisting of around 40 houses (now protected) from the Middle Ages to the late 19C. Further on in Utne, the **Hardanger Folk Museum** ⊙ is worth a visit; this open-air museum comprises several traditional local buildings and exhibitions about the way of life in the Hardanger area. Beyond Utne, the road turns south-west along the east bank of Hardangerfjord to Jondal. From there a road leads up to Folgefonn Summerski Centre on the edge of Folgefonna glacier.

Road 13 follows the east bank of Sørfjord, from Odda to Kinsarvik over a distance of 41km. Shortly beyond Odda, the **Tyssedal Power Station** ⊙, built in 1908 but with its turbines and generators still intact, offers an insight into the history of hydroelectric power in Norway with the help of exhibitions and a multimedia programme. To the east of the fjord lies the vast expanse of **Hardangervidda**, a mountain plateau from 1 000m to 1 200m high, covering an area of 7 500km², part of which is now a national park. It is inhabited by wild reindeer who, in summer, are joined on the rich grazing land by several thousand sheep, goats and horses. The century-old tracks and footpaths are used today by hikers who can stay overnight in log cabins. Good places to start from are Kinsarvik and Eidfjord *(contact the local tourist offices)*.

Lofthus and Kinsarvik – *105km and 115km respectively.* Both villages belong to Ullensvang Kommune, a traditional fruit-growing area since the 13C and today Norway's main producer; the richness of the soil, the mild winters and the long hours of sunshine in summer create the right conditions despite a latitude of 60° north. During the last two weeks of May and the first week of June, the banks of Sørfjord offer a festival of colours. **Ullensvang Kirke** ⊙ in Lofthus is a Gothic stone church built at the end of the 13C and remodelled in the late 19C. It contains a pulpit dating from the Reformation and an altarpiece from 1699. A hut used by Edvard Grieg when he stayed in the area for a year in 1877-78, can be seen in the grounds of Ullensvang Hotel on the edge of the fjord *(apply for the key at the hotel reception)*.

Kinsarvik – This is the main centre of Ullensvang Kommune and a charming holiday resort at the mouth of the River Kinso. **Kinsarvik Kirke** ⊙ is one of the oldest churches in Norway. It is said to have been built by Scottish master builders during the second half of the 12C; this is quite possible since it is a known fact that Kinsarvik exported timber to Scotland during the Middle Ages. The chancel was added later, probably in the early 13C. Inside there are traces of medieval frescoes including an unusual Last Judgement depicting St Michael holding a pair of scales and weighing the souls of those who wish to enter Paradise while devils armed with hooks try their best to interfere. There is also a pulpit painted by Peter Reimers in 1609 and an altarpiece from c 1695.

From Kinsarvik to Brimnes (133km), road 13 continues along the wild and beautiful Eidfjord. Before taking the ferry across to Bruravik, it is recommended to make a detour to Eidfjord, 11km east of Brimnes.

Eidfjord – This picturesque resort offers various possibilities of sightseeing trips within a radius of 20km. With a sheer drop of 182m, **Vøringfossen** is one of Norway's most spectacular waterfalls, situated 18km east of Eidfjord along the main road. *Drive north for 1km to Fossli, then follow the footpath to the waterfall; 1hr there and back.*

The **Hardangervidda Natursenter Eidfjord** is located at Øvre Eidfjord, near Vøringfossen; this nature centre offers information and proposes activities related to the natural environment, the culture and outdoor life on Hardangervidda *(see Sørfjord above)*. The protected mountain farm at **Kjeåsen** overlooks the fjord from a height of 600m in a beautiful Alpine setting. It can be reached by means of a picturesque twisting road which goes through a more than 2km-long tunnel *(12km north of Eidfjord)*.

From Bruravik you can drive straight to Granvin (14km) through a 7.5km-long tunnel or make a detour via Ulvik (10km north of Bruravik).

Ulvik – Ulvik is another important holiday resort of the inner Hardanger area, offering various interesting possibilities such as sightseeing flights over fjords, glaciers and waterfalls aboard a seaplane as well as boat trips on Ulvikfjord and Osafjord. The surrounding area is a bird-watcher's paradise, particularly the woodlands close to Ulvik and the salt-marsh on the shore of the fjord, most interesting at low tide, with a convenient bird-watching cottage nearby.

At Granvin, turn left along road 7 to Norheimsund (193km).

Norheimsund – The road follows the majestic Hardangerfjord which in places widens considerably, reaching impressive proportions and affording grandiose vistas. There are some lovely colourful villages like **Ålvik** along the way. Norheimsund, the main centre of the north side of Hardangerfjord, has one of Norway's three centres for the restoration of old wooden boats, **Hardanger Fartøyvernsenter**, where visitors can watch experts at work; there is also a collection of boats, exhibitions about boat-building and maritime traditions in Hardanger and a slide show. The easily accessible **Steindalsfossen** waterfall is a great tourist attraction and the café-cum-souvenir shop at the foot of the waterfall can get overcrowded in summer, but several paths offer possibilities of exploring the surrounding countryside; one of them leads right under the waterfall.

HEDDAL★★

Telemark

Michelin map 985 M 6 or Atlas Europe p 116

Situated 5km west of the town of Notodden, the rural community of Heddal owes its fame to its splendid stave church, the largest in Norway and one of the best examples of these medieval wooden buildings, still used as a parish church today.

NORWEGIAN STAVE CHURCHES

Stave churches are only to be found in Norway and they are now rightly considered as a unique national heritage. Once there were hundreds of these churches in the country, but many were torn down after the Reformation or destroyed by fire or simply rotted away through lack of care. It was only in the 19C that the architectural and historical value of stave churches became generally recognised after the painter JC Dahl published a book on the subject. Today fewer than 30 remain, mostly in the mountainous regions of the south and, although they have all been carefully restored and some have even been moved to more suitable locations, their survival is constantly threatened as the fire which destroyed Fantoft Stavkirke near Bergen in 1992 shows.

A revolutionary building technique – This kind of distinctive architecture flourished mainly in the 12C and 13C, although stave churches built during that period usually replaced a similar type of construction dating from the 11C, soon after Norway was Christianised. The early buildings barely lasted 100 years because their pillars were sunk into the ground and slowly decayed. At the beginning of the 12C a new technique was introduced which enabled the whole building to be raised above ground level and therefore to last much longer. Each wall consisted of horizontal beams at the top and bottom linked by vertical posts called staves and forming a strong frame; this frame was in turn filled in by vertical planks secured, inside grooves, in the two horizontal beams. When the four walls were assembled, they formed a solid structure on which the whole church rested.

Variations in styles – This technique was adapted to different architectural styles. At first churches were built according to a plain rectangular plan consisting of a nave and a chancel. Later on a semicircular apse was added and the central part of the nave was raised and separated from the aisles by free-standing posts to imitate contemporary stone churches; this is the plan adopted for the building of Heddal Church. Other churches, like Nore and Uvdal churches in the Numedal Valley, were constructed with a central free-standing pillar reaching right up to the top of the roof. Whatever their style, most stave churches were surrounded by an external gallery which served as a porch and a protection for the base of the walls. The roof, rising in three tiers and crowned with one or several turrets in the more elaborate cases, was covered with wood shingles and the whole building was painted with wood tar against decay, a precaution which is still taken today.

Ornamentation – The stave churches were more or less richly decorated with carvings usually illustrating various animals, either real or mythical, a practice stemming from the Viking tradition. Door frames were usually carved from top to bottom with intricate designs and those which have been saved today represent a truly original expression of Norwegian medieval art. The top of the numerous gables were also often surmounted with dragons as a protection against evil spirits. The interior of these churches is normally extremely dark as they were originally built without windows, the only source of light coming from small round openings under the roof. Yet the wealth of ornamentation is surprising: some of the pillars for instance have carved capitals just like Romanesque stone churches and walls and ceilings were often covered with frescoes in the late Middle Ages or even after the Reformation.

 ★★ HEDDAL STAVKIRKE ⊙

According to a runic inscription in the covered exterior gallery, Heddal stave church would appear to have been built in 1242 and dedicated to the Virgin Mary, but it is generally recognised that the chancel is roughly 100 years older than the rest of the church and was probably the nave of a previous church which proved too small. Heddal was altered several times but it has now been restored as far as possible to its medieval state. The main entrance of the church is through the West Portal which is the most profusely decorated with intertwined animal and foliage motifs characteristic of 13C decoration. The nave is separated from the aisles by round pillars carved with highly expressive masks and joined at the top by St Andrew's crosses and horizontal beams. The only piece of medieval furniture left in the church is a wooden chair, known as the 'Bishop's chair', decorated with skilful carvings depicting a legend of Norse mythology, which has prompted some experts to say that the chair might date from the pre-Christian period. The altarpiece is from 1667 and the walls of the nave and chancel are covered with paintings from two different periods, the more recent dating from the late 17C.

Heddal Bygdetun – Situated about 300m south of the church, the Heddal farm comprises several old buildings representative of wooden architecture in Telemark.

HURTIGRUTEN ★★★
EXPRESS COASTER
Michelin map 985 – Local map see below

King among the numerous Norwegian ferries, the Express Coaster is the lifeline of the North: half of its journey takes place north of the Arctic Circle and its arrival in the ports of the north-west coast of Norway is a daily event which regulates life in the Arctic regions. The scheduled service has been running successfully for more than 100 years and is now taken for granted but, for the men who started it, it was a daring enterprise and a demonstration of great navigational expertise.

Hurtigruten – the fast route – Before 1893, north Norway was cut off during the long Arctic winter and postal communications were interrupted during that time. Maintaining a regular mail service throughout the year was therefore the main argument put forward a century ago for launching the Express Coaster service.
In spite of being situated on the same latitude as Alaska and Siberia, Norway, and its coastal areas in particular, enjoys a much milder climate; this is due to the Gulf Stream which flows all the way from the Gulf of Mexico across the Atlantic Ocean and along the coast of north-west Europe, penetrating 1 000km into Arctic waters and keeping the sea along the coast of Norway free of ice all year round. But, until the end of the 19C, ships that sailed along the coast and round the North Cape only did so during the summer months as they feared the violent winter storms and the dark polar nights. However, the coast is lined all the way by a screen of small and large islands which have provided natural shelter to small boats for centuries, and what the pioneers of Hurtigruten did was to work out an itinerary through the maze of islands and reefs, venturing with relatively large ships through narrow sounds, even at night! Two men had enough confidence to navigate in such conditions: **Richard With**, the founder of Hurtigruten, and **Ånders Holte**, the best coastal pilot in Norway at the time, who was the first to navigate ships during polar winters.
On 2 July 1893, the first of the coastal ships, the **Vesterålen**, completed her maiden voyage by sailing from Trondheim to Hammerfest and return in less than six days. As years went by, the service was speeded up and the itinerary extended round the North Cape and to Kirkenes next to the Russian border. In order to maintain this kind of service, the Vesterålen was soon joined by other ships whose number has

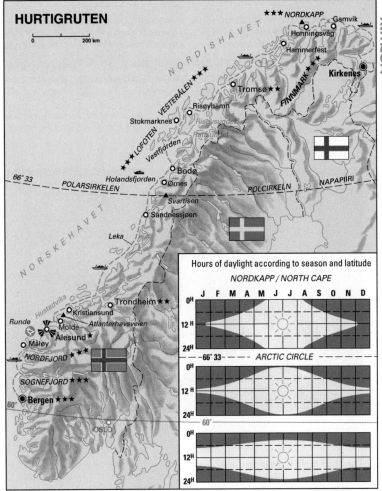

HURTIGRUTEN

0 —— 200 km

Hours of daylight according to season and latitude

NORDKAPP / NORTH CAPE

J F M A M J J A S O N D

0^H

12^H

24^H

—— 66° 33 —— ARCTIC CIRCLE —— —— ——

0^H

12^H

24^H

—— 60° ——

0^H

12^H

24^H

increased regularly ever since. Improvements in the accessibility of some ports of call were also made: the Risøysundet (Risøy Sound) between two of the Vesterålen islands, Andøya and Hinnøya was too shallow to allow large ships through and had to be dredged so that the Express Coaster could call at Risøyhamn; the way was opened in 1922. But the fishing port of Gamvik on the north coast had to wait until the mid-1980s for a proper quay to be constructed.

From the very beginning, the ships carried mail, cargo and passengers, including a growing number of tourists wanting to take part in an exciting sea voyage and experience the authentic Norwegian way of life at a pace in tune with the Express Coaster's schedule.

Some facts:

– Hurtigruten provides a daily service both ways between Bergen and Kirkenes.
– The distance between the two towns is 2 537km and there are 34 ports of call along the route.
– The Coastal ships cover a total of 1.5 million km every year. As many as 2 000 to 3 000 passengers can come on and off a single ship during one journey.
– There are 11 ships belonging to two companies. Three of the ships were launched to mark the centenary of Hurtigruten in 1993. The two oldest ships date from the 1960s but were refurbished during the 80s. The *Vesterålen* bears the same name as Hurtigruten's first ship, which belonged to Captain With's newly founded Vesterålen Steamship Company based on the Vesterålen islands. Another recent ship is called *Midnatsol* (Midnight Sun), a romantic name indeed for a ship bound for the land where the sun never sets for nearly two months in summer. The *Polarlys* and *Nordlys*, on the other hand, have been named after a phenomenon, called Aurora Borealis or northern lights, which occurs during the long polar nights: charged particles (protons) from the sun burn up as they enter the earth's magnetic field and can light up the sky for 20hr at a time.

The journey – The return journey Bergen-Kirkenes-Bergen lasts 11 days, but it is more of a round trip than a return journey because when a ship calls at a port during the night on the northbound voyage, it will almost certainly call at the same port during the day on the way south. It is, of course, possible to go on board the Coastal ships or leave in any port along the way and to bring one's car along, but bookings have to be made well in advance. There is a third possibility which consists in combining either a northbound or a southbound journey with a flight to or from one of the Express Coaster's ports of call.

On board ship the emphasis is put on comfort and informality in true Norwegian tradition and there are many opportunities to get acquainted with the Norwegian way of life.

Express Coaster – King of the Norwegian ferries

The sights – The ships skirt the coastline and manoeuvre between the islands all the way so that there is never a dull moment and some of the best scenery in Norway unfolds at a speed of about 15 knots, allowing ample time for viewing and filming. Striking sights such as the bird island of **Runde** near Ålesund can only be seen from the sea. Most stops last long enough for passengers to go ashore and visit the port of call; moreover, excursions to famous sights such as the North Cape or the impressive Svartisen glacier are organised to coincide with scheduled stops and can be booked on board ship.

All aboard – The first major stop after leaving Bergen on the northbound journey is at **Ålesund★** where 3hr allow ample time for a thorough visit of the town and a climb to the top of mount Aksla to enjoy panoramic views. The next stop is at **Molde**, in a picturesque mountain setting, the city where roses bloom in spite of the northerly latitude; passengers have the choice of continuing the voyage to **Kristiansund** across one of the few stretches of open sea known as Hustadvika or leaving the ship momentarily and taking a sightseeing trip along the spectacular Atlantic Road, **Atlanterhavsveien★**, to go back on board at Kristiansund. This fishing town, built across three islands, can be visited on the southbound journey. **Trondheim★★** is another main stop both on the way north and on the return journey and there is time for a sightseeing tour of at least part of this ancient city including an excursion to an unusual museum of musical instruments. After Trondheim comes another expanse of open sea between Stokksund and Rørvik beyond which stretches the narrow strip of land which forms northern Norway. The island of **Leka** is steeped in Norse mythology: according to legend, the mountain on the island is the virgin Leka who was turned to stone by the sun as she fled from a horseman who had watched her bathing in the nude. After crossing the Arctic Circle north of which 70% of all Norwegian fish is caught, those who are looking for a unique experience can transfer to a smaller ship which will take them along the Holandsfjord to the foot of **Engabreen** glacier, a branch of **Svartisen**, then by coach to Bodø to rejoin the Express Coaster. **Bodø** is the last port of call before the Coastal ship veers to the north-west and crosses the vast open Vestfjorden to reach the **Lofoten Islands★★★**. The Express Coaster steers its way with great prowess between the islands, through the extremely narrow Raftsundet and the Risøyrenna lined with beacons; most of the distance is covered during the night on the northbound journey, but, on the way south, there is time to admire the unique landscapes of Vesterålen and Lofoten throughout the day. There is a call at **Stokmarknes**, Hurtigruten's birthplace, where a museum relating the history of the Express Coaster was inaugurated in July 1999 *(see p 171)*. The Arctic city of **Tromsø★★** can be visited on the way north and/or on the way south; there is even time for a cable car ride with perhaps a glimpse of the midnight sun. The Express Coaster calls at **Hammerfest**, Norway's most northern town, and then at the fishing port of Honningsvåg where shore excursions are organised on the north and southbound journeys to the famous North Cape, **Nordkapp★★★**. The mining town of **Kirkenes**, where Norway's most important iron-ore mines are situated, marks the end of a long and exciting journey from fjord country to Arctic wilderness and the beginning of another as the Express Coaster turns back and heads south again.

KONGSBERG ★

Buskerud
Population 22 000
Michelin map 985 M 6 or Atlas Europe p 117

Situated 80km west of Oslo, at the heart of a mountainous region, Kongsberg lies on both banks of the River Lågen which flows south through the Numedal Valley. The bridge linking the old and the new towns spans the river at the point where it cascades over a weir in a picturesque setting dominated by the massive church tower.

The silver town – Silver deposits, discovered in the mountains west of the river, led to the foundation of the town in 1624 by King Christian IV of Denmark. The mines were worked for over 300 years before they were finally closed down in 1958. During all that time they were a source of considerable prosperity for the town; today, this is still reflected by the atmosphere pervading the district which surrounds the imposing 18C church. However, during the early 19C, there was a temporary mining recession and the arms factory was established in 1814.

Skiing tradition – More recently, Kongsberg became famous in the world of sport when its skiing champions won an impressive amount of Olympic and world Championship medals in the 1930s and 1940s. Their exploits are recalled in the town's ski museum while the modern ski centre helps to keep up the tradition.

Today Kongsberg is a modern industrial and commercial centre, anxious to preserve its heritage and conscious at the same time of having acquired a new identity as an important tourist centre of the Numedal and Telemark areas with numerous possibilities such as sightseeing excursions, skiing, trout fishing in the river and mountain lakes, a brand new 18-hole golf course and a jazz festival in June.

SIGHTS

★★ **Kongsberg Kirke** ⊘ – This edifice was built as the largest church in Norway with the most magnificent Baroque interior. The building of unusually ambitious proportions for Norway replaced an earlier church which had become inadequate when the town rapidly expanded in the 18C. The project was funded with money from the silver mines treasury. It was completed in 1761 which is the date inscribed on the front of the gable beneath the tower; just above it is the mining emblem which also appears on the church of another mining town, Røros. Although it was built in the shape of a cross, the tower surmounts one of the transepts and it was decorated inside as if it were rectangular. The altar stands in the middle of one of the long sides, with its back to the tower and the pulpit and organ above it. On the opposite wall are the royal box and smaller boxes reserved for the high-ranking officials of the silver mines. The pews on the ground floor and in the galleries were destined to the rest of the parishioners according to their social status. Among the splendid decorations there are three large Baroque chandeliers made by Norwegian craftsmen, as well as a number of valuable pieces of silver including a box and a wine jug from the previous church.
The two bells in the bell-tower were cast in Denmark; it took six men to ring the large bell which could be heard from all over town!

★ **Norsk Bergverksmuseum** ⊘ – Housed in the former building of the Silver Mining Company, in the town centre, the Norwegian Mining Museum retraces the history of silver mining in Kongsberg over 300 years with the help of models showing access to the mines and working conditions of miners, methods of extracting the silver ore etc. Quite unique is an 18C working model showing the whole process of mining and smelting silver ore. The old smelting house is located in the basement of the museum. In addition, there is a very special collection of minerals and rare specimens of pure silver with unusual shapes found at different times.

Den Kongelige Mynts Museum ⊘ – Housed in the same building, the museum contains a collection of coins minted in Kongsberg since the Royal Mint was moved to the town in 1686.

Kongsberg Skimuseum ⊘ – This is the third museum housed in the mining company's old building. Founded by Olympic and World champions Birger Ruud and Petter Hugsted, it contains a historic collection of skis and equipment as well as cups and medals won by Kongsberg skiers. There is also an extensive archive library containing books and documents about international skiing events. A recent extension contains objects and equipment used by Erling Kagge and Børge Ousland on their unaided ski expeditions to the North and South Poles as well as exhibits on the history of Alpine skiing in Norway.

A fourth museum under the same roof, the **Kongsberg Arms Factory Museum** ⊘, illustrates the town's industrial history from 1814 onwards.

Lågdalsmuseet ⊘ – Situated near the town centre, this open-air museum comprises a selection of old buildings illustrating traditional life in the city and in the villages of the Numedal Valley.

EXCURSION

★ **Kongsberg Sølvgruver** ⊘ – *Saggrenda, 8km south-west by road 11– guided tour: 1hr 20min.* The tour starts with a ride on a small train which penetrates 2.3km inside the mountain to the King's Mine, the largest of the Kongsberg silver mines.

A silver lining – Two young shepherds discovered a vein of pure silver under some loose moss in the summer of 1623; the area was soon systematically searched and Christian IV, who laid claim to the potential wealth to be derived from the discovery, invited experienced German miners to work on the site. At the end of the 18C about 80 mines employing 4 000 men were being worked at the same time. Then, at the beginning of the 19C, the mines were closed because of financial difficulties. Before they reopened, adits were dug to make work easier and more productive and the results were soon felt, a greater quantity of ore was extracted by just 400 men than ever before by 10 times that number. From 1870 the price of silver began to drop and the quality of the ore became poorer, causing the mines to be eventually closed down in 1958. Between 1623 and 1958, 1 350t of pure silver were produced, representing an average of 4t a year; this was quite an achievement when one considers that a ton of ore contained 200-500g of silver!

Kongens Gruve – The train stops at a depth of 342m below ground, at the entrance of the King's Mine, where the main air compressors were kept, supplying the drilling machines and other equipment several kilometres away. The King's Mine reaches a depth of 1 070m below ground or 500m below sea level. The main shaft is wide enough for two lifts which took four or five men down to the different levels. There is also a demonstration of the *Fahrkunst*, the first machine to carry people up and down the mine; of German design, it was installed in c 1880. The Rest Room was the place where miners spent their hour-long lunch break.

KRISTIANSAND

Vest-Agder
Population 72 000
Michelin map 985 N 4-5 or Atlas Europe p 116

Kristiansand is Norway's fifth largest town and the capital of Sørlandet, the coastal region bordering Skagerrak. One of the most important ferry ports with regular services to Hirtshals in Denmark, Göteborg in Sweden and Newcastle, it is a busy industrial and commercial centre and one of the lively white towns of south Norway, so called because of their characteristic white wooden houses.

Kvadraturen – The city was founded by King Christian IV of Denmark in 1641 at the mouth of the River Otra. The geometric plan with central market, designed by the king himself, was typical of Renaissance towns of the 17C. The centre has retained the strict layout of its streets crisscrossing at right angles which caused it to be known as Kvadraturen, a nickname still used today. In order to defend the town from a sea attack, the king built a fort on the shore of the fjord, **Christiansholm Festning** ⊘, still standing today. Industrialisation in the 20C brought prosperity to the town which extended on the east bank of the Otra.

OLD TOWN *30min*

Within the town centre the ███████ll-preserved district along the river, known as **Posebyen★** with a charming ███████ tmosphere. The white houses, some of which go back to the 17C, hav███████ window frames and doors, tiled roofs and wrought-iron handrails to ███████ eerful note to the attractive provincial scene. There are several small art ga███ in the area.

North-west of Posebyen, just a██s the E 18 motorway, lies an area of green open spaces with lakes and pleasant footpaths, called **Baneheia**.

ADDITIONAL SIGHTS

Vest-Agder Fylkesmuseum ⊘ – Situated on the eastern outskirts of town, this regional museum has an open-air section where a street of Kristiansand in the past has been recreated and typical farms illustrate rural life in Vest-Agder and Setesdal. The main building contains thematic exhibitions.

Agder Naturmuseum og Botaniske hage ⊘ – This is one of the oldest museums of natural history in Norway, founded in 1828. Completely renovated in 1990 and housed in Gimle Gård just north of the E 18 motorway, the museum now shows part of the natural history of south Norway since the last Ice Age: it illustrates how glaciers have modelled the landscape, how rocks travelled from Sweden and Denmark embedded in glaciers and it also shows the various animals living during the different climatic periods. There is a botanical garden attached to the museum.

EXCURSIONS

Kristiansand Dyrepark – *12km east*. This leisure park comprises a zoo, a theme park with an imaginary town called Kardemomme, an aqualand, a choice of outdoor activities and even theatrical shows.

The south coast between Kristiansand and Arendal – *67km east. Leave Kristiansand by E 18 towards Oslo.*

Lillesand – *28km*. This typical white town has retained much of its past charm and several elegant 18C and 19C houses, some of which are now protected, including the old customs house. Lillesand is famous for its profusion of roses and geraniums which seem to turn everyday into a festive day. The town has a new marina and a boat trip along **Blindleia** is strongly recommended. Blindleia is the name of the picturesque channel which winds its way through the islands lying just outside the harbour.

Grimstad – *47km*. Two of Norway's most prominent writers, Henrik Ibsen and Knut Hamsun once lived in Grimstad which is now a lively cultural centre whose activities culminate in summer with theatre performances, an International Ibsen Seminar and a film festival as well as concerts and exhibitions. The local museum, **Ibsenhuset og Grimstad Museum**, houses a wealth of mementoes of the famous dramatist including the old chemist's shop where he was an apprentice. Every summer the sunny white town is invaded by a crowd of enthusiasts who enjoy the sea and the islands as much as the culture.

Arendal – *67km*. This busy commercial and administrative centre was built on seven islands linked by canals and was once called the Venice of the north. The canals have been filled in but the town has retained part of its charm particularly round **Pollen**, the old harbour and at **Tyholmen**, one of the best preserved urban sites in Norway. Some impressive wooden houses built as private residences are reminders that Arendal has a long-standing tradition as a major commercial port. The town hall, **Rådhus**, is a superb example of such a house: built in 1815 in the Empire style, it is the highest wooden building in Norway. It became a town hall in 1844.

LAPLAND ★★★

See FINNMARK

LILLEHAM ★★

Situated on the eastern shore of Lake Mjøsa,   th of Oslo, Lillehammer is built
on the lower slopes of the surrounding mou   the entrance to the beautiful
Gudbrandsdalen Valley and, in spite of being on   e main touristic centres of southern Norway, it has retained the quaint appearanc   a 19C provincial town with its low
wooden houses along the main street Storgata. Yet Lillehammer has by no means
remained static; it is a modern town which has a lively pedestrian centre with pavement
cafés and elegant shops and provides plenty of night entertainment; it also organises
the annual **Vinterspillene**, the only winter musical and cultural festival in Norway as well
as **Inga låmi**, the most important women's cross-country skiing competition involving
some 8 000 participators. Moreover, Lillehammer has proved its boundless dynamism
in organising the 1994 Winter Olympic Games.

The legend of the two Birkebeiner (literally birchlegs) – The saga of Håkon
Håkonson tells the story of two brave men who saved the two year old heir to the
throne, Håkon, from his enemies and carried him to safety across the mountains overlooking Lillehammer during the winter of 1205-06. It is probable that they stayed in
Lillehammer for a night or two before embarking on their perilous journey. A romantic
picture painted in 1869 by K Bergslien shows the two heavily armed men carrying the
young prince as they ski through a blizzard. An annual cross-country ski race between
Lillehammer and Rena (56km), known as the **Birkebeiner race**, commemorates the event.

Sigrid Undset (1882-1949) – The novelist who won the Nobel Prize for Literature in
1928 for a series of novels set in medieval Norway, lived at Bjerkebæk, her home on
the outskirts of Lillehammer, from 1919 until her death in 1949. Her father was a well-
known archaeologist and from an early age she became extremely interested in history
and in particular the Norse sagas. But her hopes of a university education vanished
when her father died and she had to work to help her mother and two sisters. She
began writing in her spare time and at the age of 25 published her first novel, a realistic story set in Oslo (called Kristiana at the time). Until 1919 she wrote a number of
novels in a similar vein, depicting with great realism the ordinary life of ordinary people. In 1909 she travelled abroad and in Rome she met her future husband, a
Norwegian painter. They married in 1912 and had three children but they separated in
1919 and she went to live in Lillehammer with her children. She then embarked on her
first historical novel, **Kristin Lavransdatter**, which is usually considered as her masterpiece;
it was followed by another, **Olav Audunssøn** and it is for these two long works that she
was awarded the Nobel Prize.
In 1940, she fled to the US and throughout the war she wrote and spoke incessantly
about her occupied country. The war years seemed to drain away all her literary powers and after her return to Norway in 1945 she stopped writing altogether.
Sigrid Undseth Dagene (Sigrid Unset's Days) is an annual literary event organised in
honour of the writer.

Olympic town 1994 – In February 1994, the attention of the world was focused on
Lillehammer for 16 days, as the town hosted the 17th Winter Olympic Games. All the
sites were within a 50km radius of Lillehammer where the cross-country, ski jumping
and ice hockey events were held while the alpine events took place in Hatfjell and
Kvitfjell to the north and skating and ice hockey events were staged in Hamar and
Gjøvik in the south. A visit to the ski jumps tower and the Håkons Hall, both built for
the occasion is really worthwhile *(see Olympic sites below)*.

SIGHTS

★★ **Maihaugen: De Sandvigske Samlinger** ⊙ – Maihaugen is one of the most attractive
open-air museums in Norway, located on the slopes overlooking the centre of
Lillehammer and comprising an impressive number of timber houses scattered over
a beautiful woodland area covering 369ha. The dream of a dentist, Anders Sandvig,
to preserve rural culture came true in 1904 when Maihaugen was inaugurated.
Since then the Sandvig Collections have been extended and the museum is now one
of Europe's largest open-air museums. Nearly 150 timber houses from the
Gudbrandsdalen Valley dating from the 18C and the 19C have been reconstructed
in Maihaugen to show the unique architectural variety of the area. The rural community has been carefully recreated around the lakes and streams to give an impression of space and at the same time of unity and the good balance found between
the two is the key to the museum's success. A stave church has been brought from
Lom and refurbished as it was in the 1700s whereas the 27 buildings of a farm
complex have been re-erected in the exact position they occupied on their original
site. An urban community has been started mostly with buildings from Lillehammer;
it is situated near the museum's main building which contains workshop interiors,
an arts and crafts collection from all over the country, a hall for concerts and plays
as well as a permanent exhibition entitled *We Won the Land* which offers a novel

and highly imaginative illustration of Norwegian history with the help of models, figures and slide shows as well as striking sound and light effects.

Maihaugen is also a living museum since in summer, people and animals live at the farm Øygarden and the workshops are occupied by craftsmen.

Lillehammer Kunst-museum ⊙ – This interesting gallery, overlooking the main square and built in the shape of a grand piano, houses a comprehensive collection of Norwegian paintings from the 1830s to the present day. In addition, it holds temporary exhibitions devoted to Norwegian and foreign artists.

Norsk Kjøretøyhistorisk Museum ⊙ – This important Museum of Historical Vehicles (Norway's largest), illustrates the development of overland transport from the first sledges to modern cars.

Early 18C Norwegian tapestry

B. Gérard/EXPLORER

★**Olympic sites** – **Håkons Hall**, the ice hockey stadium (now a multi-purpose venue), situated in Lillehammer, is a splendid example of Norwegian contemporary wooden architecture. The centre includes the **Norges Olympiske Museum** ⊙ covering Norwegian participation and achievements in the Olympics. The **Lysgårdsbakkene Ski Jumping Arena** is an impressive technical achievement; the natural incline of the terrain was used in such a way that the two runs blend in with the lovely wooded surroundings. The **view**★★★ from the tower over the whole town and the lake is superb. The arena was the venue for the opening and closing ceremonies of the 1994 Winter Olympics.

Located 15km north of Lillehammer, the **Olympic Bobsleigh and Luge Track**, the only one in Scandinavia to be artificially cooled, is open to visitors who can choose taxibob, bob-rafting or luge and discover what speeding down the track feels like!.

The Winter Olympics

When on 25 November 1892 Baron Pierre de Coubertin suggested that the Olympian Games could be revived in a manner in keeping with the 20C and when the first modern games were organised in Athens in 1896 little thought had been given to winter sports which were in their infancy. With the rapid development of winter sports the International Olympic Committee, under the presidency of Baron Coubertin, decided to organise a winter Olympics (figure skating had been an official Olympic sport since 1908) which originally took place in a different site but the same year as the Summer Olympics. The first Winter Olympics were held in Chamonix in 1924 the year that Paris was host to the Summer Olympics.

The Chamonix Olympics included 16 different events – only one for women – in five different disciplines (Nordic skiing, figure skating, speed skating, ice hockey and bobsleigh; downhill skiing only became an Olympic sport in 1948) and 258 participants represented 16 nations.

The Lillehammer 17th Winter Olympics, the first to be programmed in an even-numbered year in alternation with the summer games, involved 1 737 athletes from 67 different nations competing in 61 events. These figures give a good indication of the development and ever-growing popularity of winter sports.

EXCURSIONS

The area surrounding Lillehammer offers endless possibilities of going on exciting sightseeing tours, of hiking, skiing or rafting according to the season and above all of simply enjoying the infinitely varied aspects of unspoilt nature.

Lake Mjøsa – Mjøsa is Norway's largest lake at the heart of a rich agricultural area; Eidsvoll at its southern extremity is only 70km away from Oslo and it was there that the Norwegian constitution was drawn up in 1814. Norway's first railway line was opened in 1854 between Christiana (Oslo) and Eidsvoll. Two years later, a paddle-steamer, the **Skibladner**, started regular sailings of the whole length of Lake Mjøsa, and in the 1880s there were up to 40 boats sailing across the lake. Today the *Skibladner* is the only one left and it has changed very little. Some coach tours are organised around the steamer's schedule *(inquire at the tourist office in Hamar)*.
On the eastern shore of the lake, **Hamar** has only retained of its ancient past, the romantic ruins of its cathedral. However there is an interesting railway museum, **Jerbanemuseet** ⊙, the oldest in Scandinavia, with a steam train going round the museum park in summer. The **Olympia Hall**, in the shape of a Viking ship, was built for the skating events of the 1994 Winter Olympic Games.

Hunderfossen family park ⊙ – *13km north.* This is a combination of a theme park, based on Norwegian folk tales, and an amusement park with an educational pur-pose: there is an energy centre, an oil and gas centre, a driving school for children as well as a fairy grotto guarded by a gigantic troll and a video journey across Norway.

Nordseter and Sjusjøen – *12km and 22km north-east.* These picturesque mountain resorts are on the **Birkebeinerveien** *(toll road)*, a historic route which goes down to Messelt in the Østerdalen Valley, through beautiful mountain country, past traditional mountain farms. This is one of Northern Europe's best areas for cross-country skiing with more than 300km of double tracks available every winter. Ski-touring maps are on sale at the resorts. Ski lessons and rental are provided by local sport shops.

LOFOTEN and VESTERÅLEN★★★
Nordland
Michelin map 985 CE 9-13 or Atlas Europe pp 104 and 107

These islands have for generations stirred the imagination of travellers anxious to admire their wild landscapes and to experience a simple and natural way of life which has long disappeared from our civilized world. Indeed those who are looking for unfor-gettable impressions will not be disappointed if they travel to the islands by ferry or Express Coaster from Bodø for, as the ship crosses Vestfjorden, the sight of the famous sombre **Lofoten Wall** (Lofotveggen) first looming above the sea then literally barring the horizon is far more impressive than anything one could have imagined *(see photograph p 24).* The austere and ragged mountain range stretching for 100km is a wonder of nature which appears to be rising straight out of the sea until one gets closer and grad-ually distinguishes tiny villages surrounded by green patches nestling at the foot of the craggy peaks.

Rorbuer at Mortsund

Access – The Express Coaster calls daily in both directions at Svolvær, Stokmarknes, Sortland and Risøyhamn. In addition there are ferry services between Bodø and Moskenes and between Skutvik and Svolvær. There are flights to Andenes, Stokmarknes, Svolvær and Leknes as well as Værøy and Røst, the two most southern islands. To the north, the Vesterålen are linked to the mainland by bridges and are accessible via the E 10 motorway which runs right across both archipelagos, the only remaining ferry link being Melbu-Fiskebøl.

Facts	Lofoten	Vesterålen
Area	1 227km²	2 368km²
Pop	24 000	32 000
Main towns	Svolvær	Sortland

The Lofoten and Vesterålen form two distinct archipelagos stretching in a south-west/north-east direction along the west coast of Norway, 200km north of the Arctic Circle. There are beaches and green fields full of colourful wild flowers, but the dark mountain peaks are always in sight, often overwhelmingly present. The rocks which abound on the islands were formed during different geological periods, some of them as far back as 3.5 billion years ago, others (on Andøya for instance) only 150 million years ago, with layers of coal and fossils trapped in them. Four successive ice ages and the subsequent variations in the level of the sea modelled the landscape, levelling a good layer of rich soil along part of the shoreline, leaving large stones rounded by the waves in other places and causing lakes to be formed behind the moraines left by the glaciers.

Climate – The islands enjoy a humid oceanic climate with frequent changes in the weather and relatively little difference between summer and winter temperatures. Moreover, because of the Gulf Stream, temperatures are milder than they would normally be at the same latitude; it rarely freezes even in January and in summer the average temperature is around 12°C. However, when the wind blows from the east it is cold and dry in winter or unusually hot in summer. Like other Arctic regions, Lofoten and Vesterålen are plunged into darkness during December and part of January but, on the other hand, the sun does not set in June and July. Tides are particularly strong and there are powerful currents between the islands, in particular the Moskenestraumen (or the Mælström) between Moskenes and Værøy which was known in ancient times.

Historical notes – The islands' first inhabitants were primitive hunters and fishermen attracted by the rich animal life both on land and in the sea. During the Viking period and the Middle Ages, the development of Lofoten and Vesterålen depended entirely on exporting great quantities of stockfish to continental Europe and in particular to the Hanseatic towns of northern Germany via Bergen. Excavations near Kabelvåg have revealed the existence of the oldest town north of the Arctic Circle (see Kabelvåg), a fact which confirms the importance of the islands during the Middle Ages. After Bergen lost its monopoly, there were alternating times of prosperity and decline until the second half of the 19C when herring fishing brought new wealth to the area and the population grew rapidly. Then, at the end of the century, the Express Coaster service was launched from Stokmarknes and from that time the islands were regularly linked to the mainland.

Fishing – Cod fishing has for centuries been the most important event on the islands. It takes place between January and April, when mature adult fish (between 7 and 10 years old), swim south from the Barents Sea to Vestfjorden in order to breed in warm waters from the Atlantic which are an essential factor of the eggs' development. The young are born within three weeks and they start the journey back to the Barents Sea.

During the fishing season, fishermen live in wooden cabins called *rorbuer*, which are now often let to holidaymakers during the summer. The fish are split and dried in the open air on special wooden frames all over the islands and then exported to different parts of the world. The heads are dried separately and exported to Third World countries to be made into fish soup. Whereas all the fish caught used to be dried in the past, nowadays 50% is frozen before being exported.

Hanging fish to dry

171

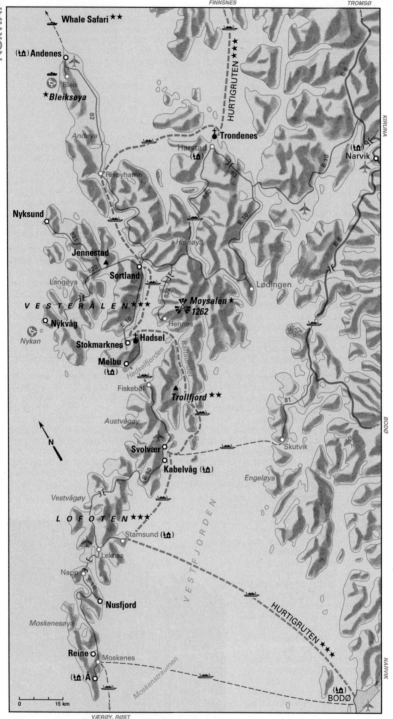

The inter-island ferry routes, crossing the many straits and sounds, are an integral part of the road network. The ferries are working vessels, the Express Coasters included, and they run regularly and leave on time.

Birdlife – The size and variety of the resident and migrating bird population make Lofoten and Vesterålen the paradise of ornithologists. Particularly fascinating are the large colonies of various species nesting on the cliffs along the west coast of the islands, facing the ocean; thousands of birds cohabit in overcrowded quarters, each species having its place on the rock face according to its size and flying ability; cormorants for instance, who are the least agile, live at the foot of the cliff. In the evening the dark cliffside disappears behind a cloud of whirling and shrieking guillemots, kittiwakes, puffins and less common gannets and fulmars.

The most famous and interesting bird cliffs are at Bleiksøya just off the coast of Andøya, Nykan near the fishing town of Nykvåg on the western side of Langøya, and on the two most southern islands of the Lofoten group, Værøy and Røst.

Food – Produce from the sea plays an essential role in local gastronomy. Specialities to look for in the islands restaurants are: *Fiskemølje*, cod's liver and roe on wafer thin toast; herring and barley soup; *Boknafisk*, a stew made with partly dried fish; seal steaks and *Finnbiff*, reindeer meat with a bilberry sauce.

SIGHTS

Selected sights are mentioned from south to north, beginning with the southern tip of Moskenesøya; the most convenient ferry link to the islands' southern part is the Bodø – Moskenes line.

Å – This fishing village situated at the extremity of Moskenesøya (the E 10 motorway ends here), is one of the most picturesque on Lofoten, having retained its typical setting: red-painted fishermen's cabins *(rorbuer)* built on stilts surround a tiny harbour, adding a touch of colour to the sombre landscape dominated by the dark blue mountain peaks. The shrill cry of sea gulls whirling over stockfish drying on wooden frames soon becomes obsessive. Many old buildings have been renovated and the village is now an open-air museum, the Norwegian Fishing Village Museum, **Norsk Fiskeværsmuseum** ⊙, recalling the days when Å was an important trading centre, during the 19C. There is a boathouse, a cod-liver oil factory, a fisherman's cabin, a bakery and other interesting buildings in and around the village.

Sakrisøy (near Reine) – In this small village, there is a very tastefully displayed collection of dolls and toys at the Dagmars Dolls Museum, **Dagmars Dukkemuseum** ⊙, containing 19C German and French dolls, post-war Norwegian dolls, as well as teddies and various other toys. Nearby, there is a row of restored *rorbuer* with wooden balconies over the harbour, furnished in a traditional way; they are let in summer, rowing boat included.

Henningsvær

Reine lies at the foot of some impressive steep mountains which attract keen climbers and the old fishing village of **Nusfjord**, which is on UNESCO's list of protected areas, is gradually being restored. After Napp, landscapes become less austere and more open with areas of grazing land alternating with moorland.

Kabelvåg – This village was the most important fishing centre on Lofoten during the 19C, but centuries ago, during Viking times, it was already an important trading centre controlling the export of dried fish. Excavations are going on in order to find out more about the oldest village in northern Norway. The archaeological site is on the grounds of the Lofoten Museum, **Lofotmuseet** ⊙, illustrating local history and way of life. **Svolvær** is Lofoten's main town.

A ferry service between Fiskebøl and Melbu links Lofoten and Vesterålen.

Melbu has a lively centre round the harbour and a museum of local history, the **Vesterålen Museum** ⊙, housed in a turn-of-the-century farmhouse and other buildings. The former Neptune herring oil and meal factory is the appropriate setting of the **Norsk Fiskeindustrimuseum** ⊙ (National Fishing Industry Museum) which illustrates all aspects of the industry from catching methods to the ready-to-eat product. There are concerts, exhibitions and activities for children. The village really comes to life in summer when the **Summer Melbu** takes place; this is a broad cultural festival which is now internationally known and includes concerts, garden parties, exhibitions, pantomime, seminars and displays of local gastronomy.

Hadsel Kirke ⊙ – The octagonal wooden church dates from 1824, but it contains an altarpiece from 1520 and a chandelier from the 12C.

Stokmarknes is an old commercial centre and the birthplace of Hurtigruten, the Express Coaster service founded in 1893. The **Hurtigrutemuseet** ⊙, housed in the new Hurtigrutens Hus, retraces the history of the service and includes MV Finnmarken, a now retired coaster dating from 1956, which offers an insight into the traditions of Hurtigruten.

The E 10 road goes through **Sortland**, the main town on Vesterålen, then road 820 on the left leads to the west coast of Langøya. Just north of Sortland, the old trading centre at **Jennestad** has remained virtually unchanged since the turn of the last century when it was the general store and meeting place of the community.

Nykvåg is a picturesque lively fishing village with a large bird rock, particularly interesting during the nesting season. Further north, **Nyksund**, deserted by its inhabitants, has become a ghost village, but not for long since one by one the buildings are being restored by young people from various European countries.

Andenes – This important fishing centre at the northern extremity of Andøya is now a NATO base but in the 16C and 17C it was the starting point of whaling expeditions. Today, there is an interesting whale centre, **Hvalsentret** ⊙, at the harbour and whale hunting has given way to whale safaris *(see below)*. The island of **Bleiksøya**, just off the coast is famous for its bird rock.

Trondenes Kirke ⊙, 3km north of Harstad, dates from c 1250; it was originally surrounded by fortifications, parts of which can still be seen today.

EXCURSIONS

The superb scenery and unique environment of Lofoten and Vesterålen offer many possibilities of exciting boat trips.

★★ **Trollfjord** – *Allow about 3hr.* This narrow fjord with almost vertical mountains on either side can only be reached by boat from Raftsundet, the long channel which separates Austvågøy and Hinnøya. In summer, there are regular excursions from Svolvær and Stokmarknes and the Express Coaster sometimes makes a detour to the fjord which is so narrow that the ships can hardly manoeuvre safely.

★ **Bleiksøya** – *Allow about 2hr – bookings at the harbour in Andenes.* There are daily boat trips from Bleik near Andenes to the bird island, which looks like a dark cone sticking out of the sea; a cave runs right through the island. Local people have kept up the tradition of egg-hunting which takes place every year in May.

★★ **Whale safari** – *Allow 7-8hr – bookings at the Whale Centre in Andenes.* Several species of whales can be observed on this trip, including the largest of them all, the sperm whale of Moby Dick fame, 20m long and weighing 60t. Season: 25 May to mid-August, daily departure at 10.30am.

Whale safaris combined with seal and seabird safaris also start from Nyksund. *Bookings from Whale Tours, Nyksund,* ☎ 76 13 11 66.

★ **Møysålen** – *Allow about 9hr including boat trip.* An excursion to the summit of the highest peak on Lofoten and Vesterålen is a thrilling experience which offers superb **panoramas** of the surrounding area. The excursion starts from Hennes on the shores of Hadselfjord.

MAGERØYA

Magerøya is Norway's most northern island with the famous North Cape at its extremity facing the North Pole across 2 000km of the Arctic Ocean.

The island looks austere and barren as its sparse vegetation consists mainly of lichen and moss; however, in spite of the extreme northern latitude, the relatively mild climate allows some species of Alpine flora and other delicate plants including small orchids to bloom in summer and add a touch of colour to the predominant dark rock. The inhabitants of Magerøya have always lived by fishing alone and do not keep livestock; consequently the only domestic animals found on the island are the Sami's reindeer spending the summer months on the island and feeding on lichen; they traditionally swim across the 3km-wide strait separating Magerøya from the Porsanger peninsula, although nowadays only the strongest animals attempt the strenuous crossing, the others being transported in landing crafts. In September the herds go back to the mainland and journey across Finnmark to the wild Finnmarksvidda plateau.

The fishing grounds around Magerøya, which are among the world's richest, have, for centuries, provided the islanders with their livelihood. Today, however, fish is not so plentiful as it used to be and many small fishing villages along the most exposed parts of the coast have been deserted, leaving just three main fishing ports located in suitably sheltered creeks, Honningsvåg in the south, Gjesvær in the west and Skarsvåg in the north; these were burnt down by the Germans during the Second World War and had to be entirely rebuilt. Fortunately, tourism has given a welcome boost to the local economy as great efforts have been made to improve roads and accommodation and provide interesting excursions for the numerous visitors which the North Cape attracts every year.

Access – There are daily flights from Honningsvåg to Hammerfest but most of the traffic between Magerøya and the mainland journeys by sea from Kåfjord at the tip of the Porsanger peninsula to Honningsvåg. Visitors are prepared for unusual scenery as soon as they leave road E 6 which continues eastwards to Kirkenes and follow E 69 due north along the vast Porsangefjord. All along the way there are striking formations of stratified rock rich in fossils, which have been sculpted by erosion into prominent shapes. Norway's largest car ferry makes 22 daily crossings, lasting 45min each, between Kåfjord and Honningsvåg.

Honningsvåg – Only the church escaped total destruction during the Second World War, but now Honningsvåg has been rebuilt and, with the largest community on Magerøya, it is Finnmark's most important fishing port and one of the main centres of piloting along the coast. The harbour is one of the busiest in the country as it is the home port of many trawlers and the regular port of call of numerous other ships in need of a pilot. Industries connected with fishing as well as shipyards for repairing fishing boats are situated all round the harbour.

Situated in the town centre, the North Cape Regional Museum, **Nordkappmuseet** ⊘, houses permanent exhibitions devoted to North Cape tourism from the 17C onwards and to the history of fishing along the coast of Finnmark and its influence on the way of life on the island. Among the annual events held in Honningsvåg the most popular are the **North Cape Marathon** which takes place in June and the **North Cape Festival**, also in June, which organises a variety of cultural activities including traditional dancing.

There are boat trips to deserted fishing hamlets, bird cliffs and other interesting sites as well as exciting adventures such as deep-sea rafting in large open rubber boats that reach speeds of over 30 knots.

Gjesvær – This small fishing village on the west coast of Magerøya is the starting point of a fascinating **bird safari★★** *(allow 2-3hr)* aboard a large converted fishing boat with a friendly captain at the helm, a young man who is more than willing to share his love and knowledge of the sea with his passengers. The destination is **Gjesværstappan Naturreservat** ⊘ situated 15km west of North Cape. This is a bird sanctuary consisting of three rocky islands, Storstappan, Kirkestappan and Bukkestappan, which are the nesting ground of thousands of birds, kittiwakes, cormorants, razorbills, guillemots, gannets, fulmars and storm petrels, not forgetting the largest puffin colony in Norway numbering some 360 000 birds. Their confident dives and spectacular aerobatics are particularly comical and the captain will confirm that puffins are quite special: they arrive on the Stappan Islands at the beginning of April, but unlike that of other species, their timing is incredibly precise; for as long as he can remember, they have been gathering round the islands every year on 6 April, arriving in waves throughout the day; then, at 6pm precisely, suddenly making for the cliffs all together and settling on ledges or in holes. The boat manoeuvres with admirable ease among the numerous skerries, some of them barely showing above the water. Seals can be seen lying in shallow waters near the reefs while high flying sea eagles prey on the nests of other species.

Fishing can be combined with bird watching for a complete and wonderful immersion in this wildly beautiful Arctic environment.

MANDAL★

Vest-Agder
Population 13 000
Michelin map 985 N 4 or Atlas Europe p 116

Mandal is the most southern town in Norway and one of the oldest on the south coast, its origins going back to the foundation of the small port of Kleven at the beginning of the 16C. It lies inside a small bay sheltered by a cluster of picturesque islands, at the mouth of the River Mandalselva famous in the 17C for the fine quality of its salmon. The architecture of white wooden houses, the cobbled streets, the pavement cafés, the street market, the colourful boutiques and the leisurely atmosphere contribute to make this seaside resort one of the most attractive white towns along the south coast. The town centre is lively throughout the summer, but never more so than in August when the **Shellfish Festival** takes place and all sorts of delicious shellfish are displayed for the delight of gourmets on a huge buffet table in the pedestrian street.

The tip of the tiny peninsula close to the town centre is a protected area with a beautiful south facing beach known as **Sjøsanden**. This stretch of golden sand, gently curving round a small open bay is framed by a row of dark green bushes covered with lovely crimson flowers in early summer.

White Town of Mandal

EXCURSIONS

Lindesnes – *38km south-west to Lindesnes Lighthouse.*
The district of Lindesnes has 90km of deeply indented coastline with tiny harbours and sandy beaches; a great number of small islands and reefs lie just off the coast. Inland there are vast expanses of moorland inhabited by elks.
The lighthouse, **Lindesnes Fyr** ⊘, stands at the most southern point of mainland Norway, 2 518km from North Cape. It has been in operation since 1655 and is open to visitors.

Vigeland, situated 11km west of Mandal on E 39, is the birthplace of **Gustav Vigeland** (1869-1943), the famous sculptor who designed the monumental park in Oslo which bears his name. The Gustav Vigeland Gallery holds exhibitions and shows films from June to September.

Vigeland's Nordic predecessors and contemporaries

Although the Danish sculptor **Bertel Thorvaldsen** (1770-1844), a brilliant exponent of neo-Classicism, was to dominate the first half of the 19C, it was the other Scandinavian countries which produced sculptors of genius a century later. Norway's **Gustav Vigeland** (1869-1943) excelled in portrait statues and figures to adorn fountains and monuments, whereas his Swedish contemporary, **Carl Milles** (1875-1955) made his name in Europe and the United States with his more idiosyncratic works. In Finland **Wäinö Aaltonen** (1894-1966) practised a more monumental style often using Finnish granite.

MÅLSELVFOSSEN

Troms
Michelin map 985 C 15 or Atlas Europe p 104

This impressive waterfall is situated in the midst of unspoilt countryside with extensive woodland in an area of natural beauty which seems quite remote from civilization yet is within easy reach of E 6, the main north-south highway, about 30km north of Bardu.

From Bardu, drive north to Elverum (19km); turn right on road 87 then left and follow the signs to Målselvfossen (11.5km).

The Målselva is a famous salmon river, the largest in Troms county. The setting of the waterfall is grandiose as the river is particularly wide at that point and huge quantities of white foamy water cascade down three gigantic steps over a distance of 600m. A very long salmon ladder was built in 1910 to enable salmon to swim upstream; in late June and early July salmon can be seen jumping up against the strong current.
There is a tourist centre high up on the steep banks of the river with cabins to let and a restaurant; the camp site, a little way further down, has an outdoor heated swimming pool. Beside salmon fishing, outdoor activities offered by the centre include riding packhorses along mountain trails, dog-sledging and rafting down the rapids of the River Målselva.

EXCURSION

Rock carvings near Storsteinnes – *70km north. There are two ways of driving to Storsteinnes: along E 6 going north or along road 87 to Skjold then along roads 857 and 858. From Storsteinnes, follow road 859 to Balsfjord Church overlooking the fjord (10.5km). From the parking, a path signposted Helleristninger leads to the site (150m).* The rock carvings, dating from the late Stone Age (between 3 000 and 5 000 years ago) and depicting animals (mainly reindeer and fish), are spread over a hilly wooded area and can be seen on large flat rocks partly covered over with moss.

NARVIK

Nordland
Population 19 000
Michelin map 985 D 14 or Atlas Europe p 104

Situated 345km north of the Arctic Circle and a few kilometres from the Swedish border, Narvik is built on a headland overlooking Ofotfjord and Rombaksfjord. Rebuilt after the Second World War, it is now a modern industrial town with a spacious centre and the second largest port in Norway. The recent decline in the export of iron ore, on which the town's economy was founded, has prompted Narvik to develop other fields of activity such as mechanical and electronic engineering, printing, waste treatment, consultancy, research and tourism.
An excellent network of communications and the nearby mountains are the essential assets on which the town is relying to become a successful summer and winter holiday resort. In summer, excursions in the surrounding region, in particular to Lofoten by express boat and to Sweden on the famous **Ofoten Railway** (Ofotbanen) are enticing possibilities. In winter, the slopes of Mount Fagernes offer the best alpine skiing in northern Norway with the most up-to-date equipment. A cable-car ride is an excellent way of appreciating Narvik's exceptional setting between fjord and steep mountains. The town's new **cable-car** ⊙ takes visitors up to 656m above sea level. Besides offering wonderful views, the place is ideal for hiking and there is a restaurant for those who wish to prolong the evening and admire the midnight sun at leisure. There is a fine golf course on the banks of the River Skjomen abounding in salmon, beneath mountains culminating at 1 500m.

HISTORICAL NOTES

Iron ore town – Narvik was founded at the end of the 19C when the unified states of Norway and Sweden decided they needed a port which was free of ice all year round in order to export the precious iron ore mined in nearby Swedish Lapland. The construction of a railway line between Kiruna and Narvik was undertaken in 1898 and took four years to complete. The 168km-long Ofoten line was built by itinerant workers known locally as *rallare* who lived in the village of Rombaksbotn, at the head of the narrow Rombaksfjord. The village burnt down in 1903 and quite a few of the workers settled in Narvik as the town prospered rapidly. Every year in March, a cultural festival celebrates the men and women who contributed so much to the town's prosperity. The old road built at the time, which led from Rombaksbotn to the Swedish border in the mountains and was known as Rallarveien, has been restored and now offers interesting possibilities of hikes or mountain-bike excursions in beautiful surroundings.

The Ofoten Line – The railway line climbs steep mountainsides for 42km from Narvik to the Swedish border, at times running along sheer precipices and going through 22 tunnels and over 9 bridges; 13 trains a day on average bring iron ore to Narvik harbour. Each wagon carries about 80t of ore and each train is made up of 52 wagons. It would take 300 lorries to transport the equivalent of a train load!

The Battle of Narvik – On 9 April 1940, the harbour was attacked by 10 German destroyers and the town occupied by German troops. The British Navy retaliated immediately and destroyed the German warships. In May, British, French and Polish troops were landed and joined forces with Norwegian troops. The Germans were forced to withdraw into the mountains and on 28 May Narvik was liberated, but German bombers managed to destroy the town centre. Unfortunately, the Allied forces had to withdraw on 8 June as the Battle of France was raging and they were badly needed on the front.

However, the Battle of Narvik was the Germans' first defeat in their onslaught on Europe and it helped occupied countries regain confidence in the final outcome of the war.

SIGHTS

Krigsminnemuseum ⊘ – The war museum is owned and run by the Nordland District of the Norwegian Red Cross. It is devoted to the Battle of Narvik in April-May 1940 and to the German occupation from June 1940 to May 1945. The collections, which are arranged in chronological and thematic order, show the participation of British, French, Polish, Norwegian and German forces and include equipment, arms, uniforms, medals, photos, drawings, maps and models.

Ofoten Museum ⊘ – This small local museum shows the spectacular development of Narvik from a single farm to a town in the space of a few years, after the construction of the Ofoten railway line.

Harbour facilities – Narvik ore terminal is one of the largest and most efficient in the world. The trains are unloaded through hatches on the underside of the wagons and the ore is separated into different grades of quality. Ships of over 250 000t can be moored at the loading quay and every year 14 million tons of iron ore is loaded on about 220 ships. In summer there are daily guided tours of the storage area and the loading quay.

NORDFJORD ★★★

Sogn og Fjordane
Michelin map 985 K 2-4 or Atlas Europe p 110

The fishing port of **Måløy** is situated on one of several islands off the west coast of Norway which command the entrance to Nordfjord, one of the most beautiful Norwegian fjords. Nordfjord penetrates inland, over a distance of just over 100km, deep into a picturesque mountainous area and stops at the foot of Norway's largest glacier, **Jostedalsbreen**.

The Coastal Steamer calls every day at Måløy, linked to the mainland by a striking S-shaped bridge, 1 224m long, which is said to sing a C note when the wind blows in a certain direction. From there, the whole length of Nordfjord can easily be visited as road 15 follows the north bank practically all the way from the coast to the head of the fjord at Loen.

This journey offers a variety of landscapes from the rugged islands at the entrance of the fjord to tiny villages along its banks, steep mountainsides, snow-capped peaks in the distance, rocky promontories reflected in the still waters and green pastures gently sloping down to the edge of the fjord; the scenery changes so rapidly that it is almost impossible to appreciate it fully in the time it takes to drive the 100km or so.

Nordfjord is also easily accessible by road from the south via Skei and Byrkjelo and from the east via Grotli or Geiranger; at the head of the fjord, peaceful resorts like Olden and Loen are excellent bases from which to explore the many facets of the area at one's own pace. There are many possibilities for walks, boat trips, excursions to the glaciers or for leisurely drives along the narrow minor roads which wind round the mountain lakes.

SIGHTS

Nordfjordeid – Situated on the north bank, midway between the coast and the head of the fjord, Nordfjordeid is the regional centre of Nordfjord, famous for its Fjord Horse Centre, **Norsk Fjordestsenter** ⊘, which takes care of about 40 fjord ponies and organises horse shows throughout the summer, as well as an annual exhibition of stallions. Events are held in a large indoor arena. Riding instruction and sightseeing tours in horse-drawn carriages are also organised. The *Fjording* is a native breed of the fjords of western Norway, specially adapted to the mountainous terrain; its lovely golden colour from head to tail and its placid nature make it very popular with visitors to the area.

Sandane – Lying at the head of Gloppenfjord, a branch of Nordfjord, Sandane is another busy commercial centre of the Nordfjord region. The **Nordfjord Folkemuseum** ⊙, an open-air museum consisting of 29 old buildings from all over the area, including a single-room dwelling with an open hearth and just a hole in the roof for a chimney.

The old **Gjemmestad Kirke**, dating from 1692, stands on the south-west shore of the fjord, 5km from Sandane along road 615.

Inner Nordfjord – The most inland part of Nordfjord and the three secluded valleys, stretching from Stryn, Loen and Olden at the head of the fjord to the foot of the massive Jostedal glacier, form Inner Nordfjord, an area of great natural beauty where mountains, lakes, waterfalls and glaciers combine to create some of the most harmonious landscapes in Norway at once remote, familiar and soothing.

From Byrkjelo in the south, road 60 climbs to 630m then winds down again on the other side of Utvikfjellet, affording splendid **views** of Nordfjord which describes a graceful S through a wild and severe landscape brightened up now and again by green river valleys and a cluster of farms and colourful villages like Utvik and Innvik.

Olden – The village, which lies on the shores of the fjord, at the lower end of a beautiful valley, is a pleasant resort with plenty of good accommodation and numerous walks and excursions. The combined drive and walk up the Olden Valley, Oldedalen, to the Briksdal glacier *(see below)* is an absolute must.

Olden's **Gammla Kirke** ⊙, dating from 1759, was built in the shape of a Greek cross on the site of a former stave church. Some of the wood from the stave church was used in the construction of the present church. The interior is very interesting, particularly the old pews with carved doors and hat stands, the altarpiece from 1772 and a Bible printed in Copenhagen in 1550.

Nearby stands **Singerheimen** ⊙, the former home of an American millionaire, **William Henry Singer**, who settled in Norway where he devoted himself to painting. Some of his best works are exhibited in his studio together with some of his furniture, books etc. Further uphill, the house is now, according to his wishes, a recreation home for nurses from the local hospital.

★★ **Briksdalsbreen (The Briksdal glacier)** – *23km south to car park, then about 4km walk or ride in horse-drawn cart – comfortable flat shoes are recommended; allow half a day.*

The drive up the Olden Valley is magnificent. The tumultuous stream which comes down from the Briksdal glacier widens into three successive lakes enclosed within steep wooded mountainsides, with the glacier's white mass visible in the distance. Silt carried by glacier-fed rivers is responsible for the characteristic green colour of Norway's lakes and fjords in summer.

At the end of the road, near the car park, there is a mountain lodge, called Briksdalsbre Fjellstove, with a cafeteria and souvenir shop; from there it is about 4km up to the foot of the glacier.

Part of the journey can be made in a two-wheeled cart drawn by a fjord horse, known as a *stolkjerre*. It is a very enjoyable experience as it allows plenty of time to admire the superb scenery as the sturdy little horse proceeds bravely up a fairly steep track with impressive hairpin bends, passing close to a thundering waterfall. The track stops short of the glacier and a narrow path makes its way through huge boulders to the bottom of the glacier which comes down from a height of 1 700m to a mere 346m above sea level. The view of this huge mass of ice split by deep crevasses and contained between two walls of dark rock like a flow of white lava, is breathtaking. In summer large chunks of ice can often be seen falling off the mass of the glacier as it calves into the stream below.

Loen – This farming community is, like Olden, a pleasant and friendly resort with hotels, chalets and camping facilities, offering many outdoor activities in beautiful surroundings. **Lovatn** and the upper valley of the River Lo are even wilder than the Olden Valley. The road which skirts the east shore of the lake is extremely narrow in parts and dominated by sheer walls of rock. These rocks are craggy and look really threatening in places; not surprisingly so since there were three landslides last century near the hamlet of Bødal, where the lake narrows considerably; each time part of Ramnefjell (Raven Mountain) fell into the lake causing a powerful wave which, in one instance, lifted the lake steamer 400m inland! The scar can be seen on the mountainside. The road stops at Kjenndalsbre Fjellstove (mountain lodge) and the rest of the journey to the foot of **Kjenndalsbreen★**, another branch of the Jostedal glacier, must be made on foot *(about 45min)*.

Stryn Summer Ski Centre ⊙ – *East of Stryn, on road 258 between Videseter and Grotli. Follow road 15 along Lake Stryn and up to the first tunnel, then bear right on the old road (258) whereas road 15 continues to Geiranger.*

Closed until 15 June, **Gamle Strynefjellsvegen★**, a national tourist road, climbs in a succession of hairpin bends to the **Tystig Glacier** and the **Stryn Summer Ski Centre**. On the way there are superb views of the valley, particularly from the **Videseter Hotel** at an altitude of 600m. There is an impressive waterfall nearby.

A ski lift and a ski tow take skiers on top of the glacier where there is a choice of alpine skiing with slalom and downhill runs or cross-country skiing on the glacier plateau. There are activities for children as well. The good quality snow, even at the height of summer, attracts many visitors and when the sun shines most people ski in shorts or bathing costumes. Beyond the ski centre, the road reaches an altitude of 1 139m and crosses a desolate barren mountain plateau, skirting partly frozen lakes on the way down to Grotli.

At Grotli, turn left on road 15, then right on road 63 to reach Geiranger.

NORDKAPP★★★

NORTH CAPE – Finnmark
Michelin map 985 A 22 or Atlas Europe p 105

The most northern point of the continent of Europe, at a latitude of 71° 10' 21" North, is an impressive promontory jutting out into the Arctic Ocean.

Its old Norse name was Knyskanes and the Russians called it Murmanski Noss, the Norsemen's Headland, but in 1553 Richard Chancellor, an English explorer trying to find the north-east passage to China, named it North Cape.

Famous visitors – North Cape had for a long time been a landmark for seafarers, fishermen, whalers and even pirates when, in the 17C it became a tourist destination; Francesco Negri, an Italian priest from Ravenna is believed to have been North Cape's first real visitor in 1665. Louis Philippe of Orléans, later to become King Louis Philippe of France, visited North Cape in 1795. Much later he sent a bronze bust of himself to the people who had made him so welcome in Masøy not far from North Cape; unfortunately it was destroyed during the Second World War but, in 1959, the French State sent a copy of the bust in white marble to the Norwegian people which has now been placed in the new North Cape building.

After the visit of King Oscar II of Sweden and Norway in 1873, Thomas Cook pioneered the first charter tour of North Cape. Until 1956 tourists used to arrive by sea, land at the bottom of the cliff and had then to face the steep climb up to the plateau. Since the building of the 34km-long road from Honningsvåg, the flow of tourists has steadily increased.

THE NORTH CAPE PLATEAU

The drive from Honningsvåg across barren hills and craters filled with frozen water, along a twisting road seemingly leading nowhere is certainly a foretaste of the unique experience to come. The plateau itself is often shrouded in mist which can clear in 5min to reveal the huge empty ocean, a vast expanse 2 000km wide from Nordkapp to the North Pole. One can walk to the edge of the cliff and get a glimpse of the sheer rock face plunging

Nordkapp – North Cape

straight into the sea 307m below. The see-through globe erected near the edge to catch the rays of the midnight sun has now become a distinctive feature of North Cape. In 1988, seven children from different parts of the world made drawings on the theme of peace and the sun which were reproduced on seven large round slabs and called *Children of the Earth* as a symbol of unity among the peoples of the world.

The first building on the plateau, an octagonal post office and champagne shop, was erected in 1898. The latest one, built by the SAS in 1988, is **Nordkapphallen** ⊙, ingeniously concealed inside the cliff. It is a welcoming place with all facilities and instructive entertainment for weary travellers.

A **video show** gives a vivid account of the changing aspects of Nordkapp and its area throughout the seasons on a 225° screen. A terrace, called the **Grotto**, dug into the rock and facing due north, offers a realistic view of the emptiness ahead; behind it is an amphitheatre with panoramic windows and a bar. Deep inside the cliff there is a small ecumenical **chapel** for meditation. On top, there is a fine **restaurant** with beautifully prepared specialities from the north, a **post office** and a **souvenir shop**.

Most people come during the period when the sun never sets (14 June to 30 July), although winter tourism is becoming very fashionable as more and more people want to see the famous northern lights and go on snow-scooter safaris across the plateau.

In summer, however, the animation is at its peak at midnight when, if the weather is clear, the view is unforgettable. But even if it is not, few people are disappointed as they are aware of having had a unique experience.

NUMEDAL★★

Buskerud

Michelin map 985 L 5-M 6 or Atlas Europe p 116

The inland mountainous region of southern Norway some 200km north-west of Oslo, is characterised by vast areas of dense forest which give way to heathland above a certain altitude and deep valleys through which run powerful streams and rivers. The steep slopes are covered with lush grass up to the forest line and the long-standing farming tradition has left a wealth of wooden rural architecture. Numedalen is no doubt the most typical and picturesque of these valleys with its beautiful old farms often built on high ground and unique stave churches.

FROM GOL TO KONGSBERG 216km – allow a day

The route chosen starts from Gol and the high pastures of the upper Hallingdal Valley and follows the Numedal Valley south to the silver mining town of Kongsberg.

Gol – This regional commercial centre is also a lively summer and winter resort centrally situated and within easy reach of Sognefjord along the Hemsedal Valley and Hardangerfjord along road 7. The old stave church was moved to the folk museum in Oslo. Among the numerous excursions suggested by the local tourist office, mountain farm visits are one of the most interesting.

Drive west on road 7 to Torpo (16km).

Torpo Stavkirke ⊙ – This is one of the oldest remaining stave churches, built in the mid-12C. The chancel, apse and outside gallery were pulled down in the 19C, leaving only the nave and side aisles. The west and south portals are beautifully carved with interwoven animal motifs. Most remarkable is the vaulting supported on carved capitals and covered with paintings from c 1260, depicting Christ with six Apostles on either side and scenes from St Margaret's life.

Ål – *26km.* The regional museum, **Rolf Nesch Museum** ⊙, consists of 25 old houses and a rare collection of rose painting ornamentation, a tradition which originated in France in the 17C and flourished in Norway, particularly in Telemark and Numedal. There are some splendid examples of it in Uvdal and Nore stave churches.

Geilo – *53km.* Like Gol, Geilo is a lovely mountain resort and the convenient starting point of numerous excursions including the remote Hardangervidda plateau.

Turn south and follow road 40 down the Numedal Valley. At Uvdal, opposite the new church, a minor road leads to the stave church (5km) and Uvdal Bygdetun (see below).

★★ Uvdal and Nore stave churches – *108km and 136km respectively.* These churches have several points in common, they were both built at the end of the 12C with a central pillar supporting the whole structure, then remodelled in the 17C and decorated by the same artist. In **Uvdal Stavkirke ★★**⊙, the earliest paintings, dating from 1656, imitate stained-glass windows surrounded by flower and fruit motifs in ochre and charcoal colours, whereas other paintings date from 1720 and include a touching Adam and Eve in naive style. The pulpit is decorated with scenes depicting four Apostles accompanied by the wrong animal, for instance St Matthew with a billy goat!

There are several splendid old farm buildings in the open-air museum near the church (Uvdal Bygdetun) and the view over the valley is beautiful.

At Hvåle, cross the river over Norefjord bridge to reach Nore Stavkirke.

When **Nore Stavkirke ★★⊘** was extended in 1683, the builders reused the panels painted in 1656, but did not bother to match them, so that the patterns do not coincide. The Dingbats painted on the panels of the north and south walls under the gallery are copied from an illustrated Bible printed in Copenhagen in 1710.

OPPLAND AND HEDMARK
Michelin map 985 JK 5-8 and L 6-8 or Atlas Europe pp 110-111 and 116-117

Situated north of Oslo, this vast mountainous region forms a triangle between Eidsvoll at the southern end of Lake Mjøsa, Geiranger in the north-west and Røros in the north-east. According to legend, the region is infested with trolls (characters in Norwegian fold tales), who live in forests and on mountains and can only be seen in the evening or at night. They look like human beings although some of them are gigantic and others quite small; they all have a very long nose and are rather ugly and all Norwegians know it is wise to keep on the right side of them as their anger is frightening!

Trolls

The counties of Oppland and Hedmark cover an area of 55 000km², with some of the most beautiful scenery inland Norway has to offer, but on a much grander scale than anywhere else. Norway's longest and broadest valley, **Gudbrandsdal**, cuts right through the region in a north-west/south-east direction, surrounded by Norway's highest mountains, the **Jotunheimen**, **Rondane** and **Dovre ranges**. To the east, along the Østerdal Valley flows Norway's longest river, the **Glomma**. South of Lillehammer lies Norway's largest lake, **Lake Mjøsa**, whereas the second largest, **Lake Femund** to the east is at the heart of a vast wilderness area,

Femundsmarka, unique in Norway *(see RØROS: Excursions)*. Dense forests cover large parts of the two counties which include several national parks, in the mountain areas and in Femundsmarka.

With such a variety of landscapes and natural environments, the area is ideal touring country and lends itself to the pursuit of exciting outdoor activities both in summer and winter. For instance, rafting down the numerous rivers coming down from the mountains and in particular down the rapids of the **River Sjoa** *(just south of Otta)*, known as the washing machine, can be an exhilarating experience; and a wilderness safari can be equally fascinating. There are more than 250km of marked ski tracks across the region from north to south, several ski arenas suitable for the whole family and many resorts such as Lillehammer in the south and Beitostølen at the foot of Jotunheimen *(for detailed information about the various possibilities, contact the tourist office in Lillehammer)*.

★★THE GUDBRANDSDAL VALLEY

The River Lågen flows through Norway's longest valley from Bjørli in the north to Lillehammer in the south over a distance of 203km. The Gudbrandsdal Valley cuts its way through the centre of the region thus allowing easy access to other areas.

A good way to visit the area is to follow E 136 and E 6 all the way, stopping in Dombas, Otta, Vinstra or Ringebu where there is good accommodation.

There are many excursions, hikes and organised tours to choose from: musk ox, elk and reindeer safaris, horse riding on mountain tracks, exploring the flora and fauna along nature trails, visiting a mountain dairy farm just west of Vinstra which started making the famous Gudbrandsdal cheese in 1863, presented to visitors with the very efficient cheese slicer invented in 1925 to go with it!

Jørundgard Middelaldersenter, situated just north of Otta at Sel, close to the pilgrim way from Oslo to Nidaros (Trondheim), is a medieval farm reconstructed for the filming of Kristin Lavransdatter, Sigrid Undset's historical novel *(see LILLEHAMMER)*. Guided tours include demonstrations of various techniques used in medieval times. There are exhibitions, music courses and concerts, an introduction to daily life during the Middle Ages in beautiful surroundings.

At **Vinstra** there is an alternative route south called the Peer Gynt Way, **Peer Gynt Veien**, named after the legendary character who inspired Ibsen's play set in the region. It runs more or less parallel to road E 6 and offers superb views of the Jotunheimen and Rondane mountains.

Ringevu stave church

Rejoin road E6 at Tretten or further south at Fåberg.

Just beyond Ringebu village, **Ringebu Stavkirke** ⊘ is an interesting 13C specimen, its austere outside appearance in striking contrast with the Baroque interior decoration including a magnificent altarpiece and pulpit, as well as a brightly painted organ and pillars.

OSLO ★★★

Population 730 000
Michelin map 985 M 7 or Atlas Europe p 117
Plan of the conurbation on Michelin map 985

Oslo is a modern city with a long history behind it. In spite of its moderate size, it has seen its international influence in the spheres of politics and business grow rapidly during the last decades and it is now becoming one of the main capital cities of the world. The town is situated at the head of Oslofjord, the only large fjord along the south coast of Norway, on low land surrounded by steep forested hills. The widely spread urban area with its green open spaces gives an impression of spaciousness and of a provincial leisurely life. By contrast, the compact town centre and the great concentration of activity within it create an atmosphere of intense living which is Oslo's greatest charm.

Oslo enjoys a temperate climate with a moderately cold winter and just the right amount of snow for good skiing conditions while spring and summer are warm with long sunny periods. Given such favourable conditions, the inhabitants enjoy being out of doors as much as possible: they like strolling in the streets or along the harbour throughout the long summer days... and nights, or crowding the numerous pavement cafés after work and eating outside late into the night with a carefree relaxed attitude which is a prominent feature of their social behaviour. As the seat of the oldest university in the country, Oslo has a strong cultural tradition, offering its visitors a wide choice of museums, a busy theatrical season and an International Jazz Festival in August.

The county of Akershus surrounds the town like a green belt with lakes, forests and picturesque villages where city dwellers can enjoy various outdoor activities in a natural unspoilt environment within a few kilometres from the town centre *(see excursions)*. In summer one of the favourite pastimes is sailing on the fjord whereas, in winter, skiing on one's doorstep is almost taken for granted. As quality of life is one of the Norwegians' top priorities, they want to be able to live in their capital city without having to suffer the usual frustrations associated with town life.

OUT AND ABOUT IN OSLO

Transport – Oslo is compact and easy to visit on foot. There is however a well integrated public transport system. The **underground** *(T-bane or Tunnelbane)* has five lines which converge on Stortinget Station. One of the underground lines takes visitors to the wonderful forest area, Nordmarka, which encircles the capital. The **tramway** system consists of five lines which converge on the city centre. There are at least 20 **bus** lines going from the bus station, beside Central Station, out to the suburbs. **Ferries** leave from Rådhusbrygga 3, in front of the town hall, and cross the busy harbour to reach the green peninsula of Bygdøy with its cluster of famous museums or sail to the islands.

Oslo Card *(Oslokortet)* – This entitles holders to free public transport, free entry to museums and discounts on other activities. It can be purchased for one, two or three days for 150NOK, 220NOK or 250NOK respectively from hotels, travel agents, post offices, the Tourist Information Centre, the town hall, and at Central Station.

Shopping – The main shopping streets are Karl Johans gate, the pedestrian precinct in the town centre and Vikaterrassen. There are numerous shopping centres to choose from: notably Aker Brygge, Paléet and Oslo City. Or try the department stores Steen & Strøm or Glas Magasinet.
Trolls, pewter ware, wooden items, and objects in painted wood *(rosemaling)*, silver jewellery, enamel ware and the richly patterned knitwear all make ideal gifts or souvenirs.

The Oslo Visitor's Channel – A 30min information programme giving day to day details on shows, concerts, exhibitions, sporting and other events taking place in the capital.

Olso on the Internet – For those who browse the Internet more information on the capital, its tourist attractions, public transport, entertainment, night-life, accommodation, restaurants and events is available from www.oslopro.no.

Sports – This city of parks and open spaces offers plenty of opportunities for the visitor who wants to relax by playing a sport. The city is well equipped with skating rinks, sports grounds and swimming pools. With the ski jump at Holmenkollen Oslo is often the venue for world championship events. The Ski Festival and the Summer Concert are both popular annual events.

Excursions – These include guided ski tours in winter, bike tours in summer or landrover trips into the forest area around the capital. Others may prefer a more leisurely horse and carriage tour of the city centre. Boat trips leave for Drøbak, the islands and the fjord to name only a few.

The port of Oslo

HISTORICAL NOTES

The Viking settlement at the head of Oslofjord was a thriving port by the time the city was officially founded by Harald Hardråde in 1048; there are still traces of this first city east of the town centre, in the park on the corner of Bispegata and Oslogate. Oslo became the capital of Norway at the end of the 13C and Håkon V built Akershus Fortress to defend the city. But several adverse factors contributed to hinder the town's normal development: first of all, the Hanseatic League, which had exclusive trading agreements with Bergen, controlled the Baltic trade, then the plague killed half the population in 1348, and later Norway was annexed by Denmark which meant that Copenhagen remained the capital of Norway for a very long time. When, in 1624, Oslo was almost totally destroyed by fire, Christian IV built a new Renaissance town near Akershus Fortress and named it Christiana. From 1814, which marks the beginning of the union with Sweden, the town developed rapidly, acquiring new public buildings. In 1905, independence gave a boost to this expansion and in 1925 it was decided, ironically on the 300th anniversary of the foundation of Christiana, to go back to the original name of Oslo.

TOWN CENTRE

The town centre is small enough to be visited on foot and it is recommended to leave one's car in one of the large car parks north of Karl Johans gate to avoid the difficulties created by one-way streets and insufficient parking places.

Oslo Rådhus ⊘ (**CY H**) – The tall red-brick town hall proudly overlooks the harbour and the fjord, its massive twin towers being a distinctive landmark for ships sailing up the fjord. It was inaugurated in 1950 to celebrate the 900th anniversary of the city's foundation. The interior decoration is a homage to Norwegian modern art and, through the themes depicted, to Norwegian history and daily life. Every year on the 10 December, the official ceremony for the award of the **Nobel Peace Prize** takes place in the town hall. The Peace Prize was established by the will of **Alfred Nobel** (1833-96), a Swedish chemist and engineer inventor of high explosives, together with four other prizes for literature, physics, chemistry and medicine to be awarded by the Swedish authority; another prize for economic sciences was introduced in 1969. Among famous Nobel Peace Prize winners were Albert Schweitzer, Willy Brandt, Mother Teresa, Lech Walesa, Andrey Sakharov and Mikhail Gorbachev.

Nearby is the **Norges Informasjonssenter** (Tourist Information Centre), which provides information about Oslo, excursions from the city and short breaks; the tourist office also has information about other tourist attractions including specific destinations, accommodation and transport in other parts of Norway. There is a gift shop displaying handicraft and applied arts, a Norwegian restaurant and a shop selling international newspapers and magazines.

P. Thompson/SUNSET

OSLO

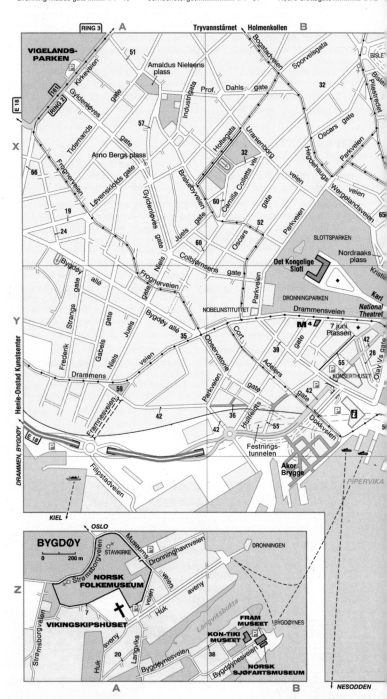

Toll road system - Bompengeringen.
Both Oslo and Bergen make a small charge for cars going into the city centres.
Single tickets and toll passes can be purchased at the toll booths.

M² Hjemmefrontmuseum
M⁴ Ibsen-museet
M³ Museet for Samtidskunst
M¹ Nasjonalgalleriet
H   Rådhuset

NORWAY

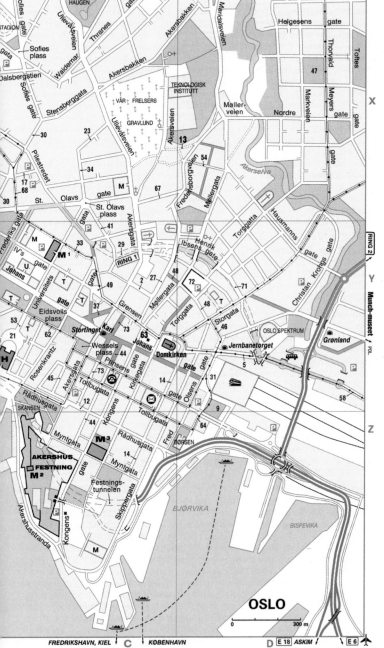

Those with passes should take the lane with a blue sign (Abonnement); those with the correct amount, the lane with the yellow sign (Mynt/Coin) and those with no change, the lane with the grey sign (Manuell).

Aker Brygge (BYZ) – Just across Rådhusplassen, along the waterfront, Aker Brygge is, with Karl Johans gate, the liveliest spot in the capital; the wharf literally disappears under a pleasant confusion of pavement cafés and restaurants overwhelmed with eager customers from 6pm onwards in summer. Moored along the quayside is the Bygdøy ferry next to a colourful assortment of fishing boats, their owners quietly relaxing on deck while they wait for strollers to buy their tempting fresh prawns. The old warehouses along the wharf have been converted into an attractive ultra-modern shopping and entertainment complex which includes theatres, cinemas, restaurants and snack-bars where one can have a quick and relatively cheap meal.

★ **Akershus Festning** ⊙ (CZ) – Still used for official functions, Akershus appears today as a renovated Renaissance castle bearing traces from the original medieval fortress. The latter was built in c 1300 by Håkon Magnusson as a royal residence and a stronghold to protect the city of Oslo to the east; it stands on a promontory overlooking the fjord. The castle was greatly remodelled by King Christian IV and in the early 17C the defence perimeter was extended, slender Renaissance towers added, the courtyard and windows enlarged, and the interior richly decorated. After it was besieged by the Swedes in the early 18C, its defences were once again reinforced. The entrance to the castle's grounds is at the end of Myntgata. On the ground of the rectangular courtyard of the castle itself, markings show where the massive medieval keep used to stand; two large halls, Olav's Hall and Christian IV's Hall occupy the top floor of the north and south wings respectively; the dungeons can also be visited.

A separate building in the grounds of the castle houses the Resistance Museum, **Norges Hjemmefrontmuseum** ★⊙ (CZ M²), which illustrates, with the help of documents, pictures, posters, models and recordings, the story of occupied Norway during the Second World War, the role of the resistance during five years of hardship and their contribution to the final victory, including the heavy water battle in the region of Rjukan in 1943-44. The location of the museum is particularly fitting since Akershus was used by the Germans during the occupation.

Museet for Samtidskunst ⊙ (CZ M³) – Inaugurated in 1990, the Museum of Contemporary Art occupies the former building of the Bank of Norway, erected between 1902 and 1907. It houses the post-war collections of Norwegian and international art previously exhibited at the National Gallery and at Norway's State Gallery.

Domkirken ⊙ (CY) – Built during the second half of the 17C and consecrated as the Church of Our Saviour, Oslo's cathedral was extensively restored in the 19C and again in 1950 so that today very little remains of the original interior except the **pulpit** and the **altarpiece** carved in the late 17C with beautiful motifs of acanthus leaves; the organ front dates from the 18C. The whole of the vaulted ceiling is covered with frescoes painted between 1936 and 1950 and the stained glass is the work of Emmanuel Vigeland, Gustav Vigeland's brother.

There is a lovely **view★★** of the city from the nightwatchman's room in the steeple added in 1850.

In front of the cathedral, on **Stortorvet** (the main square), there is a colourful flower market and the building is surrounded on the sides and rear by a row of tiny boutiques, known as **Basarhallene**, built in c 1850, and now selling handicraft and antiques. The tables and chairs of a quaint little café are precariously balanced on the uneven cobblestones.

Karl Johans gate (BCDY) – This is Oslo's most famous and liveliest street, stretching from the Central Station to the Royal Palace, right through the heart of the city. The street starts up a fairly steep hill past the cathedral on the right, then levels off just before reaching the imposing Parliament building **(Stortinget)** on the left, built between 1861 and 1866. This first part of Karl Johans gate is pedestrianised as are some of the adjacent streets. It is lined with shops of all sizes and crowded throughout the day with window-shoppers and strollers enjoying the animation. Between the Parliament building and the Royal Palace, Karl Johans gate acquires a more formal character as the shops give way to fashionable hotels and expensive restaurants and cafés. On the left, the university gardens, **Studenterlunden**, are a popular meeting place for the capital's inhabitants and on the right, at the very end of the street are the university buildings, **Universitetet**. Karl-Johansgate ends in front of the statue of Karl Johan XIV, the ex-French general Bernadotte who was king of Sweden and Norway after the treaty of 1814. Beyond the statue is the royal residence, **Det Kongelige Slott**, surrounded by a park open to the public.

★★★ **Nasjonalgalleriet** ⊙ (CY M¹) – Situated behind the university, the National Gallery houses Norway's largest collection of Norwegian and international art up to 1945. Established in 1836, the museum moved to its present premises in 1881. Since

1990, the works of artists born after 1920 have been transferred to the Museum of Contemporary Art. The collections of Norwegian and European art are exhibited on three floors.

Norwegian painting (second and third floors) is particularly well represented and gives an excellent account of the development of Norwegian art from 1814 onwards. **Romanticism** is illustrated by the landscapes of JC Dahl, one of the leaders of the movement and by *Bridal Voyage on Hardangerfjord*, a famous masterpiece by two other leading Romantics, Adolph Tidemand and Hans Gude. A period of realism inspired by French painting was followed by a return to Romanticism (neo-Romanticism) towards the end of the 19C. It was then that the name of **Edvard Munch** began to rise above that of his contemporaries. Two rooms of the museum are entirely devoted to Munch; they contain 58 of his paintings, mainly from the 1890s, such as *Moonlight, The Scream, Ashes* and *The Dance of Life*. The beginning of the 20C was dominated by Expressionist and neo-Impressionist painters such as Erichsen, Svarstad, Lund and Karsten, followed, in the period between the two World Wars, by a group of Matisse's pupils, while other artistic trends such as Cubism and German Expressionism also flourished at the same time. Several rooms on the third floor are devoted to **Danish and Swedish painting**; particularly noteworthy is the room containing works from the Golden Age of Danish painting.

The collections of **European painting**, although far from comprehensive are excellent and contain many important and representative works.

Old European Masters (ground floor) are mostly represented by Flemish (Van Dyck, Rubens) and Dutch (Ludens, Kessel) artists; there is also a remarkable *St Peter Repentant* by El Greco. However the most impressive possession of the museum in this section is the extensive collection of **French paintings of the 19C and 20C**, from Corot and Delacroix to Braque and Léger, including artists associated with 20C French painting such as Picasso and Juan Gris. Particularly interesting are *Toilette matinale* by Degas, *Bords de Seine* and *Etretat* by Monet, *Après le bain* by Renoir, *Self Portrait* by Cézanne, *Brittany 1889* by Gauguin, *Self Portrait* by Van Gogh, *The Seine in Winter* by Marquet, *Pauvre ménage* and *Guitar* by Picasso, *Le Journal* by Juan Gris, *Nature Morte* by Léger and *Siesta in the Garden* by Bonnard.

★ **Ibsen-museet** ⊘ (BY **M⁴**) – Inaugurated in 1993, this museum dedicated to Norway's most famous dramatist is housed in Ibsen's own apartment, situated only a stone's throw from the National Theatre in Stortingsgata, where so many performances of his plays have been given. The writer spent the last 11 years of his life at no 1 Arbinsgate where he wrote several of his most famous plays. The apartment has been restored to the condition it was in at the time of Ibsen's death. **Henrik Ibsen** (1828-1906) spent his childhood in Skien (Telemark), his native town, and his early youth in Grimstad on the south coast as an apprentice in a chemist's shop. His modest background greatly influenced his outlook on life and his awareness of underlying social problems. For 12 years or so he worked in the theatres of Bergen and Christiania (now Oslo), writing plays without much success. At the same time, he was concerned with his country's search for a national identity and, with his friend Bjørnstjerne Bjørnson (awarded the Nobel Prize for literature in 1903), he founded the Norwegian Company in 1859 in order to promote Norwegian art and culture. This prompted him to write historical plays set in medieval Norway with a clear message to his contemporaries and he gained some recognition from them. However, outraged when Norway did not offer to help Denmark at war with Prussia, he voluntarily exiled himself in 1864 and only returned home 27 years later to settle in Christiania. After leaving Norway he stopped writing historical plays; and instead wrote two dramas on the problem of personality which clearly reflected his doubts and anxieties about his country. One of these, *Peer Gynt* (1867), depicts a weak character who discovers that he has wasted his life and lost his identity. Although it was not meant for the stage but intended to be read, *Peer Gynt* is now considered as a forerunner of modern drama. Ibsen finally achieved recognition as an international dramatist in the 1880s with *A Doll's House* (1879) and *Ghosts* (1881); with these plays and those which followed, Ibsen created a realistic contemporary drama, exposing the real problems of society and denouncing hypocrisy. The characters he portrays come to realise that their values and their need for freedom are in opposition to their bourgeois environment and, when they do, social order is threatened. In all Ibsen's plays there is also an undercurrent of despair as individuals gradually become aware of the gulf that exists between their aspirations and what they can really expect out of life. In his last drama, *When We Dead Awaken*, written in 1899, Ibsen goes even further when the main character, an artist, expresses a pessimistic vision not only of mankind but also of himself for having sacrificed life to the pursuit of his art.

NORWAY

BYGDØY (AZ) *half a day*

The Bygdøy peninsula can be reached by car: follow road E 18 going west and take the exit for Bygdøy; turn left into Bygdøy Allé, then left again over the E 18 dual carriageway; Dronning Blancas Vei leads to Museumsveien where the Folkemuseum is situated. Alternatively, in summer, you can take the Bygdøy ferry from town hall pier no 3 (Rådhusbrygga) to Dronningen, then the museum train to the different sights and return to the town centre from Bygdøynes.
The third alternative is to take bus no 30 from Stortingsgata in the town centre.
The Bygdøy peninsula, which juts out into the fjord south-west of the town centre, is a fashionable residential area with exclusive beaches on the west side at Huk and Paradisbukta. However, a visit to Bygdøy is a must on account of its five splendid museums, each illustrating a different aspect of Norwegian culture and achievement.

★★★**Norsk Folkemuseum** ⊘ **(AZ)** – *Situated in Museumsveien – car park opposite the entrance.* Located in attractive unspoilt parkland, this museum of Norwegian cultural history going back to medieval times is the largest in the country with fascinating indoor and outdoor collections. It is one of the oldest museums of its kind in the world and celebrated its centenary in 1994. Spread over a large area, the open-air section, which is the main attraction of the museum, comprises 153 buildings illustrating rural and urban architecture from various regions, mainly from southern Norway. Farm buildings from Fjordane, Østerdal, Hallingdal and other regions, linked by a network of picturesque twisting lanes, show traditional construction techniques with variations from one region to the next. The most comprehensive and representative groups of buildings come from Setesdal, Numedal and Telemark. The museum's prize exhibit is **Gol stave church**, moved from the small town of Gol 224km north-west of Oslo, over 100 years ago. It has hardly been altered since it was built in c 1200 and still has no windows; the paintings in the apse, however, date from the 17C and include the *Last Supper* over the altar. The indoor collections are housed in the large buildings at the entrance to the museum and include folk costumes and art, toys and other items. There is also an exhibition of Sami culture.

Continue and turn right onto Langviksveien which leads to the Vikingskipshuset nearby.

★★★**Vikingskipshuset** ⊘ **(AZ)** – This fascinating Viking ship museum houses the contents of three Viking graves which were discovered around the Oslofjord between 1867 and 1904. The graves represent ship burials, a common practice in Viking times, and the museum was designed in 1913 by Arnstein Arneberg to display the three ships found in the graves; it is in the shape of a cross: the amazingly well-preserved **Oseberg ship** is exhibited in the nave just beyond the entrance, and the **Gokstad and Tune ships** each occupy one of the wings; the nave is prolonged by the **Oseberg Wing** containing other objects found in the graves. The remarkable condition of the finds is explained by the fact that the subsoil in the area is dense clay, which acted as a protection against the damaging effect of air and water. The contents of the Tune grave are very fragmentary but the Oseberg and Gokstad finds are varied and most interesting. The Oseberg grave, dating from c 834, was the oldest, the other two being some 30 or 40 years younger. All three graves were plundered by grave robbers. Even so, the finds yielded a lot of information about Viking traditions, daily life, religious beliefs, burial techniques and seafaring.

Oseberg ship

NORWAY

Viking burials – There were many gods in the Viking religion and, as in Greek mythology, they all led a life comparable to that of ordinary mortals, fighting, eating and drinking and even inviting to their table brave warriors fallen in battle. From this stems the belief that the needs of men and women after death were the same as during their lifetime and the Vikings' burial traditions, particularly rich in Norway, evolved from this belief. A dead person could be buried or cremated, but whatever the case, gifts reflecting the social status of the deceased, were placed beside the body. People from the higher strata of society were often buried in ships. The ship, which served as a coffin, was placed in a pit and the body laid on a bed in a specially constructed burial chamber. The ship was then filled with provisions and, as the case may be, with weapons, agricultural tools, jewellery, kitchen utensils etc; dogs and horses were also often sacrificed. Finally, a burial mound was erected on top of the ship. Two women were found in the Oseberg grave together with a ceremonial cart and three sledges, cooking utensils, farming and clothmaking tools, a saddle, fragments of tapestries and ample provisions. The wooden articles, in particular the cart and sledges, are beautifully decorated with intricate carvings of animal and human motifs. The finds in the Gokstad and Tune graves bear no comparison to the wealth of objects and tools found at Oseberg.

Viking ships – The careful examination of Viking ships like the Oseberg and Gokstad ships helps to explain the predominance of the Vikings as a seafaring people over well-established societies living in England, France and Ireland between AD 800 and AD 1050. Their superiority lay in their mastery of shipbuilding techniques. Their ships were fast-sailing, having a central mast rigged with a square sail so that the crew could man the oars even when the sail was up. They were designed in such a way that, even fully laden, a ship of the size of the Gokstad (24m long and 5m wide) needed only one metre draught and could therefore approach any coast and sail up any river. Moreover, Viking ships were extremely seaworthy as was demonstrated when a copy of the Gokstad ship sailed across the Atlantic in 1893. They were light weight and flexible with a solid keel and a distinctive curved bow which has become a symbol of Viking strength. With such ships, the Vikings sailed not only across the North Sea, but also across the Atlantic Ocean to Greenland and to America which was discovered by Leif Eiriksson almost 500 years before Columbus' famous journey took place. They gained invaluable experience and close examination of the Oseberg and Gokstad ships has confirmed a rapid evolution in hull design. As their building techniques improved, the Vikings built different types of ships, fast warships with large crews and slower merchant ships with smaller crews but more cargo space.

Continue along Langviksveien and turn left in Bygdøynesveien which leads to the remaining three museums on Bygdøy, all connected with seafaring.

Edvard Munch (1863-1944)

Munch *(see Self-portrait p 59)* grew up in Christiana in an environment where culture was prominent, yet far from being a happy one, his childhood was saddened by the long illnesses and subsequent deaths of his mother and young sister which left their indelible mark on him; later on, death and grief became strong leitmotifs in his paintings. During his studies he was inspired by French Realism and in 1885 he went to Paris where he began work on the *Sick Child*, a work which, although much criticised, drew attention to him as an artist. Back in Christiania, he associated with radical anarchists and wanted to paint modern man's despair. However, in 1889 he obtained a three-year travel grant and went back to Paris where he rejected Realism and was, for a time, attracted by Impressionism, but he was probably more influenced by Symbolism.

An exhibition on his works in Berlin in 1892 created a scandal, but he decided to settle there all the same. He met the Swedish dramatist August Strindberg with whom he discussed Nietzsche and philosophy generally and who greatly influenced his creative mood. In 1893 he exhibited some of his best-known works, part of the cycle, *The Frieze of Life*, in which the main themes are love, death, darkness and anxiety and *The Scream* through which he became a forerunner of the Expressionist movement.

In 1896 he was back in Paris at a time when Symbolism was flourishing; there he successfully devoted more time to lithography.

Upon his return to Norway, he painted several monumental landscapes of Olsofjord, but as a result of a tragic love affair he had a nervous breakdown in 1908 and definitively broke with his former anarchist friends.

In 1909 he finally settled in Norway and decorated the new auditorium of the Oslo University, choosing the sun as his main theme. His interest in the growing labour movement led to the famous *Workers on their Way Home* (1913-15). From 1916 onwards he lived in isolation in his house outside Oslo and in the latter part of his life he painted sensuous landscapes with bold colours which indicated that he might have come to a more serene vision of life.

NORWAY

★★ Frammuseet ⊙ (BZ) – This very interesting museum houses just one huge exhibit, the **polar ship Fram**, purposely built in Larvik by Colin Archer for the Norwegian explorer, **Fridtjof Nansen**, (1861-1930) who, at the age of 27, had acquired fame by crossing the Greenland ice cap on skis and who aimed to get as close to the North Pole as possible across the Arctic Ocean, with the help of polar currents. The ship's special features included completely smooth sides to prevent ice from clinging to the hull as well as a tight network of oak beams and braces to reinforce the hull from the inside; the rudder and propeller could also be pulled up when the ice closed in on the ship. Nansen commanded the first expedition which left Norway in 1893. The *Fram* managed to reach the latitude of 86o north and was immobilised by ice during three successive winters, having to sustain enormous additional weight when huge amounts of ice crashed on deck; she returned to Norway in 1896, having drifted west with the currents as predicted. Nansen later became a respected statesman, first as ambassador to Britain, then as Norway's delegate to the League of Nations where he successfully conducted several humanitarian missions. He was awarded the Nobel Prize for Peace in 1922.

The *Fram's* second expedition was headed by Otto Sverdrup who had crossed the Greenland ice cap with Nansen and commanded the *Fram* on her first voyage. This time several new islands were discovered north of Canada.

On her third journey, the *Fram* took **Roald Amundsen** to the Antarctic and he subsequently reached the South Pole, the first man ever to do so *(see TROMSØ: Polarmuseet)*. The ship was away for two years (1910-12) on an oceanographic expedition along the coast of Antarctica.

★★ Kon-Tiki museet ⊙ (BZ) – This museum is also concerned with extraordinary sea voyages, but of a totally different kind since it is devoted to the expeditions led by **Thor Heyerdahl** (born in Larvik in 1914) whose aim was not to discover new lands but to retrace the probable routes followed by ancient civilizations. In 1947 Heyerdahl sailed from Peru to Polynesia in a raft made of balsa wood to prove that the people of Polynesia originally came from South America. The raft, which he called **Kon-Tiki** *(see photograph p 477)*, was an exact replica of those made by South American Indians in pre-Inca times. The Kon-Tiki is displayed in such a way that it is possible to see its underside. Later on, archaeological expeditions to the Galapagos islands and Easter Island provided more evidence to support Heyerdahl's ethnological theories but they are still contested today in certain scientific circles.

The other boat exhibited, called **Ra II** and made of papyrus, was used by Heyerdahl in 1970 to cross the Atlantic from Safi in Morocco to Barbados, in a successful attempt to demonstrate that ancient Egyptians could have crossed the Atlantic and influenced the culture of Central American Indians.

★★ Norsk Sjøfartsmuseum ⊙ (BZ) – Opened in 1974, this modern maritime museum occupies two separate buildings. The open-plan main building houses various collections and exhibitions which include models, paintings, parts of recovered shipwrecks, navigational instruments, fog cannons, galleys, archaeological finds etc and are arranged according to various themes: living conditions on board; in the harbour; navigation; lighthouses and beacons; pilotage and sea rescue; passenger transport; ancient and medieval shipping; the age of discovery; colonies and wars; sailing ships of the 18C and 19C; polar explorations; from paddle-steamer to tanker.

The separate **Boat Hall** shows the evolution of fishing boats with original samples from around the country, including a fully rigged *fembøring* from the north which has several features in common with Viking ships, as well as river boats and a Sami boat. The polar vessel **Gjøa**, in which Roald Amundsen sailed through the Northwest Passage in 1903-06, is exhibited in the museum's large outdoor area facing the sea.

ADDITIONAL SIGHTS

★★ Munchmuseet ⊙ – *Leave by Grønland* (DY). In his will, Edvard Munch left all his works to the city of Oslo, a gift which, together with later additions, represents a huge collection of 1 100 paintings and 18 000 prints, drawings, letters etc. The museum was inaugurated in 1963 but, in view of the size of the collection, works are shown in rotation. In addition, a great number of paintings are sent to temporary exhibitions in Norway and abroad. However, there is always a representative selection of major works on display and so that, after a visit to the superb Munch collection in the National Gallery, a tour of the Munch Museum will fully satisfy admirers of his work.

★**Vigelandsparken** (AX) – *Main entrance in Kirkeveien.*
One of the most visited sights in Oslo, this formal park forms part of the vast Frogner Park situated north-west of the town centre. It was designed by **Gustav Vigeland** (1869-1943), Norway's most famous 20C sculptor, who worked on it for nearly 40 years but died a year before its completion. The park contains 227 monumental sculptures by Gustav Vigeland on the theme of man's destiny, from childhood to adult life. Beyond the imposing wrought-iron gates lies the bold and forceful expression of Vigeland's vision of Life, massive realistic figures of men, women and children, ordinary people caught in different scenes of daily life. Past the bridge and its groups of bronze figures and the allegorical central fountain, one reaches the culminating point of the park, a terraced mound with a central column surrounded by groups of figures depicting various aspects of the relationship between people such as fighting, loving etc. Climbing up the column, the monolith, is a mass of intertwined figures all striving to get to the top, symbolising the struggle of life, a recurrent theme in Vigeland's work.

The Vigeland-museet ⊘ is situated to the south of the park in Nobelsgate. It is housed in the artist's former studio house built for him by the city of Oslo, where he lived and

The Monolith by Gustav Vigeland

worked from 1924 to 1943. It contains nearly all his works, drawings, woodcuts and plaster casts, including the models and the moulds of the sculptures in the park.

★**Holmenkollen** – *About 10km north-west of the town centre. From Vigelandsparken, turn left onto Sørkedalsveien, then right onto Holmenkollveien which you follow all the way up to the ski jump and ski museum.*
There has been a ski jump on this hill overlooking Oslofjord since 1892 but the name of Holmenkollen acquired world fame when the Winter Olympic Games were held there in 1952. Modernised several times, the ski jump continues to be used for international competitions and every year in March it is the venue of the Holmenkollen Ski Festival; one of the most popular events, the Holmenkollen March, a cross-country skiing race in which thousands of skiers take part, has a spectacular finish at the foot of the ski jump. From the top of the ski jump tower there is a superb **view** of Oslo and the fjord.
The **Skimuseet** ⊘ shows the development of skis from prehistoric times; the collections also include clothing and equipment, in particular from the Nansen and Amundsen polar expeditions, and an old workshop showing the traditional way of making skis.

Continue along Holmenkollveien, turn left onto Voksenkollveien, then right onto Tryvannsveien where there is a car park.

Tryvannstårnet ⊘ – *Express lift.* From the observation room at the top of the television tower, 588m above sea level, the **view** extends to the Swedish border and over the whole of the Oslofjord.

Damstredet (CDX 13) – An old-world atmosphere pervades this quaint district, once a residential suburb, where the 19C wooden houses have been tastefully restored and are now mostly occupied by artists.

Continue down the street and turn right onto Møllerveien.

There are pleasant walks along the banks of the River **Akerselva**, right down to the town centre.

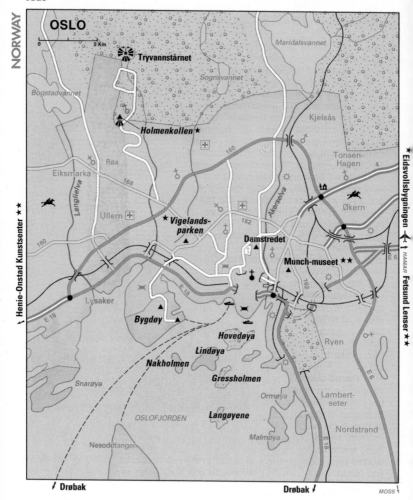

EXCURSIONS

Oslofjord offers various boat trips to the islands and the peninsula of Nesodtrangen or leisurely drives along its shores.

The west bank of Oslofjord

★★ Henie-Onstad Kunstsenter ⊘ – *At Høvikodden, 12km south-west. Leave by E 18* (AY) *to the west.* This modern art centre is beautifully situated on the wooded west shore of the fjord. It was inaugurated in 1968 to house a gift of 300 works of art from the Norwegian ice dancer Sonja Henie (1912-69) and her shipowner husband Niels Onstad. Since then the collection has increased considerably and now represents Norway's largest collection of international modern art. Changing exhibitions throughout the year enable the centre to display the works in rotation. The main trends of the 20C are well represented: Cubism with Braque, Juan Gris and Picasso, Surrealism with Miró and Ernst, the CoBrA Group with several works of its founder Asger Jorn and of Karel Appel, as well as the different movements of abstract painting. The trophies and medals won by Sonja Henie are exhibited in a special room. In keeping with the wishes of the founders, the art centre offers a lively programme of various cultural activities in the fields of music, dance, theatre, cinema, and poetry.

Asker Museum ⊘ – *Continue along E 18 to Holmen and turn right to Hvalstad, then follow signs to the museum.* The museum comprises art collectors Otto and Tilla Valstad's bequest to Asker municipality, including their home and several buildings which they had moved and rebuilt on their property to preserve them (a *stabbur* or traditional storehouse, three houses, a smithy and a small chapel); a gallery was specially erected to house the paintings and drawings collected by the couple together with the works of Otto, who was also an artist. Other artists settled in this secluded area which, at one time was known as the artists' valley.

Round trip north-east of Oslo *About 175km – allow one day*

Leave Oslo north along E 6 towards Gardermoen Airport and Hamar, exit at Råholt and continue to Eidsvoll Verk, then follow signs for Eidsvollbygningen.

★ **Eidsvollbygningen** ⊘ – The so-called Eidsvoll Building was the home of Carsten Ankers, a much-travelled and successful industrialist who bought Eidsvoll Verk (steel works), had the original house extended and lived in it from 1811 to 1823. The house became part of the Norwegians' national heritage in 1814 when they decided to have their own constitution following the Treaty of Kiel according to which Denmark ceded Norway to Sweden. Negotiations went on between Christian Frederik, the heir to the Danish throne, who was sympathetic to their cause, and a handful of influential patriots. The constitution was written and signed on 17 May (now Norway's National Day) by a National Assembly of 112 members who met in the ballroom, where the wooden benches they used are still in place. Christian Frederik's apartments have been furnished and decorated as they were at the time. The owner's own quarters are also included in the visit. The house became public property in 1837, was turned into a museum in 1914 and restored in 1964. *Café and shop in a separate building on the side of the house.*

Rejoin E 6 and drive north to Minnesund then turn left on road 33 towards Gjøvik; after 3km, turn right when you see the sign "Smaragd-Gruvene, Byrud Gård".

Byrud Gård ⊘ – The farmland stretches along the wooded banks of Lake Mjøsa. It is owned by a young couple who make their visitors very welcome *(parking opposite the farmhouse)*. The *stabbur* (storehouse) contains a collection of minerals from all over Norway as well as handicraft which can be bought. The former emerald mines are located on the shores of the lake about 2km from the farm through attractive woodland *(parking halfway)*. It is possible to go into the disused mines and observe the different layers of rock going back several million years. Over a distance of 100m, the shores of Lake Mjøsa are covered with loose stones discarded when the mines were being worked; it is still possible to find emerald chips in the rubble but what visitors appreciate most of all is the peaceful environment, the beautiful view of the lake and its surroundings, the lovely walk along the forest track and the warm hospitality of the hosts.

Return to Minnesund and follow road 177 south along the east bank of the River Vorma.

The road twists its way through rolling countryside, unspoilt and densely forested in parts yet not wild, with colourful hamlets scattered around. The brightly painted houses with their white-wooden balconies and front awnings are characteristic of the rural architecture of southern Norway.

At Vormsund, turn left on road 2 before the bridge over the Vorma and drive for about 2km. Nes Kirkeruiner is signposted on the right.

Nes Kirkeruiner – The ruins are those of a church built in c 1100 with stone from the Mjøsa area *(free access)*. The church burnt down in 1567, was re-erected and extended only to be struck by lightning in 1854. It was never rebuilt after that but the stonework was restored in 1958 after a long period of neglect and is now the venue of concerts and festivals. The site, which is freely accessible all year round, is magnificent: the park surrounding the church lies on high ground overlooking the confluence of the Vorma from Grudsbrandalen and the Glomma from Østerdalen, two of Norway's mightiest rivers. Picnic tables are available to visitors who wish to enjoy the **beautiful view★★**.

Go back on road 2, cross the bridge and turn left on road 177 towards Arnes, then right before the bridge onto road 173 which follows the west bank of the Glomma; at Sørumsand, the road crosses the river; follow road 172 south and cross the river again on reaching Fetsund. Just beyond the bridge, follow signs to Fetsund Lenser.

★★ **Fetsund Lenser** ⊘ – This unusual open-air museum was set up for the preservation of a timber boom used to collect and sort out timber floated down the River Glomma until it finally ceased operating in 1985. The museum includes 2.5km of floating paths, a forge, an exhibition showing a model of the site with logs chained together to contain others, tools used by workers to handle floating logs, steer them or untangle them, individual stamps belonging to timber owners, which also indicated where the timber was to be sent. There is also a brand new **Nature Information Centre** linked to the museum by a nature trail on land and on water. The small rustic **cafeteria** serves delicious tiny sandwiches made with brown bread, cucumber and a local white fish (smoked) and pike. Down river, within a short distance of Fetsund Lenser, the Glomma flows into Lake Øyeren through the largest inland estuary in Norway.

Continue north-west along road 22 to Lillestrøm then turn left on road 159 which joins the E 6 leading back to Oslo.

Timber floating on the Glomma

The practice of timber floating, going back to medieval times, increased considerably from the 16C onwards when timber export (particularly to England and Holland) flourished. Forest owners then felt a need to organise a joint transport system. Places like Fetsund Lenser acted as cooperatives for forest owners upriver, who marked their timber with their own stamps. Up to 300 workers were employed at Fetsund during the season which lasted from May to September. These men performed a skilled and dangerous task, steering the logs with a kind of hook fixed at the end of a long pole and often untangling huge piles which might give way at any time. At its height, Fetsund Lenser sorted out 14 million logs in one season!

When the river could no longer compete with faster road and rail transport, the whole process finally came to a halt in 1985. In 1989, Fetsund Lenser was declared a protected area and Fetsund Lensemuseum was officially opened in 1990.

Boat trips round Oslofjorden

Inner fjord archipelago – Several islands close to Oslo's harbour are easily accessible by ferry from Vippetangen Brygge just south of Akershus Festning *(frequent service)*. On the nearest island, **Hovedøya**, the romantic ruins of a Cistercian abbey, built by English monks from Kirkstead, stand in delightful landscaped surroundings with attractive bathing spots. The ferries call at several other islands, **Lindøya**, **Nakholmen** and **Gressholmen**, all fairly close to one another, but also at **Langøyene**, further south, which has good beaches.

Fjord cruises ⊙ – More or less extensive sightseeing tours of the fjord depart several times a day in summer from Rådhusbrygge 3, in front of the town hall. There is a 50min tour of the harbour with close-up views of Akershus Festning and some of the nearest islands. Or there is a 2hr trip further south along the fjord, between the islands off the west coast. There is also a choice of evening cruises.

Drøbak (AY) – *By express boat from Aker Brygge or by road along the east shore of the fjord, via road E 18/E 6 then right at Horgen and follow road 153 (40km).* This lively old market town has retained some charming wooden houses mostly from the 19C. At the beginning of the 20C, several artists, including Christian Krohg (1852-1925) and Frits Thaulow, used to work there in summer; since then, Drøbak has had a regular inflow of artists which account for the numerous art galleries and handicraft workshops. Among them, right in the town centre, **Tregaardens Julehus** ⊙ (Christmas House) sells every kind of Christmas decorations and traditional characters you can imagine in a red and green fairy-tale setting. The white wooden church dating from 1776, has an interesting Baroque interior.

★ **Follo Museum** ⊙ – *Turn right off 153 just as the road begins to twist down to the town and follow signs to the museum (800m from main road).* This open-air museum, opened in 1968, is located in a lovely wooded unspoilt setting; it includes the Korsegården coaching inn dating from the 1730s, a farmhouse from 1812, a cottager's home from around 1700, and a school house from 1869. Concerts and various activities take place during the season. The museum is also responsible for preserving the coastal culture of Akershus county and has acquired several boats of historical interest.

Monet in Norway

In 1895 when Monet was 55 he spent three months in Norway, where he was frustrated in his attempts to capture the magical effects of the snow.

In the artist's own words "it is impossible to see finer (light) effects elsewhere; the effects of the snow are absolutely unbelievable but incredibly difficult to capture".

Irascible and impatient as ever, anxious and depressive, annoyed by too many visitors, impatient with the passing time and changing seasons, continually dissatisfied with his work, Monet nevertheless managed to complete 28 canvases during his stay, including *Houses in the Snow*, *The Fjord at Christiana* and *Mount Kolsaas*.

Oscarsborg Festning – The fort stands on an island in Drøbaksundet, just where the Oslofjord widens before reaching Oslo. This strategic position brought sudden fame to the fortress in April 1940, when the German battleship *Blücher* was sunk by the fort's cannon and torpedo battery, thus allowing the royal family and the Norwegian government time to leave Oslo. Fifty years later to the day, Norway invited men from both sides, who took part in the battle, to meet for the first time on friendly terms.

POLARSIRKELEN
ARCTIC CIRCLE – Nordland
Michelin map 985 F 10-12 or Atlas Europe p 107

The Arctic Circle is the parallel of latitude 66o 33' north. This imaginary line crosses the Norwegian territory just north of Mo i Rana, an area of glaciers and barren plateaux; north of it are the Arctic regions and their fascinating specificity explains the magical appeal which the Arctic Circle exerts on most people.

In Norway there are basically two ways of crossing the Arctic Circle. The first is near the coast, when following road 17 between Steinkjer and Bodø; the Arctic Circle is crossed aboard the ferry linking Kilboghamn and Jektevik; the scenery is beautiful but the event passes almost unnoticed as the captain merely announces on the loudspeakers "we are now crossing the Arctic Circle". The second and by far the most dramatic way is inland, along the International E 6 road linking Oslo to the North Cape. The **Arctic Circle Centre** ⊘ is situated by the roadside, on the desolate Saltfjellet plateau, 650m above sea level, with wide open views over vast expanses of snow and rock. Monuments on either side of the round building, which looks like an igloo, mark the imaginary line. In summer the area surrounding the centre is partly free of snow and ice and on the patches of barren earth people from all over the world erect tiny stone mounds, no doubt making a wish as they leave these fragile mementoes of their visit; some even write their name and country on bits of paper which are carried away by the wind whereas the anonymous stone mounds last a little longer before crumbling down to be erected again by other passers-by. Inside the centre, it is warm and cosy: there is a souvenir shop, a cafeteria, exhibitions of north Norwegian art and industry and of stuffed animals living in Arctic regions including Europe's largest polar bear, a video show entitled *Nord Norge* (North Norway) and a post office to ensure that postcards sent round the world bear the Arctic Circle stamp! Outside the building there is a memorial to Russian and Yugoslav prisoners captured during the Second World War.

LAND OF THE ARCTIC CIRCLE

The Arctic climate and the presence of the Saltfjellet mountain range have a significant combined effect on the region around the Arctic Circle and act as a barrier to some species of flora and fauna: elms and ash trees for instance do not grow north of the Arctic Circle and are replaced by conifers and birch trees. In the same way, snakes are not to be found north of Saltfjellet, although other animal species commonly found in temperate climates are plentiful north of the Arctic Circle, in particular, foxes, beavers, royal eagles and dolphins.

Most of the area around the Arctic Circle forms the Saltfjellet/Svartisen National Park, a region of natural unspoilt and wild beauty which can be best explored using the nearby town of **Mo i Rana** as a base. The drive from the Arctic Circle Centre to Mo i Rana over a distance of 80km through the Dunderlandsdal Valley is extremely picturesque as the scenery changes from barren rocks and snow to green alpine landscapes with a mountain stream gradually getting wider and cattle grazing on grass covered slopes topped with dark fir trees.

★**Svartisen** – *32km north of Mo i Rana. Drive north on E 6 to Røssvoll and turn left following the signs; a 20min boat trip will take you across Lake Svartisvatn, then a 3km-long trail will lead you to Østerdalsisen glacier, which forms part of Svartisen.* Svartisen is Norway's second largest ice-covered area (370km²), divided into 60 different glaciers, the most famous being Østerdalsisen. In spite of heavy and regular snowfalls on the plateau, the glacier is still receding, revealing a fascinating landscape. The view of this huge mass of ice slowly disintegrating into tiny icebergs which drift imperceptibly on Lake Østerdalsvatnet is highly impressive.

Grønligrotta – *20km north of Mo i Rama. Follow the same directions as above; however you will reach the cave 10km after turning left (guided tours every hour between 10am and 7pm from mid-June; café and accommodation available; the area is ideal for hiking enthusiasts).* Grønligrotta is a natural limestone cave with a huge chamber, narrow passages and an underground river rushing through it as well as stalactites and stalagmites. Another similar cave nearby, **Setergrotta**, is recommended for the more adventurous.

RV 17★★★

Road 17, which runs on land and sea along the coast of Helgeland from Steinkjer in the south to Bodø in the north, offers an exhilarating journey from Høylandet onwards, through strange and captivating landscapes, and a most rewarding encounter with an authentic Norwegian coastal area. There are 460km of totally unspoilt nature and spectacular scenery in which the basic elements of sea, rock and sky are constantly recomposed like the changing patterns of a kaleidoscope. Stretches of twisting road, hugging the contours of the land and linked by six ferries and many bridges, make their way between sea and sky and, most of the time, the view extends across vast barren expanses to craggy peaks in the distance.

Helgeland has an extraordinary coastline, deeply indented and low-lying, with mountains on one side and thousands of islands of all shapes and sizes on the other. This wide belt of islands and skerries was probably formed by the pounding of the waves combined with severe frost which caused the rocks to split and break up during successive ice ages. The numerous fjords and sounds, often very narrow and going in all directions, are sometimes spanned by graceful bridges which are real works of art, but the most familiar sight is without question the ferry: it is an integral part of the scenery, faithfully fulfilling the essential task of linking with each other and with the mainland several hundred inhabited islands.

The area has been populated since prehistoric times and the austere and strange beauty of the landscape undoubtedly played on people's imagination since landmarks such as Torghatten rock island and the Seven Sisters mountain peaks have a prominent place in the fantastic world of the Nordic sagas. Today, the population of the Helgeland coastline is divided into small communities whose life is regulated by ferry timetables. There are no real towns along the coast, the largest municipality being Sandnessjøen with 7 500 inhabitants. However, without being luxurious, accommodation is plentiful and there are hotels of moderate size, guesthouses, inns, motels and camp sites all the way; the choice is greater though in Brønnøysund and Sandnessjøen, closely followed by Glomfjord, Ørnes, Nesna, Lovund, Sleneset and Saltstraumen. The opportunities for discovering the area's unique natural environment are numerous, from walking, climbing and cycling round the islands to going deep-sea fishing, diving etc.

The road surface is generally good and there are ample picnic areas. Ferries are punctual and synchronised and the journey should be planned taking timetables into consideration to avoid long delays at crossing points. There are altogether six ferry crossings between Høylandet and Bodø. It is just possible to do the whole journey in two days, but four days or more will allow time for excursions and trips to the islands.

FROM HØYLANDET TO BRØNNØYSUND

147km and a 20min ferry crossing – allow 1 day. Driving north along E 6 from Trondheim, turn left on road 775, 6km beyond Grong then right at Høylandet where you join road 17.

Foldereid – Approximately 10km before reaching Foldereid, the road becomes very picturesque as it follows the south bank of the narrow fjord lined with steep walls of sheer rock on both sides. At Foldereid, there is a tidal current abounding in fish, known as Kollstraumen.

Holm-Vennesund: ferry crossing 20min – approximately every hour.

Vik – The fascinating coast road starts at Vennesund where the landscape changes dramatically and as far as the eye can see it becomes a confusion of islands, some barely rising above the sea, others outlining their strange shape against the changing sky, some consisting only of bare rock, uncannily smooth and rounded like the back of some aquatic monster, others covered with a meagre vegetation of small trees, bushes, moss and short grass. In Vik, the local museum, **Sømna Bygdetun** ⊘, illustrates fishing traditions in south Helgeland.

Brønnøysund – The small harbour is particularly lively when the Coastal Steamer arrives late in the afternoon. At the local cinema, a slide show provides a good introduction to the area *(details from the tourist office).*

An elegant bridge spanning Brønnøysound leads, 15km further on, to the foot of **Torghatten**, a 256m-high rock in the shape of a hat, with a hole right through the middle. An ancient legend tells how, one night, Hestmannen, the son of a powerful king, was chasing Lekamøyen, a young girl from Leka, and fearing she might escape him, shot an arrow in her direction; but the king of Sømna, who was watching, threw his hat in the path of the arrow and saved the girl. The arrow pierced the hat and at that moment the sun rose and everything was petrified.

The real explanation is much less poetic: the hole is in fact due to the erosion of the sea when its level was much higher at the end of the last Ice Age.

A footpath leads to the hole *(20min)* which is 35m high, 20m wide and 160m long.

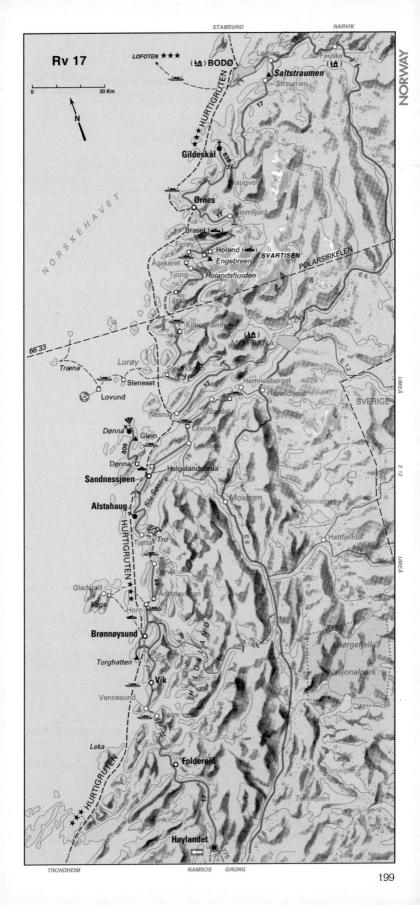

Various boat trips are organised from Brønnøysund to the archipelago just off the coast and to the island of **Vega** *(express boat from Brønnøysund or regular ferry from Horn)* which has been inhabited for 10 000 years and where traces of Stone Age dwellings have been found; there is an easy to follow marked trail with information panels *(3km)*. There are also interesting possibilities for bird-watchers on the moors.

FROM BRØNNØYSUND TO SANDNESS

64km and 2 ferry crossings – allow half a day

Brønnøysund to Forvik – A continuous screen of islands in the distance blocks the view to the open sea. Between the islands and the coast, there are peaceful enclosed bays and picturesque coves, almost dry at low tide. From time to time, cultivated patches break up the wilderness as do a few isolated farmhouses and picturesque villages with their whitewashed wooden churches.

Horn-Andalsvågen: ferry crossing 15min – approximately every 1hr 30min.
Forvik-Tjøtta: ferry crossing 60min – approximately every 2hr.

Among ancient rock carvings on the island of **Tro** *(ferry from Forvik or Tjøtta)*, is the famous skier who was chosen as the emblem of the Lillehammer Winter Olympic Games in 1994.

Alstahaug Kirke – *19km north of Tjøtta.* Built in the 12C, the church was considerably extended in the 19C. **Peter Dass**, who was vicar at Alstahaug in the late 17C, wrote *Nordlands Trompet*, a vibrant poem in which he described the region and the hard life of the local people. The **vicarage** in which he lived is now a museum dedicated to his memory.

Between Alstahaug and Sandnessjøen, the deep blue outline of the mountain range known as the Seven Sisters, **Sju Søstre**, forms an impressive barrier on the horizon. The highest peak culminates at 1 072m and all seven of them can be climbed without special equipment *(marked paths)*.

Sandnessjøen – Port of call of the Coastal Steamer, Sandnessjøen is a good base for excursions *(bicycle hire)*, in particular to the island of **Dønna** *(30min crossing)*. From the ferry port a road leads to the north of the island; at **Glein** there is an ancient fertility symbol, a marble phallus, dating from AD 400-600; it stands on a huge burial mound of the same period. At the extremity of the island stands **Dønnes Kirke**, near Dønnes Manor, on a site occupied since Viking times; the oldest part of the church goes back to the 11C. From the top of **Dønnesfjell**, which can be reached by car, there is a superb **view** of the coast of Helgeland, the islands and the mountains.

FROM SANDNESSJØEN TO ØRNES

210km and 3 ferry crossings – allow 1 day

A 1 065m-long bridge, **Helgelandsbrua**, links Sandnessjøen to the mainland. The road skirts the Leirfjord then turns north at Leirosen. The mountainous area between Leirosen and Bardal to the north-east is ideal for leisurely walking.

Låvong-Nesna: ferry crossing 30min – every 1 or 2hr.

Sleneset and Lovund – At Stokkvågen ferries leave for Sleneset where it is possible to rent a *rorbu* (fisherman's cabin) and to go sailing on a *fembøring* (large traditional boat).
The ferry goes on to Lovund, where 200 000 puffins nest in the spring and spend the summer months raising their young. It is also possible to visit an oyster farm, and to see the remnants of a Stone Age settlement.
From Stokkvågen, you can also go as far out to sea as the archipelago of **Træna**, level with the Arctic Circle, inhabited since prehistoric times; it comprises 1 300 islands and skerries and has a population of only 500.

Kilboghamn-Jektvik: ferry crossing 60min – 5 crossings daily.
Ågskaret-Forøy: ferry crossing 10min – every 1 or 2hr.

Svartisen – After Forøy, the road follows the northern shore of **Holandsfjord**; from **Braset** *(9km from Forøy)*, it is possible to see the **Engebreen**, a branch of the Svartisen glacier, which comes right down to the fjord, only 20m from the water. Small boats take passengers from Braset to the glacier *(15min)*.
From the head of Holandsfjord, a 7.6km-long tunnel leads to Glomfjord and road 17 carries on along the coast to the picturesque village of **Ørnes**.

FROM ØRNES TO BODØ

125km – allow half a day. 38km north of Ørnes, at Skaugvoll, take road 838 on the left and drive for about 9km.

Gildeskål Kirke – The name suggests that the site was used in pre-Christian times for the practice of a pagan cult. The church was built in c 1130 by the brother of a Crusader and extended in the 18C.

Saltstraumen – This impressive maelstrom is caused by the strongest tidal current in Norway: 400 million m³ of water rush through a narrow sound less than 150m wide at a speed which can reach 28 knots; every 6hr the current is reversed *(parking beyond the bridge)*.

Bodø – Principal town of the county of Nordland, Bodø was founded at the beginning of the 19C but was destroyed in 1940. Today it is a modern commercial centre with a busy harbour and a regular service to the Lofoten Islands across the vast Vestfjorden.

Paris-North Cape Auto-Photo Rally
Every summer in the month of August since 1988 almost 200 competitors head for adventure on the roads and tracks of Scandinavia. The Paris-North Cape Rally is not based on speed, although there are checkpoints, but on each team producing a written report, photographs or video footage on selected themes. To add to the excitement there are several sporting activities (mountain biking expedition, orienteering race, rafting, a mountain climb, downhill skiing) along the 12 000km route. The rally is open to everyone with a vehicle. There are no age limits but endurance and a good spirit of adventure are essential!
To follow the rally day by day Internet www.Infinit.net/Raid

RØROS★★
Sør-Trøndelag
Population 4 000
Michelin map 985 J 8 or Atlas Europe p 111

Røros is a former copper mining town tucked away in the mountains of eastern Norway, 150km south-east of Trondheim and close to the Swedish border. The town and its immediate surroundings form such an authentic and well-preserved cultural environment that, in 1984, it was officially entered on UNESCO's World Heritage list.
Røros lies at the heart of a mountainous region with open varied landscapes of pine and birch forests, bogs, streams, rivers and a great many lakes. The continental climate ensures a low humidity level, hot summers and very cold winters, the coldest in the whole of Norway. When the mines closed down, Røros turned its activities to the other raw material which is plentiful in the area, wood, and to the preservation of its cultural heritage. Today the town can look forward to an expanding tourist trade not only based on its mining history but also on a wide choice of excursions, guided tours to Sami reindeer herds as well as outdoor summer and winter activities such as angling, canoeing, skiing and dog-sledging.

K. Pesjak/PRESSENS BILD

Røros

HISTORICAL NOTES

In spite of its remoteness, the Røros region has been inhabited since the Stone Age as lakes, rivers and forests were rich hunting grounds for prehistoric men. In medieval times, pilgrims on their way from Sweden to the famous Nidarosdomen in Trondheim went through Røros which, by then, was at the centre of an agricultural area inhabited by dairy and sheep farmers and probably by nomadic Sami.

The copper town – Copper ore was discovered in 1644 by a local farmer, Hans Olsen Aasen, whose farm was situated west of the church. Two years later, the Copper Works, established on the banks of the River Hyttelva, were granted a royal charter by Christian IV; this gave them exclusive rights to all mining activities in the area within a 40km radius of the original mine situated just a few kilometres north-east of Røros. These activities demanded an extensive use of wood inside the mines and at the smelting works and deforestation began on a large scale. Huge logs were floated down rivers and across lakes and a canal system was set up in the 18C linking Lake Femund and Lake Feragen. The charter also stipulated that local farmers had to work for the copper company in addition to their farming activities. At the same time, immigrants from nearby communities, attracted by the possibility of finding work, settled in Røros and mining experts were called in from Germany. The town developed rapidly and the imposing church built at the end of the 18C testifies to its prosperity. Unlike other wooden towns, Røros was spared destruction by fire and has survived almost intact until today. The Copper Works finally closed down in 1977 after 333 years.

Summer farming – Many people, whose main farm was in the valley or in Røros itself, practised summer farming on high land close to the town. They used the land as summer pastures and for growing hay stored for winter use. It gradually became the custom for farmers to spend some months up on their summer farms and they built cottages for themselves as well as barns to store their hay and byres for their cattle. Today this practice has almost disappeared but some areas, like Småsetran, on the outskirts of the town, still retain their special character.

RØROS KIRKE ⊙

The church dominates the whole town not only because of its position high up on the hillside at the top of Kjerkgata, but also because it is by far the tallest and most imposing building in Røros, a constant reminder of the economic wealth derived from over 300 years of copper mining. The first wooden church built in 1650 only lasted 130 years as it was found to be too small. The present stone-built church was completed in 1784 after only five years. There is a striking contrast between its whitewashed outline and the dark brown and red wooden houses around. The clock at the top of the tall square tower is surmounted by the mining company's emblem. The Late Baroque interior is reminiscent of that of the church in Kongsberg, a silver mining town in southern Norway. The pulpit stands over the altar and the organ right above it. There are seats for 1 600 people at ground level and up in the galleries with separate boxes for the rich and a royal box. The flags displayed inside the church represent the mining company's private army with an appropriate colour scheme, blue for the miners working underground and cream for those working above ground. The church is furthermore decorated with portraits of famous company directors, preachers and other prominent personalities.

SMELTHYTTA ⊙ (THE SMELTING WORKS)

Near the church on **Malmplassen**, the vast open yard where load after load of copper ore used to arrive and be weighed on a wooden weighbridge before being processed. Smelthytta is a replica of the original building, dating from 1888, which was destroyed by fire. When the copper works closed down in 1977, the Norwegian government bought the land and the buildings to turn them into a museum illustrating mining and smelting techniques with the help of beautiful handmade models.

Nearby is the bell, **Hyttklokka**, which used to sound the beginning and the end of each shift at the smelting works.

The slag heaps, **slegghaugan**, occupy a large area on the other side of the River Hyttelva, their austere sombre mass now part of the Røros landscape. At the foot of the slag heaps there is a short street called **Sleggveien**, lined with small timber cottages where poor workers and craftsmen used to live without as much as a patch of grass or a yard. Five of the buildings along the street, which date from the early 19C, are now owned by the Røros Museum.

The area immediately surrounding the smelting works is relatively barren as smoke from the furnaces destroyed all vegetation.

BERGSTADEN

The old town known as **Bergstaden** lies below the church and the smelting works; it is an extensive ensemble of unique wooden houses built with thick logs and sometimes clad with weather boarding. Traditional red and ochre are still the dominant colours and the whole housing area has retained its remarkable unity. The two main streets, **Kjerkgata** and **Bergmannsgata**, stretch from the main Oslo road uphill to the church and the smelting works. Kjerkgata is lined with a variety of craftshops selling silverware, glassware, ceramics etc whereas Bergmannsgata is more residential. The large houses situated at the bottom of the hill, furthest from the smelting works, were built for the mine's directors and the town's dignitaries, whereas the humble grass-roofed cottages surrounding the works were lived in by miners and labourers employed at the smelting works. The River Hyttelva, which is more of a mountain stream than a river, rushes through the town, past the copper works and down to the Printing Press Museum, **Pressemuseet** ⊙, housed in the building formerly occupied by the newspaper *Fjell-Ljom*; it illustrates obsolete printing methods with the help of machinery left behind by the newspaper and various equipment from other regions.

EXCURSIONS

Småsetran and Olavsgruva (the Olav Mine) – *13km north-east. Leave Røros on road 31 towards the Swedish border.*
As the road skirts the slag heaps on the left, it is close to the Småsetran on the right, a delightful summer farm area with overgrown meadows, lanes lined with trees and stone walls and wooden farm cottages now used as summer residences.

The Olav Mine is situated further along the same road.

The **Olavsgruva** ⊘ consists of two adjacent mines, Nyberget Mine, one of the oldest in the area and Crownprince Olav's Mine, one of the last ones to be worked. Part of the mine was restored and opened to the public in 1979 and the museum situated at the entrance was inaugurated two years later.
Extensive guided tours take visitors through the two mines and along the way special effects give a vivid account of life and work inside the mines until they were closed down, including the different methods of extracting the ore by fire, compressed air-drilling or explosion. Among the interesting exhibits there is a mining-dog, a buggy used to carry the ore, miners' lamps and special wooden seats used by the miners during their breaks. The visit ends 50m below ground in a large hall called Bergmannshallen (miners' hall) where concerts and theatre performances are held.

Kvitsanden and Skårhammardalen Canyon – *3km west.*
Kvitsanden is an area of drift sand formed at the end of the last Ice Age when the glaciers melted and rivers carried large amounts of sand and gravel. The area is partly barren and partly covered with pine trees, heather and bushes. This landscape, so unusual in a mountainous region, is now protected by law.

Continue past Kvitsanden and turn left towards Os.

The road following the west bank of the River Glåma leads to a wild canyon 1.2km long and 30m deep with very steep sides, which was probably dug by a river formed during the melting of the ice at the end of the Ice Age. Strolling along the path running the whole length of the canyon, one can sense the peaceful atmosphere which pervades this secluded area.

Ålen – *36km north. Leave Røros on road 30.*
Situated in the village, the Norwegian gallery of Nature Photography, **Norsk Naturfotogalleri**, houses a permanent exhibition of prize-winning photographs and temporary exhibitions of works by well-known Norwegian nature photographers. Several slide presentations are also organised.
Outside the village there is an open-air farm museum, **Bygdemuseum**.

Narjordet – *25km south.*
In this village, there is a splendid old farmhouse, **Oddentunet**, which has been preserved in its original state with its unusual decorations both outside and inside.
Nearby, a path leads from the main road to an old watermill in working order.

Lake Aursunden – *Round tour of 92km – allow half a day. Leave Røros on the northbound road 30, then bear right towards Glåmos, keeping to the right of the railway line; turn right again and follow the north shore of Lake Aursunden.*
Pastures and meadows alternate with birch forest and bogs with a rich flora including some rare species as well as an interesting and varied fauna with such large animals as roe-deer and elks which can be seen grazing on farmland particularly in the evening. Three areas on the northern shore of the lake have been established as nature reserves.
Protected since 1983, the **Molinga Naturreservat**, at the western end of the lake, is an area of marshland particularly rich in wildlife. It is the nesting place of several species of duck including mergansers and of various wading birds such as cranes, as well as reed buntings, arctic terns etc. The reserve is also a sanctuary for migrating birds who use it as a resting place, while they wait for the snow to melt in their nesting areas.
A little further east, the Sakrisodden flora preservation area, **Sakrisodden Plantefredningsområde**, was established in 1981 as a sanctuary for a very rare plant, the Siberian aster, which blooms from mid-July to mid-August.
At the eastern end of the lake, the **Sølendet Naturreservat** is a mixed area of birch forests and bogs particularly rich in plant life, including many kinds of orchids.

Lake Femund – *34km south-east to Sørvika.*
During the summer season, there is a regular boat service on Norway's third largest lake, between Sørvika in the north and Femundsenden in the south, with several stops along the way. Situated between the eastern shore of the lake and the Swedish border, the **Femundsmarka Landscape Protection area** and the **Femundsmarka**

National Park (Nasjonalpark) cover a vast remote region, wild and uninhabited except for nomadic Sami, with pine forests, many lakes and streams, a real paradise for anglers and nature lovers. The park is accessible by road from the southern end of Lake Femund *(109km from Røros to Femund then 37km to Elgå on the eastern shore of the lake; from Elgå a minor road leads to the mountain lodge Svukuriset 10km to the north).* The lodge is a good starting point for walks and fishing trips in the Femundsmarka National Park.

SETESDAL★★
Aust-Agder
Michelin map 985 MN 4 or Atlas Europe p 116

Setesdal is the name of the long and deep valley of the River Otra cutting through high mountain plateaux on its way south to the Skagerrak into which it flows at Kristiansand. Streams rushing down the steep mountainsides become waterfalls whereas the river, tumultuous in its upper course, suddenly widens into a succession of narrow lakes (called fjords) swollen by melting snow in late spring. Road 9 follows the east and west banks alternately, affording lovely views along the way, going through small villages and past scattered farms which offer many examples of traditional rural architecture such as log houses and *stabbur*, the name given to the typical raised store-houses found in southern Norway. Setesdal is also one of the most colourful and interesting regions to visit because of its particularly rich folklore which includes beautifully embroidered and decorated costumes *(bunad)*, violin playing, folk dancing and handicrafts, especially wood-carving and jewellery-making.

Valle – Set against a splendid background of steep mountains, Valle is the main centre of the upper Setesdal Valley. There are various craftshops including several jewellers. The Setesdal Museum, **Setesdalmuseet** is a cultural regional museum which holds various exhibitions illustrating Setesdal's traditions. Also part of the museum is a well-preserved old farm, **Tveitentunet**, which comprises several old buildings from the 16C and later. Another farm, 12km north of Valle at Rygne-stad, is an open-air section of the Setesdal Museum, illustrating daily life on a farm through the ages; among the interesting old buildings, there is a 500-year-old storehouse, **Rygnestadloftet**.

FROM VALLE TO KRISTIANSAND
150km along road 9 – allow half a day

From the upper Setesdal Valley almost down to the sea, the scenic road offers constantly changing landscapes set against a background of omnipresent mountains. Just outside Valle, Hallandsfossen is one of the many waterfalls along the way. A few kilometres further on, a new road from Brokke to Suleskar in the upper Sirdal Valley has shortened the journey from Oslo to Stavanger by 100km.

Ph. Roy/EXPLORER

Stabbur

Hylestad and Helle – Those two villages close to each other are well known for their fine silver jewellery and for their technique of filigree work which has been passed on from generation to generation. **Hylestad Kirke**, dating from 1838, is one of several octagonal churches in Setesdal built during the first half of the 19C.

Byglandsfjord – Just beyond Ose, the River Otra widens to form the first of two successive lakes, **Araksfjord**. The road runs along the west bank, affording beautiful views at Frøysnes, and then crosses over to the east bank at Storstraumen, where the lock has recently been restored and where the long and tortuous Byglandsfjord begins. The fjord's silvery water shimmering in the sun offers a striking contrast with the dark mountains casting their shadow over it.

Grendi Church – This octagonal wooden building typical of the region dates from 1827. There is a runic stone in the churchyard.

Evje – This is the main commercial centre of the lower Setesdal Valley. The area is rich in rare minerals and the **Setesdal Mineralpark** ⊘, situated at Auesneset, 5km south of Evje, is an impressive exhibition centre set into the rock which provides a very appropriate setting for the collections of minerals from the area and from other parts of the world. There is also a marked mineral path which leads to several mines in the area *(details from the tourist office in Evje)*.

At **Hornnes** and **Hægeland**, there are two more octagonal wooden churches dating respectively from 1828 and 1830.

SIGDAL ★★

Buskerud

Michelin map 985 LM 6 or Atlas Europe p 116

The Norwegians call it **Kunstnerdalen**, the Valley of Artists, because many well-known and much-travelled painters such as Munch, Thaulow, Krohg, Kittelsen, Skredsvig, Tidemand and Gude, whose works now hang in the National Gallery in Oslo, discovered the valley of the River Simoa in the late 19C and early 20C and were inspired by its peaceful rural landscapes. Their vivid imagination was triggered by the wild scenery which becomes steeped in mystery when mist spreads its thick mantle over the dense forests reflecting in the still waters of Lake Soneren. Two of these artists, Theodor Kittelsen and Christian Skredsvig settled in the valley and a visit to their homes helps to explain the fascination of this still unspoilt region so close to the capital. For this is indeed the main attraction of the area where traditional rural activities have created a rich folk culture praised by the artists who made Sigdal their home and now preserved by the local museums.

Road 287 starts from Åmot *(75km west of Oslo via Drammen and Hokksund)* and follows the River Simoa right through the Sigdal region (Sigdal is derived from the old Norwegian form of the name Simoa) then winds its way past the Norefjell mountains before veering north towards Bromma where it joins the more familiar Hallingdal route from Oslo to the fjords. This itinerary offers an insight into an authentic aspect of Norwegian rural culture and traditions, with many interesting things to see and do on the way and a wide choice of unassuming but comfortable country inns should you feel like spending a night or two in the area or tasting the tantalising specialities of the local cuisine.

From Åmot follow road 287 for 4km to Blaafarveværket.

★★ **Blaafarveværket** ⊘ – This former industrial complex built near the cobalt mines which were worked from the end of the 18C until the end of the 19C narrowly escaped destruction in 1968. Since then, a private foundation has gradually restored various buildings spread over a distance of 8km and turned them into a fascinating cultural museum, concerned with the technical and social history of cobalt mining and with the century-old artistic connections of Blaafarvevæeket.

Glasshytten (Glassworks) was the main factory turning crushed cobalt into blue pigment, a complex process which is explained in detail; at its peak in the 1830s, the works produced 80% of the pigment used by all the glass and porcelain manufactures in the world. This meant a workforce of almost 2 000 men and a particularly large community for such a rural area; many different buildings were erected, some of which have been saved, including **workers' lodgings**, a **school**, a **grocery store** and the **technical director's house** (Nyfossum). Nearby is the mighty **Haugfoss waterfall** which powered the crushing of the ore brought down in horse-drawn carts from the **mines** 7km away. Cobalt ore was extracted from open-cast mines as well as underground galleries. One of the by-products of the processing of the ore was arsenic extracted by torrefaction.

The artistic connection goes back to 1883, when the first Open Air Academy for Norwegian artists, based at the house of the building contractor of the works, took place. Among the participants were Edvard Munch and Fritz Thaulow whose painting of Haugfoss Waterfall now hangs in the National Gallery in Oslo.

There is an annual exhibition of Norwegian or Nordic art in a gallery next to the glassworks and a permanent exhibition of Theodor Kittelsen's works at the cobalt mines *(see Theodor Kittelsens Hjem below)*.

There are picnic tables and benches in the park and the Barrelmaker's Inn serves hot and cold meals.

Continue along road 287 to Prestfoss (23km).

★**Prestfoss, Sigdal og Eggedal Museum** ○ – This museum is devoted to local rural culture and history and here also the accent is on authenticity. Part of the museum is a collection of 13 buildings, farmhouses and outbuildings, gathered in a carefully chosen rural setting, which helps to recreate country life in the past. Typical rural activities connected with traditionnal crafts and entertainment for visitors of all ages, including live animals and dancing on the village green, bring life to the museum in summer. The exhibition building, inaugurated in 1978, contains an outstanding collection of national costumes from the 19C onwards and an even more impressive collection of folk music instruments, beautifully inlaid fiddles, lurs (similar to trumpets), Norwegian cithers, mouth harps etc; the detailed explanations are full of anecdotes and recorded extracts of each instrument add a concrete touch to the visit. In addition, visitors are able to try different instruments and small concerts are given daily from 1 July to 15 August. Other interesting exhibits include a horse-drawn sledge (1795) and skins with printed motifs made with tree bark (either birch or alder).

The **Folkemusikksenteret** nearby houses important archives concerning folk music in the county of Buskerud and holds music courses, meetings, concerts, exhibitions throughout the season.

If you happen to travel through during the weekend, you could make an interesting detour from Prestfoss to Krøderen *(15km north-east along a minor road)*, where **Krøderbanen** ⊘ awaits to take you on a 26km journey to Vikersund on the Tyrifjord. The steam engine and its wooden carriages travel on a standard-gauge track which formed part of the main Oslo-to-Bergen line before this section was diverted eastwards to Hönefoss. The railway is run by enthusiastic volunteers who maintain the rolling stock during their spare time. Krøderen station is a splendid example of a 19C railway station comprising a station building and a separate freight building now housing an exhibition on the history of the line with the original ferry connection.

Continue along road 287 which skirts the west bank of Lake Soneren; 8km from Prestfoss there is a car park on the left for visitors to Lauvlia. A signposted path leads to the house.

★**Theodor Kittelsens Hjem, Lauvlia** ⊘ – Theodor Kittelsen moved here, on the shores of Lake Soneren, with his large family in 1899. He decorated the house himself with carvings and painted motifs. The surroundings, in particular Mount Andersnatten rising above Lake Soneren a few kilometres to the north, inspired this poet of nature to paint some of his most famous landscapes in which strange shapes and shadows were turned by his vivid imagination into trolls, animals and fairies. The exhibition of Kittelsen's works in Lauvlia changes every year.

Drive on to Eggedal.

The road climbs further up the valley and the scenery gradually changes as the area becomes more mountainous; the river is now a powerful foaming mountain stream. The wooden rural achitecture seems less elaborate and colourful than in the southern part.
In Eggedal, take a pause at the family run **Eggedal Borgestue**, an authentic country inn decorated with rose-painting (a speciality of southern Norway) and serving traditional Norwegian cuisine. Whitefish and salmon are almost always on the menu; marinated elk and lamb are served with a herb-flavoured cream sauce, chopped apples and cowberries. The main dish might consist of elk stew with mushrooms and vegetables and the meal could end with a very light cloudberry cake.

From Eggedal, follow the minor road towards Tempelseter for 2.5km then turn left along an unsurfaced track and continue for another 1.5km.

★**Christian Skredsvigs Hjem, Hagan** – The house where Christian Skredsvig lived from 1894 until his death in 1924, stands on the heights overlooking the whole valley. It grew from a barn into a family home and was lived in after his death until 1960. The furniture and paintings (his own and those of his friends, an impressive collection of some 150 works) have been left as they were during his lifetime. This much-travelled artist who studied in Copenhagen, Munich and Paris where he won an award at the 1881 salon, found inspiration for his landscapes and animal paintings in the rural scenery of Sigdal, yet, his was a much more realistic style than that of Theodor Kittelsen.

Beyond Eggedal, road 287 skirts the sunny side of the **Norefjell** range, long known for its wonderful Alpine and cross-country skiing, now becoming increasingly popular in summer time: it offers a choice of exciting hikes, cycle tours and horse-riding trips and the area is excellent for fishing and hunting (equipment can be hired); in addition there are a number of convivial inns and hotels up in the mountains.

SOGNEFJORD★★★

Sogn og Fjordane
Michelin map 985 K 2-4 or Atlas Europe p 110

With a total length of 205km, Sognefjord is the longest and one of the most impressive Norwegian fjords. It stretches inland in an east-west direction and spreads its arms to within a short distance of Jotunheimen, Norway's highest mountain range, and Jostedalsbreen, Norway's largest glacier. About halfway, near Høyanger, the fjord reaches its greatest depth, 1 308m. It is quite wide from the coast to Balestrand, affording grand open vistas, but it gets narrower east of Balestrand and some of its arms, such as the Nærøyfjord stretching south to Gudvangen, are very narrow indeed. This inner Sognefjord is the most attractive as it reveals the full extent of its changing moods, in turn grandiose, enigmatic, wild, austere, bright and colourful. It is at its best in late spring, particularly in the region of Leikanger, when the fruit trees are in blossom and form an idyllic picture against a background of snow-capped peaks. Moreover, the Sognefjord area lends itself to all sorts of outdoor activities, mountain walking, riding, mountaineering, alpine skiing, cycling, sailing etc.

Sognefjord is easily accessible by air from Oslo *(regular flights to Sogndal)* or by boat from Bergen on one of the Express Coaster's fast services to Sogndal and Flåm deep inside the fjord, with several stops along the way. It is also possible to travel to Sognefjord by train along different routes, the most interesting being undoubtedly the Myrdal-Flåm line *(see BERGEN: Norway in a Nutshell)*. Several roads lead to Sognefjord from the north, the south and the east, but two of them offer particularly fine views over the fjord. The first is road 13 which leads from Voss in the south over Vikafjell (986m) down to Vik on the southern shore of the fjord. The second is road 55, known as the Sognefjell road, which climbs from Lom in the north-east up to the highest pass in Norway (1 440m) then winds down to Skjolden at the head of Lustrafjord, the inner-most arm of Sognefjord. Road 55 then follows the northern shore of Sognefjord almost all the way to Lavik and is most picturesque along Lustrafjord *(see overleaf)* and between Sogndal and Balestrand.

SIGHTS

Vik – Situated on the southern shore of the fjord, this lively regional centre is famous for its stave church, the **Hopperstad Stavkirke** ⊘, dating from c 1130, which has regained its medieval appearance and is therefore very dark inside *(see illustrations pp 52 and 53)*. However, it is still possible to admire the fine Gothic altarpiece surmounted by a baldaquin. A ski festival takes place in May on the slopes of Vikafjell combined with cultural events in the village.

Balestrand – Balestrand has a long-standing tradition of welcoming visitors from all over the world and understandably so for it is picturesquely situated in a bend of Sognefjord, and at the entrance of the secluded Fjærlandfjord. It appears to be completely surrounded by snow-capped mountains and the expanse of still water stretching in front of the harbour looks like an enclosed lake so that the ferry suddenly appearing in the distance cannot fail to cause a surprise. The splendid wooden **Kviknes Hotel**, built in Swiss style, has been standing on the very edge of the fjord since 1877 and artists have been coming to Balestrand since the 1820s.
The village is the starting point for several excursions by boat and coach, in particular to Nærøyfjord and Gudvangen, the Jostedal glacier and Urnes stave church.

Fjærland – Until 1987, Fjærland's only means of communication was the ferry sailing from Balestrand and Hella, the whole length of Fjærlandsfjord. Since then, a tunnel beneath the Jostedal glacier has linked the village to Skei and road E 39 going north.
Situated 3km from the ferry terminal, the Norwegian Glacier Centre, **Norsk Bremuseum** ⊘, provides a wealth of varied information about glaciers with the help of interactive models and a fascinating 20min film shown on a giant semicircular screen.

Aurlandsfjord – This arm of Sognefjord stretches south and divides into two branches; one of them, Nærøyfjord, is the narrowest fjord in Norway with high mountains on either side. The only way to see Aurlandsfjord is from the deck of a ferry. It is possible to make an exciting tour combining car and ferry journeys, starting from Kaupanger on the northern shore of Sognefjord where there is an impressive stave church built in 1184 and remodelled in the 17C. A ferry sails from Kaupanger along the beautiful Nærøyfjord to Gudvangen; another ferry goes all the way round to Aurland and from there a 45km scenic mountain road leads to Erdal, affording breathtaking views of Aurlandsfjord. There is another short ferry crossing from Revsnes back to Kaupanger *(allow one whole day; the mountain road is not suitable for caravans)*.

Lustrafjord – Road 55 follows this other arm of Sognefjord all the way to Skjolden. Just before Hafslo, a minor road on the right leads to the small village of Solvorn where there is a ferry service across the fjord to **Urnes Stavkirke** ★★⊘, the oldest and one of the most beautiful stave churches in the country, built between c 1130 and 1150, now on UNESCO's World Heritage list. It has a unique doorway carved with intertwined dragons and snakes directly inspired by Viking art. Inside it is richly decorated with carvings of animals, human figures, dragons and centaurs on the columns and the capitals. There is also a fine Baroque altarpiece depicting the Crucifixion.
Further along road 55, at Gaupne, road 604 on the left leads to Gjerde *(30km)* where there is a **Glacier Centre** ⊘ which provides a wealth of information about glaciers over the last 20 000 years and organises guided tours on the glacier and in the surrounding national park.

STAVANGER ★

Rogaland
Population 105 000
Michelin map 985 N 2 or Atlas Europe p 116

Norway's fourth largest town is situated on a peninsula jutting out into the North Sea in a landscape of jagged coastline, sheltered by a screen of islands, typical of the Norwegian west coast. If Stavanger is today the prosperous regional capital of south-west Norway, it owes it entirely to its own unfailing determination and its faculty to adapt to changing circumstances. Ever since its humble beginnings, the town has always relied on the North Sea to provide it with essential resources and ensure a healthy economic growth.

In the early 12C, Stavanger was only a village of farmers and fishermen and a modest trading outpost along the coast when, in 1125 the bishopric of St Swithun was founded and the cathedral built. While the town was growing into a thriving cultural centre, its increasing economic wealth was based on herring fishing. At the same time, shipbuilding developed to such an extent that by the end of the 18C, Stavanger had an important fleet of merchant ships sailing to all parts of the world from the Baltic to the Mediterranean and the West Indies. When herring became scarce in the 19C, it was replaced by brisling and the city soon possessed an impressive number of canneries. Today North Sea oil has given a new boost to the local economy which is now involved in all aspects of the oil industry from the construction of oil rigs to the refining and transport of crude oil. This activity has in turn prompted the growth of the service industry and Stavanger has acquired a new international dimension.

The economic boom is reflected by the town's cosmopolitan atmosphere, its lively night-life and growing number of ethnic restaurants. However, the old harbour still has a definite traditional Norwegian flavour and the old town has managed to retain a certain old-world charm in spite of becoming a little too much like a museum.

The culminating point of Stavanger's cultural activities is the International Chamber Music and Dance Festival in August, with concerts in the cathedral and the town's concert hall.

★★ DOMKIRKEN ⊙ 45min

Bishop Reinald came all the way from Winchester in England bringing with him relics of St Swithun to whom the cathedral, built between 1125 and 1135, was dedicated. The Romanesque edifice was partially destroyed by fire in 1272 and rebuilt with a much larger chancel in Gothic style flanked at the very end with twin square towers whereas a vast porch at the west end replaced the original tower and gave the church an imposing façade. At the Reformation, the cathedral was deprived of all its treasures, including the bells, several altars and, of course St Swithun's relics. The last restoration took place from 1938 to 1942 and tried to recreate the medieval character of the cathedral which is today one of the best preserved medieval churches in Norway.

Interior – The cathedral's overall length is 65m and the chancel alone is 21.5m long. Inside, the first impression is one of striking contrast between the simplicity of the nave, with its massive round pillars and square capitals, and the delicate ornamentation of the chancel with its slender engaged columns and richly carved corbels supporting the elegant ribbed vaulting. In the nave, some of the capitals are carved with scenes from the Bible including fabulous creatures such as griffins and dragons, often depicted in medieval times.

The extremely ornate Baroque pulpit leans against the last arch of the nave; it is a masterpiece of woodcarving illustrating the Old Testament from the Creation to the Flight into Egypt and is surmounted by a baldaquin celebrating Christ's victories in a blaze of glory. At the beginning of the chancel there is a Gothic font with an 18C silver cover. Light pouring into the chancel through the tall windows plays on the intricately carved motifs and heads of medieval kings. At the eastern end of the chancel, there is a beautiful modern stained glass dating from 1957. The extremely elegant bishop's portal on the south side of the chancel is worth seeing from the outside and comparing with the two simpler Romanesque portals on the north and south sides of the nave.

★ GAMLE STAVANGER 1hr 30min

At the head of the old harbour, **Vågen**, which is now a colourful marina with one or two picturesque sailing ships, the fish market held every day until 4pm is always extremely lively and attracts a crowd of on-lookers fascinated by the huge quantities of bright North Sea prawns and other shellfish on sale. Nearby, the Maritime Museum, **Sjøfartsmuseet** ⊙, illustrates the importance of the sea in the development of the town through 200 years of shipping history with the help of various exhibits, models and interesting reconstructions of shops and a shipping office.

The **old town** is situated on the west side of Vågen, up a steep slope overlooking Strandkaien. It was originally a working class district, built at the end of the 18C when sardines were the town's main source of prosperity and canneries employed a lot of people. Some 170 houses, dating from the 18C and 19C, have been restored and are now protected. A stroll along the narrow cobbled streets is an authentic and most pleasant journey into the past: the white-washed wooden houses usually have creepers growing in boxes on their doorsteps and are sometimes separated by tiny terraced gardens; old-fashioned lamp-posts complete the quaint setting. The houses are all inhabited and the district has now become rather exclusive.

In Øvre Strandgate, the Canning Museum, **Hermetikkmuseet** ⊙, housed in one of the old canneries illustrates the various stages of the brisling canning process at the end of the 19C and the beginning of the 20C.

Norsk Oljemuseum *Kjeringholmen*

The new Norwegian Petroleum Museum stands in Stavanger harbour like an oil rig about to be tugged out to sea. The fascinating interactive displays illustrate the development of the thriving Norwegian oil industry, explain technological advances and describe the importance of oil in our society and replaces it in the perspective of the history of energy. Scale models are used to show the hugeness of the Troll platform, 100m taller than the Eiffel Tower! There is a diving bell and the first Norwegian remote-controlled underwater vehicle; working conditions on an oil rig are also vividly depicted and the story of Norwegian oil is presented in a film entitled Seaborn. *Shop and café serving light meals.*

EXCURSIONS

The beauty of the Stavanger region lies in the striking contrasts between open, rugged and often barren seascapes and the spectacular fjord and mountain landscapes in which impressive rocks seem to have been hewn with a gigantic axe.

The first two excursions can form part of a longer itinerary along the coast to the famous western fjords or they can easily be combined into a whole day tour using Stavanger as the starting point.

Nordsjøvegen: The coast road from Stavanger to Haugesund – *70km north and a 1hr 10min ferry crossing. Leave on the northbound E 39.*
The coast road is constantly being extended by tunnels linking the islands and the length and number of ferry crossings are being reduced. A recent extension from Randaberg to the tip end of Rennesøy has involved the construction of two tunnels under the sea bed; the longest is the Byfjord Tunnel, 5 830m long, which goes down to 45m under the sea bed.

However, leave E 39 on the left to take the ferry to Skudeneshavn. Ferry crossing: Mekjarvik to Skudeneshavn – 70min – 6 times a day.

Skudeneshavn is an extremely picturesque and well-preserved seaside village with quaint old warehouses lined along the wharf at the harbour and charming white timber houses lining the narrow streets. As its name implies, the island of **Karmøy** acts as a screen against the sea: its rugged coastline is matched inland by the heath-covered undulating terrain.

At Avaldsnes, Olav's Church, **Olavskirken** ⊙, dating from 1250 has hardly changed since it was built.

Ryfylkevegen: The Ryfylke Road – *160km north-east to Sand and two short ferry crossings. Drive south to Sandnes then turn left on road 13 towards Lauvvik. Ferry crossing: Lauvik to Oanes – 10min.*

Between Oanes and Tau, the scenic road skirts the coastline.

About 20km from Oanes, a road on the right leads to Preikestolen Lodge where there are parking facilities. From there it takes about 2hr to walk up to the Pulpit Rock.

★ **Preikestolen** – The Pulpit Rock owes its name to its shape since it is completely flat on top with a sheer drop down to Lysefjord, 600m below; the exhilarating experience is matched by the breathtaking **view**★★★ over the fjord and the islands.

Between Tau and Hjelmeland, the road goes through a mountainous area, offering fine views over wild barren landscapes. The early 16C **Årdal Gamle Kyrkje** ⊙ in Hjelmeland is famous for its beautifully decorated interior.

Ferry crossing: Hjelmeland to Nesvik – 10min.

After Nesvik, the road follows the **Jøsenfjord** closely, then turns to the north-west as it climbs away from the fjord, it affords lovely views of the narrow stretch of water. Before reaching Sand, a minor road on the left offers the possibility of a pleasant detour to the seaside village of **Jelsa**, with its wooden houses and Renaissance **Jelsa Kirke** ⊙.

At Sand, there are three possibilities: take the ferry to Ropeid (10min) and drive on to Ølen and Haugesund (see above) or to Sauda and Røldal (road 520) or continue on road 13 to Odda and Sørfjord, a narrow arm of Hardangerfjord.

★ **Lysefjord** – *There are organised 3hr and 6hr trips from Stavanger (details from the tourist office). There is also a combined car and ferry excursion which takes all day – 135km east along E 39, road 45, then a minor road to Lysebotn – 4hr ferry crossing, booking necessary.*

From Suleskar on the Sirdal plateau, an extraordinary road descends by means of 27 hairpin bends 900m down to Lysebotn at the head of Lysefjord, affording magnificent views of the fjord. The ferry sails beneath the Pulpit Rock *(see above)* and the view is as amazing from below as it is from above.

STIKLESTAD

Stiklestad – Nord-Trøndelag

Michelin map 985 E 8 or Atlas Europe p 111

Stiklestad is one of the most famous historic sites in Norway, where an event marking a turning point in Norwegian history took place almost 1 000 years ago. The battle which was fought on 29 July 1030 between King Olav Haraldsson's army and the far superior army of some local kings had no particular significance from a military point of view but Olav's death during the battle was to change the course of history and Stiklestad is generally considered as heralding the end of the Viking period and the beginning of the Middle Ages.

Stiklestad a national event – The reason why the battle took place was straightforward enough and certainly not novel; it was yet another attempt by a Viking overlord to submit rebellious local chiefs and unify Norway under his supreme rule, at the same time imposing the Christian faith on his subjects. In Viking times Nord-Trøndelag was an important region from an economic and military point of view and it was essential for Olav's prestige as an overall king to impose himself in that area. The king lost the battle, but his death changed his defeat into a victory with far-reaching consequences.

Olav's death was immediately looked upon as the martyrdom of a missionary for the cause of Christianity and he became at once a saint and a symbol of the Norwegian nation. Several kings before him had tried to Christianise Norway and only partially succeeded, but from 1030 onwards, Christianity spread quickly and churches and monasteries were founded with the result that the practice of writing in Norwegian became generalised. Moreover, the unification of Norway under a supreme king was made easier for Olav's successors because he had aroused admiration and respect.

St Olav – Although the king was never officially canonised, his cult spread far and wide not only in Scandinavia but across the North Sea to England where there were

still some Viking kingdoms, and churches dedicated to St Olav were built in many places. Pilgrims came from far away to see his grave in Nidaros Cathedral in Trondheim as well as the place where he fell at Stiklestad. The miracles he had accomplished during his lifetime were recorded, reinforcing the legend that had grown round his name. Throughout the centuries, St Olav has continued to play a unifying role by keeping the nation's hopes alive in difficult times.

The St Olav Play – Every year on the anniversary of the battle, a pageant is staged at the open-air theatre in Stiklestad, with 350 participants, in front of 20 000 spectators; it depicts the king's last few days before his death against the background of the battle and tries to give an account of life, beliefs and ideas at the time through the different characters.

The St Olav Play

SIGHTS

Stiklestad Nasjonale Kultursenter ⊘ – Inaugurated in 1992, this ultra-modern National Cultural Centre houses an exhibition entitled Stiklestad 1030 which illustrates the background of the battle through a series of scenes based on archaeological finds in the area, some of which are on display.

★ **Stiklestad Kirke** ⊘ – The Romanesque edifice, dating from 1150, replaced a wooden church, built on the spot where King Olav is believed to have fallen; the nave was extended in 1500. During restoration work carried out for the 900th anniversary of the battle, 16C frescoes were discovered on the walls of the nave, which depict various biblical stories including the Passion on the northern wall. The soapstone font dates from the 12C.

The paintings in the chancel were commissioned for the 900th anniversary of the battle; they are the work of Alf Rolfsen and illustrate the sequence of events throughout the day in successive scenes: the king and his men before the battle, the king leaning against the stone as he is dying, and Christ appearing with a sword in one hand and a lily in the other; the last scene is set at night after the battle, a blind man regains his sight when the king's blood touches his eyes and Tore Hund, one of the two warriors who mortally wounded the king, witnessing this miracle decides to make a pilgrimage to the Holy Land to find peace.

Stiklestad Museum ⊘ – This small open-air museum illustrates local village life in the past with regular demonstrations of traditional working methods in a dairy farm, at the forge, at the baker's, at the mill etc. The buildings date from the 17C, 18C and 19C and include a watermill, a *stabbur*, a carpenter's cottage and even a sauna from the beginning of the 18C.

TELEMARK ★

Michelin map 985 M 4-6 or Atlas Europe p 116

A mountainous region at the heart of southern Norway, Telemark is famous the world over as the birthplace of skiing. Snow-capped mountains, dense forests, deep valleys and lakes but also sunny coastline and islands form the varied scenery of this beautiful area rich in contrasts, which has retained many of its traditions, its dialect, its costumes, its folk music and dancing, displayed during the Telemark Folk Festival in Bø, its sturdy log houses and its handicraft superbly represented by delicate silver work, woodcarving and weaving.

Birthplace of Telemark skiing – The flame for the Winter Olympic Games held in Lillehammer in 1994 was brought all the way from Morgedal, the birthplace of **Sondre Norheim**, Norway's first skiing hero whose statue proudly stands in the village centre. The torch was lit in the house where he was born in 1825. He modified the traditional shape of skis and the bindings in order to experiment with new techniques which were later universally adopted. During a skiing exhibition in Oslo in 1868, he demonstrated his revolutionary equipment and the new possibilities it offered, such as the Telemark turn used to change direction or stop short and the Telemark landing used in ski jumping to absorb the jolt. Sondre Norheim can therefore rightly be considered as the father

of modern skiing. In 1884, he emigrated to the US and helped to promote skiing as a sport in his adopted country.

It is not widely known that the word slalom *(slalåm)* comes from the Telemark dialect and means the track down the slope; it was originally a cross-country race run over fields and hills and among trees and shrubs *(see Skiing the Scandinavian way p 439).*

The **Norsk Skieventyr** (Norwegian Skiing Adventure) Centre in Morgedal, devoted to the history of skiing, includes a replica of Sondre Norheim's cottage and workshop and offers a thrilling skiing experience through a film projected on three screens. *Shop and cafeteria.*

M. Nanes/PRESSENS BILD

Telemark skiing

The heavy water battle – The town of Rjukan at the foot of the imposing Gausta mountain, in north Telemark, suddenly became famous during the Second World War when it found itself at the centre of a fierce battle for the control of heavy water essential in the production of atomic bombs. The heavy water was being produced and stocked at Vemork power station and the Germans intended to ship it to Germany; the Allies decided to sabotage the power station and the carefully prepared raid, which took place in February 1943, was a complete success but within a few months the plant was producing heavy water again. This time Allied planes completely destroyed the factory; production was halted but the stocks were intact and the Germans decided to ship them immediately to Germany; however the ferry carrying the heavy water across Lake Tinnsjø was blown up by the Resistance in February 1944. The battle lasted one year and cost the lives of 30 British soldiers and 40 Norwegian civilians.

The old power station, situated 7km west of Rjukan, now houses the Industrial Workers Museum, **Norsk Industriarbeidermuseum** ⊙, with special exhibitions about the heavy water battle and hydroelectric power.

Along the Telemark Canal – Inaugurated in 1892, the Telemarkskanalen stretches from Skien on the south coast to Dalen at the heart of Telemark, for a distance of 110km, with 18 locks on the way, all stone built and still mostly operated by hand. At Ulefoss, the canal divides into two branches, the shortest one going north to Notodden near which is the famous Heddal Stavkirke, the longest going west to Dalen, at the foot of the Hardangervidda plateau.

There are boat trips along the canal starting from Skien and lasting half a day or a whole day, including the return trip by coach.

Even though the road does not follow the canal closely all the way to Dalen, the journey by car is still very interesting since the scenery changes continually.

Skien to Dalen – 160km – allow at least half a day. Drive north along road 36 to Ulefoss, then follow road 359 to Bø where you rejoin road 36; continue on the main road to Brunkeberg (Morgedal is just 5km north-west, see p 49) then take road 41 to Vrådal and turn west on road 38 to Dalen.

Skien is Telemark's most important town and Henrik Ibsen's home town. The house where he spent his childhood, **Nordre Venstøp**, is situated in Gjerpen, a northern suburb of Skien. This is where the young Ibsen first tried his hand at playwriting and directing with a puppet theatre he had made. Moreover, the attic at Venstøp is the dark attic of his famous play the *Wild Duck*. The **Telemark Museum** ★⊙ lies at the centre of a park. The main building is a former manor house dating from the beginning of the 19C; it contains extensive collections of folk art from Telemark, including a splendid interior decorated with rose-painting, a speciality of the area. Also in the museum are Henrik Ibsen's reconstructed apartments. The open-air museum consists of buildings representative of the architectural styles of various parts of the county.

Vrangfoss lock, lying between Ulefoss and Lunde, is the most impressive along the canal, with its five sluices and level drop of 23m.

Telemark Sommarland, in Bø is an aqualand complex with a difference, it is equipped with a wave generator powerful enough to create surf waves comparable to real ones.

From **Seljord**, a picturesque small town overlooking a lake, the road winds its way between steep forested slopes to **Kviteseid** on the shores of another lake; white-painted farmhouses have balconies decorated with flower boxes and there is almost always a *stabbur* nearby; a suspension bridge spans the lake and the road climbs in a succession of hairpin bends, offering lovely views of the lake.

Between Vrådal and Dalen, the road skirts Vråvatnet then rises through the mountains to come down again, revealing picturesque views of **Dalen** and its lake. **Eidsborg Stavkirke** ⊙ is situated 5km north of Dalen on road 45; built in the 14C, it was restored in 1927 when 17C frescoes were discovered. Nearby is the **Lårdal Bygdemuseum** ⊙, consisting of two old farms and their outbuildings; one of these bears a runic inscription dating from c 1300.

TROMSØ ★★

Troms
Population 47 000
Michelin map 985 C 15-16 or Atlas Europe p 104

The setting of north Norway's largest city is unique and is responsible to a great extent for the undeniable charm the Arctic city exerts on its visitors.

Tromsø is situated on the flat and relatively small Tromsøya Island (10km long) in the middle of a wide channel, between the mainland in the east and the deeply indented Kvaløya Island taking the brunt of the westerly storms. Completely surrounding Tromsøya Island, the blue, snow-capped mountains on Kvaløya and on the mainland reflect the strange white Arctic light which throws a silvery shimmer on the still waters of the sound and adds a touch of magic to the ethereal scenery.

Well north of the Arctic Circle, at a latitude of 70° north, Tromsø enjoys the midnight sun for two months in summer, but it is plunged into darkness from mid-November to mid-January, when only the striking polar lights brighten up the sky from time to time. It is no wonder then that 21 January, the day when the sun first shows above the horizon, is a festive day in Tromsø. Winter lasts from November until May and the cooling effect of the snow, which remains well into June, prevents the arrival of warm weather until July. Summer lasts for just two months but the midnight sun warms the earth so quickly that visitors sometimes witness with astonishment what local people call tropical nights, when the temperature never drops below 20°C. Throughout the long winter, the town's inhabitants store enough energy to survive with very little sleep during the summer and enjoy themselves well into the night in the numerous restaurants, cafés, pubs and discotheques.

HISTORICAL NOTES

Tromsø became an ecclesiastical centre when the king built a little wooden church in 1252, but the town remained economically dependent on Bergen throughout the Middle Ages and never really developed until it obtained its charter in 1794. At the beginning of the 19C, trade with Russia and the profits from hunting expeditions in the Arctic at last brought about Tromsø's economic independence. The mid-19C was a period of economic boom and, through its growing shipping trade, the town came under continental influences and earned itself the name of Paris of the North. At the same time, Tromsø became a cathedral town, an administrative and educational centre, as well as the base for research expeditions in the Arctic (see Polarmuseet below).

Tirpitz – Wounded by allied bombing, the legendary German battleship *Tirpitz* took refuge in the Tromsø sound in October 1944, seeking the protection of the surrounding mountains and still relying on the efficiency of her tremendous fire power. However, on 12 November, she was attacked by 32 Lancaster bombers and hit several times; she caught fire, exploded and sank, causing the death of around 973 of her crew. The wreck was removed in the 1950s.

1960 saw the inauguration of the Tromsø Bridge (Tromsøbrua) connecting the town to the mainland and in 1972 the world's most northern university was officially opened by King Olav. Some of its research work is of international importance as, for instance, the current study of Arctic atmosphere. Tromsø's economy is still based on fishing, but in recent years tourism, fish farming and high technology have developed considerably; the town is opening up again to the outside world and becoming one of the five main congress cities in Norway.

SIGHTS

Town Centre – Unfortunately in 1969 a fire destroyed some of the traditional wooden houses in the town centre. However there are still enough of them left for the town to have retained some of its 19C atmosphere. Partly pedestrianised, Storgata is the main shopping street and there are interesting buildings on Sjøgata, Vestregata, Havnegata and along the harbour.

Built in 1861 and surmounted by a tall spire, the yellow and grey-painted **Domkirken** ⊘ is one of the largest wooden churches in Norway.

Opened in 1978 and housed in an old customs warehouse, the **Polarmuseet** ⊘ retraces the history of hunting, trapping and polar expeditions in the Arctic with the help of various exhibits, and vivid reconstructions of hunting scenes, a trapper's hut etc. Subjects treated are whaling in the 1600s, fur trapping in the 1700s, sealing from 1700 until today, polar bear, musk ox and walrus hunting. A special room is devoted to the famous explorer Roald Amundsen (1872-1928) and his various expeditions to the North Pole and to the South Pole which he reached in 1911, more than one month before Robert Falcon Scott who died on his way back.

TROMSØ

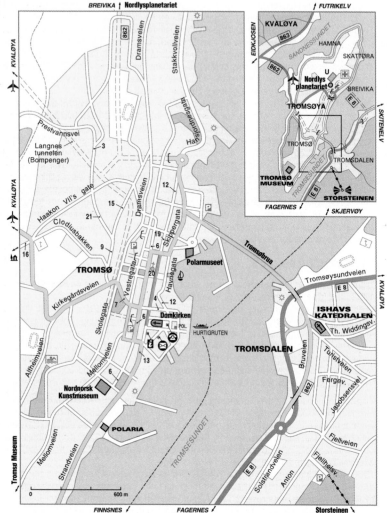

Nearby in Sjøgata is the **Nordnorsk Kunstmuseum** ⊘ (Art Museum of Northern Norway) opened in 1985. The museum's aim is to show the development of Norwegian art in relation to the general trends of international art and to generate interest more specifically in northern Norway's contribution. The permanent exhibition is devoted to figurative art and sculpture from 1800 to the 1980s, with works by JC Dahl, Peder Balke, Knut Baade, Harriet Backer, Edvard Munch, Odd Nerdrum, Bjorn Ransve, Knut Roe and Nils Aas. Applied arts are also represented. The museum stages five or six temporary exhibitions every year.

Nearby is the oldest house in town, dating from the early 19C.

South of the city centre, **Polaria** ★⊘, inaugurated in 1998, offers visitors an interesting polar experience (walk through the polar night) and provides useful interactive information on the polar regions based on current Norwegian and international research. Aquariums contain arctic fish and various fauna including wild seals.

★★ **Ishavskatedralen** ⊘ – *On the mainland.* The Arctic Cathedral is undeniably the finest building in Tromsø, a masterpiece of modern architecture combining glass and concrete in a simple yet very effective geometric design and making use of the Arctic light to create the impression of an iceberg pointing its sharp edge to the sky. The church looks striking from across Tromsø Bridge, with the imposing outline of Tromsdalstind (1 238m) in the background. The triangular façade is entirely made of plain glass panels and, at the other end, a huge stained-glass window lights up the altar with warm, bright colours.

C. Boisvieux

Ishavskatedralen – Arctic Cathedral

Storsteinen – The **cable-car terminal** is nearby. The **ride★**, which only takes a few minutes, is well worth it, especially late at night in summer, if the weather is clear. The cable-car climbs to the top of Storsteinen, the big rock, 420m above sea level, affording superb **views★★★** of Tromsø, the sound, the two bridges and the snow-capped mountains on Kvaløya.

★ Tromsø Museum ⊘ – *See inset.* Situated in Folkeparken, at the southern end of Tromsøya, the museum is now a university institute. It is divided into seven departments, those relating to nature on the ground floor (geology, zoology and botany) and those relating to culture on the first floor (archaeology, Sami ethnography and cultural history).

North of the town centre, the Northern Lights Planetarium, **Nordlysplanetariet** ⊘, shows a film entitled Arctic Light, about northern lights and the midnight sun, on a 360° screen.

TRONDHEIM ★★

Sor-Trøndelag
Population 145 000
Michelin map 985 I 7 or Atlas Europe p 111

Nestling inside the curve of the deep Trondheimsfjord, at the mouth of the River Nidelva, Norway's third largest town is also one of the oldest cities in the country which grew in the shadow of its famous cathedral and has always played an essential part in the spiritual and cultural life of the country. Because of its central position, Trondheim is often called the gateway to the north, a role which it has already assumed in times of difficult communications when it became the starting point of Hurtigruten's regular service along the coast, and which is even more important today in view of the rapid development of northern counties, particularly Finnmark, relying on fast communications.
The town centre is quite compact, tucked away on a small triangle almost entirely surrounded by water, which is part of its charm. The wide avenues, cut through the old districts during the late 17C in order to reduce the risk of fire spreading quickly, create an impression of space which emphasises the calm provincial atmosphere pervading the town. It is worth going up to **Kristiansten Festning** (Z), standing on a hill east of the cathedral, to get an overall **view** of Trondheim and the fjord.

HISTORICAL NOTES

Nidaros – Determined to unite the kingdom of Norway under his rule, the Viking king, Olav Tryggvason founded the town of Nidaros, at the mouth of the River Nidelva, in 997 and built a royal residence there thus making it the first capital of Norway. At the same time he built the first Nidaros church in an effort to convert the people to the new Christian faith.

NORWAY

Saint Olav – Olav Tryggvasson had only partially succeeded in his double task of unification and conversion and 30 years later rebellious Viking chiefs, who were particularly powerful in Trøndelag, forced another Christian king, Olav Haraldsson to flee his kingdom. He returned in 1030 but was killed at the battle of Stiklestad, about 100km north-east of Nidaros (Trondheim). What he could not achieve when he was alive was accomplished through his being declared Holy. He was buried in Nidaros and pilgrims from the whole of Scandinavia and beyond came to visit his shrine. This constant flow of visitors brought prosperity to the town which developed rapidly and work on the present Nidaros Cathedral began in 1070.

Spiritual capital of Norway – The importance attached to St Olav's shrine made the Nidaros church particularly powerful and its influence grew unchallenged throughout the Middle Ages, when it became the custom for the kings of Norway to be crowned in the cathedral. Once established, the tradition continued even after the Reformation. The ceremony of the coronation has now been discontinued in Norway, but the present king, Harald V, went to Trondheim in 1991 for his formal consecration during a service in Nidaros Cathedral.

Trondheim – Throughout the Middle Ages, the town saw its harbour activities increase, but the Reformation slowed down economic growth for a while and in 1681, Nidaros, which had been renamed Trondheim, was devastated by a fire and parts of the old town destroyed. General Caspar de Cicignon, the descendant of a French Huguenot who had emigrated to Norway, redesigned the town centre with broad straight avenues, just as it is today. At the same time he built Kristiansten Festning on high ground overlooking the city to protect the town from Swedish invasion.

The university is outstanding in the arts as its Museum of Music History at Ringve, famous throughout the country, testifies; moreover, following the foundation of the Norwegian Institute of Technology in 1910, Trondheim has developed into one of the most important centres of high technology in the country but tradition is not about to be superseded by modern trends and every year a cultural festival takes place around 29 July, in honour of St Olav who still occupies a special place in the hearts of the Norwegian people.

***NIDAROSDOMEN ⏱ (Z) *1 hr*

The cathedral holds within its walls the history of Trondheim and of the kingdom of Norway and it is still regarded today as the country's national sanctuary.

After the battle of Stiklestad, King Olav Haraldson was buried under the high altar of the original wooden church built by one of his predecessors, King Olav Tryggvasson. Rumours having spread rapidly of miracles connected with his grave, Olav was declared a saint and his remains were placed in a precious shrine. Then King Olav Kyrre decided to replace the wooden church by a stone one dedicated to Christ and work began in 1070. Pilgrims flocked to the church in growing numbers and soon the need arose for a larger building especially when in 1153 Nidaros, which had until then been the seat of a bishopric, became an archbishopric by papal decree. This meant that the city was the ecclesiastical centre not only of Norway but also of Iceland, Greenland, the Faroes, the Orkneys and the Isle of Man.

The oldest parts of the cathedral were built in Romanesque style before the end of the 12C by the second archbishop, Eystein Erlendsson: the original stone building was extended by the addition of a transept and a chapter-house. There followed the building of the octagon and the chancel but this time in Gothic style and the nave which replaced the Romanesque nave was completed in c 1300.

Although the cathedral was damaged by fire on several occasions, it was always repaired or partially rebuilt and until the Reformation it remained a famous destination for pilgrims from all over Northern Europe and the traditional burial place of Norwegian monarchs. However, at the Reformation it was robbed of all its treasures and the cult of St Olav was prohibited by the Evangelical-Lutheran church which became and still is the state church of Norway. The archbishopric was abolished and the cathedral reduced to the status of parish church in 1585. Restoration work began in 1869 and today the cathedral takes an active part in the cultural life of the city, being at the centre of St Olav's Festival.

Tour – Built of grey soapstone, the cathedral stands in a harmonious green setting, in the bend of the River Nidelva. The impressive façade facing west is decorated with rows of carved figures representing saints and kings; the main portal is surmounted by an ornate tympanum, but the most striking feature is probably the magnificent **rose window**.

The interior is vast and the impression of loftiness is increased by the predominance of perpendicular lines: the massive pillars of the nave are surrounded by engaged columns whereas slender columns joined by elegantly carved arches separate the nave from the chancel. The capitals are richly carved, one of them in particular, situated at the entrance of the octagon, on which seven very expressive heads can be seen. Apart from the rose window mentioned above, the stained-glass windows in general have superb colours.

Nidarosdomen

The **crown jewels** used for the coronations of the kings of Norway prior to the abolition of the ceremony in 1906 were first shown to the public in 1988 and are now on display in the **North Chapel** on the west front. They were made in Sweden during the 19C except for the crown worn by the heir to the throne which was made in Norway.

ADDITIONAL SIGHTS

★ **Erkebispegården** ⊘ (Z) – Situated close to the cathedral, the archbishop's palace was built at the same time by the second archbishop, Eystein Erlendsson; it remained the archbishop's residence until the Reformation. It then became the official residence of Danish governors before being taken over by the army; at that time the Great Hall was used to store grain and the roof was raised. The oldest part of the palace is Østhuset dating from 1160 to 1170, which contained the reception halls. Vesthuset, built in c 1230, contained the archbishop's private apartments and his office. The two buildings were joined by a tower with an arched doorway, which was later demolished and the palace was extended several times, particularly in the 15C when it was also fortified. It was finally restored in 1975 and is now used as accommodation for official guests.

★ **Gamle Bybro and wharves** (Z) – Just north of the cathedral, the old town bridge, **Gamle Bybro**★, was built in 1861 to replace an earlier construction of the late 17C. From the bridge there are lovely **views**★ of the gabled warehouses along the river, mostly red and brown wooden buildings on stilts dating from the 18C.
There are also some old houses along Kjøpmannsgaten (YZ) behind the warehouses. Most of them are now lively pubs or restaurants.

★★ **Nordenfjeldske Kunstindustrimuseum** ⊘ (Z M¹) – Established in 1893, the Museum of Applied Arts houses various collections illustrating major international art trends, the emphasis being on contemporary handicrafts and design.
Part of the collection is exhibited on three floors and there are in addition about 20 temporary exhibitions a year.
The **historical collections** on the lower floor are displayed in chronological order from 1500 to 1990; they include furniture from Norway but also from England, Holland and north Germany as well as a large collection of old silver from Trondheim, 18C Norwegian glass and tapestries from Gudbrandsdalen.
The **Arts and Crafts Movement**, led by William Morris at the end of the 19C, is illustrated by collections of printed textiles, metal craft, ceramics and glass, most of which were purchased in the 1890s.
The **Art Nouveau Collection** consists mainly of exhibits illustrating the French Art Nouveau style, many having been acquired at the 1900 World Exhibition in Paris. On the ground floor there is a room devoted to the Belgian architect Henri van de Velde.

TRONDHEIM

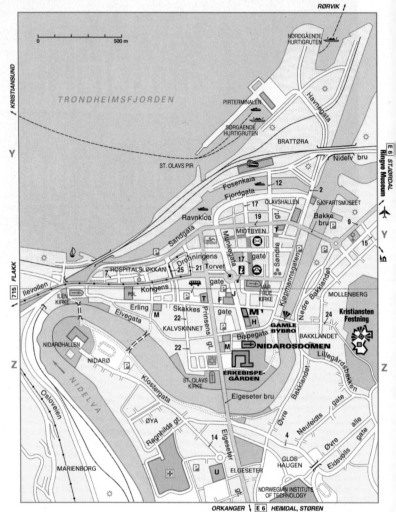

The **Modern Collection** includes objects made after 1945 from Europe, North America and Australia. Scandinavian design from 1950 to 1965 and from the 1980s is well represented. Of particular interest is the Scandinavian-design interior entirely by Danish architect Finn Juhl in 1952, which can be seen on the ground floor.

Hannah Ryggen's Tapestries, in all 20 wall hangings, are grouped together in one room; they are very representative of her artistic output from 1920 to 1969. Born in Malmø, Sweden, in 1894, Hannah married the Norwegian painter Hans Ryggen and settled in Ørlandet near Trondheim. She died in 1970.

The **Costume Collection** includes items from the end of the 17C down to today. The Rococo period is particularly well represented as are the 1920s and 30s while the contemporary collection is continually expanding.

The **Japanese Collection** includes pottery, lacquer, metal work, textiles etc.

The **Jewellery collection** consists of about 300 pieces of jewellery of contemporary international design.

★★ **Ringve Museum** ⊘ – *Leave to the east by Innherredsveien* (Y). This fascinating museum of musical instruments is housed in the splendid 19C Ringve manor house situated on the Lade peninsula, 3km north-east of the town centre, and overlooking the city and the fjord. The compulsorily guided tour of the museum includes demonstrations by students of some of the instruments, often rare specimens. Unusual and rare instruments include 18C Norwegian Aeolian bells, a superb harpsichord by Jacob Kirkman, London 1767, a grand piano from 1783 by Johann

Andreas Stein, whom Mozart visited in 1777, a piano harp by Christian Dietz, made in Brussels in the late 19C, a Norwegian zither from Telemark, an Amati violin from 1612, a German theorbo (a member of the lute family) from 1700, an attractive black 18C French harpsichord with a landscape painted on the inside of the lid, an unusual 18C square piano, barrel organs, miniature instruments, a large collection of non-European instruments, an American jukebox from 1948, beautifully decorated fiddles from Hardanger etc.

Ringve Museum

EXCURSION

Boat trip to Austrått Hall – *Allow half a day. Departures from Fosenkaia* (Y), *near the station.* A catamaran sails from Trondheim along the fjord to Brekstad where a coach takes visitors to Austrått for a guided tour of the 17C hall with traces of a medieval building. There are beautiful samples of wrought-iron work, Baroque furniture, and medieval woodcarvings in the chapel.

ÅLESUND ★

More og Romsdal
Population 37 000
Michelin map 985 J 2-3 or Atlas Europe p 110

The discovery of Ålesund comes as a surprise, partly because of its amazing setting and of its Art Nouveau architecture. The town is built right out into the Atlantic Ocean, at the centre of a group of islands. It grew on the shores of a sound from which it gets its name and gradually spread to five islands now all linked by bridges. Other islands further out to sea are also linked by bridges and, more recently, by tunnels under the sea bed; indeed, all along the coastline between Ålesund and Kristiansund, an incredible number of bridges daringly rising and twisting in all directions, real feats of engineering *(see Atlanterhavsveien below)*, have put their imprint on the seascape.

The Art Nouveau town – The islands have been inhabited since the Stone Age by fishermen attracted by the unusual abundance of fish. The area's first famous inhabitant was Rollo, the Viking chief who became the first duke of Normandy and was the ancestor of William the Conqueror; he is said to have come from the island of Giske west of Ålesund. However, pressure from Bergen and Trondheim prevented Ålesund from being given town status until 1848. In January 1904, during a raging storm, Ålesund was devastated by fire: the town centre was practically razed to the ground and, by morning, 10 000 people were homeless. Help poured in from many countries, the German Emperor William II being particularly generous. The town was rebuilt within three years in the fashionable style of the time, Art Nouveau. Today Ålesund takes pride in being the town with the most of and the best-preserved Art Nouveau domestic architecture in Western Europe.

Today Ålesund is a tasteful blend of modern architecture and of a unique heritage from the turn of the last century. The town centre nestles round the lively old fishing harbour, Brosundet, usually cluttered with a colourful array of small fishing and pleasure boats. There are picturesque steps going down to the water and warehouses built on the very edge of the water. It is possible to buy fresh fish and prawns along Skansegata. Many buildings are decorated with spires, turrets and elaborate carvings, in true Art Nouveau style, with now and again a few typically Norwegian touches such as dragons heads etc. The most interesting streets are the pedestrianised **Kongensgate** as well as **Apotekergata, Kirkegata** and **Løvenvoldgata**. There are **guided tours** ⊘ of the Art Nouveau town in summer.

East of the town centre, a winding road climbs through a lovely residential district to the top of **Mount Aksla**, a promontory overlooking the town, and ends at Fjellstua (the Mountain Lodge), from which there is a stunning view of the town and the various islands *(access also via 418 steps from the park at the foot of the mountain)*.

Located at Tueneset, some 3km west of Ålesund, **Atlanterhavsparken** ⊘ (the Atlantic Sea Park) houses large sea aquariums built into the coastline; the largest contains 4 million litres of water and a diver can be seen moving about among the Atlantic fauna. There are also hiking trails, diving areas, a cafeteria and a souvenir shop.

EXCURSIONS

Giske Island – *Toll road.* Giske is now linked to Ålesund and the mainland by bridges and tunnels. On the island the lovely small Romanesque **Giske Kirke** ⊘ is built of marble as a family chapel. It was restored during the 18C and the pulpit and altarpiece date from that period.

Beyond Giske, at the tip of Godøy Island, stands Alnes lighthouse taking the full brunt of the Atlantic weather. Nearby is the picturesque fishing village of Alnes.

Runde Island – *40km to Ulsteinvik and 4hr boat trip to and round the island.*
Further out to sea, south-west of Ålesund, the island of Runde is one of the most famous bird rocks in Norway. More than half a million birds belonging to 40 different species nest on the cliffs and can be observed from March until August. The sanctuary is highly protected and strict regulations enforced.

★ **Atlanterhavsveien (Atlantic Road)** – *150km to Kristiansund.* Atlanterhavsveien is the name given to an 8km-long road (including eight bridges), built off the coast south of Kristiansund, using a string of islands as stepping stones. The result is amazing: the flat, barren islands and skerries and the omnipresent sea combine to create an unforgettable impression of vast open spaces and of a road leading towards an elusive horizon which gets further and further away.

Ålesund

Riddarhilmen with Gamla Stan in the background, Stockholm

P. Thomson/SUNSET

Sweden

ARVIKA

Värmlands län – Population 26 700
Michelin map 985 M 9 or Atlas Europe p 118

Arvika is a cultural centre attractively set on the shores of Glafsfjorden. It was by the small lake of Racken that a group of artists gathered at the turn of the last century to capture the northern light. The local sculptor and craftsman **Christian Eriksson** (1858-1935) was the founder of the **Rackstad Colony**. The members of the group were attracted by the unspoilt beauty of the surrounding countryside in line with the National Romantic movement of the time. The group also put great store by craftsmanship. Eriksson, his brothers and his father, were all skilled cabinet-makers. Eriksson travelled to Stockholm, Hamburg and Paris to study as a sculptor and it was only in 1894 that he returned to Arvika to settle. **Gustaf Fjæstad** (1868-1948) captured the silence of the white winter landscapes in his works, many of which were reproduced in beautiful tapestries woven by his wife **Maja Fjæstad** (1873-1961). Other members included **Fritz Lindström** (1874-1962) a portrait and still-life painter who often captured the Värmland landscapes in a bewitching twilight and **Björn Ahlgrensson** (1872-1918).

★ **Rackstadmuseet** ◷ – *Before entering Arvika from the east, turn right at the roundabout (still road 61), then first right again (signposted).* This spacious and well-lit museum, an annexe to the Eriksson family home, was inaugurated in June 1993 and is devoted to the artists of the Rackstad Colony. The exhibition hall displays a selection of the group's works, which are representative of Swedish art at the turn of the last century, and their craft work is on show in the basement.
The studio, **Oppstuhage★**, stands to the south-east of the Rackstad Museum and is now a small Christian Eriksson Museum with monumental and small sculptures in granite, marble, bronze and wood.

Trefaldighetskyrkan ◷ – *Follow Torggatan, the entrance is in Tingsgatan.* This majestic white church was designed in Jugend style in 1911 by Ivar Tengbom (1878-1968) and is another place to admire works by the Rackstad artists and craftsmen.

Såguddens Museum ◷ – *5min walk from the car park outside the Tourist Information Centre.* This old farmhouse, surrounded by 17C to 19C cottages, has a museum with some well-preserved Dalecarlian paintings. Musical evenings are organised in summer.

Brunskog ◷ – *Skutboudden Heritage Centre.* This open-air museum comes to life with an old world festival **Gammelvala** during the last week in July when the villagers turn the clock back 100 years.

EXCURSION

Klässbols Linneväveri ◷ – *18km in the direction of Säffle by road 175. The last 1.5km is a minor road.* Ever since 1920 damask linen has been woven in this **mill**, the only remaining one in Scandinavia. Beautiful tablecloths and napkins are woven to traditional designs as they were 70 years ago. The company produces the damask cloths for the Nobel Prize banquets in Stadshuset in Stockholm.

BIRKA ★

Stockholms län
Michelin map 985 M 14 or Atlas Europe p 119 – Local map see STOCKHOLM: Outskirts

Birka on the island of Björkö in Lake Mälaren, is a World Heritage Site. The settlement of Birka was the greatest Viking market place of all, between 800 and 960 AD, and archaeological excavations have revealed trading connections with the East via Russia and Byzantium.
It was to this trading settlement that **Ansgar**, the first Christian missionary of note, sailed in 829 AD in his attempt to convert the heathen Svíar (Svear). He paid a second visit in 852 but met with a much more hostile reception, as many had already reverted to paganism. After the saint's death in Bremen in 865 there is no evidence of missionary work in Sweden until the 11C, by which time Birka had declined whereas Sigtuna and Visby had become the new centres of Baltic trade.

The site today – It is hard to imagine the appearance of the town where 700 to 1 000 people lived, worked and traded within the semicircular earth ramparts. The exact site is known as the Black Earth area. Beyond the walls there are a large number of **grave fields**, the largest contains about 1 600 burial graves. The **Museum** ◷ recreates life in Birka 1 000 years ago and the displays include many of the finds from the site.

From the hilltop, with a **monument** (1834) commemorating Ansgar's mission, one can more readily appreciate Birka's strategic location on Lake Mälaren. The small **Ansgar Chapel** (consecrated in 1930), a short distance away, has three sculptures by Carl Eldh (1873-1954) and several paintings by Olle Hjortzberg (1872-1959).

BOHUSLÄN★★

Västra Götalands län

Michelin map 985 O-N 8 or Atlas Europe p 118

The remoteness and wild beauty of Sweden's west coast, north of Gothenburg, with its indented coastline, inlets and islets, rocks and skerries and colourful fishing villages, make this province a popular destination with Swedes and foreigners alike. Tourism has taken over from the fisheries as the mainstay of the coastal economy.

For a stay in Bohuslän – It goes without saying that Bohuslän should be seen from the sea and there is a wide choice of cruises locally. For those who prefer to hoist their own sails or man their own motor boat there is a good selection of boat and yacht hire outlets to choose from.

For the landlubbers, although hotels do exist, this is an area for trying other types of accommodation, a stay in a farmhouse or one of the smaller boarding houses, a rented cottage or even one of the archipelago youth hostels.

For an active holiday – Sea angling, deep-sea diving, canoeing, freshwater fishing and swimming are all popular activities in Bohuslän. Those who prefer cycling can pedal the 290km of the **Bohuslän Way** from Svinesund near the Norwegian border to Gothenburg. Hikers are also catered for with the 360km long-distance path, **Bohusleden**, between Strömstad and Lindome. Local Tourist Information Centres will provide leaflets and maps on all the above activities.

GOTHENBURG TO SVINESUND

220km – E 6 is the main route north but it is well worth the time and trouble to make detours to some of the coastal villages and offshore islands. Leave Gothenburg to the north by E 6 and then take road 155. The ferry between Hjuvik and Hönö takes 12min and leaves every 30min.

Öckerö; Hönö and Rörö – *See GÖTEBORG: Excursions.*

Return to road E 6 and head northwards to Kungälv.

★★ **Bohus Fästning** ⊘ – On the southern outskirts of Kungälv the ruins of a mighty fortress can be seen on an island in the Nordre älv. King Håkon of Norway built the stronghold of Bohus, from which the province takes its name, in 1308 as a strategic strongpoint from which to defend this marshland area. The fortress played an important role in the Nordic Seven Years War (1563-70) and later the Danish King Christian IV fortified the site – as part of an overall campaign to strengthen Danish fortifications in Skåne and on the Sound – with star-shaped fortifications and bastions around the inner castle which was transformed into a Renaissance palace. After the Treaty of Roskilde in 1658 the fortress passed to Sweden and with the loss of its strategic role it fell into ruins. The massive drum tower named Fars Hatt (Father's Hat) is the only one of the four corner towers to remain. Today the inner courtyard is the stage for concerts and other entertainment in summer.

Kungälv – Kungahälla was the name of the original settlement which occupied a riverside site 5km further west. During the Middle Ages it was an important Norwegian town and it suffered repeated destruction. In 1613 Kungälv was rebuilt on Fästningsholmen, at the foot of the mighty Bohus Fortress, and then in 1676 the town was moved to its present site, where it developed as a single street due to its restricted site. Today Gamla Torget, Östra Gatan and Västra Gatan, with their pleasant pastel-painted wooden buildings (18C-19C), comprise the picturesque centre of town. The simple exterior of the white wooden **kyrka** ⊘ erected in 1679 conceals a colourful Baroque interior.

Continue for 28km on road 168. Cars are not allowed on this group of islands and there is a car park just before the ferry. The ferry takes 7min.

★★ **Marstrand** – From a 13C settlement the town developed into an important trading centre and herring fishing port in the 16C. By the mid-19C Marstrand had a growing reputation as a spa but its heyday came at the end of the 19C when King Oscar II (1829-1907) started the fashion for this resort. With its sprucely painted wooden buildings, its narrow winding lanes full of the bustle of boutiques and restaurants and the activity of its marina with its bobbing yachts and dinghies, it is the quintessential Bohuslän resort. Today this popular resort is a Mecca for yachtsmen, international races and a popular annual regatta. The town is dominated by the massive outline of its fortress **Carlstens Fästning** ★⊘ which took 200 years to build and the help of 200 prisoners and inmates to complete. Building started shortly after the Treaty of Roskilde and in 1719 it was captured by a combined Danish-Norwegian fleet under Admiral Peter Tordenskiøld, who used it as a base from which to attack Nya Elfsborgs Fästning guarding the channel to Gothenburg.

Return to road E 6. Just south of Stenungsund leave E 6 for road 160, signpost Tjörn-Orust.

The road follows Hakefjorden to the bridge of **Almöbron★** (Tjörnbron) and after the first traffic lights on the island (café and tourist information point) there is a breath-taking **panorama★★★** to the right of three fjords and a scattering of islands.

To visit Tjörn take road 169 to the left in the direction of Skärhamn and Rönnäng.

★★ Tjörn – Both the islands of Tjörn and Orust, with their special light, have been an inspiration for artists, notably Karl Nordström, one of the Varberg School and two of the so-called Göteborg Colourists, Ragnar Sandberg and Ivan Ivarsson. The west coasts are punctuated with colourful fishing villages where red-wooden boathouses and sheds line the harbours and a twisting maze of lanes winds through tightly packed white-painted houses. The small offshore islands can be reached by local ferries.

★★ Skärhamn – This is the island's main community and it acts as one of the home ports to the Swedish navy and is a centre for freighters. **Skärhamns Sjöfartsmuseum** ⊙ is a small maritime museum.
The island of **Klädesholmen★★** is connected to the mainland by a bridge and ever since the 16C the islanders have made their livelihood from fishing and even today the cottage industry of canning herring is their main activity.
Passenger ferries leave from Rönnäng. The white buildings of **Åstol★★** huddle together on bare rock behind a quayside lined with colourful boathouses. Freshly smoked mackerel is an appetising local delicacy.

Road 160 follows the north coast of Tjörn with the ever-changing views of cliffline and seashore as far as the bridge of **Skåpesundsbron**. There is a good view from the car park.

Orust – Wooded heights and farmland alternate on this island with a reputation for its boat building tradition. Kungsviken and Henån are the main centres. Although plastic hulls are the rule now, there is still a master boat builder who specialises in wooden boats.

Käringön – This fishing hamlet can be reached by passenger ferry from Hälleviksstrand or by boat from Lysekil and Uddevalla.

Gullholmen – *Passenger ferries leave from Tuvesvik.* The island has been inhabited since the 13C and its houses cling more tightly together than anywhere else in Bohuslän. Down by the harbour **Skepparhuset** ⊙ is a skipper's house from 1893, with all its traditional furnishings and household utensils, adjoining boathouse, fishery museum and sail-maker's loft.
Beyond the main community of Henån (3-4km), there is another look-out point with good **views** just before the bridge of **Nötesundsbron** leading to the mainland.

At the intersection of roads 160 and 161 turn left in the direction of Lysekil (Fiskebäckskil).

The medieval **kyrka** of **Bokenäs** with its cobbled porch floor dates from the 12C. The semicircular apse and the absence of windows in the north wall are typical features of the period. Both the tower and interior paintings were 18C additions.

Continuing westwards a ferry takes cars, free of charge, over Gullmarsfjorden. A little further on at the T-junction take road 162 left to Lysekil.

★★ Lysekil – Lysekil developed rapidly during the herring boom in the late 18C but by the mid-19C it had acquired a growing reputation as a bathing resort and some of its spa buildings still remain. The main street runs alongside the south harbour, base for the fishing fleet, which supplies the local canning industry. For information on boat trips, evening cruises and a fishing jaunt on a working boat enquire at the Tourist Information Centre *(Södra Hamngatan 6). Continue along Södra Hamngatan.*

Havsbadsområdet – Lysekil's early importance as a holiday resort is reflected in its seafront: the red and yellow **Curmanska villan** in an old Nordic style was the summer residence of the doctor who recommended the health resort to so many of his patients; the richly decorated bathhouse, dating from 1864, and the turreted Assembly Rooms, **Societshuset** (copy of the original building) are to be found in Havsbadsparken. The **Havets Hus** ⊙ (at the far end of Södra Hamngatan) has a small museum – an annexe to the Marine Research Centre in Gothenburg – devoted to the marine life of the offshore waters and those of Gullmarsfjorden. Follow the sign-posts to **Vikarvet** ⊙ *(Turistgatan)* where the museum depicts the local fishing and quarrying industries.

Take the path to the left behind Vikarvet then turn left again in the direction of the piers.

★ Stångehuvud – This pink granite Bohus headland is curiously enough home to more than 250 species of plants and is often included in both botanical and geological field trips.

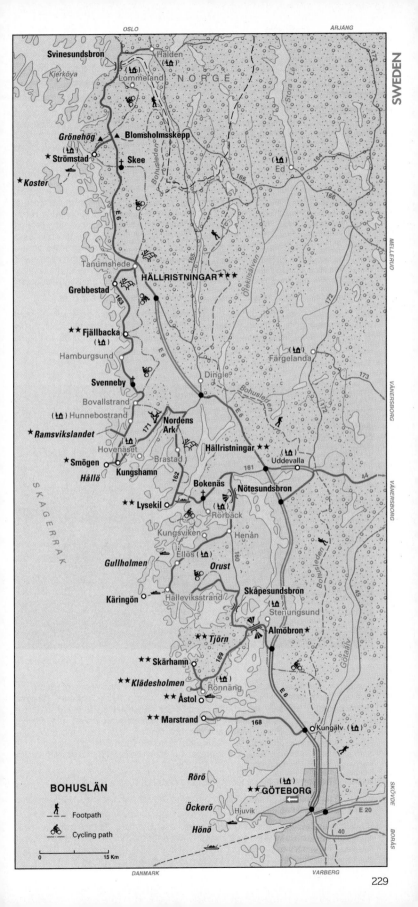

The old herring fishing town (Gamlestan) was centred around the north harbour. The 1901 church in Bohus granite, high on its hilltop site, served as a landmark for seamen.

Returning along road 162 turn right at Brastad and follow the signpost Backa Hällristning.

★★ Hällristningar – The Backa **rock carvings** are at the roadside. The first important carving portrays, among other figures, a life-sized figure of a man with a raised axe. Circular forms or sun-wheels are depicted in another carving about 600m further on. The sun and seasons of the year were of great importance to the people of the early Bronze Age.

Continue on road 162 in the direction of road E 6. Turn left onto road 171 towards Kungshamn.

Nordens Ark ⓥ – *The sanctuary is part of an estate (Åby Säteri) which lies close to road 171.* The Nordic Ark sanctuary for endangered species was founded in cooperation with the Jersey Wildlife Preservation Trust, as a refuge and breeding ground for animals threatened with extinction. The surrounding countryside provides a splendid natural setting for the enclosures and visitors can catch glimpses of animals (Arctic foxes, wolverines, otters, snow leopards, Przewalski horses and eagle owls) from the wooden walkways. One of the projects is to re-establish the comical puffin, emblem of the sanctuary, in its old breeding grounds off the Bohuslän coast.

Continue 100m beyond the entrance to Nordens Ark to a small car park.

Åby – Another fascinating display of **rock carvings** portrays ornate boats with serried ranks of passengers, some of whom are wielding oversized spears and axes, a row of men with ritual headgear who are probably involved in a ritual dance and some unique animal tracks.

Road 171 leads to Smögen.

Smögen

★ Smögen – *The island is linked to the mainland by a bridge.* An important fishing village where trawlers unload their catch and where **shrimp auctions★ (Smögen: Fiskmarknaden)** ⓥ are daily attractions. Over 2 000t of fish and seafood are sold here annually. The wooden pier, **Smögenbryggan**, is very popular with visitors as it fingers seawards between visiting boats and the boathouses, now converted into boutiques, cafés and restaurants, where you can taste the fresh Smögen shrimps. Smögen faces its twin village of **Kungshamn** – a mainland seaside resort and fishing port – across the narrow strait.

Hållö – This barren island famed for its rare flora is a nature reserve.

Continue on road 174 for about 7km; a road to the left leads across the Soten Canal to the nature reserve.

★ Ramsvikslandet – This is another nature reserve where the outcrops of pink Bohuslän granite are washed by the mighty waves of the Skagerrak on the west and the peaceful waters of the Soten Canal in the east. After the bridge turn left to see the rugged cliffline and right for the camp site and beach.

Follow road 174 along the coast and 3km beyond Bovallstrand turn left in the direction of Hamburgsund.

Svenneby – A timbered porch was added in the 18C to this early-12C Romanesque **kyrka** ⊘ with its rectangular nave and narrow apse. The magnificent ceiling **paintings★★** date from 1741. Part of a crucifix and other sculptures are rare items from the 13C.

Continue along road 163.

★★ Fjällbacka – Lobster, crayfish, oysters and crab are some of the specialities of this fishing port which is also known as the favourite summer retreat of the film star **Ingrid Bergman**. A bronze statue commemorates the actress in the square which also bears her name.

All along this coast the arable land is interspersed with rocky outcrops.

Grebbestad – Another resort famous for its oysters and lobsters.

Road 163 joins E 6 at Tanumshede. Keep to the right and after about 400m turn right again. From Tanum Church signposts indicate the way to the rock carvings.

★★★ Hällristningar: rock carvings in the Tanum Area – Tanum is renowned for its rock carvings from the early Bronze Age (1 500-500 BC) and is now a UNESCO designated World Heritage Site. Carvings in northern Scandinavia characteristically show hunting symbols whereas those of the southern regions, including Bohuslän, more often depict agricultural motifs. It is quite possible that the originals were painted in red ochre. Some carvings have been re-painted to make them easier to decipher. The significance of the carvings is unclear but both animals and human beings – woman with long hair and man with his sexual organ – are portrayed. In most cases figures should be regarded as separate pictures but at times several are grouped together in a scene.

Vitlycke – *2km south of Tanum Church.* The rock carvings here depict various rudimentary boats, axe-wielding figures and the love couple. The **Vitlycke Museum** ⊘ gives background information on the carvings, the carvers and their way of life. The full-scale Bronze Age farm gives some idea of what life was like at the time.

Aspeberget – *Continue for another 500m; the carving is another 100m beyond the roadside car park.* In this procession of carvings the visitor can distinguish several figures, a row of sturdy bulls followed by a man, perhaps the herdsman, a ploughman, an archer and a big four-wheeled cart drawn by two animals.

Litsleby – *Another 500m on, then turn right (signpost Tegneby). After another 800m the car park and carvings are on the left.* A more than 2m-tall figure of a man brandishing a spear has been chiselled over earlier carvings.

Fossum – *4km east of Tanum Church by road 163 following the signpost Hällristningar. Car park on the right-hand side of the road and the carvings lie on the other side of the road some 10m further on.* Here the figures are tightly grouped together. There are many almost identical ships and several hunting scenes.

Continue northwards on E 6 then turn right onto road 164 and follow the signs for Skee kyrka for 2km.

Skee – The Romanesque **kyrka** ⊘, dated c 1150, has an apse and three doorways

C. Boisvieux

Vitlycke rock carvings

typical of this period. The **chancel★★** is a gem of Romanesque architecture. The Lübeck reredos dates from the 1490s although its Baroque frame and base were added in 1686. The **Skee Madonna**, placed on an altar to the left, is of dark soapstone and dates from the 13C. The statue's original position was above the west doorway. The ceiling paintings date from a 1924 restoration.

★Strömstad – This established seaside resort was Norwegian until 1658, when it was promoted as a new trading centre. Today the harbour is busy with ferry traffic to Sandefjord *(just over 2hr)* in Norway and the town is a lively shopping centre, but it is fresh prawns and lobsters *(fish market 7am Tuesdays to Fridays)* that have made its reputation. Take one of the regular ferries to visit the **Koster Islands ★**⊙ (Nord-Kosteröarna and Syd-Kosteröarna) where cars are prohibited. Sweden's most westerly inhabited islands enjoy the tempering effects of the Gulf Stream resulting in lush vegetation and a rich fauna.

Make for the junction of road 176 and E 6.

The burial mound of **Grönehög**, 6m high and 45-50m across, dated from c AD 500.

Once back on road E 6 turn right.

Blomsholmsskeppet stone ship and stone circle – *From the car park a path to the left – 200m – leads to the stone ship and a path to the right – 250m – leads to the stone circle.* A large stone setting in the shape of a ship, 42m long and 9m wide, with a stern stone 4.3m high. The ship and the surrounding small burial stones date from the Iron Age or possibly the Migration Period (AD 400-600). The stone circle from the Migration Period measures 33m in diameter.

The 420m-long single span bridge of **Svinesundsbron**, connecting Sweden with Norway, was built between 1939 and 1942 across the narrow strait and opened to traffic four years later.

DALARNA★★★

Dalarnas län
Population 288 000
Michelin map 985 KL 11-12 or Atlas Europe pp 112 and 118-119

Dalarna represents all that is quintessentially Swedish, colourful costumes, lively dancing and music, especially at Midsummer, and always with a beautiful rural landscape in the background. Today the Dalecarlian folklore traditions attract many visitors to the area.
The old-world villages of Dalarna have remained untouched by land reforms and their community spirit remains strong.

Summer pasture farms – In the past the animals were taken up to the summer farms for grazing and simple buildings were erected to shelter animals and farm folk and to store winter fodder. As a rule these summer farms were owned jointly by several families. In Dalarna the system of summer farms reached its peak in the 1870s and 80s and slowly declined from the beginning of the 20C. Today these summer farms are

Dalecarlian painting from Skansen, Stockholm

enjoying a revival and although most offer few home comforts, with no electricity and running water, they are popular with visitors who want to get a taste of life in the old days, see the butter being churned and taste the traditional sweet butter *(messmör)* and cheese *(mesost)* as well as other farm products and a true country brew of coffee. These farms are often isolated and the access roads leave much to be desired.

Arts and crafts – Around the turn of the last century folklore societies were formed to revive old crafts and today numerous craftsmen keep alive the traditions of basket-making, weaving, pottery-making and iron-working.

Midsummer procession

Costumes – Dalarnans take great pride in their regional costumes. Each village has its own colours and patterns and the women's costume includes a multitude of accessories each with its own special significance. All festivities, especially the Midsummer celebration, are the occasion for Dalarnans to don their colourful outfits.

Folk music – One of the oldest musical traditions was the calling home of the animals to the sound of the female voice or a horn. The fiddle was the most popular instrument often accompanied by the keyharp and the clarinet until the accordion took over. Great gatherings of musicians *(spelmansstämmor)* have always been part of the local musical scene and today they attract thousands of visitors.

Dalecarlian painting – Floral decoration has always been used to decorate cupboards and chests but towards the end of the 18C itinerant artists began to decorate rural homes all over Dalarna. Biblical scenes, often taken from the Bible of the Poor, were given Dalecarlian settings with figures in local costumes. One of the best-known artists was Winter Carl Hansson (1777-1805) who worked at Daniel's Homestead in Bingsjö. Collections of Dalecarlian paintings are to be found in Falun and Leksand.

Festivals – The villages of Dalarna are known for their traditional summer festivities, including the raising of the maypole, accompanied by folk music and dancing and in some cases a traditional open-air play.

Midsummer celebrations – Midsummer is celebrated in Dalarna with more gusto than elsewhere and maypoles are raised during a period of several weeks. They often remain up throughout the year only to be redecorated with fresh flowers and greenery the next year.

Music at Lake Siljan – For nine whole days the entire area around Siljan resounds to the sound of music from early morning to late at night during this great celebration of folk music.

Rättvik Folklore Festival (Rättviksdansen) – Every second year this international festival of folk music and dancing attracts musicians and dancers from all over the world.

Church boat races – Around Lake Siljan it was usual to row to church and whenever two boats met on the lake a race was on. Annual races between Midsummer and the end of July keep this time honoured tradition alive.

LAKE SILJAN AND SIGHTS ON ITS SHORES

Siljan – Lying at a height of 161m above sea level Lake Siljan is part of the so-called Siljan Circle (Siljansringen) which was supposedly formed 360 million years ago when a meteorite crashed earthwards creating this huge depression which in addition to Siljan contains lakes Orsasjön, Skattungen and Oresjön. The area is renowned for its beauty and the communities of Leksand, Rättvik, Mora and Orsa cherish the old Dalarnan folklore traditions and they attract many tourists.

Leksand, Mora and Rättvik – *See under each entry.*

Orsa – This town marks the end of agricultural land with the great wilderness beyond. Lying 12km to the north-west in the direction of Fryksås is the Grönklitt bear park, **Grönklitts Björnpark** ⊙, where the bears live in their natural forest habitat. Just 1km further on is the summer pasture farm of Fryksås, a reminder of a past way of life. Some of the old cottages are for visitors who can enjoy the beauty, peace and quiet of this rural setting.

From Siljan to the Norwegian frontier

Älvdalen – Älvdalen lies in the valley of the River Österdalälven, surrounded by thick forests and beyond stretches Sweden's most southerly wilderness. It also lies on the copper trading route, Kopparleden, which stretched north-westwards from Falun to Røros in Norway. The mountainous wilderness area is the natural habitat of bear, lynx, beaver, elk and wolverines. The local tourist offices organise elk and beaver safaris as well as fishing excursions. There are many summer pasture farms in the vicinity.

The volcanic rock porphyry has been worked at Älvdalen since 1788 and a porphyry works, **Nya Porfyrverket** *(across the river in the direction of Sälen)*, still makes small items, ornaments and jewellery. In the centre of the village the **Porfyrmuseet** ★ⓥ includes a large collection of porphyry ware and a geological section. Another famous item associated with Älvdalen is the Hagström electric guitar, favoured by such stars of the pop world as Björn Ulveus of ABBA, Elvis Presley and Frank Zappa. A former accordion factory now houses a collection, **Hagströmsamlingen** ⓥ, of its famous accordions and electric guitars. Behind the church is an unusual tithe barn (kyrkhärbre).

Särna – Like Idre, Särna is also a gateway to the wild mountainous wilderness beyond. Both villages were originally Norwegian and only became Swedish in 1644 when the local pastor from Älvdalen claimed them on behalf of Queen Christina. The event is commemorated by a stone alongside the church. The old church, **Särna Gammelkyrka** ★ⓥ *(100m beyond the present day white church)* is in the typical Norwegian tradition and dates from the 17C. The interior is beautifully decorated; the pulpit was the work of the conquering clergyman. Nearby are several timbered buildings, **Särna Gammelgård**, dating from the 18C.

★★ **Njupeskär** – *30km by road 70 then left in the direction of Mörkret. A path leads from the car park to the waterfall.* Fulufjället is a flat topped massif rising to a height of 1 044m. The main attraction of the area is one of Sweden's highest waterfalls, **Njupeskär**★★ with a total drop of 125m. The other long-distance footpaths in the area are for the well-equipped as the terrain can be quite difficult.

Idre – The genuine mountain village and popular ski resort attracts many summer visitors for a wide range of sporting activities from fishing, hill walking, white-water canoeing to riding. The mountain resort of **Idre Fjäll**, on the slopes of Nipfjället, is an ideal family resort with something for skiers of all levels. The **Städjan-Nipfjället Nature Reserve**★★ is dominated by the characteristic volcanic-shape of Städjan (1 131m). A road leads up to a height of 1 000m on the highest peak of Nipfjället (1 191m), where there is a breathtaking **panorama**★★★ of the surrounding mountains which are often shrouded in clouds.

Grövelsjön – The road ends at Grövelsjön, on the border with Norway and it is here that the true wilderness begins. Visitors come to enjoy the overwhelming silence and beauty of nature or to follow in the footsteps of Linnaeus who crossed by Grövelsjön to Røros in 1734. The STF (Swedish Touring Club) Tourist Station provides accommodation for hikers for whom there is a wide choice of marked trails and footpaths, ranging from 2hr to tours lasting several days. Lake Grövelsjön at a height of 762m is Sweden's highest lake.

DROTTNINGHOLM ★★★

Stockholms län
Michelin map 985 M 14 or Atlas Europe p 119
Local map see STOCKHOLM: Outskirts

SWEDEN

The magnificent royal residence of Drottningholm with its palace, theatre, gardens and Chinese pavilion is included on the UNESCO list of World Heritage Sites. As the palace stands on the island of Lovön on Lake Mälaren one of the best ways to arrive is by boat *(1hr trip from the quay in front of Stadshuset in Stockholm)*. This way visitors will have a good view of the splendid entrance front. Since 1981 Sweden's royal family has occupied the south wing.

History – The architect **Nicodemus Tessin the Elder** (1615-81) was commissioned in 1662 by the Dowager Queen Hedvig Eleonora, King Karl X Gustav's widow, to design a palace similar to the great Baroque palaces of France and the United Provinces. The imposing Baroque interior is to a great extent the work of his son, **Nicodemus Tessin the Younger** (1654-1728). In 1744 Princess Lovisa Ulrika of Prussia, the sister of Frederick the Great, received the palace as a wedding gift on her marriage to King Adolf Fredrik. Carl Hårleman added a storey to the wings and the interior was refurbished in the fashion of the time by Jean Eric Rehn (1717-93), the true originator of the Gustavian style; the furniture was by the cabinet-maker Georg Haupt (1741-84). In Sweden as elsewhere the reaction to Rococo favoured a stricter neo-Classicism or Gustavian style as it was known and it was to some extent a Swedish variation of the French style under Louis XVI.

Court life at Drottningholm enjoyed its heyday under Queen Lovisa Ulrika and her son King Gustav III. The present royal family have made Drottningholm their main residence.

★★★**Drottningholms Slott: Apartments** ⊙ – In spite of later alterations Baroque decoration prevails. The majestic **staircase** has abundant stucco decoration by the Italian master Giovanni Carove. Other outstanding artists have contributed to the interior decoration. The State Apartments are open to the public. Note in particular Hedvig Eleonora's state bedroom designed by Tessin the Elder and completed in 1683. The colour scheme was black and gold until 1701 when the Dowager queen ended the official period of mourning and changed it to the present shade of blue. Also of interest is Queen Lovisa Ulrika's beautiful **library** which is a fine example of the Gustavian style by Jean Eric Rehn.

★★**Court Theatre** – *The theatre can be viewed during guided tours only.* This gem of Baroque architecture was designed by Carl Fredrik Adelcrantz for Queen Lovisa Ulrika, to replace the previous one destroyed by fire. The inaugural performance was held in 1766, however it was under her son Gustav III that this little theatre knew its golden age. Gustav was a great patron of the arts and he was determined to create a Swedish musical tradition. In 1773 he founded the Royal Music Academy and then the Royal Opera. The purity of line, the harmony of its proportions and the delicacy of its blue and white decor make this a masterpiece of Gustavian interior decoration. Every detail is intact including its intricate wooden machinery by Donato Stopani. In 1791 the architect and scenery painter, Louis Jean Desprez added the ballroom.

Opera and ballet performances are given in summer.

The premises for a lyrical masterpiece

King Gustav III (1742-92) was the son of Adolf Fredrik and Lovisa Ulrika of Prussia, sister to Frederick the Great. The little prince was given a French upbringing and it was not long before he began to show a preference for the Caps but made efforts to reach a compromise between the warring Hat and Cap parties. As a true enlightened despot he adopted interventionist policies and after the coup of 1772 the assembled estates were obliged to accept the new constitution drawn up by the king and his advisors. Then again in 1783 he pushed through further reforms which greatly displeased the Swedes and brought about a mood of conspiracy. On the occasion of a masked ball on the night of 5 March 1792 the noble assassin, Ankarström, a former captain in the king's guard, shot the king at close range; Gustav III died a fortnight later. In 1833 the Paris opera house staged the opera Gustav III or The Masked Ball with lyrics by Scribe and music by Auber. In 1859 Verdi used the same theme in his opera Un Ballo in Maschera but Neapolitan censorship was strongly opposed to portraying a regicide on stage. Verdi changed the setting to Massachusetts, the year to 1700 and Gustav III became Riccardo, Duke of Warwick, the governor of Boston.

SWEDEN

Theatre Museum ⊘ – *Admission fee for both the theatre and the museum to be paid here.*
Duke Karl's Pavilion is the setting for an exhibition on European theatre since the 16C with a section on the Drottningholm Court Theatre.

★★**Gardens** – In 1681 Tessin the Younger began to plan the strictly symmetrical Baroque garden flanked by avenues of lime trees. The intricate pattern of the parterre nearest the palace has been replaced by lawns edged with boxwood. The Hercules Fountain, like all the bronze work in the gardens, was the work of Adriaan de Vries and was brought to Sweden as the spoils of war from Prague in 1648 and Denmark in 1659. Beyond is the water garden with its 10 water jets and boxwood lined lawns. The entrance front garden has been laid out to the original design. The landscaped park with two ornamental pools, canals, islands and bridges in the English fashion, was landscaped as a contrast to the formal gardens in 1780.

Drottningholm

★**Kina Slott** ⊘ – *In the south-east corner of the park.* This Chinese Pavilion with its exotic silhouette is the Swedish version of the Grand Trianon; it replaced an earlier building (1753) for Lovisa Ulrika. Carl Fredrik Adelcrantz designed this chinoiserie fantasy from 1763 to 1767. Jean Eric Rehn excelled in his designs for the red, green, yellow and blue rooms with lacquered panels, abundant decorations and showcases displaying delicate Chinese objects.

ESKILSTUNA

Södermanlands län
Population 88 700
Michelin map 985 M 13 or Atlas Europe p 119
Local map see STOCKHOLM: Outskirts

Eskilstuna stands on the banks of the River Eskilstunaån, between Lake Mälaren and Lake Hjälmaren. The town developed as an industrial centre specialising in mechanical engineering in the 19C although its industrial origins go back to the era of the iron forges.

★★**Rademachersmedjorna** ⊘ – *West end of Rademachergatan.* In 1658 King Karl X Gustav engaged Reinhold Rademacher, a merchant from Livonia, to found an ironworks and supply the kingdom with cutlery, needles, stirrups etc. The town's present reputation for manufacturing fine cutlery, surgical instruments and stainless steel is the heritage of this past tradition. Today, six of the forges are maintained as living museums, where a coppersmith, knifesmith, goldsmith, engraver and ironsmith demonstrate their craftsmanship.

Faktoriholmarna – In the 17C these islets were already the scene of industrial activity and from 1813 to 1969 a factory produced firearms. The **Faktorimuseet** ⊘ now houses an exhibition on Eskilstuna's industrial heritage. The displays in the former firearms factory **Vapentekniska Museet** ⊘ outline the development of firearms from the 17C musket to the automatic weapons of today.

EXCURSION

★★**Sigurdristningen** ⊘ – *10km to the north-east, follow signposts to Sundbyholm and just before the entrance to the castle of the same name take a minor road to the right.* The **Sigurd Carving**, to the memory of a dead hero, dates from the 11C and depicts some dramatic episodes in the Scandinavian version of the Teutonic epic poem *Nibelungenlied*. One scene shows how the hero Sigurd managed to thrust his sword through the body of the dragon Fafner whose body is covered with runes.

C. Boisvieux

FALKENBERG
Hallands län
Population 39 000
Michelin map 985 P 9 or Atlas Europe p 123

This picturesque town, once famed for its ceramics and shoe industry, is even better known for its salmon fishing. It is common to see anglers fishing in the River Ätran right in the centre of town. The **old town★** *(southern end of Storgatan)* has retained much of its medieval charm, with quaint low wooden buildings from the 18C and 19C lining the narrow cobbled lanes. **Skrea Strand** to the south is the most popular beach.

★**Tullbron** – Stone bridge erected between 1756 and 1761.

★★**St Laurentii kyrka** ⊙ – *Southern end of Storgatan*. This 13C whitewashed church, dedicated to the patron saint of artisans, acquired its tower in the 1780s. It has a most delightful **interior** where the light pastel colours set off the richly painted nave vaulted ceiling with its heavenly blue background. The central painting depicts Judgement Day. Fragments of 17C wall paintings have been revealed. The baptismal font is dated 16C and the ash-wood pulpit from 1978 shows Jesus raising Jairus' daughter from the dead. Note the votive ship.

★**Törngrens Krukmakeri** ⊙ – *Under the railway bridge then left once past a green house*. The Törngren family continues a 200-year-old tradition in ceramic making. The workshop, housed in the same humble buildings since 1789, produces the same patterns and designs, which have been the hallmark of seven generations of potters.

Falkenbergs Museum ⊙ – *Further down Storgatan*. A granary from the 1860s houses collections on Falkenberg's handicrafts and industry during the last century, highlighting the 1950s.

FALUN ★
Dalarnas län
Population 55 000
Michelin map 985 L 12 or Atlas Europe p 119

Also called the Copper Town, the fame of this administrative and cultural centre in the county of Dalarna lies in a gaping hole called the Great Pit. It was probably as early as the Viking Age that the massive deposits of copper, thereafter called the Great Copper Mountain (Stora Kopparberg) were first discovered. The first written proof dates, however, from 1288. The heyday, of the Falun Mine coincided with the Great Power period of Sweden. At times the mine accounted for about half of the total global production, and with over 1 000 workers the mine was Sweden's largest industrial employer in the 17C. Stora Kopparberg also became the corporate name for Sweden's (maybe the world's) oldest company, its history tracing back to the 13C. Its name has recently been

237

changed to simply Stora (Great). During the 18C copper no longer occupied a key position in the Swedish economy, but Falun remained an important producer of copper far into the 19C. By 1641 Falun had acquired its town charter and the new town centre grew around the Main Square (Stora Torget) and the Falu Kristine Kyrka *(see below)* and the town hall. The miners and the foundry workers had their own districts, and in the wooden quarters some small timber houses still remain *(east of the river, on both sides of Åsgatan northwards past Södra Mariegatan).*

Falun is also an international skiing centre. In 1954 and 1974 the world ski championships were held at the Lugnet ski stadium.

Falu Red Ochre

The red colour that embellishes houses and cottages, and the Swedish landscape, is a side-product of copper-mining. The production of Falu Red Ochre started in the early 17C, and is still very much in demand. Nobody would ever deny that the red-coloured Swedish cottage has become a national symbol. In the early 17C only churches and mansions were painted red, but during the period of Great Power it was important to present a pleasing appearance, and the red colour became more frequent.

SIGHTS

A guided tour of the mine complex every 15min takes 50min. In English and German every day. Call in advance if guided tours are required in French or Italian. Temp +5°C. Waterproof cape and safety helmet are provided at the entrance. Warm clothes and sturdy shoes are recommended. Access from the entrance building in the open space in front of the Stora Museet.

★★ **Falu Koppargruva** ⓥ – *West of the river, a few minutes from the town centre in the direction of Borlänge and Leksand. Straight ahead at the roundabout.* "Sweden's greatest wonder, but as awesome as hell itself", was the account that the famous botanist Carl von Linné gave about this mine when visiting it in 1734. The imposing opencast mine called the Great Pit was given its present shape by an extensive cave-in in 1687, when galleries and chambers collapsed to a depth of 300m, a result of the mining technique itself, since work was mainly carried out in large chambers opened up one beneath the other. Ever since then the Great Pit, around 100m deep and up to 400m wide, has been a major tourist attraction. A lift carries visitors down to a depth of 55m. The tour (about 600m) takes in some of the oldest galleries and chambers, the Creutz Shaft, where work first started in 1662. A tradition exists whereby all drifts are given names. The General Peace, named after a shortlived peace treaty between Britain and France in 1801, is an enormous working chamber of a type common in mines during the 17C. In the Christmas Gift, so named because ore was found at Christmas time, visiting royalties have written their names on the wall.

★★ **Stora Museet** ⓥ – The nearby Company Museum is of considerable interest with its outstanding collections from the technical and industrial past, including Christopher Polhem's ingenious inventions. **Polhem** (1661-1751), the father of Swedish mechanics, did much important work for Stora and the mine, using mechanical devices (the Mechanical Alphabet). The history of the various methods of iron production is illustrated in paintings and scale models. A collection of minerals and cases containing metal plates for printing money (1650-1717) and huge copper coins (1718-59) are fascinating.

★★ **Dalarnas Museum** ⓥ – *Falugatan westwards from the main square and across the river.* This museum introduces the visitor to the very special traditions of the county. Exhibitions deal with folklore, painting and music chiefly, but also local tradition represented by some of the genuine old colourful **folk costumes★★** with their accessories. The fascinating **Dalecarlian paintings★★** are the very soul of the museum. **Folk music★★** has a long-standing symbolic value in Dalarna, and one section is devoted to these traditions, where both the sound of fiddlers, folk singers and girls blowing traditional horns, like small alp-horns, may be enjoyed. **Selma Lagerlöf's study and library★★** have been recreated in this museum. She lived and worked for long periods in Falun.

★★ **Falu Kristine kyrka** ⓥ – This triple aisled basilica was built between 1642 and 1659 and is a testimony to Falun's importance in the 17C. Visitors are immediately struck by the impressive Baroque decoration; the blue and gold colour scheme dates from the 1905-6 restoration. The pompous altarpiece and the golden pulpit were made in 1669. The marble baptismal font and the gallery organ both date from 1906. The choir organ (1982) was an attempt to reconstruct an earlier organ, built in 1724 by Johan Niclas Cahman, who has been called the Father of Swedish organ building.

EXCURSIONS

★★ Carl Larsson-gården, Sundborn ⊘ – *13km north of Falun, first by road 80 in the direction of Gävle, then in the direction of Svärdsjö and Sundborn. In the village of Sundborn follow signposts for Carl Larsson-gården.* The unconventional home of **Carl Larsson** (1853-1919) and his large family is one of Sweden's most visited tourist attractions. The Larssons gave their home an entirely new decorative style and the dark interiors of the 19C were replaced with bright, warm colours. Carl Larsson's wife, Karin, turned from painting to the world of textiles and her tapestries and embroideries may be seen throughout the house. Much of the furniture was designed by Karin and made by the village carpenter. Carl himself contributed murals and portraits of their seven children to the decorative schemes and these figure in a series of watercolours known as the *House in the Sun*.

Carl Larssons Porträttsamling ⊘ – Twelve detailed portraits, depicting local people, are displayed in the Congregation House next to the church. Some of them have been exhibited in Helsinki, Tokyo, Peking and New York. The artist's comments about the people portrayed are available in English, German and French.

Sundborns kyrka ⊘ – In a restoration in 1905, the interior decoration of this red-painted wooden church was done by Carl Larsson.

★ Bjursås – *20km by road 80 in the direction of Rättvik, at Bjursås signposted Dössberget.* Old homestead buildings housing the local history **museum** ⊘ are attractively sited on the mountain of Dössberget. There is a spectacular **view★★** of Bjursås Church and the surrounding landscape of lakes and forests. **Stadigstugan★★★** was the home of the Dalecarlian painter Mats Stadig (1786-1862), and the walls and roofs are graced with his wall paintings in splendid colours *(see Dalecarlian Painting p 232).* Utensils and materials used by him may be seen in Dalarnas Museum in Falun.

GOTLAND★★

Gotlands län
Population 58 000
Michelin map 985 O15 or Atlas Europe p 119

The Pearl of the Baltic lies 80km off the east coast of Sweden and enjoys an exceptionally mild climate, making it a favourite holiday spot with Swedish people. Some 120km long and 56km at its widest point, Gotland's 770km-long coastline consists mainly of shingle beaches along with the occasional stretch of golden sand (**Tofta** south of Visby, **Sudersand** on Fårö and **Ljugarn** on the east side of the island) or lush meadows covered with wild flowers stretching down to the sea, which has eroded the local limestone to form great cliflines, sea caves and offshore sea stacks *(raukar).*

A mild climate and fertile soil make the island famous for roses, orchids (36 of Sweden's 46 species of orchids are to be found on the island) and a wealth of wild flowers.

Of the other smaller islands **Fårö** is paradise to the film director Ingmar Bergman, politicians and other prominent personalities; the great sandy expanse of **Gotska Sandön** is a defence area (restricted access for foreigners); whereas **Stora Karlsö** and **Lilla Karlsö** are bird sanctuaries populated from March to early August by colonies of guillemots and razorbills which breed on every nook and cranny of the steep cliff faces.

Raukar – limestone stacks, Fårö

MERCANTILE CENTRE

The island has been inhabited for over 7 000 years and grave fields, grave mounds, Bronze Age stone ship settings and picture stones were left by successive settlers. In the pre-Viking period the island was a base for the penetration of Eastern Europe. The Gutarna were able seafarers and peaceful traders and by AD 700 (pre-Viking era) dominated the Baltic trade and had forayed south to the Caspian Sea in search of new markets and trade with Byzantium.

By the late 12C German merchants trading on the island of Gotland had already organised themselves into a merchants' association which represented the beginning of the **Hanseatic League**. The delightful town of Visby and 92 marvellously decorated medieval churches are the heritage of the great period of prosperity (12C-early 14C). A century later Visby had declined as a trading centre and its role had been taken over by the trading towns of the southern Baltic. Visby's golden age was drawing to a close and the year 1361 was a turning point in the island's history when it was captured by the Danish king, Valdemar Atterdag. With a few breaks the island then remained under Danish control for 300 years.

Picture stones and churches – Gotland has a rich heritage of Viking picture stones and medieval churches. The finest features of the churches are the square west towers, which gradually became more elaborate – the finest are by Egypticus. There are also some lovely fonts by masters such as **Byzantios**, **Majestatis** and **Sigraf** and wall paintings.

Events

Medieval Week – In early August Visby once again becomes a Hanseatic town, with Hanseatic merchants, monks, jesters and craftsmen all over town.

Gotland Chamber Music Festival – In the first week of August, Swedish and foreign artists participate in this festival.

Stång Games – In the first week of July there are competitions in ancient games, which were popular with islanders in the past.

Shakespeare in Roma Cloister – Shakespeare's works are performed in the setting of a ruined 12C Cistercian monastery.

★★VISBY Population 20 000

Cars are not allowed within the walled city in summer so it is best to leave the car in one of the car parks near the following gates, Söderport, Österport and Fiskarporten.

When seen from the sea the City of Roses and Ruins seems to rise in tiers out of the water. The magnificent medieval walled city and the ruins of its great churches are the heritage of Visby's glorious Hanseatic past.

In the Viking Age Visby was a stronghold and trading post swarming with life and provided the ideal base for the eastern expeditions. By the mid-12C German merchants had settled in the town which again enjoyed a key position in the Baltic trade. In the 13C Visby had a population of 8 000, a third of which were Germans and by the 14C the town was a leading and prosperous member of the Hanseatic League. During the 15C Danes and Germans fought for possession of the town and in 1525 the Lübeckers attacked and burnt much of the town.

Visby is included on the UNESCO list of World Heritage Sites.

★★★**Ringmuren** – The city walls, stretching over 3.4km, are interspersed by towers and gates and consist of a sea wall and a land wall. The **sea wall**, 5.3m high, parallels the shoreline and dates from the late 13C. It incorporates several gateways and a mid-12C gunpowder tower, **Kruttornet** ★⊙, which stood sentinel over the old harbour (now a park, Almedalen). The crenellated **land wall**, 6m high, had an archers' gallery and three landward entrances, **Norderport** (view of Visby), **Österport** and **Söderport**. Of the original 29 towers, 27 remain. In the early 14C the walls were heightened and at the beginning of the next century a stout fortress, Visborg, was built in the south-west corner. Little remains of this powerful stronghold since its demolition by Danish troops in 1679.

★★**Domkyrkan** – When visiting the cathedral one gets some idea of the former splendour of the other churches, now in ruins. The church was founded by German traders and soon became the parish church for the German community in Visby. The original basilica (1175-1225) was extended and remodelled into a hall-church (1230-60). Then again in the early 14C the towers were heightened.

Norderport, Visby

The ruined medieval churches – Today the many medieval churches remain as impressive ruins with unique outlines. Most of them were built and remodelled between the early 13C and the mid-14C. During the Lübeckers assault in 1525 they destroyed all the other churches, except the Domkyrkan, which belonged to the German community.

Medieval city – The medieval network of streets has remained within an area delimited by the three main streets, **Strandgatan**, **Mellangatan** and **Sankt Hansgatan**, all lying parallel to the coast and connected to one another by endless cobbled lanes. Due to a lack of space the storehouses were built upwards and houses were built over the lanes. Some of these storehouses can still be seen in Strandgatan. The 13C **Gamla Apoteket** or Old Pharmacy at no 26 is the best preserved. The 17C half-timbered **Burmeisterska Huset** once belonged to a Lübeck merchant.

Stora Torget – The lively main square was where Valdemar Atterdag exacted a ransom from Visby in 1361, an event which has become the highlight of the popular **Medieval Week** in August. The square is lined by restaurants and boutiques selling Gotland crafts. Adelsgatan is the main shopping street.

★★ **Gotlands Fornsal** ⊘ – Gotland's Historical Museum displays a good collection of picture stones (AD 400-1100), a typical storehouse and the gracious Öja Madonna, a 13C polychrome wooden sculpture *(see Excursions: Öja Church)*.

Botaniska Trädgården – The garden was originally laid out in 1856 by The Society of the Bathing Friends who recommended sea bathing and the growing of medicinal herbs to combat prevailing sickness. The garden now boasts a collection of over 2 000 plants from all over the world. The rose garden is a delight and the ivy covered ruin by the entrance was the west tower of Sankt Olofs kyrka.

EXCURSIONS

West coast north of Visby – *27km by road 149; follow the signs for Snäck and then Kappelshamn. Turn left for Brissund.*

★ **Krusmyntagården** ⊘ – This attractive herb garden, in the true monastic tradition, displays a large selection of medicinal plants *(plants for sale)*.

Lummelundagrottan ⊘ – *Follow the signs for Grottan.* This is the only cave with limestone formations open to visitors in the Nordic countries and is therefore very popular.

Lickershamn – This fishing village claims the highest *rauk*, namely **Jungfrun** (Maiden), as it towers 12m above the clifftop.

North to Fårö – *55km by road 148.*

Bro – The church has an interesting 1300 doorway and a font by Sigraf.

Tingstäde – Predominantly Romanesque frescoes in the tower and a 12C font.

Lärbro – Lovely Gothic church with an unusual octagonal tower.

Beyond Rute there is a restricted military zone and foreigners must stick to road 148 until they reach Fårö Church.

Bunge – The open-air museum, **Bunge Friluftsmuseum** ★★⊙, stands alongside the village church. This fine collection of buildings is divided into the 17C farm (to the left), the 18C farm (to the right) and the 19C farm further east. There is also a fine collection of picture stones.

The ferry across Fårösund takes 10min.

Fårö – Sheep Island is the island paradise of the film director Ingmar Bergman and other well-known personalities. The north-western shores of Fårö have an amazing number of surrealistic **raukar** near the shingle ridge of Gamlehamn, between Digerhuvud to the small fishing hamlet of Helgumannen and at Langhammars. Sandy beaches prevail on the east side at **Sudersand** where there is an impressive inland sand dune, Ulla Hau, 15m high.

Källunge and Dalhem – *30km. Leave Visby by road 147 then right to Källunge.*

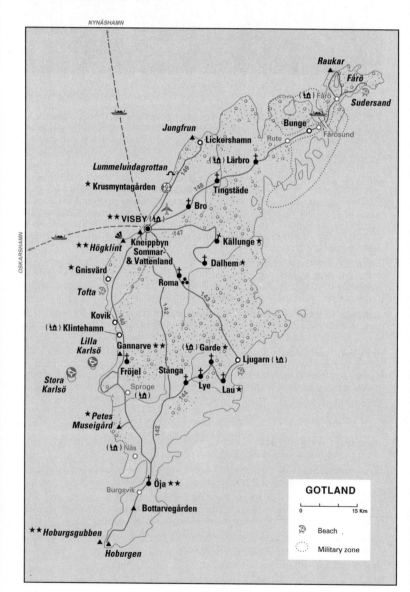

Källunge – The Romanesque nave and west tower of the **kyrka** ★ⓋⒹ are dwarfed by the grandiose Gothic chancel.

Continue by local roads to Dalhem.

Dalhem – This **kyrka** ★Ⓥ is one of the largest with its great tower rising to a height of 50m. Note the sculptures of the west doorway by Egypticus and the **stained-glass windows★★** in the chancel.

Ljugarn – *66km. Leave Visby by road 143.*

Roma – The church displays typical Gotland features and nearby are the ruins of a Cistercian monastery church.

Continue to Ljugarn on the east coast.

Ljugarn – The island's second largest town is a port and seaside resort. On the coast to the north of the town there are more weirdly shaped rock stacks *(raukar)*.

Take road 144 then a local road to Lau.

Lau – This impressively large **kyrka** ★Ⓥ comprises an early-13C triple-aisled nave extended by an equally large chancel dating from 1300 and the result is a harmonious ensemble. The **triumphal cross** is mid-13C whereas the **mural** depicting the Last Judgement dates from 1520.

Take the local road north to Garde.

Garde – The 11C **kyrka** ★Ⓥ, with its medieval enclosure wall and four lich-gates, is known for its murals which show a strong Byzantine influence.

Take road 144 to Lye.

Lye – This large well preserved **kyrka** Ⓥ is known for its **stained-glass windows★★**.

Continue on road 144.

Stånga – The village is known for annual games in July when athletes compete in traditional sports not unlike Scotland's highland games. The limestone reliefs embedded in the wall alongside the south doorway of the **kyrka** Ⓥ are said to be the work of Egypticus.

The west coast south of Visby – *110km. Leave Visby via Söderväg and Toftavägen to take road 140 in the direction of Klintehamn. Follow signs to Kneippbyn.*

Kneippbyn Sommar– & Vattenland Ⓥ – **Villa Villekulla** is the house that featured in the films of Astrid Lindgren's Pippi Longstocking stories. The house is now part of a large attraction park but this chaotic, crazy and cosy place is a paradise for Pippi fans.

Follow signs to Högklint.

Högklint – From this clifftop, 48m above sea level, there is a spectacular **view★★** of Visby in the distance.

Return to road 140; take the road to the right signposted Gnisvärd Kyrka. There is a boat grave on the left.

★ **Gnisvärd** – This was one of the west coast's largest fishing hamlets and a serried rank of curing huts and net-drying stands are still to be seen.

Kovik – This old fishing hamlet on its sandbank has a fishing museum. The small chapel commemorates those who lost their lives at sea.

Klintehamn – Boats leave from the harbour for the nature reserve on the island of Stora Karlsö.

Gannarve – The Bronze Age **stone ship setting★★**, 29m long and 5m wide, is only one of two that remain.

Fröjel – The **kyrka** Ⓥ stands in a splendid clifftop site quite apart from the ruins of its defensive tower (north of the churchyard). Notice the remarkable **stone labyrinth** in the churchyard west of the church.

16km detour via Djupvik and Hammarudd.

★★ **Scenic coastal route** – The minor road south from the late-19C fishing hamlet of Djupvik offers splendid views of the sea and the offshore islands of Karlsö.

Take the side road to the right signposted Petes.

★ **Petes Museigård** Ⓥ – *In Hablingbo.* This large 18C farmhouse is now a museum and the barn has an interesting display on building traditions.

Lansmuseet Gotlands Fornsal

Öja Crucifix (detail)

Return to road 140 and continue on road 142 to Burgsvik then turn left.

Öja – The sturdy **kyrka** ★★⊙ tower was the work of a 14C master mason, Egypticus. The **Öja Crucifix**★★★ was originally surrounded by a wealth of carved figures. The Virgin on the left is a replica of the original **Öja Madonna** now in the Gotlands Fornsal, Visby.

Return to road 142 and continue south.

Bottarvegården ⊙ – In Vamlingbo. This character-istic south Gotland farm (1844), a huddle of turf-covered buildings, is now a museum.

Take the minor road that follows the coast between Kettelviken and Hoburgen.

★★Scenic route – The tradi-tional arable landscape divided up by dry-stone walls gives way to sparkling views of the sea, and green swards bright with wild flowers, the yellow buttercup (April and May) is followed by the deep blue echium vulgare (June and July).

Hoburgen – This headland is famous for its limestone formations, in particular the striking **Hoburgsgubben**★★, Old Man of Hoburgen.

GRIPSHOLMS SLOTT★★

Södermanlands Län
Michelin map 985 M 14 or Atlas Europe p 119
Local map see STOCKHOLM: Outskirts

The delightful little town of Mariefred and its illustrious neighbour **Gripsholms Slott**, with its important portrait collection, are situated on an inlet on Lake Mälaren which pro-vides a popular approach by steamboat, on the trusty old SS *Mariefred* plying between Stockholm and Mariefred.

The attractive town of **Mariefred** with its cobbled streets and wooden houses grew around a Carthusian monastery (Pax Mariae) founded in 1493 by the lord of Gripsholm.

In the 18C Gustav III encouraged his worthy neighbours, the townspeople, to build 2-storey houses like the Gustavian town hall dating from 1784 on Rådhustorget.

The builder of the first fortress (14C) on the island site was Bo Jonsson Grip a state councillor but it was Gustav Vasa who erected the present impressive castle, a hexag-onal building round an inner courtyard with circular towers at four corners. Over the centuries his successors have altered and redecorated the castle, notably Gustav III who took up residence in 1772 and started the great portrait collection.

Gripsholms Slott ⊙ – Since 1822 the castle has been the home of the **national por-trait collection** numbering some 4 000 works from the 16C onwards; 16C-17C (Gustav Vasa-Karl XII) on the first floor; 18C (Fredrik I-Gustav III) on the second floor; 19C-20C on the third floor portraying writers, contemporary politicians and artists, with for instance Greta Garbo by Einar Nerman and a bronze bust of Ingrid Bergman. Foreign portraits are found in a special suite of rooms on the first floor.

The second floor is the main storey and most of the interior decoration dates from the 1770s and 1780s. The largest room in the King's Apartment is the council chamber, **Rikssalen**, completed in the 1590s but refurbished several times since then. Gustav III's beautiful white drawing room, **Runda Salongen**, in the Theatre Tower was designed by Jean Eric Rehn the true originator of the Gustavian style. Gustav III's fascination with the theatre resulted in another elegant Gustavian theatre, **Slottsteatern**, with its 18C machinery. This intimate theatre in the strict neo-Classical style was the masterpiece of Erik Palmstedt (1741-1803).

Gripsholm

GÄLLIVARE-MALMBERGET

Norrbottens län
Population 21 700
Michelin map 985 E 17 or Atlas Europe p 108 – Local map see LAPPLAND

Arriving from the south through endless forests, the visitor will suddenly catch sight of a town spread out ahead: Gällivare and its twin, the mining town of Malmberget. They lie 70km north of the Arctic Circle.

GÄLLIVARE

Dundret – Altitude 820m. *9km south by road 45, after 5km follow the sign Dundret, Toppstuga.* Even in the 19C the mountain of Dundret was recommended as a suitable spot to see the Midnight Sun (2 June to 12 July – a café on the summit opens from 9pm to 1am). The **panorama★★★** reveals Malmberget to the north, the peak of Kebnekaise to the north-west, the national parks of Sarek and Padjelanta to the west, the valley of the River Lule with the Norwegian mountains visible on the horizon. The large timber building half way down the mountain is called the Bear Trap, Björnfällan, and to reach it go back down to road 45 and continue in the direction of Gällivare until you come to the sign Dundret, Björnfällan. Built of 400-year-old pine trees from northern Finland, it was designed by the Finnish architect Esko Lehmola the designer of President Kekkonen's sauna. The building is part of a holiday centre with different facilities including downhill and cross-country skiing.

Lappkyrka ⊙ – *The sign Lappkyrka is east of the white wooden church; follow the road alongside the church and continue straight ahead to cross the railway line then turn right at the signpost Gamla Kyrkan.* This simple wooden church and belfry stand on the bank of the River Vassara with Dundret in the background. It was built with money raised by the Swedish people, a silver one-penny coin from every family, by decree of King Frederick, which accounts for its second name Friedrich. When it was first built between 1747 and 1754 most of the members were Sami thus the epithet Lapp Church.

"The Pensive Lapp" – *Close to the white church, but on the other side of Lasarettsgatan westwards.* The inscription on this granite monument reads "This land was mine in bygone days. Bless my land in days to come".

Hembygdsmuseet ⏱ – This local heritage museum is housed on the second and third floors of the red-brick school building. The museum has Sami handicrafts for sale. Tourist Information Centre on the first-floor.

Hembygdsområdet ⏱ – *In the direction of Jokkmokk immediately before the River Vassara follow the sign camping then continue past the sports camp.* Collection of buildings from the late 19C and early 20C as well as a Sami camp.

MALMBERGET

5km north of Gällivare take Parkgatan which becomes Malmbergsleden.

Mining – Malmberget literally means ore mountain; along with Kiirunavaara they are Sweden's largest reserves of iron-ore. The earliest finds date back to the middle of the 18C but commercial exploitation was delayed due to transportation difficulties and conflicts with the Sami who considered the mountain holy. Mining actually started in the 1860s by several Englishmen who also financed the railway link with Luleå harbour; the first wagon left for Luleå in 1888. The mines were then taken over by Luossavaara-Kiirunavaara AB (LKAB). The population rose from 147 to 7 000 in the space of eight years (1891-99). At present six million tonnes are mined annually from a seam of iron ore 850m down.

MINE TOURS

These start at the Tourist Information Centre and in addition to a visit to the mine they take in the museum or the shanty town.

Gruvtur LKAB: Iron Mine – *3hr.* This tour begins with a visit to the **Gruvmuseet** ⏱ or Mining Museum where the displays illustrate 250 years of mining and a slide show gives an insight into mining conditions today. The next part of the tour includes a 35-40km bus trip to see the various production sites and a visit 815m underground to the ore face. The scoops of the electrically powered trucks, large enough to hold a VW Golf, have a loading capacity of 120t.

Aitik-turen: Copper Mine – *3hr 30min.* This tour begins with the Kåkstan or shanty town *(see below)* and then continues for 16km to Aitik, an enormous open-cast mine (2.5km long, 800m wide and 300m deep). This is the largest European copper mine still operating and Sweden's largest gold mine with an annual production of 2t of gold.

Kåkstan ⏱ – *Follow the signs to Kåkstan from the Statoil petrol station.* Early prospecting and mining attracted would-be-miners from far and near and very soon the pit was surrounded by a shanty town which was moved gradually further away as the pit increased in size. Today the buildings have been re-erected on the original site. Activities are organised in summer and just before Christmas.

Gropen – *East of the shanty town.* The mine divides Malmberget in two and houses are moved as the pit moves progressively outwards.

GÖTA KANAL★★

Västra Götalands län, Östergötlands län

Michelin map 985 N 11-13 or Atlas Europe pp 118-119

The Göta Kanal, as it crosses Sweden from Gothenburg in the west to Stockholm in the east, is a relaxing way to discover a cross-section of Swedish landscapes and towns, not to mention the Swedes themselves, always great sailors.

For yachtsmen this is serious sailing country as the journey includes several stretches of open water in the lakes of Roxen, Boren, Vättern, Viken and Vänern, where it is possible to explore the islands and shores.

Many were to ponder the idea of a waterway from coast to coast, linking the great Lake Vättern and Lake Vänern, until Baltzar von Platen (1766-1829) a naval officer and leading politician, had the foresight and energy to see the project through. Building started in 1810, the year the Swedish Parliament approved the plan, on what was to be the country's biggest ever construction project. For 22 years as many as 58 000 conscripted soldiers laboured to build the 190km waterway between Mem and Sjötorp. With the Göta Älv, the Trollhätte Kanal, Lake Vänern and Lake Vättern the canal formed a waterway 398km long. The inauguration ceremony took place in 1832 in the presence of the king and royal family but the guiding spirit, Von Platen, had died three years earlier.

The canal greatly improved Sweden's communications as steamers carried both passengers and goods, however the railways soon rivalled water transport and the canal became a popular tourist waterway.

Berg on the Göta Canal

C. Boisvieux

Some statistics – Over the canal's total length of 190km there are 58 locks; the average depth is 3m and the width on the surface varies between 7m and 26m. The canal is open to general traffic from early May to mid-October. In some sections where the lock-keeper has several bridges and locks in his charge a delay is inevitable. Some bridges have fixed opening times depending on local traffic, other bridges are remote controlled. Some may want to hire their own boat and sail at their own pace, others may want to travel more leisurely by taking one of the **cruise boats** and the energetic can cycle on the towpaths (144km from Sjötorp).

SOME SIGHTS ALONG THE WAY FROM WEST TO EAST

★★ **Gothenburg** – See GÖTEBORG.

Trollhättan – The strong running Göta Älv flows from its source in Lake Vänern to Göteborg and into the Kattegatt a total distance of 82km. The one impediment to this important link between Vänern and the west coast was the roaring falls at Trollhättan. To overcome this obstacle **Christopher Polhem** (1661-1751) planned a series of locks but it was 1800 before the first lock was built. The opening of the Göta Kanal in 1832 with its larger capacity meant that the Trollhätte waterway had to be extended. In 1844 the system included one lock in three flights. A new system was built in 1910. Take the opportunity to visit one of Polhem's locks (Ekeblad), the **Kanalmuseet**, as well as the present-day locks *(slussar)* now used by 3 500 cargo ships and 65 000 leisure craft annually. The impressive Olidestationen, a granite power station dating from 1910 is Sweden's oldest hydroelectric power station. The Energy Centre (Energihuset Insikten) gives an insight into the world of energy.

Vänern – Sweden's largest lake has a lovely shoreline, numerous islands and sandy beaches. Other sights described on the shores of Vänern are Lidköping, Läckö Slott, Mariestad and Karlstad.

★ **Vättern** – Sweden's second largest lake stretching 160km from north to south and 31km wide. *See VÄTTERN and VADSTENA.*

GÖTEBORG★★

GOTHENBURG – Västra Götalands län – Population 454 000
Michelin map 985 O 8 or Atlas Europe p 118

Not without reason, Gothenburg has been designated by Swedes themselves as Sweden's most friendly town. Sweden's second city and gateway to the west is favourably located on the west coast equidistant from three Scandinavian capitals, Stockholm, Copenhagen and Oslo. With strong maritime traditions Gothenburg at the mouth of the River Göta is Scandinavia's number one seaport and a bustling commercial centre.

The city boasts excellent facilities for conferences, trade fairs, sporting events and rock concerts but it is its cosmopolitan, lively and friendly welcome that makes it so popular as a venue. An international Travel and Tourism Fair (TUR) in spring and a Book Fair in the autumn attract visitors to the exhibition centre, **Svenska Mässan**. Shoppers may enjoy Northern Europe's largest indoor shopping centre, **Nordstan**. Scandinavia's largest stadium, **Ullevi**, with a seating capacity of 47 000, and **Scandinavium**, with 12 500 seats, the second largest indoor arena after the Globe Arena in Stockholm, are stages for events ranging from rock concerts to sports events. The annual Gothia Cup is the world's greatest junior football tournament, with about 25 000 participants from 52 countries.

HISTORICAL NOTES

The original settlement was founded by King Karl IX at Hisingen to the west of the River Göta but when it was destroyed in 1611 by the Danes and the Norwegians, Sweden was cut off from the sea. To avoid a repetition of this, King Gustav II Adolf founded a new town on the present site in 1619 and granted it a charter two years later. Due to the strategic nature of the site and its difficult clay subsoil the king enlisted the help of Dutch engineers to build his new town. The early town had a decidedly Dutch look about it with its geometric street pattern, canals, walls and city fortifications. The Kronhuset, Skansen Kronan and Skansen Lejonet all date from this period. The Swedish East India Company was founded in 1731 (Dutch 1602) and the late 18C was a period of prosperity as the merchants traded in cargoes of tea, porcelain, silk and spices from the Far East. Herring fishing also thrived in the second half of the 18C on the west coast and combined to make Gothenburg a prosperous centre of commerce and shipping. When the Napoleonic Wars (late 18C-early 19C) occasioned the continental blockade Gothenburg became a port of transit for British goods to the European markets. Good commercial relations were established and many Scottish merchants (Dickson, Chalmers and Carnegie) settled in the town and handsomely patronised cultural and social institutions. The town's prosperity increased with the coming of the railway and the building of the Göta Canal (1822-32). For many of the Swedish emigrants on their way to America between 1850 and 1870 the sight of Gothenburg on the horizon was often the last cherished view of their native land. In the early 20C Gothenburg became a busy industrial town with heavy engineering, shipbuilding and maritime transport (Stena Line). Gothenburg is headquarters to some of the most prestigious flagships of Swedish industry such as Volvo, SKF ball bearings, Hasselblad cameras, Saab Ericsson Space.

SIGHTSEEING IN GOTHENBURG

Transport – Gothenburg is built on a bed of clay which precludes a subway, however, the city boasts a tram network which functions as well as any underground system. The blue and white **tram cars** are named after personalities with Gothenburg connections. Tickets, timetables, routes and fares for buses and trams are available at travel information centres (Tidpunkten) at Brunnsparken, Drottningtorget, Nils Ericssons-platsen or Folkungabron. The tram/bus drivers also sell tickets. Enquiries ☎ 031-80 12 35.

In summer **Lisebergslinjen** (vintage trams) ☉ operate between Central Station and Liseberg.

The **paddan** ☉ or flat-bottomed boats are a fascinating way to discover this maritime city as they glide along the canals past stately canalside buildings and under 20 bridges. The boats leave from the bridge at Kungsportsplatsen.

Göteborg Sightseeing organises **boat trips** from Lilla Bommen to Nya Älvsborgs Fästning and Vinga.

With a **Göteborg Card** (Göteborgskortet) you are entitled to free boat and tram rides, free parking at municipal car parks, a free sightseeing tour, free entry to the amusement park and museums, discounts in certain shops and restaurants. The card can be purchased at tourist information offices, the amusement park, Pressbyrån kiosks, hotels and camp sites.

Shopping – The main shopping areas are Nordstan, Avenyn, Linnégatan and in Haga. Look out for the tax-free sign in the windows (not for EU members).

Entertainment – For more information on what's on ☎ 031-61 25 00. Information and tickets to sports events, concerts and theatres are available from Scandinavium ☎ 031-81 10 20.

Further information about the city on the internet: www.gbg-co.se or by e-mail: turistinfo@gbg-co.se

MARITIME GOTHENBURG

The waterfront
from Götheborgs Utkiken south to Älvsborgsbron

When the shipyards closed down in the 1970s the harbour lost much of its activity. Some of the shipyards have been redeveloped as housing schemes easily reached by ferries crisscrossing the river. The former Eriksberg owned shipyard which faces Majnabbe harbour is now the site for an interesting project, the rebuilding of the *Götheborg*, **Ostindiefararen Götheborg** ⊘, at the Terra Nova Shipyard. The Swedish East India clipper *Götheborg* ran aground and sank with her cargo of tea, porcelain, silk and spices from Canton as she was entering Gothenburg harbour in 1745. Much of the cargo has been recovered and the present project entails the building of a replica of the sailing ship dating from 1738. Recovered sections of the clipper and 18C shipbuilding manuals have been scrutinized to provide new drawings for the future *Götheborg*. The keel was laid in June 1995 and the ship is scheduled to be launched in 2002. Later the clipper will set off on a research and trade expedition to Canton following the traditional 18C route.

Similar rescue operations

The Mary Rose – Four-masted vice flagship of Henry VIII's fleet sank off Portsmouth on 19 July 1545. Built in 1509 and raised in 1982 *(see The Green Guide Great Britain)*.

Batavia – Dutch East India merchant ship. Built in 1628 and ran aground off Australia on her maiden voyage *(see The Green Guide The Netherlands: Lelystad)*.

Vasa – A warship the pride of Gustavus Adolphus' navy. Built in 1628 and sank in Stockholm harbour on 10 August 1628 on her maiden voyage. She was raised in 1961 *(see Stockholm)*.

Kronan – Warship of the Swedish navy which was twice the size of the *Vasa*. Built between 1665 and 1672 she exploded and sank fully equipped and manned in 1679. She was rediscovered in 1980 *(see KALMAR)*.

The port is actually composed of several harbours, with a total capacity of 30 million tonnes of cargo: the oil harbour handling 18 million tonnes of crude oil annually; Skandiahamnen harbour, the largest container terminal in Scandinavia and also the ferry terminal for passenger traffic from England via Norway; Älvsborgshamnen harbour for the roll-on/roll-off cargo; and the Innerhamnen harbour with its roll-on/roll-off berth, the largest banana import harbour in Scandinavia, to meet the high Swedish consumption of 20kg per person annually.

Götheborgs-Utkiken ⊘ **(BT)** – *Enter from the north side*. This red and white office skyscraper is a striking example of unconventional architecture of the late 1980s by Ralph Erskine (b 1914) an Englishman resident in Sweden. A lift whisks visitors 86m above sea level to the café with its breathtaking **panorama★★** of the city and its harbour.

Lilla Bommens Hamn (BT) – This basin is the departure point for a variety of local excursions (Elfsborg, Vinga, Marstrand and Hisingen) and evening cruises organised by Börjessons Restaurang & Utflyktsbåtar. The four-masted barque *Viking* (1906) made her last voyage in 1948, then served as a sail training ship between 1957 and 1994. Following restoration the sailing ship is now fitted out as a restaurant, hotel and cafeteria, providing entertainment during the summer. There is also a marina for visiting boats.

Göteborgsoperan ⊘ **(ABT)** – *Packhuskajen*. The nautical lines of Gothenburg's new opera house, inaugurated in 1994, are highly appropriate for its waterfront site. The architect Jan Izikowitz's design has visitors entering through the bows to reach the semicircular glass walled foyer with its superb panorama of the river, harbour and shipping, an auditorium resembling a funnel and the fly house, a ship's bridge. The opera has a permanent orchestra, choir, soloists and ballet company who perform in about six new productions every year. For the opening performance Karl-Birger Blomdahl's 1959 space fantasy *Aniara* was an appropriate choice to test the advanced stage technology and the acoustics. The conducted tour takes visitors to the wings, backstage, workshops and rehearsal rooms.

Göteborgs Maritima Centrum ⊘ **(ATU)** – *Packhuskajen*. The maritime park with historic vessels and boat displays brings to life Gothenburg's seafaring past. Enter via the ferry *Dan Broström* named after a well-known shipowner. The ferry also provides facilities for a café, souvenir shop and seafood restaurant.

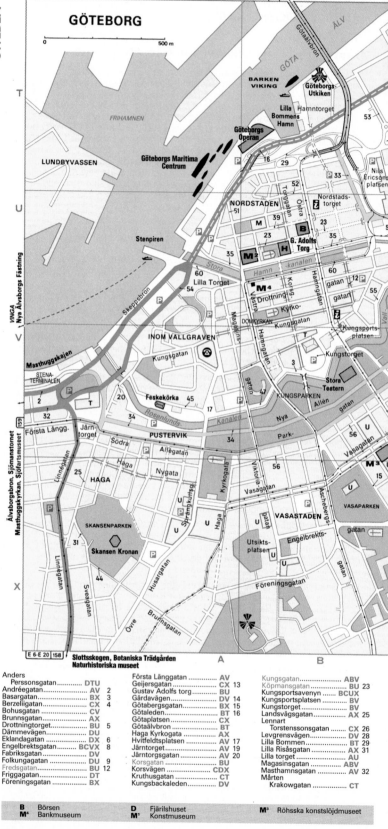

SWEDEN

GÖTEBORG

0   500 m

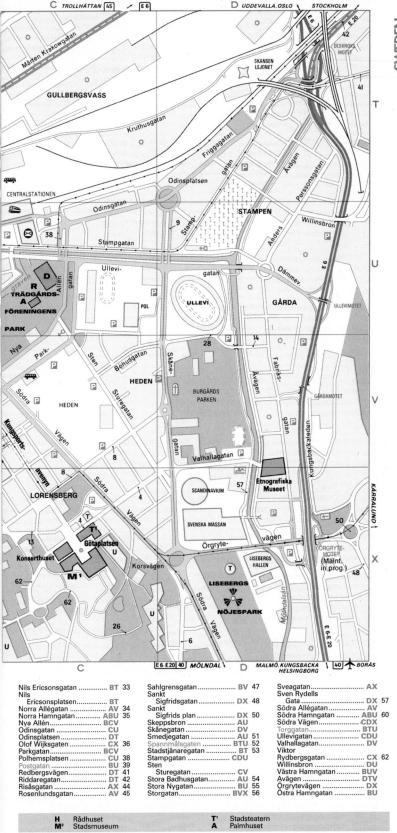

H	Rådhuset	**T'**	Stadsteatern
M²	Stadsmuseum	**A**	Palmhuset

The floating museum of 11 ships includes the destroyer *Småland*, the submarine *Nordkaparen*, a lightship and tug boats. The Göta canal boats are berthed here when not in service: *Juno* built in 1874, *Wilhelm Tham* built in 1912 and *Diana* built in 1931.

The first stone pier **Stenpiren** (AU) dating from 1845 is graced by a copy of Carl Milles' **statue** in memory of the many Swedish emigrants to the New World. The original statue in the American town of Wilmington, Delaware, is a memorial to the Swedish community that settled there in 1638. **Masthuggskajen** (AV) is the location for the Stena Line's Denmark terminal.

Frederikshaven is 3hr away.

Masthuggskyrkan – *Stigbergstorget*. The church is one of the city's most distinctive landmarks as it stands high on a mound which affords a good view of Göteborg. The church built between 1914 and 1919 by Sigfrid Ericson is an excellent example of Swedish National Romantic architecture. When the bells first rang out it was to mark the start of the First World War.

★ **Interior** – This very unusual three-aisled hall-church is reminiscent of ancient Nordic wooden architecture, its high middle aisle dressed with timber beams. The white-washed walls are in striking contrast to the wooden interior. Each pillar is carved in a different fashion and the one supporting the southern gallery is called the Tree of Life. Note the model of an East India clipper which is on loan from the Sjöfartsmuseet. The lamps of cast iron are crested with dragon heads. The frame of the Byzantine style **altarpiece** was the work of Sigfrid Ericson and the wooden sculptures by Ninnan Santesson were added in 1923. The triumphal crucifix by the same artist is from 1925.

Gathenhielmskulturreservatet – This preservation area of 1 and 2-storey wooden houses and their gardens is typical of the city's residential areas prior to 1850. **Gathenhielmskulturreservatet** belonged to the renowned privateer Captain Lars Gathenhielm and is typical of the type of wooden house common in Gothenburg before recurring fires swept through the city between 1794 and 1813.

★ **Sjöfartsmuseet** ⊘ – *Stigbergstorget*. Amid the smell of pitch pine this maritime museum celebrates Göteborg's East India trade, the life of seafarers and the development of ships and shipping by means of paintings and model ships. One of the main attractions is the East India merchant ship *Finland*. The collection of figureheads is quite impressive. In the **Aquarium** both Nordic and tropical species can be admired.

Sjömanstornet – This 49m-high tower stands next to the museum with the entrance facing the river. It is surmounted by the statue of a patiently waiting seaman's wife, *Woman by the Sea*, a memorial to the seamen who lost their lives in the First World War. From the top *(spiral staircase with 192 steps or lift)* there is a splendid **view**★★ of the city and the harbour.

The transatlantic liners have been replaced by luxury cruisers at **Stigbergskajen**. The *SeaCat* – a catamaran – takes passengers to the Danish town of Frederikshavn in 1hr 45min.

Fiskhamnen – Enjoy the scene of early morning **Fiskauktion** (fish auctions) ⊘ here on Tuesdays to Fridays. The auction only lasts 15 to 30min. Beyond **Majnabbehamnen** is Stena Line's Germany terminal and the journey to Kiel lasts 14hr.

Klippans kulturreservat – *Carnegiekajen, enter from Adolf Edelsvärds gata*. This harbourside preservation area was already a port in the 17C and it makes an ideal place for a stroll. Many of the buildings are associated with the East India Company and the period of prosperity in the 18C. Carnegie brewery was an important activity in the 19C. This was the site of the original 14C Älvsborg Fortress until it was replaced by the new fortress in the 17C. Services are still held in the Birgitta Chapel which dates from 1857. A pier-restaurant overlooks this part of the harbour.

Älvsborgsbron – The impressive suspension bridge, opened in 1966, connects the suburb and site of the original settlement, Hisingen, to Gothenburg. Standing 933m long with the roadway 45m above the river and a main span of 417m, the bridge affords a fine **view** of the harbour and inlet.

CENTRAL GOTHENBURG

Gustaf Adolfs Torg (BU) – Since 1621, when the city was founded, this has been the centre of the city and was called Grand Square until 1854 when the statue of King Gustav II Adolf was unveiled. A plan of the town in 1644 is inlaid in the cobbled square. The pillared building to the north is the former stock exchange, **Börsen** (BU B), dating from 1849 and today it is the setting for civic receptions and banquets. Next door is **Wenngren's House**, a mansion built in 1759 for the city councillor of the same name. The third storey was a later addition. Adjoining this is the **Stadshuset** built a year earlier in 1758 as an armoury but it has since seen service as a guard-house and a fire station. Today the two buildings are home to the city councillors and administrators. The **Rådhuset** (BU H) on the west of the square was built in 1672 to designs by Nicodemus Tessin the Elder. Later alterations include the columned façade and north wing to designs by Gunnar Asplund.

★**Kungsportsavenyn** (BCVX) – Known to Gothenburgers as Avenyn the pulsating artery of Gothenburg stretches from Götaplatsen northwards for almost 1 km to the canal and Kungsportsplatsen. The tree-lined boulevard with its cafés and restaurants has become the living room for locals from early spring to autumn.

Stora Teatern (BV) – This musical theatre, specialising in light opera, musicals and ballet, is one of Sweden's oldest, as it was inaugurated in 1859.

Götaplatsen (CX) – The cultural heart of the city is located at the southern end of Avenyn and most of the buildings date from 1923 to 1935. Carl Milles central statue **Poseidon Fountain**★★ is the powerful symbol of maritime Göteborg. Grouped around the square are Göteborgs Konstmuseum *(see below)*, **Stadsteatern** (CX T1) with its repertoire of drama and comedies and the **Konserthuset** (CX) home to the Göteborg Symphony Orchestra under the baton of Neeme Järvi. The concert hall boasts excellent acoustics and is used by Deutsche Grammophon for recordings.

Haga (AX) – *Tramcar 1, 3 or 4 to Järntorget.* Around the 1640s fishermen and other workers favoured this area beyond the fortifications and by the middle of the 19C it had become a working-class area.
Many of the houses date from this period when two wooden storeys were added to a stone-built ground floor to get round fire regulations stipulating that no wooden house could be more than 2-storeys high. Haga Nygata, the main street, is lined with shops and cafés.

Feskekörka (AV) – *Overlooks Rosenlundskanalen; tramcar to Järntorget.* This indoor fish and seafood market has a restaurant in its eaves. Built in 1874 its church-like outline has earned it its nickname of Fish Church. Morning is the best time to visit. Fish shops are closed on Mondays and restaurants don't usually serve seafood or fish on Sundays and Mondays as fishermen don't go out at weekends.

Feskekörka

MUSEUMS

★★★**Göteborgs Konstmuseum** ⊘ (CX M¹) – *Götaplatsen.* This important art museum includes holdings of 19C and 20C Scandinavian art, 17C Dutch and Flemish art, 16C-18C Italian and Spanish art, 19C and 20C French art as well as contemporary international art. The highlights are Scandinavian art from the 1880s and 1890s and the **Göteborg Colourists** (Göteborgskoloristerna) who were active between 1930 and 1950. The new Hasselblad Centre for photography and the Stena Room for exhibitions of contemporary art are to be found on the refurbished and extended ground floor.
A lift takes the visitor up to the **Fürstenberg Gallery**★★★ named after the influential benefactor Pontus Fürstenberg (1827-1902). The first room displays a survey of works by Scandinavian artists who lived in Paris and Grez-sur-Loing in the 1880s. The room on the left covers the National Romantic period (1890s): Richard Bergh, Nils Kreuger, Karl Nordström, Prince Eugen and Bruno Liljefors. The innermost room contains interesting works by Carl Larsson. The room on the right regroups

works by artists from the 1880s notably Ernst Josephson's *Näcken* – a Nordic water sprite – and Peder Severin Krøyer's painting depicting a happy group of artists in Skagen, Denmark. The octagonal **Arosenius Room★★★** is noteworthy for its delightful and humorous pictures by Ivar Arosenius (1878-1909). The two rooms beyond contain the works of the **Göteborg Colourists**. These are characterised by a colourful lyricism. Distinctive individualists, these artists never really formed a group. Preceded by Karl Isakson (1878-1922) and Carl Kylberg (1878-1952), they are represented here by Ivan Ivarson, Inge Schiöler and Ragnar Sandberg.

Collections on this floor include works by Sigrid Hiertén (1885-1948), her husband Isaac Grünewald (1889-1946), Nils Dardel (1890-1976) and Einar Jolin (1889-1946). These painters were disciples of Matisse between 1908 and 1911 and belonged to a new generation in Swedish art.

★★ Röhsska Konstslöjdmuseet Ⓥ (**BVX M³**) – This arts and crafts museum was opened to the public in 1916 following a bequest made by the Röhss brothers. The main entrance to the Swedish National Romantic style building is flanked by two marble lions from the Ming dynasty (1368-1644). The basement has a collection of textiles whereas the ground floor is reserved for temporary exhibitions of modern art and crafts. On the first floor the display covers European handicrafts (17C-19C). The very latest in Nordic and international design has its place here. The second floor follows the stylistic developments in furniture, silver, glassware, porcelain and textiles. A section traces the development in publishing from the earliest manuscripts. The third floor is devoted to East Asian art.

Etnografiska Museet (**DVX**) – The ethnographic museum has a unique South American collection with some lovely prehistoric Peruvian Paracas textiles.

Göteborgs stadsmuseum Ⓥ (**BU M²**) – *Norra Hamngatan 12*. The dignified canalside house, Swedish **East India House★★**, was constructed between 1750 and 1762 to serve as headquarters, warehouse and auction room. The company was declared bankrupt in 1809 and formally liquidated four years later but it was only in 1861 that the premises were assigned to the Gothenburg museums. Following a recent refurbishment the museum will house three different museums under one roof.

Archaeology: From prehistoric times up to the Viking period.

History: The city's history and changing fortunes over the centuries are outlined by these collections. The section on Oriental porcelain is particularly fine. Also included are period interiors, furniture, household utensils, costumes, handicraft and medieval and ecclesiastical collections from western Sweden.

Industry: Collections recount the industrial development and heritage of the Göteborg region.

★ Naturhistoriska museet Ⓥ – *Slottsskogsparken. Leave by road 158* (**AX**) *to the south.* Gothenburg's oldest museum was founded in 1833 and its extensive collection includes two whale skeletons, a cachalot stranded on the coast in 1988 and a young blue whale stranded in 1865.

Skansen Kronan Ⓥ (**AX**) – *Tramcar 1 to Prinsgatan; the entrance is on Risåsgatan.* This is one of two small fortresses built to protect the city in the 17C. Its roof is crested with a golden crown. It has been converted into a military museum, **Militärmuseet**, with displays of weapons and uniforms from the 17C up to the Second World War. From the tower there is a good view of the city.

Bankmuseum Ⓥ (**BU M⁴**) – *Södra Hamngatan 11*. Right in the heart of the business district, on the canalside, Chalmerska Huset dating from 1805-7 was occupied by a bank at the turn of the last century and now a green marble chamber houses a fine collection of coins and medals.

PARKS AND GARDENS

As early as 1746 Linnaeus called Gothenburg "the prettiest city in the whole land".

★★ Liseberg Ⓥ (**DX**) – *Tramcar 5; enter from Örgrytevägen*. Sweden's number one tourist attraction is much more than an amusement park. Switchback rides, dizzy loop-the-loops, the roller coaster, the noise, the fun, the music and the excitement are all there, moreover it includes a pleasant green setting with colourful flower beds, many sculptures, bandstands, ballroom dancing, cafés, restaurants and theatres making it an enjoyable outing for all the family. The amusements of Liseberg Cirkus are for small children.

★★ Trädgårdsföreningen Ⓥ (**CU**) – *Entrance in Södra Vägen*. Since the park was laid out by the horticultural society in 1842 it has always been popular as a meeting place. It has its own crystal palace in the Palm House, **Palmhuset★★** (**CU A**), built by a Scottish company in 1878 (refurbished in the 1980s). Each season offers special delights: camellias in February, orchids from March to April while the giant waterlily is at its best in July. The rose garden, **rosariet★★★**, is a particular delight with around 7 000 bushes representing 2 600 species, some of which are quite rare.

Early July and late August are the two main flowering periods. Green and brown labels indicate plants for sale or rare species not for sale respectively. In the butterfly house, **Fjärilshuset**, (**CU D**) 200 to 300 pairs of delicately patterned wings flutter among the visitors and plants.

★★ **Botaniska Trädgården** ⊙ – *Carl Skottsbergs gata 22A, tramcar 1, 2 or 7. Leave by road 158* (**AX**). These botanical gardens were opened to the public in 1923 and they now have kilometres of winding paths, wide expanses of lawn, woodland, arbours such as the Bamboo Grove, the Japanese Dale and the Rhododendron Valley in addition to well-kept flower beds of bulbs, summer varieties or perennials and greenhouses. Every nook and cranny of the splendid **Rock Garden★★★** with its cliffs, rugged rocks, ponds, rivulets and cascade is the rooting place for one of the 5 000 plants from every corner of the globe.

★★ **Slottsskogen** ⊙ – *Tramcar 1 or 2 to Linnéplatsen. Leave by road 158* (**AX**). Slottsskogen is another extensive area of winding paths and great grassy areas, perfect for picnics and a leisurely walk. Various cottages from the different Swedish provinces, an azalea valley at its best in June, a children's zoo, a belvedere, cafés and restaurants all add to the enjoyment of the park. The Naturhistoriska Museet *(see above)* stands in the north-east corner of the park.

OUTSKIRTS

Volvo Museum ⊙ – *Leave by road 159* (**AV**). The museum retraces the history of Sweden's number one car manufacturer, since its foundation in 1927, when the first Volvo ÖV4 came off the production line in the Gothenburg factory. Amid the lines of prototypes, experimental vehicles and trucks, look out for the special favourite the PV444, more commonly known as the people's car.

Boat trips – Many of the islands of the southern archipelago are restricted areas for foreigners. However Vinga in the outer archipelago, and Marstrand, Rörö and Öckerö in the northern group may be reached by boats from Lilla Bommen (**BT**) from July to mid-August.

Vinga – The skerry of Vinga is the westernmost point of the archipelago and its lighthouse is well-known to seafarers. The island has excellent opportunities for fishing and bathing. A small museum is devoted to one of Sweden's most popular poets and composers Evert Taube (1890-1976).

★ **Öckerö Archipelago** – *The archipelago can be reached by boat from Gothenburg or by car; 17km by E 6 to the north and then road 155. A car ferry, free of charge, operates every 30min between Hjuvik and Hönö.* This group includes 10 inhabited islands. The islands are a paradise for cyclers and surfers who have the choice of the open sea or sheltered bays. Hälsö, Öckerö, Hönö and Fotö are linked to each other by bridges.
On **Öckerö** the whitewashed 15C **Kyrka** ★⊙ has a delightful interior and it is neighbour to the red buildings of a homestead museum. **Hönö** takes pride in its fishing museum, **Fiskemuseet** ★⊙ *(at the far end of Hönö harbour)* which maps the history and development of fishing, the fisherfolk and their way of life. The most northerly island and nature reserve of **Rörö** offers excellent possibilities for bathing.

★ **Nya Älvsborgs Fästning** ⊙ – *Leave by road 159* (**AV**). Also known as Nya Elfsborgs Fästning. The New Älvsborg Fortress strategically located on an island at the entrance to the harbour was erected between 1653 and 1670 to replace the old Älvsborg Fortress and to protect the newly founded town from Danish attacks as the first half of the 17C was a time of constant warfare. In 1570 and 1613 Sweden was forced to pay a ransom, known as the **Älvsborg Ransom**, for the return of the old fortress. Again in 1719 Gothenburg was attacked by the combined Danish-Norwegian fleet under the command of Admiral Peter Tordenskiøld but after a four-day siege they had to beat a retreat. In the 18C the fort served as a prison. The little chapel has become a popular place for weddings.

EXCURSIONS

★★ **The Golden Coast** – The attractive granite coast to the north with its islands and skerries is ideal sailing country. *See BOHUSLÄN.*

★★ **Göta Canal** – *See GÖTA KANAL.*

Coast of Halland – The coastline south of Gothenburg down to Hallandsåsen (a ridge stretching inland from the coast and forming a natural border with Skåne), is characterised by flat open landscapes along with sweeping bays and miles of sandy beaches lined by dunes. The beaches at Skummeslövsstrand and Mellbystrand attract many holidaymakers.

Kungsbacka – The market town of Kungsbacka with its attractive town centre of pastel coloured wooden houses makes an excellent excursion centre.

Take road E 6 south and turn off at the Fjärås junction then follow signs to Äskhult.

★ **Äskhult** – This hamlet regrouping four farmsteads around a courtyard gives an accurate picture of life in the 18C. In the early 19C, 35 people lived here but between 1890 and 1914, 25 emigrated to the United States. No children were born in the hamlet in the 20C and the last villager died in 1964.

Continue on road 939.

★ **Tjolöholms Slott** ⊘ – The property not only includes a big house but boasts the usual attributes of an English estate such as an estate village in the true Swedish tradition, a chapel and an entrance lodge. The Tudor style manor was built between 1898 and 1904 for a wealthy Gothenburg merchant, James F Dickson, who unfortunately did not live to see his dream come true. The vast rambling interior of the castle has all the comfort and conveniences that money could provide in the late 19C. Opulence is the byword from the Moorish smoking room, the oak panelled study, the Jacobean dining room to the royal bedchamber but it is the ingenious showers which give cause for amazement. The carriage museum, **Vagnmuseum**, displays a comprehensive collection of carriages and harness including the famous vacuum cleaner, whereas the adjoining indoor riding school is now a cafeteria. The surrounding parkland slopes gently down to the shore.

HALMSTAD ★

Hallands län
Population 83 600
Michelin map 985 or Atlas Europe p 123

The largest town and administrative centre of Halland grew from a settlement at the estuary of the River Nissan and is now a manufacturing centre with an active port. Halmstad is closely associated with a group of artists of the same name and known for its lovely sandy beaches, the most popular one being **Tylösand** 8km to the south-west. Like much of the surrounding countryside Halmstad was Danish until the signing of the Treaty of Roskilde in 1658. The medieval town quickly became a military stronghold with its walls and bastions girdled by a moat and was soon able to fulfil its strategic role in the line of Danish defences against Sweden. The castle is where the Danish king, Christian IV lavishly entertained King Gustav II Adolf for seven days in 1619. The very same year a fire swept through the city and in the rebuilding King Christian IV (1588-1648) left a strong imprint on the town with his work on the castle, north gate and layout of the old town with Stora Torg at its centre. When Halland finally became Swedish Halmstad lost its importance as a garrison town and then when the army withdrew in the 18C the walls were razed and the moat filled in.

The Halmstad Group – The Halmstadgruppen comprised six artists, the brothers Axel and Erik Olson, their cousin Waldemar Lorentzon, Stellan Mörner, Sven Jonson and Esaias Thorén. These post-Cubists first gathered here in 1929 and their art was to develop towards a particular form of Nordic Surrealism deeply rooted in the landscapes of Halland. They remained active until the 1980s.

Stora Torg – Since 1926 the pride of the main square has been Carl Milles' great fountain group **Europa and the Bull**★. On the south side the medieval interior of **Sankt Nikolai kyrka** ⊘ makes an ideal setting for the rich colours of some fine 20C **stained-glass windows**★★★. The tall windows are the work of Einar Forseth (1892-1988), designer of the golden mosaics in Stockholm's Stadshuset and the mosaic paving in Coventry Cathedral. The Halmstad Group artist, Erik Olson (1901-86), designed the two smaller circular windows. Take the time to study the wealth of pictorial detail.

The half-timbered **Three Hearts Inn** dates from the 18C. Tradition has it that the three crowned hearts were a gift from King Christian – whose own coat of arms included a single heart – to the townspeople for their stout defence of the town during a Swedish siege in 1563. Today the crowned hearts are part of the city's coat of arms. The granite monolith on the steps of the Rådhuset commemorates the meeting of Christian IV and Gustav II Adolf in 1619.

★ **Halmstad Slott** – Christian IV commissioned the Dutchman Hans van Steenwinckel to build the castle in 1620 as part of the town's defensive system. It now serves as the county governor's residence and is not open to the public.

Berthed alongside the bridge is the square rigger **Najaden** ⊘ dating from 1897; she spent part of her life as a training ship.

SWEDEN

Storgatan – The pedestrian precinct stretching from Stora Torg to Lilla Torg boasts several sculptures notably the soldier **91 Karlsson** a popular Swedish comic character. Also at the Lilla Torg end of the street are the north gate, **Norre Port**, dated 1601 and remnants of the city walls, **Norre Katt**.

★ **Museet i Halmstad** ⊘ – *Follow the river northwards past the park of Norre Katt.* The main point of interest in this regional museum (prehistoric and maritime sections) is the collection of **painted wall hangings**★★ *(bonader)* on the first floor. These naive folk paintings, typical of the region, usually portray biblical scenes but both the costumes and settings are from the 18C and 19C. These cloth or paper wall hangings decorated the walls and ceilings of peasant cottages during festivities especially at Christmas. Similar works are found in Dalarna. Art in Halland, the exhibition on the second floor, comprises works by the members of the Halmstad Group *(see above)*.

Miniland ⊘ – *2km to the west in the direction of Tylösand.* Seventy four scale models of famous Swedish buildings, such as the royal palace of Stockholm and the cathedral in Uppsala, attract crowds of children and their parents to this Sweden in Miniature. The latest arrival on the scene is Globen, the famous spherical arena in Stockholm. In the Country of Fairytales (Sagolandet) meet all the favourite characters from Swedish tales.

EXCURSIONS

★★★ **Coastal Road Northwards** – *This road covers about 40km before rejoining road E 6 south of Falkenberg. 2km beyond Halmstad airport Mjällby is signposted to the left.*

★ **Mjellby Konstgård** ⊘ – This attractive art centre in the heart of the countryside was set up by the daughter of Erik Olson, one of the Halmstad Group *(see above)*. She herself had spent 17 years in Paris in close touch with the artistic community and on her return she decided to create a centre devoted primarily to the Halmstad Group with temporary exhibitions of the great masters (Le Corbusier, Léger, Sonia Delaunay and the French Surrealists) that she had met *(the restaurant follows the opening hours of the centre)*.

Return to the main road.

Heagård Konst & Hantverk ⊘ – This great barn has been converted into an exhibition centre for arts and crafts *(some of the articles are for sale)*.

2km north of Gullbrandstorp at Lingalax the salmon smoke-house follow the signpost Naturreservat.

★ **Haverdal Naturreservat** – Over half of this nature reserve is drifting sand with a 4km-long and 30m-wide belt lying parallel to the shore backed by a line of dunes stabilised by a cover of marram grass. Take the steep path to scale the 36m-high Big Sandhill, **Stora Sandkullen**. From the top there is a good **view** of the reserve and the coast. Note the gnarled and twisted forms of the wind-sculptured trees of the pinewoods.

Return to the main road and after several kilometres turn left at the signpost Haverdalsstrand then after about 500m turn right onto Skallbergsvägen a minor road leading uphill.

Skallen – This steeply rising headland, covered with juniper and heather, provides an excellent **view**★★★ of the coastline and the sea. Towards the end of May the beach to the north is a mass of bright-pink thrift plants.
The drive takes you through an open countryside of heathland and pastures grazed by cattle. The rocky shoreline makes a striking contrast to the sandy beaches further south.

★ **Steninge** – The village had a glassworks from 1873 to 1917. From the café (Göstas Café) there is a pleasant view of the heathlands and the sea.

Svedinos Bil– och Flygmuseum ⊘ – *Ugglarp.* The car and plane museum is easily located by the two aircraft standing outside. Crammed with old cars and planes it attracts enthusiasts of all ages.

Laxbutiken ⊘ – *Heberg junction on road E 6.* With a selection of salmon, prepared in 30 different ways, this shop entices visitors to sample the delicacies of Halland *(take away or taste on the spot)*.

HELSINGBORG

Skåne län
Population 115 000
Michelin map 985 P 9 or Atlas Europe p 123

Throughout the centuries two great castles have faced each other across the 4km-wide straits of Öresund. Helsingborg was founded in the 11C and placed strategically to control the straits and today the Danish town of Helsingør is only 25min away by ferry. Helsingborg is a busy port, commercial and administrative centre.

For many centuries this was Danish-held territory and the 17C was a sombre period in the town's history as it was caught up in the incessant warfare between Sweden and its neighbour Denmark. The Swedes captured the town at least six times before the Treaty of Roskilde (1658) returned the lost provinces to Sweden. The city suffered most in the period which followed known as the Scanian Wars (1675-79) when the Danes tried to recapture Skåne.

The **Battle of Helsingborg** in 1710, when Magnus Stenbeck routed the Danes, finally put an end to the wars.

★**Kärnan** – *Stortorget*. In the 14C the Danes built this stone keep to replace an earlier wooden one. It was part of an elliptical castle with an enclosure wall hence its name Kärnan Swedish for kernel. The stronghold was demolished in the 1680s and the 34m-tall keep with its stout walls and external staircase tower is all that remains. The **panorama** from the terrace *(146 steps)* takes in its counterpart, Helsingør, on the far shore and the island of Ven *(see below)* a little further to the south.

Sankta Maria kyrka ⊘ – *South Storgatan*. The original 12C sandstone church was replaced in the 15C by the present red-brick Gothic building. The stepped gable tower was added in the 16C.

Take particular note of the **reredos** (1450) by a north German craftsman, the Renaissance **pulpit** (1615) and the medieval **baptismal font** in grey limestone by the Gotland School. The remains of 15C mural paintings by the Helsingborg Master are to be seen in the ambulatory where there are also some fine **stained-glass windows★★**. The two on the right by Martin Emond illustrate the history of Helsingborg, the third and fourth by Einar Forseth portray the Father and the Virgin and Child whereas the pair on the left by Erik Olson represent the Son and the Holy Ghost. The windows called River of Life and Tree of Life in the north transept both date from 1953 and are by Ralph Bergholtz.

★★**Vestry and Silver Chamber** – The first contains a priceless array of church vestments and the second houses Christian III's Bible from 1550 and a number of exquisite silver items from the 17C to the present day.

Ven – Boats leave several times a day for this island where the famous Danish astronomer, **Tycho Brahe** (1546-1601) lived between 1576 and 1596. He built both a castle, now grass-covered ruins, and an observatory *(see HELSINGØR)*.

EXCURSIONS

Kullen Peninsula – This windswept headland jutting westwards into the Kattegatt is a place to be visited for its fishing villages.

Leave to the north by Drottninggatan.

★**Sofiero** – The castle was built for Queen Sophia, the wife of King Oskar II, and then passed as a wedding present in 1905 to their grandson, the Crown Prince Gustav Adolf and his bride Princess Margaret of Connaught (d 1920). Margaret like her father the Duke of Connaught was a great gardener. The **gardens** ⊘ *(a plan is available at the entrance)* have one of the finest collections of rhododendrons and azaleas. The Rhododendron Path starts in the ravine below the castle and ends by the ornamental pool. Discover part of the Crown Princess Margaret's Flower Walk just as it was when she planned it over 80 years ago.

Now make for road 111 in the direction of Höganäs.

Viken – The picturesque fishing village is now one of Helsingborg's elegant suburbs.

Höganäs – Höganäs is the cradle of the Swedish ceramics industry. The town grew from a small fishing village in the 16C to a coal mining community with the discovery of the local coal seams in the late 18C. When in the 19C clay was extracted from the mines it was used to produce bricks and then earthenware and stoneware. Several companies still continue to produce salt-glazed stoneware.

The **Höganäs Museum och Konstgalleri★** ⊘ has a chronological display of local pottery on the ground floor and more than 60 contemporary Nordic artists have contributed to the display of stoneware objects in the basement. Note in particular the humorous biblical figures by Åke Holm (1900-80). A special exhibition for children is devoted to the famous cartoon character, Bamse, the strongest bear in the world.

Höganäs Saltglaserat AB ⊘ – *Going towards Mölle take Bruksgatan to the left then follow the signs.* "He arrived like a snow squall one April evening, with a Höganäs bottle on a leather strap around his neck." This was how August Strindberg described the arrival of Carlsson in his novel *The People of Hemsö*. The company was established in 1832 and initially produced yellow-glazed earthenware before changing to salt-glazed stoneware. The stoneware was highly popular and there is hardly a Swedish home which doesn't have a Höganäs pot. Today production continues on a small scale following traditional methods, everything being still made by hand.

BodaNova-Höganäs Keramik ⊙ – A huge pyramid of pots marks the building where household stoneware items have been made since 1910.

Continue in the direction of Mölle.

Krapperup – This large estate once belonged to the Gyllenstierna family. The small museum and gallery *(in the roadside building)* and the remarkable **gardens** ⊙ are open to the public. The gardens offer a fine view of the moated castle originally built in the 16C but greatly altered in the late 18C. The star, which spangles the façades, figures in the family's coat of arms.

Mölle – Built on a hillside, the small summer resort was popular with Danes and Germans at the turn of the last century. Mölle's notoriety for its sinful way of life, as a place where mixed bathing was permitted, attracted enthusiasts from all over Europe. The Kaiser Wilhelm II and his wife were two of the most famous patrons.

★★★**Kullaberg** – The headland, with its cliffs dropping sheer into the sea, divides the bay, Skälderviken, to the north from the straits of Öresund. Paths follow the cliff edge *(care is required)* leading to Kullen lighthouse which rises 88m above the sea. This 1900 version replaced an earlier 16C one. Half way along the path a signpost (Ransvik) leads to a café dramatically set on the cliff edge with excellent views across the straits to Denmark.

Left off the main road.

Himmelstorp – The old Skåne farmstead, now a café, is the starting point for a 15km walk *(waymarked by painted stones; walking shoes are necessary as there is somes crambling at the end)* to **Nimis**, a collection of driftwood works of art on the shore.

Return to the main road and turn right at the next T-junction, just before the left turn-off for Arild.

Brunnby Kyrka ⊙ – The 12C Romanesque church is known for the 15C **paintings** on the aisle vaulting. They are some of the best-preserved works by the Helsingborg Master.

Arild – The old fishing village of small houses and gardens is a picturesque resort which has been popular with artists for almost a century.

Flickorna Lundgren ⊙ – *Skäret, look for the signpost.* The 260-year-old summer cottage belonged to the Lundgren family with their seven daughters. In 1938 they decided to refurbish it as a coffee house and have never looked back. The garden with its splendid view of the bay is the ideal place, amid the sea of flowers, to sample the pastries which "taste like angels sing".

HÄLSINGLAND★★
Gävleborgs län
Michelin map 985 J-K 11-13 or Atlas Europe p 101

Although adjacent to Dalarna, Hälsingland belongs to northern Sweden, Norrland as the Swedes call it, which in itself represents almost half the country and yet is very sparsely populated. Beautiful unspoilt nature and wilderness areas rich in fauna and flora are what most people associate with the north of Sweden and Hälsingland is certainly no exception with its great variety of landscapes; there is an abundance of lakes and forests everywhere, imposing blue mountains to the west and the Orsa Finmark wilderness area on the border with Dalarna, two powerful rivers flowing down from the mountains to the Baltic and linking a string of lakes on the way, and, in total contrast, there is the coast along the Gulf of Bothnia, its sheltered creeks, numerous islands, sandy beaches and above all its charming fishing villages. But that is not all for Hälsingland has another treasure, its cultural heritage.

A rich cultural heritage

Flax-growing brought prosperity to Hälsingland in the 18C and farmers began building large farmhouses, elaborately decorated to reflect their newly acquired wealth. Many of these farmhouses from the late 18C and 19C have survived; some are still privately owned but can be visited, others have been turned into heritage farms or museums.

Wooden castles – These imposing farmhouses were often built on high ground, on the top of hills or on south-facing slopes, with cultivated land running down into the valley and pastureland covering the humid lowland areas. At first, large farms consisted of several buildings surrounding a square courtyard. From 1800 onwards, gardens surrounded the main house.

The **house** itself was usually two-storeys high with an elaborate porch and moulded cornices, a style which was modelled on that of manor houses. A verandah was sometimes added round the turn of the last century. The house consisted of one living and working room for all the family and one or several bedrooms, other rooms being used for storage and for entertaining on festive days. Ceilings and walls would generally be decorated with painted motifs (flowers, vines, draperies), in some cases with landscapes or lively scenes.

In early days, outbuildings were built like log cabins; barns and storehouses were often located outside the courtyard so that they would be protected in case of fire. Storehouses were sometimes three-storeys high and rested on short wooden stilts.

Forest cabins – In striking contrast, people who lived and worked in the dense forest of the western part of the region and lumberjacks who prepared timber for floating down rivers such as the Ljusnan could only afford to live in simple log cabins.

Traditions and events – Music and dance are everywhere in Hälsingland, with groups of fiddlers in almost every village and a wide choice of folk festivals in summer. The best-known event is undoubtedly the **Hälsingehambo**, an annual dance festival which takes place in the lower Ljusnan Valley and involves around 1 000 dancers in colourful regional costumes. One of the most important jazz festivals in Sweden is organised every year in the little town of Svabensverk, south of Edsbyn.

There is also a strong **handicraft** tradition in Hälsingland, in particular in the area round the Dellen lakes, north-west of Hudiksvall. Delsbo, where there is a magnificent 18C heritage farm, is the place to find objects made of silver, wood and birch bark. Bjuråker and Hedvigsfors to the north are also interesting handicraft centres. Hälsingland Museum in Hudiksvall contains Alfta tapestries dating from the 16C and 17C as well as a collection of painted furniture. Inland, the town of Bollnäs has an interesting exhibition of handicraft from the area.

Excursions ⓥ

The Coast – There is plenty to see between **Söderhamn** in the south and Sörfjarden in the north: idyllic fishing villages such as Skärså, Stocka and Mellanfjärden, numerous islands, medieval churches at Trönö and Enånger, old boathouses in **Hudiksvall**, the Hornslandet peninsula and its fine sandy beaches.

The Voxnan and Ljusnan valleys – This is the area which has the highest concentration of Hälsingland farmhouses. Drive down the Voxnan Valley from **Edsbyn** to **Bollnäs** where the rivers meet then up the Ljusnan Valley to Ljusdal. Edsbyn has one of the largest heritage farms; do not miss the old flax mill in **Växbo**, just north-east of Bollnäs and the mountain pasture farm at Svedbovallen south-west of **Järvsö**.

Forests and wilderness areas – West of Ljusdal along road 84, at **Lassekrog**, there is a log-cabin settlement and log-floating museum. South from there along road 296 or 310, **Los** offers guided tours of its ancient cobalt and nickel mine. Further west, the **Hamra National Park** is a paradise for nature lovers.

Outdoor activities ⓥ

The many rivers and lakes offer a variety of activities from swimming and canoeing in many places, with varying degrees of difficulty, to rafting down the River Ljusnan; fishing for pike, salmon trout, perch and char can be a rewarding pastime in mountain streams and lakes or in the Voxnan, one of the best-preserved rivers in Sweden. The forested mountainous areas to the west also provide a wealth of activities like mountain hikes, riding trips, berry picking in wild forests or even taking part in a beaver safari! There is plenty to do along the coast as well, such as swimming off one of the fine sandy beaches, fishing along the coast or from one of the numerous islands or going on an exciting grey-seal safari. And for those who prefer to take it easy, there is a choice of boat trips along the coast or on several of the lakes, some of them aboard picturesque old steamers.

HÄRNÖSAND

Västernorrlands län
Population 27 000
Michelin map 985 J 14 or Atlas Europe p 112

Härnösand, at the mouth of the Ångermanälven, is partly built on the island of Härnön.

Härnösands Domkyrka ⊘ – The handsome neo-Classical porticoed cathedral was built between 1842 and 1846 during the bishopric of Frans Michael Franzén poet and hymn-writer to replace an earlier building burned down in 1721 when the Russians sacked the town. The Baroque altar and altarpiece, both dating from 1728, are the work of David von Cöln. The baptismal font is a piece of Spanish Rococo silverware dated 1777.

One of the sculptures in the adjoining municipal park is a 1910 work by Carl Milles depicting Franzén, the poet-bishop, with his two muses, his daughters. To the south of the cathedral is Östanbäcken, an area of wooden houses.

Murberget ⊘ – *2km in the direction of road E 4, signposted Murberget.* This open-air museum with its farmhouses and cottages, summer farm, church and inn is set in a delightful wooded area. In summer the museum becomes a hive of activity with craft demonstrations and festivities. The regional museum, inaugurated in 1994, has an interesting collection of arms and armour.

★★HÖGA KUSTEN

This part of the Swedish coast stretching from Härnösand to Örnsköldsvik, is known as the High Coast and boasts a succession of dramatic clifftops *(see Skuleberget below)*, bays and inlets, islands and skerries, wooded heights and arable valleys. The beauty of the area has attracted many artists and craftsmen and some of the workshops and studios are open to visitors *(further details from the Tourist Information Centre in one of the following towns: Kramfors, Lund, Skule or Nordingrå).*

★ **Höga Kusten Bron** – The High Coast Bridge is Sweden's longest bridge and the seventh longest in the world. The 1 800m long suspension bridge was built over four years and inaugurated in 1997. Spanning the River Angerman 40m above water lever, the bridge forms part of a new section of the E4 European motorway which includes 35 new bridges and shortens the distance between Härnösand and Örnsköldsvik by 44km. At the northern end of the bridge stands Hornöberget, an information centre and hotel with a restaurant offering a breathtaking view.

The Nordingrå peninsula, midway along the Höga Kusten, is known for its many colourful fishing villages which can be visited from Nordingrå.

★★ **Nordingrå** – The town stands on the shores of a lake, once an inlet, and the imposing ruins of its church testify to its importance during the Middle Ages. The 19C **kyrka** ⊘ has a lovely 16C altarpiece from Brussels, an item commissioned for the earlier church. A picturesque row of **church stables** leads down to the lake. The area is known for its **fishermen's chapels**: these simple wooden buildings were too cold to serve as churches in winter and some doubled up as warehouses. Examples can be seen in the villages of Norrfällsviken, Bonhamn and Barsta where the **chapel**★ has been preserved as it was in 1666. The two islands of Ulvön are famous for the Swedish delicacy, fermented Baltic herring *(surströmming)*; the tins should be opened outside. It is definitely an acquired taste.

In the village of **Häggvik** *(3km from Nordingrå)* the **Café Mannaminne** ⊘ is used for concerts and exhibitions; a series of local museums are housed in adjoining buildings. The **Villa Fraxinus** ⊘ *(10km from Nordingrå)* has a beautifully landscaped **garden**★ in complete harmony with the surrounding countryside.

Skuleberget – 294m. The striking profile of this mountain is easy to pick out as you drive along road E 4. An ancient shoreline not far below the summit shows just how much the land has risen isostatically (285m) since the Ice Age. The Skule climbing trails take about 1hr 30min each, but one is more difficult. A café on the summit *(chair-lift)* and wonderful views reward those who make the climb to the top.

Further along the road is the visitor centre, **Skule Naturum** *(3km north of Docksta)* for Skuleskogen National Park and the Skuleberget.

JOKKMOKK ★

Norrbottens län

Population 6 500

Michelin map 985 F 17 or Atlas Europe p 108 – Local map see LAPPLAND

The municipality of Jokkmokk is Sweden's most extensive after Kiruna, as it stretches from the high mountains in the west to the bogs and ancient pine forests of Muddus National Park in the east. Jokkmokk has always been a political and cultural centre for the Sami and was for a long time their winter gathering place; today it is famous for its Winter Market. The Arctic Circle passes about 14km to the south of Jokkmokk and is clearly marked by a multilingual sign: Polarsirkelen, Polcirkeln and Napapiiri.

Jokkmokk Winter Market – Ever since 1605 people have come from far afield for the market on the first Thursday, Friday and Saturday in February to trade in handicrafts. The population increases tenfold and hotel rooms have to be booked a year in advance! An Autumn Fair is held on the last Friday, Saturday and Sunday in August.

Storknabben – *At the eastern end of the village, east of Ájtte take the narrow forest road for the final 2km to the top*. This is an ideal viewing point to watch the Midnight Sun between 15 June and 7 July. There is daylight, however, all night long from May through to July on the other hand between 20 and 22 December the sun never rises above the horizon.

★★★Ájtte Svenskt Fjäll – och Samemuseum ⊙ – *At the eastern end of the village. The museum provides information on the national parks and trails of the region.* This exciting and unorthodox museum inaugurated in 1989 focuses on the cultural heritage of the Sami and their mountain homelands from an ecological point of view. The museum is in direct contrast to the Silver Museum at Arjeplog and here the shape of the rooms and the wall decorations are as important as the items on display. Outside the visitor can discover Sami huts, storehouses *(Ájtte)* and mountain flora. The permanent exhibition tells the story of the Sami *(Sápmi* is Sami for their homeland), their myths, religion, traditions and their reindeer. Other sections cover the different aspects of their homeland.

The Alpine Garden nearby presents the mountain environment and Alpine vegetation.

Edvin "Sarek" Nilsson Naturfoto ⊙ – *The yellow building at the junction of roads 97 and 45*. The majestic landscapes of the Sarek massif, the delicacy of the flora, a lone bear or a herd of reindeer are all splendidly captured by the photographer Edvin Nilsson who is famous for his books and documentary films on the Swedish national parks.

Workshop of Lars Pirak ⊙ – *Jarregatan 4. Follow Storgatan right through the village until you come to a slight bend in the street and Jarregatan is on the left. Workshop and display of art and handicrafts in the basement of the red-brick house with the sign Lars Pirak Konstnär.*

The work of this Sami artist and craftsman is to be found in museums all over the world. Sami art and Shamanism are his greatest sources of inspiration and mountains and reindeer are recurring motifs in his work.

EXCURSIONS TO THE NATIONAL PARKS

Northwest to Sarek and Padjelanta – *120km to Kvikkjokk by road 45. Before leaving fill up the petrol tank as there is only one petrol station along the route at Årrenjarka holiday village 20km before Kvikkjokk.* The road follows the Lilla Luleälven and as you near Kvikkjokk high mountains appear on the horizon.

Linnaeus in Lapland

During Linnaeus' trip in the area he was joined by a third traveller making a trip into Norway for some *brännvin* (eau-de-vie) and Linnaeus describes the descent towards the green valleys and coastal plain of Norway:

"When we had at long last reached the bottom it was a great relief for my weary body! I had left behind the ice-covered rocks to enter a warm valley with shimmering colours (I sat down to eat some wild strawberries); instead of snow and ice I saw green smiling meadows (nowhere else had I seen such long grass); instead of the atrocious weather there was a marvellous smell of clover in flower and of other plants. *O formosissima aestas!* Oh! how beautiful and what a summer!"

Kvikkjokk – Road 805 ends here and beyond there is the endless wilderness of the Sarek and Padjelanta national parks, home to the golden eagle, bear, lynx and wolverine. Daily flights from Kvikkjokk take visitors to some of the more outlying wilderness areas of the national parks.

Sarek – This national park covers a mountainous area where the peaks rise to around 2 000m and glaciers are common, where heathland occurs between 800 and 1 200m and deep valleys and screes are common. Only experienced hikers and climbers should tackle the trails in this park.·

Padjelanta – Even further west than Sarek, this is Europe's largest national park and it covers the plateau area around Lake Virihaure and Lake Vastenjaur. As early as 1732 Linnaeus recognised its importance from a botanical point of view and it has always been an important grazing area for the reindeer herds of the Sami. This park is more suitable for the less experienced and shorter treks can be organised.

North-west to Stora Sjöfallet – *160km by road 45 to just beyond Porjus then follow the sign for Stora Sjöfallet.* The Great Lake Falls National Park is easily reached by car. As you drive alongside the lake of Stora Lulevatten the high mountains soon loom into sight. The great hydroelectric scheme, centred on the immense Suorva Dam and attendant underground power stations, has transformed the rivers and ribbon lakes of the area into great reservoirs. However, much of the park including the fells, which it was created to protect, and the mountain of Akka has remained unspoilt.

North to Muddus – *The park lies to the east of Porjus.* This national park was created to safeguard the ancient forests, bogs, gorges and lakes. Bear, lynx and wolverine roam freely and during the breeding season (15 March to 31 July) the central part of the park is out-of-bounds for visitors.

★**Vuollerim 6000** ⊘ – *42km to the east by road 97. Once in Vuollerim follow the sign for Stenåldersbyn. Allow 3hr for a guided tour including the excavation site.* The small village of Vuollerim stands at the confluence of the River Lilla (little) and River Stora (great) Luleälven. Excavations have brought to light a 6 000-year-old Stone Age village and the custom-built museum displays finds from the archaeological site. One of the dwellings has been reconstructed outside and there are demonstrations of ancient methods of cooking and handicraft.

JULITA ★★

Södermanlands län

Michelin map 985 M 13 or Atlas Europe p 119
43km south-west of Eskilstuna by road 214

Julita Gård och Museum ⊘ (manor and museum), on the shore of Lake Öljaren, is now home to the Swedish Agricultural Museum.
In the 12C Cistercian monks founded a monastery which was dissolved and rased in 1535. It then became royal property, a manor was built and an ordnance factory (1627-65) established which supplied King Gustav II Adolf with cannon during the Thirty Years War. The estate changed hands several times until the beginning of the 20C when it passed to **Lieutenant Arthur Bäckström** (1861-1941) who was influenced by the ideas of Artur Hazelius of Skansen fame. With the cooperation of the Nordiska Museet, to which he bequeathed the estate, and the Historiska Museet he created an open-air museum.

★★★**Stora huset** – The beautiful 3-storey yellow manor dates from 1750. Two detached wings of a later date face each other across the courtyard. The house is as it was during the lifetime of the last owner Arthur Bäckström and many of the fine pieces of furniture were the work of the estate carpenter.
The coach house now contains a collection of 19C and 20C carriages and Bäckström's office just as it was.

Park – The lovely park with its stately old trees has a rose garden, an attractive gazebo and the delightful Åttkanten down by the pier. Originally a wash-house it was transformed into a guesthouse in the 20C. South of the stables is the abbot's house where the ground floor is 13C whereas the upper one was added in the 18C. The role of the Nordic Gene Bank for plants is outlined in the exhibition illustrating genetic engineering for plants in the greenhouse whereas other experiments to safeguard old and local varieties can be seen in the kitchen and herb gardens. Bäckström created a mini Skansen with cottages, museum and chapel to conserve the country's cultural heritage. The estate also had a dairy, a brickworks, lime kiln, tobacco-drying barn and fire station, which is now a small museum.

KALMAR ★

Kalmar län
Population 59 000
Michelin map 985 P 13 or Atlas Europe p 123

Kalmar is famous for its castle, the long-time guardian of Sweden's southern frontier. There have always been close connections between the expanding industrial city of Kalmar and the agricultural island of Öland, now linked by the magnificent Öland Bridge and today many Ölanders commute daily to Kalmar for their work.

The Union of Three Northern Crowns – The town has always been associated with the **Kalmar Union** (Kalmarunionen) signed here in 1397. This vast territorial union between the kingdoms of Denmark, Norway and Sweden stretched from the Atlantic seaboard to the Karelian isthmus and was a remarkable achievement at a time when dynastic rivalries and civil wars were rife elsewhere. Queen Margrethe of Denmark headed the union which was intended to counter the growing influence of the Hanse in the area. The union proved hard to maintain, with growing internal struggles between the nobility and the royal power, and following the Stockholm Bloodbath and Gustav Vasa's accession it was dissolved in 1523.

The city was often exposed to attacks and sieges during these troubled times but it was during the Kalmar War (1611-13) that it was most badly damaged and after a devastating fire in 1647 the town was moved away from the castle to its present island site on Kvarnholmen.

★★★KALMAR SLOTT ⊙

For five centuries this castle with its fortifications and strategic location guarding the Kalmar Sound was one of the strongest and most disputed fortresses in Sweden. During the period when the south of Sweden was in Danish hands the fortress at Kalmar was known as the key to Sweden because of its immense strategic value.

The original keep dated from the 12C and was a part of a string of defensive churches and keeps from Öland to the mainland. It was King Gustav Vasa who strengthened the fortifications and rebuilt the castle in the 16C and his sons transformed the interior into a Renaissance palace. The castle became a symbol of royal power and a favourite residence of Swedish kings and the splendid State Apartments with their lavish decor reflect the pomp and glitter that was associated with this period. After the Treaty of Roskilde the castle lost its importance to Karlskrona.

Kalmar Slott is quartered by four round towers crowned by gored cupolas and tapering finials. Gable ended bastions project from the wings and a larger square tower and turreted cupola rise above the rest. Bare walls contrast with the delicate roofscape.

Of particular note are King Erik's Bedchamber (1555-62) with its sumptuous decoration and the chapel with attractive 16C barrel vaulting.

City Centre – *Park the car down by the harbour in front of the museum.* The best-preserved remains of the walls, **Kalmar vallar**, face the harbour and include the Bastion Johannes Rex and south gate, Kavaljeren. Once through the gate the small square of **Lilla Torget** surrounded by 17C buildings and a part of the wall has a truly medieval character. Västra Storgatan leads to Stortorget where the 17C **Rådhuset** faces across to the church in the middle of the square. **Domkyrkan** ⊙ is a misnomer as it is no longer a cathedral. Nicodemus Tessin the Elder designed the church in 1660 and gave it a Roman Baroque appearance after a visit to Rome.

Länsmuseet ⊙ – A refurbished steam-mill is home to the county museum. The relics from the royal flagship **Kronan** are the highlight of this museum. The ship exploded and sank in a battle off the coast of Öland in 1679. Of the 800 on board only 42 were saved. The wreck was rediscovered in 1980 7km offshore at a depth of 26m. The *Vasa* in Stockholm is perhaps the best-known 17C ship and the most well preserved but the *Kronan* has yielded the most important collection of finds. These include 18 bronze cannon, some lovely wooden sculptures, pewter plate, earthenware pitchers, the ship's bell, navigational instruments and gold items. The exhibition on the fourth floor presents **Jenny Nyström**'s enchanted world of elves and pixies which have become traditional motifs on Swedish Christmas cards.

Krusenstjerna – *200m west of the castle; enter from Stora Dammgatan.* Furnished 19C house, secluded in its own garden behind a high wooden fence. This marks the site of the old town.

KARLSHAMN

During the Scanian Wars (1675-79) Karl XI settled the devastated areas with loyal Swedes and founded the town of Karlshamn as a mark of Sweden's intentions. The town was originally planned as the base for the Swedish Navy as it had the largest deep-water harbour on the south coast but it proved too difficult to defend. Karlshamn developed into a trading centre instead.

A **Baltic Festival** (music and cultural events) is organised in July with the participation of other Baltic countries.

** **Karlshamns Kulturkvarter** ⓥ – *Drottninggatan/Vinkelgatan*. These historic buildings house some interesting museums and galleries.

Karlshamns Museum – *Enter from Vinkelgatan*. There are sections on folklore (art and costumes), local industry, maritime activities and on the art of painted ceilings. Another room commemorates the local songwriter Alice Tegnér (1864-1943) who is known for her children's songs.

Go into the courtyard.

In the **Stenhuset** there are displays of organ fronts, wall decorations and wrought-iron work. **Holländarhuset**, which was once a centre for Dutch merchants on their trips to Sweden has now been converted into dwelling quarters and a workshop. The tobacco shed, **Tobaksladan★★**, is now a small museum devoted to the local tobacco industry which dates back to the 17C. In the 18C the Swedes quickly took to snuff and the tobacco industry flourished. In 1915 the remaining 40 factories were taken over by the Swedish Tobacco monopoly. The **art gallery** *(on the far side of Vinkelgatan)*, in addition to regular exhibitions on contemporary Swedish art, has some good examples of mural paintings and lovely painted ceilings which came from the town hall.

** **Punschmuseet** – Arak or Arrack liquor is of two types, that distilled from the juice of the coconut palm or that distilled from rice and molasses. Punch making is explained with the help of equipment from a 19C distillery.

Turn left onto Drottninggatan.

** **Skottsbergska gården** – This perfect example of an 18C merchant house contains fine furniture and wall paintings.

Follow Prinsgatan then Hamngatan until you pass a small marina.

Make for the harbour and Hamnparken with Axel Olson's famous **monument★★** in memory of all those who emigrated to America; the statue represents the main characters, Kristina and Karl-Oskar, of Vilhelm Moberg's great work *The Emigrants*. The film version starred Max von Sydow and Liv Ullman.

A promenade passes **Villa Utsikten**, a café in a pleasant setting with an excellent view of the firth of Karlshamn and the 17C island citadel guarding the approach to the town. The promenade continues for another 2km to reach the small harbour where salmon, smoked eel and mackerel are sold.

EXCURSIONS

Mörrum – *10km to the west by road E 22. Follow the sign for Laxens Hus.*
The River Mörrum has been famous for its salmon fishing ever since the 13C and even today it provides good sport for fishermen (1 April to 30 September). The current record for a salmon is just under 25kg (1991). The salmon aquarium, **Laxens Hus** ⓥ, shows salmon and trout at different stages.

* **Sölvesborg** – *22km to the south-west by road E 22*. The oldest and smallest town in the province of Blekinge received its city charter in 1445 but it was probably founded in the 13C. The town has a certain medieval character with its narrow, winding streets and closely packed houses. The imposing silhouette of the 13C brick-built **St Nicolai kyrka** ⓥ marks the centre of town. In summer it is a busy resort with a selection of beaches to choose from (Listershuvud) and good sailing locally.

Eriksbergs Naturreservat ⓥ – *About 10km to the east by road E 22. Follow the signposts first for Åryd and then for Eriksberg. 14km drive along the trail. Visitors are requested not to leave their cars except at the manor and at certain lookout points. Recorded commentary available in English and German.*
The reserve is home to about 800 animals such as red and fallow deer and European bison. The drive takes the visitor through deciduous woodland, past vast tracts of coniferous forest and a small lake with the rare **red water-lily**. The facilities at Eriksberg manor include a children's zoo, a museum, a cafeteria and an impressive collection of hunting trophies including antlers.

KARLSKRONA

Blekinge län
Population 60 000
Michelin map 985 P 12 or Atlas Europe p 123

SWEDEN

The city was founded by royal command (Karl XI) in 1680 as a base for the Swedish Navy and even today the town's activities are predominantly naval with its naval base and shipyard. Karlskrona spreads over some 30 islands and the smell of the sea is everywhere. Most of the archipelago is a military zone but foreigners may join a guided tour *(enquire at the Tourist Information Centre)*. With its strong maritime tradition Karlskrona has often been the host port for the international Cutty Sark Tall Ships' race.

Stortorget – King Karl XI's statue stands in the centre of this vast square which is the venue for a **Lövmarknad**, on the day before Midsummer's Eve. Nicodemus Tessin the Younger designed both Baroque churches, the first, **Fredrikskyrkan** ⊙, (1720-58) named after King Frederick is embellished with pilasters whereas the second church, **Trefaldighetskyrkan** ⊙ (1697-1749) was used by the German community which continued to worship here until 1846.

★ **Blekinge Läns Museum** ⊙ – The main building of the local museum (fine art, furniture and handicrafts) is an elegant Baroque mansion, Grevagården, dating from 1705 and adjoined by a lovely garden. Other buildings in the grounds illustrate stone carving, shipbuilding and fishing.

Fisktorget or Fiskbron – This was the site of the old covered market and the fishing boats tied up along the quayside. Today it is the landing-stage for boats touring the archipelago.

Björkholmen – This was where the original community of naval craftsmen settled. The cottages stand gable-on to the steeply sloping streets. The streets running from east to west are named after famous Swedish admirals, and those going from north to south after different types of ship.

Amiralitetskyrkan ⊙ – The Royal Admiralty Church, built entirely of wood, was the city's first place of worship when it was consecrated in 1685 five years after the city was founded. The church is well known for its unusual **poor-box** which represents Rosenbom, a character from *The Wonderful Adventure of Nils*. It was Rosenbom who hid Nils under his hat.

Kungsbron – In the past when it was normal to arrive by sea the King's Bridge was the prestigious gateway to the city. The statue represents Erik Dahlberg the original town planner who gave the city its broad streets and spacious squares fronted by monumental buildings. The pink building was the Governor's Residence. The **Bastion Aurora** was part of the fortifications built around the naval dockyard. The fully rigged *Jarramas* is now a café and organises musical entertainment in summer.

★ **Marinmuseum** ⊙ – The new Naval Museum on the island of Stumholmen traces Sweden's naval heritage. Two exciting exhibits are the wreck visible through the panoramic window of the underwater tunnel and the reconstruction of a replica of a post yacht. The museum also boasts two good collections of figureheads and ships models (18C-19C). The mine-sweeper *HMS Bremön* is moored alongside the museum as part of the open-air section.

EXCURSIONS

Ronneby – *25km to the west by road E 22*. The healing properties of the waters in Ronneby were discovered in 1705 but it was the 19C before it gained fame as a cosmopolitan spa and played host to the elite of Europe. When fire destroyed the spa buildings a new conference and recreation centre was built. Some of the elegance and style of the past is still to be glimpsed in the few remaining spa buildings in **Brunnsparken**. A converted industrial building, the **Kulturcentrum** ⊙, now houses the Tourist Information Centre and an exhibition hall.
Tosia Bonnadan, which literally means farmers crazy day, is a popular fair which draws crowds to the town.

★★ **Heliga Kors kyrka** ⊙ – The church enjoys a prominent site on a mound in the centre of town. Latter additions to the original 12C Romanesque building include the 13C transept and the late-15C stout west end tower. Interesting 15C and 16C **paintings** have been uncovered in the chancel and south transept; note the danse macabre on the south chancel wall. The beautifully carved 3-storey **altarpiece** dated 1652 and the painted and gilded **pulpit**★ (1620s) are both Baroque. The later is a good example of elegant Danish woodcarving from the reign of King Christian IV. Erik Olson of the Halmstad Group designed the two 1955 **stained-glass windows** in the chancel.
A heavy oak door showing traces of fire and axe marks is a reminder of the Ronneby Bloodbath in 1564 when the Swedish king, Erik XIV captured the town.
To the west of the church is the charming old quarter, **Bergslagen**, with its winding streets, steep alleyways and picturesque houses. Both **Möllebackagården** ⊙ (Kyrkogatan) and **Mor Oliviagården** (by the rapids) have displays of handicrafts.

KARLSTAD ★

Karlstad stands at the mouth of the River Klarälven as it runs into Lake Vänern. The town was founded in 1584 by Count Karl, later to become King Karl IX, on the site of an early trading centre and meeting place of the people's court, known as the Tingvalla.

There is nothing more Swedish than Värmland – Great forests, rushing torrents, placid lakes and small farms are all part of the typical Värmland landscapes which have enchanted and inspired musicians, authors and poets. The jazz musician Stan Getz composed his own version of the Värmland folk song, *Värmlandsvisan*, and called it *Dear Old Stockholm*. The 500km-long River **Klarälven** (Trysilelva in Norway) rushes over rapids or winds a curving course through the landscapes of Värmland to **Lake Vänern**, Sweden's largest lake (140km wide and 75km long). This inland sea boasts an archipelago of no less than 22 000 islets and rocks.

Activities – The abundance of lakes and inter-connecting waterways makes Värmland ideal for boating, sailing, canoeing, white-water rafting or being different and taking the slow way, drifting down the river on a raft of logs. The adventurous can discover Värmland by cycle-trolley on disused railway tracks. The forests provide good elk hunting and visitors can choose between a gun or a camera to shoot the king of the forest but be prepared for a close encounter with a lynx, bear or wolf. Värmland is the trotting kingdom of Sweden with a choice of race tracks for a day at the races. Arvika's is the oldest, Årjäng's is in a delightful setting, Mysen's is in Norway and the last is at Karlstad.

Värmland specialities – The best-known is perhaps the Värmland sausage whose main ingredients are minced pork or beef, onions and potatoes. *Nävgröt* or oatmeal porridge usually accompanies roast pork and whortleberries. Other local delicacies include fillet of elk, venison, Vänern salmon, char from the Klarälven, chanterelle mushrooms and cloudberries.

Events – The province is known for its Midsummer celebrations, the fiddlers' gathering and FA Dahlgren's folk comedy *Värmlänningarna* at Ransäter and the Fryksdalsdansen (folk dancing) in Sunne.

SIGHTS

Residenstorget – *Overlooks the river.* The square is dominated on the east side by the County Governor's Residence and has a **statue** of the city's founder, King Karl IX, by the Värmland sculptor Christian Eriksson.

Kvarteret Almen – *Further west on the south bank of Västra Älvgrenen.* Fires swept through the city in 1616, 1719 and 1865 and this district of classical wooden houses is one of the rare areas to have been spared. The first building to come into view acted as the governor's residence between 1793 and 1809 and at the time was considered to be one of the most handsome residences.

Karlstad Sunbeam – *North of Residenstorget at the eastern end of the bridge of Västrabron.* Karlstad is remembered above all for the Karlstad Sunbeam a waitress who radiated happiness and hospitality. Her **statue** stands to the north of Residenstorget.
At the other end of the bridge stands a **statue** of another local personality, the writer Selma Lagerlöf by Arvid Backlund (1895-1985).

Värmlands Museum ⊙ – *Northwards along the riverside to the park of Sandgrund.* The elegant Museum of Värmland in its pleasant riverside setting was the work of Cyrillus Johansson (1884-1959) and extended by Carl Nyrén (b 1917). The holding includes a collection of local art and artefacts of cultural and historical interest.

Domkyrkan ⊙ – *V Kyrkogatan, north-east of Residenstorget.* This small cruciform cathedral with its bright and spacious interior was consecrated in 1730. Only the roof and the upper part of the tower were destroyed by fire. The gilded **coat of arms★** above the door in the porch is surrounded by the symbols of Christ.

LITERARY EXCURSIONS

Fryksdalen – **Mårbacka and Rottneros** – *The total length of the drive is 84km whereas Mårbacka is 70km north of Karlstad. Leave by E 18 to the west, then turn onto road 61 in the direction of Arvika. Beyond Kil look for the road to Östra Ämtervik which follows the west bank of Nedre Fryken before crossing between the two lakes and continuing up the east side of Middle or Mellan-Fryken.*
This excursion takes visitors into the Fryk Valley with its long lake, really three lakes, made famous by the novels of Selma Lagerlöf, and through typical Värmland countryside on the way to two important attractions.

★★ **Mårbacka** ⊙ – The writer **Selma Lagerlöf** (1858-1940) was the first woman to win a Nobel Prize for literature in 1909 and the province of Värmland is the setting for many described in her novels. The long lake of Löven and the manor of Lövdala of her novels are in fact Lake Fryken and her own lakeside home. For anyone interested in the writer a visit to her home is a must. In 1907 she was able to repurchase her beloved home, which her family had to give up when she was still very young, and she stayed here until her death. All the rooms have been refurbished as they were when she lived there.

Selma Lagerlöf's study, Mårbacka

Continue for 10km in the direction of Sunne, then turn southwards onto road 45 to follow the west bank of Mellan-Fryken. After 2km turn left.

The Kinship Monument, **Stamfrändemonumentet★**, a granite map of Värmland crested by an eagle, was erected in 1953 to commemorate the exodus of Swedes to America and the influx of Finnish immigrants to Värmland in the 17C. There is a spectacular **view★★★** of Lake Fryken surrounded by wooded heights.

Drive a further 2km south of Sunne.

★ **Rottneros** – This manor is known to many as the Ekeby Manor of Selma Lagerlöf's epic novel the *Gösta Berling's Saga* published in 1891. The old manor dating from the 13C was destroyed by fire and the present building dates from 1931. However it is the splendid 40-acre **park ★★**⊙ and its many **sculptures★★** which deserve all the attention. These include works by such Scandinavian artists as Christian Eriksson, Carl Milles, Carl Eldh and Gustav Vigeland.

★ **Alsters Herrgård** ⊙ – *Leave Karlstad by road E 18 to the east following signposts to Alster, then Frödings Minnesgård and finally Herrgård.* This manor was the birthplace of one of Sweden's greatest and without doubt most popular poets, **Gustaf Fröding** (1860-1911). The manor was built in 1772 and is now a museum to the memory of the poet with an exhibition devoted to Värmland's literary heritage. An interesting chart shows how the various Värmland writers were related to one another.

A nature trail, Frödingleden, leads to the small dell which was an unending source of inspiration for Fröding's poetry.

Drive under the viaduct and follow signs to Frödingdungen and Frödingstenen.

In the nearby birch grove which was the subject of one of his poems there is Christian Eriksson's memorial stone to the poet inscribed with one of his most famous poems.

KIRUNA

Norrbottens län
Population 26 000
Michelin map 985 E 17 or Atlas Europe p 108 – Local map see LAPPLAND

The ore mountain of Kirunavaara, right in the centre of town, is a prominent but appropriate landmark for the bleak mining town of Kiruna which has contributed so much to Sweden's prosperity. It was an almost insurmountable task to open a mine, build a city and then a railway in this arctic outpost at the beginning of the last century. The resulting irregular town plan is adapted to the terrain and the street network is designed to check the high north winds.

Kiruna is also famous for its space research station at **Esrange** *(see opposite)* and the Geophysical Institute investigating the phenomena of the aurora borealis, cosmic radiation, earth magnetism and earthquakes. Kiruna is the seat of the Swedish Sami Parliament.

Kiruna makes an excellent excursion centre for exploring the high mountains to the west and especially the Kebnekaise massif with Sweden's highest peak 2 114m above sea level. In clear weather the massif is visible from central Kiruna.

Snöfestival – Kiruna, the winter city with crisp low temperatures and magic darkness illuminated by the northern lights, organises a popular **Snow Festival** where visitors can admire the results of the **snow sculpture competition** which takes place during the last weekend in January.

Aurora borealis – The constant darkness always fascinates people from abroad as does the possibility of seeing the **northern lights** flickering in the clear cold nights from October to February.

During the 28 days between 9 December and 5 January, when the sun never rises above the horizon, it doesn't mean complete darkness but a beautiful sort of twilight when the sun is less than 6° below the horizon. The sparkling white mantle of snow also helps to lighten the darkness.

Midnight sun – During the period of eternal daylight, all night long from early May through August, the best time to look for the complete sun is between 28 May and 14 July and the best place is from the summit of Luossavaara, the former ore mountain now a ski centre. Drive to the end of Hjalmar Lundbohmvägen.

STRIKING IT RICH IN KIRUNA

The founding father – Although the deposits at Kiruna had been known for some time they had never been assessed when the geologist **Hjalmar Lundbohm** (1855-1926) arrived in 1890. Following his investigations and the discovery of the rich vein of iron ore he developed open-cast mining on a commercial scale and became manager of Luossavaara-Kiirunavaara Aktie-Bolag (LKAB). Although he was a wealthy man for the time, he had a strong social conscience and took an active part in establishing a town plan for Kiruna as he had been appalled by the shanty town which had grown up around Malmberget. He was a close friend of some of the foremost artists and writers of the time, Prince Eugen, Christian Eriksson, Albert Engström, Carl Larsson and others.

The Mine – By the end of the 19C mining had started on a large scale and in 1903 the Ore Rail (Malmbanan) was built to Narvik in Norway as an outlet for the ore. Unlike Malmberget this is one large vein 4km long, 100m wide and 2km deep and it produces about 200 million tonnes of iron ore annually from the working face 775m down. By the end of the 20C it will probably be 1 000m down. Thirteen trains with 52 wagons export 52 000t of ore daily. In summer there are guided tours to a **visitors' mine** 375m below ground.

★★ Kiruna kyrka: The Shrine of the Nomadic People ⊘ – Hjalmar Lundbohm commissioned Gustaf Wickman to design a church in the shape of a Sami tent. The free-standing **bell-tower** in front of the church is supported by 12 props and Hjalmar Lundbohm's tombstone on the south side has an inscription by Albert Engström, "For the benefit of the Nation he exposed the treasures of the mountain and created the city". The gilt bronze **statues** standing sentinel around the roofline were the work of Christian Eriksson and they represent man's various states of mind: despair, shyness, arrogance, piety and trust on the north side and humility, love, sorrow, melancholy and devotion on the south. The **relief**, above the main door, depicting groups of Sami beneath the clouds of heaven was also the work of Eriksson. The wrought-iron decorations on the double doors were by Ossian Elgström.

Interior – The spacious interior with its dark timber walls does indeed remind one of the interior of a Sami hut. The visitor's attention is immediately drawn to the **altarpiece** by Prince Eugen representing Paradise as a Tuscan landscape. Christian Eriksson made both the **cross** with Sami praying at its base and the metal sculpture of **St George and the Dragon**.

★★**Kiruna Stadshus** ⓥ – The edifice, designed by Arthur von Schmalensee, was inaugurated in 1963. The tower of cast iron was designed by Bror Markland and the carillon of 23 bells rings out at noon and 6pm every day. The door handles of birch and reindeer horn are by Esaias Poggats and are inspired by the Sami magic drum. In the main hall the floor is Italian mosaic, the walls are of Dutch handmade bricks and the woodwork is Oregon pine. The hand-knotted hanging entitled **The magic drum from Rautas** was made to the designs of the artist Sven X:et Erixon. The upper part depicts the midnight sun at Lapporten whereas the lower part is rich with the glowing colours of autumn. The birch and reindeer horn sculpture by the Sami artist Lars Sunna shows the magic drum between two mountain peaks. The wall mosaic in the café was by Bruce Carter and is entitled *Four Dancing People in the Sunrise*. To the left before entering the conference room (konferensrum) is Christain Eriksson's bust of Hjalmar Lundbohm and inside the same room is a work by Helmer Osslund, *Autumn Colours in the Mountains*. The council chamber (sessional) has more paintings by Osslund and a large picture of the ore mountain Kiirunavaara by Sixten Lundbohm the nephew of Hjalmar Lundbohm.

Hjalmar Lundbohmsgården ⓥ – This timber house was the home of Hjalmar Lundbohm *(see The founding father above)* and today it serves as a cultural centre with displays concerning Kiruna, including Lundbohm's study.

Samegården ⓥ – Cultural centre and meeting place for the Sami community of Kiruna. In summer the basement **museum** organises an arts and crafts exhibition. The door handles by Lars Sunna are in the shape of the magic drum *(see illustration p 8)*.

EXCURSIONS

★★**Jukkasjärvi** – *See LAPPLAND*.

Esrange – *45km in the direction of Jukkasjärvi. Guided tours; group visits only apply to the Kiruna Tourist Information Centre.* Rocket base and space research centre which sends between 10 and 20 rockets annually into space.

Nikkaluokta – *70km west of Kiruna, leave by Hjalmar Lundbohmvägen.* Sami village near Kebnekaise (2 111m). A Tourist Information Centre and a restaurant are housed in the modern building of interesting design. The former provides information on boat trips on Lake Ladtjojaure, a 19km trail to **Kebnekaise Alpine Centre** from where there are guided ascents of Kebnekaise and guided tours to the glacier research centre of **Tarfala**. One of the most popular stretches of the Kungsleden long-distance footpath is from Abisko south to Kebnekaise and Nikkaluokta.

★★★**Nordkalottvägen: from Kiruna to the Norwegian border** – *See LAPPLAND*.

LAPPLAND★★★

SWEDISH LAPLAND – Norrbottens län, Västerbottens län, Jämtlands län, Västernorrlands län

Michelin map 985 D-G 11-20 or Atlas Europe pp 104-109

Swedish Lapland coincides with the most northerly county, Lappland, a sparsely populated area where the land rises from east to west to the mountain area bordering the Norwegian frontier and the highest peak, Kebnekaise. The area of Sami settlement extends down as far as northern Dalarna. Of the 70 000 estimated Sami in northern Scandinavia 17 000 live in Sweden but they are a minority even in their settlement area.

The Sami established a viable culture adapted to the harsh living conditions of the north – all based on the reindeer. The Sami lived in family groups *(siidat)* and their society was hinged on the good will of the gods and the wisdom of the elders. The shaman *(noaidi)* with his special gifts could make contact with the gods and look into the future with the aid of a drum. When the Christianisation of the Sami began in the 17C their spiritual leaders were persecuted and the Sami were forced to renounce their old religion and surrender their sacred drums to the travelling missionaries. The early missionaries attempted to put Sami children into permanent schools; the first one was set up in Lycksele in 1632. Then early in the 20C special nomad schools were established however today Sami children can choose between local schools or government sponsored Sami schools. Luleå has a teachers' training school for Sami-speaking students, Jokkmokk has a folk school and Umeå a chair in Sami language.

G. Lacz/SUNSET

Beware of Reindeer

Drive with care in Lapland as reindeer have little road sense (some even head straight for vehicle headlights). Any accident involving a reindeer must be reported to the local authorities as compensation is due for all animals injured or killed on the road. Reindeer represent a herder's wealth and it is discourteous to ask him how many he owns!

The Land of the midnight sun – For visitors the land of the midnight sun is one of the much publicised marvels of these northern latitudes, but the native Sami have to cope with a winter period of darkness when the sun never appears above the horizon. This period of darkness varies from two months in the Arctic's lower regions to four months in the higher latitudes *(see HURTIGRUTEN: inset on local map)*. The northern lights, or **aurora borealis**, are a spectacular feature of the polar nights.

Reindeer breeding – A new law was passed in 1971 to regulate reindeer breeding and now the activity is organised into 43 Sami villages. Roughly 35% of Swedish territory is given over to reindeer breeding and at present approximately 300 000 head of reindeer live on the area.

Laponia – In 1996, part of this vast country, was added by UNESCO to its World Heritage list under the name of Laponia. The area which extends westwards from Gällivare and Jokkmokk covers an area of 94 000km² and includes four national parks (Muddus to the east, Stora Sjöfallet, Sarek and Padjelanta to the west) and two bird sanctuaries (Sjaunja and Stubba). Laponia was chosen on account of its natural uniqueness and beauty and of its cultural wealth since the area has been occupied continuously by the Sami people from time immemorial (one of the oldest archaeological sites of northern Sweden is situated at Kårtejaure in Stora Sjöfallet National Park). In national parks and nature reserves, the public right of way, *Allemansrätten (see Introduction: Great wilderness areas)*, is restricted by certain regulations concerning mountain biking, riding, keeping dogs on a leash, lighting a fire and camping *(more information in local tourist offices or on the Internet: www.environ.se)*.

The sights described under this heading go far beyond the county of Lappland, but they have been regrouped geographically – along valleys or roads – for convenience, because of the great distances involved. The map below includes the sights described under Lappi (Finnish Lapland) and Finnmark (Norwegian Lapland).

BLÅ VÅGEN Road E 12

The good surfaced Blue Road runs from the Gulf of Bothnia up the valley of the Umeälven then winds up the valleys of the Vindel Mountain range in Sweden where it offers many far-reaching views before arriving at Mo i Rana on the Norwegian coast. Beyond the Gulf of Bothnia the final stretch in Finland, known as the Sininen Tie, goes from Vaasa to Joensuu. When driving through the Swedish section from east to west it is a slow progression towards the mountains with colours changing from blue-lilac to rose-brown. Between Lycksele and Storuman it is mainly forested countryside with many ribbon lakes and the peak with the characteristic outline to the north of the road before coming to Tärnaby is Ryfjället (1 412m), the emblem of the Tärna Mountains. Beyond the snow-capped mountain range comes into view.

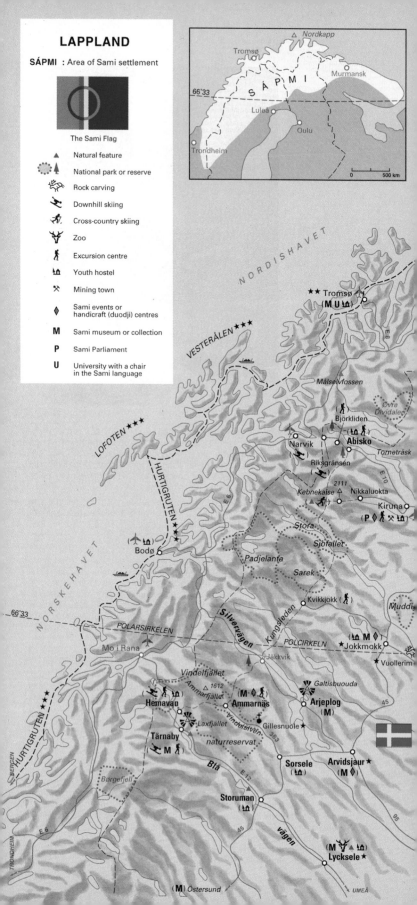

LAPPLAND

SÁPMI : Area of Sami settlement

The Sami Flag

▲ Natural feature

🌸▲ National park or reserve

🐾 Rock carving

🎿 Downhill skiing

🎿 Cross-country skiing

🦌 Zoo

🚶 Excursion centre

🏠 Youth hostel

✗ Mining town

◊ Sami events or handicraft (duodji) centres

M Sami museum or collection

P Sami Parliament

U University with a chair in the Sami language

△ Nordkapp

Tromsø
SÁPMI
Murmansk
66°33
Luleå
Oulu
Trondheim
0   500 km

NORDISHAVET

★★ Tromsø 🏠 (M U 🏠)

Målselvfossen

Övre Dividalen

Björkliden
(🏠 🎿) Abisko
Narvik
Torneträsk
Riksgränsen
Kebnekaise △ 2111 Nikkaluokta
Kiruna
(P ◊ 🎿 ✗ 🏠)

Stora
Sjöfallet

Padjelanta

Sarek

VESTERÅLEN ★★★

LOFOTEN ★★★

HURTIGRUTEN ★★

(✈ 🏠) ★★
Bodø

NORSKEHAVET

Kvikkjokk (🎿)

Muddus

(🏠 M ◊)
★ Jokkmokk

66°33
POLARSIRKELEN

Silvervägen
Kungsleden
POLCIRKELN
★ Vuollerim

Mo i Rana

Jäkkvik

Vindelfjället
△ 1612
Ammarfjället
(M ◊ 🎿)
Ammarnäs

Galtisbuouda
Arjeplog
(M)

Hemavan
🎿 🚶 🏠

Laxfjället
🎿
Gillesnuole ★

Tärnaby
🎿 M 🎿

naturreservat

Vindelälven

Sorsele
(🏠)

Arvidsjaur ★
(M ◊)

Blå
E 12

HURTIGRUTEN ★★★

Børgefjell

Storuman
(🏠)

vägen

(M 🦌 ▲ 🏠)
Lycksele ★

(M) Östersund

UMEÅ

BERGEN

TRONDHEIM
E 6

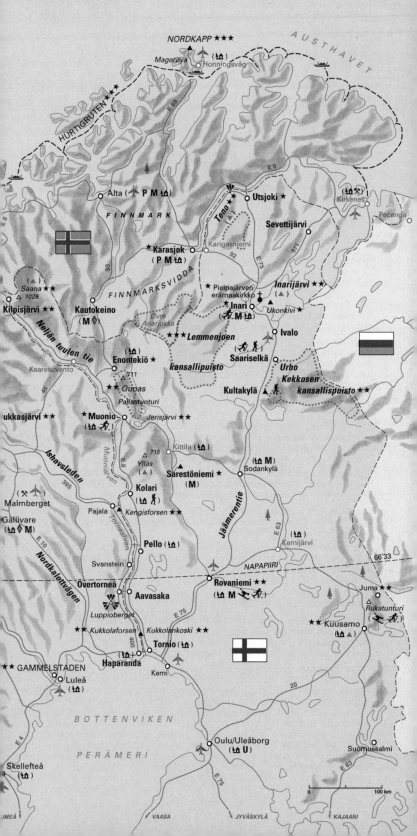

NB: Although we are in the heart of reindeer country it has been decided not to reveal the whereabouts of Santa Claus

*Lycksele Population 13 800

Lycksele lies on both banks of the River Umeälven and is popularly referred to as Lappstockholm and the immense Sami tent (restaurant) confronting the visitor on his arrival in town is a good reminder that this is the gateway to Swedish Lapland and Sami culture.

★★★**Lycksele Zoo** ⊘ – *Cross the river, turn right after the bridge, then first left and follow the sign for Djurpark and after 1.2km turn left again onto Brännbergsvägen.* This immense zoo specialises in Nordic fauna with 36 species and around 120 animals in all. Feeding time is often the best time to catch a glimpse of the animals as some of the enclosures are so big that it is not always easy to get a close look at them. Feeding times are as follows: elks, bison and musk oxen at noon; bears, wolves and lynx at 2pm; seals, otters and other marine animals at 10am and 3pm.

★★**Gammplatsen** ⊘ – *After the bridge continue along the river bank for another 700m then follow the sign for Gammplatsen.* The original site of Lycksele became an open-air museum in 1945. Take the time to visit the lovely Margareta Chapel and its belfry down by the river, then the Museum of Hunting, **Jaktmuseet** beside the car park. There is a lovely collection of Sami woodcarvings on the first floor. The forestry museum, **Skogsmuseet**, evokes the hard physical labour involved in lumbering and logging. Ruselegården is a small café.

Storuman Population 7 359

Storuman is beautifully located on the lake of the same name and is now an important road junction at the intersection of E 12, road 45 and the Wilderness Railway. Not far from the camp site is **Kåtakyrkan** ⊘, a chapel built to look like a traditional Sami hut. The former railway hotel, **Järnvägshotellet** ⊘ *(entrance in Stationsgatan)*, today houses a library but is decorated with some lovely Dalecarlian paintings. For a lovely **view**★★ of Lake Storuman and the isles of Luspholmarna against a mountain backdrop drive past the Toppen Hotel then look for the signpost Utsikten. To visit the **isles of Luspholmarna**★★★ turn right beyond the Tourist Information Centre then right again. Again there are splendid **views** of the isles from the approach road.

Stensele kyrka ⊘ – *5km to the east by road E 12.* Of the many large wooden churches in the north of Sweden, this one, dating from 1886, is one of the biggest and it boasts one of the smallest books. A magnifying glass and tweezers are necessary to read The Lord's Prayer in seven different languages. The church also has one of the best-preserved examples of Queen Christina's 1646 Bible.

Tärnaby Population 630

The mountain village and ski resort of Tärnaby, at the northern end of Lake Gäutajaure, makes an ideal excursion centre for discovering the wilderness area of the Vindel Mountains Nature Reserve. However it has another claim to fame as the home of slalom champion Ingmar Stenmark.

Fjällvindens Alpinarium ⊘ – *Ground floor of the Hotel Fjällvindens Hus, east of the town centre.* This **Ski Museum** displays cups, medals and other items relating to the skiing exploits of two slalom champions, Ingmar Stenmark and Stig Strand.

Laxfjället – *4km east of the bridge. Either walk up from the car park or take the chair-lift from Fjällvindens Hus.* The drive up to the car park of the Tärnaby slalom course affords splendid **views**★★★.

Samegården ⊘ – *6km to the east.* The **museum** (and café) run by Sami has in the basement a collection of photographs, costumes, baskets, bowls and other items like the bridal crown of horn, the sledge with a lid. Horn handicrafts and decorated Sami knives are on sale.

Hemavan Population 225

Like its sister village of Tärnaby *(see above)* to the south-east Hemavan is a tourist resort in the heart of mountainous moorland country. This is the starting point of the **Kungsleden**, long-distance footpath as it sets off northwards through Ammarnäs and ends 500km later at Abisko *(see below)*.

Tärna Fjällpark ⊘ – *1.5km out of the village.* This striking, mushroom-shaped tower with its golden dome stands right up against the mountainside and serves as a visitor centre for the Vindel Mountains Nature Reserve (Vindelfjällens Naturreservat). The visitor centre will also be able to tell you how to get to the Sami's Holy Mountain, Atoklinten. In the ground floor display entitled Kingdom of the Senses, **Sinneriket**, light, sound and smell are used to evoke the surrounding mountain environment and its wildlife. There is a splendid **view**★★★ of the surrounding countryside from the 10th floor café. An enclosed footbridge leads from this floor straight onto the flank of the mountain and the world's northernmost **Botanical Garden** specialising in mountain and Alpine flora. One of the stars is a new species of orchid created in 1987 called Brudkulla. From the garden it is possible to follow one of several trails, including the first kilometre of the Kungsleden.

VINDELÄLVEN From Sorsele to Ammarnäs – Road 363

Most Swedish rivers, to a greater or lesser extent, have been harnessed to provide hydroelectric power. The Vindelälven is one of the few large rivers that has remained unspoilt, largely due to an important campaign by conservationists and it is considered the flagship for future projects. The river is almost 500km long with numerous stretches of falls and rapids. The calm sections between the turbulence of rapids and falls are known as *sel* and the word is found in many place names as it was along these stretches that the first people settled.

Sorsele Population 3 524

Like Storuman, Sorsele is a central community set mainly on a midstream island. The Tourist Information Centre will provide information on the possibilities for fishing, canoeing, and shooting the rapids locally.

The name of the roadside village of **Hemfjäll** means village with a view and roadside signs invite drivers to stop and enjoy the view. The river rushing over **rapids** may be seen from the road at Björkheden and Järnforsen.

★**Gillesnuole** – *60km north-west of Sorsele*. A path leads to an old Sami chapel hidden amid trees, on the north-west shore of Lake Storvindeln. It was built in the 1750s and it is still accompanied by its belfry, a memorial stone, a log shed, raised on four posts as well as a Sami hut. Church weekends are held three times in summer.

Ammarnäs Population 280

This remote mountain village standing on the shore of Lake Gausträsk at the foot of Ammarfjället (1 612m) was only linked by road to Gillesnuole in 1921 and to Sorsele in 1939. With a population of barely 300, of which half are reindeer tending Sami, the village is now popular as a centre for adventure activities into the remote fastness of the Vindel Mountains Nature Reserve. Walkers and hikers can take the short cut south to Hemavan *(see above)* and Tärnaby *(see above)* via the Kungsleden.

Vindelfjällens Naturreservat – With an area of 5 500km≤ the Vindel Mountains Nature Reserve is one of the largest in Europe; it was designated to safeguard a fragile mountain and forest environment. Within the boundaries of the reserve there are many high peaks, hundreds of lakes, the mighty Vindelälven, a varied fauna including wolverine, bear, lynx and Arctic fox – the emblem of this reserve – a bird sanctuary, a rich flora with everything from orchids to brushwood and a resident herd of 25 000 reindeer.

Wilderness Express

275

★**Workshop of Margareta Grahn** – *Just before Ammarnäsgården take the road to the right and after 200m a steep road on the left leads to a greenhouse.* A Sami woman sells beautiful, authentic Sami handicrafts *(Sameslöjd Sámi Duodji)* from her workshop to the left of the greenhouse. The materials are roots, pewter, skins and textiles whereas wood and horn are traditionally used in Sami handicrafts made by men.

Potato Mound – *Turn to the right at the T-junction, then continue to the end of the road.* This remarkable mound never ceases to fascinate visitors. Since the beginning of the 19C the almond potato, thus named because of its shape, has been grown in terraces. A path on the north side leads to the top of the mound.

Ammarnäs kyrka – *Close to the mound.* This fine timbered Sami chapel was built in 1858 to replace the one at Gillesnuole. It was remodelled in 1912. Note how some of the tombstones are simple boulders.

★**Lappstan** ⊘ – *South-west of the church.* Sami huts and sheds from Gillesnuole were moved to the present site in 1911. They are used by the Sami during three annual festivals.

Samegården ⊘ – *Right at the T-junction, then first left to the grey building beyond the ICA shop.* A Sami collection is displayed in this Sami hut and there are also temporary exhibitions of art and handicrafts.

Hembygdsgården ⊘ – *Right at the T-junction, then continue to the end of the road; it is to the right.* This homestead museum traces the history of the Swedish settlers by means of objects and photographs.

Excursions

North Ammarnäs – *4km to the north, follow signposts to N Ammarnäs.* After about 2km stop at the bridge to admire the Vindelåforsen where the river rushes over flat stratified rocks. Continue to the mountain village through which the Kungsleden passes. An easy path 4.5km long leads to an old mountain farm known as the Eagle's Nest, Örnboet. The last occupants left in the 1950s. The cottages and their contents give some idea of what life was like in this remote corner of Sweden in the 19C.

Ammarnäsgården – *Coming from Ammarnäs turn left at the T-junction.* A central building, in addition to providing accommodation, also houses the Tourist Information Centre and the visitor centre, **Naturum**, for the Vindel Mountains Nature Reserve. Lapplandsafari organises a number of excursions and safaris into the mountains, fishing expeditions to the River Laisälven or white-water rafting on the River Vindelälven. All the necessary equipment can be bought or hired on the spot.

SILVERVÄGEN Road 95

The Silver Road stretches from Skellefteå on the Gulf of Bothnia to Bodø on the west coast of Norway. In the 17C ore was mined around Nasafjäll and transported by reindeer sleigh and then boat to the east coast of Sweden. Mining ceased in 1810. The road was only surfaced in 1972.

★**Arvidsjaur** Population 7 716

Arvidsjaur was an early road junction, trading centre and meeting place along the Silver Road on the way to the mine at Nasafjäll. Today it is a typical small Swedish town offering the basic necessities to locals and tourists in summer.

★★★**Lappstan** – *In summer there are guided tours daily from the end of June to July; one of the huts serves coffee and sells dried reindeer meat.* This is the oldest and best-preserved Sami church village dating from the 17C. Church villages were a common feature in Sami territory. The nomads built huts where they could stay overnight when they gathered for religious festivals. Here at Arvidsjaur there were three distinct districts: one for the Sami huts and storehouses, another for the church cottages and stables of the Swedish settlers and a third for the tradesmen's market cottages. Only the Sami district remains and the huts are still used during the great Sami festival on the last weekend in August.

Hembygdsmuseet ⊘ – *3km west by road 951, signposted Hembygsgård.* The 100-year-old former vicarage now houses the local heritage museum.

Arvas – The red-timbered building is occupied by the Sami tourist organisation, **Sita Sameland** (*sita* is Sami for communion). The organisation provides information on the Sami and organises guided tours of Lappstan *(see above)* as well as excursions locally to give visitors an insight into the Sami way of life and traditions and in particular the life of a reindeer herder. During three weeks starting from Midsummer night tours are organised to see the branding of new born calves. Each herder has his own mark – a distinctive nick in the calf's ear.

Arjeplog Population 3 615

Arjeplog occupies a group of headlands and islands between Lake Uddjaure and Lake Hornavan – at 226m the deepest lake in Sweden.
The town organises an international chamber music festival **Lapplands Festspel** *(end of June and beginning of July)* and a **Square Dance Festival** around Midsummer. On Midsummer's Eve the dancing is held on the summit of Galtisbouda *(see below)*.

★★Silvermuseet ⊘ – Einar Wallquist (1896-1985), the Lapp doctor, first came to Arjeplog in 1922 and in addition to his medical work, he began collecting simple everyday objects and exquisite pieces of silver. He founded the museum in 1965 in the former Sami school (1854). The museum shop, in the former classroom, sells Sami handicrafts. The rooms at the back are where the teacher lived and Dr Wallquist's study can be seen through a glass partition. In the basement a series of show cases display the splendid silver collars, belts, ornaments, drinking bowls and spoons which have given the museum its name. The oldest items are Norwegian and date from the 15C. The collection also includes Sami handicrafts, a storage hut on runners (*skiedja* in Sami) and other objects commonly used by the nomadic Sami. The **magic drum** is of particular interest as it was one of few to be saved when the Sami were christened by force and their drums destroyed. The first-floor display of simple unadorned utensils of the Swedish settlers make a striking contrast to the richly decorated Sami utensils.

Skeppsholmen Saamiland ⊘ – *From the centre of Arjeplog follow the signpost for Skeppsholmen.* A narrow footbridge leads to an islet in lake Hornavan where Sami huts *(härbren)* and storehouses have been regrouped as in a typical Sami camp. The huge tent-shaped hut *(kåta)* serves as a meeting place for the two groups of mountain and forest Sami which today constitute the Arjeplog Sami Association. The camp enjoys a peaceful setting standing as it does surrounded by water with the mountain of Galtisbuouda in the background.

Arjeplogs kyrka ⊘ – This rose-coloured cruciform church dating from 1763 stands on the site of an earlier one consecrated by Queen Christina in 1641.

Galtisbuouda – *15km to the east of Arjeplog in the direction of Arvidsjaur; after 3km look for the signpost Galtisbuouda; an asphalt road leads to the top and the final 5km are quite steep.* From the top one can fully appreciate the beauty of the network of lakes spreading out around Arjeplog. On a clear day the **panorama★★★** extends 100km on all sides to take in the peak of Ammarfjället to the west, Pieljekaise to the north-west and the snow-covered Pårte Massif in the Sarek National Park.

Linnaeus in Lapland

During his 1732 visit to Lapland Linnaeus never actually reached Abisko and there are some doubts if he even made it to Jukkasjärvi but he described his ascent of Vallevare near Kvikkjokk:
"Here, there are no longer any trees – nothing but mountains, all higher than their neighbour and covered with frozen snow. There are neither paths nor trails and no sign of living habitations. The bright green of summer seems to have been banished (from nature's palette) relegated to the deepest valleys. No birds are to be seen, other than the ptarmigan which run hither and thither with their young in the valleys... I climbed to the highest point to see the midnight sun... Then I sat down to sort through and describe the plants which I had gathered (and he lists 30)..."

★★★NORDKALOTTVÄGEN From Kiruna to the Norwegian border – road E 10

The more recent North Calotte Trail was designated in 1993 in the presence of the Swedish and Norwegian monarchs and the Finnish president. **North Calotte** – skull cap – refers to the polar cap of Norway, Sweden, Finland and Russia north of the Arctic Circle. In 1984 a road was opened through one of Europe's last wilderness areas, from Kiruna via Riksgränsen on the Norwegian frontier to Narvik. Until then the railway built in 1903 to export the iron ore was the only cross-border link. It makes a spectacular drive with the glistening blue waters of Lake Torneträsk enclosed by imposing mountains on both sides.

★★Jukkasjärvi Population 1 000

Since Jukkasjärvi is the most northerly village on the River Torneälven it has always welcomed travellers from afar. Today Jukkasjärvi is an ideal centre for fishing, canoeing and white-water rafting on the rapids of the River Torneälven in summer whereas winter brings the choice of dog-sledging, scooter-safaris, and cross-country or downhill skiing.

Altarpiece by Bror Hjorth

Arctic hall – The village is known for its spectacular winter hotel built each year using more than 1 500t of ice. This giant igloo also houses a gallery, restaurant, bar, jazz club, exhibition hall and church in addition to sleeping accommodation – sleeping bags and reindeer skins are provided for the hardy. Indoor temperatures remain between -3°C and -8°C regardless of the temperature outside. Around April and May the sun starts its work of demolition.

Jukkasjärvi kyrka ⊘ – The wooden church down by the river dates from 1726, although further additions were made in the late 18C. The porch has several inscriptions made by travellers notably one in Latin by three Frenchmen dating from 1681: "Raised in Gaul, we have seen Africa, tasted the Holy Waters of the Ganges, and travelled our own Europe; so driven by fate and travelling by land and sea we finally stood here at the pole where the world ends". The remarkable **altarpiece★★** is a brightly coloured triptych carved in teak by **Bror Hjorth** in 1958. It depicts Lars Levi Laestadius preaching a sermon to the people. The figures are naive but the message is clear as is the tone of the preacher. The drops of blood from Christ's side and brow become red flowers as they fall, Mary has the midnight sun for a halo and the panel culminates in the leap of a Sami woman who has found salvation. A winter landscape and a night sky lit by the stars and the aurora borealis form the background.

Kiruna and Esrange – See *KIRUNA: Excursions.*

Mattarahkka – *5km west of Kiruna.* The Sami flag flutters a welcome to this Sami handicrafts centre where young Sami women continue the age-old traditions of craft making. The workshops are all connected to the exhibition and shop.

Torneträsk – At 72km long and 9km wide this is one of Sweden's longest lakes. The name in Sami means forest by the big water. Boat trips leave from Abisko tourist station.

Abisko Population 120

The mountain village of Abisko *(98km west of Kiruna)* on the south bank of Lake **Torneträsk** is right in the heart of the Swedish wilderness, its main attraction. Abisko is the northern starting point of the **Kungsleden** a 500km-long mountain trail for skiers and walkers which goes south to Hemavan *(see above).*

Abisko Turiststation ⊘ – *2km west of the village. Facilities include a youth hostel, holiday chalet village, camp site, food shop and hire of sports equipment.* The visitor centre, **Naturum**, has displays on local flora, fauna, geology and the Sami.

Saunas in the past

The Swedish word for sauna *(bastu)* means bath hut and at one time communal bathhouses existed all over Sweden until they were closed as being unhealthy and places of iniquity. Northern Sweden preserved the tradition of the sauna and by the 1930s saunas had once again spread to the rest of the country. The oldest type is the smoke-sauna.

SWEDEN

The centre organises walks to a nearby Sami camp to enjoy the bird life (May and June), the flowers (July), the autumn colours (August to mid-September) and boat trips on the lake.

Nearby is **Abiskojåkka★★**, a canyon-like feature, as this mountain river flows into the lake. The geological strata are clearly visible and it is possible to pick out a yellowish-white dolomite known as Abisko marble.

Njulla – 1 169m. A cable-car leads up to a height of 900m from where there is a grand **view** of the well-known landmark **Lapporten** (Lapp gateway) and its striking outline to the south-west of Abisko. Njulla also makes an ideal viewing point for the midnight sun *(31 May to 16 July)*.

Abisko National Park – The park lies to the west of Abisko and is one of the main tourist attractions of the area. The park with a total area of 77km2 was designated in 1909 and is known for its rich mountain flora, in particular the many rare species of orchids. Lemmings, bears, elks, martens, lynxes and wolverines may be seen.
Further north near Björkliden where the road curves round between mount **Njulla** (1 169m) and the lake, the visitor will discover traffic lights; these are in fact avalanche warning lights. The sign recommends motorists to maintain a steady speed of 60kph when the warning lights are not on.

★ **Rakkasjåkka** – *Between Björkliden and the traffic lights; parking space on either side of the bridge.* A wild mountain torrent *(jåkk)* rushes down to Lake Torneträsk. Follow the path down the steep slope to the shingle shore of Torneträsk.

Björkliden – *10km north-west of Abisko.* This holiday centre on Lake Torneträsk offers accommodation and all kinds of adventure tours into the great expanses of the surrounding wilderness areas.

Riksgränsen – This ski resort on the boundary with Norway offers good summer skiing. An auditorium, located next to the hotel, stages a permanent **slide show** ⊙ on Lapland through the seasons by the well-known Swedish nature photographer, Sven Hörnell.

Lapporten

ISHAVSLEDEN Road 400

The Tornedalen has always been a culturally and linguistically unified area until the 1808-9 Swedish-Russian War divided the valley. The River Torneälven in Swedish (Tornionjoki in Finnish) flows from its source at Abiskojåkka into Lake Torneträsk then joins the River Muonioälven south of Pajala, before entering the Gulf of Bothnia. The Mounioälven forms the border with Finland from Treriksröset, where the Finnish, Swedish and Norwegian borders meet southwards. For over 100 years this was one of the great timber floating rivers.

SWEDEN

Haparanda Population 10 666

The treaty of 1809 ceded Finland to Russia and in the process the Swedish-speaking Tornedalen was divided in two. Haparanda was founded in 1842 as a substitute for the lost merchant town of Tornio. A monument to the victims of the 1808-9 war stands near the Finnish border.

Haparanda kyrka ⊙ – *Follow Västra Esplanaden, turn right at Köpmansgatan then left onto Östra Kyrkogatan.* The church's modernity has made it a discussion point ever since it was consecrated in 1967. The dark, copper-clad exterior makes a direct contrast to the light, airy interior. The strange bell-tower stands on the site of the original wooden church which was destroyed by fire in 1963.

***Kukkolaforsen** – *15km north of Haparanda.* The rapids overlooked by rickety wooden jetties and attendant fishing huts and watermills make an all too familiar scene. Ever since the Middle Ages whitefish *(sik)* have been caught in the traditional way with haaf nets from the rickety jetties built for this purpose. Between mid-June and mid-September the visitor can enjoy freshly grilled fish. The **Sikfesten** or White Fish Festival is held on the last weekend in July.

Övertorneå Kyrka

Luppioberget – *9km south of Övertorneå; a road leads to the top.* There is a magnificent **view***** of the Tornedalen (Torneälven/Tornionjoki).

Övertorneå – *Matatengivägen runs right through the village and joins road 400 on the other side.* The polygonal **kyrka*** is one of the best-preserved 18C churches in these northern regions. The bell-tower has paintings above each doorway and the church's interior is richly decorated with more paintings. Both the pulpit and chancel parclose are beautifully carved. Among the many medieval wooden sculptures is a delightful **Madonna in a Mantle**** which opens like an altarpiece.

At Niskanpää the road crosses the **Arctic Circle**.

Svanstein – *15km north of the Arctic Circle. Follow the sign for Konst och konsthantverk.* The main building, Dränglängan, once reserved for the farmhands, houses sculptures in wood by Rolf Suup. A genuine old-fashioned **smoke sauna*** can be seen in the grounds.

****Kengisforsen** – *7km south of Pajala follow the sign for Kengis; the last 2km are gravel.* The road passes the 1830s Kengis Manor, the only surviving building of a once flourishing iron foundry, on its way to the spectacular rapids.

Pajala – *Road 400 leads eastwards, then left onto Soukolovägen.* The town is known as the home of **Levi Laestadius** (1800-61), the founder of an evangelical movement which had a wide following in northern Scandinavia. His home **Laestadii pörte** is open to visitors and the old vicarage has an exhibition on his life and his religious movement. During the latter years of his life he lived in a simple wooden hut at the vicarage of Pajala. Laestadius was also a notable botanist, scientist and a great advocate of temperance.

LEKSAND★★

Dalarnas län
Population 15 500
Michelin map 985 L 12 or Atlas Europe p 119

The bustling little community of Leksand at the southern end of Lake Siljan is the regional centre for the commune's 90 villages and has a reputation for cherishing past traditions in particular the Maypole Festival. From the Sunday preceding Midsummer to mid-July the colourful maypoles are raised in most of Leksand's 90 daughter villages. Every year now for more than half a century, Rune Linström's morality play *The Road to Heaven (Himlaspelet)* is performed in the open-air theatre, and if the Swedish tongue is impossible, the colourful local costumes and spirited performance of the actors make it an enjoyable event all the same.

During the reign of King Gustav Vasa Leksand was the scene of the **Bell Uprising** (Klockupproret). To help repay the crown's debts to the Hanseatic town of Lübeck it was decreed that the second largest bell from every church in the country was to be handed over to the king. The uprising was soon quelled and the church bells confiscated.

SIGHTS

Parking places are available outside the cultural centre and at Leksand's old heritage buildings, next to the church.

Leksands Kulturhus ⊙ – *Norsgatan west end between the town's information centre and the church.* In the basement of the cultural centre is a fascinating museum devoted to Dalecarlian painting and local costumes.

★**Leksands kyrka** ⊙ – The cream and white-stone church stands in a peaceful site by the lake. The turquoise interior makes a perfect setting for the ornate gilded pulpit (1757) and the 15C triumphal crucifix.

EXCURSIONS

★★**Ljusbodarna** ⊙ – *20km south-west of Leksand in the direction of Dala-Järna. After 10km, signpost to the left; bumpy gravel road.* In this old-fashioned setting, some 25 buildings are assembled, the oldest of which dates from the 17C. Four families stay here in the summer with their cows and goats. Upper (Övre) Ljusbodarna *(to the right before entering Lower Ljusbodarna)* contains a row of old wooden buildings.

★★**Alfvéngården** ⊙ – *At Tibble. 2.5 km to the east in the direction of Sågmyra. Immediately on the approach at Tibble, Alfvéngården is signposted (small sign beyond the maypole). Drive into the village, then left.* In this delightful village with its red-timbered houses, the composer and conductor **Hugo Alfvén** (1872-1960) found a haven for the last 15 years of his life. Alfvén represented National Romanticism, and his repeated use of the delicate tones and gradations in Swedish folk music has contributed to a revival in folk music. His orchestral works, romances and choral works are pure pleasure to music-lovers, and of his five symphonies, he himself preferred the fifth one. Alfvén also devoted himself to painting (watercolours) and writing (his memoirs fill four volumes). The three rooms on the ground floor are open to visitors.

★★**Tällberg** – *12km north of Leksand in the direction of Rättvik.* This pretty little village with its typical Dalarnian houses is located on a gentle hillside which slopes down to the lakeside. Tällberg attracts crowds of visitors each summer, causing the narrow village road to become jammed with cars. Domestic arts and crafts flourish here. **Holens Gammelgård** ⊙ *(drive uphill from the maypole)* is a homestead museum with an enchanting **view★★** of the area.

Jobs Handtryck ⊙ – *Västanvik, 6km west of Leksand, on the road to Siljansnäs. The right turn for Jobs Handtryck comes abruptly, shortly after Västanviksbadet.* The workshop produces beautiful handprinted cotton and linen fabrics with the pattern inspired by Swedish summer flowers.

Siljansnäs Naturum ⊙ – *15km north-west of Leksand. On the approach to Siljansnäs, go right towards the church and follow the road (a right bend) to the top of Björkberget.* In this little village, the belvedere (128 steps) of Björkberget (Birch Mountain, 344m above sea level) provides a splendid **panorama★★★** of Lake Siljan and the surrounding countryside *(view indicator)*. A nature room, Naturum, houses a flora and fauna exhibition.

LIDKÖPING

Västra Götalands län
Population 37 000
Michelin map 985 N 10 or Atlas Europe p 118

This pleasant little town lies at the head of a bay on Lake Vänern with the Kålland peninsula to the west and the mountain of Kinnekulle to the east. The medieval merchant town stood on the east bank of the River Lidan until it was destroyed by fire. The few red-wooden houses around Limtorget are all that remain.
In 1670 Chancellor Magnus Gabriel de la Gardie decided to build a new town on the opposite bank of the river and today the old and new squares are linked by a footbridge. In the chancellor's **Nya Torget** the focal point is without doubt provided by his **hunting lodge** which he had transported from his estate to serve as town hall. The red-wooden building, crested with the figure of Justice, now houses the Tourist Information Centre and a café. The square is a popular meeting and market place.

★★ **Rörstrands porslinsfabrik** ⊙ – The original porcelain manufactory was founded near Stockholm in 1726, making it Europe's second oldest porcelain factory after Meissen. In 1936 the workshops were transferred to Lidköping where they have produced a wide assortment of tableware and decorative items. The Blue Fire line was designed in 1951 by Hertha Bengtson who had also been a designer for the Rosenthal Group in Germany. It has become a classic and is found in many Swedish homes.

> **Rörstrand and Arabia – hallmarks of fine porcelain**
>
> The Finnish company Arabia was a subsidiary factory of Rörstrand when it was opened near Helsinki in 1874. In 1916 it became a separate concern.

Visitors can tour the workshops then visit the **museum**★★ with its fine collection of porcelain which is a delight to the eye and finally be tempted by the displays in the showroom.

EXCURSIONS

Läckö Slott – *25km to the north. Leave by Kållandsgatan, which becomes Läckögatan and then follow the signposts to Läckö Slott.* The winding road to Läckö leads through the quiet countryside of the Kålland peninsula and continues over narrow sounds to the two northerly islands which themselves are fringed by many smaller isles and islets.

Spiken – In this small fishing hamlet – the only one on Lake Vänern – the visitor may choose between a variety of freshly smoked fish. Smoked burbot is the local speciality.

Läckö Slott ⊙ – The white walls, towers and turrets of this castle rise out of the waters of Lake Vänern like a fairytale castle. The original 12C episcopal castle was destroyed by fire. The next castle, built in the 15C, was gradually extended and modified but it was Magnus Gabriel De la Gardie in the 17C who transformed his new seat into the Baroque palace we see today. De la Gardie took great pains to embellish the apartments and their most notable features are the painted ceilings. Once they had finished working on the castle the artists, later known as the Läckö School, went on to decorate local churches.

★★ **Kinnekulleleden** – *About 45km to the north-east; leave by road 44 in the direction of Mariestad and after 14km turn left towards Husaby.*
The drive leads through the surrounding arable countryside past medieval churches and manors to the summit of the oval plateau of Kinnekulle (306m) on the shores of Lake Vänern.

Husaby – The dominating feature of the village church is the stout defensive tower, flanked by circular staircase turrets. The tower was probably built around 1100 as a free-standing keep although it may have adjoined an early timber church. The present Romanesque stone-built church was a later replacement.
About 100m up the road is St Sigfrid's Spring and legend has it that it was here that Sweden's first king, Olof Skötkonung, was baptised in 1008 by the English missionary, St Sigfrid.

Continue to follow the signs to Kinnekulleleden. To reach the summit turn right at the church in Medelplana and take the direction for Högkullen.

Kinnekulle – On the summit there is a Tourist Information Centre, restaurant and café. A further 900m has to be climbed on foot to reach the top of Högkullen (306m) and the observation tower. The tower affords a spectacular **panorama**★★★ over Lake Vänern with Lidköping to the south at the head of its bay, straight ahead the island of Kållandö and far away on the other side of the lake the county of Dalsland. Away to the east is the fertile plain of Västergötland with the mountain of Billingen in the background.

LINKÖPING ★

Östergötlands län
Population 132 000
Michelin map 985 N 12 or Atlas Europe p 119

As early as the 12C Linköping was an ecclesiastical centre and it soon acquired a reputation as a seat of learning. Today it is the administrative capital of Östergötland, a modern industrial town and a university city with a teaching hospital and an Institute of Technology. It is a pleasant town set in the heart of a fertile agricultural region.

Östergötland – The land of the Eastgoths lies between Lake Vättern in the west and the Baltic Sea in the east. It is a fertile agricultural area intermingled with forests, lakes and waterways and some of Sweden's largest estates are to be found here.

★ **Domkyrkan** ⊙ – This is one of Sweden's loveliest churches. The earliest building on the site dated back to the 1120s but the present one was begun in 1232 and was extended and remodelled over a period of 300 years. Majestic and harmonious are apt descriptions of the interior which is the setting for furnishings from every century as in the true medieval tradition. The 20C is particularly well represented with the 1934-36 altarpiece by the Norwegian artist Henrik Sørensen, the etched-glass windows (1995) of the Lady Chapel, Mariakoret, and the 1987 altar screen depicting events from the life of the Virgin and the tapestries portraying the Creation of the World (1938).

Östergötlands länsmuseum ⊙ – Archaeology, European and Swedish paintings are the main themes but items not to be missed are the **Königsmarck embroideries★** of 1680.

EXCURSIONS

★ **Gamla Linköping** ⊙ – *3km, leave by the C-ring in the direction of Mjölby and follow the signposts for Gamla Linköping.* Some 80 buildings dating from 1695 to 1887 have been removed from the town centre and re-assembled here. The charm of this open-air museum is that a community of around 50 people – mostly craftsmen – lives and works on the site bringing life and authenticity to the homes, museums and workshops.

Flygvapenmuseum ⊙ – *6km away in Malmslätt. Leave by road E 4 to the west in the direction of Ryd.* This is the largest collection of military aircraft in Sweden with exhibits ranging from 1912 models with rotary engines and speeds of 80-100kph to present-day aircraft capable of Mach 1.

LULEÅ

Norrbottens län
Population 71 000
Michelin map 985 G 19 or Atlas Europe p 108 – Local map see LAPPLAND

Luleå takes its name from the Sami word for eastern water *(Luleju)* and it is now the most important town in northern Sweden. It occupies a pleasant site on the banks of Luleälven whereas the central area covers a strip of land fringed with marinas and a leisure area, **Gültzaudden**, at the extremity with riverside walks and sandy beaches. Luleå was the first Swedish town to build an indoor shopping mall in the 1950s to the designs of Ralph Erskine.

A false start – By the early 14C seafaring colonisers had settled along the coast and the rivers and the main settlement in the area was inland at Gammelstad. It was given its founding charter by King Gustav II Adolf in 1621 but when the navigable channel to the coast began to silt up the town was moved, by royal decree, to its present coastal site (Lule Nystad) in 1649. The church and its attendant church village became known as Lule Gammelstad, Luleå Old Town.

Luleå became a busy port at the end of the 19C with the discovery of iron ore inland at Kiruna and Malmberget and the subsequent building of the railway from Gällivare in 1895.

Norrbottens Museum ⊙ – *Enter from Storgatan 2 in Hermelin park.* The museum provides a picture of the people, their work and daily life in north Bothnia. On the second floor there is a major collection of Sami artefacts.

Teknikens Hus ⊙ – *4km, follow the sign for Högskolan or Porsön.* The House of Technology is part of the university campus and it gives children and parents a hands-on insight into industrial technology.

Domkyrkan ⊙ – This red-brick Gothic church is the third one on the site and its 63m-tall spire is a local landmark. The gilt work on the inside glass doors is known as the Tree of life.

The Archipelago – There are about 100 islands in the Luleå Archipelago and many of them are inhabited. The long beach and the restaurant at Sandön are popular with the locals as a recreation area. Boat trips leave from the south harbour, Södra Hamnen and others from Norra Hamnen, picturesque with its red-wooden ware-houses, bound for Hindersön and other small islands.

★★★GAMMELSTAD

Gammelstad or old town was the original site of Luleå before it was moved down-stream in 1649 when its harbour no longer served its original purpose. It is now the site of the largest church village in Sweden, which was built 450 years ago. The church village traditions are still very much alive and even today the church cottages are occupied by the parishioners during the important church festivals, as they have been for centuries.

Gammelstad

Gammelstads kyrka – This impressive church in the Scandinavian Late Gothic style is built with massive blocks of red and grey granite with brick ornamentation on the gable. Although the church was built during the first half of the 15C the vaulting dates from the 1480s. A wall with several gates surrounds the churchyard. The northern gate is as it was whereas the northern section of the wall is now a nest-ing place for hundreds of sand martins. The tower at the western end was added in 1851 as a ceremonial entrance in direct line with the altar but the parishioners continued to use the old entrance. The building against the south wall of the church is the parish tithe barn.

Interior – This splendid, lavishly adorned church, the largest medieval church in Norrland, was intended to serve as the episcopal see when it was consecrated in 1492. The frescoes in the chancel were revealed in 1909 when the whitewash was removed and they are, in all probability, the work of one of Albertus Pictor's pupils and date from around 1492. The carved and gilded altarpiece was made in Antwerp. The triumphal crucifix is a splendid medieval masterpiece with an evan-gelist and symbol at each end of the cross. The sandstone baptismal font from Gotland is even older than the church itself. The carved choir stalls are also medieval. The memorial tablets on the walls and the sumptuous pulpit decorated and gilded in the local Baroque style were the work of a local carpenter, Nils Fluur during the early 18C. The organ is a modern piece of craftsmanship from the famous local organ makers, Grönlund Company.

Church villages

For more than 500 years people from Luleå have travelled to Gammelstad to hold markets, district court sessions, weddings and funerals but above all to celebrate church festivals. It has also become customary for people to stay in their cottage near the church for several days. There were originally 72 church villages in the north of Sweden but today only 18 remain; six of these are Sami church villages.

Church village – The main street Gamla Hamngatan runs from the square north of the church to the harbour. The best church village buildings are to be seen in the area to the south-west of the church. One of the cottages in Framlänningsvägen is open to the public. The humble dwellings of craftsmen and labourers are crowded side by side with the more spacious homes of the rich, while church cottages and stables are squeezed in between them all. In 1817 there were as many as 350 stables but many disappeared with the advent of the car and now only five remain. Three are to be seen behind the cottages on the south side of Gamla Hamngatan.

Hägnan Open-Air Museum – The museum, with its various homestead buildings down by the original harbour, organises summer demonstrations of various rural skills. The Gammelstad **Festival of Folk Music** in mid-June is attended by folk musicians from the Arctic regions of all the Scandinavian countries.

LUND★★

Skåne län
Population 97 000
Michelin map 985 Q 10 or Atlas Europe p 123

Sweden's second oldest university town, Lund is a charming town where buildings from different periods line the narrow streets.

With its lively student population (around 30 000), the streets and squares are often the venue for colourful traditions and unique customs such as Tegnérplatsen (**BY 61**) where students don their caps ceremoniously every year on 30 April to celebrate the arrival of spring.

Probably founded by the Danish Viking king, Svend Forkbeard (Sven Tveskägg) about 990, Lund became a bishopric in 1050 and in 1104 archbishopric for the Nordic countries. As an established Danish religious centre churches and monasteries flourished – there were 27 in all – however the advent of the Reformation in the 1530s brought an end to the days of ecclesiastical glory. The power of the medieval Danish church was crushed and most of the town's religious establishments were demolished. By the **Treaty of Roskilde** of 1658 Halland, Skåne and Blekinge – the diocese of Lund – passed to Sweden and it was of critical importance to establish a Swedish academic institution in this former Danish province. The University of Lund was founded in 1666. The Danes and Swedes continued to fight over the territory until the **Treaty of Lund** in 1679 marked the end of the **Scanian Wars** (1675-79).

★★★DOMKYRKAN (BY)

This imposing twin-towered, grey-sandstone cathedral is the finest example of Romanesque architecture in Sweden. Building was initiated in the 1080s by King Knut II and consecrated in 1145. The initial plan, showing a strong Anglo-Norman influence, was followed by a period of Lombard decoration (arcading and carving). The 1130s **apse★★★** is a masterpiece of Romanesque architecture with its Lombard arcading and third tier gallery. The north and south doorways have some of the finest Lombard carving; on the tympanum of the south doorway is the *Agnus Dei* surrounded by the symbols of the Evangelists all linked by trailing foliage.

Legend of the Giant Finn

The master builder was said to be St Lawrence himself and being too weak to continue he was obliged to engage a giant to do the work. The giant demanded St Lawrence's eyes as tribute if he couldn't discover the giant's name before the cathedral was finished. St Lawrence happened to overhear the giant's wife singing a lullaby, revealing his name. St Lawrence hurried back to the church and just as the giant was putting the last stone into place he said "Finn, put that stone in better". In his rage the giant rushed into the crypt and grabbed hold of one of the pillars and tried to make the church collapse.

Interior ⊘ – To the left on entering, the remarkable **astronomical clock** dating from the 14C continues to draw crowds with automata coming to life as the clock strikes. After 300 years of inactivity the clock was restored to working order in 1923. The German master Johannes Ganssog made the fine Renaissance **pulpit** in black marble and alabaster in 1592. The graceful sculpture of the Virgin in the north transept dates from the first half of the 14C. The seven-armed bronze candelabra in the south transept is from the late 14C. A relief (c 1510) by Adam van Düren in the south wall portrays the Virgin Mary and the patron saints of the cathedral; St Lars and Knut the Holy. The beautifully carved oak **choir stalls★★★** (c 1370) are Gothic in style whereas the reredos is probably a north German piece from c 1400. The 20C works include, the painted-glass windows (1930) of the apse and transept by Emanuel Vigeland and the **mosaic★★★** of the apse vault representing the Resurrection. The Danish artist Joakim Skovgaard produced the Venetian glass mosaic of Christ between 1925 and 1927 in the true Byzantine tradition. Malmö Konstmuseum has a section on the artist and this particular work.

★★★**Crypt** – *Enter from either side of the chancel steps.* The pillars of the early-12C crypt are carved with zigzag and twisting patterns but two, often referred to as the Finn columns, recall the legend of the Giant Finn.

The monumental Renaissance tomb chest in front of the altar was made by Van Düren for Lund's last archbishop and is a monument to Lund's 400 years as an ecclesiastical centre (1104-1519).

ADDITIONAL SIGHTS

Lundagård (BY) – *North of the cathedral.* In the Middle Ages this park was where the bishops had their fortified residence and the only building associated with those times is **Kungshuset** (BY K); a red-brick building with a circular tower, which now houses the lecture halls. It dates from 1580 to 1584 and was built for the Danish king but when the university was founded in 1666 King Karl XI gifted it to the university. The park as we see it today was designed by Carl Hårleman in the mid-18C.

Universitetsplatsen – It was during the 19C century that Helgo Zetterwall gave this square its present appearance with a series of dignified buildings. The white Classical style building on the west side, **Universitetsbyggnaden** (BY U), stands opposite the Students' Union, **Akademiska Föreningen** (BY A), whereas **Palaestra** (BY P), originally for gym and music, on the north side looks over the large central **fountain** to Kungshuset.

Tegnérplatsen (BY 61) – This square takes its name from the central **statue** of the Swedish national poet, **Esaias Tegnér** (1786-1846) who was first a student and then professor at the university. At the east end of the square, behind Sankt Annegatan stands the main building of Kulturen *(see below)* whereas the south side is framed by the **Historiska museet** ⊘ (BY M¹) *(entrance on the east side).* The History Museum is home to impressive collections of items from the Stone, Bronze and Iron Ages as well as the Cathedral Museum, **Domkyrkomuseet ★**⊘ (BY M²) *(enter from Kraftstorg in summer or through the History Museum all the year round)* with its fine collection of precious vestments from the 13C onwards and a good section on the history of the cathedral.

★★**Kulturen** ⊘ (BY) – This museum right in the centre of Lund was founded in 1882 and transformed into an open-air museum in 1892 only one year after Stockholm's Skansen. The museum boasts good collections of textiles, ceramics, glass and silverware and an interesting display of finds from Lund's archeological sites. Start with the main building which has recently been rearranged.

An underground passage leads to the open-air section beyond Adelgatan.

The buildings represent the four estates of the realm: nobility, burghers, clergy and peasants. Immediately on the left is the late-14C Deacon's House. The orange nobleman's house contains a good collection of china and silver (in the basement). The large 3-storey building illustrates the development of middle-class furniture in a series of 16 rooms. The Schlyter House, to the west, is devoted to craftsmen's guilds (handicrafts) and has four workshops. The farming section is to the east. The wooden church dates from 1652.

★★**Skissernas Museum: Arkiv för dekorativ Konst** ⊘ (BX M³) – *Finngatan 2.* This unusual Museum of Sketches, looking rather like a studio, has a large collection of about 20 000 preliminary sketches for public monuments; its aim is to illustrate the entire creative process. The international collection holds works by Henri Matisse, Fernand Léger, Sonia and Robert Delaunay, Jean Bazaine and the leading Mexican mural artists, Orozco and Diego Rivera. The Swedish collection offers an exciting survey of 20C artists, including drawings by the museum's first donator, Prince Eugen, for the Stadshuset in Stockholm, and avant-garde artists such as Sigrid Hiertén, Isaac Grünewald and GAN. The international sculpture hall is dominated by various models for Henry Moore's *Hill Arches*.

LUND

SWEDEN

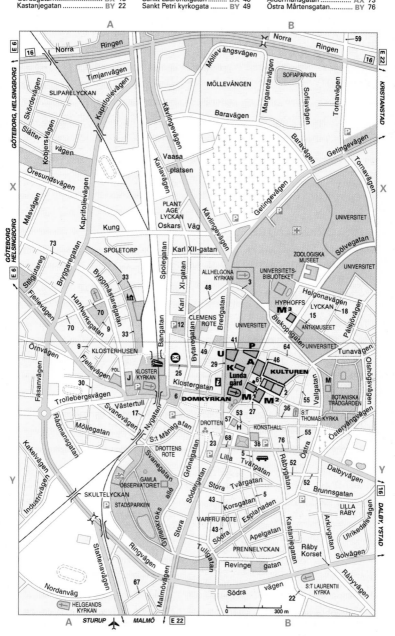

A	Akademiska föreningen	K	Kungshuset	M³	Skissernas museum: Arkiv
M²	Domkyrkomuseet	P	Pælestra		för dekorativ konst
M¹	Historiska museet	U	Universitetsbyggnaden	

*The **Michelin Green Guides**, **Belgium**, **Germany** and **Netherlands**,*
are informative travel guides,
which aim to make touring more enjoyable
by highlighting the natural features,
historic sites and other outstanding attractions

MALMÖ ★

Skåne län

Population 248 000

Michelin map 985 Q 9, 10 or Atlas Europe p 123

Sweden's third city faces the Danish capital across the 25km-wide sound of Öresund. With the completion of the Öresund fixed link, the taunt that Malmö is but a suburb of København will become more of a reality.

Malmö is a lively cultural centre and takes pride in its active theatrical tradition. The Malmö Festival in mid-August is a highly popular party event with a good mix of theatre, art, exhibitions and gastronomy as is the annual equestrian week when the main square is transformed into a show-jumping arena.

Möllevångs Torget is the scene of a daily fruit and vegetable market well worth a visit whereas fresh fish is sold on Banérskajen lined with old fishermen's huts.

The city developed in the 13C from a fishing village to an active trading centre and the German merchants who settled here called it Elbogen (elbow) after the curve of the coast at that point. In 1360 the Danish king, Valdemar Atterdag conquered Skåne which was the start of almost 300 years of Danish rule. In the late 1520s the Reformation had made more headway in Denmark and the town became one of the centres of reformist activity in Denmark. Malmö enjoyed a great period of prosperity in the first half of the 16C when it was still under Danish sovereignty and the ambitious burgomaster Jörgen Kock. It was then the second Danish city after Copenhagen! Following its union with Sweden the town suffered an economic decline but its fortunes revived with the building of the port in the late 18C and the coming of the railway in 1860.

HISTORIC CENTRE

The old town is delimited by a girdle of early-19C canals which replaced the moats of the earlier fortifications. The medieval character of the central area has been well preserved.

★**Stortorget** (BY) – The main square dates from the 1530s during the city's period of prosperity and in the centre stands an **equestrian statue** of Karl X Gustav who reunited Skåne, Blekinge and Halland with Sweden in 1658. The fountain (1964) is the work of Stig Blomberg. A Dutch Renaissance town hall, **Rådhuset** (BY **H**), dating from 1546 but remodelled by Helgo Zetterwall in the 1860s, borders the east side of the square, and to the north there is the early-17C governor's residence, **Residenset** (BY **D**). The impressive 1523 **Jörgen Kocks Gård★** (BY **B**) with its stepped gable looking north onto Västergatan is the only remaining one of three which belonged to the burgomaster and powerful master of the mint Jörgen Kock. The old pharmacy, **Apoteket Lejonet** (BY **A**), dates from 1571.

★★**Lilla Torg** (BY) – The attractive cobbled square is lined on two sides by some fine half-timbered buildings dating from the 16C-18C. For centuries this was the scene of a lively market, however at the beginning of the 20C a covered market replaced the booths and stalls. Today a more recent market building also accommodates a number of restaurants.

At no 9 Lilla Torg the **Form/Design Centre** ⊘ (BY **E**) displays the best in Swedish and Scandinavian design (architecture, design and arts and crafts).

★**Sankt Petri kyrka** ⊘ (BY) – The imposing brick church was built in the early 14C when Malmö was under the sway of the Hanseatic League and modelled on Lübeck's Marienkirche. The interior is bright and lofty with slender pillars supporting ogive vaulting. The 15C **Krämarkapellet★★** or tradesmen's chapel is the only part of the church to have retained its medieval murals. The others were lost during an over zealous restoration in the 19C. Some of the pre-Reformation furnishings have been retrieved notably the 15m-tall **retable★** (1611), an exquisitely carved sandstone and black limestone **pulpit** (1599) and the octagonal **baptismal font** (1601) both by the same craftsman, Daniel Tommisen.

Malmöhus slott: Malmö museer ⊘ (AY) – The earliest fortress was built on this site by Erik of Pomerania in the 1430s. Later it served as the Danish mint, and then it became a royal residence for visiting Danish royalty. Once under Swedish sovereignty in 1658 the fortifications were strengthened and the castle was given an outer moat and bastions.

From the 18C on, the castle lost its strategic significance and it was used as a prison from 1820 to 1914. In 1937 three ranges were built around the courtyard to house the collections of the city museums.

Naturmuseum – *Ground floor.* The natural history museum covers the geology, landscape, flora and fauna of Skåne and includes an aquarium and a tropicarium in the basement.

Stadsmuseum – *First floor, on the right.* Displays illustrate the history of Malmö.

★★ **Malmö Konstmuseum** – *Second floor.* The collection highlights Nordic art during the 1920s and 1930s with artists such as Carl Fredrik Reuterswärd and Christian Berg and the works of Max Walter Svanberg (b 1912) also attract attention. There are also many works by the landscape painter Carl Fredrik Hill as well as works from young Nordic artists from the late 1980s and 1990s and an extensive collection of Russian works from the 1890-1914 period.

Go through the handicrafts section on the first floor to reach the **Skovgaard Room** with Joakim Skovgaard's (1856-1933) great **cartoon** for the golden apse mosaic in Lund Cathedral. In the same room is the late-15C **organ** from Sankt Petri kyrka *(organ concerts in spring and autumn).*

Across the road.

Kommendanthuset (AY) – The Commander's house was part of the 18C arsenal.

Tekniska museet och Sjöfartsmuseet ⊙ (AY) – The Technical Museum, on the left, deals with local industries, the history of aviation and steam and combustion engines. The Maritime Museum, to the right, outlines the history of Skåne's harbours, lighthouses and beacons.

Hippodromen (BY **T**) – *Kalendergatan 12.* The imposing Art Nouveau building with its 12-gored dome has recently been refurbished as Malmö Dramatiska Teater and is better known as the Hipp Theatre. Originally it housed a circus (1899-1922), then it became a theatre until 1950 and finally a place of worship. The restaurant is a remarkable example of Art Nouveau.

Malmö Musikteater (AZ) – *Fersens Väg.* The theatre was inaugurated in 1944 and produced mainly plays, ballets, operas and musicals until 1992. The 1950s were the theatre's heyday when **Ingmar Bergman** directed such well-known actors as Max von Sydow, Bibi Andersson, Harriet Andersson and Ingrid Thulin.

★ **Rooseum** – **Center for Contemporary Art** ⊙ (BY) – *Gasverksgatan 22.* An electricity generating station from the turn of the last century was transformed in 1988 into an elegant museum. This was the brainchild of the art collector Fredrik Roos (1951-91) who aimed to present contemporary art movements through thematic exhibitions. The gallery has met with considerable international success.

Parks and gardens – With its many canals, parks and gardens Malmö is a pleasant city. The **Kungsparken** (AY) and **Slottsparken** (AY) together with the castle grounds form over 50ha of greenery crisscrossed by canals and pathways.

The extensive garden known as **Pildammsparken**★★ (AZ) was laid out for the 1914 Nordic Exhibition. To the south of the Margareta Pavilion (Paviljongen), in memory of the late King Gustav VI Adolf's first wife, is an open-air theatre (Frilufts Teater) used in summer to stage dance, theatrical and musical performances.

EXCURSION

★★ **Svaneholm** – *40km east of Malmö; leave by E 65* (CZ) *south of the plan. Signposted to the north just before Skurup.* This imposing Renaissance castle dating from 1530 has been home to several prominent families but the most colourful owner was without doubt Baron Rutger Macklean (1742-1816) an enlightened landowner who introduced the rotation of crops to Sweden. The displays include furniture, textiles, costumes, paintings, arms and tools.

The Öresund Fixed Link

The newly completed fixed link between Sweden and Denmark will be an important tie-up in the transportation network between Sweden and Denmark and also between Scandinavia and Europe. It comprises a four-lane motorway, a double-track railway as well as a two-level high bridge. The toll station is located at Lernacken to the south of Malmö. All ferry services have ceased to operate except the Helsingør-Helsingborg crossing. The crossing takes approximately 20min by car and 30min by train, from city centre to city centre.

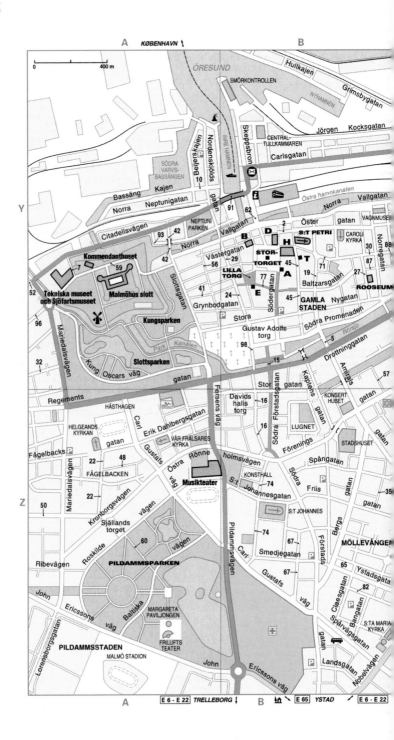

MALMÖ

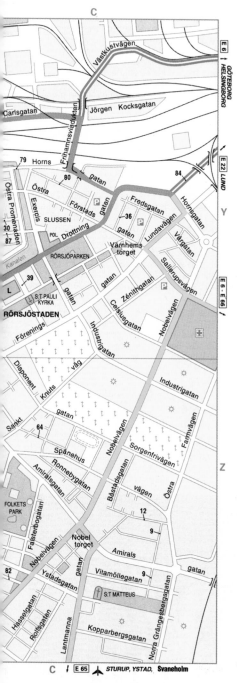

A Apoteket Lejonet
E Form/Design Center
T Hippodromen
B Jörgen Kocks Gård
D Residenset
H Rådhuset

MARIESTAD

Västra Götalands län
Population 24 500
Michelin map 985 N 10 or Atlas Europe p 118

Mariestad is attractively set on the eastern shore of Lake Vänern. It is an ideal centre for short excursions on the canal and boat trips on the lake. Mariestad takes its name from Maria von Pfalz, the first wife of Duke Karl, later King Karl IX.

The Renaissance **Domkyrka** with its elegant tower surrounded by slender turrets was built between 1593 and 1625. Duke Karl is said to have built this church to rival that of his brother, Johan III's in Skara and the architect is said to have used Willem Boy's drawings for Sankta Klara Kyrka in Stockholm as his model. South of the cathedral the two most interesting streets, **Västerlånggatan** and **Kyrkogatan**, are lined with attractive wooden buildings dating from the 17C to the 19C.

Three wings of the governor's residence, on its island site, now house the **Vadsbo Museum** which traces the history of the town from earliest times to the present.

MORA★★

Dalarnas län
Population 21 000
Michelin map 985 K 11 or Atlas Europe p 112

In the heart of Dalarna, Mora is a busy resort both in summer and winter. Both King Gustav Vasa and Anders Zorn have close associations with the town and are commemorated by statues. The statue of King Gustav Vasa (1903) by Anders Zorn marks the finishing point of the Vasaloppet and the statue of Zorn the artist with paintbrush in hand, done by Christian Eriksson in 1936, stands near the church.

Anders Zorn (1860-1920), one of Sweden's foremost artists, was also an eminent etcher and sculptor. Zorn achieved international fame with his portraits of famous people but today he is best remembered for his paintings of nude women bathing. Zorn was a great art collector and he and his wife Emma were among the most ardent champions of folk traditions.

★★ **Zorngården** ○ – *Vasagatan to the west of the church.* Zorn's home has remained unaltered since it was completed in 1910 and it is a good example of interior decoration of the period. The great Viking style room on the first floor was where the Zorns entertained their many artist friends. Beyond the heart-shaped lawn with its statue *(Morning Bath)* are the three wooden buildings, one of which served as Zorn's studio.

Vasaloppet ○

Every year on the first Sunday in March this gruelling 90km cross-country ski race has more than 14 000 participants. The first race was held in 1922 to commemorate Gustav Vasa's escape from his persecutors in the 16C when he fled on his skis from Mora to Sälen. The first race was won in 7hr 32min 49sec and the fastest ever time was 3hr 48min 55sec in 1986.

Dahlskog/Pressens bild

★★ Zornmuseet ⊘ – The main features are works by Anders Zorn himself: water-colours, oils, etchings and sculptures. Also exhibited are works by his friends, such as Bruno Liljefors, Carl Larsson, Ernst Josephson and Karl Nordström. Silver and Dalecarlian paintings from the artist's personal collection are also on display.

★★ Zorns Gammelgård och Textilkammare ⊘ – *In the direction of Malung. A few hundred metres beyond the railway crossing Zorns Gammelgård is signposted to the left.*

Zorn brought together the 40 odd timber buildings, which go to make up this open-air museum of summer pasture farmsteads so typical of the area. The furnishings and tools are authentic and the whole gives a good idea of rural life in the past. The **Zorns textilkammare** regroups an interesting collection of textiles.

Vasaloppsmuseet ⊘ – The museum of the great Vasaloppet skiing race is appropriately located near the finishing line. The film *(25min with subtitles in English)* and displays present the course, the competitors and champions, the records, equipment and traditions.

EXCURSIONS

★ Sollerön ⊘ – *14km to the south by roads 45 and 64. Once in Sollerön bear left at the church and follow the sign Hembygdsgård.* During the Viking Age this small island was the site of a Viking settlement. A signposted trail (a golden sun and Viking ship on a blue background) illus-trates finds made during excavations. The islanders have maintained the boat building traditions of their ancestors and most of the present-day church boats are built here. The summit of **Gesundaberget** (514m with a chair-lift) commands an extensive **view★★★** of Sollerön and Lake Siljan fringed by its wooded heights.

Souvenirs from Dalarna

★ Nusnäs – *10km to the south-east by road 70.* This is a little village where that famous Swedish souvenir, the Dala Horse, is manufac-tured. With its coat of vivid colours it has become some-thing of a national symbol. The **workshops** ⊘ are open to the public.

Våmhus – *13km; leave Mora by road 70 in the direction of Älvdalen and after 5km turn right for Våmhus.* The women are known for their hair-plaiting work and in the 1840s they travelled as far afield as Russia, England and Germany to sell their unusual wares.

The men were skilled in the art of basketwork and examples of both crafts can be seen in the **Sivarsbacken Hemgårdsmuseum** ⊘ just out of the village on the Orsa road.

NYKÖPING
Södermanlands län
Population 49 000
Michelin map 985 N 14 or Atlas Europe p 119

Nyköping, the administrative capital of Södermanland, lies on the coast 102km to the south-west of Stockholm. Assembled around the market square of Stora Torget and its Ragnar Östberg fountain are the 13C church, the yellow and white 18C court house and the 19C governor's residence. The small River Nyköpingsån lined by weeping willows and rhododendrons meanders through the town, pausing here and there, to show off with a cascade. A pleasant riverside **walk** follows the river banks between Storgatan and Nyköpingshus and continues to the harbour from where **boats** leave for the archipelago. The harbour area, with its red-wooden warehouses, now decked out as shops and cafés, is where locals and visitors tend to congregate.

★ **Nyköpingshus** ⊘ – *On the west bank, follow signs to Slottet. Enter through the old gatehouse opposite the youth hostel.* In the 16C Karl IX, Duke of Södermanland, pulled down the original 12C keep to make way for a sumptuous Renaissance palace which was destroyed by a fire in 1665. The palace was never repaired and today the remains, which still stand, serve other purposes. The **Renaissance gatehouse**★★ is one of these remains and the second is the king's tower, **Kungstornet**★★, with exhibitions on its three floors tracing the history of both town and castle. The ruins of the original keep with its legendary dungeon can be seen in the north-east corner of the courtyard. The courtyard is the scene for the re-enactment of the **Nyköping Banquet** each year in July. Another smaller courtyard is overlooked by the 18C old governor's residence, Gamla Residenset, which houses **Södermanlands Museum** ⊘ with displays on social history and costumes.

The Nyköping Banquet

During the 14C there was a fratricidal struggle for the Swedish crown between the sons of Magnus Ladulås. King Birger invited his pretender brothers, Erik and Valdemar, to a banquet but had them cast into the dungeons where they starved to death. The historical play *(see below)* recounts the gruesome story.

To the south-east of the castle is a 17C peat and bark roofed cottage **Tovastugan** ⊘ which now serves as a café. The real point of interest is the beautiful decoration (1641) in the true tradition of ornamental painting.

EXCURSIONS

Trosa – *To the north by E 4 and road 218 towards the coast.*
The idyllic little town of Trosa knew great glory around the turn of the last century when it became the select retreat for Stockholm's high society. For centuries fishing was the main source of income and the skerry-dwellers who lived in small villages out on the skerries during the fishing season built the same type of dwelling in town. The best place to see them is to the west of the river. Take a stroll down by the River Trosaån to see a selection of summer residences with their Toddy-verandahs. The harbour area with its restaurants and craft shops is a lively area frequented by locals and visitors *(guest marina)* alike. At the corner of Västra Långgatan and Garvaregränd a tanner's cottage and workshop, **Garvaregården**, is open to visitors *(café and entertainment in summer)*. A pocket-size museum presents the history of Trosa as a trading and craft centre and fishing port.

★ **Kolmårdens Djurpark** ⊘ – *35km west along E 4 (exit signposted).*
In this zoo and safari park, the largest in the Nordic countries, 400 baby animals are born every year! The Dolphinarium is particularly popular and a show takes place four or five times a day in summer. Entertainment for children includes the Magic Forest adventure trail and Grandma's Kitchen which serves children's favourites such as pancakes etc.

ROSLAGEN★★
Uppsala län and Stockholms län
Michelin map 985 M 14 or Atlas Europe p 119

SWEDEN

The coastal area to the north of Stockholm is known as Roslagen and is a popular summer retreat for Stockholmers. The area is known for its **foundry villages** and its many **medieval churches** (1150-1300). When in the 15C the wooden ceilings were replaced by brick vaulting the latter was usually painted over with decorative patterns and scenes from the Bible. The main source of inspiration was the *Biblia Pauperum*, the well-illustrated *Poor Man's Bible*.

★★ **Vallonbruken: Walloon Ironworks of Uppland** – The Swedish mining industry had its roots in the mining district of Bergslagen where small privately owned ironworks and mining communities flourished as early as the 16C and 17C. The area flourished as an ironmaking centre with the ready availability of raw materials yielded by outcrops of high-quality iron ore, charcoal from the forests and water power. The ironworks were originally privately owned, often by Dutch-speaking families (De Geer and De Besche) from the United Provinces, whereas many of the skilled workers were Walloons (certain family names such as Martinelle, Gauffin, Mineur remind us of these early immigrants). The ironworks used the high-quality iron ore from the **Dannemora Mine** *(mining ceased in 1991)* to produce a quality pig iron which soon became world famous and was exported to Sheffield for the manufacture of tools and cutlery.
The itinerary follows roads 276 and 76 with several detours.

★★ **Wira Bruk** ⊘ – *17km north-east of Åkersberga by road 276. Turn left at the church in Roslags-Kulla.*
The ironworks date from the 1630s and the foundries were kept busy supplying the arms and armour for the Thirty Years War. The local smiths were known for the Carolean rapier. The forges and village buildings date for the most part from the 18C and 19C and have been well restored.

Norrtälje – This attractive town is the administrative centre for Roslagen and the area's maritime past is illustrated in the **Roslagens Museum** ⊘ *(Hantverkargatan 23)*.

Grisslehamn – *Detour: leave road 76 at Söderby-Karl and follow road 283 northwards.* This little fishing and ferry port *(ferries to the Åland island of Eckerö)* on the island of Väddö grew up around a postal and customs post established on the postal route from Stockholm to Finland. Mail was carried in rowing boats across the Åland Sea to the small port of Storby on the island of Eckerö and when the sea was frozen over the boats were hauled across the ice. The postal service by boat ceased in 1876 but a rowing race between the two ports commemorates the service. The village was home to the popular artist and author **Albert Engström** (1869-1940) who is best-known for his amusing portrayal of Roslagen's old folk. From his harbour side home a path winds through the woods to his **studio** ⊘ (Albert Engströms Ateljé) perched on a clifftop.

Häverö kyrka – *Once back in Älmsta take the road to Hallstavik.* This church dates from around 1300 and probably occupies an ancient place of worship as it is surrounded by grave fields. The **paintings** have not been quite so carefully restored as at Edebo. The beautiful reredos dated 1500 is the work of an Antwerp craftsman.

★ **Edebo kyrka** ⊘ – *On road 76.* Careful restoration has revealed some splendid **paintings**★★ dating from 1515 by the Edebo Master, who was influenced by Albertus Pictor. The warm reddish greens and yellows give a golden shimmer to the interior. The 14C font is from the Gotland workshops.

Hargs bruk – *Further on road 76. The storehouse is located 3km from the village; follow the signs for Hargshamn and Järnboden.* This foundry village was founded in 1668 although its mansion *(not open to the public)* and park date from the 1760s. The storehouse, **Järnboden**, is used as an exhibition area for modern art in the summer.

Östhammar – A quaint little town with well-preserved 18C wooden buildings.

Gimo bruk – *Detour: 13km south-west of Östhammar by road 288. Drive through the village and look for the signpost to Gimo Herrgård.* This foundry village was founded by royal decree in 1615 but it was during the management of Louis de Geer that it knew its greatest prosperity. The elegant Gustavian-style mansion dating from 1770 was again the work of Jean Eric Rehn. It has now been transformed into a conference centre.

★ **Öregrund** – *Detour: leave road 76 at Lindersvik.* Narrow lanes lead to the heart of this pretty town where the harbour is overlooked by an ancient lighthouse, a 15C church and its 18C belfry.

★ **Forsmarks bruk** ⊘ – *North again on road 76.* In 1646 Willem de Besche acquired the long-established ironworks at Forsmark (1570) with its three forges. The ironworks prospered and continued to operate until 1898.

The village at Forsmarks Bruk

The Gustavian-style **mansion** (1774) was designed by Jean Eric Rehn and given an English landscape park. Rehn also planned the symmetrical layout of the village with the two poles of authority, the manor and the church (1800), at either end of the main street lined with low white buildings. The church tower affords a fine view of the village. The granary next to the inn serves as a **museum**.

★★ **Lövstabruk** ⊘ – *17km north of Forsmark on road 76.* Lövstabruk (or Leufsta as it was once known) was purchased by Louis de Geer in 1643, the same year that he bought Österbybruk ironworks. It was a model village and became the centre of the De Geer mining empire. This status is reflected in the stately **mansion★** with its elegant interior decoration by Jean Eric Rehn and its beautiful Baroque garden. The west side of the main street is lined by the immaculate yellow and white trimmed dwellings of the smiths, echoed opposite by the mansion. The **kyrka** was completed in 1727 and takes pride in its famous Baroque **organ** made by Johan Niclas Cahman in 1728.

★★ **Österbybruk** ⊘ – *28km from Lövstabruk by a minor road. Drive through the village then follow the signpost for Herrgården.* Österbybruk is the oldest and most complete foundry village probably explained by its proximity to the Dannemora iron-ore outcrop. A simple smelting forge existed as early as 1443 but the real boom began when Louis de Geer acquired the estate in 1643. The exhibition in the **Walloon Forge★**, the last remaining one of its kind, brings to life the working conditions of the past. The 2-storey **mansion** dates from 1758 to 1785 and is used as an exhibition centre in summer.

Bruno Liljefors, an artist internationally known for his scenes of Nordic fauna, lived in the mansion from 1917 to 1932. He transformed the old laundry to serve as his studio, **Liljeforsateljén** ⊘, and the view from the window is often depicted in his paintings. A selection of his works is on permanent display. The west wing contains the chapel and an inn occupies the east wing. The stables and warehouses have been refurbished as handicraft shops. The park was laid out by Carl Hårleman. The Caroline **bell-tower** (1700) is a typical feature of an Uppland foundry village.

Foundry villages

The foundry villages *(bruk)* were laid out to a set pattern and were characterised by their uniform colour and building materials. Although a certain spirit of improvement prevailed in these new industrial villages, the established order was maintained with the workers or smiths occupying small neat 1-storey houses along the main street *(bruksgata)* whereas the proprietor resided in a stately manor.

Today, all the forges have been closed down but these model villages are an important part of Sweden's industrial heritage.

RÄTTVIK ★★

This small town between Leksand and Mora is closely associated with Dalecarlian culture and traditions and is best-known for the **Rättvik Folklore Festival**, a biennial event. The tradition of rowing to church in longships, **Kyrkbåtsrodd**, has been revived in the summer months. On Midsummer's Eve and Midsummer's Day the local ladies team, dressed in their traditional finery, row the 18.5m-long boats on the 25min trip across the lake to church in Rättvik. The town has become an important classical music centre since **Dalhalla** ⊙, an abandoned limestone quarry situated 10km out of town, was turned into an open-air amphitheatre with a seating capacity of 3 500 and excellent acoustics which draw the finest international musicians *(concerts and operas from late May to late August)*.

★ **Rättviks kyrka** ⊙ – As in Leksand, this large white church, known as the kneeling bride, stands on the lake shore, making it easy to reach by boat. The original 13C church was rebuilt in the 17C and given a tower a century later. Although the **triumphal cross** dates from the 14C, the **altarpiece** and **Dalecarlian paintings** on the organ loft are 18C. The 87 **church stables★★** huddled closely together are a reminder of times when people went to church in horse-drawn conveyances.

★★ **Rättviks Gammelgård** ⊙ – *150m north of the village centre in the direction of Lake Siljan.* This homestead museum has a farmhouse, summer house and guesthouse arranged around the same courtyard. The furnishings, Dalecarlian decorative paintings and costumes are all typical of the region.

Rättviks långbrygga – *Behind the tourist office.* The original wooden pier 628m long was built in 1897. Ice slowly wore away the supports and with the funds raised by the sale of the old planks an identical pier was inaugurated in 1992.

Vidablick: tower ⊙ – *Take road 70 to the south then turn off to take road 80 in the direction of Falun; after 500m turn left onto Vidablicksvägen.* The Vidablick viewing point 190m above the lake offers a spectacular **view★★★** of Lake Siljan and the surrounding area.

EXCURSIONS

Danielsgården ⊙ – *38km to the north by road 301 in the direction of Furudal, then east to Bingsjö.*
Unique paintings by the Dalecarlian artist **Winter Carl Hansson** decorate this homestead which was one of the three largest in the 18C. Hansson arrived in 1799 and it took him three years to complete the paintings. The most interesting paintings are to be found in the summer house where an Ages of Man can be seen showing the road from the cradle to the grave.
Carl Larsson was often a guest of the Daniel family and a great admirer of Dalecarlian painting and several of his watercolours portray the Daniel family in their home surroundings.

SIGTUNA ★

Stockholms län
Population 33 700
Michelin map 985 M 14 or Atlas Europe p 119
Local map see STOCKHOLM: Outskirts

From being the country's earliest capital Sigtuna then became an important religious centre and finally replaced Birka as the main Baltic trading place. The ruins of St Lars, St Pers and St Olofs Kyrkor date from around 1100 and are interesting as Sweden's earliest stone-built churches. Today Sigtuna is a pleasant garden city on the shores of Lake Mälaren and has again acquired a reputation as a religious centre.

Take the time to wander around and enjoy the atmosphere of the historic part with its medieval lanes and wooden houses and a rich sprinkling of rune stones.

★ **Stora Gatan** – This has been the town's main street since the Middle Ages and today it is lined with colourful 19C wooden buildings, picturesque shops and cafés. The local museum, **Sigtuna Museum** ⊙, at no 55 displays the finds from the town's Viking and medieval archaeological sites.

Sigtuna

C. Boisvieux

Lundströmska gården ⊙ – *At no 39*. It belonged to the parents of one of Sigtuna's most famous sons, **Vilhelm Lundström** (1869-1940). Lundström was a tireless patron and promoter of Swedish culture overseas as founder of the Swedish Cultural Institutes. The miniature Rådhuset in Stora Torget dates from the 18C.

The Dominican friars abbey church, **Mariakyrkan** ⊙, was consecrated in 1247. It is believed that the monks introduced the technique of building with bricks to Sweden.

SIMRISHAMN ★
Skåne län
Population 20 000
Michelin map 985 Q 11 or Atlas Europe p 123

This is the heart of Österlen and Sweden's most colourful town where cobbled streets twist between charming low buildings. From quite early on the town was under the influence of the Hanseatic League and by the 14C merchants from Lübeck dominated the herring trade. Simrishamn prospered during the reign of the Danish king, Christian IV (1588-1648) but the Scanian Wars soon put an end to this as the town was sacked by both sides. Prosperity returned in the 19C with the fishing boom and the growth in the cereals trade. Simrishamn is still one of Sweden's largest fishing ports, handling as it does 25 000t annually of mostly herring, cod and eel.

A wander through the historic centre – *Leave the car in the harbour area*. Pass the Tourist Information Centre then take Strandvägen where the garden, **Sjöfartsplatsen**, on the right is dotted with works of art made of debris from shipwrecks. **Gösta Werners Museum** ⊙ beside the Svea Hotel on the left displays the works of the artist Gösta Werner who specialised in seascapes and mariners and their way of life. Turn onto Stora Rådmansgatan to enjoy the colourful sight of the trimly painted houses with red-pantile roofs. Then look towards the church *(see below)* towering over the houses in **Lilla Torg**, at the heart of the old quarter. Both **Stora Norregatan** and **Östergatan** are lined with neat little 19C houses brightly painted with carved wooden doors and pot plants on the doorsteps. Take the lane, Klockaresträddet, towards the church then go round it to enter the main square, Stortorget. Storgatan to the right leads to Hafreborg *(see below)* whereas the part of Storgatan to the left is a pedestrian precinct which leads back to the harbour. Follow the latter for a short distance before turning right onto Dammgatan then left onto **Strömmens sträddle** a winding street where the tanner Ström once had his house and workshop. A small tanning museum, **tannerymuseet** ⊙ explains the craft of tanning hides. Continue down the street to the harbour, a bustling spot in summer.

★ **Hafreborg** ⊘ – *Storgatan, behind the green fence.* An old granary is home to Österlen's museum on local history with its interesting sections on **peasant art★★**, costumes and **bridal silver★★** (first floor) and local lacemaking traditions (second floor). The third-floor exhibition covers fishing and navigation.

Sankt Nicolai kyrka ⊘ – The mellow colour of the stonework of the older parts contrasts with the 15C brick porch. The gaily painted furnishings stand out well against the pristine white interior. The **altarpiece** and **pulpit** date from the reign of Christian IV (1588-1648) hence the C4 (CIV) monogram on the pulpit.

On the south side of the church is Carl Milles' sculpture, **The Sisters**, which is a detail from his *Fountain of Faith* in the Falls Church Cemetery, Washington, United States.

SKELLEFTEÅ

Västerbottens län

Population 75 000

Michelin map 985 H17 or Atlas Europe p 108 – Local map see LAPPLAND

Skellefteå, on the banks of Skellefteälven, is a busy services centre for the local farming, mining and forestry industries.

★★★ **Nordanå Kulturcentrum** – Along with Gammelstad this old **church village** is one of the best-preserved examples in Sweden. When the Reformation stipulated that parishioners should attend church every Sunday, church villages grew up around the church. Bonnstan today counts 116 houses, three stables and a shed. Following two fires in 1672 and 1835 the village was moved to its present site. The larger houses usually comprised eight rooms, four on each floor but only three remain. Compulsory church attendance ended in 1850 but the tradition of meeting in the church villages was to continue for several decades. By the 1920s public transport had improved and it was no longer necessary to spend the night in the church village.

The houses are all still privately owned and the church village comes to life again on Midsummer and the church holiday a week later.

Skellefteå landsförsamlings kyrka ⊘ – The white neo-Classical church consecrated in 1800 stands on the banks of Skellefteälven. Of the numerous wood carvings, the **Skellefteå Virgin★** of walnut wood is a rare example of a wooden statue to have survived from the Romanesque period.

Lejonströmsbron – The road behind the church leads to the longest wooden bridge in Sweden still in use.

Skellefteå Museum ⊘ – The local collection has sections on archaeology, mining, forestry and agriculture as well as coins. On the second floor neatly carved wooden figures illustrate the Work of the Seasons *(Möda för föda)*.

SKOKLOSTER★★

Uppsala län
Michelin map 985 M 14 or Atlas Europe p 119
Local map see STOCKHOLM: Outskirts

Skokloster overlooks an arm of Lake Mälaren and makes an ideal destination for a day's outing from Stockholm. It may be reached by road *(E 18 and road 269)* or by boat from the capital. The grounds make the perfect spot for a picnic *(picnic baskets are available from the café)*.

From abbey to stately home – A Cistercian abbey was founded here in the early 13C. All the buildings except the church and the canon's house were demolished in the 16C. The estate was acquired in 1611 by Field Marshal Herman Wrangel, whose son Carl Gustav Wrangel was to become a Grand Marshal and Grand Admiral during Sweden's period as a Great European Power. The latter commissioned the same architects who were working on his Stockholm residence, Wrangelska Palatset, to build this grandiose home worthy of his new wealth, power and status.

Skokloster

★★ **Skoklosters Slott** ⊘ – Nicodemus Tessin the Elder and Jean de la Vallée collaborated with the German architect Caspar Vogel to build this great Baroque castle (1654-76). It is striking for its whiteness and its symmetry, as the four ranges surrounding a courtyard, are quartered by octagonal corner towers capped by cupolas and lanterns.
The interior is richly decorated with fine stucco ornamentation, wall and ceiling paintings and makes a perfect setting for the priceless collections of paintings, textiles, glass, ceramics, silverware and notably arms.

Skoklosters kyrka ⊘ – Although this brick chapel dates from the 13C many of the furnishings are of later date. The pulpit with its beautifully carved figures, the baptismal font and the altarpiece are from Oliva Abbey near Gdansk. The wooden sculpture of the Virgin and Child and the triumphal crucifix both date from the 13C. The Wrangel burial vault dates from 1639.
To the east of the chapel is a remarkable **rune stone** with two equestrian figures which are reputed to be older than the inscription (AD 1000).

Skoklosters Motormuseum ⊘ – *Beside the car park.* The oldest vehicle in this display of over 40 cars, dates from 1898.

Skåne is Sweden's most Danish county being the immediate neighbour to Copenhagen and 600km distant from Stockholm. For almost 300 years this was Danish territory until the Treaty of Roskilde (1658) pronounced otherwise. However the following years were turbulent with the Scanian Wars as the Danes tried to recapture Skåne and peace only came with the Battle of Helsingborg in 1710. Patriotic Scanians maintain that Skåne should be an independent kingdom and are proud to fly their own flag. The local dialect has a distinctive Danish twang which leaves few indifferent and is the source of many a friendly dispute.

Landscape – Inland the flat rolling countryside is interrupted by three north-west/south-east ridges (Romeleåsen, Söderåsen and Linderödsåsen) and dotted with prosperous and well-tended farms, striking white churches and great expanses of yellow fields of oilseed rape. There is no fringing archipelago as further north but two islands are worth a visit, Ven and Väderö. Coastal interest lies mainly in the three peninsulas, Bjäre and Kullen in the north and Falsterbo, Sweden's most south-westerly point.

Tasting tempting titbits – Skåne is known for its gastronomic traditions and the famous Swedish *smörgåsbord* was a local invention. It is served especially on Sundays in many of Skåne's traditional inns (*Gästgivaregårdar*) where an elaborate buffet occupies a large table in the centre of the dining room. Guests are free to help themselves as often as they like but there is an order to be followed. Traditionally the order should be: pickled herring prepared in various ways; a couple

> ### St Martin's Day or Martin Goose – 11 November
>
> St Martin's Day is particularly popular in Skåne where they hold traditional goose banquets. Black soup (*svartsoppa*) made with goose-blood and spices is followed by roast goose. Martinmas marks the end of the autumn work and is associated both with St Martin of Tours and Martin Luther who is celebrated the day before.

more fish courses like cold smoked salmon, cold smoked and boiled eel, fried herring and sardines in oil; then the meats include cold roast turkey, duck and goose, boiled ham, sliced beef; the cheese board follows; then come fruit salads, fresh fruit, cream pastries all rounded off with the *spettekaka*, a traditional Skåne dessert. This yellow meringue-like pyramid-shaped sweet is usually made from eggs, sugar and flour, baked in front of an open fire. The eel season is in September and October and a true eel feast should be graced by seven different dishes of cooked eel. In Skåne the geese are fattened for St Martin's Day (11 November).

SOUTH COAST AND ÖSTERLEN

Skanör and Falsterbo – These twin towns sited on Sweden's south-western peninsula are popular holiday resorts known for their marvellous white beaches. Falsterbo grew with the herring fishing and both were important trading centres during the Hanseatic period. Falsterbo in particular has preserved its medieval aspect and its church has some fine medieval sculptures. Falsterbo Museum has an enlightening section on Hanseatic times. Skanör on the other hand has a charming cobbled Rådhustorget and an 18C town hall.

Trelleborg – The town prospered in the Middle Ages with the herring fishing and today it is an important terminal for ferries to the German ports of Travemünde (7hr), Rostock (5hr) and Sassnitz (3hr 30min) on Rügen.

★**Smygehuk** – Sweden's most southerly point is where the young Nils Holgersson bids farewell to the wild geese. The feathered heroine Akka is commemorated by a **statue**. The harbour once a limestone quarry, is lined with fishing sheds and smoking houses. A path leads eastwards, passing on the way a lime kiln, to the large white **Merchants' Warehouse**, an imposing reminder of past prosperity. It was initially built to store grain, however it served as store for smugglers' booty and now houses an arts and crafts exhibition.

Smygehamn – The tiny hamlet prospered with first the fishing industry and then the lime industry. The 19C cottages are popular as holiday homes.
The way to the east, **Österlen**, is a term that was coined in the 19C and the area is known for its wealth of art galleries and workshops (there is an annual open week at Easter time).

★**Ystad** – See YSTAD.

Kåseberga – 8km from road 9. One of the many delightful fishing villages where a smoked-fish sandwich can be sampled while admiring the view out to sea. A 15min walk up a steep hillside path takes you to **Ales stenar★★★**, the burial site of the

Chieftain Ale, which is marked by this 67m-long **stone ship setting** comprising 58 stones. The stem and stern stones are 3.3m and 2.5m tall respectively. The setting was buried under sand until 1956.

Return to Kåseberga and turn right before following the sign for Sandhammaren and then the sign for Dag Hammarskjölds Backåkra.

★ **Backåkra: Dag Hammarskjöld's Memorial House** – The old farmstead Backåkra standing on the Kåseberga ridge was purchased by the former United Nations Secretary General in 1957 and the area was designated a nature reserve a year later. Following his untimely death in a plane accident, the estate was made over to the Swedish touring club. With few exceptions the furniture, works of art and other objects belonged to Hammarskjöld.

★ **Sandhammaren** – The shifting dunes and sand banks of the south-eastern point of Skåne are part of a nature reserve. This stretch of coast has some of the best beaches in Sweden.

Skillinge – Another fishing village with narrow winding alleys and charming cottages.

In Gislöv go in the direction of Järnestad then follow the signpost for Glimmingehus.

★ **Glimmingehus** – Adam van Büren built this majestic edifice between 1499 and 1509 for a Danish nobleman and it has all the accoutrements of a respectable fortress (stout walls, tiny windows, loopholes, a wide moat and machicolations). The fortress was abandoned when its living quarters were judged too spartan and inconvenient and it became a granary inhabited only by rats. In *The Wonderful Adventures of Nils* Selma Lagerlöf recounts the epic fight between the grey and the black rats of Glimmingehus and how Nils lures away the grey ones by playing his enchanted pipe, which he had received from the owl who lived in the tower of Lund Cathedral.

★ **Simrishamn** – *See SIMRISHAMN.*

Kivik – *18km north of Simrishamn.* Set in the heart of orchard country of apple and pear trees the village of Kivik is known for its cider production but more so to Swedes for its burlesque market. The foreign visitor will be intrigued by the famous **Bronze Age monument**, a remarkable burial cairn 75m across. The burial chamber is lined with eight slabs engraved with enigmatic carvings. The grave was discovered in the 18C and extensively restored even rebuilt in the 1930s.

STOCKHOLM★★★

Stockholms län
Greater Stockholm population 1 750 000
Michelin map 985 M 15 or Atlas Europe p 119
Plan of the conurbation on Michelin map 985 – Local map see Outskirts

Venice of the North, Queen of Lake Mälaren or The City that Floats on the Water all these epithets aptly evoke the special charm of the city on water. Stockholm is built on 14 islands between two great stretches of water, Lake Mälaren to the west and the Baltic to the east. These islands are part of the larger Stockholm archipelago of 24 000 rocky skerries. It follows that one of the most appropriate ways to discover the city is to experience it from the water by taking one of the sightseeing boats from beside Nybroplan or Stadshuskajen.

The best overall views of Stockholm can be had from the heights of Södermalm in the southern part of the city, the Stadshuset Tower and Kaknästornet.

HISTORICAL NOTES

In the 13C the island of Stadsholmen was only a third of its present size as the waters of Lake Mälaren and the Baltic were so much higher. Although the past 700 years have seen the land rise isostatically about 3m, most of the additional land in the old town was reclaimed by man.

Stockholm's location between lake Mälaren and the Baltic Sea made it ideal for both trade and defence. The Regent Birger Jarl is said to have founded Stockholm in 1252 and built the necessary fortifications: two towers linked by walls to encircle the city. By the end of the 13C the Franciscan friars had also established their monastery on the island.

Merchants from Lübeck had been trading in the provinces around Lake Mälaren since the end of the 12C, and a new trade agreement was to mark the beginning of Hanseatic times, which lasted until the end of the 15C.

In 1336 Magnus Eriksson was crowned in the city although it was not yet the capital.

SWEDEN

The period of the **Kalmar Union** (1389-1523) was characterised by a continuous power struggle between the leading protagonists and antagonists of the union. A few dramatic events were to mark this period, notably the **Battle of Brunkeberg** in 1471, when the Swedish hero Sten Sture defeated the Danish king, Christian I *(see Storkyrkan)*, and the **Stockholm Bloodbath** in 1520, when following the coronation of Christian II of Denmark, 82 people were executed.

Three years later the young Gustav Vasa, having won back territory in the south, made his entry into Stockholm and was crowned king of an independent Sweden. His reign brought an end to the Kalmar Union. Stockholm became the centre of Sweden's administration and the city grew beyond its old walls and new fortifications had to be erected. The neighbouring districts grew in importance, and in 1573 they were granted the same charter as the city.

It was during the reign of Gustav II Adolf (1611-32) that the central administration was located in the city. On his death on the battlefield of Lützen, Sweden was an empire and Stockholm its capital in all but name. The official declaration only came in 1634.

It was thus in the 17C that before Sweden acquired the status of a Great Power, and Stockholm's position as a capital was on a par with the other European capitals. Trade and shipping prospered.

In 1640 the rectangular network of streets, which still remains, was laid out. Stone buildings and imposing palaces in the German-Dutch Late Renaissance style were erected, most of them located on Blasieholmen, Riddarholmen and around the Royal Palace. With a population that increased from 9 000 to 43 000 in only 46 years, Stockholm became a densely populated, and also a dirty and unhealthy metropolis.

During the so-called **Era of Liberty** (1718-72), trade and production developed and art and science prospered. The construction of the Royal Palace in the 18C was a major commission, and its architectural style became a model for other buildings throughout Sweden.

The reign of King Gustav III (1771-92) was marked by a rich and varied cultural activity, reflecting his passion for art, theatre and French culture. He initiated Stockholm's first Opera House (later replaced by a new building). Academies were founded, and poets and writers of prose gathered round the king. The most famous troubadour **Carl Michael Bellman** (1740-95), wrote poetry about the ordinary people who frequented the taverns and markets of Stockholm.

New scientific inventions such as steam-power, gas and dynamite, paved the way for the industrial revolution in the 19C. Newly acquired wealth in the wake of industrialization is revealed in the waterfront dwellings of Stockholm's stylish thoroughfare, Strandvägen.

At the beginning of the 20C the population had increased to 300 000 and the suburbs were growing rapidly.

TIPS FOR STOCKHOLM

Arriving by air – Stockholm Arlanda airport is situated 40km north of the city centre and until recently visitors had to face a long bus journey or an expensive taxi fare, but now a new train service, the Arlanda Express, links the airport directly to the Central Station.

Stockholm's Tourist Centre is located in **Sweden House** (☎ 08-789 24 90), opposite the NK Department Store. The **Excursion Shop** (☎ 08-789 24 15) in the same office, provides package-tours and organised excursions, as well as the **Stockholm Card**, which entitles the holder to free transport, parking, a sightseeing tour and admission to a number of attractions. The **Accommodation Booking Office** (Hotel Centralen, ☎ 08-789 24 25), in Central Station will help you to find a hotel room. It is advisable to obtain the monthly publication *Stockholm This Week* which contains information about shopping, attractions and events, as well as opening hours and admission fees to the museums.

Transport – An efficient and integrated public transport system with an underground railway, which is much more than a mere means of transport *(see overleaf)*, and frequent buses cater for the traveller. Timetables and maps can be obtained on board the buses or at SL's (Stockholm's Local Traffic) information centre in Central Station. A ferry boat plies between Skeppsbron and Djurgården all the year round with an extra summer service from Nybroplan. *(For trips to the Archipelago and Lake Mälaren, see Stockholm Archipelago.)*

Sightseeing tours – **By bus:** several trips in double-decker panoramic buses are organised daily from April to early October (departure from the Opera House) by City Sighteeeing, Skeppsbron 22, 111 30 Stockholm, ☎ 08-587 140 30.
By boat: Under the Bridges of Stockholm or the Royal Canal Tour show the fascinating side of the island city and its complex network of waterways (daily departures from Strömkajen or Nybroplan). There is also a combined bus and boat tour. Information and bookings from Stockholm Sightseeing. Skeppsbron 22, 111 30 Stockholm ☎ 08 587 140 20.

Walking tours: Old town Walkabout is a 1hr 30min guided walk through Gamla Stan starting daily from the Opera House.

Ekoparken – There are boat tours to different part of this National City Park: round Djurgården daily from April to mid-December; round Brunnsviken north of the city centre daily from late June to early August (last tour in English); daily shuttle to the Fjäderholmarna Islands to the east of Djurgården from May to mid-September. For further information ☎ 08-587 140 40.

Entertainment – During recent decades, Stockholm has become an international metropolis. The city enjoys a bustling street life with a high density of restaurants (700), many of them serving food from a variety of countries. A thriving café society, staged entertainments in parks and gardens *(free of charge)* contribute to the outdoor life in summer. Stockholm is also rich in cultural activities, with a wide selection of museums, theatres, art galleries and music performances. Concerts are held not only in such traditional settings as the Berwald Hallen or the Konserthuset (the Concert Hall), but even some museums play host to various kinds of music. Musical creativity has also found a niche in Stockholm's many churches. Concerts there range from an oratorio or a mass – such as Händel's *Messiah* or Mozart's *Requiem*, to the rhythmical sounds of a gospel choir. Half a million Swedes are members of some sort of choir. Jazz has enjoyed a revival with the young, and Sweden takes pride in its excellent artists. *Club Fasching (Kungsgatan 63)* offers modern jazz, whereas the pub *Stampen (Stora Nygatan 5)* is the venue for traditional jazz and Swing. Two internationally renowned festivals attract crowds of visitors from near and far, the **Stockholm Water Festival** during the second week in August, and **Stockholm International Jazz & Blues Festival** in July. In addition to *Stockholm This Week*, the Friday issue of the daily newspaper *Dagens Nyheter*, contains a section called *På Stan* (On the Town), which provides information about literally all that is going on, where and when; concerts, museums, art galleries, restaurants, movies (with their original soundtracks with Swedish subtitles) excursion tours etc. Although it is written in Swedish, the advertisements give valuable, understandable information, even to foreign visitors.

Eating out – **In the city centre**: the triangle formed by Birger Jarlsgatan and Nybrogatan up to Östermalmstorg has a high concentration of cafés, snack bars and restaurants. For a light lunch, go into Östermalms Saluhall (covered market) on the corner of Nybrogatan and Humlegårdsgatan, where individual stalls sell an array of fish, meat, vegetables and cheese and offer a choice of Smørgasbord (Scandinavian sandwich), salads and snacks served directly at the counter or on tables laid out inside the market hall.

Gamla Stan also boasts many restaurants, some of them established in picturesque old houses; try Markattan at Stora Nygatan 43, where the fish is excellent, or Fem Små Hus (16C vaulted premises) at Nygränd 10, a tiny side street, or again Den Gyldene Freden, at the southern end of Österlånggatan, serving typical Swedish cuisine.

Shopping – Like all big cities, Stockholm has a great variety of shops from small boutiques to large stores. Certain streets or areas in the city centre tend to specialize in one kind of shop: department stores are located in Hamngatan while quaint expensive boutiques line the narrow streets of Gamla Stan. As for the pedestrianised Drottninggatan, the rendezvous of Stockholm youth, it is lined with individual shops, a good many of which sell trendy clothes. Many design shops are situated in the area backing Strandvågen.

★★★GAMLA STAN

The old town comprises **Stadsholmen**, the original site of Stockholm, **Riddarholmen** with its law courts, **Helgeandsholmen**, which is entirely taken up by the Swedish Parliament building, and tiny **Strömsborg**, which was still an unpopulated islet in the 18C. The oldest city wall (1250), a simple stone wall, which gave the city its characteristic shape of a heart, ran inside **Österlånggatan** and **Västerlånggatan**, the two long streets. The picturesque medieval lanes, at right angles to these streets were originally piers and harbours, which pushed seawards as land reclamation proceeded. By the end of the 14C a new city wall replaced the old one and the Long Streets were now inside the walls. Foreign trade was handled at the southern end of today's **Skeppsbron**. The principal exports were copper and iron, which were weighed at **Järntorget** (**AZ 21**) (Iron Square). Goods were loaded for export in the harbour of Kornhamn, the present **Kornhamnstorg** (**AZ 29**) on the Mälaren side of the island. With its maze of wooden buildings the city was ravaged repeatedly by fires. The rebuilding took on the 17C character which still remains.

«The World's Longest Art Gallery»

At the foot of the escalators awaits a world of caverns full of colour and form. Seventy-three of the 100 stations are embellished with paintings, sculptures, mosaics, or engravings, executed by more than 125 artists. **T-Centralen** is the hub of the network (descriptive leaflet available). The tunnels and platforms of the blue line have been hewn out of igneous rock, its prehistoric surfaces now decorated with modern colour. On the Hjulsta branch of the blue line, the stark white **Rissne** Station offers information on world history in pastel shades, the terracotta-coloured Rinkeby Station is adorned with golden mosaics, **Kungsträdgården** recreates an archaeological site, Tensta basmany paintings of animals as well as ceramics in the form of birds.

Stockholm Tunnelbana Underground

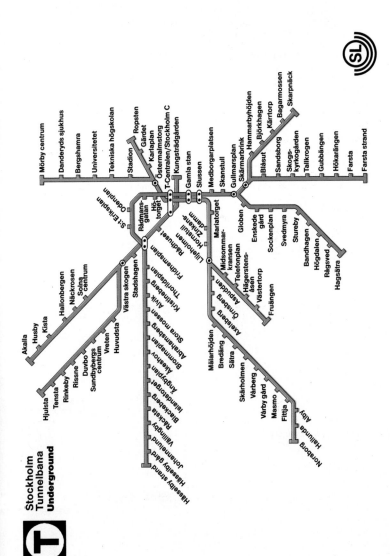

Kornhamnstorg

P. Wysocki/EXPLORER

Gamla Stan is a pedestrian's paradise, but beware, its uneven cobblestones are hard on the feet, so it is advisable to wear comfortable walking shoes. Once you cross Riksbron or Vasabron into the old town, you step into a cosy old-world atmosphere where narrow streets are lined with oddly shaped houses almost touching one another in places. The three main streets converging towards the narrow southern end of the old town, Stora Nygatan, Österlånggatan and above all the central Västerlånggatan are lined with picturesque and often exclusive boutiques (selling art, antiques, clothes, toys etc) as well as dimly lit cafés and restaurants at all prices.

★★Kungliga Slottet (AZ)

History – The original Royal Palace of Stockholm, known as Three Crowns (Tre Kronor), evolved over the centuries from a keep, erected around 1200, to a heavily fortified fortress under King Gustav Vasa; it was later given a lavish Renaissance exterior during the reign of Johan III. Three generations of the Tessin family played leading roles in Swedish art and architecture, all three were associated with the Royal Palace. Designs for a completely new building were drawn up by Nicodemus

Skeppsbron

Tessin the Elder (1615-81) in the 1660s. But it was his son, Nicodemus Tessin the Younger (1654-1728), strongly influenced by the Classical architecture of Rome, who carried through a reconstruction in the Roman Baroque style of the north wing of the palace. The death of Karl XI in 1697 coincided with a disastrous fire which destroyed all but the north wing of the old palace; this was to become the nucleus for a completely new palace in Italian Renaissance and Roman Baroque styles. Building work began but Karl XII became embroiled in the Great North War and the palace project was to take more than 50 years to complete. Carl Gustaf Tessin (1695-1770) took over from his father and supervised the completion of the palace. The real lead was, however, taken by Carl Hårleman (1700-53), who adhered very closely to the original plans. The royal family moved into their new abode in 1754 although interior decorating continued until the 1770s.

Exterior – The present palace stands four square, an imposing quadrangle around a cobbled central courtyard. Two wings, enclosing a garden terrace, jut out towards the east and the waterfront. A semicircular outer courtyard on the west front provides the setting for the changing of the guard. The north, or main, front, on the riverside, is preceded by two ramps.

Interior – This stately palace with its 608 rooms is quite a hive of activity as at least 200 people work there. Although the King and the Queen have their offices there, and the palace is used regularly for State occasions, visitors may still discover the splendour of its lavish interiors. Although the Baroque exterior lost its fashionability during the long period of building, the interior reflects the French Rococo style, introduced to Sweden by Carl Hårleman.

★★ **Royal Apartments** ⊙ – ⊺ *Gamla Stan. Entrance via the west arch (Västra Valvet).* The **State Apartments** *(second floor of the north wing)* have the oldest interiors of the palace, rooms decorated in the 1690s by famous French artists to the designs of Tessin the Younger. Karl XI's Gallery provides a sumptuous setting for official banquets, and beyond is the brilliant ballroom, known as the White Sea. In Gustav III's State Bedchamber the French Rococo decor was the work of Jean Eric Rehn. Carl Hårleman designed the **Bernadotte Apartment** *(first floor of the north wing)*. The Pillared Hall is the scene of the honours ceremonies whereas the investiture of foreign ambassadors takes place in the eastern octagonal cabinet, one of the finest Rococo rooms. The **Guest Apartment** *(west wing)* was also designed by Jean Eric Rehn. The work was carried out in the years 1760 to 1770, and the decoration of the main rooms reflects the development in style from French Rococo (main bedchamber) to Gustavian classicism *(see DROTTNINGHOLM)*.

Rikssalen – *Entrance via the western arch (Västra Valvet).* The Hall of State is a harmonious combination of Tessin's strict Classicism and Hårleman's delicate Rococo. Queen Christina's silver throne is a rare piece of silver furniture, which was fashioned for her coronation in 1650.

Changing of the Guard – *West courtyard.* A ceremonial changing of the guard takes place at noon on weekdays and 1.10pm on Sundays and holidays.

★★ **Livrustkammaren** ⊙ – *Enter from Slottsbacken.* The palace vaults make the ideal setting for the unique collection of the Royal Armoury, which was founded in 1628. Magnificent State coaches, ceremonial armour, weapons, coronation robes, the costume worn by Gustav III at the fatal masked ball *(see Gustav Adolfs Torg)*, and much more are displayed.

P. Thompson/SUNSET

★★Skattkammaren ⊙ – *Entrance via the south arch (Södra Valvet).* In the Royal Treasury visitors may enjoy the glittering splendour of Sweden's royal regalia. The magnificent crown, sceptre, orb and key of State from King Erik XIV's coronation in 1561 are still regarded as the principal emblems of State. Further additions include a princely crown, added as recently as 1902. King Oskar II was the last king to be crowned in 1873. Nowadays the crowns are symbolically placed beside the royal couple on very special occasions.

Museum Tre Kronor ⊙ – *Entrance opposite the bridge of Norrbro.* The cellars of the north wing house the Three Crowns Museum, where visitors can see vestiges of the old Three Crowns Palace.

Slottskyrkan ⊙ – *Entrance via the southern arch.* The original Baroque Palace Chapel was given Rococo decoration by Carl Hårleman in 1754.

Slottsbacken (AZ) – Palace Hill, sloping steeply down to the waterfront, affords good views of the imposing museum buildings across the water.
The Architect Royal, Tessin the Younger, built a splendid palace of his own **Tessinska Palatset** (AZ **A**) *(facing the south arch of the Royal Palace)* opposite the royal one. It was to form part of a suitable backdrop for the palace, but Karl XII's interminable wars put paid to this scheme. The Tessin palace is the official residence of Stockholm's County Governor.
Down by the waterside is Sergel's famous **statue** of Gustav III.

Skeppsbron (AZ) – For centuries this was Stockholm's front window, the first view of the city when approached from the sea. Today it has become one of the city's busiest traffic arteries linking northern Stockholm to the southern part. The long line of imposing waterfront buildings is a heritage of the 17C and 18C, when Skeppsbron was a row of trading houses owned by rich merchants, who were nick-named Skeppsbro Aristocracy.

★★Walk through the Old Town

★★Storkyrkan ⊙ (AZ) – ⏺ *Gamla Stan. Entrance from Trångsund.* The present Great Church or Stockholm Cathedral, serving as royal wedding and coronation church, was the only parish church in the Middle Ages. Dating from at least 1279, the church was consecrated in 1306. The exterior received its Baroque façade and lantern tower in the 1740s to harmonise with the neighbouring Royal Palace. The interior is a result of extensions, carried out in the 14C and 15C. This hall-church in the Late Gothic style, with high star vaulting and sturdy pillars in red brick, is graced with sumptuous Baroque furnishings. Both the **pulpit** (c 1700) and part of the north **gallery** (1686) with its gilded ornamentation are by Burchardt Precht, a German immigrant, who also made the grandiose **royal pews** to the designs of Tessin the Younger. Behind the southern royal pew an amusing **monument** (1933) by Carl Milles commemorates the three generations of the Tessin family. The magnificent **silver altar** encrusted with ebony dates from around 1640. The most spectacular work of art is, however, the extraordinary 15C group of **St George and the Dragon★★★** a monument to the Swedish victory over the Danes (the Dragon) in 1471 at the Battle of Brunkeberg. Carved in oak by Bernt Notke, a master sculptor from Lübeck active in Stockholm from 1483 to 1498, it is regarded as one of the most exquisite medieval sculptures in Northern Europe. Careful observers may see that the dragon's ruff consists of elk antlers. Alongside the monument of St George (Sten Sture) is the figure of a princess (Stockholm) on a base in the shape of a pinnacled castle. The sculpture was commissioned by the hero himself, the Viceroy Sten Sture the Elder. On the south wall, close to the entrance, is another interesting item; the **Parhelion painting** of Stockholm, dating from 1535; it shows the city under a halo phenomenon (a copy is on view in the Medeltidsmuseet).

Walk southwards to Stortorget.

Ornamental doorway, Stortorget

C. Boisvieux

★Stortorget – Stockholm's oldest centre, the Great Square, on the highest point of the island, was a noisy place of trade in medieval times. The streets leading off the square, paths in the 12C, were trodden by porters who carried the merchandise being transhipped between the Baltic and Lake Mälaren. The square was also a place of execution and in 1520 the site of a most dreadful event, the **Stockholm Bloodbath**, when almost 90 people were beheaded or hanged. The square is characterised by the elegant house façades which date from the 17C and 18C. The large building in Late Rococo style is the **Börsen**, Stock Exchange, which was built in 1776 on the site of the old town hall. This is also where the 18 members of the Swedish Academy meet regularly. The Academy was founded by King Gustav III in 1786. It is from here that the name of the Nobel Prize Laureate for Literature is revealed to the international press. The square is a delight during the Christmas fair in early December when visitors peruse the gaily decorated stalls with a glass of *glögg* to keep warm.

Walk down Köpmangatan to Köpmantorget.

Köpmangatan (AZ 35) – This street, lined with antique and curiosity shops, is the oldest street name on record (1323) in Stockholm. As late as the 13C it ended at a city gate on the waterfront then level with Österlånggatan.

Make a detour onto Själagårdsgatan.

Brända Tomten (AZ 8) – When a corner building burnt down in the late 1730s, it was decided to leave the space free for wheeled-vehicles to turn. Brända Tomten means burnt site.

Retrace your footsteps to Köpmangatan.

Köpmantorget – The city's east gate was demolished in 1685. A bronze casting (1912) of Bernt Notke's **St George's monument** in the cathedral adorns this square.

Turn right onto Österlånggatan.

The Stockholm Bloodbath – 1520

This event has caused endless controversy among historians concerning the motifs of the participants, the nature of the charges and the validity of the sentences. Christian II may well have seized on the complaints of the outraged Archbishop Trolle to rid himself of his opponents, the Sture party. During the investigation Sten Sture's widow had revealed the existence of the estates' plotting in 1517. Outraged the king declared the participants heretics and of the 82 who were executed on 8 November there were not only leading members of the Sture party (including Eric Vasa, father of the future king and his son-in-law Joakim Brahe), but also members of the council and the episcopacy. The misdeeds of the bloody tyrant and cruel unchristian were shouted from the rooftops and his reputation was forever stained.

★**Österlånggatan** (AZ) – Outside the first city walls, Österlånggatan and Västerlånggatan enclosed the original heart-shaped city. Österlånggatan was linked by narrow lanes and vennels to the docklands and it was usually thronged with sailors and dockers, who frequented the local inns, taverns and ship's chandlers. Today Österlånggatan is a pleasant shopping street with craft shops, fashion boutiques and galleries.
At no 51 is situated the oldest and most famous tavern in Sweden: **Den Gyldene Freden** (AZ **S**) (The Golden Peace). The tavern started business in 1721, when the peace between Sweden and Russia finally put an end to the wars of Karl XII. The tavern has been a favourite with Stockholm poets since the 18C. The artist Anders Zorn bought the building in 1919, later to bequeath it to the Swedish Academy, who hold their traditional Thursday suppers here.

Järntorget (AZ 21) (Iron Square) – The much loved poet and troubadour, **Evert Taube** (1890-1976), stands on the eastern pavement of the square looking skywards with his back to the building that housed the Bank of Sweden, the oldest national bank in the world, between 1680 and 1906.

Västerlånggatan (AZ) – A counterpart to Österlånggatan, this busy street with a mix of boutiques and restaurants is often very crowded.
The narrow alley **Mårten Trotzigs gränd** at no 81 with its steep stairway clearly demonstrates the difference in level between the plateau of Stadsholmen and the shore of Lake Mälaren.

Continue along Västerlånggatan, then turn right onto Tyska Brinken.

Tyska Brinken (AZ 73) (German Hill) – The names of the streets around the German Church remind us of the German influence in the Middle Ages when the Hanseatic League held sway.

★**Tyska kyrkan** ⊙ (AZ) – ⊺ *Gamla Stan.* In 1565 the Finnish community was given the German guildhall, by then in abeyance, and they extended it to make a church which at first they shared with the German community. In 1601 the latter took over the church dedicated to St Gertrude – the patron saint of wayfarers, merchants and sailors – and its present richly ornate appearance dates from this period. The ebony pulpit (1660) is decorated with carved alabaster figures of the apostles and a kneeling figure of an angel supporting the whole. The splendid royal gallery in the corner with all its angels, gilding and ornamentation is more like a theatre box. It was the work of Tessin the Elder who was a member of the parish.

Continue along Prästgatan or take the parallel street, Skomakargatan, which returns to Stortorget.

Prästgatan (AZ **48**) (Priest Street) – This long and silent street inside the earliest city wall has retained its medieval character. The beams protruding from the gables all along the street were formerly used to hoist supplies to the apartments or merchandise to the attics for storage.

Turn left onto Storkyrkobrinken. The building straight ahead is Riddarhuset.

Bondeska Palatset (AZ **B**) – *To the right of Riddarhuset.* Designed by Jean de la Vallée and Tessin the Elder between 1662 and 1673, this palace has housed the Supreme Court since 1949.

★ **Riddarhuset** ⊘ (AZ **R**) – 🚇 *Gamla Stan.* With its two waterfront pavilions, this graceful palace of the House of Nobility, a reminder of Sweden's Great Power status, is regarded as one of Stockholm's most beautiful buildings. The House of Nobility, where the aristocrats, as one of the four Estates that governed the country, met regularly, was erected between 1641 and 1674 in Baroque style, designed by among others Simon and Jean de la Vallée. The pale red brick with a colossal order of grey-sandstone pilasters is further adorned with pediments and lush garlands of fruit, in harmony with the curved, now green with age, copper roof.

Riddarhuset

The **Great Hall**, its walls tightly covered with no less than 2 326 coats of arms and Mother Svea (Moder Svea), who symbolizes Sweden, hovering above (ceiling painting – 1675 – by David Klöcker Ehrenstrahl) makes a captivating setting for evening concerts in the summer. Riddarhuset remains the property of the Swedish nobility.

RIDDARHOLMEN (AZ) **(KNIGHTS ISLAND)**

The island of the knights and nobles is a remarkable oasis of peace. A Franciscan monastery was established on the island in the 1270s; it was dissolved in 1527. During Sweden's period as a Great Power in the 17C, noblemen (Wrangel, Sparre and Stenbock) were granted plots on the island, where they built stately mansions and palaces.
Today just a few privileged people live on the island and the mansions and palaces are now government offices.

★ **Riddarholmskyrkan** ⊘ (AZ **K¹**) – Riddarholmskyrkan is the Swedish pantheon and Stockholm's only surviving medieval monastic church. The Franciscans started building work around 1270 and the great brick-built church was given two aisles and cross-vaulting in the French tradition; it was consecrated around 1300. Over the centuries chapels were added and after the great fire in 1835 the church acquired its unusual lattice-work spire which makes it one of Stockholm's most recognisable landmarks.

Once inside the main points of interest are the burial chapels. On the north side of the chancel is the Carolean Chapel on two levels. The two recumbent figures in front of the High Altar are of two medieval kings, Karl Knutsson Bonde and Magnus Ladulås, founder of the monastery. On the south side of the chancel are the Gustavian and Bernadotte Chapels with their imposing sarcophagi.

All around the walls are the coats of arms of the Knights of the Seraphim Order (founded in 1748), Sweden's highest order of chivalry.

Gamla Riksdagshuset (AZ) – *Birger Jarls Torg 5, south of the church.* From 1834 to 1866 the non-aristocratic Estates (clergy, burghers, peasants) gathered in this building, which then became the first home of the Parliament until 1905 when the assembly moved to the imposing Riksdagshuset on Helgeandsholmen.

Birger Jarls Torg (AZ) – This cobbled triangular square, surrounded by palatial buildings, has taken its name from the statue of Birger Jarl.

Stenbockska Palatset (AZ J) – This elegant red edifice received its present aspect under the direction of Tessin the Elder. Since 1971 it has been the seat of the Supreme Administrative Court (Regeringsrätten).

Wrangelska Palatset (AZ C) – This palatial residence, with its private harbour on Lake Mälaren (Riddarfjärden), was designed in the early 17C by Tessin the Elder and Jean de la Vallée for Carl Gustav Wrangel *(see SKOKLOSTER)*. It was damaged by repeated fires and little now remains of its former glory. When the Royal Palace was destroyed by fire in 1697, it was this palace that served as a temporary residence for the Royal family until 1754. The Court of Appeal (Svea Hovrätt) has occupied the building since 1757. The south tower, the oldest part of the building, was originally part of Gustav Vasa's fortification system *(see below)*.

Descend the hill to the waterside.

Evert Taubes Terrass (AZ 13) – The popular troubadour is commemorated by a **statue** *(to the right)*. A splendid **panorama★★** opens out across the bay of Riddarfjärden, with the bridge of Västerbron straight ahead, Stockholm's red-brick Stadshuset to the right, and the heights of the southern district to the left. The white **yacht**, *Mälardrottningen*, moored to the left, once belonged to the American millionairess Barbara Hutton and now serves as a unique and popular floating hotel.

Birger Jarls Torn (AZ D) – *Opposite Stadshuset.* Like the south tower of Wrangelska Palatset, this tower was part of Gustav Vasa's fortifications, built around 1530.

★★★VASAMUSEET ☉ (DY)

Buses 44 or 47 or take a ferry from Slussen in Gamla Stan to the landing-stage beside the amusement park. Vintage trams operate between Norrmalmstorg and Djurgården.

Sails set, flags flying... – On a summer Sunday afternoon, 10 August 1628, the pride of King Gustav II Adolf's Navy set out on her maiden voyage. As the *Vasa* left the quay below the royal palace she listed heavily and sank, only 20min after leaving her berth. For over 300 years she lay deep in the mud of Stockholm harbour until Anders Franzén with his simple lead-core sampler and a great deal of perseverance located the mighty warship. Then began a salvaging operation which captured the imagination of the world.

The historical context – Gustav II Adolf, the Lion of the North, was determined to gain control of the Baltic and its trade and protect Sweden from a perceived Polish and Imperial German threat. To these ends he required a strong navy and had recently commissioned four new warships (1625). Master Henrik Hybertsson supervised the building of the warships and for two and a half years activity was intense in the shipyards at Skeppsgården to build Sweden's most powerful warship ever.

Why did the Vasa sink? – The royal inquiry did not disclose its findings but it is generally held that the basic design fault stemmed from the last-minute addition of a second gundeck. This addition raised the centre of gravity and made the warship highly unstable.

Salvage and preservation – The low salinity level of the brackish water and the deep layer of mud in Stockholm harbour ensured the excellent state of preservation of the oak woodwork. The shipworm *(teredo navalis)* does not live under such conditions. Once the intricate salvage operation was complete then began the complicated process of preservation.

STOCKHOLM

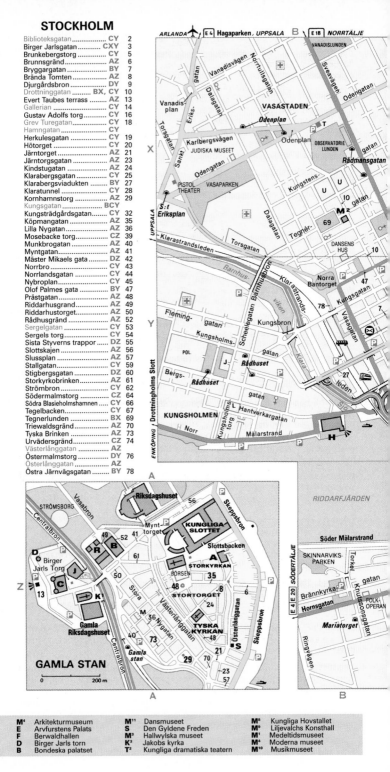

Help us in our constant task of keeping up-to-date.
Send your comments and suggestions to
Michelin tyre PLC
Tourism Department -
38 Clarendon Road - WATFORD Herts WD1 1SX

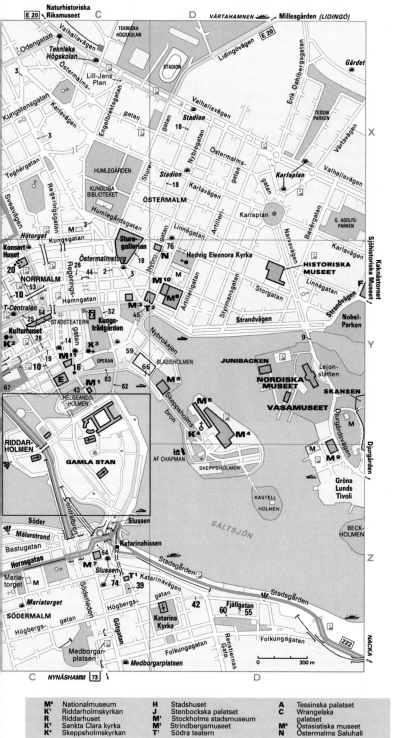

SWEDEN

M⁹	Nationalmuseum	H	Stadshuset	A	Tessinska palatset
K¹	Riddarholmskyrkan	J	Stenbockska palatset	C	Wrangelska
R	Riddarhuset	M⁷	Stockholms stadsmuseum		palatset
K²	Sankta Clara kyrka	M²	Strindbergsmuseet	M⁶	Östasiatiska museet
K⁴	Skeppsholmskyrkan	T¹	Södra teatern	N	Östermalms Saluhall

*Each year the **Michelin Red Guide Europe**
revises its many town plans which show
- through-routes and by-passes
- new roads, one-way systems and car parks
- the exact location of hotels, restaurants and public buildings.
This up-to-date information makes town driving less stressful.*

313

The museum – As you enter, the dim lighting adds an extra dimension to the awe-inspiring outline of the ship defiantly pointing its prow towards you. The custom-built museum is on several levels with the Vasa propped up inside a central pit. The entrance is at waterline level; next to it is an auditorium used for regular showings of an introductory film. Further inside and all round the ship there are exhibitions on different subjects connected with this splendid warship: the inquest which took place at the time including a 10min film entitled Why did the Vasa sink, a 1:10 model of the Vasa as it was when it was built, chronological displays of the salvage operation in 1961, a study of the sculptures decorating the ship and of the different styles of the craftsmen who carved them, naval warfare at the time, Sweden in 1628 and the Skeppsgården shipyard in 1627.

The Vasa (1628)

C. Boisvieux

Some statistics
length: 69m
height from keel to mast head: 53m
cannons: 64
iron bolts: 8 558
wooden nails: 20 000
sails: approx 1 275m²
crew: 145
soldiers: 300

The craftsmen – The 700 sculptures and ornaments, which can be admired from the different levels, are unpainted because the original colours are still being investigated. The carvings were the work of three foreign artists, the best known being Mårten Redtmer. The decoration – wild men, Roman warriors and emperors, heraldic beasts – is typical of the effusive 17C architectural style then in favour. Many of the decorated doorways in Gamla Stan display the same motifs. The two most imposing pieces are the national coat of arms and the lion beak head holding the corn sheaf *(vasen)*, symbol of the Vasa dynasty.

★★★ SKANSEN ⊘ (DY)

Skansen open-air museum was founded in 1891 by Artur Hazelius (1833-1901) to show how people from different regions of Sweden lived and worked in the past. Although Sweden was still at that time primarily a rural society, Hazelius foresaw the changes that would follow industrial development. In addition, to complete the cultural historical exhibition, a zoological section was added, including livestock and wild Scandinavian animals – bear, wolf, lynx and moose.

Skansen, the world's first open-air museum, is Sweden in a nutshell. The physical layout of the site represents geographical reality and consequently the Sami Camp, from the north of Sweden, lies to the north of Skansen beside the enclosures of the Scandinavian animals. Here also is the Summer Pasture Farm from Älvdalen. The seven houses of the Delsbo Farmstead from Hälsingland show how a fairly wealthy farmer, with forestry as a supplementary income, lived in the middle of the 19C. The Mora Farmstead from Dalarna, where all the principal buildings are of genuine log cabin construction, is built around the four sides of a yard. One of the four store-houses to the right of the yard is from the 14C. The Älvros Farmstead from the south-east of the province of Härjedalen is a typical northern Swedish farm. The buildings are of timber and are roofed with wood and birch-bark. The house of Bollnässtugan overlooking the market square is from the province of Hälsingland. The interior decoration includes examples of wall and ceiling paintings from the late 18C, an artistic tradition which is common to central and northern Sweden. To the north-east is the Finn Settlement with its sooty black huts and further on the Ironmaster's Farmstead with houses from the mining district of Ljusnarsberg in the province of Västmanland. The house and the two large barns are built of logs and roofed with birch-bark and turf. The five iron chimneys are characteristic of the building style in the mining districts. The farmstead shows what conditions were like in the early 18C. Further south is the Kyrkhult Farmhouse from the province of Blekinge, a low turf-covered log cabin, between two high storehouses, a common feature in the south of Sweden. Oktorp Farmstead is an enclosed courtyard built on the same principles. Although in reality it dates from the early 18C its furnishings are late 19C. The Skåne Farmstead is also of the enclosed type and it originated from the parish of Hög in western Skåne. All the buildings have thatched roofs. The houses are mostly half-timbered and the interiors are in the style of the 1920s. The Swedish Manor is typified by Skogaholms Herrgård from Närke, originally a 17C building, but remodelled in the Louis XVI or Gustavian style when it was rebuilt in the late 18C.

Other aspects of Swedish life are represented by the Assembly Hall or Folkets Hus and the meeting house of the Mission Church as well as Väla School from the 1840s when education became compulsory. Two landmarks stand out, the Håsjö and Hällestad belfries and Seglora Church from Västergötland. The church was built around 1730 mostly of heavy logs with wall and roof covered with red-painted oak shingles. The tower and sacristy were added around 1780. The ceiling is decorated with paintings dating from 1735. The Rococo altarpiece was added in 1780. The pulpit (1700), organ (1777) and the church bells (14C and 1759) are from other churches.

Skansen is not only rural history but the urban areas contain residential and working environments from the 1760s to the beginning of the 20C.

HELGEANDSHOLMEN (ISLAND OF THE HOLY SPIRIT)

Riksdagshuset ⏱ (AZ) – 🚇 *Gamla Stan. Guided tours (1hr) take visitors through the buildings, entrance on Riksgatan 3A.* The pillared edifice, with the statue of Moder Svea on the Norrbro side, is the 1905 Parliament building and the building to the west housed the Bank of Sweden between 1906 and 1975. When a unicameral system was introduced in 1971 the two buildings were refurbished and linked by passageways. On the guided tour visitors are given an insight into the history and working of Parliament as well as the Swedish Constitution. The early-20C Parliament building is a unique mixture of old and new and visitors are able to see both chambers.

★★ **Medeltidsmuseet** ⏱ (CY M¹) – 🚇 *Kungsträdgården. In front of the Riksdagshuset take the stairs down from Norrbro.* The site of the underground Museum of Medieval Stockholm was established when excavations for a car park under the Swedish Parliament uncovered portions of Stockholm's medieval (c 1530) town wall, now incorporated into the museum. This delightful walk-through museum portrays the development of the city from its foundation by Birger Jarl and the treaty with Lübeck, the early religious houses to the prosperous years of the Hanse.

Carl Milles' sculpture, **The Sunsinger**, erected in 1926, can be seen opposite the entrance.

NORRMALM (CY)

Norrmalm, the district north of the old town and part of central Stockholm, was originally an island, and for a long time it was dominated by the Brunkeberg gravel ridge, running north south to the east of Drottninggatan, dividing the district in two. Gradually earth was excavated from the ridge, and little now remains of it. In the 17C a rectangular network of streets was laid out and the simple dwellings were replaced by palaces and burghers' residences.

City Centre – *Area between Kungsgatan in the north, Sveavägen in the east, Sergels Torg in the south and Drottninggatan in the west.* Whereas the rest of Stockholm takes pride in its exceptional beauty, the City Centre, no more than 40 years old, has met with much criticism. In an enthusiasm of modernity in the 1950s and 1960s the heart of the city, including 17C, 18C and 19C buildings, was razed, to make way for a new business district of banks and local authority buildings, centred on Sergels Torg.

Kulturhuset ⏱ (CY) – 🚇 *T-Centralen. South side of Sergels Torg.* This concrete and glass Cultural Centre, designed by one of Stockholm's leading modernists, Peter Celsing (1920-74), is the venue for cultural activities and exhibitions. Reading rooms provide Swedish and international newspapers.

Hötorget (CY 20) (Hay market) – Today a lively fruit, vegetable and flower market replaces the old hay and cattle market. The outdoor market is supplemented by an underground food hall, **Hötorgshallen**, with a wide variety of Swedish and international foodstuffs.

Konserthuset (CY) – *East side of Hötorget.* Shadowed by the five trumpet blasts, or skyscrapers, the blue Concert Hall with its imposing granite columns, crested with Corinthian capitals, dominates the Hay Market. The architect Ivar Tengbom's 1926 concert hall building shows a strong Classical influence.

In front of the Konserthuset is Carl Milles' masterpiece *Orpheus*, which also shows a certain Greek influence. Its stone steps have become a popular meeting place.

Drottninggatan (BCY **10**) – The main northern thoroughfare in bygone times, paved even in the 1630s, forms part of the old rectangular network of streets. In the early 19C, this was Stockholm's High Street and today its southern end passes the cabinet building **Rosenbad**, and is then continued by the bridge Riksbron to Gamla Stan. Today, Drottninggatan is to a great extent a pedestrian precinct lined with shops and the stalls of street traders.

Sankta Clara kyrka ⊙ (CY **K²**) – 🚇 *T-Centralen. Klara Västra Kyrkogata, opposite Åhléns Department Store.* St Clara's is located on the site of the former Franciscan St Clara nunnery, which owned all the property on Norrmalm until 1527, when it was confiscated by King Gustav Vasa, and the nunnery was pulled down. The present cruciform church was constructed in 1577-90 by the Dutch master-builders Henrik van Huwen and Willem Boy. Damaged by fire in 1751, the church was restored under the guidance of Carl Hårleman, and was given a low, capped tower. The majestic tower that we see today, with its 108m-tall spire, was erected in the 1880s, designed by Helgo Zetterwall. The church boasts Stockholm's largest carillon (35 bronze bells of different sizes), which chime daily at 9am, noon, 3pm, 6pm and 9pm.

At the northern exit of the churchyard a life-size statue of the poet **Nils Ferlin** (1898-1961) reminds us of the writers who once lived in these bohemian quarters, with its mix of pubs, cafés and newspaper offices, before the area was demolished in the 1950s and 1960s.

★ **Strindbergsmuseet** ⊙ (BX **M²**) – 🚇 *Rådmansgatan. Drottninggatan 85.* This small fourth-floor flat, known as The Blue Tower, is where the famous author **August Strindberg** (1849-1912) spent the last years of his life. The apartment and sixth-floor attic library, looking like stage scenery, and the contents have been preserved as they were at his death. He is said to have written over 20 books and initiated the Strindberg Feud during the four years he spent here.

August Strindberg 1849-1912, Sweden's Zola

It was the Swedish artist Carl Larsson who said that Strindberg was Sweden's Zola.

Strindberg sought abroad, in Paris, Berlin and elsewhere, the fame that the citizens of Stockholm refused him and twice he turned his back on his native city and went into voluntary exile. In *Old Stockholm* the young Strindberg proclaims his love for his native city and on his return from his second exile he again professes his love for the Stockholm archipelago in *By the Open Sea* and *The People of Hemsö.*

Although ignored throughout his lifetime by the Swedish Academy on his 63rd birthday in 1912, the year of his death, he was awarded the Anti-Nobel Prize for Literature by popular subscription.

Gustav Adolfs Torg (CY **16**) – Facing the Royal Palace, this square with its equestrian statue (1790) of King Gustav II Adolf is flanked to the west by the Crown Prince's Palace, **Arvfurstens Palats** (CY **E**), which is now the Ministry of Foreign Affairs. When it was built in the late 18C this French Classical style building formed an imposing ensemble with the former Opera House on the east side and the Royal Palace to the south. The building standing on the east side of the square today, known as the **Operan**, replaced Adelcrantz's lavish Rococo masterpiece when over zealous developers tore it down in 1891. It was the opera-loving King Gustav III who founded the original opera house on the site and tragically it was there that he was assassinated in 1792 during a masked ball. The incident inspired Verdi to write his opera *The Masked Ball.*

Dansmuseet ⊙ (CY **M¹¹**) – 🚇 *Kungsträdgården. Gustav Adolfs Torg 22-24.* Originally founded in Paris in 1933 by a Swedish art collector, Rolf de Maré, the Dance Museum opened in the Royal Opera House in Stockholm 20 years later when part of the Paris collection was transferred there. It took possession of its new premises on Gustav Adolfs Torg in spring 1999 and its first temporary exhibition was devoted to Toulouse-Lautrec who immortalised Paris' night-life at the turn of the last century. The museum, which is also a research institute, illustrates the history of dance (in its widest meaning) throughout the world with the help of films, videos, costumes, masks, posters, artistic expression, books and documents. The Folk dance archives are an internationally recognised source of information. There is a shop and a café with a fine view of the surrounding area.

Kungsträdgården (CY) **(King's Garden)** – In the early 17C the King's Garden was a royal kitchen garden, where fruit and vegetables were grown. In the 18C it became a stately garden in the Baroque style, encircled by walls and accessible only to the royals. After the death of King Gustav III, the walls and gates were pulled down and the garden was opened to the public. Today the King's Garden has become the living room of Stockholmers, where all kinds of activities, such as chess and boules, take place among leisurely strollers. The garden was extended to the south in 1825 when the stately palace of Nonesuch (Makalös) burnt down. In the centre of the southern part stands a famous statue of King Karl XII.

In the south-west corner of the park stands **Jakobs kyrka** (CY **K³**) designed by Willem Boy and completed in 1643. The southern part of the garden looks onto the east front of the Opera House with its distinguished restaurant, Operakällaren. Its nightclub, Café Opera, is known for its clientele of celebrities – and its long queue.

* **Hallwylska Museet** ⊙ (CY **M³**) – ⊡ *Kungsträdgården. Hamngatan 4. Guided tours in English at 1pm.* Right in the middle of the city, squeezed in between restaurants and cafés, stands a stately home from the beginning of the 20C, the former abode of the Countess Wilhelmina von Hallwyl. The rooms and furniture evoke different periods whereas the decoration, panels and floors bear witness to the exquisite craftsmanship of the time. The collection includes priceless paintings, tapestries, arms, armour, china, silver and glassware. The residence was donated to the nation after the death of the countess and opened to the public in 1938. Summer evening concerts in the central courtyard are highly appreciated events.

Blasieholmen (CDY) – In the 17C palatial homes were erected on this peninsula with a view of the Royal Palace. The waterfront is now dominated by the Nationalmuseum and the elegant Grand Hotel. Since the middle of the 19C Strömkajen became a mooring place for boats arriving from the archipelago. Skeppsholmen to the south is reached by a narrow bridge.

** **Nationalmuseum** ⊙ (DY **M⁵**) – ⊡ *Kungsträdgården.* Sweden's foremost art museum, housed in a large Italian Renaissance style building (1866), comprises works of a high international standard from the Early Renaissance to the beginning of the 20C. The largest single collection of Swedish paintings and representative works from the other Nordic countries, as well as an interesting selection of applied arts are presented. Carl Gustaf Tessin, who was engaged in the completion of the Royal Palace, was a devoted art collector, and he laid the foundations of the fine collection of 18C French paintings, which is now the pride of the museum. Dutch 17C painting is well represented and includes Rembrandt's monumental *Batavians Oath of Allegiance*, which was originally painted to decorate Amsterdam's city hall. The huge murals in the entrance hall by Carl Larsson culminate in *The Entry of Gustav Vasa into Stockholm (opposite the staircase on the first floor)*. His final mural, *Midwinter Sacrifice*, was refused by the museum and ended up in Japan; it has since been bought back by Sweden *(second floor)*. Atrium, the museum's new restaurant, situated in the piazza-style inner courtyard, serves high-quality meals and snacks.

KUNGSHOLMEN (BY) (KING'S ISLAND)

West of Norrmalm. Take the pedestrian underground passageway.

King's Island, laid out in the late 17C as a workers' and craftsmen's district, is now a prosperous mix of residential and administrative buildings, home of the police headquarters, law courts and, on the western part of the island, the tall buildings of Sweden's major newspapers. Kungsholmen boasts Stockholm's best-known landmark, the Stadshuset.

Pedestrians may enjoy pleasant walks along the north shore of Lake Mälaren, **Norr Mälarstrand**. Sightseeing boats for the lake leave from Stadshuskajen east of the Stadshuset.

** **Stadshuset** ⊙ (BY **H**) – ⊡ *T-Centralen. Guided tours only. The tower is open May to September.* This highly distinctive red-brick city hall with its green copper roofs is one of the city's best-known landmarks. **Ragnar Östberg's** (1866-1945) designs took 12 years to complete (1911-23) and the finished result is a pre-eminent example of the National Romantic style. The buildings are arranged around two courtyards, an open one with a view through the arcade over the terraced garden to the lake and an indoor one. The plain square corner tower 106m tall is crowned by an open lantern topped out by a bulbous dome delicately crested with the three gilt crowns of the Swedish coat of arms. From the tower's observation platform (365 steps) there is a spectacular **view★★★** in all directions. The plain brickwork provides the perfect background for a wealth of decorative details: sculpted figures and groups, ironwork, tapering spires and finials.

Interior – The guided tour starts in the covered courtyard or as it is known the **Blue Hall★★★** (Blå Hallen) with its majestic staircase and ground-floor arcades. The architect's original intention was to paint the hall blue, but on seeing the beautiful shades

C. Boisvieux

Gyllene Salen, Stadshuset

of red of the bricks, he changed his mind. The Blue Hall makes a stately setting for the annual Nobel banquet. The members of the city council meet in the **Council Chamber** (Rådssalen) with its pinewood roof resembling that of a Viking longhouse. Civil marriages take place in the **Oval Room** (Ovalen), decorated with fine Beauvais tapestries. The plainer **Prince's Gallery** (Prinsens Galleri) takes its name from Prince Eugen, whose large al fresco painting depicts the same fantastic view as may be seen from the windows of the gallery. Clad in 18.6 million mosaic cubes in gold and in painted glass, the **Golden Hall★★★** (Gyllene Salen) offers the most sumptuous interior. The young artist Einar Forseth was inspired by the golden mosaics of Ravenna and he persuaded the architect to grant him the commission of decorating this room. The result is stunning. The window bays to the left illustrate events from Swedish history and the bays to the right depict celebrated Swedish people. The gigantic Mälaren Queen (Mälardrottningen) holding Stockholm's most important buildings on her lap, dominates the northern wall. Important guests enter the city hall via the tower of the **Hundred Vaults** comprising 100 intricate little vaults.

The **Engelbrekt Monument**, raised on a column in the south-east corner of the garden *(viewed from Stadshusbron)* is the work of Christian Eriksson (1932) and depicts Engelbrekt, a 15C Swedish national hero.

In the summer, at noon and at 6pm, a procession of St George and the Dragon emerges onto a small balcony, while a carillon plays a medieval tune. The St George group above is another work by Christian Eriksson.

SKEPPSHOLMEN (DYZ) (SHIPS' ISLAND)

Skeppsholmen may be reached by bus 65, leaving from the Central Station (Vasagatan). The nearest underground station is Kungsträdgården, exit Kungsträdgården.

The island of Skeppsholmen was the home base of the Swedish Royal Navy from the 1640s to 1958 and today the island has a unique sense of timelessness and peacefulness.

In more recent times the naval premises have been taken over by cultural institutions.

As you cross Skeppsholmsbron, embellished with two royal crowns, admire the **view** to the left of Strandvägen stretching away to the east, and on the other side the imposing form of the Royal Palace with Gamla Stan clustered beyond.

Berthed to the right, below the red form of the Admiralty House, which dates from 1650, is **af Chapman**, a 100 year schooner, named after Sweden's master shipbuilder Fredric af Chapman (1721-1808). The clipper was refurbished and now serves as a highly popular youth hostel and café. Secured by a bridge to the south side of Skeppsholmen is Citadel Islet, **Kastellholmen** (DZ). The present fort on the hilltop was erected in 1848 on the site of an earlier one.

As the road climbs slowly you can see emerging on the left, the octagonal cupola-crested form of **Skeppsholmskyrkan** (DY K⁴) with the long low building of the Östasiatiska Museet behind *(see below)*.

★ **Östasiatiska Museet** ⊘ (DY **M⁶**) – *To the left after the bridge.* The Museum of Far Eastern Antiquities, accommodated in a long, narrow building, was originally a warehouse for the artillery. Collections of art and archaeological objects from China, Japan, Korea and India, from the Stone Age to the late 19C, include one of the most eminent collections of Chinese art outside Asia.

Large colourful sculptures herald the presence of the two new museums. Picasso's *Déjeuner sur l'herbe* (1962) and Niki de Saint-Phalle's and Jean Tingueley's *Le Paradis* (1966) are joined by Per Kirkeby's *Byzantine Labyrinthe* (1998).

Moderna Museet; Arkitekturmuseum ⊘ (DY **M⁴**)

The Spanish architect José Rafael Moneo has designed Stockholm's building project of the century: the new **Moderna Museet** and the **Arkitekturmuseum**. Little other than the lanterns of the pyramidal roofs will disturb the present skyline as the buildings and their colour scheme blend harmoniously with the traditional Swedish architecture and unspoilt environment of Skeppsholmen.

Inside, although some of the rooms are below ground, Moneo's unerring sense for the contents has ensured settings with a unique character which owes much to the contribution of light.

From the entrance foyer, common to both museums, the **Modern Art Museum** on the left, starts with the temporary exhibition areas. Beyond are three sections on one level, separated by light wells and divided into square and rectangular rooms where light streams in through the lantern roofs. These are the custom-built home of the museum's collections of Swedish and international modern art, displayed in chrono-logical order, which are strong in selective quality while covering the main trends of the 20C up to the present day. Stairs from the main foyer lead down to the prints and photographs, away from the harsh light of day, lecture rooms, studios, archives etc. Scandinavia's largest art bookshop is on the right of the foyer and the stylish restaurant at the back of the building offers one of the finest views in Stockholm.

★★ Moderna Museet's Collections

First section: International art from the first half of the 20C – Fauvism is represented by Matisse *(Moroccan Landscape, Apollo)* and some of his Swedish students, including Grünewald *(The Crane)*, next to Munch *(Girl seated on a bed, Strindberg)*, Expressionists such as Kandinsky *(Improvisation no 2 Funeral March)* and Emil Nolde, as well as Modigliani *(Seated Woman wearing a Blue Dress)*. Other major artists represented in this section include Sonia Delaunay *(Self-portrait)*, Vlaminck *(Landscape)*, Picasso *(A Woman* and the famous *Guitar Player)* and his cubist friends Braque *(Still Life with Violin)*, Juan Gris *(Landscape near Céret)* and Picabia *(First Meeting)*. Dada and Surrealism are represented by significant works by Max Ernst *(The Imaginary Summer)*, Joan Miró *(The Toys)* and Salvador Dali *(The Enigma of William Tell)*. The last room in this section is devoted to works by Erik Olson *(Red figure)*, Fernand Léger *(The Camper)*, Picasso *(The Spring)* and includes a large sculpture by R Duchamp-Villon *(the Large Horse)*.

Second section: Art from 1945 to 1970 – The first room presents Movement in Art, a cen-tral theme in 20C, art with mobiles by Calder, Duchamp, PO Ultvedt and Jean Tinguely, next to contrasting works such as *Untitled Gold Monochrome* by Yves Klein, *Still Life in the Studio* by Giacometti and *Hat with a Bow* by Jean Dubuffet. The end of this section is devoted to the beginning of Pop Art with Martial Raysse *(Green France)* and Erró *(Foodscape)*.

Niki de Saint-Phalle's overwhelming *King-Kong* is exhibited in the space separating the second and third sections.

Third section: contemporary art – This section starts with the continuation of Pop Art with, among others, several works by Andy Warhol from the late 1960s *(Electric Chair, Flowers)*. The 1980s are represented by Richard Long, Ola Billgren *(Easterly Panorama)*, Ulf Rollof *(Lead Mattress)* and others. The display ends with the 1990s characterised by a great variety: *Sperm Piece* by Kiki Smith is a tableau comprising 731 pieces of crystal; note also Gerhard Richter's *Bach 1-4* and several video works, photographs etc.

In its new premises *(to the right of the main foyer)* the **Museum of Architecture** has the space to mount its permanent collection, which concentrates on the last 100 years, and function as an archive for blueprints, photographs and models. Other facilities include seminar rooms, studios, offices and workshops. The library, furnished with the best in Swedish design, contains some 25 000 volumes.

SÖDERMALM (BCZ)

Rich in its contrasts, this district offers unparalleled panoramas, charming wooden quarters and modern creations (Bofill's Bow). Bounded by a ridge, running parallel to Söder Mälarstrand, Södermalm was initially called the Ridge Island (Åsön). The first settlers on this island were fishermen, seafarers and craftsmen. At the end of the 17C noblemen and wealthy burghers erected stately summer residences here.

But in the 18C small factories were built around lake Fatburen *(see Bofill's Bow)* and the area rapidly became working class. It is only during the last few decades that it has become fashionable to live here, and today an apartment on Södermalm is highly prized.

Old main streets – In medieval times **Götgatan** (CZ) was the main thoroughfare leading south out of Stockholm. Today, as you look southwards, there is an immense golf ball, the spherical **Globe Arena** (Globen), a popular venue for sporting events and concerts.

Hornsgatan was the other main thoroughfare which led west out of the city. The cobbled lanes of **Hornsgatspuckeln** (in the vicinity of Maria Magdalena Kyrka) are lined with small galleries of good repute.

Slussen (CZ) – It is hardly noticeable that this area forms a bridgehead between two islands. It takes its name from the locks, which separated the brackish waters of the Baltic (known locally as the Salt Sea) from the fresh water of Lake Mälaren. The first lock was constructed in the 1640s, and was replaced a century later by a newer version by Christopher Polhem. A new 19C lock became obsolete in 1935, when shipping was diverted further south and the area became an intricate traffic junction.

Stockholms Stadsmuseum ○ (CZ **M⁷**) – Ⓣ *Slussen.* The City Museum is located in an Italian Baroque building, designed by Tessin the Elder to serve as the town hall for southern Stockholm. The exhibitions on the first floor present Stockholm in the 17C, when it was a capital of a Great Power and then as it was during the lifetime (18C) of the poet Bellman when squalor, poverty and cramped conditions prevailed. The second-floor exhibits portray 20C Stockholm as a multicultural city with a population of over a million, whereas the floor above presents the rapidly growing industrial city of the late 19C and Sweden's first Industrial Exhibition of 1897.

Panoramas and Picturesque Quarters East of Slussen

Buses nos 46, 48 and 53 take you from Slussen to Renstiernas Gata, from where a flight of steps (the lower) leads to Fjällgatan. Those with more time to spend (30min in either direction) may enjoy a walk via Mosebacke Torg and Katarina kyrka, which takes visitors through 18C quarters and offers numerous vistas of the city. Walk uphill if you will via Urvädersgränd (from Götgatan, the second street to the left) or choose the easy way out, the Katarina Lift. Both ways end up in Mosebacke Torg.

Urvädersgränd no 3 (CZ **74**) – The troubadour Carl Michael Bellman (1740-95) occupied two small rooms in this building where he wrote many of *Fredman's Epistles.* The steep cobbled street is a reminder of medieval times.

Katarinahissen (CZ) – By this lift, a masterpiece of technology when it was constructed in 1883 (rebuilt 1935), visitors are quickly brought up to the heights of Södermalm.

Mosebacke Torg (CZ **39**) – This square is dominated by Stockholm's oldest theatre, **Södra Teatern** (CZ **T¹**), erected in 1859, and a red water-tower, dating from 1895. The archway to the right of the theatre leads to **Mosebacke Terrass**, a popular place in summer. The captivating **view** from here inspired August Strindberg to create the opening passage of his masterpiece *The Red Room (Röda Rummet).*

Walk in the direction of the water tower. Follow Fiskargatan and then turn left onto Svartensgatan. Descend the sloping cobbled street. (High heels are not to be recommended.) At the end of Svartensgatan, Katarina kyrka suddenly appears quite close on the right.

Katarina kyrka (DZ) – A landmark, this church in the form of a Greek cross, raises once again its great Baroque cupola, which collapsed when the church caught fire in 1990. The original church, designed by Jean de la Vallée, dated from 1656 to 1690.

Now follow Mäster Mikaels Gata to the east.

Mäster Mikaels Gata (DZ **42**) – The eastern part is lined with picturesque wooden houses in pink, grey and red. This street formed part of Fjällgatan until Renstiernas Gata was blasted through the ridge around the turn of the last century.

Continue eastwards through the leafy glade, descend the flight of steps called Albert Engströms Trappor onto Renstiernas Gata. Cross the street and climb the steps to Fjällgatan.

Fjällgatan (DZ) – On the ridge of Stigberget, this street is lined with a row of old timbered houses and stone buildings, erected in the 18C in various colours and shapes. The enthralling **panorama★** it offers of Stockholm has become famous: from left to right Skeppsbron with its row of buildings (the church towers belong to

Tyska Kyrkan, Storkyrkan and Sankta Klara Kyrka), the Waxholm Company's fleet of white steamers moored in front of the Grand Hotel, *af Chapman* berthed at Skeppsholmen, the round fortress of Kastellholmen and to the right of it, across the water, the amusement park Gröna Lund, the twinkling light of the Kaknästornet, and the vast area of Djurgården.

Fringed by pocket-size gardens, a flight of steps which climbs to Stigbergsgatan, took its peculiar name of **Sista Styverns trappor** (DZ 55) (Last Penny's Steps) from a tavern, which once stood by the steps.

The Steps lead to Stigbergsgatan. Go to the right.

Stigbergsgatan (DZ 60) – At the west end of this street are a few low red, timber buildings, so typical of Södermalm. At no 21 the Pulley-Maker's House, **Blockmakarens hus,** is a humble dwelling dating from 1730, which has been carefully restored and turned into a museum *(☏ 08-700 05 00, the City Museum, for information about opening hours).*

Descend the flight of steps at the end of the street and return to Renstiernas Gata.

★★**Åsöberget (Åsö Ridge)** – *The promenade on the Åsö Ridge and around Sofia Kyrka takes about 1hr. Bus 53 to Erstagatan (second stop after turning onto Folkungagatan). In low traffic approximately a 10min ride from the Central Station. Continue on foot in the same direction and turn right onto Sågargatan.* A strong sense of bygone days pervades the picturesque quarters in the vicinity of Lotsgatan and Skeppargränd, not far from the bustle of Folkungagatan.

Continue along Lotsgatan, round the edge of the cliff and return by Åsögatan to Skeppargränd. For Sofia kyrka, keep to Åsögatan and turn left onto the flight of steps at Klippgatan.

Sofia kyrka – A central tower, surrounded by smaller turrets, emerges above the other buildings. The church was built in 1906 on a Greek cross ground plan in the Romanesque style with rounded arches and a large central dome.

Pretty red **cottages** perch on the hillside, a sharp contrast to the concrete blocks of the city.

Return by bus no 46 (from Bondegatan) to Slussen.

Panorama and Picturesque Quarters West of Slussen

Underground to Mariatorget, exit Torkel Knutssonsgatan. Go to the right, cross Hornsgatan and climb Ludvigsbergsgatan (to the left). Turn left onto Gamla Lundagatan (through the gap between the houses), and continue up the hill.

★★**Skinnarviksberget (Skinnarvik Ridge)** – It may be difficult to imagine yourself right in the middle of a busy capital when walking this well-trodden road, now worn and lined with low old buildings, which in the 18C were the dwellings of flayers and tanners. Further up, the road narrows to become a path, which ends on Skinnarvik Ridge with a splendid **panorama★** of the city. This is Stockholm's highest point, 53m above sea level, with a view of Norr Mälarstrand, the Stadshuset, Sankta Klara Kyrka, the five skyscrapers at Hötorget, Riddarholmen and Gamla Stan. The large red-brick building at the foot of the hill is the 1850s München Brewery. On the west side of the cliff a flight of steps descends into **Yttersta Tvärgränd,** a unique part of the city with stone buildings dating from the 18C and 19C.

The underground station of Zinkensdamm is across the street.

Bofill's Bow – *Medborgarplatsen* (CZ). 🔁 *Medborgarplatsen* or *Mariatorget*. This was once the site of a small lake, Lake Fatburen, which by the middle of the 19C was filled in to provide the site for Stockholm's first railway station, Stockholms Södra. The area is now given over to modern housing estates, in particular the very interesting semicircular Bofill's Bow, which is named after its Spanish architect, Ricardo Bofill. The Bow and its four pavilions were erected between 1989 and 1992, as a Versailles for the people. They are an expression of Post-modernism adapted to the Nordic mood.

Långholmen – *Approached by car from Söder Mälarstrand or the bridge of Västerbron. Parking places available on the island.* In the shadow of the busy Western Bridge (Västerbron), Långholmen, an old prison island, lies separated from Södermalm by a narrow stretch of water. The island offers pleasant walks and bathing opportunities, both from the rocks and from a small sandy beach. The former prison, in use until 1987, has been transformed into an unusual youth hostel.

SWEDEN

ÖSTERMALM

Kungliga Dramatiska Teatern (CDY T²) – *Nybroplan*. Sweden's National Theatre was founded by King Gustav III in 1788. The present Royal Dramatic Theatre with its white marble façade, was built in 1901-08 in the Art Nouveau style. From 1963 to 1966 Ingmar Bergman was the director, and he still occasionally directs plays here.

Kungliga Hovstallet ⊘ (DY M⁸) – *Next to the Royal Theatre. Entrance from Väpnargatan*. Horses, coaches and carriages used by the royals are on view in the royal stables.

Musikmuseet ⊘ (DY M¹⁰) – Situated next door to Kungliga Hovstallet, the Music Museum is housed in an austere 17C building stretching along Sibyllegatan, still known today as the Crown Bakery since it was used as such for over three centuries. In 1935, it was classified as a historic building and in 1974 the decision was taken to convert it into a Museum of Music. The architect (Kjell Abramson) partially rebuilt the interior but left the exterior intact. The museum contains instruments from the 13C onwards, including a large collection of Swedish folk instruments, printed and manuscript scores, concert programmes, photographs, press cuttings and letters. The Musikmuseet is also an interactive museum with a sound room where some of the instruments can be played by visitors as well as a sound workshop, musical games for children, instrument building etc.

Strandvägen from Djurgårdsbron

Strandvägen (DY) – The mansions and palatial houses of Stockholm's fashionable esplanade were built at the end of the 19C in eclectic styles for industrialists, timber barons and press magnates who had amassed their wealth in Sweden's recent industrialisation. Beyond Djurgårdsbron to the right, Strandvägen curves past the **Nobel Parken**, with specimens of most of Sweden's deciduous trees.

Berwaldhallen (DY F) – The site for this concert hall, named after Sweden's first great symphonist Franz Berwald (1796-1868), was blasted out of the granite hillside. The auditorium has superb acoustics.

Diplomatstaden – As its name suggests, diplomats' town is an elegant district where many of the embassies and consulates are to be found.

English Church – *Strandvägen 76*. The Anglican Church of St Peter and St Sigfrid has been represented in Stockholm since the 17C. This church was built in 1866 and moved stone by stone to its present site in 1911. The Congregation consists of English-speaking people of many denominations and nationalities.
A fine **promenade** stretches along the north side of the Bay of Djurgårdsbrunnsviken, past the National Maritime Museum *(see below)* and on to northern Djurgården.

Sturegallerian (CXY) – *Stureplan*. In 1883 this was a bath house. In 1989 the huge block of buildings was transformed into a luxury shopping mall, stretching to the three surrounding streets. The bathing establishment was rebuilt after a fire in 1985, as an exclusive health club with pool, sauna, beauty parlours...

Östermalmstorg (DY 76) – On the west side of this square stands a covered market hall, **Östermalms Saluhall** (CDY N), where all kinds of delicacies are on sale. On the south side is **Hedvig Eleonora kyrka** (DY), designed by Jean de la Vallée in the 17C.

★★**Historiska museet** ⊘ (DY) – *Narvavägen 13-17.* ⓣ *Karlaplan or Östermalmstorg.* The Museum of National Antiquities boasts one of the most precious collections of gold in Europe. The **Gold Room★★★** (Guldrummet, *an underground vault to the right of the entrance*) displays 50kg of gold and 250kg of silver treasures, totalling over 3 000 objects, which date from about 2 000 BC until about AD 1520. The collection of gold items includes exquisite collars and medallions of finest filigree work. A copy of the Sigurd Carving *(see p 236),* is engraved on the floor.

Finds from the Stone, Bronze and Iron Ages (Forntid, from 14 000 BC) and the **Viking Age** (Vikingatid, AD 800-1050) are exhibited on the ground floor. The **Medieval Period** (Medeltid, 1050 to early 16C) displays on the first floor include a rich collection of polychrome sculptures and altarpieces as well as textiles from Swedish churches and monasteries.

★★DJURGÅRDEN

In the summer private cars are restricted on southern Djurgården. Visitors may take bus 44 or 47, the latter continues past Skansen to Waldemarsudde. A pleasant approach is by ferry from Slussen or Nybroplan, which arrives near the amusement park. Vintage trams run between Norrmalmstorg and Djurgården.

For centuries Djurgården has been a popular recreation area. The name, which literally means animal farm, dates from the 16C when the area was royal hunting grounds. Southern Djurgården is an island, about 4km long and 1km wide, separated from northern Djurgården by Djurgårdsbrunn Bay and canal.

The western part of the island, nearest the city, is occupied by trim gardens, restaurants, museums, the amusement park Gröna Lund and Skansen, the popular open-air museum.

The rest of the island is a large park, enjoyed by walkers, joggers, riders, picnickers and other outdoor enthusiasts. The southern shores overlook the seaway into Stockholm and visitors may enjoy the sight of innumerable boats of all types.

A **promenade** *(east of Djurgårdsbron)* curves along the shore of Djurgården Bay, past several sculptures and through a **blue gate**, one of the many blue-painted gates, which punctuated the fence around Djurgården.

Western and southern Djurgården

★★★**Vasamuseet** – *See p* 311.

★★**Nordiska museet** ⊘ (DY) – *Djurgårdsvägen 6-16.* This magnificent building, built like a Renaissance palace and completed in 1907, hosts the largest museum of cultural history in Scandinavia. A counterpart to nearby Skansen, the Nordiska Museet was founded by Artur Hazelius, a scientist and teacher, who started collecting in 1872 to preserve the old rural heritage which was dying out as industrial society

Pippi Longstocking

Astrid Lindgren's World

The grand old lady of Swedish children's literature was born in 1907 in Vimmerby, an ancient market town at the heart of Småland, some 300km from Malmö, Göteborg and Stockholm. The successful author, who has delighted children all over the world throughout the second half of the 20C, has also contributed to Vimmerby's tourist appeal. Several films of her books were set around Vimmerby and **Astrid Lindgren's World** opened in 1981; since then, the fairy-tale park, with settings from Astrid Lindgren's stories, has grown and now attracts some 300 000 visitors a year. Children can play with live characters (Emil, Pippi, Ronja etc) and re-enact scenes from her books. There are also theatrical performances in summer, Astrid Lindgren's films at the cinema, restaurants, cafés and shops. Information available from Vimmerby Turistbyrå ☎ 0492 31010.

took over. This museum houses collections from all over Sweden, describing life and work from 1520 to the present day. The Sami culture is presented in the basement. On entering the Great Hall on the ground floor, attention is drawn to the big statue of King Gustav Vasa, carved in oak by Carl Milles in 1925. This floor, with book shop, restaurant and a children's play world, is devoted to temporary exhibitions, which relate to Swedish culture and history. The first-floor exhibits folk art, textiles, table settings, traditional toys and fashion. Also on the first floor is a new permanent exhibition entitled Strindberg at Nordiska Museet, presenting August Strindberg both as a painter (16 of his paintings are displayed) and as an author with several of his original manuscripts including one of his most famous plays, Miss Julie. His association with Nordiska Museet goes back to the early 1880s and his interest in Hazelius's project. Displays on the second floor describe the developments in Swedish housing.

★**Junibacken** ⊘ (**DY**) – Situated on Djurgården Island, near the Vasamuseet and the Nordiska Museet, Junibacken is a museum of another kind; here there is fantasy, laughter, excitement, surprises, mischief...in other words it's a children's paradise! The concept was based on children's books and in particular on old favourites by Astrid Lindgren. The activity and cultural centre opened in 1996 and has proved a great success with families and schools. From the entrance hall, one steps through a huge book into a world of fantasy full of fun and poetry with wonderful settings. The Story Train leaves from Vimmerby Station (Astrid Lindgren home town) and takes its passengers through the Swedish countryside and dark forests to meet some of Astrid Lindgren's best known characters. After the 10min ride children can try lots of amusing things and get up to as much mischief as they like in Pippi Longstockings' house, Villekula Cottage. Junibacken also stages one yearly exhibition about a children's story writer and there is a well-stocked multimedia shop with computers and games for children to try and a pleasant cafeteria with a fine view.

Liljevalchs Konsthall ⊘ (**DYZ Mᵉ**) – Djurgårdsvägen 60. This art gallery, housed in an elegant neo-Classical (1916) building, concentrates on contemporary works.
Next door is a popular café, **Blå Porten** (the Blue Gate). The Archer high on his granite pedestal is a sculpture by Carl Milles.
East of **Gröna Lunds Tivoli** (**DZ**) is **Djurgårdsstaden** where some of the buildings were the homes of 17C seafarers, ships carpenters and chandlers.

★★**Prins Eugens Waldemarsudde** ⊘ – Terminal of bus 47. Prince Eugen (1865-1948) made the place on Djurgården his permanent residence from 1905.

The perfect setting, overlooking the seaway to Stockholm, and the interesting collections combine to make this a pleasant visit where the works by the artist Prince and his artistic friends bring to life the Nordic art scene at the beginning of the 20C. Look for the portraits of the Prince's mother, *Queen Sofia* and the *Prince* himself by Zorn; a *Self-portrait* by Larsson; the terracotta bust of Prince Eugen by Eriksson; Bergh's drawings of *The Committee of the Artists' Union*; Josephson's controversial work, *The Water Sprite*; and works by the Prince. The gallery contains the Prince's own collection with works by Nordic artists (Josephson, Zorn, Nordström, Bergh, Liljefors and Munch) and sculptors (Milles, Eldh, Johnsson and Eriksson).

Go via northern Djurgården, by car or by bus 69, in the direction of Blockhusudden to reach Thielska Galleriet.

★★**Thielska Galleriet** ⊘ – *Sjötullsbacken 6.* The wealthy banker **Ernest Thiel** (1859-1947) commissioned the architect Ferdinand Boberg to build this residence where he and his second wife, by then ostracized by Stockholm society, created a home decorated with paintings on every wall. The couple were socially restricted to his new wife's friends who were mainly artists, writers and composers and Thiel initially purchased from these contemporaries who not unexpectedly belonged to the Independent Artists Union (f 1886). The result is a unique collection of animal paintings by Bruno Liljefors, nudes by Anders Zorn, works by the group's spokesman, Richard Bergh, examples of the blue paintings by Eugen Jansson, numerous Larssons, winter scenes by Gustaf Fjæstad, several Strindbergs all with tormented skies and one by Prince Eugen (compare his *Night Cloud* with the twilight scenes by Jansson).

Later Thiel extended his collection to include foreign works in particular an important group by Edvard Munch. The immense carved sofas with matching table and chairs *(first floor)* were made by Gustaf Fjæstad. In 1924 Thiel went bankrupt and the Swedish State bought the gallery and opened it to the public.

★**Rosendals Slott** ⊘ – *Rosendalsvägen 41.* A number of lavish interiors, illustrating the Swedish adaptation of the French Empire style, may be enjoyed in this summer palace, erected between 1823 and 1827 for King Karl XIV Johan.

Rosendals Trädgård – *Rosendalsterrassen, across the road.* A shop and a café provide fruit and vegetables that are biologically grown in this market garden.

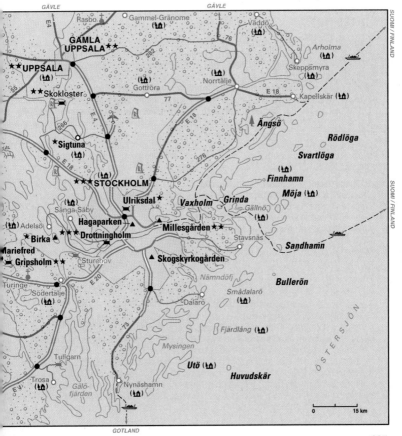

Northern Djurgården

Reached by bus 69 or by car (follow Strandvägen, which becomes Djurgårdsbrunnsvägen).

The vast area of northern Djurgården is actually called the Barn Meadow (Ladugårdsgärdet) or simply the Meadow (Gärdet). A Kite Festival in May is an annual event, which attracts large crowds.

Kaknästornet ⊘ – An exceptional **panorama★★★** of the city, is offered from this 155m-high telecommunications tower.

Three museums stand in a row on the north shore of Djurgårdsbrunn Bay.

Folkens Museum – Etnografiska ⊘ – This Ethnographic Museum gives an insight into how people used to live outside Europe. The first floor presents exhibitions on North and Central Africa, India, North America and Mongolia. The ground floor is devoted to temporary exhibitions. In the garden, a **Japanese tea house** is open to visitors in the summer.

Tekniska Museet ⊘ – The National Museum of Science and Technology appeal to all ages and is one of Sweden's most popular museums. The Machinery Hall displays steam-engines, cars, aircrafts etc. On the ground floor are the permanent exhibitions on the history of the iron and steel industry in Sweden. In the **Teknorama** *(straight through the Machinery Hall plus another 50m)* visitors may test their own technical skill. The History of Electric Power is outlined in a wing of the main building *(to the left of the ground floor)*, and the Museum of Telecommunications (**Telemuseum**, *to the right*), traces that story, from beacon fires to today's global digital network. The upper floors of the main building present exhibitions about engineering technology, technology in the home, the graphic industry and the history of chemistry.

Sjöhistoriska museet ⊘ – Designed by Ragnar Östberg, this white, slightly curved building (1938) houses the National Maritime Museum, which traces Swedish shipbuilding, marine defence and commercial shipping from the 17C to the present. A unique collection of model ships from the 17C and 18C is normally featured on the ground floor, where visitors may also see the stern, complete with cabin from King Gustav III's schooner *Amphion*.

OUTSKIRTS

Hagaparken – ⊡ *Odenplan. North of the city and east of the busy E 4, direction of Hagaparken. Entrance via the North Gates. Walk eastwards.* Stretching about 2km along the shores of the small Baltic bay of Brunnsviken, this English landscape park was laid out for King Gustav III, and is an excellent setting for the pavilions and temples. The remarkable **Copper Tents** (Koppartälten) were erected in 1787. The **Bird and Butterfly Houses** (north of the Copper Tents) are home to 300 tropical butterflies and 130 exotic birds. Further east stands the masterpiece **Gustav III:s Paviljong** ⊘ (1792), its interior graced with fine detail in the Gustavian style. The **Echo Temple**, dates from the same period and was built to serve as dining room on summer evenings. The present king of Sweden and his sisters spent their childhood in **Haga Manor** dating from 1804. This landscape forms part of **Ekoparken**, which stretches from Djurgården to Ulriksdal, a green oasis of unspoilt nature on the outskirts of the city.

★★ **Millesgården** ⊘ – ⊡ *Ropsten. About 5km from Norrtull. Follow Valhallavägen southwards and turn left in the direction of Lidingö. Keep to the centre lane on the Lidingö Bridge (direction Herserud). At the traffic lights after the bridge, go to the right (Millesgården and Foresta) and follow the road uphill for 500m to Millesgården's car park.*

High atop steep cliffs stands this outdoor museum, the home of the sculptor **Carl Milles** (1875-1955) and his wife Olga. An attractive arrangement of sculptures and harmoniously arranged Italian-style terraces, fountains with rippling water, steps

---

Carl Milles 1875-1955

Sweden's most sought-after sculptor in the 1920s, Carl Milles was even more highly acclaimed in the United States, where he spent 20 years (1931-51) at the Cranbrook Academy of Art in Michigan. Milles was influenced by Auguste Rodin and served as his assistant during his seven years in Paris at the end of the 19C. He was also inspired by the art treasures of Classical Greece and Rome, and Greek mythology often provided Milles with motifs. In his big fountain compositions, he devoted himself to the ample movements of the Baroque style, a true successor to Lorenzo Bernini. Milles depicted his figures in flight or leaping, and they all seem to defy the laws of gravity.

C. Boisvieux

Bergs Brygga in the Stockholm archipelago

and columns, coupled with a diversity of vegetation and a splendid **view** across the water to Värtan, terminal for the Finland ferries, makes Millesgården a work of art in its own right.

Most of the sculptures are replicas of works to be found elsewhere in Sweden and abroad. Thus the museum provides an exemplary survey of the artist's creations.

Terraces – Particularly noteworthy is the beautiful *Susanna Fountain* (upper terrace), framed by weeping willows. It received the Grand Prix at the World Fair in Paris in 1925. From the middle terrace with its long granite colonnade we can see *The Sunsinger*, cresting a pillar. The *Aganippe Fountain* (1955) was executed for the Metropolitan Museum in New York, but recently moved to South Carolina. The three figures mounted on dolphins symbolize the arts. When designing the lower terrace, Milles wanted his sculptures to be seen as silhouettes against the sky, raised high on columns. *The Hand of God* (1954) is one of Milles' most well-known sculptures, which may be found reproduced in different parts of the world. The *Fountain of Europe and the Bull* (original in Halmstad) and the powerful *Poseidon* (original in Göteborg) have become symbols of these two cities. In *Man and Pegasus* (1949) on a weightless flight through the Universe, Pegasus is said to symbolize the artist's genius. The original may be found in Des Moines, USA, and there are replicas elsewhere in the world. One of Milles' major works in the US is the *Fountain of Faith* (1949-52) on the outskirts of Washington D.C. It regroups more than 30 figures. Replicas of some of them are on view on a small terrace near the *Angel Musicians* (1950).

Interior – The main building, dating from 1908, was made into a museum in 1936. The Gallery displays some of Milles' works in bronze and marble, and in the Red Room a large collection of Milles' early small sculptures are presented. Olga and Carl Milles were avid collectors of art, and paintings by Camille Pissarro and Maurice Utrillo may be found in the Music Room. In the Monk's Cell a collection of Chinese sculptures, and in the long Eastern Gallery a great number of Antique sculptures and fragments have been installed.

Skogskyrkogården (Woodland Cemetery)– Ⓣ *Skogskyrkogården (12min from T-Centralen on the Farsta line). Turn right and follow the signs.* The Holy Cross Chapel at the Woodland Cemetery was the last great work of **Gunnar Asplund** (1885-1940), Sweden's foremost advocate of Functionalism and the cemetery is now listed as a UNESCO World Heritage Site. On approaching the cemetery visitors are filled with a sense of awe as the large plain cross rises, like a beacon, above the low chapels to the left and the undulating lawns to the right. The smooth, unadorned surfaces and pure geometrical lines of the chapel, in keeping with the precepts of Functionalism, blend so perfectly with the surrounding landscape.

SWEDEN

★★★ SKÄRGÅRDEN (STOCKHOLM ARCHIPELAGO)

Stockholm takes pride in a unique archipelago – known as the garden of skerries – with tremendously varied nature, ranging from the lush vegetation of the inner archipelago to the windswept barren cliffs of the outer skerries. Starting right in the centre of Stockholm, the archipelago extends for about 70km out into the Baltic Sea, and measures approximately 140km from north to south.

The archipelago numbers no less than 24 000 islands and skerries, of which only 150 are inhabited all year round, but there are about 50 000 summer houses and chalets. It is the favourite holiday and weekend retreat of Stockholmers. Many artists and writers have been attracted by the charm of the archipelago which has been immortalized in print by August Strindberg in *The People of Hemsö* (Kymmendö) and in paint by artists such as Bruno Liljefors and Anders Zorn.

Getting around

There is a wide choice of boat cruises and excursions to the islands of the archipelago and further details can be obtained from the Excursion Shop in Sverigehuset *(see p 303)*. Many of the islands have youth hostels but these are very popular and it is advisable to book in advance.

The Waxholm Company (Waxholmsbolaget) offers a regular ferry service to all parts of the archipelago all year round. The company's fleet comprises some 20 boats ranging from fast modern crafts to the faithful old steamers *S/S Storskär* and *S/S Norrskär*, favourites with the locals. Information on schedules and tours can be obtained at the company's terminal on Strömkajen near the Grand Hotel, departure point for the cruises. An Inter-Skerries Card *(Båtluffarkort)* is valid for 16 days and offers unlimited travel on cruises with Waxholmsbolaget.

The Strömma Canal Company (Strömma Kanalbolaget) boasts one of the world's oldest fleets of classic boats, still in regular service. Some have good restaurants on board, and the evening trips also include dancing and entertainment. The boats leave from Nybroplan, close to the Kungliga Dramatiska Teatern. boat trips for **lake Mälaren** and lakeside towns, such as Mariefred and Sigtuna, leave from Stadshuskajen.

Selection of islands

Vaxholm – Pop 8 385. This idyllic town with attractive shops and tourist facilities, is a pleasant introduction to the skerries. Once a vital strategic location, commanding the eastern approach to Stockholm, Vaxholm's **fortress** on a small island opposite the town, is a reminder of the town's military role. Part of the fortress dates from the 16C.

Grinda – Typical of the inner archipelago, this verdant island, less than 2hr from Stockholm, is a popular spot to go for a swim or a stroll.

Möja – *Youth hostel.* One of the largest islands of the middle archipelago, Möja, has about 250 year-round residents, still engaged in the traditional archipelago occupations of fishing and farming. Möja is not the place to go for a swim, but rather for walks. In its largest community, a little village called Berg, you will find a café, shops offering archipelago handicrafts, and a small museum.

Finnhamn – *Youth hostel.* Finnhamn, which comprises three islands, lies at the point where the northern archipelago opens up to the barren cliffs of the outer skerries. Ramblers may enjoy the narrow paths, and sun-lovers the smooth rocks or the small sandy beaches.

Sandhamn – *Hotels, restaurants and other services.* Perhaps the best-known destination, Sandhamn has been the meeting point for seafarers since the 18C, and today it is popular with the yachting fraternity. The village with its narrow alleys and tightly packed houses is well worth exploring.

Utö – *Tourist information, bicycle rental, youth hostels, hotel, restaurants, café, bakery and shops.* Far south in the archipelago, Utö has a resident population of about 200. The island is a popular destination for cycling. Utö claims the oldest iron mine in Sweden; its deep shaft may still be seen. A small mining museum, and the miners' 18C homes also remain from this period.

Ängsö – *Ask in the Excursion Shop for information on sailing schedules.* The only skerry with the status of a National Park. As its name (Meadow Island) implies, Ängsö is a miniature floral paradise, with a very rich bird life.

Rödlöga and Svartlöga – *Departure from Nybrokajen.* These two islands lie quite some distance away in the northern archipelago and they are particularly popular with yachtsmen.

Bullerön – *Served by special tour boats. Ask for information.* Located in the outer archipelago, Bullerön has a unique environment. The artist Bruno Liljefors came here to study its bird life. His hunting lodge is open to visitors.

Huvudskär – *Shuttle ferry from Dalarö, south of Stockholm, twice weekly.* Due to its remote location on the periphery of the archipelago, this bare low-lying group of islands with smooth rock-surfaces, has remained a secluded spot.

Stockholm's Ekoparken a unique national city park

The world's first national city park, Ekoparken, has aroused great public interest and the organised boat trips leaving from Brunnsviken's six jetties are very popular; from April to mid-September boats leave at hourly intervals between 10am and 9.30pm. This recently designated national city park offers both cultural and natural attractions and takes in such well-known sites as the palace at Ulriksdal, Hagaparken with its royal follies, the island of Djurgården and the islands of Fjäderholmarna with their exceptionally rich flora and fauna *(for sightseeing tours of Ekoparken, see Tips for Stockholm p 304).*

STRÄNGNÄS★

Södermanlands län
Population 29 000
Michelin map 985 M 14 or Atlas Europe p 119 – Local map see STOCKHOLM

Strängnäs on the southern shore of Lake Mälaren played an important role in the history of the nation. It was in Strängnäs that the new faith was introduced to Sweden when the young deacon **Olaus Petri**, a preacher of Lutheran doctrines, converted the Archdeacon of Strängäs, Laurentius Andreae, to his cause. It was Andreae who proclaimed Gustav Vasa king of Sweden in 1523 and Olaus Petri became one of the king's closest advisers. Although the king was not unsympathetic to the new doctrines the driving forces behind his policy were the elimination of the power of the church and the strengthening of royal authority.

★★ Domkyrkan ⊘ – The cathedral was consecrated in 1291 and when building work stopped in 1342 only the naves and aisles up to the chancel had been completed. In the mid-15C the chancel was added and it was Carl Hårleman who added the Baroque cupola to the 15C tower.

Following the Reformation the side chapels became burial chapels. From west to east on the south side: the Lady Chapel built in 1404 is sometimes referred to as the Fresco Chapel due to its remarkable mural paintings; the **Gyllenhjelm Chapel**, beyond the south porch, with its 17C stucco decor, is a monument to an illegitimate son of King Karl IX; the last chapel on the south side has more murals. At the end of the 17C it became the burial chapel for the nobleman Stenbock and the huge wooden monument with Death as the principal figure is his memorial. The murals on the chancel arch date from the 15C when the chancel was added. The elaborate star vaulting of the chancel contrasts with the simpler cross-vaulting of the nave. At the high altar there is a magnificent **reredos★★★** (1490) a masterpiece of Brussels art. When open it portrays the Passion of Christ in seven large and seven small scenes and when the doors are closed a series of paintings with motifs from the Christmas cycle of the ecclesiastical year appear. Completely closed the reredos shows the Annunciation and the Last Judgement. The **monument** to King Karl IX is crowned by the statue of a wooden horse carrying a suit of gilt copper armour and surrounded by attractive railings (1597). Another popular monument is Willem Boy's effigy of Princess Isabella (1580), the daughter of King Johan III, who spent all her life in captivity in the dungeon of Gripsholm. The decoration of the Baptismal Chapel on the north side, opposite the Lady Chapel, dates from 1910 but the **baptismal font** is 14C; the **reredos** (1515) is from the Brussels workshop of Jan Borman whereas the predella is thought to have been made in Antwerp.

Cathedral precincts – **Gyllenhjelmsgatan** with its low wooden houses was laid out by royal command in the 1640s to provide a suitable approach to the cathedral. The medieval network of streets has been preserved to the west. **Lillgatan** is lined with red-painted houses from the 17C and 18C. The building on the left just before Lion Gate, which marks the entrance to the churchyard, was the diocesan printing house in the 18C and it now houses **Strängnäs Museum** with its local history collections. To the right of the gate is the medieval consistory building, today the chapter-house.

The **Roggeborgen** close to the cathedral chancel was originally the episcopal residence but in 1626 it became Sweden's second college after the one in Västerås (1623). It now houses a library with over 70 000 books as well as manuscripts. The State Hall is supposedly where Archdeacon Andreae proclaimed Gustav Vasa king of Sweden. The pink building to the south of the cathedral has served as episcopal residence since the 17C. Coffee is now served in the former church stables, **Kyrkstallarna**.

Café Grassagården ⊘ – *Kvarngatan 2*. This is a burgher's homestead dating from 1638 where the main house faces the courtyard and the outbuildings overlook the street. Most of the other buildings are 18C. For most of its life the premises were run as a public house (at the end of the 17C Strängnäs had 17 public bars and Mariefred boasted 32). It is now a **museum** with musical entertainment and a café in July.

Continue up Kvarngatan past more burghers' houses to an old mill, **Kvarnen**, from where you can enjoy the **view** of Strängnäs in its lakeside setting.

Olaus Petri

Olof Petersson was born in Örebo in 1493 and studied at Uppsala and Leipzig and under Luther at Wittenberg between 1516 and 1519. In 1529 he published *The Swedish Handbook* and participated in a translation of the Bible with his brother the archbishop of Uppsala. Gustav Vasa feared that Olaus Petri and Laurentius Andreae, the leading forces of the Swedish Reformation, were working too much against the royal power. Eight years later Petri fell from grace and was condemned to death for high treason. Pardoned by the king, Petri spent the rest of his life studying theology and literature. He died in 1552.

STRÖMSHOLMS SLOTT★

Västmanlands län
Michelin map 985 M 13 or Atlas Europe p 119
Local map see STOCKHOLM: Outskirts
10km south of Hallstahammar by road 252

Strömsholms Slott is attractively set in lush green parkland where venerable millenary oaks provide shade and shelter for the grazing horses. King Gustav Vasa built the castle in 1556 on a royal estate with the intention of making it a stud farm. In the 17C it became an equestrian centre with a riding school and finally, for a period of 100 years (1868-1968), it served as the Military Riding Academy. It is still a popular centre for equestrian events; the National Dressage Competition and the Swedish Grand National (flat race) are two of the greatest crowd pullers. A colourful jousting tournament takes place towards the end of July.

★**Strömsholms Slott** ⊘ – The castle was a favourite retreat for several dowager queens. The architect royal Nicodemus Tessin the Elder was commissioned to build a new castle which was completed in 1681 but only furnished between 1767 and 1776. The interior decoration is essentially Gustavian. Again in the first half of the 19C Strömsholm renewed its connections with royalty when it became a country retreat for the royal family. The large collection of paintings includes works by the Swedish Stubbs, David Klöcker von Ehrenstrahl, one of the foremost painters during Sweden's period as a Great Power. The summer concerts are popular with music lovers.

Strömsholms Kanal – The canal, built between 1777 and 1795, is Sweden's second oldest (Hjälmare Canal is older) and second longest canal (Göta Canal is longer). The 110km-long navigable stretch goes form Smedjebacken in Dalarna to Strömsholm on Lake Mälaren and in the process flows through no less than 14 lakes and 26 locks raise the canal 100m. It is open to navigation from mid-June to mid-August.

SUNDSVALL

Sundsvall lies between the Indalsälv and Ljunga half way up the eastern coast of Sweden. The two rivers were important logging rivers and the town rapidly became the centre of the Swedish forestry and timber industries.

Timber merchants and barons – By the 19C Sundsvall was already a prosperous sawmilling town and the timber merchants and barons had acquired a reputation for their high living. In striking contrast to the mill owners, the sawmill workers lived in appalling conditions. The **Sundsvall Strike** in 1879 was Sweden's first major industrial conflict. The authorities retaliated in a very harsh manner and the outcome was the emergence of a strong labour movement.

On the same day in 1888 both Sundsvall and Umeå was destroyed by fire. The mill owning aristocracy (Träpatronerna) invested in the rebuilding of the new stone town (Stenstaden). The massive scale of rebuilding offered work opportunities for many newcomers.

SIGHTS

Stenstaden – The stone town rose like a phoenix from the ashes, surrounded on all sides by simple wooden houses and cottages. Storgatan, Stora Torget and Esplanaden are lined by impressive **mansions★** in a variety of architectural styles resembling Italian Renaissance palaces or French and German castles.

Knaust Hotel – *At Storgatan 13.* This hotel dates from the heyday of the timber barons and it is best-known for its grand staircase.

★★ Kulturmagasinet ⊘ – Four harbourside warehouses dating from the turn of the last century have been ingeniously made into a single unit by glazing over the intervening streets. The cultural centre includes the Sundsvall Museum (local history, handicrafts, art etc), the Town Library, the Medelpad Archives (a research centre on local and family history), the Children's Cultural Centre and Café Skonerten.

EXCURSIONS

Alnö – *11km north by road E 4.* This volcanic island with its many sandy beaches is connected to the mainland by a 1 024m-long road bridge. Turn left after the bridge to reach **Alnö kyrka** ⊘ dating from the 12C with its medieval murals. The new church has a richly carved wooden baptismal font. It is a pleasant drive to the picturesque fishing village of **Spirkarna** in the south of the island.

Indalsleden (Indal Trail) – The valley of the Indalsälven is known for its splendid scenery and the riverside road 86 offers numerous views of rolling pastures, lush vegetation, steep-sided valleys and wooded slopes with here and there midstream islets. The river has been harnessed for hydroelectric power and at times the crisscrossing of power lines may intrude on the scenery.

Liden – *55km west of Sundsvall, look for the sign Kyrka 1km and Vättaberget 4km.* The **kyrka** ⊘ dating from 1483-1510 was abandoned for over 50 years before it was restored (1911-28). The wooden lych-gate (1693) is all that remains of a timbered enclosure around the church. Vildhussen *(see below)* was buried here in 1798; his burial stone stands in a corner of the churchyard.

Vättaberget – *Altitude 381m.* The road to the top *(café open in summer)* offers splendid views of the meandering river.

★ Döda Fallet – *100km north-west of Sundsvall.* Planks lead over the rocks of the so-called Dead Falls which were once known as Storforsen or the Great Falls. On the night of 6-7 June 1796 the river burst its banks to follow a canal which had been dug by a timber merchant from Sundsvall, Vildhussen, to float his logs past the falls. Within 4hr of bursting its banks the river had emptied Lake Ragundasjön. A play adapted from a novel about Vildhussen is staged in the open-air every summer.

UDDEVALLA
Västra Götalands län
Population 49 000
Michelin map 985 O 8 or Atlas Europe p 118 – Local map see BOHUSLÄN

Uddevalla is Bohuslän's main town and a modern centre of commerce and industry (textiles, paper, wood processing and shipbuilding). Initially known as a trading centre, the herring fishing in the late 18C brought prosperity to the port.

★★ **Bohusläns Museum** ⊙ – *A red-brick building facing the car park beside the bus station. The restaurant on the ground floor serves traditional Swedish dishes.* Three white wooden gabled buildings overlook the quay and River Bäveån where it flows into Byfjorden. The spacious interior consists of a ground floor, housing temporary exhibitions, and a mezzanine showing the history of Bohuslän in photographs. The main exhibition on the first floor depicts the province's natural environment, the life of the fisher folk, farmers, town dwellers, quarrymen and other industrial workers through the centuries in a series of tableaux.

EXCURSION

★ **Gustafsberg** – *4.5km to the south by road E 6.* The drive provides splendid views of the fjord on the way to the charming village of Gustafsberg, a time-capsule from another age. The trim, gaily painted, ornate houses date from the village's heyday as a spa in the mid-19C. The baths were closed in 1970 and the spa building has been converted into a youth hostel.

ULRIKSDALS SLOTT ★
Upplands län
Michelin map 985 M 14 or Atlas Europe p 119
Local map see STOCKHOLM: Outskirts

Ulriksdals Slott is attractively set on a small Baltic bay.

Ulriksdals Slott ⊙ – Hans Jakob Kristler built a 2-storey palace in Dutch-Renaissance style between 1639 and 1644. The main building was given two detached single-storey wings, ornately carved doorways and saddleback roofs. In the 1720s Carl Fredrik Adelcrantz gave the palace a distinctly Baroque appearance. The interior decoration dates in part from the reign of King Karl XV (19C) and partly from the reign of King Gustav VI Adolf (1882-1973) who lived here for part of the year. His sitting room was fitted out with furniture by Carl Malmsten.

★ **Slottskapellet** – *Further down towards the lake.* This 1865 chapel shows a strong oriental influence. The interior is richly decorated with carved and painted ornaments and a fine collection of stained glass from King Karl XV's private collection.

Orangerimuseet ⊙ – *Along the north side of the park.* Nicodemus Tessin the Younger designed the Orangery in 1693. In 1988 it was opened as a museum to house the National Art Gallery's collection of Swedish sculpture from 1700 to the early 20C.

Kröningsekipaget ⊙ – *To the left of the road.* The main attraction in the stables is the carriage used by Queen Christina on her coronation journey to Stockholm in 1650. The carriage itself is a replica whereas the lavish textiles are original.

Confidencen ⊙ – *Across the road.* This building was planned in 1671 as a combined riding school and hostelry. Carl Hårleman redesigned the exterior in the 1740s and soon afterwards Queen Lovisa Ulrika had the interior refurbished as a theatre. The work directed by Carl Fredrik Adelcrantz was completed in 1753 which makes it even older than Drottningholm's Court Theatre (1766). Between May and September concerts, ballets and opera performances are given in the restored theatre.

UMEÅ

Umeå is often referred to as the town of the birches. When the town centre was destroyed by a devastating fire on Midsummer's Eve in 1888 the new urban plan included avenues of birch trees to act as fire breaks. Umeå has Sweden's most northerly university with a Department for Arctic Cultural Research and also has a reputation for its lively theatrical and musical traditions. The **International Festival of Chamber Music** takes place in June and the popular **International Jazz Festival** is held in October.

Gammlia Friluftsmuseum ⊘ – *At the junction of road E 4 with E 12 follow road E 12 eastwards and once under the viaduct turn left and then take the second on the right, Gammliavägen which leads steeply uphill.* This **open-air museum** was first inaugurated in the 1920s. Of particular interest are the farmstead with all its attendant buildings, the Helena Elisabeth Chapel which is popular for weddings and the manor of Sävargården *(now a restaurant)* from Sävar ironworks. The museum is a hive of activity in summer when craftsmen are in residence and the presence of the animals adds an authentic note.

Västerbottens Museum ⊘ – The various museums deal with the cultural heritage and history of Västerbotten. First floor: displays evoke the life of early Swedish settlers in Lapland at the end of the 17C; the seasonal activities of the nomadic Sami; the **Swedish Ski Museum**★ including the world's oldest ski dating from 3 200 BC; hunting and fishing in the Bering Strait based on material collected during the Vega expedition led by the famous explorer AE Nordensköld in 1878-80. The second floor exhibits outline the town's history. The university's Museum of the Graphic Image, **Bildmuseet**, occupies the basement. The low red-wooden building on its own, houses a **Maritime Museum** with sections on seal hunting, the boats used and the hunters' way of life.

At the corner of Storgatan and Östra Kyrkogatan stands the neo-Gothic **kyrka** ⊘ with some unusual 19C German **glass-paintings**★★. The park, **Vänorts parken**, in front of the church regroups benches, lamps and plants from Umeå's twin towns: Petrozavodsk in Russia, Helsingør in Denmark, Vaasa in Finland, Harstad in Norway, Saskatoon in Canada and Würzburg in Germany.

Trädgård i Norr – *Down by the river in front of the town hall.* Five themed gardens demonstrate how even in these northern latitudes – where summer is a fleeting season – plants thrive. The longer hours of daylight compensate for the brief growing season.

UPPSALA★★

Recognized from afar by the silhouettes of its massive red-brick castle and the slender dark spires of its cathedral, Uppsala is the ecclesiastical capital of Sweden and an academic centre with the oldest university in Scandinavia. The west bank of the Fyrisån is dominated by the cathedral, the university and the castle, whereas the east bank has developed as a modern business district. The presence of a large student population (around 20 000) makes this a lively town especially on the **30 April** (Sista April) when they celebrate the arrival of spring.

Uppsala was the birthplace of Ingmar Bergman and the setting for his film *Fanny and Alexander.*

HISTORICAL NOTES

In the 11C Östra Aros (eastern estuary) was a trading post. After the cathedral at Gamla Uppsala was damaged by fire the see was transferred to Östra Aros (1273), a new cathedral was built and the relics of St Erik translated.

CATHEDRAL PRECINCTS

★★**Domkyrkan** ⊘ (BY) – Uppsala Cathedral is Sweden's most famous Gothic creation and was for 300 years Sweden's coronation church. Compared with other European cathedrals of the 13C this one has a remarkably simple layout. Construction probably started around 1270 and progressed slowly until the consecration in 1435. It was Estienne de Bonneuil, a French master mason who gave the cathedral its High Gothic character. The cathedral was destroyed by fire on several occasions. Although rebuilt at the beginning of the 18C it was heavily restored in the late 19C. Some of the original Gothic work is visible in the doorways.

UPPSALA

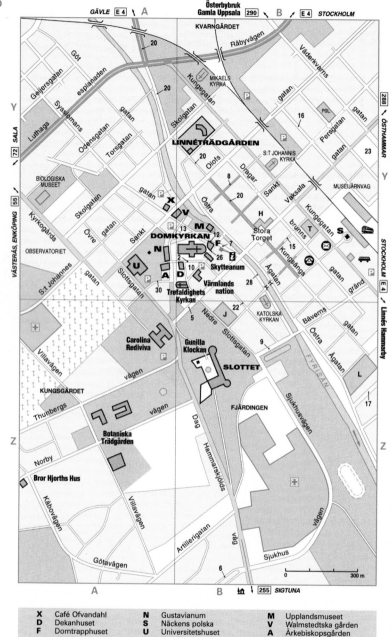

Interior – *Enter by the west door and go in an anticlockwise direction.* The marble **tomb** of the philosopher Emanuel Swedenborg (1688-1772) stands in the second chapel off the south aisle. Both the **Chapel of Prayer** and the **Chapel of Peace** have some fine tapestries. Note the memorial to Dag Hammarskjöld, Secretary General of the United Nations and Nobel Peace Prize winner (1957). Eleven Swedish kings and one queen were crowned under the **Coronation Vault** between 1441 and 1719. The exquisite Baroque **pulpit★★★** (1710) was carved by Burchardt Precht to designs by Nicodemus Tessin the Younger. The resplendent 3m-high **altar cross** in silver and crystal dates from 1976. The medieval **Lady Chapel** is the resting place of King Gustav

Vasa and his first two queens. The tomb chest (1562-83) was executed by the Dutchman Willem Boy. 19C frescoes record important events in the life of Gustav Vasa. The **Finsta Chapel** boasts one of the cathedral's most renowned treasures, the gilt silver **reliquary of St Erik★★★** (1579) the patron saint of Sweden who was killed fighting the Danes in the vicinity of the cathedral. The black marble **tombstone** from Tournai marks the burial place of the parents of St Birgitta. The couple are surrounded by their seven children and Birgitta is on the right at the bottom. The octagonal silver gilt **shrine** (1990) encircled by delicate ironwork contains relics of St Birgitta. In the **Sture Chapel** note the Flemish reredos made in Brussels in 1520. The **Jagellonic Chapel** is the memorial chapel for King Johan III's first queen, the Polish princess, Katarina Jagellonica. The small canopied tomb chest dating

Helga Trefaldighets Kyrka

II. Bohin/EXPLORER

from 1590 was the work of Willem Boy. The marble sculpture of the reclining figure of King Johan is a 16C Dutch work. Note above the memorials of their native cities, Cracow (Kraków) and Stockholm. Note the **tombstone** of Carolus Linnaeus.

★★ Museum ⊘ – *In the porch take the lift to the left.* The north tower houses an outstanding collection of rare textiles (12C-20C), church vestments, the royal burial regalia from the Vasa tombs and the Sture costume of the murder *(see Slottsruinen below).* A gold embroidered brocade robe dated 1400 is said to have belonged to Queen Margrethe, the ruler of the united kingdoms of Denmark, Norway and Sweden. Two of the chasubles are attributed to Albertus Pictor who was also known to be a pearl embroiderer.

Walk round the south side of the cathedral and past the east end.

The seven **rune stones** on the right have 11C inscriptions. The building on the right, **Skytteanum (BY)**, incorporates part of the medieval town wall with visible traces of a former gateway. The late-13C tower, **Domtrapphuset (BY F)**, straight ahead was also part of the town wall.

Go down the steps (Domtrappan) and then turn immediately right onto Valvagatan. Continue along this narrow lane passing through an arched passageway formed by Skytteanum.

Exactly 12 of the 13 student clubs, representing different Swedish regions, are to be found on the west bank and their elaborate 19C architecture adds interest to the area. Beyond the 17C Oxenstiernska huset is the Värmland Student Club, **Värmlands nation (BY)**, which was designed in 1930 by Ragnar Östberg, the architect of Stockholm's famous Stadshuset.

As you climb up Biskopsgatan pass on the left stands the Dean's House, **Dekanhuset (BY D)**, and then the Archbishop's House, **Ärkebiskopsgården (AY A)**.

Helga Trefaldighets kyrka – Holy Trinity Church was built on the site of an earlier wooden church and was finished in c 1343; the west front tower was a 14C addition. The paintings in the old porch and the transepts are said to be by Albertus Pictor and his pupils.

Gustavianum ⊘ **(AY N)** – *Enter from University Park.* The Gustavianum, named after its benefactor King Gustav II Adolf, was built on the site of the medieval episcopal palace and served as university buildings from the 1620s to 1887. The distinctive feature is the sun-crested cupola which throws light onto an **anatomy theatre★★** (1663) devised for public dissections by the naturalist and medical scientist

Anatomy Theatre, Gustavianum

Olof Rudbeck (1630-1702). The **Museum Gustavianum** presents an exhibition on the history of the university as well as a section on Swedish prehistory and the Middle Ages. Also on view is the famous **Augsburg Cabinet of Curiosities★★** gifted to King Gustav II Adolf in 1632 by the city of Augsburg. This elaborate ebony cabinet, encrusted with gem stones, had many drawers and pigeon-holes and was intended for the display of precious objects.

★Universitetshuset ⊘ **(AY U)** – The University of Uppsala was founded in 1477 by Archbishop Jakob Ulvsson and it was initially administered by the Catholic Church and specialised in higher education for the clergy. It was closed in 1515 because of political unrest. The Gustavianum served as the university building from the 1620s to 1887 when the present building was inaugurated. The entrance hall and lecture theatre are worth a visit.

University Park – Lying in front of the building, this park has several rune stones and a **statue** of **Erik Gustaf Geijer**, historian and poet, who was professor at the university from 1816 to 1847.

Walk down Sankt Olofsgatan towards Sysslomansgatan.

Across the street is the **Café Ofvandahls (AY X)**, a favourite meeting place for students since the beginning of the last century.
Nearby is **Walmstedtska gården** ⊘ **(ABY V)**, the late-19C home (six rooms and kitchen) of a university professor.

Upplandsmuseet ⊘ **(BY M)** – The Uppland Museum occupies the university's old watermill. This local museum has sections on the medieval town, the cathedral and student life. The folk exhibits include two items typical of Uppland, a keyharp and rya rugs.

Sankt Eriks gränd leads back to Domtrappan.

Famous alumni

In the 17C and 18C the university boasted such famous graduates and professors as Olof Rudbeck (1630-1702) naturalist, author and medical scientist, Anders Celsius (1701-44) known for his invention of the Celsius thermometer (1742) and Carl von Linné. Other famous students included Emmanuel Swedenborg (1688-1772) and August Strindberg (1849-1912).

ADDITIONAL SIGHTS

Carolina Rediviva ⊘ **(AZ)** – The University Library is Sweden's largest with more than two million volumes and 30 000 manuscripts. Its greatest treasure *(on display to the right of the entrance)* is the famous Silver Bible **Codex Argenteus★★**, written in silver and gold letters on 187 leaves of purple parchment about AD 520 in Ravenna. Other valuable items are the *Codex Uppsaliensis*, which is the oldest manuscript of Snorre Sturlasson's *Edda*, around 1300. *Carta Marina*, a map of the northern seas printed in Venice in 1539, was drawn by Olaus Magnus, Sweden's last Catholic archbishop.

★Slottet ⊘ **(BZ)** – When King Gustav Vasa began building this castle he had just broken with the Catholic Church and wished to emphasise his own power by building his fortress on the ridge overlooking the cathedral. It was a royal custom to be crowned in the cathedral and to celebrate the event in the castle, which was also the scene of Queen Christina's abdication in 1654. Gustav Vasa's sons turned the castle into a royal residence. The castle suffered two major fires and the present appearance dates from 1757 when Carl Hårleman redesigned the exterior.

Today the county governor occupies part of the building. The Hall of State, **Rikssalen**, was restored by Ragnar Östberg and it is now popular for banquets and other festivities.

Slottsruinen – These ruins are all that remain of Gustav Vasa's original fortress. A dramatic event took place in 1567 when King Erik XIV in a fit of rage had members of several important families imprisoned in the castle's dungeons then put to death. The event is called the **Sture Murders** after three of the victims. Several tableaux with waxwork figures recreate scenes from 1567. The Gunilla bell, **Gunilla-klockan**, is named after King Johan III's second wife. She gifted the bell to the castle chapel and today the bell plays an important part in the celebrations of 30 April when the students gather and welcome spring with a speech and songs.

Botaniska Trädgården ○ (AZ) – *West of the castle.* Olof Rudbeck laid out this palace garden in 1670, and Carl Hårleman remodelled it after the French manner in the 18C. In 1787 it became the university's botanic garden.

★**Linnéträdgården** ○ (BY) – *Svartbäcksgatan 27.* The residence of **Carolus Linnaeus** – Carl von Linné – (1707-78), father of our system of botanical classification, is now a museum adjoining his own botanical garden with 1 600 different plants. Originally this botanical garden belonged to the university and was laid out by Olof Rudbeck in c 1655. The plants in the two sections on either side of the central path are arranged in 44 beds according to Linnaeus' system with annuals on one side and perennials on the other. When he was appointed Professor of Medicine and Botany in 1741 he persuaded the university to extend the garden and build the orangery, which Carl Hårleman designed.

Bror Hjorths Hus ○ (AZ) – *Norbyvägen 26, west of the botanical gardens.* **Bror Hjorth** (1894-1968) is one of Sweden's best-known 20C artists. His sculptures and naive, expressive oil paintings in bright colours clearly show that he was inspired by Swedish folk art and African sculpture. The works on display throughout the house and studio include the sketches for the altarpiece of the church in Jukkasjärvi.

The artist's monumental bronze, **Näckens polska**★ (BY S), provides a striking splash of colour in front of Central Station. According to popular belief the spirit Näcken lives in rivers and streams to make the water sing. Näcken is seen playing his fiddle while Huldran the Siren of the Woods listens to his music. On top two young people are dancing a country reel; the erotic undertones of the work have been the subject of lively discussions.

EXCURSIONS

★★**Gamla Uppsala** – *5km to the north by road 290* (BY) *in the direction of Österbybruk.*

The burial mounds were the graves of chieftains or princes from the pre-Viking Ynglinga dynasty. King Egil and the three princes Aun, Egil and Ådil are mentioned in the opening passages of *Beowulf.* Around 1070 Adam of Bremen gave a detailed description of the pagan temple on the site, however, by 1130 the episcopal see at Sigtuna was transferred to Gamla Uppsala where it remained until 1273 when it was again transferred to nearby Östra Aros, later known as Uppsala.

The present-day church probably stands on the site of the pagan temple.

The archaeological site includes the three **Royal Mounds**★★★ and the very eroded Court or Thing Mound (Tingshögen to the east) but also 250-300 graves.

Linnés Hammarby ○ – *13km. Leave by Kungsgatan* (BY). *Turn onto road 282 in the direction of Edsbro. After 3km turn right towards the Danmark Church. From there an old village road winds its way to Linnés Hammarby.*

Linnaeus' 18C country estate is surrounded by flower beds, shrubs and trees tended by the great botanist himself. The house has little of the original furniture although the study still has evidence of his scientific work. Copies of some of his most famous works *Flora Lapponica* (1737, translated in English as *Lachesis Lapponica* 1811), *The Journey to Scanica* and *Species Plantarum* (1753) are on view. Many of his students used to visit him at his summer home and Linnaeus held impromptu lectures in the pavilion north of the house where he held forth from a peculiar rostrum called the study horse to his enraptured audience. His manuscripts and herbarium are now preserved by the Linnean Society at Burlington House in London.

★★**Vallonbruken** – **Walloon Ironworks of Uppland** – *See ROSLAGEN.*

Härkeberga Kyrka ○ – *38km south-west of Uppsala by road 55 then a local road.* The **mural paintings**★★★ by **Albertus Pictor** (fl 1445-1507) attract people from near and far to this medieval church. The paintings date from the end of the 15C when brick vaulting replaced the original wooden ceiling. Contrary to other churches, where the paintings were whitewashed, these are extremely well preserved and are considered to be some of the finest examples of the painter's work. His style is realistic and although the figures are powerful and vigorous the work expresses a delicate sensitivity. The paintings bring to life legends and biblical scenes in a well-established order with the Trinity above the altar, Mary and Christ's childhood in the chancel, events from the Old Testament on the vaulting of the nave and the Passion of Christ on the walls whereas the porch is often reserved for moralising tales and scenes with the devil. The colours have darkened with the passage of time.

Albertus Pictor (fl 1455-1507)

Albert the Painter, as he was sometimes called in Sweden, was a painter and embroiderer who decorated more than 30 churches in the provinces of Uppland, Södermanland and Västmanland in the late Middle Ages. He had a large workshop and no doubt employed several journeymen and apprentices on his numerous projects. The lively, expressive paintings, in a new realistic style, portrayed scenes from the Old and New Testaments; the woodcuts in *The Poor Man's Bible* no doubt provided the main source of inspiration. Unfortunately many of these paintings were whitewashed in the 17C and 18C and the rare examples of Pictor's work which remain are a highly prized part of Sweden's heritage. The church at Härkeberga has some of the best paintings.

VADSTENA ★

Östergötlands län
Population 7 700
Michelin map 985 N 11 or Atlas Europe p 118

Sweden's patron saint, St Birgitta, brought fame to this charming little town, on the shore of Lake Vättern, which was to become an important pilgrimage centre in the Middle Ages earning itself the name of Rome of the north.

Take the time to wander round the medieval town centre with its narrow streets and many delightful buildings and make a stop in Storgatan at the shop with a collection of local handmade lace.

St Birgitta or Bridget (1303-73) – Birgitta was of noble birth, a daughter of the royal Folkunga dynasty and lady in waiting to Blanche of Namur, queen to Magnus Eriksson from whom she received a royal seat. Birgitta was mother to eight children. After the death of her husband in 1344 she decided to start a new life and it was during a stay in Alvastra, beside the monastery, that she had the vision of her vocation (1344-49). In 1349 at the time of the Black Death she travelled to Rome where, with the exception of a pilgrimage to the Holy Land, she spent the rest of her life.

St Birgitta was a woman of outstanding willpower and great vitality who campaigned for the return of the popes to Rome, dictated her revelations to her confessors and established the rules for the new monastic order. This was approved by Papal Bull in 1370 three years before her death. Her canonisation was pronounced in 1391 and three years later she was declared Sweden's patron saint.

The Bridgettine Order – Birgitta had decided quite early on that the site of her first convent for both men and women would be her property in Vadstena. Building work began seriously in the 1360s but the church was only consecrated in 1430. Birgitta's daughter Katarina was abbess when the convent was consecrated in 1384. The convent flourished and daughter houses were founded in other Scandinavian countries (Mariebo and Mariager in Denmark and Nådendal in Finland) as well as other European countries (England, Germany, Netherlands and France).

The Bridgettine houses in the Nordic countries were dissolved at the Reformation with the exception of Vadstena. Persecution began in 1543 and the convent was dissolved by royal decree several years later (1585 or 1595) when the last members fled south to Germany or Poland. Birgittine nuns returned in 1935 and a new convent was established in 1973 and 1992 saw the first consecration of nuns in the church since the Reformation. Today there are three branches of the order: a medieval branch, a Spanish one and a modern one (created in 1911) often referred to as the Hesselblad branch. The first and the third have daughter houses in the Nordic countries.

Today the Church of Sweden uses the abbey church.

ABBEY AND PRECINCTS

Leave Stora Torget to the north by Torggatan which leads onto Lasarettsgatan.

★★★ **Klosterkyrkan – of plain construction, humble and strong** ⊘ – The plan specified a nave with a narrow chancel, which oddly enough lies to the west. The lack of ornamental decoration recalls the simple but expressive style of the Cistercian order. The abbey church is built of blueish limestone from Omberg and the tall windows and sturdy buttresses are the only ornaments to a plain exterior. The spacious interior leaves a powerful impression. The beautiful star vaulting is supported by octagonal limestone pillars. The church is known for its collection of **late medieval sculptures.** Two of these, placed against pillars at the entrance to the nave, depict St Birgitta: the one on the left the **Portrait Birgitta** and on the right **St Birgitta in ecstasy** which was very popular with pilgrims. The Brussels altarpiece (c 1520) at the high altar, represents the Assumption and Coronation of the Virgin and is an outstanding work of art. The **Birgitta Triptych** showing St Birgitta presenting her revelations to two cardinals was made in Lübeck in 1459 whereas the **Birgitta Reliquary** (behind the high altar) dates from the time of her canonisation in 1391. The translation of Birgitta's remains took place in 1393, 20 years after her death.

Bjälboättens Palats ⊘ – *To the north of the abbey church.* This was the original property, gifted to Birgitta by King Magnus Eriksson, around which she built her convent. Birger Jarl had built the palace in the 1250s which became the seat of the Bjälbo family. Following the dissolution of the convent these buildings served various purposes and today they house a hotel and conference centre. The chapterhouse, dormitory with a small exhibition and **Birgitta's Prayer Room** on the first floor can be visited during a guided tour.

Slottet ⊘ – It is ironic that Gustav Vasa the first Lutheran king and instigator of the dissolution of the monasteries should have chosen Vadstena as the site for his Renaissance palace which his sons embellished. Its stout walls and moat did stalwart service during the Nordic Seven Years War (1563-70) and only time and decay caused its ruin.

15C statue of St Birgitta

VARBERG ★

Hallands län
Population 52 000
Michelin map 985 O 9 or Atlas Europe p 123

Already in the Middle Ages the fortified town of Varberg played a strategic role but its importance increased when it became a link in the formidable frontier defences of Denmark. The town was moved to its present site following a fire in 1666, the year of the Great Fire of London. In the 19C Varberg found fame as a fashionable spa and bathing resort. Today there are ferry connections with Grenå in Denmark.

Varberg School – Three artists, **Richard Bergh** (1858-1919), **Nils Kreuger** (1858-1930) and **Karl Nordström** (1855-1923), influenced by Gauguin and Van Gogh worked at Varberg between 1893 and 1896. The three artists had been firm friends since they had studied together at the Fine Arts Academy in Stockholm and they had been part of the Swedish artists colony at Grèz-sur-Loing in France. The symbolism and the synthetism of Gauguin provided the catalyst for their work as a group in Varberg and greatly influenced the artists of the Swedish National Romantic movement at the turn of the last century. A room in the Varbergs Museum *(see below)* is devoted to the work of these artists.

Reminders of times past – Among the reminders of its days as a fashionable spa are the **Societetsparken** *(to the west of the railway)* which is still the venue for summer entertainment as in the good old days and the Assembly Rooms, **Societetshuset**, now used as a restaurant and an exhibition hall. The **bathhouse** has been refurbished and visitors can now enjoy warm saltwater baths. **Apelviken**, just out of town, is where they first took the waters and today it is the place for seaweed baths. The cold water **bathhouse** is the rectangular wooden building quartered with Moorish cupolas down by the shore, to the right of the fortress.

On Wednesdays and Saturdays the **main square** is the scene of a lively market where as in the past flowers and vegetables are to be found alongside displays of the colourful fabrics from the local weaving mills. In the 19C travelling salesmen *(knallar)* traded in these textiles. The statue in the centre of the square called *Bathing Youth* was the work of Bror Marklund.

Visitors may join **fishing boats** on their trips to the deeper waters of the Kattegatt. In summer one of the warehouses down by the harbour comes to life as a **workshop**, Västkusthyttan, for handmade glassware.

★ VARBERG FORTRESS

The first fortification on the rocky promontory dated from the 1280s; it was enlarged in the 14C and became a royal stronghold under King Magnus. The castle suffered greatly during the struggle for Baltic supremacy between Denmark and Sweden but it was the Danish king, Christian IV who commissioned Hans van Steenwinckel the Elder to build an Italian Renaissance fortress complete with bastions and ramparts between 1595 and 1617. This popular Dutch architect was responsible for other strongholds in the Danish line of defence: Halmstad and Bohus as well as Akershus in Norway. With the signing of the Treaty of Roskilde in 1658 the castle was ceded to Sweden and with the loss of its strategic importance it soon fell into disrepair. It then served as a prison from 1848 to 1881.

Fortress ⊙ – Once through the lower gateway on the left is a small **Kommunikationsmuseet** ⊙ in what was King Karl XI's stables and officers' quarters, now private homes. The yellow building to the right was built in the mid-19C to serve as a prison and now does service as a youth hostel where hostellers can try a cell for the night. The 1612 middle gateway leads to the inner courtyard.

Länsmuseet Varberg ⊙ – *The museum occupies the north and west wings of the castle.* In the King's Hall, which is now used for temporary exhibitions of arts and crafts, the Nordic kings met in 1343. Highlights include the bullet that is said to have killed Karl XII at Fredrikhald Fortress in Norway in 1718 and the **Bocksten Bog Man★** with his medieval clothes (1360). He was found in 1936 perfectly preserved by the peat. Another room is devoted to the Varberg School *(see above)* and glassware by some of Sweden's foremost glass artists Simon Grate, Ulrika Hydman-Vallien and Edvin Öhrström.

EXCURSIONS

Apelviken – *3km to the south. Leave by Västra Vallgatan.* This very popular beach can be reached on foot *(4km)* by a path which starts just south of the fortress and follows the curve of the bay. Pass on the way the Kurorten Hotel where seaweed baths or therapy can still be enjoyed. A little further on you come to the great sandy beach.

Getterön – *4.5km to the north. Take Hamnvägen to the west of the railway line through an industrial zone before following signposts for Getteröns naturcentrum to the left.* Over 300 different bird species have been observed on this nature reserve which is internationally known to ornithologists. Between 1 April and 15 July only the observation tower and the nature exhibition, Naturum, are open to the public.

VÄSTERÅS ★

Västmanlands län
Population 124 000
Michelin map 985 M 13 or Atlas Europe p 119
Local map see STOCKHOLM: Outskirts

SWEDEN

The commercial and administrative centre of Västerås enjoys a strategic location on lake Mälaren with boat connections to Strängnäs and to other islands and sites in and around the lake (Birka, Tidö Slott and Engsö Slott). The town also lies on the King's Road which links Oslo to St Petersburg and in so doing crosses Norway, Sweden, Finland and Russia.

An early trading settlement was founded on the estuary of the River Svartån and given the name of Västra Aros (western estuary), later simplified to Västerås. With the growth of copper and iron mining in the Bergslagen area (centre of Swedish mining) Västerås soon developed as an important port for exporting ores and by the end of the Middle Ages it was one of Sweden's most important cities. In 1527 Gustav Vasa summoned the *riksdag* to meet in Västerås, sometimes known as the first Reformation Parliament, where he submitted his plan to curtail the powers of the church and to redistribute the wealth of the church.

> ### The Reformation in Sweden
>
> Following his participation in the Stockholm Bloodbath (1520) the hated archbishop of Uppsala, Gustav Trolle, fled in the footsteps of his master King Christian II to exile in the Low Countries. In the summer of 1523 Gustav Vasa was elected king and his early reign was plagued by troublesome subjects and tussles with the church leadership. In his effort to eliminate ecclesiastical power Gustav Vasa chose to nominate Swedish bishops. Pope Clement VII retaliated by negotiating for the reinstatement of the hated archbishop. The king's refusal finalised the break with Rome. In 1527 he summoned the *riksdag* to meet in Västerås (later known as the first Reformation Parliament) where he submitted a lengthy proposition to drastically curtail the powers of the church and redistribute its wealth. A year later the Council of Örebro adopted Lutheranism as the established religion of Sweden.

Domkyrkoplatsen – Cathedral square is dominated by the statue of the 17C bishop of Västerås, Johannes Rudbeckius, by Carl Milles and bordered by the bishop's residence and Sweden's first school which was founded in 1623.

★★★ **Domkyrkan** ⊙ – The cathedral was built in the 13C but subsequent additions and alterations have modified its initial aspect. The spire was by Nicodemus Tessin the Younger. Of particular interest amid the wealth of memorials are the black Carrara marble monument *(south side of the ambulatory)* on a base of red Öland sandstone to King Erik XIV and the imposing Brahe Mausoleum in black and white marble with its figures in alabaster, the last resting place of the count of Visingsö and his wives. There are three excellent Flemish altarpieces: in the large baptismal chapel from Antwerp (early 16C); at the high altar from Antwerp and in the Chapel of the Apostles by Jan Borman in Brussels (c 1500). The paintings on the base are by Jan van Coninxloo also from Brussels. The triumphal crucifix is early 14C.

To the north is the district known as **Kyrkbacken**, or church hill, full of character with wooden buildings once the home of craftsmen and workers.

Fiskartorget – The **Rådhuset** with its unusual bell-tower stands on the site of a 13C Dominican Monastery which was destroyed at the Reformation. The chimes of the bells are in contrast to the sonorous sounds of the cathedral's bells. The golden *Bull*, placed on high on a column to the left, symbolises force whereas *The Cave of the Winds*, in front of the main entrance, is by Eric Grate (1896-1983). The old court house next door dates from the 1850s, and now houses Västerås **Konstmuseum** ⊙ with an interesting display of mainly Swedish 20C art.

Take the footbridge to cross the river.

Turbinhuset ⊙ – The small brick Turbine house was built in 1891 and a year later it was equipped with three turbines and put into operation by the electrical engineering company Asea. In 1988 Asea merged with the Swiss company Brown Boveri to form the multinational group Asea Brown Boveri.

Västerås Slott ⊙ – *Slottsgatan, on the west bank of the river.* The original 13C fortress was strategically sited at the mouth of the river. It has been remodelled on several occasions and what we see today is the result of Hårleman's work in 1737. It once served as the county governor's residence and today it houses the **Västmanlands läns Museum** ⊙ *(enter from the courtyard)* with interesting historical displays. The public can visit the Hall of State.

EXCURSIONS

★ Anundshög and Engsö slott – *East by road E 18. After 5km turn off in the direction of Badelunda.*

★ Anundshög – This remarkable burial ground has Sweden's largest burial mound – 14m high and 60m across the base – which probably dates from AD 400-700. The two **stone ship settings** 53m and 50m long respectively and three smaller settings all date from AD 1 000. In the Middle Ages (1050-1500) when the site became the meeting place for the people's court *(tingvalla)* the king arrived by the old road (Eriksgata) lined with **rune stones** and rows of smaller stones when travelling between the western estuary (Västra Aros means Västerås) and the eastern estuary (Östra Aros means Uppsala).

Return to road E 18 and continue for another 20km.

★ Engsö Slott ⏱ – A castle was originally built on the island site in the 1480s and extended in the 1630s but it was Carl Hårleman's (1700-53) rebuilding that gave it its present aspect. He added a fourth storey, two new wings and laid out the park, all in the Rococo style. The 14C **chapel** with its beautiful 14C murals also has a Hårleman addition, the cupola.

Engsö Naturreservat ⏱ – The nature reserve covering several islands in Lake Mälaren through its visitor centre, **naturum**, describes the evolution of the local landscapes from the isostatic uplift to the evolution of crofting communities and their farming methods.

Friluftsmuseum ⏱ – *5km to the west by road E 18 then follow signposts to Vallby.* This open-air museum with some 40 houses and cottages from various parts of Västmanland recreates life in the past (17C-19C).

Tidö Slott ⏱ – *13km to the south-west of Västerås.* This 17C palace on the banks of Lake Mälaren was another of the great residences built when Sweden was a Great Power. It was the chancellor Axel Oxenstierna who commissioned the building in 1625.

The Carriage Museum, **Vagnmuseet★**, is an outstation of the Royal Armoury in Stockholm. It displays a collection of state coaches, funeral carriages and elegant equipages from the 18C and 19C. Many were made in the carriage workshops run by the royal stables.

★ Sala Silvergruva ⏱ – *37km north, 2km from the town.* The silver mine was worked for 400 years, until 1908. The mine belonged to the Crown and, in the 16C, King Gustav Vasa personally supervised its improvement. During the next three centuries, new shafts were opened and, in the 1830s, the deepest shaft reached 318m. There are guided tours (1-2hr) to different levels (40m and 60m) and various shafts and galleries are explored. The admission charge includes a film and a visit to the mining museum.

VÄTTERN ★

Michelin map 985 N-O 11 or Atlas Europe pp 118-119

Europe's fifth largest lake, and Sweden's second largest lake after Lake Vänern, at almost 2 000km², is clear, deep (max depth 128m) and cold. Road E 4 follows the east shore and provides breathtaking views across the lake. It is notorious for rough water when strong winds blow.

EAST SHORE From Jönköping to Motala

112km – by E 4 motorway to just south of Ödeshög and then road 50 beyond.

★ Gränna – This delightful village with its cobbled streets and painted wooden houses is known for its **striped peppermint rock** *(polkagrisar)*, which the visitor can still see being made. Gränna is also home to the **Andrée Museum** with a display of items from the Swedish scientist, Salomon August Andrée's (1854-97) intrepid attempt to fly over the North Pole in a balloon in 1897. The flight ended in disaster and the three balloonists perished trying to walk back to civilization. Their frozen bodies and other items were found 33 years later on Spitzbergen. Gränna has become the main ballooning centre in Sweden.

★ Visingsö – *25min by ferry from Gränna harbour.* This charming agricultural island was a political centre in the 12C and 13C. From 1561 to 1680 the local countship of Visingsborg was in the hands of the Brahe family. To the right of the harbour are the ruins of the Brahe family seat, **Visingsborg Castle.** Further north **Brahe kyrka** was begun in 1564 by Count Magnus Brahe and completed in 1636 by his grandson Per

Brahe the Younger. The church treasures many items belonging to this famous family. **Kumlaby kyrka** dating from 1135 with a typical nave, chancel and apse layout is simple and beautiful.
The terrace affords a good viewpoint *(18 dark narrow steps followed by 60 wider and better-lit ones)*.

9km north of Gränna by road E 4.

Per Brahe the Younger built a country retreat, **Brahehus**, for his wife in 1650 using stone from Alvastra Monastery. Standing as it does on a clifftop it provides good views of Visingsö and the other family properties.

Continue on road E 4 then turn left for Rökstenen.

★ **Rökstenen** – *It stands quite close to road E 4.* This famous Rök rune stone, erected in 9C AD in memory of a Viking chief's son, carries a long and complicated runic inscription. The adjoining exhibition gives some explanations in Swedish.

Alvastra klosterruin – Only ruins remain of the monastery founded by the Cistercians in 1143 close to the mountain of Omberg. Sweden's first monastic community prospered to become the richest and most powerful Cistercian monastery. Following the Dissolution the stones were carried away as building material.

Strand – This house attractively set on the shore of Lake Vättern was the home of the feminist writer **Ellen Key** (1849-1926) who was one of the first to call for women's suffrage.

Omberg – 10km long, 3km wide and 263m high, this ridge ends in a scarp face which drops vertically into the lake.

Motala – The Östergötland section of the Göta canal starts in Motala where Von Platen is buried.

VÄXJÖ

Kronobergs län
Population 73 000
Michelin map 985 P 11 or Atlas Europe p 123

Växjö, in the heart of the wooded wilderness of Småland, was an episcopal see as early as the 12C. Today Växjö organises a series of festivities for visiting Swedish-Americans on **Minnesota Day**.

★★ **Utvandrarnas Hus** ⊘ – The Swedish Emigrant Institute was founded in 1965 and took possession of its custom-built home three years later with ample space for the largest European archives on emigration and a library of more than 25 000 volumes. 1846 to 1930 were the years of the great exodus when 1.3 million people, almost one quarter of the population, left Sweden for America. The majority came from the stony and infertile province of Småland.

The Kaboka service by Ulrica Hydman-Vallien, Kosta Boda

Documents and books from the archives and library and a database can be consulted in the reading room where the staff are happy to assist *(small research fee for non-members)*. Various displays cover the many aspects of Swedish emigration to North America, Australia and European countries. One room is the study of **Vilhelm Moberg** (1898-1973), the Småland-born writer who told the story of some of the early emigrants in four *Emigrant* novels, which have been translated into many languages. The sculpture by Axel Olson shows two of the novels' most famous characters Karl-Oskar and Kristina. Carl Milles' fountain is a tribute to the emigrants (copy of the one in Karlshamn).

Smålands museum ⊘ – *Next to the House of Emigrants*. Pride of place goes to the comprehensive **glass collection★★★** presented both chronologically and alphabetically. There is also an interesting collection of coins and medals.

Domkyrkan ⊘ – The cathedral was largely rebuilt in 1958-60 in an attempt to recreate its medieval appearance. The contemporary furnishings are of particular interest especially the bronze cross (formed by 11 plates) which reflects the light streaming through the purple stained-glass windows. The golden mosaic at the far end of the south transept is the work of the artist Bo Beskow. Look for the spot on the floor of the nave which marks the burial place of St Sigfrid (d 1045), a missionary sent by King Ethelred of England to evangelise the Norwegians and Swedes.

★ GLASRIKET (THE GLASS KINGDOM)

Sweden enjoys a worldwide reputation in glass design and production and Småland is Sweden's glass-making country. Fifteen firms are located deep in the forests between Nybro and Växjö. Many of them started as ironworks which explains the traditional layout *(bruksmiljön)*. Most of the glassworks have developed their own unique style.

Most glassworks welcome visitors Mondays to Fridays 9am to 3pm to watch the skilled glass-blowers twirling the red-hot glowing bulbs of molten glass. The seconds shops are a good place to look for that special souvenir or gift. The following is a selection of glassworks.

★★ Orrefors ⊘ – *Road 31, 17km north-west of Nybro*. Since the establishment of the glassworks here in 1898 production has been concentrated on classical design in full lead crystal and decorative items in colour with an advanced design. Orrefors was one of the first companies to employ designers and they were soon to become one of the world's most renowned glassworks. Two of the artists who were active at the beginning of the last century were Simon Gate the portrait and landscape painter and Edvard Hald who had worked with Matisse. An exhibition outlines the Gate-Hald period.

★★ Åfors ⊘ – *Road 25, 33km west of Nybro. After Eriksmåla follow signposts for Åfors. Showroom and shop*. Three designers with very different styles have left their stamp on Åfors glass: Gunnel Sahlin whose creations are a symphony of colour and shape; Ulrika Hydman-Vallien whose works of art are to be found in art galleries throughout the world; and her husband Bertil Vallien who is best-known for his sand-cast glass sculptures.

★ Kosta Boda ⊘ – *Road 28, 42km north-west of Nybro. Go right through the village of Kosta. Showroom and shop*. The Kosta glassworks were founded by two generals, Koskull and Staël von Holstein, (the name derives from the first letters of the founders' names) and date from 1742 which makes them the oldest. Their output ranges from artistic pieces to high-quality tableware.

★ Strömbergshyttan – *30km east of Växjö by road 25*. Here visitors may watch the delicate art of hand painting in Lindblom's glass painting studio. Beyond the silversmith's red cottage in the distance is a lovely Doll Museum. To the left is **Studioglas Strömbergshyttan** ⊘ where there is an exciting display of the audacious pieces produced in the workshops.

Lessebo – *42km east of Växjö by road 25. Continue right through the village until you come to a yellow and red-stone building on the left*. The people of Småland are also known for their skill in papermaking. In this paper mill, where handmade paper has been manufactured in essentially the same way since 1693, a guided tour takes visitors through the different stages of production. The guided tour ends in the showroom with a manuscript of August Strindberg, who preferred handmade paper.

YSTAD ★

Skåne län
Population 26 000
Michelin map 985 Q 10 or Atlas Europe p 123

Ystad is an enchanting medieval town with over 300 half-timbered houses and the ferry port for Bornholm.

Medieval town – Start from Lilla Västergatan, once the main route into town, noting on the way **Kemmerska Gården**, parts of which date from the 16C. Stortorget is over-looked by **Sankta Maria kyrka** ⊘ a 13C Romanesque basilica with numerous subsequent alterations. Interesting features include the sumptuously decorated altarpiece (1733) and the remarkable Renaissance **pulpit★★** by a north German craftsman.

The town watchman still blows his horn *(lur)* on every quarter from 9.15pm until 3am and the fire watch still watches over the sleeping town.

Also on the square is the **Latinska skolan** c 1500, a late 18C half-timbered house, Krookshuset which is painted yellow and **Gamla Rådhuset** completed in 1840. Take Stora Norregatan north to Sladdergatan where on the left is **Änglahus** with its 1630s street front. Diagonally opposite stands the 15C **Brahehus**. Sladdergatan on the right leads to the 13C hall-church, **Sankt Petrikyrkan**, which was once part of the Franciscan monastery. The friars were expelled at the Reformation (1530s) and today the cloisters house the **Ystads Stadsmuseum** ⊘ with a local history section and attractive display on bridal costumes (18C-19C) with their silver decorations. A narrow lane, Bäckahästgränd, leads to the town's smallest square, Tvättorget, surrounded by half-timbered houses. In the pedestrian Stora Östergatan, note on the right the stepped gables of **Birgittahuset**. At the corner of Pilgränd is the oldest half-timbered house, **Pilgrändsgård**, dating from the 1480s. Continue south to Sankt Knuts Torg and the **Ystads Konstmuseum** ⊘ with a representative collection of Swedish and Danish 19C and 20C art as well as a military section.

ÖLAND ★

Kalmar län
Population 24 000
Michelin map 985 O-P 13 or Atlas Europe p 123

Sweden's smallest province is the island of Öland which presents an unbroken horizon as it stretches 140km along the mainland coast. The 14km-wide island is connected to the mainland by a magnificent new bridge *(see below)* which is an important link for the many islanders who work in Kalmar.

Agriculture is still the main source of income and endless limestone walls enclose and separate fields and farms. Many islanders fish for their own requirements and commercial fishing only began in the 20C. Limestone quarries appear here and there but it is tourism which has become one of the most important sources of income and the annual summer invasion of tourists is not without causing a strain on the island and some congestion. The west coast all along road 136 is where all the holiday homes and tourist facilities are concentrated.

Windmills are a characteristic feature of the island which is known as the Island of the Sun and Winds and only 400 remain of the 2 000 which existed in the 19C. The post mill, where the body turns with the sails round a heavy wooden post, is the most common type.

Nature – The island is a great limestone plateau with thin soil and the south is known for the Stora Alvaret a great expanse of treeless heath known for its rather barren aspect. It is however an area of interesting flora known for the many orchids which flourish here and the yellow *potentilla fruticosa (Ölandstok)* and the Öland Rock Rose *(Ölands solvända)* which when they flower in late spring and early summer form a brightly coloured carpet. The latter flower is the emblem of Öland.

History – The island is known for its immense Iron Age forts, 15 in all, but only a few have been fully excavated. These ring-forts served as a place of refuge in times of unrest and possibly also as a place of ceremonies and meetings. Some of the forts (Eketorp and Gråborg) were still in use during the medieval period.

Island delicacy – Öland flounder served fresh or smoked.

Sightseeing on Öland

Although cars now cross without difficulty, it is an island to take at a leisurely pace, ideally by bicycle. Start with the visitor centre, **Träffpunkten Öland** ⊘ which combines the Tourist Information Centre, the historium with a 12min-slide show and short historical commentary *(in English and German)*. The naturum identifies the special plants worth looking for.

SWEDEN

★★**Öland Bridge** – With a total length of 6 072m, it straddles Kalmar sound in 155 spans, making it Europe's longest bridge. The bridge was opened in 1972 and from a viewpoint *(parking space)*, 42m above sea level, there is a breathtaking **panorama**.

NORTHWARDS

86km to Byxelkrok by road 136

Halltorps hage – *Follow signpost at Eketorp*. Half way down to the seashore this grove where hornbeam, oaks and hazel trees predominate is the habitat for the rare oak buck.
A tract of heathland or Alvaret stretches away to the right.

★**Borgholms Slottsruin** ⊘ – The ruins of this once mighty castle still rise imposingly over the heathland. Like Kalmar Castle it too guarded the sound and served as Sweden's southernmost outpost against Denmark. The remains of the original fortified circular tower are to be seen in the north-west corner of the inner courtyard. King Johan III built a fortified castle, with four ranges around a courtyard and a stout tower at each corner but it suffered greatly during the Kalmar War (1611-13). Then King Karl X Gustav commissioned Nicodemus Tessin the Elder to remodel the fortress to create a Baroque palace. Building was interrupted in 1709 and a fire in 1806 reduced the rest to ruins.

Solliden ⊘ – This Italianate villa was built between 1903 and 1906 as a summer residence for the royal family. The beautiful park is open to visitors for several hours a day in summer.

★**Borgholm** ⊘ – The island's capital was founded in 1816 when the castle, which gave its name, was already a ruin. The main street Storgatan leads down to the bustling harbour.

Sandvik – *Turn left, 2 km from the main road*. Sandvik is the centre for limestone quarrying. The huge 8-storey windmill, **Sandviks kvarn** ★⊘, has a 24m sail span. Visitors can still marvel at the original wooden mechanism.

Källa kyrka ⊘ – *2km off the main road to the right*. This is the only remaining example of a medieval defensive church with three storeys. The vaulted place of worship on the ground floor had a living area above with the top floor as the ultimate place of refuge.

Byrum Raukar – *Turn left at Högby Church roundabout and after 200m turn right to Byrum*. There is an impressive array of limestone **sea stacks**★ *(raukar)* just offshore.

Böda Kronopark – Road 136 goes through this crown park comprising 6 000ha of primeval conifer trees, many covered with ivy. The splendid sandy **Böda Sand** beach is a paradise for bathers as it curves round Böda Bay on the east side of the island. Offshore the great dome-shaped form of the isle **Blå Jungfrun** rises 86m above sea level making it a well-known landmark in Kalmar Sound. The pink granite rocks polished by glaciers are extremely smooth and inviting.

Neptuni Åkrar – *2km north of Byxelkrok*. Linnaeus gave these raised shingle beaches their name of Neptune's Fields. Today they are covered with the abundantly flowering *echium vulgare (Blåeld)*.

THE EAST COAST AND THE SOUTH

74km south from Borgholm

A gang of seven windmills lines the road in the village of **Störlinge**. However the most attractive ones are to be found at Lerkaka where one might be open to visitors.

★★**Himmelsberga Museum** ⊘ – *23km south-east of Borgholm and 2km off the east road*. Himmelsberga open-air museum is a fine example of a traditional farming village where the courtyard farmsteads lined the main road. Implements, furnishings and household goods are typical of the 18C and 19C.

★★**Ismanstorp** – *5km from the main road and a further 500m on foot from the car park*. This Iron Age fort dating from AD 400 is 125m in diameter. Inside its circular wall, 3-4m high, are the foundations of 88 houses, some standing against the wall and others huddled in an irregular fashion in the centre of the fort. The wall has no less than nine gates which leads archaeologists to believe that it may have been a market place or a cult centre.

★★**Gråborg** – *On the road between Färjestaden and North Möckleby a signpost indicates Gråborg 1km*. The island's largest fortified fort was built in AD 400-500. Its immense walls, up to 6m high and 11m thick describe a circle with a circumference of 640m and a diameter of 200m. The ruins of a chapel dated 1200 stand outside the fort to the north. The arch of a gateway is all that remains of late-13C fortifications.

SWEDEN

★★ **Eketorp** ⊘ – Many years of archaeological research have traced the history of this fort set in the heart of heathland. Three phases of settlement have been revealed which cover 1 000 years of settlement from AD 300 (Migration Period) to 1300. A large section of the outer wall has been rebuilt and visitors can visit houses, byres and storehouses. Archaeologists have also been able to identify the animals that were husbanded at the time. A selection of the many finds brought to light are now on display in the **museum** where simple everyday objects are found alongside skilfully worked jewellery and weapons.

Karl X Gustav's Wall – Beyond the last building in the village of Näsby stands the deer dyke built in the 1650s to keep the deer on the royal estate of Ottenby. The wall stretches, as straight as a die, across the southern tip of the island.

Ottenby – This property, which once belonged to the crown, stretches the whole width of the island.
The oak and birch wood of **Ottenbylund** to the south-east has a herd of fallow-deer whose ancestors were originally imported from England by King Johan III. The grassy meadows and long beaches are the haunt of wading birds (ruff and avocet) and resting places for visitors such as geese, ducks and waders on their spring and autumn migrations.
The southernmost point of the island takes pride in Sweden's tallest lighthouse, **Långe Jan**, 42m high. The climb *(195 steps)* to the top is rewarded by a grand panorama.

Return by the west coast.

Immediately north of Ottenby estate farm is a vast burial ground, also scattered with rune stones, between the road and the coast.
The burial ground 3km to the north of Degerhamn has a great variety of graves, stone ship settings and upright megaliths thus indicating a long period of settlement (1000 BC-AD 1050).

Linnaeus at Eketorp

Linnaeus visited Eketorp on 8 June 1741 during his tour of Öland and described it as follows "Eketorp Fort was visited, with its rough, dilapidated walls, 2.5km from the eastern shore and formerly one of the most magnificent in this country. For it was a musket shot in diameter, with a well in the middle which never dries up. Undoubtedly these forts were places of refuge for the inhabitants, before the invention of powder and shot".

ÖSTERSUND

Jämtlands län
Population 60 000
Michelin map 985 111 or Atlas Europe p 112

Östersund has a perfect location on the shores of Lake Storsjön with the mountains of Oviksfjällen in the background and it can also claim to be not too far from the popular ski resorts of Åre and Storlien. In July the town organises the Chamber Music Festival and the Great Lake Festival (Storsjöyran).

Lake Storsjön – a rival for Nessie – Like Loch Ness in Scotland, Lake Storsjön, the fifth largest stretch of inland water in the country, has its own monster the **Great Lake Monster** (Storsjöodjuret). Many sightings have been recorded and some of the equipment used to try and capture the monster in the 19C is displayed in the museum. Storsjöodjuret has resisted all attempts at capture and now enjoys the status of a protected species since a local law in 1986 made it illegal to kill, injure or capture any of the species in Lake Storsjön. The monster in the shape of an Ö has become the symbol of Östersund. The steamer **S/S Thomée** built in 1875 makes regular sailings on the lake during the summer.

SIGHTS

★★ **Jamtli** ⊘ – *Beside road E 14 in the direction of Trondheim.* This popular open-air museum – with at least 60 buildings – takes visitors back in time to the years 1895 and 1929. Costumed participants, animals, well-tended gardens and crops serve to create an appropriate environment and capture an authentic note.

Jämtlands Läns Museum ⊘ – A brand new building (1995) marked by a 22m-high tower houses the collections which date from 1886. The outstanding item is the remarkable **Överhogdal Tapestry**★★★ woven during the Viking Age (AD 800-1000). It depicts people, deer, reindeer, dogs, four and eight-legged horses, trees, boats and houses.

Open-air museum Jämtli Historieland

The folk art section including strange **fiddle cases**, and the Sami exhibition, focusing mainly on reindeer, are both interesting. There is also the section on the Great Lake Monster *(see above)*.

EXCURSIONS

★★ **Frösön** – *A footbridge and road bridge lead to the island.* The island which takes its name from Frö or Frej, the fertility god, was a place of sacrifice in ancient times. The island has many burial mounds and Sweden's most northerly rune stone, the **Frösö Stone** *(turn left after the bridge, then first right to follow the sign for Runsten)*. The inscription recounts that Östman, Gudfast's son, Christianised Jämtland in the middle of the 11C and built the bridge.

★★ **Sommarhagen** ⊘ – *6km from Östersund, follow signs for Sommarhagen.* Initially this was the summer residence of the celebrated composer and music critic, Wilhelm Peterson-Berger (1867-1942), before it became his permanent home from 1930 until his death. A prolific composer, he was best loved in Sweden for his piano compositions. Every July his best-known work, *Arnljot*, the opera about the freedom loving Viking is performed on the meadows of Frösön *(further details and bookings from Östersund Tourist Information Centre)*.
The composer stipulated that the house should be brown and not the traditional red so that it would merge more easily with the surrounding countryside. The music room resembles a Viking hall.

Frösö kyrka ⊘ – *8km from Östersund, follow the signs.* This church in its idyllic island setting is very popular for weddings. The white-painted stone church, dating from the 12C, has a delicate blue and gold interior colour scheme. The detached **belfry** (1754) is characteristic of Jämtland. Wilhelm Peterson-Berger's tombstone stands near the south wall of the church.

Östbergets utkikstorn ⊘ – *3km from the bridge.* The tower on Östberget (468m) offers a splendid **view** from the observation deck of the surrounding countryside of forests and lakes rimmed by mountains.

Östersund to Åre

Road E 14 parallels this **Pilgrim Way** along quite a few stretches. St Olav was a typical wandering Viking before he made himself ruler of Norway and became the national hero saint. This pilgrim way retraces his journey from Novgorod to Stiklestad in Norway where he lost his life in battle. After his canonisation many pilgrims travelled to the shrine of the sainted king in Nidaros (Trondheim).

★★ **Alsensjön** – *39km detour around the lake. Take road E 14 in the direction of Trondheim and after 27km at Kingsta follow the sign Alsen 21km. Return to road E 14 at Mörsil.*

This delightful drive takes in attractive views of the glistening lake; wooded hills and little red and white houses and a white church complete this picture.

Shortly after Undersåker Church follow the sign for Ristafallen, then 500m on a narrow road.

Like the falls of Tännforsen, the **Ristafallen★** have never been harnessed for hydroelectric power.

Åre – Sweden's pre-eminent winter sports centre, nestling at the foot of Åreskutan (1 420m) on the shore of lake Åresjön, hosted the World Championships in 1954 and many World Cup Competitions. As early as 1880 it was a health resort in great favour with the British aristocracy and it was the Swiss resort of Davos which served as a model, hence the grandiose spa hotels and guesthouses. The funicular linking the town centre to the cable-car dates from the early days of the resort in 1909, and the **cable-car** takes visitors up to a height of 1 274m from where there is an 800m walk to the summit and the café. The splendid **panorama★★★** reveals delightful lake and mountain scenery in all directions.

The 12C **kyrka**, rebuilt in 1736, has an unusual 14C statue of St Olav *(see TROND-HEIM)* wearing a three-cornered carolean hat. He was given this unusual headgear in the 18C when his crown disappeared. The finely carved bench was used as a resting place by pilgrims on their way to the saint's shrine in Trondheim.

The **Åre Guides** *(behind the Konsum store)* organise a wide range of outdoor activities for discovering the surrounding wilderness. These include fishing or boat trips, hiking, horseback riding on Iceland ponies, canoeing or white-water rafting and even gold panning.

5km west of Duved, follow the sign for Tännforsen; once beyond the river follow the sign for a further 8km.

The foaming falls of **Tännforsen★★** with a 38m drop are the source of the River Indalsälven.

Njarka – *20km west of Duved.* A Sami camp has been rebuilt on the shore of Lake Häggsjön where in summer a Sami couple take visitors round the different huts and sheds and demonstrate the skills of a reindeer herder.

Kolovesi National Park, Finland

F. Jourdan EXPLORER

Finland

AHVENANMAA ★★

See ÅLAND at the end of the Finnish section

EKENÄS/TAMMISAARI ★

Etelä-Suomi
Population 11 500
Michelin map 985 M 20 or Atlas Europe p 120

The charming south coast town of Ekenäs has developed from a small fishing community on a narrow peninsula jutting out into the Gulf of Finland. The town received its charter in 1546 from Gustav Vasa in the hope that it would rival the Hanseatic city of Reval (now Tallinn). Although it never became a great seafaring or trading centre Ekenäs has grown to become the main resort and cultural centre in the west of Uusimaa. Over 80% of the population is Swedish speaking.

It was the idyllic atmosphere of this peaceful seaside resort with its well-preserved historic core that attracted the artist **Helene Schjerfbeck** (1862-1946). She spent over 20 years in the town.

The medieval centre, **Barcken★★** (Barckens udde), down by the water's edge is an irregular network of narrow lanes bordered by mainly 18C and 19C wooden houses. One of the more typical streets is Linvävaregatan/Liinankankurinkatu. The handsome town hall on the north side of the market place was designed by T Höijer in 1882.

> **Ekenäs Museum / Tammisaaren museo** ⊘ – *Gustav Vasas gata / Kustaa Vaasan katu 13.* Borgargården, the main building is furnished in the fashion of a wealthy burgher's home in the late 19C. The house at the far end of the courtyard dates from 1730.

> **Kyrka / Kirkko** ⊘ – *Stora kyrkogatan.* In 1839-42 the Italian architect Carlo Bassi worked on the restoration of the interior of this 17C granite church; the result is a rather surprisingly light, neo-Classical decor.

> ★**Ramsholmen Nature Reserve** – This relatively small reserve (50ha) comprises the islands of Ramsholmen and Högholmen and the peninsula of Hagen, which belong to the highly attractive Ekenäs archipelago *(boat trips from Norra Hamnen harbour).* These recreational areas are all accessible from the town by footpaths and footbridges. The yacht-shaped house in Snäcksundsvägen was designed in 1970 by Alvar Aalto for his friend, the art critic and great sailing enthusiast, Göran Schildt.

EXCURSIONS

★**Snappertuna** – *15km east of Ekenäs.* The mighty form of the castle of **Raseborg / Raasepori** ⊘★ stands on a rocky outcrop overlooking the River Snappertuna. The original fortress was built in the 14C and by the 15C it had become an important strategic and administrative centre greatly coveted by Danes, Swedes and pirates alike. By the mid-16C the castle was in a ruinous state and was abandoned until an initial restoration was undertaken in the 1890s.

A footpath *(300m on foot or 2km by car)* leads to **Forngården**, an authentic 18C farmhouse from the island of Halstö.

In the centre of Snappertuna the wooden **kirkko** ⊘ dates from 1688. The interior is beautifully decorated with paintings, especially the pulpit (1701) and galleries.

ESPOO/ESBO

Etelä-Suomi
Population 200 000
Michelin map 985 L 21 or Atlas Europe p 121 – Local map see HELSINKI: Excursions

Helsinki's western neighbour was only designated in 1972 but it is now the second largest city in Finland. It lies on the centuries old Great Coastal Road which led from Turku to Vyborg, and the lands of Espoo have a long history with some of the country's oldest cultural traditions. Great and prosperous manor houses were a typical feature of the scenery until the early 20C, when the growth of the capital transformed the neighbouring areas. The town of Espoo differs from a traditional one in that it was planned around several urban centres, each with their own trading, banking, educational and basic medical services. Some 86% of its housing dates from the 1960s or later.

SIGHTS

Espoon kirkko ⊘ – *Kirkkotie at Espoon Keskus, the administrative centre of Espoo.* The beautiful 15C grey-stone church, a triple-nave building, was transformed into a cruciform church in 1821-23. The many **mural paintings★** from the late Middle Ages depict biblical scenes from the Creation to the Last Judgement.

Tapiola – *10km west of Helsinki by road 51*. This Garden City dating from the early 1950s is a good example of contemporary urban planning. The most prominent young architects of the period participated in the project to create a harmonious mixture of flats, semi-detached and single-family houses around the commercial and recreational **central area**★ designed by Aarne Ervi (1910-77). The more recent Espoo Cultural Centre (Espoon Kulttuurikeskus) (Arto Sipinen, 1989) on the left behind the central pool blends perfectly with Ervi's elegant architecture. The massive commercial buildings adjoining the original centre on the left side date from the 1980s.

★**Otaniemi / Otnäs** – *2km east of Tapiola*. The main part of Otaniemi consists of the red-brick buildings of the Helsinki Institute of Technology campus designed by Alvar Aalto in the mid-1950s. The **main building**★ in the centre of the campus takes the form of a hemicycle. The library is the low building in front of it, and the whole makes a unique architectural ensemble. The Dipoli Congress Centre (Raili and Reima Pietilä, 1966) is an interesting multiform building of concrete, wood and copper designed to blend seamlessly with its natural environment.

★**Gallen-Kallelan museo** ⊘ – *Gallen-Kallelantie 27, 02600 Espoo; the road to the museum branches off Kehä I, 200m west of Tarvontie.*
This was the Jugendstil-inspired home-cum-studio of Finland's greatest painter of the National Romantic Period, **Akseli Gallen-Kallela** (1865-1931). The castle-like building, located in a beautiful conservation area on Laajalahti Bay, was planned to the last detail by the artist himself and built in 1913. The main exhibition covering the life and work of Gallen-Kallela includes paintings, graphics, applied art, stained glass, reliefs, posters, photographs, tools, artist equipment etc. Many of his most remarkable works are displayed in the Ateneum in Helsinki. The museum organises regular exhibitions on the painter and his contemporaries in collaboration with various European museums as well as exhibitions of contemporary art.

HAMINA ★★

Etelä-Suomi
Population 10 500
Michelin map 985 L 24 or Atlas Europe p 121

This remarkable little fortified town with its barracks has preserved its Renaissance-style radial town plan, drawn up in 1722 by General Axel von Löwen. Hamina lies quite near to the Russian border and its history has been closely associated with the fluctuations of the latter; the town has known Swedish, Russian and Finnish rule. Today this Finnish Baltic port, the European Union's most easterly port, is consolidating its position as fulcrum of expanding trade links between East and West.

★★**Old Town Centre** – The charming **town hall** ★⊘, built in 1798 and altered in the 1840s, stands like a jewel in the octagonal central square. Standing opposite is the round Orthodox **St Peter and St Paul Church** (1837) by the Italian Visconti who had also worked in St Petersburg. The belfry is an 1863 addition in the neo-Byzantine style then so popular in Russia. Behind the town hall is the Lutheran **church** (1843) a pure neo-Classical work by CL Engel.
Eight avenues radiate from the central square and there are two ring roads the smaller or inner one (Pikkuympyränkatu) and the larger or outer one (Isonympyränkatu). 18C circular bastions and moats mark the outer limits of the town.

The changing border

In the early 14C south-west Finland was under Swedish control; in 1595 the northern territories of Kainuu and Lapland also passed to Sweden and in 1617 it was the turn of Karelia and areas around the Gulf of Finland.
In 1809 Finland acquired autonomous status under Russia and in the years that followed regained certain territories on its eastern frontier. Then in the Second World War Finland once again lost territory, including a large part of Karelia, to the Russians.

FINLAND

HANKO/HANGÖ ★

Etelä-Suomi
Population 11 500
Michelin map 985 M 19-20 or Atlas Europe p 120

Renowned for its sandy beaches, rocky skerries and colourful gingerbread houses Finland's southernmost town has a cheerful holiday atmosphere. The large marinas provide moorings for the thousands of visiting yachts in summer and the Hangon Regatta (first weekend in July) is the most prestigious sailing event.

Hanko has always enjoyed a certain strategic importance; for hundreds of years it was at the intersection of the old King's Road and the Great Post Road (Stockholm to St Petersburg). In the 18C the Swedes built fortifications which were destroyed by English and French battleships during the Crimean War. In 1940 the Russians commandeered the peninsula as a naval base; the Finns recovered it the following summer.

★ **Itäsatama (eastern harbour)** – In summer life revolves around the marina and the many seafront restaurants and cafés of the eastern harbour. The Finns are a seafaring people and everyone has a boat of some description; sailing is a way of life with them and even the family pets join in.
Granstedt Park beside the harbour is the setting for **Hangon museo** ⊙ which organises changing exhibitions.

★ **Gingerbread Houses** – *Situated along Appelgrenintie.* In the late 19C when Finland was part of Czarist Russia, Hanko was a popular bathing resort and many of the Russian nobility and wealthier citizens built these fanciful summer residences.

★ **Casino** – *Appelgrenintie.* The handsome white casino building was refurbished by Gustaf Strengell in 1910. Today it is a popular summer restaurant.

Vesitorni ⊙ – *Vartiovuori.* From the top of this 50m tall water tower *(lift)* there is an impressive **view** of the coast and the offshore skerries.

★ **Hauensuoli** – This natural haven (Pike's Gut) in the narrow sound between the islands of Tullisaari and Kobben can only be visited by **boat** ⊙ *(boats leave from the eastern harbour).* It was a local tradition that navigators, noblemen, soldiers and merchants carved their names or emblems on the rocks. The Archipelago's Visitors Book contains over 600 carvings.

Neljän Tuulen tupa ⊙ – *4km east by the coastal road.* The House of the Four Winds was purchased as a summer retreat by Mannerheim in 1928 (now a tea room).

The Winter and Continuation Wars

When the Second World War broke out the Scandinavian countries were determined to preserve their neutrality. In the early days Finland had serious reasons to doubt the Soviet Union's intentions after the Russo-German non-aggression pact, the partitioning of Poland and the acquisition of bases in the Baltic states. The Soviet Union's request for islands in the Gulf of Finland to close the gulf to an attack on Lenningrad was met by a Finnish counter-proposition but when the first bombs fell on Helsinki the Finns were left in little doubt as to the Soviet Union's intentions. The **Winter War** covers the Finn's desperate 100-day struggle in 1940 against overwhelming odds. Mannerheim's white-clad troops manoeuvred in the wilderness areas – often on skis – and harassed the Soviet divisions along the long Finnish front. Against such odds the outcome was inevitable and negotiations were rapidly followed by a peace treaty on 12 March 1940. The terms were hard, Finland lost the islands inside the gulf, her fourth largest city Viipuri along with the entire Karelian Isthmus and a second area of the same extent to the north of Lake Ladoga. Roughly 12% of the Finnish population had to be evacuated and resettled.

The extension of the Second World War during the years 1941-44 was known as the **Continuation War**. Norway and Denmark had passed under German control and the Finns wavered between fear of a Russian occupation and hope of a German occupation of Sweden. Mannerheim's army, equipped from German sources, regained much of the lost territory and Finland was reluctant to incur German reprisals (five sixths of all food imports came from Germany) but when the great Russian offensive came, during the Western allies landing in Normandy, Mannerheim was in a better position to sue for an armistice, which he did on 19 September 1944. The Finns had to expel the German troops who as they retreated left an area of totally devastated territory. Finland had to cede the Petsamo area, which shut Finland off from the Barents Sea, and lost for a second time territory regained during the Continuation War.

354

HELSINKI/HELSINGFORS ★★★

Etelä-Suomi
Population 540 000
Michelin map 985 L 21 or Atlas Europe p 121
Plan of conurbation on Michelin map 985

Helsinki "Daughter of the Baltic" is appropriately named as the sea is ever present in continental Europe's most northerly capital. The city presents many facets from its formal neo-Classical showpieces, the imaginative volumes and decoration of Art Nouveau to the pure lines of modern architecture all against a backdrop of sea and forests. Helsinki was one of nine cities chosen as European City of Culture for the year 2000.

HISTORICAL NOTES

Rival to Tallinn – In 1550 King Gustav Vasa of Sweden founded a new town at the mouth of the River Vantaa to compete with the flourishing Hanseatic town of Tallinn across the Gulf of Finland. The city did not grow as expected and in 1640 it was relocated to its present position by the sea. The Great Northern War raged between Sweden and Russia from 1700 to 1721. In 1713 the city was taken by the Russians and remained in their hands until 1721. Then in 1742-43 came a new period of Russian occupation. As part of the Swedish kingdom the years 1746 to 1809 were a period of considerable prosperity during which the great sea fortress of **Suomenlinna** (Sveaborg) was built to protect the eastern frontier of the kingdom and the town. Around 1805 the fortress had a larger population than Helsinki. The fire of 1808 wreaked great damage in a city with many wooden houses. For Finland the 1808-9 war was a historic turning point as it meant a final break with Sweden and unification with Russia to become part of her empire as an autonomous Grand Duchy.

Capital of the Grand Duchy – The Grand Duchy was granted the right to keep the Swedish Constitution dating from 1772 and the Lutheran religion. However in 1812 Helsinki was proclaimed capital as Turku was deemed to be too close – geographically and politically – to Sweden. The until then insignificant merchant town required some rebuilding after the 1808 fire and replanning to fill its new role as capital. The result was the town's unique neo-Classical centre. In 1819 the Senate was transferred from Turku and in 1828 the university followed suit. Although the building of the new centre had been achieved by 1852 the reign of Alexander II (1855-81) was a period of prosperity for the capital city. The town grew slowly – the population had multiplied by 25 by the end of the 19C – and consolidated its position as the cultural and political centre of Finland.

Capital of an independent state since 1917 – Although Lenin's government recognised Finland's sovereignty on 4 January 1918, the capital soon had to endure the dramatic turns of the Civil War. However the new-born independence was secured and on 16 May 1918 CG Mannerheim led a parade of his troops along the main street that was later to bear his name. Helsinki's new commercial centre developed in the vicinity of Mannerheimintie. In 1930 the handsome new building of the Stockmann department store was completed, to be followed a year later by the new Parliament House.

During the Continuation War the capital was bombarded, on three consecutive occasions in February 1944, but the damage was limited, the greatest loss being the destruction of the university's Ceremonial Hall.

In 1946 Greater Helsinki was created with the incorporation of the smaller surrounding communities.

By 1952 when Helsinki organised the Olympic Games the capital was gaining a reputation for its bold, modern, post-war architectural achievements and as the Geneva of the North for hosting international conferences: the Strategic Arms Limitation Talks (SALT) between the Soviet Union and the United States in 1970 followed in 1975 by the 35-nation Conference on Security and Cooperation in Europe (CSCE). Helsinki is the country's number one tourist centre with a lively student population. In addition to the nation's principal university, it has some 18 institutions of higher education. But it is also a working capital with five busy harbours.

Main Events – *Some of the most outstanding events in the city's calendar are:*

March	Helsinki Biennale of contemporary music
30 April 1 May	May Day celebrations
June	Folklore event in Senaatintori organised by a different province each year
12 June	Helsinki Day to commemorate the founding of the city in 1550
June	Midsummer Eve celebrations at Seurasaari
August	Helsinki City Marathon
Aug-Sep	Helsinki Festival
October	Baltic herring market
December	Christmas Market in Esplanadi and at Hakaniemen tori
31 Dec	New Year's Eve Festivities on Senaatintori

SIGHTSEEING IN HELSINKI

Public transport – Helsinki sprawls in rural fashion over peninsulas and islands and the main sights are widely dispersed. The public transport system (trams, buses and underground) is practical and efficient. A flat rate of one ticket (10FIM on trams and buses; 8FIM from R-kiosks) is charged and transfers are allowed within 1hr of the time stamped on the ticket. Multi-trip tickets (10 trips) are available for 75FIM.

Underground: one line only. The service runs Mondays to Saturdays 5.33am to 11.23pm and Sundays 6.38am to 11.23pm.

Buses: city buses are easy to recognise by their blue colour; they operate over 150 lines and run until 1.30am in the morning.

Tramways: green-yellow tramcars operate on the 9 lines.

Ferries and boats: most of the departures are from Kauppatori.

Yellow Line Airport taxi: a shared taxi service (up to eight passengers) operates between the city and Helsinki-Vantaa airport 20km to the north. Fixed rate regardless of the distance travelled.

The Helsinki Card – This card gives access to museums and other places of interest and grants free travel on buses, trams, the underground and local trains. Other offers include a free sightseeing tour as well as reductions for theatre and concert tickets and discounts in some shops. The card is available for 24hr (120FIM), 48hr (150FIM) and 72hr (180FIM) and is accompanied by a booklet with details of the various offers. The card can be obtained at the **City Tourist Office** ⊘, the railway station, R-kiosks in the city centre and most hotels.

Shopping – The main shopping area is delimited by Mannerheimintie, Esplanadi and Aleksanterinkatu. Esplanadi is a design showcase with such famous names as Arabia, Aarikka and Marimekko. The shopping centre Forum at Mannerheimintie 20 and the shopping mall Kluuvi at Aleksanterinkatu 9, both regroup shops and restaurants and the department store Stockmann, Aleksanterinkatu 52, is well worth a visit. Kämp Galleria (entrances; Kluuvikatu 4, Pohjoisesplanadi 33, Milonkatu 1 and Aleksanterinkatu 42) is a recently opened shopping centre on three storeys with some 50 elegant boutiques, cafés and restaurants. A multitude of smaller shops and boutiques (furs and jewellery) are to be found in the same area. Shops are generally open weekdays from 9am to 5pm or 6pm and Saturdays 9am to 2pm or 3pm although the large department stores stay open until 7pm or 8pm on weekday evenings and to 5pm or 6pm on Saturdays. Many shops are also open on Sundays (opening times vary). Visitors from non-EU countries can enjoy tax-free shopping whereby they can reclaim the VAT. A passport is required for this operation. One of the particularities of northern countries is that alcohol can only be purchased from State liquor monopoly shops (Alko).

Market and market hall – Market Square at the eastern end of Esplanadi is the place to go for leisurely window-shopping and mingling with the crowds any morning including Sunday. North of Market Square along Unioninkatu and Silta-saarenkatu to Hakaniemi metro station is Hakaniemi Market Hall, housing 100 tiny shops on two storeys which sell a variety of delicacies, souvenirs, Finnish design, handicrafts, etc.

Credit cards – The following international credit cards are generally accepted: American Express, Diners Club, Eurocard, MasterCard and Visa.

Entertainment – Procure a copy of *Helsinki this Week* (from the tourist office at Pohjoisesplanadi 19, next to Market Square) to find out what is on at the Finnish National Opera in its seaside setting, at Finlandia Hall home to the Helsinki Philharmonic Orchestra and the city's other concert halls (Hall of Culture, Sibelius Academy of Music and the House of Nobility) or even at the Temppeliaukio Church with its excellent acoustics. The main centres for theatrical productions are the Finnish National Theatre (performances in Finnish) and Helsinki City Theatre (also dance performances), or the Swedish Theatre (performances in Swedish). The Alexander and Savoy theatres present musicals. Institutional theatres are usually closed in July when the open-air theatres take over. In the city's many cinemas films are shown in their original language with Finnish and Swedish subtitles. Film showings usually start at 6pm and 9pm. Night-life is concentrated in the discotheques and night-clubs, which are often in the bigger hotels.

Tickets for concerts and theatre performances can be obtained from TourExpert in Helsinki City Tourist Office *(see address above)*, Lippupalvelu (Ticket Service), Mannerheimintie 5 and Tiketti, Yrjönkatu 29C, which are open Mondays 9am to 8pm, Tuesdays to Fridays 9am to 5pm and Saturdays 9am to 2pm.The high point of the city's arts scene is the annual Helsinki Festival (late August and early September) with its multitude of concerts and exhibitions.

Sports – There is also a wide selection of sporting events from trotting at Vermo to ice hockey at the ice rink and athletic events or football matches at the Olympic Stadium.

Saunas – Most hotels and summer hotels, as well as swimming pools, have saunas. Other saunas open to the public are Finnish Sauna Society at Vaskiniemi on the island of Lauttasaari and as a curiosity, the smoke sauna in the Krapihovi Hotel in Tuusula.

Beaches – Hietaranta is perhaps the most popular beach west of the city centre along Hietaniemenkatu, but the beaches on the islands are a special attraction: Pihlajasaari, Seurasaari, Suomenlinna or Uunisaari are served by waterbuses. The temperature of the sea often reaches 20-22°C in July and August. There is a large open-air swimming pool at the Swimming Stadium (Uimastadion) behind the Olympic Stadium, and of course the Serena Leisure Centre in Espoo with its giant pools, chutes, restaurants etc.

Café terrace on the seafront, Helsinki

Cafés, pubs and restaurants – Cafés and pubs are popular with Finns especially those on the seafront (Café Ursula, Ehrenstömintie) or in a garden setting (Kappeli and Happy Days summer terraces in Esplanadi) or as part of a museum (Café CaraMelle in front of City Museum, the Café Amos in the museum of the same name or the Kiasma Café in the Museum of Contemporary Art), hotel (Café Socis in the Seurahuone Hotel near the railway station) or bookshop (Akateeminen in Esplanadi); at times the style is more central European with coffee, rich cakes and appropriate background music. Why not also try the newly renovated Lasipalatsi *(see p 364)* which houses three elegant cafés.

The choice of restaurants is wide but try Havis Amanda, Unioninkatu 23 by Kauppatori and Savoy, the rooftop restaurant with a Functionalist interior (1937) by Alvar Aalto. Or be tempted by the Russian specialities at Bellevue near Uspenski Cathedral or Alexander Nevski, Pohjoisesplanadi 17. Kosmos, a smoky artists' restaurant in the spirit of the 1920s, in Kalevankatu is known as a cosy watering hole, as well as the more elegant Bulevardia in Bulevardi by the Alexander Theatre restored to its original Functionalist splendour (1939) by Kaisa Blomstedt in 1985. One of the latest arrivals on the Italian scene (and already renowned) is Toula at Ratakatu 9, a building designed by Alvar Aalto. In total contrast, try Zetor, Kaivokatu 10, serving Finnish country style cuisine.

Sightseeing bus tour (free with the Helsinki Card) which starts from Fabianinkatu, Esplanade Park daily at 10.45am and lasts 1hr 30min or hop on the 3T tram on its double loop itinerary (a leaflet describes the main sights along the route). This way you can sightsee and rest at the same time. But the real treat for any visitor is to take one of the boat trips – water is the city's natural element – around the offshore islands starting from Market Square, such as Helsinki by Sea run by the Royal Line ☎ 622 1113. The cathedral and waterfront buildings backing Market Square and the Art Nouveau buildings further along the waterfront are seen to their best advantage from the sea against a background of rock and dark fir trees. Among the different guided walks of the city on offer are Jugend Helsinki and Helsinki's Russian past.

A visitor to the Finnish capital should try to see the different aspects of Helsinki. Senaatintori and Kauppatori squares are the heart of the official centre created for its new role as capital of Finland.

Katajanokka behind Uspenski Cathedral is worth a visit to glimpse the inventiveness of Art Nouveau. Helsinki is also known for its modern architecture.

The unexpected – Winter brings a frozen sea from February to April which becomes a playground for muffled Helsinkians who brave the cold to ski, ice-walk to the normally sea-bound islands, to fish or take a plunge after the ritual sauna. Even in summer the ice-breaker fleet makes an interesting outing. Another touch of the unusual is provided by the family ritual of washing carpets in the sea. In July the appearance of strawberries on the market stalls causes a rush of Helsinkians to savour the taste of berries which have ripened slowly.

Life in Helsinki – The Finns are an outdoor-loving people and with the approach of summer they spend the long summer evenings jogging, cycling, swimming, boating, fishing or just being outside as a family. In winter, when the sea is frozen over, many take to their skis for a promenade round the islands.

NEO-CLASSICAL HELSINKI

When Helsinki acquired the status of capital of an autonomous Grand Duchy, building work began on the master plan elaborated by the city planner, **Johan Albert Ehrenström** (1762-1847) in collaboration with the German-born architect **Carl Ludvig Engel** (1778-1840) who had worked in both Tallinn and St Petersburg. The first official building was Senate House (1818-20) and when fire destroyed the university in Turku it was transferred in 1828-9 to Helsinki. The main building was completed in 1832 and the library in 1840. The existing burghers' houses on the south side of Senaatintori Square were altered to harmonise with the overall design. By 1839 the cathedral was completed, however the Czar ordered the removal of the Guardhouse at its foot and a massive flight of stairs facing south was built to replace it. Today the square and its steps are popular with visitors and locals alike and it is the scene of several celebrations such as New Year's Eve festivities.

★★★**Senaatintori / Senatstorget** (DY 53) – The familiar silhouette of the cathedral's white form and green domes dominates the Helsinki skyline from the north side of the square. Engel worked on the cathedral between 1830 and 1839 from his original drawings of 1818, but the whole ensemble including the stairs and the remodelling of the burghers' houses was not completed until 1852.

★★**Tuomiokirkko / Domkyrkan** ⊘ (DY) – The stark white beauty of the Lutheran cathedral's interior and the plain woodwork of the pews are the perfect foils for the delicate gold decoration of the curved organ, the pulpit trims and the surrounds of the altarpiece. The statues portray three Lutheran theologians, Martin Luther, Felip Melanchthon and the Finnish Reformer and translator of the Bible **Mikael Agricola** (1508-57). During his translation work on the Bible, Agricola created the first rules for written Finnish and is therefore called the Father of Finnish literature.

Tucked in behind the cathedral is the delightful Holy Trinity church, **Pyhän Kolminaisuuden kirkko / Treenighetskyrkan** (DY K¹), *(Unioninkatu 31)* dating from 1827. Its elaborate finery is in stark contrast to its imposing neighbour, but it was this one that was in keeping with the Helsinki of the time.

Helsinki's kiosks

These often colourful permanent stands dotted about the city, in parks and at street corners, reflect the various styles which characterise Helsinki's architecture. Introduced at the end of the 19C, they come in all shapes from the tall podium-like specimen in true National Romantic style to the Early Functionalist pillar-box or the 1950s' blockboard model with a large bright awning. The latest model to intrude on the cityscape was designed by the a.men architectural office. Its neutral cubic shape with two glass sides and two wooden ones makes it unobtrusive enough to blend with its surroundings, unlike the Café Compass kiosk on the waterfront, designed in 1994 by Jyrki Ylä-Outinen to draw the attention of passers-by. Originally intended as refreshment stands, kiosks have become retail outlets for a variety of goods from newspapers to tobacco, ice cream, drinks, rolls of film etc.

Arranged around the square are a series of buildings, all the work of Engel. To the east is the Senate House, **Valtionneuvoston linna / Statsrådsborgen** (**V**), now home to the State Council, facing its counterparts, the main university building and the University Library, **Yliopiston kirjasto / Universitetsbiblioteket** (**R**) with its dome. On the south side are the burghers' houses which were raised by one storey to match the others. To the south-east corner is **Sederholmin talo** ⊘ (**DY E**) with its mansard roof. This former burgher's house dating from 1757 is now arranged as a museum with period interiors from the 18C and 19C. In the centre is the **statue** (1894) of Czar Alexander II by Walter Runeberg.

★★ **Kauppatori / Salutorget** (**DY 26**) – As its name suggests a bustling market (produce in the morning and souvenirs on summer afternoons) occupies Market Square on the edge of south harbour. The port is also a hive of activity with the constant toing and froing of the sightseeing boats as they pass the towering shapes of the huge Baltic ferries berthed on either side of the harbour.

From east to west the Empire frontage facing the harbour includes:

- the Presidential Palace, **Presidentinlinna / Presidentens slott** (**DY F**), was built as a private mansion in 1818 by Engel's predecessor, Pehr Granstedt (1764-1828), for a merchant named Heidenstrauch. In 1837 the city fathers purchased the house to transform it into an imperial residence and in 1854 Czar Nicholas I resided here. The mansion is now reserved for official functions only;

- the Supreme Court, **Korkein Oikeus**, is another work by FA Sjöström from 1883;

- the town hall, **Kaupungintalo**, by Engel was for quite some time a luxury hotel, the centre of Helsinki's social and cultural life. When the hotel closed in 1913 it was taken over by the city council. The pediment carries the city's coat of arms.

In front of the latter is the **Havis Amanda Fountain** (1908) by Ville Vallgren. This well-known statue is the centre of May Day activities when students crown her with their white graduation caps. Further to the east, facing the Swedish Embassy, is the

Tuomiokirkko

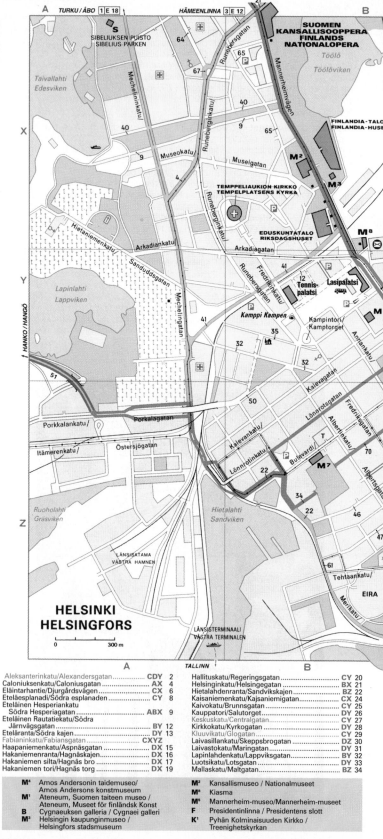

FINLAND

A TURKU / ÅBO 1 E 18   HÄMEENLINNA 3 E 12   B

SIBELIUKSEN PUISTO
SIBELIUS-PARKEN

SUOMEN
KANSALLISOOPPERA
FINLANDS
NATIONALOPERA

Töölö

Taivallahti
Edesviken

Töölöviken

FINLANDIA - TALO
FINLANDIA - HUSET

Museokatu
Museigatan

TEMPPELIAUKION KIRKKO
TEMPELPLATSENS KYRKA

EDUSKUNTATALO
RIKSDAGSHUSET

Arkadiankatu
Arkadiagatan

Hietaniemenkatu

Sanduddsgatan

Tennis-
palatsi

Lasipalatsi

Lapinlahti
Lappviken

Kamppi Kampen

Kampintori /
Kamptorget

Kalevagatan

Lönnrotsgatan

Porkkalagatan

Porkkalankatu /

Kalevankatu /

Östersjögatan

Itämerenkatu /

Lönnrotinkatu

Bulevard /

Ruoholahti
Gräsviken

Hietalahti
Sandviken

LÄNSISATAMA
VÄSTRA HAMNEN

EIRA

Tehtaankatu /

Merikatu /

HELSINKI
HELSINGFORS

0   300 m

A   TALLINN   B

LÄNSITERMINAALI
VÄSTRA TERMINALEN

M⁴ Amos Andersonin taidemuseo/
        Amos Andersons konstmuseum
M¹ Ateneum, Suomen taiteen museo /
        Ateneum, Museet för finländsk Konst
B Cygnaeuksen galleria / Cygnaei galleri
M³ Helsingin kaupunginmuseo /
        Helsingfors stadsmuseum

M² Kansallismuseo / Nationalmuseet
M⁵ Kiasma
M⁹ Mannerheim-museo/Mannerheim-museet
F Presidentinlinna / Presidentens slott
K¹ Pyhän Kolminaisuuden Kirkko /
        Treenighetskyrkan

360

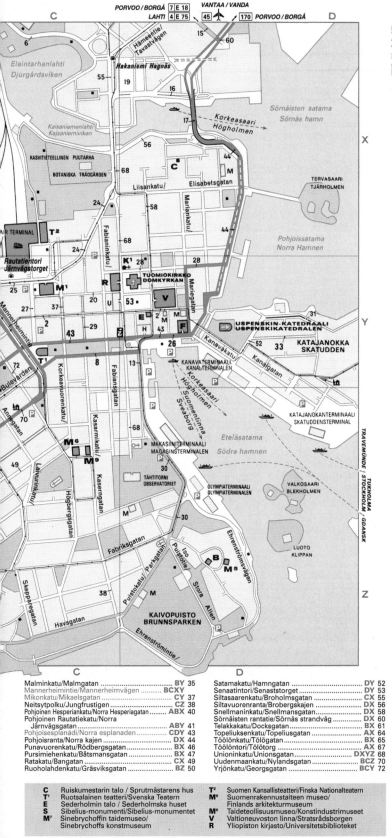

FINLAND

361

Czarina's Stone, **Keisarinnan kivi**, in commemoration of Czarina Alexandra Feodrovna's visit to the Grand Duchy in 1833. The obelisk is crowned by the Romanov's double-headed eagle.

★★ **Esplanadi** (**CDY 8/43**) – The central park, bordered by an avenue on each side and leading west from Kauppatori to Mannerheimintie, was laid out in 1831. The ornate neo-Renaissance buildings along the northern avenue (Pohjoisesplanadi) by T Höijer date back to the 1880s. **Hotel Kämp** at no 29, which once welcomed such illustrious guests as Jean Sibelius and Akseli Gallen-Kallela, has been completely renovated and turned into Helsinki's first five-star hotel under the name of Sheraton Kämp. Some of the leading Finnish design and fashion shops are to be found on Esplanadi. Hidden amid the trees at the east end is the elegant form of the **Kappeli** restaurant and café (1867). Further west is the **statue** of Finland's national poet **JL Runeberg** (1804-77) sculpted by his son Walter. The west end of the garden is marked by the semicircular form of the Swedish Theatre (1866), **Ruotsalainen teatteri / Svenska Teatern** (**CY T**[1]) for plays and musicals in Swedish.

THE NEW CITY CENTRE - A REVIEW OF 20C ARCHITECTURE

The 20C brought independence to Finland, and Helsinki as the capital gained even more importance. Construction work continued up to and during the Second World War, when the capital played its part in rehousing the 400 000 evacuees from the Karelian territories ceded to the Russians. Then again between 1950 and 1970 the city had to accommodate large numbers of Finns from the rural areas – as many as 16 000 a year – and the population almost doubled. Alvar Aalto (1898-1976) had devised in 1964 a master plan for a new city centre on the shores of Töölönlahti. Although only a small part of the plan – Finlandia Hall – was realised during his lifetime his idea of a chain of cultural buildings bordering the bay is slowly becoming reality; the new opera house was inaugurated in 1993 and the Museum of Contemporary Art by the American architect, Steven Holl, opened its doors in 1998.

★★ **Rutatieasema / Järnvägsstation** ⊙ (**CX**) – *Rautatientori*. The original competition entry (1904) by the Gesellius, Lindgren and Saarinen partnership was in the true National Romantic style but by the time Saarinen completed the commission in 1914 it was more in the spirit of international Art Nouveau. The railway station is one of the landmarks of the capital and for specialists it alone justifies a visit to the city. The main entrance on Kaivokatu is flanked by the massive and solemn-faced

> ### European Art Nouveau landmarks
>
> The railway station ranks alongside the works of Berlage in the Netherlands, Guimard in France, Gaudi in Spain and Mackintosh in Scotland.

figures sculpted in the true National Romantic tradition by Emil Wikström. A large painting of Lake Pielinen by Eero Järnefelt adorns the end of the station restaurant.

★ **Euskuntatalo / Riksdagshuset** ⊙ (**BX**) – *Mannerheimintie*. The massive red-granite Parliament House (1931) was designed by Professor Sirén to house the unicameral Parliament with its 200 members. The interior is purity of line and Finnish Functionalism at its best, especially the cafeteria. The main chamber, decorated with five statues by Wäinö Aaltonen, is circular with columns rising the height of the two galleries under a dome of compressed sugar cane pulp.

★★ **Finlandia-talo / Finlandia-huset** ⊙ (**BX**) – *Mannerheimintie 13e*. Helsink's main concert hall and conference centre was thrown into the limelight when its Italian-marble facing failed to stand the hard weather conditions and acid rain. After much controversy and debate, it was decided to replace it at great expense with smaller and thicker slabs of Carrara marble. And, for a while at least, the building has regained its original appearance. Finlandia Hall was planned as part of a new city centre on the shore of Töölönlahti by **Alvar Aalto**. Of his original plan only the main building was completed in 1971, the congress wing was added in 1975. Its long low-lying form in white Carrara marble makes a striking contrast to the National Museum and the Parliament House opposite. The main façade of this white marble-clad building overlooks Töölönlahti Bay and the railway yard. In addition to the main concert hall (1 700 seats) there is a chamber music hall (340 seats), a terrace hall (200 seats) as well as conference and committee rooms. The Helsinki Agreements in 1975 and more recently the International Press Centre for the meeting of presidents Clinton and Yeltsin during the 97 Helsinki Summit were held in this hall. It is home to the Helsinki Philharmonic Orchestra and the Radio Symphony Orchestra; a total of 97 concerts were given in 1998.

FINLAND

E. Baret

Wikström's figures on the Rautatieasema

★★ Kansallisooppera / Nationaloperan ⊘ (**BX**) – *Helsinginkatu 58 on the corner with Mannerheimintie*. The sleek new opera house designed by the architectural partnership of Hyvämäki, Karhunen and Parkkinen gleams with white ceramic tiles and Finnish granite, in its setting on the shore of Töölönlahti Bay. In addition to the main auditorium with its 1 364 seats and its state-of-the-art machinery there is a smaller 500-seat theatre for experimental work and additional rehearsal space. The opera house was inaugurated in 1993 with the first Finnish performance of Aulis Sallinen's *Kullervo* commissioned for the opening. The repertoire is strongly rooted in the great classics such as Verdi's *Don Carlos*, Puccini's *Tosca* and Wagner's *Das Rheingold*, but the Finnish National Opera is also well known for its productions of modern Finnish operas.

★★ Temppeliaukion kirkko / Tempelplatsens kyrka ⊘ (**BX**) – *Lutherinkatu 3*. This circular Church in the rock was designed in 1960 by the brothers Timo and Tuomo Suomalainen. Although it was not built until 1968-69 it rapidly became one of the city's main attractions, renowned for its ingenious engineering and architectural solutions. The natural-rock inner walls are prolonged by stone built ones and capped by a shallow copper dome with a fringe of concrete rafters between which daylight streams into the interior. The church has excellent acoustics and is often used for concerts.

A. Koening/EXPLORER

Temppeliaukion kirkko – "Church in the rock"

FINLAND

Suomen Kansallisteatteri / Finska Nationalteatern (CX T²) – *Asema-aukio.* The Finnish National Theatre was founded in 1872 and the red-roofed, grey-granite, castle-like building was built in 1910 in the purist National Romantic style by Onni Tarjanne. The first-ever play in the Finnish language had been premiered only three years previously.

The **statue** in front of the theatre shows a pensive father of the Finnish novel, **Aleksis Kivi** by Wäinö Aaltonen. Kivi wrote the first novel in the Finnish language *The Seven Brothers* (*Seitsemän Veljestä,* 1870), a realistic and very humoristic tale.

Lasipalatsi (BY) – This Functionalist building situated on the west side of Mannerheimintie, opposite the railway station, was renovated in 1998 to be sued as a culture and media centre as well as a meeting place for Helsinkians who come in for a spot of lunch in one of the cafés or a refined traditional meal at the Restaurant Lasipalatsi. In an effort to bring new technology into people's daily life, the centre offers free access to the Internet in a branch of the city's library, a youth information centre, another information centre for Swedish-speaking Finns and an unusual café, run by the Cultural Office of the City of Helsinki, where the tables have inbuilt screens enabling customers to surf on the net. There is also a television studio whose activities can be watched by all those interested, a giant-screen cinema, an information centre on the European Union, a bookshop with a book-on-demand service (the book is printed for you in about 30min), several shops and cafés.

Are public saunas on the way out?

Statistics speak for themselves: 50 years ago there were 122 public saunas in Helsinki, today there are only three. Yet public saunas are a traditionally important aspect of Finnish culture since they are seen as a means of socialising. Are the Finns then about to give up one of their deeply rooted customs? Nothing is less sure and the answer is not yet anyway for someone has come up with a new idea: a sauna bar combining the traditional sauna experience with convivial drinking, eating, listening to music and relaxing. Saunabaari in Eerikinkatu is open to groups during the week and to the general public on Sundays and Mondays. If the idea catches on, public saunas in Helsinki will not disappear but simply undergo a mutation!

MUSEUMS IN THE IMMEDIATE VICINITY

★★ **Ateneum, The Museum of Finnish Art** ⊘ (CY M¹) – *Kaivokatu 2.* The Ateneum Art Museum's main collection is hung chronologically and gives an excellent introduction to Finnish art from the 18C to the 1960s. The early portraitists Nils Schillmark and Isak Wacklin are followed by the self-taught Von Wright brothers. The majority of their works are still-life paintings (Wilhelm's *Hanging Wild Ducks* and *Fighting Capercaillies*) but their forays into other genres are not without interest (Magnus' image of Helsinki slumbering under the snow, *The Liljestrand House in Winter,* and Ferdinand's peaceful scene of *The Garden at Haiminanlahti*). Several Finnish artists were introduced to landscape painting at the Düsseldorf School (Werner Holmberg, Munsterhjelm and Lindholm). Fanny Churberg's vigorous works broke with this tradition. Edelfelt's *A Child's Funeral* (1879) is acknowledged as Finland's first Realist work of art and his Parisian works *(Luxembourg Gardens and Louis Pasteur)* with their Impressionist influence are in direct contrast to the mainstream of Finnish art then so influenced by Finnish folklore. However his *Queen Bianca* (1877) based on Topelius' tale *The Nine Silver Coins* and his *Women Outside the Church* show how even he yielded to the influence of Karelianism. The artist Victor Westerholm inclined towards Impressionism (*Fruit Trees in Blossom, Suresnes,* 1890) and in reaction to the current Karelianism and National Romanticism founded a colony at Önningeby in the Åland islands. The supreme Realist was Akseli Gallen-Kallela, probably Finland's greatest artist. His large scale masterpieces include an early work *The Boy and the Crow,* the lovely *Imatra in Winter* and his works from the 1890s which were so influenced by the national epic *Kalevala (Aino Myth, Lemminkäinen's Mother, Kullervo's Curse and The Fratricide).*

Look out for the works of the most famous Finnish woman artist Helene Schjerfbeck (1862-1946) and the haunting works by the symbolist Hugo Simberg (1873-1917).

★ **Amos Andersonin taidemuseo / Amos Andersons konstmuseum** ⊘ (BY M⁴) – *Yrjönkatu 27.* The printing magnate and patron of the arts, **Amos Anderson** (1878-1961), had the building erected in 1912-13 as an office and a home for himself by the architects WG Palmqvist and Einar Sjöström. He later bequeathed the premises and his valuable collections to the State and the museum was inaugurated in 1965. His summer home at Söderlångvik in the Turku archipelago has a collection of personal items and his art collection.

The Amos Anderson Museum was renovated in 1998-99, when an original exhibition area on three levels was created on the ground floor and the former attic was turned into additional exhibition space occasionally used as an auditorium. The tasteful renovation using top-quality materials includes elegant wood flooring throughout, stainless steel washrooms and a lift as well as the brick-and-concrete loft conversion.

The **ground floor** houses temporary exhibitions devoted to invited artists such as Susanne Gottberg, whereas the **top floor** stages themed exhibitions such as Eros and the art of Gustav Vigeland. The museum's collections, which are mainly devoted to 20C Finnish art, are displayed on the intermediate floors.

5th floor – The chapel contains painted wood panels from and early-19C German church. One room is devoted to Henry Ericsson, a friend of Amos Anderson, another to the latter's theatre mementoes and another two are furnished as they were during his lifetime, with 18C Swedish and 19C Russian furniture. Other rooms display paintings from the first half of the 20C, namely from the 1920s and 1930s.

4th floor – This floor, devoted to the 1960s and 1970s, also displays new acquisitions and holds changing exhibitions. In addition, there is a small art library with an Internet terminal for use by visitors.

3rd floor – This floor contains Finnish and foreign art from 1900 to 1920, including works by Magnus Enckell, leader of the Impressionist group, and AW Finch, an English artist who settled in Finland.

On the ground floor, there is a museum shop and Café Amos, a popular place for both visitors and the general public.

⋆⋆ **Kiasma** ⊘ **(Museum of Contemporary Art)** (BX M⁸) – *Mannerheiminaukio 2.* Opened in May 1998, Kiasma won international acclaim for its striking architectural style, even before its permanent collection was displayed. Situated right in the city centre, the new museum stands in a key position between the Art Nouveau station, the Functionalist Parliament House and Alvar Aalto's white-marble Finlandia Hall, three buildings with distinctive architectural styles. The American architect, Steven Holl, designed a structure which in no way interferes with its neighbours yet immediately draws attention to itself. On the outside, zinc, titanium and copper was used on the roof, whereas some of the walls are aluminium clad and others are lined with acid-reddened brass; in addition, the building has several glass walls which let in natural daylight. Some controversy arose over Kiasma's nearest neighbour, Marshall Mannerheim's equestrian statue, but Helsinkians had to admit in the end that the new building does not impair the great man's image. The interior is a multi-level space with five overlapping storeys connected by ramps, staircases and lifts. In the main hall, there are information booths, the Kiasma Theatre, the Kiasma shop and the Kiasma Café with access to Kiasmanet providing the latest information about the museum's activities. The walls and ceiling of the exhibition area are white to convey simplicity and tranquillity. In contrast, the floor is made of dark-grey concrete.

Kiasma, the Museum of Contemporary Art

Exhibited for the first time during the summer of 1999, the collection of contemporary art spans the period from 1960 onwards, offering a good overall view of the main international trends (Minimalism, Pop Art, Arte Povera, German neo-Expressionism, Italian Trans-Avant-Garde, American painting of the 1980s, English sculpture) through 61 works by 38 artists including paintings, sculptures, installations (*Monument* by Christian Boltanski, *Untitled (Igloo)* by Mario Merz) and graphic art. In addition, Kiasma organises several temporary exhibitions every year, major solo exhibitions on the fifth floor, smaller ones in Studio K and exhibitions involving the use of media technology in Kontti.

★★ **Kansallismuseo / Nationalmuseet** ⊘ (**BX M²**) – *Mannerheimintie 34*. The recently renovated museum building was designed by Herman Gesellius, Armas Lindgren and Eliel Saarinen in the early 1900s. The architecture contains allusions to Finnish medieval churches and castles together with elements of Art Nouveau. The **frescoes** (1928) in the entrance hall by Akseli Gallen-Kallela illustrate the legends of the *Kalevala*.

The National Museum of Finland presents with its rich archaeological, cultural history and ethnological collections the development of Finnish life from prehistoric times to the present. The most important attractions include a prehistory exhibition, a display of medieval art, the armoury, the Jakkarila Hall, which depicts 18C manor life, and a traditional chimneyless cabin. There is also a new section on coins and medals.

Helsingin kaupunginmuseo / Helsingfors stadsmuseum ⊘ (**BX M³**) – *Karamzininkatu 2*. When Hakasalmi Villa, now home to a branch of the Helsinki City Museum (whose main centre is in Sofiankatu, opposite the cathedral), was built between 1843 and 1847, it was outside the city boundary. The exhibitions relate to Helsinki's history.

Tennispalatsi (**BY**) – This complex situated west of Mannerheimintie, close to the railway station houses two museums, a 14-screen cinema, restaurants, bars and cafés.

★ **Kulttuurien museo / Kulturernas museum** ⊘ – *Salomonkatu 15*. The Museum of Cultures, inaugurated in 1999, is a branch of the National Museum of Finland. The extensive collections featuring items from all over the world have been gathered by Finnish explorers, missionaries, scientists and art collectors. Among them, the Finno-Ugric collection is particularly famous. By showing the great diversity of cultures throughout the world, the museum aims to encourage multicultural education and tolerance. There is no permanent exhibition but temporary ones including travelling exhibitions from Finland and abroad. One of the two opening exhibitions was devoted to Marshall Mannerheim's expedition along the Silk Road to Central Asia and China in 1906-08 and illustrated by the many items he collected on the way. The other one, called *The Stars*, presented rare treasures from the museum's collections.

Helsingin kaupungin taidemuseo / Helsingfors stads konstmuseum ⊘ – *Salomonkatu 15*. Also inaugurated in 1999, this is one of the City Art Museum's two venues for its temporary exhibitions of Finnish and foreign art from various periods.

Architectural variety for a young capital city

Within its short lifespan as a capital city Helsinki has acquired a reputation for architectural sophistication. Most, but not all, of the creative responses were provoked by periods of national change or even crisis. CL Engel used neo-Classicism to provide a suitably dignified centre (Senate Square, the Observatory and the Naval barracks) for the fledging capital of the Grand Duchy. In the 1880s and 90s T Höijer favoured a neo-Renaissance style (Esplanadi and Ateneum).

The international wave of Art Nouveau was applied in the National Romantic spirit in the first decades of the 20C by the architects Gesellius, Lindgren, Saarinen and Sonck.

National Romanticism was an expression of the vigorous national feeling and struggle for independence during the last oppressive years of Russian rule.

Architecture passed from a new phase of Classicism in the 1920s to the era of Finnish Functionalism in the 1930s. The post-war period was marked by a new generation of architects (Ervi, Revell, Penttilä and Pietilä) with their modern projects and some of the most remarkable creations of the father of modern Finnish architecture, Alvar Aalto (House of Culture and Finlandia Hall).

FINLAND

★KATAJANOKKA/SKATUDDEN (DYZ)

The rocky headland dividing north and south harbours was originally an area of warehouses and naval barracks. Walk up Luotsikatu to admire the decorative motifs used by the Art Nouveau architects at the turn of the last century. **No 1** Tallberg House and **no 5** are full of inventiveness. On the northern side is the berth of the imposing **ice-breaker fleet★** overlooked by the frontage of Engel's naval headquarters, now occupied by the Ministry of Foreign Affairs.

★★ **Uspenskin katedraali / Uspenskikatedralen** ⊘ **(DY)** – The gleaming onion domes of this red-brick building, standing high on a rocky mound, serve as the counterpart to the Lutheran cathedral. The cathedral dates from 1868 when there was a large population of Russian officials and is one of the adornments of Russian Helsinki. The very ornate interior (mosaics, gilded and highly colourful iconostasis and icons) is in direct contrast to the sobriety of the Lutheran cathedral.

Art Nouveau doorway

Ch. Bastin - J. Evrard

WATERFRONT DISTRICTS

Helsinki is first and foremost a city on the Baltic and the Finns' deep feelings for the sea underline most social activities.

To get a real feel of life in Helsinki, take a stroll along the waterfront from the marina right round to Market Square, along the promenade which skirts the Eira district and Kaivopuisto. Many Finns own a pleasure boat and, at the end of summer, you can see whole families watching them being hauled out of the water and lined along the coastline, just behind the waterfront promenade, in readiness for the hard winter when the sea freezes. The view along the way is magnificent with rocky islands of all sizes scattered as far as the eye can see, some of them smooth like the back of some sea monster gleaming in the sun and barely showing above the water. As one comes within sight of Market Square, huge ferries, several storey high, can be seen moored within a short distance of the white Lutheran cathedral and red-brick Orthodox cathedral, both overlooking the harbour. As one gets nearer, one can spot the crowd taking a leisurely stroll among the tiny stalls on Market Square.

The round tour takes just over 1hr, more if you stop at one of the kiosks or waterfront cafés to enjoy the sun and the lively atmosphere.

Kaivopuisto/Brunnsparken (DZ)

In the 19C the Kaivopuisto spa was the haunt of Russian princes and dukes who came for health cures and today foreign diplomats have taken over its secluded and leafy streets. It is an ideal district for a pleasant stroll to see a variety of 19C wooden villas.

★ **Cygnaeuksen galleria / Cygnaei galleri** ⊘ **(DZ B)** – *Kailiolinnantie 8*. The summer home of **Professor Fredrik Cygnaeus** (1807-81) – once so typical of Kaivopuisto Park in the mid-19C – houses his collection, representative of the art of the 19C. The works illustrate his associations with other artistic and literary personalities of the period: the sculptor Carl Eneas Sjöstrand, the painter Albert Edelfelt *(The Burnt Village)*, the landscape painter Werner Holmberg and many others.

★ **Mannerheimmuseo / Mannerheim museet** ⊘ **(DZ M⁵)** – *Kalliolinnantie 14*. For many **Carl Gustaf Mannerheim** (1867-1951) was the chief figure in Finland's struggle for independence. He was Marshal and Commander-in-Chief of the Finnish Army during the 1939-40 and 1941-44 wars and then President from 1944 to 1946. Uniforms, medals, documents and photographs illustrate the life, expeditions and campaigns of this great military leader and statesman. In the dining room hangs a portrait of the Marshal, at the age of 62, painted by his friend Akseli Gallen-Kallela.

Eira

This district on the seafront was planned in the 1900s as a residential area and today there are still numerous Art Nouveau gems to be discovered. The **Eira Hospital** (1905) by Lars Sonck is a National Romantic masterpiece whereas the neighbouring **Villa Johanna** (1906) by Selim Lindqvist represents international Art Nouveau.

ADDITIONAL SIGHTS

★**Olympiastadion** – *Eteläinen Stadionintie 3. To the north by Helsinginkatu* (**BX**). The Olympic Stadium was designed by Yrjö Lindegren and Toivo Jäntti in a Functionalist spirit for the ill-fated 1940 Olympic Games. It was 1952 before Helsinki was to welcome the Olympics. The 72m-tall **tower** gives a great **view**★★ of Helsinki laid out in its forested and lake-strewn setting. The sports museum, **Suomen Urheilumuseo** ⊙ *(entrance 50m beyond the tower)*, illustrates the evolution and moments of glory of Finnish sport.

The **statue** by Wäinö Aaltonen, in front of the main entrance, represents the Finnish long-distance runner **Paavo Nurmi** (1897-1973) often known as the Flying Finn. He competed in three Olympics and won nine gold and three silver medals during the 1920s and it is often jokingly claimed that he ran Finland onto the world map!

Sporting Finns

With the tradition of *sisu* (inner strength) the Finns have always been keen sportsmen and determined competitors like the 23 Finnish (although they were still competing under the Russian flag) medal winners at the Stockholm Olympics in 1912. Other medal winners include the runner, Hannes Kolehmainen, the amazing Paavo Nurmi, and his more recent successor Lasse Viren, the long-distance runner who won four gold medals.

Finns have been victorious in other disciplines: the skier Eero Mäntyranta and the ski-jumper Matti Nykänen, the javelin thrower Seppo Räty and the rower Pertti Karppinen.

★★ **Taideteollisuusmuseo / Konstindustrimuseet** ⊙ (**CZ M⁶**) – *Korkeavuorenkatu 23.* The ground-floor collections of the Museum of Art and Design trace the development of Finnish design from the Karelianism of the 1880s and 90s through Art Nouveau (Walter Jung, Albert Finch) and its more National Romantic applications (Eliel Saarinen, Gallen-Kallela) to Functionalism (Alvar and Aino Aalto), the Rationalist movement and the successful years of Finnish design from the 1950s and 1960s until today. Finnish glassware is given a prominent place with such famous items as Alvar Aalto's Savoy Vase dating from 1936, for which he claimed to draw his inspiration from Finnish lakes, Tappio Wirkkala's post-war Kantarelli Vase or Timo Sarpaneva Orkidea Vase from 1953. The permanent exhibition is renewed every two years. In addition, the museum organises two themed temporary exhibitions every year; for instance Living Rooms from the 1950s to the 1990s showed the evolution of economic prosperity since the Second World War as well as the changing styles from Functionalism to Minimalism and the return to natural materials.

Suomen rakennustaiteen museo / Finlands arkitekturmuseum ⊙ (**CZ M⁹**) – *Kasarmikatu 24.* Backing on to the Museum of Art and Design, the Museum of Finnish Architecture, founded in 1956, is one of the oldest of its kind in the world. Its main fields of activity are exhibitions and archives. Several **exhibitions** of variable importance are organised every year; some of them travel within Finland and abroad. One of the recent exhibitions entitled En route! displayed a collection of drawings by famous and less famous Finnish architects travelling abroad, among them Selim A Lindqvist, Eliel Saarinen, Armas Lindgren, Väinö Vähäkallio and Alvar Aalto. The **archives department** contains an extensive collection of photographs as well as original drawings by Finnish architects and models of famous buildings including the official presidential residence in Helsinki, St-Michael's Church in Turku and Toronto town hall. These models can be seen by the public on the second floor of the building *(open weekdays only)*. In addition to exhibition catalogues, the museum also publishes various books including a series entitled Acanthus, in English and Finnish, aimed at international readers. One of the latest publications was *Alvar Aalto in Seven Buildings*, published for the centenary of the architect's birth.

Sinebrychoffin taidemuseo / Sinebrychoffs konstmuseum ⊙ (BZ **M⁷**) – *Bulevardi 40*. The Finnish National Gallery's collection of foreign art is housed in an 1840s building which was erected as the home and offices of the Sinebrychoff family of brewing fame. The collection features Early Renaissance Italian, Dutch and Flemish works, as well as French, Spanish and English paintings. The museum also has good collections of miniatures, porcelain and icons. The original rooms of the family home are distinguished by their refined decor.

★**Sibelius-monumentti / Sibelius-monumentet** (AX **S**) – *Sibeliuksen puisto just west of Mechelininkatu; bus 18 from the railway station*. The sculptress Eila Hiltunen worked six years on this intriguing steel pipe monument erected in 1967, ten years after the great composer's death to commemorate his life's work.
The bust on the rock to the right was added several years later by the same artist. The gleaming bay behind and the splendid birch trees make a superb setting for this impressive work of art.

Ruiskumestarin talo / Sprutmästarens hus ⊙ (DX **C**) – *Kristianinkatu 12*. It is well worth the trip to see one of the few remaining wooden houses, known as the Burgher's House, which were typical of pre-1812 Helsinki. Although the buildings date from 1818 the furnishings are from the 1860s. Of particular interest in this four-roomed dwelling are the folding beds, the original brick stove in the bed-chamber and the half-year's supply of bread hanging in the kitchen. The smaller dwelling has photographs of old Helsinki.

ENVIRONS

Arabian museo / Arabias museum ⊙ – *Hämeentie 135. Leave by road 170 (DX) to the north-east. Tram 6 or buses 71, 74 or 76. Free transportation in summer from the city centre*.
A small porcelain factory was established in Arabia on the outskirts of Helsinki in 1873. Arabia's products have played a major role in creating the Finnish and Scandinavian reputation for design: quality, purity of line, originality and Functionalism. During the **factory tour** visitors have an opportunity to see the production processes and finished products. A **museum** *(ninth floor)* covers the century of production and the **factory shop** is the place to let temptation take over.

★★**Seurasaari / Folisö** ⊙ – *Museum and recreational park on the island of Seurasaari. Bus no 24 goes directly from the city centre*.
The open-air museum was founded in 1909 by Professor AO Heikel and the idea was to collect typical wooden buildings from the different provinces in order to display various traditions of timber construction and traditional ways of life. Today the museum presents almost 100 different buildings dating back mostly to the 18C and 19C. The **Niemelä Tenant Farmhouse** (7) is a good example of how the sauna, often the first building to be built, served as a temporary home until completion of the rest. **Karuna Church** (8) dating from 1686 is the oldest building. Beyond are the **church boats** (9) and a replica of the writer **Aleksis Kivi's cottage** (10). The Karelian farmhouse **Pertinotsha** (19) is of round log construction. The **Antti Farmstead** (25), with its two enclosed yards, shows the standard of living of a wealthy family working an arable farm in south-west Finland. The **Lapland village** (27) is a special curiosity with its storehouses perched on poles to deter marauding animals. For those who are in Helsinki for midsummer, Seurasaari is the right place to see the traditional Midsummer's Eve Celebrations.

★**Urho Kekkonen museo / Urho Kekkonens museum** ⊙ – *Tamminiemi, Seurasaarentie 15*. This early-20C villa was donated to the State in 1940 by the editor and publisher, Amos Anderson. Other presidents Risto Ryti and Carl Gustaf Mannerheim used Tamminiemi as their official residence. It is however with Urho Kekkonen (1900-86) that Tamminiemi is most closely associated. Kekkonen lived here from his election as president in 1956 until his death. The exhibits recall the life and main political events of his four-term presidency (1956-81). Works of art rival with official presents and Finnish works include Essi Renvall's gilded relief *People at Work*, Aimo Kanerva's watercolours so loved by Sylvi Kekkonen and Akseli Gallen-Kallela's *Dusk*. The Russian painter Ilja Glazunov has portrayed Kekkonen's home village and the President himself.

★★**Suomenlinna / Sveaborg** ⊙ – *Ferries ply between Kauppatori (DY **26**) and the islands. A restaurant is open all the year round and several restaurants and cafés are open in summer*.
When the fortress of Sveaborg was built on the group of six islands just offshore from the settlement of Helsinki it was Sweden's largest fortress designed for the defence of the entire eastern frontier. The greatest fear then, was that Russia would annexe Finland. The construction project, supervised by Augustin Ehrensvärd (1710-72), was the biggest ever undertaken and involved the building of four separate fortresses each on their own island including 8km of defensive walls and room for over 1 000 guns. Sveaborg became the base of the coastal fleet and garrison

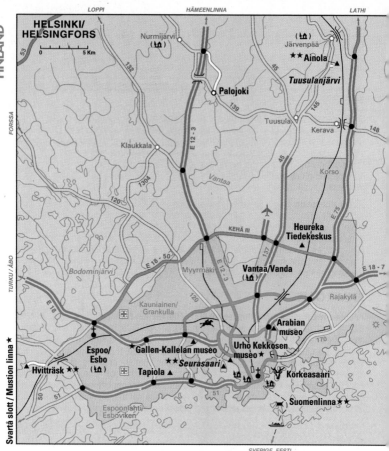

town whereas the open-sea fleet remained at Karlskrona, Sweden. In 1805 the fortress had a total population of 4 600, making it Finland's second largest town after Turku with 11 300, and an important cultural centre. In 1808, like the rest of Finland, it fell to Russian hands and was assigned the role of protecting Finland's new capital. At the time of the Crimean War (1853-56) it was by then vastly outdated and it suffered greatly during a Franco-British naval attack. The Russian era in Suomenlinna ended in 1918 and the Gibraltar of the North was renamed Suomenlinna or Fort of Finland.

Today, although the islands are home to some 900 people, they serve mainly as a recreational and cultural area. There are several museums and restaurants, a visitor centre, guided tours, a multimedia show on the history of the fortress and art exhibitions during the summer. Suomenlinna is included on the UNESCO list of World Heritage Sites.

Korkeasaari / Högholmen – *Ferry service from Kauppatori* (**DY 26**). *Café open in summer*. This offshore visit makes a pleasant outing, so go for the boat trip as well. The zoo is one of the northernmost and specialises on animals from cold or mountain areas.

★ **Akseli Gallen-Kallelan museo** – *See ESPOO / ESBO.*

EXCURSIONS

★★ **Hvitträsk** ⊙ – *30km west by road 51 to join the ring road, Kehä Ring III, and head north then follow the signs.*
The three most prominent architects of the early 20C in Finland, Eliel Saarinen, Herman Gesellius and Armas Lindgren, built this castle-like masterpiece of the National Romantic period in the years 1902-4. The wooded hill by the deep and clear Lake Vitträsk offered an ideal site for the artists seeking a return to nature in the spirit of the period.
The house was the meeting place for many of the great names of the early 20C: the composers Jean Sibelius and Robert Kajanus, the Russian writer Maxim Gorki and artists like Gallen-Kallela and the Norwegian Edvard Munch – all young and of fiery

spirits. The Saarinens lived in the house until 1923 when they left for the United States following Eliel's success in the competition for the headquarters of *The Chicago Tribune*.

The **main building★★**, now the museum, was the home of **Eliel Saarinen** (1873-1950) leader of the team; it included the architectural office which connected it to Armas Lindgren's home. The house is not only an architectural conception but according to the principles of the National Romantic movement, it was also a work of art. Thus the interior and the furnishings were designed in the National Romantic spirit by Saarinen himself and his wife Loja Gesellius who wove the textiles. Other contemporaries also contributed; Akseli Gallen-Kallela painted the **frescoes★** in the dining room and Olga Gummerus-Ehrström designed the stained-glass windows.

The northern wing was the home of **Armas Lindgren** (1874-1929) but the building burned down in 1922 and was rebuilt in 1936 according to plans by Eliel Saarinen's son Eero; it has been refurbished as a hotel. The dark log-building, now the restaurant, was the home of **Herman Gesellius** (1874-1916) who married Mathilda, Eliel Saarinen's first wife. Gesellius' sister Loja was Saarinen's second wife. By the time Eliel Saarinen moved to the United States in 1923, he and his family owned the entire estate. Hvitträsk became the property of the Finnish State in 1981.

Follow the path from beside the restaurant or the stairs from behind the main house down to the lakeside and a typical log-sauna built in the 1960s to the designs of Reima Pietilä.

Both Eliel and Loja Saarinen are buried in the forest of Hvitträsk as they had wished, although they never returned to live permanently in Finland.

★ Mustion linna / Svartå slott ⊘ – *74km by road 51 in the direction of Hanko.*
The wealthy ironworks owner **Magnus Linder II** (1751-1801) commissioned Erik Palmstedt, city architect of Stockholm, to design the wooden manor house (1783-92). The elegant **Gustavian interiors★★** include the Ladies Salon on the first floor with remarkable murals (1790) by Louis Jean Desprez, Gustav III's favourite architect and the splendid Ballroom with *trompe-l'œil* murals.

The manor stands in a beautiful park, landscaped in the English manner by Fridolf Linder (1823-96) in the 1860s. The trees include such exotic species as walnut and cork.

The white building (1867) to the left has been refurbished as a hotel and the neo-Gothic carriage-shed houses a restaurant. A bridge leads over the River Svartå to the **ironworkers dwellings★**, charming red-painted wooden houses, which have been renovated to provide more hotel rooms. The wooden manor **church★** dates from 1757.

Palojoki – *37km to the north by E 12-3 to the Nurmijärvi exit then south in the direction of Tuusula as far as the village of Palojoki.*
The home country of the Father of the Finnish novel **Aleksis Kivi** (1834-72) has to a large extent preserved its fields and meadows crisscrossed by streams and brooks, so familiar to every Finn through the novel *Seven Brothers (Seitsemän veljestä)* written in the 1860s. The birthplace of Aleksis Kivi, **Aleksis Kiven syntymäkoti**, has

Interior, Hvitträsk

mementoes of the writer and his father who was a village tailor. The garret upstairs was Kivi's favourite hideaway from where he admired the view of the valley of the River Palojoki.

★★ **Porvoo / Borgå** – *See PORVOO / BORGÅ.*

The Tuusula Lake Road – *This round tour of 77km takes in the Tuusulan Rantatie, the road that runs along the eastern shore of lake Tuusula. Leave Helsinki by road 45 in the direction of the airport, beyond Tuusula the road becomes 145.2km before Järvenpää follow the sign to Ainola.*
This excursion takes the visitor to the heart of the province of Uusimaa and the banks of Lake Tuusula (Tuusulanjärvi). At the beginning of the 20C the area was popular with artists and writers who in the spirit of the National Romantic movement advocated a return to nature. The region has retained a certain charm despite the fact that numerous new satellite towns have been developed around the original villages.

★★ **Ainola** ⊘ **(Sibelius' home)** – *Alongside road 145.* The site was chosen by Eero Järnefelt, the house built by Lars Sonck and by 1904 **Jean Sibelius** (1865-1957), his wife Aino Järnefelt (after whom the house was named) and their two daughters could move in. The beauty and peace – disturbed only by birdsong – of his new environment inspired the composer throughout his long lifetime until his death at the age of 91 in 1957. One of the first works he wrote here was his *Third Symphony.*
Both Sibelius and Aino have found their last resting place in the garden surrounded by their apple and pine trees.

★★ **Interior** – The Steinway grand piano in the drawing room was a present from his friends on his 50th birthday in 1915. Hanging on the wall nearby is Albert Edelfelt's drawing of the composer aged 38 when he moved to Ainola and to the left of the glass-fronted cabinet is a *Winter Landscape* (1915) by Sibelius' friend and neighbour, Pekka Halonen. The library is furnished in the Functionalist style of the 1930s and the composer's armchair has pride of place. On the far wall are two **watercolours★★** (1894) by Gallen-Kallela representing Sibelius and his composition *The Saga.* The study cum bedroom was where the composer chose to work from 1940 when he could no longer tackle the stairs. Lying on the table are the ever-familiar Borsalino hat and walking stick.

Drive 2km back the same road before turning right to Rantatie, following the lakeside road.

★ **Halosenniemi** ⊘ – The artist **Pekka Halonen** (1865-1933) designed this impressive pinewood house for himself in 1902. He was no doubt influenced by his friends' studio-homes, notably Emil Wickström's in Visavuori and Akseli Gallen-Kallela's wilderness studio Kalela in Ruovesi. The interior is simple, functional and somewhat spartan, the decorative work on the doors was by his cousin Arttu. The ground floor was reserved for the studio, the dining room and the kitchen and the other family rooms were upstairs. Pekka Halonen studied at the Académie Julien in Paris between 1891 and 1892 and in 1904 he was a student in Gauguin's studio. Halonen was essentially an illustrator of Finnish people and nature and became well known for the immense beauty of his winter scenes. The majority of his works are in private collections but changing exhibitions here give visitors some idea of his art.

Continue to Rantatie.

Aleksis Kiven kuolinmökki ⊘ – This extremely modest cottage was the home of Kivi's brother, Albert Stenvall. When the author fell ill he came to stay with his brother and family and it was in one of these small rooms that he spent the last months of his life. He died on 31 December 1872 aged only 38. He had created the masterpieces of Finnish prose and drama which were later to make him Finland's national writer. He alone may have foreseen the immortality of his life's work and just before he died he whispered in the ear of his brother, "I live, I live!".

Vantaa / Vanda – *15km north by road 75. The centre lies close to the Kehä Ring III.* The Heureka science centre, **Heureka Tiedekeskus** ⊘, with its hands-on approach offers a fascinating introduction to scientific phenomena. The spherical screen of the Verne Theatre with its very realistic panoramic views is an added attraction.

Ideas for an excursion from Helsinki

Regular ferries ply between Helsinki and the emerging **Baltic states** where each of the capitals has its own style. Another popular cruise takes in the **Baltic capitals** (Tallinn, Copenhagen and Stockholm).
The splendours of **St Petersburg** are only hours away by boat. Arrive by sea to discover the romantic charm of Peter the Great's capital on the Neva, also admire the majestic façades of its 18C palaces and the masterpieces of its museums. Or try the impossible and get tickets for the ballet.

HYVINKÄÄ

Etelä-Suomi
Population 41 000
Michelin map 985 L 21 or Atlas Europe p 121

The industrial town of Hyvinkää stands on a pine-covered ridge 50km to the north of Helsinki. By the early 19C the town had acquired a growing reputation as a health resort and it became fashionable for Russians to come and take the waters. In 1862 the first Finnish railway was opened here and Hyvinkää rapidly grew to be an important rail junction and industrial centre (railway workshops, woollens and quarrying).

Suomen Rautatiemuseo ⊙ – The Finnish Railway Museum was founded as early as 1898 and the star exhibit of the collection is the **imperial train★**, custom-built in Finland for Czar Alexander II in 1875.

HÄMEENLINNA/TAVASTEHUS ★

Etelä-Suomi
Population 46 000
Michelin map 985 L21 or Atlas Europe p 120

The oldest inland town in Finland stands to the south of Lake Vanajavesi on the edge of the Lake District *(local map see JÄRVI-SUOMI)*. It is known for its medieval castle and the beautiful Aulanko National Park. However its greatest claim to fame is as the birthplace of the great composer **Jean Sibelius** (1865-1957).

SIGHTS

★ Hämeen Linna ⊙ – *Kustaa III:n katu 6, 1km north of the centre – allow 1hr*. This medieval castle was built at the end of the 13C to strengthen the kingdom against the growing threat from Novgorod. By the 18C the original fortress had grown to its present size. The abundant use of brick is an indication of the castle's importance; brick was expensive and as such only used on worthy enterprises. Shortly after a visit by King Gustav II Adolf in 1626, Governor General Pehr Brahe founded the town of Hämeenlinna. During Russian rule in the 19C the castle was turned into a prison. Extensive restoration has taken place since 1960, and the castle now houses an exhibition relating the prehistory of Häme.

Sibeliuksen syntymäkoti ⊙ – *Hallituskatu 11*. **Jean Sibelius** (1865-1957) spent his childhood and youth in this Empire style family house. His father was a doctor but all the members of the family were talented musicians. The exhibited items are associated with the composer's childhood and his family.

16C frescoes in Hattulan kirkko

373

Taidemuseo ⓥ – *Viipurintie 2 at the foot of the bridge.* The nucleus of the art gallery's **collection★** is formed by works from Vyborg (Viipuri) Art Gallery, which were evacuated in 1939. There are paintings by the greatest Finnish artists of the Golden Era: Gallen-Kallela, Schjerfbeck, Järnefelt and Simberg. The contemporary art collection of Henna and Pertti Niemistö includes Finnish paintings and sculptures from the 1950s to the present day.

EXCURSIONS

★ **Aulanko** – *4km north along Aulangontie.* The Aulanko National Park comprises a hotel and recreation complex and it is the last stop on the Silver Line lake cruises. The beautiful Aulanko Nature Reserve was founded by Colonel Hugo Standertskjöld in the late 19C. From the 30m-high **belvedere** ⓥ on the hilltop there is a splendid **view★** of the surrounding countryside. From the foot of the tower 322 steps lead down to a charming sculpture *Family of Bears* by Robert Stigell (1905).

★★ **Hattulan kirkko** ⓥ – *8km north by road 57.* This brick church from c 1320 is a delightful example of a Finnish medieval church. The **frescoes and murals★★** were painted in the years following 1510 and mainly illustrate scenes from the life of Christ. They resemble those of Lohja Church and show some similarities to the work of the Swedish master Albertus Pictor of Uppland. Pay particular attention to the wooden religious sculptures, notably the **Triumphal Crucifix★** and the group **Carrying the Cross★★**, supposedly from the 16C.

Riihimäki – *32km south by E 12; Tehtaankatu 26.* There are two interesting sites standing side by side on the outskirts of this important rail junction and industrial town. The first being the Glass Museum of Finland, **Suomen Lasimuseo ★**ⓥ, which displays the historical development of glass-making and a valuable collection of Finland's finest pieces of glass. The second being the Finnish Hunting Museum, **Suomen Metsästysmuseo** ⓥ, which illustrates the hunting methods used by Finns from the Stone Age to the present.
Across the street, Tehtaankatu, is a handicrafts village, the Hyttikortteli, where the small shops all have attractive displays.

★★ **Visavuori: Emil Wikströmin museo** ⓥ – *25km north-west by E 12; follow the signpost Emil Wikströmin Museo.*
The charming studio (1903-12) and home (1903) of the sculptor **Emil Wikström** (1864-1942) stand in a splendid setting on the banks of Lake Vanajavesi. The items on display include the original plaster casts and drawings for sculptures which decorate many of Finland's public buildings. The artist was also a keen astronomer and he had a small observatory built above his studio. The log house and the studio are good examples of the National Romantic style.
The Silver Line cruises also stop here.

IISALMI
Itä-Suomi
Population 24 000
Michelin map 985 I 24 or Atlas Europe p 115 – Local map see JÄRVI-SUOMI

Located in a beautiful site by Lake Porovesi the town is an important half-way stop between Kuopio *(84km to the south)* and Kajaani *(88km to the north).* During the Finnish War of 1808-9 bitterly fought battles were won on the banks of the Koljonvirta stream north of the town. There the troops of Colonel Sandels (1764-1831) defeated the enemy forces – said to be seven times superior in numbers – led by the dreaded Russian Prince Dolgorouki (1780-1808).

Evakkokeskus (Iisalmi Evacuation Centre) ⓥ – *Kirkkopuistonkatu 28.* This Orthodox Karelian Cultural Centre was opened in 1989 in a building showing strong Russian Byzantine influences. The role of the centre is to conserve and explain the cultural heritage of northern Karelia, ceded to the Soviet Union first in 1940 and again in 1944; a library completes the collections of religious and other items.

IMATRA

Etelä-Suomi

Population 34 000

Michelin map 985 K 25 or Atlas Europe p 121

The recent and very modern town of Imatra lies at the heart of Finland's most industrialised region, on the banks of the broad and busy River Vuoksi which flows from Lake Saimaa into the immense Lake Ladoga on the Russian side.

SIGHTS

Imatrankoski – These rapids were once the country's main tourist attraction and they were a constant source of inspiration to Finnish artists such as Gallen-Kallela and Edelfelt. The falls with a drop of 24m were harnessed in the 1920s for a hydroelectric scheme and today this power station alone provides 11% of all Finland's hydroelectric energy. In summer the water is allowed to flow freely during a daily 30min **display** ★⊘ and once again the falls become spectacular as the waters thunder over the rocky lips to become a mass of foaming water.

The impressive Art Nouveau hotel, **Valtionhotelli**, overlooking the falls, was built in 1903 within the boundaries of the beautiful park, Kruunupuisto, classified as an area of outstanding scenic beauty in 1842 by Czar Nicholas I (1796-1855).

★ **Kolmen Ristin kirkko** ⊘ – *9km to the north-east.* The white, sculptural church of the Three Crosses (1950s) by Alvar Aalto is easy to identify with its tall slender belfry in the form of a down-shot arrow. On the altar three crosses replace the usual altarpiece. Of the 103 stained-glass windows only two are identical.

INGÅ/INKOO

Etelä-Suomi

Population 4 800

Michelin map 985 L 20-21 or Atlas Europe p 120

This small coastal resort triples its population in summer when many holidaymakers from the capital are attracted by the beautiful scenery and the peaceful islands.

Ingå kyrka / Inkoon kirkko ⊘ – This 13C-15C church in the centre of the village is dedicated to St Nicholas the patron saint of sailors (votive ship hanging from the ceiling). The mural on the north wall depicts a **Dance of Death**★. The free-standing **belfry** (1740) with its tiered roof was the work of Johan Friedrich Schulz, a master builder, from Brandenburg in Prussia.

★ **Fagervik Museiväg (Museum Road)** ⊘ – *12km west by road 110.* The Great Coastal Road from Turku to St Petersburg followed this stretch of road. Today the road goes through the grounds of Fagervik Manor (1773) (private) passing the foundry and red-ochre workers' houses (18C-19C) then on via a shady lane to the small wooden church, built by JF Schulz in 1737.

JOENSUU

Itä-Suomi

Population 51 000

Michelin map 985 J 26 or Atlas Europe p 115 – Local map see JÄRVI-SUOMI

Joensuu is less glamorous than its festive neighbour, Savonlinna, but it makes a perfect centre for exploring the land of the *Kälevala* – Finland's great folk epic. A busy trading centre grew up where the estuary of the great logging river, the Pielisjoki, flowed into Lake **Pyhäselkä**. Today Joensuu is still an industrial town but it has acquired a new dimension as the cultural capital of north Karelia, the land of bards and poets. The high standards and authentic atmosphere of the annual **Joensuu Song Festival** *(June)* have contributed to make this an international event of considerable importance.

SIGHTS

Kaupungintalo – *Rantakatu 4 by the riverside.* The red-brick town hall with its tower has become the landmark of the town. It also houses the Municipal Theatre and a restaurant. The building (1914) was designed by Eliel Saarinen and is one of his early Constructivist works, together with Lahti town hall and the Helsinki railway station of the same period.

Ortodoksinen Pyhän Nikolaoksen kirkko ⊘ – *Northern end of Kirkkokatu.* The timbered Orthodox church of St Nicholas dating from 1887 is one of the most beautiful examples of its kind. The impressive 19C **iconostasis**★ was painted in St Petersburg.

Taidemuseo ⓥ – *Kirkkokatu 23*. The art gallery has three particularly interesting holdings: Finnish 19C-20C paintings including Albert Edelfelt's *The Parisienne*, one of the works from his Paris period in the 1880s, a superb collection of 18C Russian **icons★** as well as an interesting section on Chinese art.

Pohjois-Karjalan museo/Carelicum ⓥ – *Koskikatu 5, close to the Joensuu market square*. This cultural and tourist centre has a permanent exhibition entitled Karelia – Both Sides of the Border, which is based on the theme of Karelia's historic position at the very centre of an East-West power struggle. There are also regular temporary exhibitions of local or regional interest, a tourist information centre, a café and gift shop.

Tori ⓥ – There is a distinctly Karelian atmosphere about the market place with its colourful stalls and it is a good place to taste the delicious Karelian pasties *(Karjalan piirakka)* made of rye dough and filled with rice or mashed potatoes. The lively **Jarmanka flea market** is to be found at the western end of Rantakatu, beside the bustling passenger harbour.

EXCURSIONS

★ **Ilomantsi and Petkeljärven kansallispuisto** – *72km east by road 74, and a further 21km to Petkeljärvi National Park*.
This excursion takes you through great tracts of dense pine and birch forests which yield grudgingly to get another watery expanse.

★ **Ilomantsi** – Finland's easternmost locality is an Orthodox stronghold. This was also the homeland of popular poets and bards who passed the folk tradition from generation to generation by singing it in the form of poems. The rune singer was accompanied by a zither-like instrument, the **kantele**. Elias Lönnrot procured most of the poems of the *Kanteletar* collection during his travels in the region in 1838. Lönnrot said of the local houses "There is a kantele hanging on every wall". In 1964 a traditional-style log-cottage, the Rune-Singers' Lodge, **Runonlaulajan pirtti ★**ⓥ, was built on Parppeinvaara hill as a tribute to the folk-poetry tradition. Here the visitor may enter the magic world of the bards as talented musicians perpetuate the tradition.
Further on in the village, at the very end of Kirkkotie is the Orthodox church of St Elias, **Pyhän Eliaan kirkko** *(from the main road take Kalevalantie on the left through the village until it ends at Kirkkotie)*. The handsome wooden church stands in a rural setting. The most important annual feast day is the Prazdnik of St Elias, **Pyhän Eliaan praasniekka★** celebrated on 20 July in honour of the church's patron saint, the prophet Elijah.

★ **Petkeljärven kansallispuisto** – *21km east of Ilomantsi village*. The road to the national park's visitor centre, **Opastuskeskus**, turns right just before the memorial commemorating the battle of Oinassalmi, one of the most difficult engagements in the Winter War of 1939-40. The park's trails vary in length and difficulty. The most demanding is the 90km-long Wolf's Trail (Susitaival), however the park's varied landscapes may be admired from one of the shorter trails such as the Taitajan Taival (26km) or from the nature trails (6.4km and 3km), which are suitable for children and the elderly.

★ **Uusi Valamo (New Valamo Monastery)** ⓥ – *65km west by road 23*. Tradition has it that in the 12C the Greek monk **Sergius** settled on the island of Valamo in Lake Ladoga. A monastic community grew around him, and by the end of the Middle Ages Valamo Monastery had become a major centre of Orthodox tradition. During the Winter War of 1939-40, the territory was annexed by the former USSR and the monastery was deserted. The few monks that could escape took a handful of their invaluable holy icons with them and moved westwards until they found a new home in Heinävesi commune in the summer of 1940. The new Valamo Monastery is today the centre of Orthodox religious life and culture in Finland. The **new church★** was consecrated in 1977. The precious **sacred objects★★** such as the miraculous icon of the Mother of God of Konevitsa, and the holy icons from the old Valamo Monastery can be admired in the church.
In July **cruises** are organised from Valamo to the Orthodox convent of Lintula, which has a similar history. The cruise takes visitors through canals and locks in beautiful lakeland scenery.

★★★ **Koli: panorama** – *See PIELINEN*.

JYVÄSKYLÄ

Länsi-Suomi
Population 76 000
Michelin map 985 J 22 or Atlas Europe p 115 – Local map see JÄRVI-SUOMI

The important road and rail junction, industrial town and provincial capital of Jyväskylä is situated at the northern end of Lake Päijänne. Internationally Jyväskylä is known as the venue for the world championship **Thousand Lakes Rally** and for its modern architecture. It was here that the first Finnish-language secondary school was established in 1858 to be followed in 1863 by a Finnish Teachers' Training College. Today the University of Jyväskylä carries on this educational tradition and is proud of its **campus★** with several buildings by Alvar Aalto (1898-1976). It was here that Aalto started his career and he designed, in all, around 30 buildings, many of them in the administrative and cultural centre, such as the Municipal Theatre (completed in 1982).

SIGHTS

★ Alvar Aalto museo ⓥ – *Alvar Aallon katu 7*. The museum building designed by Aalto himself and completed in 1973 stands beside the university campus and the Museum of Central Finland. It houses a comprehensive display of the architect's works from vases and furniture to town plans.

★ Keski-Suomen museo ⓥ – *Alvar Aallon katu 7*. The Museum of Central Finland is in an earlier building (1960) by Aalto with an extension (1990) by Alvar Aalto & Co. Two permanent exhibitions cover the cultural heritage and history of central Finland and the town of Jyväskylä. Scale models of Jyväskylä from 1805, 1880 and 1952 illustrate the city's development.

Suomen käsityön museo ⓥ – *Kauppakatu 25 next to the pedestrian street*. The small Craft Museum of Finland is devoted to crafts from 1700 to 1990 with a section of Finnish national costumes.

Kansallispukukeskus ⓥ **(National Costume Centre of Finland)** – *Gummeruksenkatu 3*. A valuable collection of national costumes is on display in the small exhibition room of the National Costume Council which is responsible for research activities and public relations.

Vesilinnan Näkötorni ⓥ – *Stairs from Harjukatu behind the bus station, or by car from Pitkäkatu on the northern side of the park*. A superb panorama of the Jyväskylä area can be had from the top of the Vesilinna water tower (34m) set high on Harju ridge, which is famous for its pine trees.

Thousand Lakes Rally

A classic in the international rallying calendar, this race is sometimes dubbed the Finnish Grand Prix. It was for long considered an exclusively Scandinavian race due to the unique character of the gravel roads with their spectacular bumps. The rally takes the form of daily loops from its home base, the university town of Jyväskylä.

The event is highly popular and some 200 000 to 300 000 spectators flock to see the Flying Finns prove their skills and claim the honours. In the race's 44 years Timo Makinen has won it four times, Hannu Mikkola five times, Ari Vatanen twice, Timo Salonen twice, Juha Kankkunen twice and Tommi Mäkinen twice. In recent years Didier Auriol was one of the rare non-Scandinavians to win.

Laajavuori – *4km north from centre.* A winter sports centre with a ski jump **(tower** ⊘**)** dedicated to the legendary ski jumper Matti Nykänen, world champion from 1982 to 1989. Every year in August Laajavuori comes to life as the coordination centre for the Thousand Lakes Rally.

EXCURSIONS

★★ **Petäjävesi: kirkko** – *32km west on road 23.* This masterpiece of vernacular timber architecture (1763-64) by the master carpenter Jaakko Klemetinpoika Leppänen, is now on the UNESCO list of World Heritage Sites. The plan is a cross with equal arms, and above the high, angular vaults rises an octagonal dome. The vault edges are decorated with red-ochre ornaments but otherwise the interior is of bare, unpainted pinewood patinated with age. The splendid **pulpit★★** supported by a primitive St Christopher and decorated with angels is even older than the church. The windows were enlarged in 1821 by the master carpenter's grandson Erkki, who also built the handsome **belfry★** which is joined to the church by a narrow passageway. Both the church and the belfry are roofed with triangular shingles.

★ **Säynätsalo and Muurame** – *Round trip of 30km to the south. Leave Jyväskylä by E 63-9.*

Säynätsalo – Säynätsalo consists mainly of 11 islands in Lake Päijänne, of which the largest, namely Säynätsalo, Lehtisaari and Muuratsalo are interconnected by bridges. Alvar Aalto had his summer residence on Muuratsalo, which is now a highly desirable residential area. The main point of interest, apart from the superb scenery, is the **Civic Centre★** (1952), a red-brick complex around a beautiful patio with the Council Chamber building rising as a tower high above the offices and the library. This complex is one of Aalto's major works.

Muurame – *16km west of Jyväskylä.* Alvar Aalto's design for the church, one of his earliest, shows a strong classical Italian influence. Close to the village centre across the main road (E 63-9) is the **Sauna Village ★**⊘, an open-air museum displaying an impressive collection of traditional saunas, including several smoke-saunas, from all over the country.

Kivikauden kylä ⊘ – *60km north, on Summassaari Island in the middle of Lake Summanen.* Excavations on this Stone Age site have located a group of 18 prehistoric dwellings. The reconstruction represents a dwelling site of the Comb-Ware Culture from c 3 000 BC. Finds from the site show how these lake-dwellers depended for their livelihood on hunting and fishing.

JÄRVI-SUOMI ★★
LAKELAND
Michelin map 985 JK 21-26 or Atlas Europe pp 115 and 120-121

Finnish lakeland with its shimmering lakes and forests is for many the most familiar and the most beautiful aspect of Finland. Over 10 000 years ago the retreating ice sheets moulded Finland's bedrock and created an amazing lace-like pattern of lakes, ridges and rocks which is characteristic of the central and eastern parts of the country. The thousands of lakes are often interconnected by straits, canals or rivers and form whole lake systems interrupted here and there by morainic ridges.

Up to the late 19C, when the road network was poor, waterways offered the best means of transport: in summer by boat and in winter on ice by skis or horse-drawn sleighs. The true heart of Finland is best seen from a boat and today it is possible to take a cruise from nearly all localities within lakeland. Trips can last anything from 1hr up to several days.

Lakeland proper is the area delimited by the towns of Tampere, Kuopio, Joensuu and Lappeenranta *(see under these names)*, however the main tourist centres within the area are Tampere, Savonlinna, Mikkeli and Lahti. The two most extensive lake systems of Päijänne and Saimaa are connected by waterways to most of the smaller lakes.

PÄIJÄNNE

This immense lake is Finland's third largest after Lake Inari and Lake Saimaa and it ribbons its way southwards from Jyväskylä to Lahti (120km). Lakes **Vesijärvi** to the south, **Ruotsalainen** to the east and Jyväsjärvi to the north are also part of the Päijänne system. The shoreline is highly indented and sheltered bays and inlets are backed by rocky escarpments or gently rolling arable land whereas the lake itself is dotted with a large number of islands *(see JYVÄSKYLÄ)*. It is an unspoilt countryside of lakes and forests. Lake Päijänne lies between road E 75-24 and road 59, which separate at Lahti but meet again at Jyväskylä. The most beautiful scenery however is often found by trying the smaller winding lakeside roads. Full day **cruises★★** operate between Lahti and Jyväskylä.

Jyväskylä – *See JYVÄSKYLÄ.*

★★ **Petäjävesi: Church** – *See JYVÄSKYLÄ: Excursions.*

★ **Säynätsalo** – *See JYVÄSKYLÄ: Excursions.*

★ **Muurame: Sauna Village** – *See JYVÄSKYLÄ: Excursions.*

Kivikauden kylä – *See JYVÄSKYLÄ: Excursions.*

Lahti – Lahti lies at the southern end of Vesijärvi on the edge of the Salpausselkä ridge which marks the southern limit of lakeland. The town grew rapidly in the 20C from a small rural village into a modern business centre with over 95 000 inhabitants. Apart from business and trade, Lahti is known as an important venue for winter sports events and its three ski jumps (114m, 90m and 64m high) have become its most distinctive landmarks. In summer, the highest one serves as a viewing platform, **Näkötorni** ★ ⊙. The sports centre includes a ski museum, **Hiihtomuseo** ⊙.

Lahti's two most exciting buildings make an interesting contrast: the town hall *(Harjukatu)* was designed in 1912 by Finland's first internationally known architect, Eliel Saarinen and it faces northwards to Alvar Aalto's brick-built church, **Ristin kirkko** ⊙ *(in the park off Kirkkokatu)* dating from 1978.

Hollola – The splendid stone-built **Hollolan kirkko** ⊙, dedicated to the Virgin Mary, was completed in the 1480s. The tall gables are richly ornamented with decorative brickwork. The **star vaulting**★ is an example of how local masons adapted the German Gothic style. Some of the superb 15C **sculptures**★ probably came from Germany. Note the remarkable sculptured panel on the 4m-high pinewood **door**★, representing St Hubert on a hunting trip.

Verla Mill Museum ⊙ – *25km north of Kuusankoski, near the town of Jaala.* The pulp and paper mill built in 1882 on the site of an earlier mill lies on both banks of the River Kymi. The neo-Gothic industrial premises are characteristic of mills in operation in the Nordic countries and northern Russia in the late 19C and early 20C. After it closed down in 1964, the mill complex, which comprises the owner's residence with its park, the mill itself and the workers cottages on the other side of the river, was turned into a museum illustrating the life of the mill workers and their families as well as the impact of the industrial activity on the surrounding countryside. Verla Mill is now on UNESCO's World Heritage list.

Hartola – *1km to the south of Hartola city centre and a short distance from road 4.* The **Itä-Hämeen museo** ⊙ or Eastern Häme Museum was founded by Maila Talvio (1871-1951), a well-known literary personality, in Koskipää Manor which once belonged to her sister. The lovely green and white **manor house**★ (1828) on the banks of the River Tainionkoski is in pure Empire style. The collections depict the life and history of the wealthy manor owners and of the peasants of the region. The yellow building, Pyhäniemi, was the original 18C manor and houses the **Artcastle Hollola** ⊙ with temporary exhibitions in summer.

Joutsa: Talomuseo ⊙ – *2km to the north of the village of Joutsa.* Two hundred-year-old farmstead buildings, including storehouses, barns, stables and sauna, are regrouped in the traditional manner around the courtyard and provide an attractive setting for a local history museum.

★ **Jämsä** – *At the intersection of roads E 63-9 and E 75-24.* The small town by the River Jämsänjoki is known for its beauty spots and the Himos winter sports centre. The excellent road and waterway connections have contributed to the development of a flourishing paper industry and business centre. The **scenery**★★ between Jämsä and Korpilahti *(30km north-east)* is exceptional and the drive along the hilly and winding minor road *(no 610)* from Korpilahti over to the eastern side of Lake Päijänne is worthwhile. The Saimaa system has a good network of ferry services linking the various lakeside towns (Lappeenranta, Savonlinna, Mikkeli and Imatra). Boat trips enable visitors to fully appreciate the beauty of the scenery – which is not always possible from the road.

★ **Tampere** – *See TAMPERE.*

Näsijärvi lake system and sights – *See TAMPERE: Excursions.*

SAIMAA

In the land of a thousand lakes, lake Saimaa is the largest, with an area of 1 400km², and claims to be the lake of a thousand islands. The great terminal moraine, known as the Punkaharju ridge, separates Saimaa from the other lake systems to the north.

Joensuu – *See JOENSUU.*

★ **Ilomantsi and its Orthodox traditions** – *See JOENSUU: Excursions.*

★ **Petkeljärvi: National Park** – *See JOENSUU: Excursions.*

Valamo: monastery – *See JOENSUU: Excursions.*

Lake Pielinen – *See PIELINEN.*

★**Kuopio** – *See KUOPIO.*

Lappeenranta – *See LAPPEENRANTA.*

★**Saimaan kanava** – *See LAPPEENRANTA: Excursions.*

★**Lauritsala: Church** – *See LAPPEENRANTA: Excursions.*

Ylämaa: Spectrolite Village – *See LAPPEENRANTA: Excursions.*

Mikkeli – Surrounded by waterways connected to Lake Saimaa, Mikkeli has developed from a 15C market place into a modern commercial town with a population of 32 000. The sacristy, **Kivisakasti** ⊙, *(Porrassalmenkatu 32A)* is all that remains of a medieval church; it houses a collection of religious items. The water tower, standing high on Naisvuori hill, has been the town's outstanding landmark since it was built in 1911; the observation platform of **Naisvuoren näkötorni** ⊙ affords a good overall view of the town.

Mikkeli played an important strategic role during the wars of 1939-40 and 1941-44, when the Finnish Army made its headquarters in a local school at Päämajankatu 1-3. The school buildings now house the Headquarters Museum, **Päämajamuseo** ★⊙, where Marshal Mannerheim's **study**★ is spartan but typical of Finland's great military leader. A 19C neo-Classical ensemble at Jääkärinkatu 6-8 houses the Infantry Museum, **Jalkaväkimuseo** ⊙, which depicts the development of the Finnish infantry regiments from 1881 to the present. Many of the buildings in the area are still occupied by the army.

★★**Punkaharju Ridge Area (Harjualue)** – *East of the village of Punkaharju. See SAVONLINNA: Excursions.*

★★**Savonlinna** – *See SAVONLINNA.*

★**Rauhalinna** – *In the village of Lehtiniemi. See SAVONLINNA: Excursions.*

★★**Retretti: Art Centre** – *See SAVONLINNA: Excursions.*

★**Kerimäki: Church** – *See SAVONLINNA: Excursions.*

★**Varkaus** – The town developed during the 19C around scenic rapids and vast forests at the intersection of Lake Saimaa waterways, providing favourable conditions for the forest industry. Today this town of 25 000 inhabitants is a centre for high technology and processing industries. Some of the industrial sites represent the best in industrial architecture from the 1920s to the present. The Lutheran **kirkko** ⊙ (1939) by Martti Paalanen is a rare example of a Functionalist church with touches of classicism. The interesting fresco *Thy Kingdom Come* (1954), on the wall behind the altar, is by Lennart Segerstråle (1892-1975).

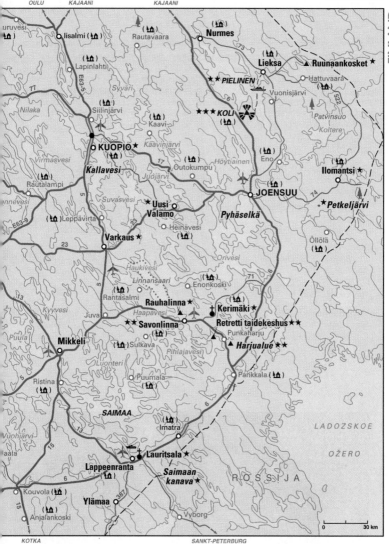

The Museum of Mechanical Music, **Mekaanisen musiikin museo** ★⊙ *(Pelimanninkatu 8)*, presents a collection of over 200 instruments including gramophones, street organs and orchestrions from the 19C to the present. Complete the visit by trying the nice café-restaurant in the side-building furnished in the same spirit.

The most forested country in Europe

Over two thirds of Finland is covered by forests; the majority of the trees are conifers (pine and spruce) but deciduous species (birch, oak, maple and ash) grow in the south-west. Tar distillation and exportation were followed by sawmilling in the 1800s, then in the mid-19C the cellulose and paper industries took over and by the beginning of the 20C forest industry exports amounted to over 85% of Finland's total exports. Although Finland's industrial sector has witnessed a certain diversification the forestry industry continues to earn more than a third of the country's export income. One Finnish family in five owns some forest which means that two thirds of Finnish forests are privately owned.

KAJAANI

Oulu

Population 37 000

Michelin map 985 H 24 or Atlas Europe p 115

The administrative and cultural centre of the Kainuu district was founded by Per Brahe on the banks of the River Kajaaninjoki in 1651, at the foot of Kajaani Castle. The castle itself fell into ruins in 1716 during the Great Northern War, but the solid grey-stone foundations are still visible. In the 19C Kajaani grew in importance when the heavily forested Kainuu district became the world's most important tar-producing area. The tar was shipped from Kajaani across Lake Oulujärvi and along the river in large rowing boats to the seaport of Oulu on the Gulf of Bothnia.

SIGHTS

Castle Ruins and Tar Lock ☉ – *By the Linnansilta bridge*. A pleasant walk stretching the river bank from the 17C castle ruins along the tar canal to the lock-keeper's cottage, **Lussitupa.**

Luterilainen kirkko ☉ – Twenty-four local carpenters built the church in 1896 to the neo-Gothic designs of Jacob Ahrenberg. The many decorative carvings are exceptionally rich. The 1925 altarpiece is by a local artist, Toivo Tuhkanen.

Kainuun museo ☉ – *Satamakatu 4*. The small provincial museum has an interesting scale model to explain the process of tar distilling, the province's main activity for over a century.

EXCURSION

★ **Paltaniemen kirkko** ☉ – *9km north-west by road 880 (airport road)*. This church was built in 1726 and is richly decorated with an astonishing series of **frescoes** ranging from the Creation to the Last Judgement; the latter, above the main door, is the best preserved. The frescoes were painted between 1778 and 1781 by Emanuel Granberg.

Frescoes in Paltaniemen Kirkko

KEMI

Lappi
Population 25 000
Michelin map 985 G 21 or Atlas Europe p 109

Situated at the mouth of the mighty River Kemijoki at the northern end of the Gulf of Bothnia, Kemi is a major export harbour. Until recent times timber from Lapland was floated down the river to the town's timber processing plants. Although road transportation finally took over in the 1990s, the tall chimney-stacks of the paper and cellulose mills still stand as a heritage of another age. Tourism continues to play a growing role in the town's economy.

** **Jäänmurtaja Sampo** ⊘ – *7.5km south-west in Ajos harbour.* A visit to the ice-breaker *Sampo*, which is capable of breaking a 15m-tall wall of ice, makes a fascinating experience even in summer. *Sampo* is the world's only ice-breaker to spend her early retirement in the tourism industry; she served for 25 years in the Finnish ice-breaker fleet. The 4hr **ice-breaking cruises**★★★ *(from mid-December to mid-April)* offer an unforgettable experience. The seaways of Finland are kept open all year round by a fleet of nine ice-breakers based in Helsinki.

Jalokivigalleria ⊘ – *Kauppakatu 29 by the seafront.* A comprehensive collection of gems and carefully made replicas of the world's most famous pieces of jewellery as well as an exhibition of jewellery making techniques are displayed in this interesting gallery. A small collection of traditional Sami jewellery from Lapland adds to the interest of the visit.

KEURUU ★

Länsi-Suomi
Population 13 000
Michelin map 985 J 21 or Atlas Europe p 120 – Local map see JÄRVI-SUOMI

Keuruu is beautifully set on four islands at the northern end of Lake Keurusselkä. Although set in the heart of a traditionally agricultural region Keuruu is now an important industrial centre.

★ **Vanha kirkko** ⊘ – *At the junction of road 23 and Keuruuntie road leading to the centre.*
This charming church from 1758 was built by Antti Hakola (1704-78) and is one of the finest 18C wooden churches. The interesting decorative paintings also date from the late 18C and illustrate scenes from the Bible. The original altarpiece representing Christ on the Cross is said to be by the Swede Johan Backman the Younger.
Alongside the churchyard wall on the north side lies a 21m-long **church boat**★ (19C) with 15 pairs of oars, which could transport 80 passengers. The boat was used by worshippers from outlying villages.

EXCURSIONS

★ **Pihlajaveden vanha kirkko** ⊘ – *23km north-west by road 23 and then right onto road 6211. Leave the village by the narrow Erämaakirkontie.*
This beautiful red-ochre church stands in the heart of the forest and is one of central Finland's wilderness churches. It was built in 1781 by master Matti Åkerblom for the local tenant-farmers who were

A Lake in the Wilderness (1892)
by Akseli Gallen-Kallela

The Gösta Serlachius Museum of Fine Arts, Finland

keen to have their own place of worship. The resulting church and onion-shaped tower surpassed by far the initial commission but it remains a good example of wooden architecture of the period.

★★ Gösta Serlachiuksen taidemuseo ⊙ – *34km south in the village of Mänttä.*
This important art collection belonged to one of the most prominent figures of the Finnish paper industry **Gösta Serlachius** (1876-1942). Joenniemi Manor by the lakeside was designed in 1935 by Jarl Eklund (1876-1962) whereas the wonderful **parkland★** was laid out by the Dane Paul Olsson. Near the car park is a life-size statue of an elk by Jussi Mäntynen (1886-1967).

Interior – The European paintings, on the ground floor, include valuable works from the Renaissance to the Impressionist period. Note Juan de Zurbaran's (1620-49) *Still-life with Basket of Fruit and Cardoon* and Gerbrandt van den Eeckhout's (1621-74) *Abraham meeting Melchizedek* (1648). The former library is decorated with the monumental mural by Lennart Segerstråle (1892-1975) .

The masterpieces of the **Golden Age★★** of Finnish art are in the first-floor rooms. One of the finest is *The Symposium* (1894) by Akseli Gallen-Kallela (1865-1931) showing the painter with composers Jean Sibelius, Robert Kajanus and Oskar Merikanto in a late-night session. The portrait of the composer Gustav Mahler (1907) is one of Gallen-Kallela's best-known portraits. In addition, several of his *Kalevala* inspired paintings can be seen here. Also on display are some of the most remarkable paintings of Albert Edelfelt (1854-1905), Eero Järnefelt (1863-1937), Magnus Enckell (1870-1925), Hugo Simberg (1873-1917) and Pekka Halonen (1865-1967).

Finally the wine cellar in the basement is of special interest because of the hilarious frescoes by the Swede Irina Bäcksbacka when she was only 16, illustrating the drinking songs of Carl Michael Bellman. The fine woodcarvings are by the Finnish master woodcarver Hannes Autere (1888-1967).

KOKKOLA/KARLEBY

Länsi-Suomi
Population 36 000
Michelin map I 20 or Atlas Europe p 114

In 1620 King Gustav II Adolf founded a town on the Ostrobothnian coast and it soon grew to become a major seaport known for its shipbuilding and tanning industries. As the land rose the harbour no longer had the depth of water necessary for ocean-going vessels and Kokkola lost its maritime trade. Today Kokkola is essentially a commercial and service centre for its hinterland.

★★ Mannerheiminaukio – The attractive main square is graced by a statue of liberty, *Vapaudenpatsas*, (1920), by J Munsterhjelm in front of the Empire-style **town hall** (1845) by Helsinki's architect Carl Ludvig Engel.

★★ Historiallinen museo ⊙ – *Pitkänsillankatu 28, at the corner of Läntinen Kirkkokatu.* The picturesque wooden building with its attractive shingle roof was the Karelby Pedagogium in the 17C. A small museum illustrates Kokkola's maritime history.

Old Town – *Delimited by Rantakatu, Pitkänsillankatu and Läntinen Kirkkokatu.* The grid-iron layout dates from the 1660s although the oldest houses are 18C. The English Park, Englantilainen Puisto, has a 19C paddle steamer, which was taken as a war trophy in 1854 during the Crimean War, when the British Fleet tried to create a diversion by attempting to land along the Finnish coast. The Halkokari naval battle took place off Kokkola in 1854.

Kaarlelan kirkko ⊙ – *Elisabetintie in Kirkonmäki 2km south of the city centre.* This late 15C church was enlarged in the late 18C by the progressive Finnish thinker Anders Chydenius (1729-1803). In addition to holding high office in the church, Chydenius was also an important statesman during the Enlightenment and contributed to improving popular education. Next to the church is the wooden vicarage dating from 1736 and a tiny local history museum containing some of Anders Chydenius' personal items.

EXCURSION

★ Väinöntalo ⊙ – *In Evijärvi 60km south-south-east.* A typical late-18C farmhouse from central Ostrobothnia, also known as the lakeland of Ostrobothnia. The museum comprises 19 separate buildings in all, of which the 2-storey main building contains authentic furnishings of the period. The cupboards and clocks with decorative flower-paintings are characteristic of the region.

Kaustinen – *42km south-east.* The little Ostrobothnian village is the venue for a superb international **Folk Music Festival★★** which is organised annually during the second fortnight in July. The Folk Music Centre in the heart of the village comprises a small museum of traditional instruments.

FINLAND

* **Jakobstad / Pietarsaari** – *38km south-west by road 749 (Seven Bridges Road) connecting the larger coastal islands.* The home town of the national poet **JL Runeberg** (1804-77) was founded in 1652 by Ebba Brahe, the widow of the famous soldier Jakob de la Gardie (thus the Swedish name Jakobstad meaning Jakob's town). The town, with a population of 20 000, still has a slight Swedish-speaking majority of 55%. The old seafaring and shipbuilding traditions are illustrated in the attractive museum at **Malmin talo** *(Isokatu 2).* The old wooden town **Skata★** grew during the industrialization of the town in the early 19C and it is now a historic preservation area. On the outskirts of the town there is an old hunting and fishing chalet, the **Runebergintupa,** which once belonged to the poet.

* **Kalajoen hiekkasärkät** – *60km north.* Smooth dunes of fine sand extend for 5km along the shore of the glittering Gulf of Ostrobothnia and are backed by a beautiful pine forest on the landward side. A holiday village offers a wide variety of recreational facilities.

KOTKA
Etelä-Suomi
Population 56 000
Michelin map 985 L 23-24 or Atlas Europe p 121

This major port and industrial centre (together with the neighbouring town of Karhula) for eastern Finland, is located on two islands at the mouth of the River Kymi on the Gulf of Finland. On one of the main logging routes, Kotka developed with the growth of the timber trade and ancillary industries and is today the number one port for exporting timber.

The past – Ever since the Dark Ages, when Kotka was a trading post and overwintering stop for the merchant Vikings travelling on the Amber Road, trade has been vital to the town. The naval battles of Ruotsinsalmi (1789 and 1790) engaged the maritime might of the Russian and Finnish-Swedish fleets; the second battle was reputedly Europe's greatest naval engagement with over 500 ships involved and the victory for the Finnish-Swedish fleet reversed their previous defeat. However the town of Kotka (eaglet in Finnish) was only officially founded in 1878 by Czar Alexander II in part to counteract the Swedish garrison town of Loviisa further to the west.

SIGHTS

Kotkansaari – The Island of the eaglet is the site of the old town and it is here that the bustle of the port is at its busiest. Every August the harbour area is the scene of the Sea Festival (Kotkan Meripäivät) when visitors can enjoy dancing and singing in the true maritime tradition. The town's oldest building is the Orthodox **St Nicholas' Church** ⊙ (1795); it was the only one to survive the attack during the Crimean War. The Lutheran red-brick church, on the hill in the centre, is a typical late-19C neo-Gothic construction by J Stenbäck (1898).

* **Langinkosken Keisarillinen kalastusmaja** ⊙ – *7km north.* Langinkoski Imperial Fishing Lodge, a 2-storey log-cabin, was built in 1889 for Czar Alexander III, grand duke of Finland. He and his consort, Danish-born, Empress Maria Feodorovna enjoyed the simple life and salmon fishing in the fast-flowing waters of the Langinkoski rapids. The lodge is furnished with the original imperial furniture. A path through the national forest park leads to the Czar's private chapel.

KRISTINESTAD/KRISTIINANKAUPUNKI ★★
Länsi-Suomi
Population 8 800
Michelin map 985 J 18 or Atlas Europe p 120

This picturesque seaside town is one of the very few old Finnish towns never to have been destroyed by fire. The town was founded in 1649 by the governor **Per Brahe,** who named it after his wife Kristina and the Swedish queen of the same name. It has been an important commercial and service centre for the Swedish-speaking communities of the coast.

* **Old Town** – The old district, around the central market square, with its colourful wooden houses dating from the 17C and 18C and its narrow streets and lanes has retained much of its original character. The narrowest lane has the curious name of Cat Whipper's lane (Kattpiskargränden). At the top of Kyrkogatan is the charming wooden **Ulrika Eleonora kyrka** ★⊙ dating from 1700. The spire leans gently towards the town hall (1856) on the left by EB Lohrman. The two tiny wooden buildings (1687 and 1720) on the other side once served as customs houses.

EXCURSIONS

Närpes / Närpio – *16km north*. This predominantly (94%) Swedish-speaking community produces 60% of Finland's tomato crop. Närpes has been a pioneer in greenhouse production in the near Arctic conditions of northern Finland. This successful venture brought considerable prosperity to Närpes and the town centre was redeveloped in the 1960s and 1970s. The attractive wooden houses and stables of the old church village line the main street leading to the 15C church.

Lappfjärd / Lappväärtti – *7km east*. The size of **Lappfjärd kyrka** ⊘ is surprising for this small suburban community. The red-brick church (1851) by Lohrman can seat 3 500 and has an unusual wooden cupola.

KUHMO

Oulu – Population 13 000
Michelin map 985 H 26 or Atlas Europe p 115

The wilderness locality of Kuhmo extends over an area of 5 000km2 of which 80% is forest belonging to the northern coniferous zone or the Taiga. Hiking and canoeing are the best ways to discover the mysterious silence of these wilderness areas.

The town centre comes alive during the second fortnight of July when the **Kuhmo Chamber Music Festival**★★ attracts visitors and musicians from all over the world.

SIGHTS

★**Kuhmo-talo** ⊘ – The Kuhmo Arts Centre by Matti Heikkinen was inaugurated in 1993 to provide the highly successful chamber music festival with its own premises. The facilities include two multi-purpose concert halls, teaching facilities for music and dance, rehearsal and dressing rooms as well as exhibition space.

Kirkko ⊘ – The large wooden church (Jacob Rijf, 1816) has a cruciform plan and a large central cupola. The belfry by Carl Ludvig Engel was added in 1862.

Kalevala-kylä ⊘ – *Allow 1hr 30min for the circuit*. The Kalevala Village offers an insight into local folklore and traditional skills and crafts, through demonstrations and exhibitions. It brings to life the mythical tales of the national epic, the *Kalevala*, and in fact it was in these regions that **Professor Elias Lönnrot** (1802-84) finally put together his collection of old folk poetry and named it the *Kalevala* in 1834. The first edition of the *Kalevala* appeared in 1835.

The romantic idealisation of Karelia – Karelianism – became an important symbol of Finnish identity.

Kalevala – poem and national epic

Dr Elias Lönnrot (1802-84) put his signature to the foreword of his work entitled *Kalevala* or *Old Poems of Karelia from the Ancient Times of the Finnish People* on 28 February 1835. The date has become **Kalevala Day**, a celebration of Finnish culture.

The edition of 1835 is known as the *Old Kalevala*. In 1840 he published *Kanteletar (The Spirit of the Kantele)* and he prepared an expanded second edition of *Kalevala* (1849). The latter contained 50 poems and 22 795 lines and is known as the *New Kalevala* and was to be the final form of his work.

The content – This epic is based on folk poetry – old lyric poems, wedding poems, incantations, proverbial phrases and additions by Lönnrot himself – and recounts the life and feats of the heroes of old folk poetry. The background is the struggle for power and wealth between two rival tribal communities (Kalevala and Pohjola). The former symbolised Finland and the latter a realm of darkness and evil.

The principal heroes are:

Väinämöinen – a great wise man, rune singer and leader of his tribe;

Ilmarinen – the smith and forger of the vault of heaven, Väinämöinen's companion;

Lemminkäinen – an inconstant ladykiller and reckless adventurer;

Joukahainen – a young Sami and fledgling wizard who loses to the leader in a magical singing duel and seeks revenge;

Kullervo – son of a slave and tragic avenger in a family feud;

Louhi – the mistress of Pohjola and strong ruler of her tribe;

Aino – maiden sister of Joukahainen, courted by the old Väinämöinen;

Jlmatar – a divine being who gives birth to Väinämöinen;

Lemminkäinen's mother – her motherly love brings her son back to life.

KUOPIO ★

Itä-Suomi
Population 86 000
Michelin map 985 J 24 or Atlas Europe p 115 – Local map see JÄRVI-SUOMI

The town was founded in 1782, by order of King Gustav III, on the shore of the wide and beautiful Lake **Kallavesi** in an area of endless forests and waterways. The 19C saw a rapid development in inland navigation, which greatly contributed to the town's prosperity. Kuopio is a busy provincial capital, an important university town and a good centre for boat excursions.

SIGHTS

★★ **Ortodoksinen kirkkomuseo** ⊙ – *1.3km north-west of the centre, at Karjalankatu 1.* The collections of this unique Orthodox Church Museum came in large part from the monasteries of Valamo, Konevitsa and Petsamo, all ceded to the Soviet Union after the Second World War. The upper gallery displays **sacred objects and icons★★★** exhibited in seven rooms surrounding the main hall. Some of the most valuable objects are the silver **cenotaph of St Arseny★★**, founder of Konevitsa Monastery (room I), and the **cenotaph of St Sergius and St Herman★★**, founders of Valamo Monastery (room VII). Two particularly lovely icons among the remarkable icon collection are the **Annunciation★★** and the **Nativity of Our Lady★★** (both in room VII). The ground-floor exhibition displays a fascinating collection of **liturgical vestments**.

Tuomiokirkko ⊙ – *In Snellmaninpuisto.* A combination of Gustavian and Empire styles gives this 1815 Lutheran cathedral its own special charm. It is surrounded by a beautiful park.

Tori – The bustle of Kuopio **market** ⊙ is often accompanied by accordion players or other folklore events. The local speciality, *kalakukko*, a pasty of fish and pork baked in a rye crust, is on sale here or in the busy market hall, Kauppahalli, on the Kauppakatu side of the square.

Kuopion museo ⊙ – *Kauppakatu 23.* The ground floor of this Art Nouveau building is reserved for changing exhibitions. The permanent displays include items from the history and natural history collections.

Kuopion korttelimuseo ⊙ – *Kirkkokatu 22.* The Old Kuopio Museum comprises a group of early 19C wooden houses and it illustrates the history of life and housing in the town from the 18C to the 1930s.

JV Snellmanin kotimuseo ⊙ – *Snellmaninkatu 19.* The nationalist, philosopher and statesman **Johan Vilhelm Snellman** (1806-81) lived in this house between 1845 and 1849 when he was the local headmaster before he embarked on his political career. He became an important figure in the Finnish national awakening of the mid-19C. The museum contains furniture and personal items.

★★ **Puijon näkötorni** ⊙ – *3.5km north-west of the centre.* The 75m-high observation tower on its forested hillside is the town's outstanding landmark. It provides a fantastic **view★** of the typically Finnish landscape of lakes and forests. The revolving panoramic restaurant is on the 12th floor; the viewing platform can be reached by stairs from the 13th floor.

KUUSAMO ★★

Oulu
Population 18 500
Michelin map 985 G 26 or Atlas Europe p 109

Kuusamo is located on the highlands of north-eastern Finland, an area of ravines and canyons where lazy flowing rivers become seething rapids. The forests of Kuusamo are still home to bears and wolves and a large variety of smaller predators such as foxes, raccoons, minks and ermines. The magnificence of the wilderness areas has been immortalised by numerous artists, but above all by Akseli Gallen-Kallela (for example the *Herd-boy at Paanajärvi*, 1892) who maintained that this was the ideal Finnish scenery. In the centre of Kuusamo, beside road 5, is the **Karhuntassu Tourist Centre** ⊙ which provides information on a variety of activities from hiking and rapids shooting to skiing trips in winter.

EXCURSIONS

★ **Rukatunturi** ⊙ – *25km north-east*. In summer Ruka Fell which rises to a height of 491m is a lovely beauty spot. The summit can be reached by chair-lift and the more adventurous can take a summer toboggan downhill. The famous Bear's Ring trail *(see below)* for experienced hikers ends at the foot of Ruka Fell. In winter Ruka is one of the most popular Finnish winter sports centres (28 pistes and 18 ski-lifts) and the first down-hill skiers can be seen on the slopes by mid-October. There are also some 180km of marked cross-country skiing tracks.

★★ **Oulangan kansallispuisto** – *56km north*. The Oulanka National Park, situated in northern Kuusamo, covers an area of 270km2 and boasts some of the region's most extraordinary natural sites. The Oulankajoki is a powerful river flowing eastwards at an average height of 133m above sea level. **Kiutaköngäs★★** is a magnificent 600m-long stretch of rapids where water rushes over red-granite rocks. A path from the **Information Centre** ⊙ leads to the falls and the round trip is only 2km. The Bear's Ring (Karhunkierros) is an 80km-long hiking trail which lies within the national park. The trail passes the finest canyons and rapids and shelter is provided by wilderness cabins. The hiker should reserve four to six days depending on his physical condition. Prior to departure always leave your itinerary and schedule with the local information centre.

★★ **Juuma** – *50km north*. This hiking and camping resort lies on the edge of the wilderness on the banks of the River Kitkajoki. The Bear's Ring hiking trail passes the famous **Niskakoski** and **Myllykoski rapids★★**, both crossed by a rope bridge. There are more powerful rapids at **Aallokkokoski** and at **Jyrävä**, both within the boundaries of the national park. A 7km path, part of the Bear's Ring, makes it possible to visit these sights on a day trip. The adventurous **rapids shooting★★** on the River Kitkanjoki is a white-knuckle experience not to be missed.

★ **Julma Ölkky: Canyon Lake** – *66km south*. See SUOMUSSALMI: Hossa.

A wilderness retreat for a famous artist

Following Gallen-Kallela's second visit to Paris in the spring of 1892 and the luke-warm reception given to his work *Aino*, he spent some time in Kuusamo rebuilding his inspiration and strength. The painting *The Great Black Woodpecker – Virgin Landscape*, 1893 *(Palokärki, Erämaa)* is a direct result of this stay. Pekka Halonen painted a similar canvas in 1899 *Karelian Scene – Virgin Landscape (Erämaa, Karjalainen maisema)*.

LAPPEENRANTA

Etelä-Suomi
Population 57 000
Michelin map 985 K 25 or Atlas Europe p 121

This lively town on the southern shore of Lake Saimaa has grown, since the post-war period, to replace Vyborg (Viipuri) lost to the Soviet Union in 1944, as the cultural and commercial centre of southern Karelia. The beautiful location and good waterway connections along the Saimaa canal have contributed to the growing importance of tourism.

Linnoitus: sights within the fortress area – Work on the fortress started in 1721 and was still not completed when the Russians captured the town in 1741. Work then continued under Prince Suvorov, but when Finland became a Grand Duchy in 1809 and the frontier moved eastwards, the fortifications lost their strategic value. The fortress area has been transformed into a leisure and cultural centre.

Ratsuväkimuseo ⊘ – Uniforms and weapons of the Finnish Cavalry are on display in the town's oldest building dating from 1772.

Majurska ⊘ – The former Young Officers' Club houses a cosy cafeteria arranged as a 19C army officer's home.

★ **Ortodoksinen kirkko** ⊘ - The Church of the Protection of the Virgin Mary is the oldest Orthodox church in Finland, built by the Russians in 1785. The 17C **icon**★ in the middle of the north wall bears the same name as the church.

Etelä-Karjalan taidemuseo ⊘ – Changing exhibitions alternate with the south Karelian art museum's permanent collection of mainly local artists' works.

★ **Etelä-Karjalan museo** ⊘ – The former artillery depot houses the south Karelian local history collections (period rooms and costumes). The main attraction is however the Vyborg section with an interesting scale model of Vyborg as it was just before the outbreak of war in the autumn of 1939.

Tori ⊘ – Delimited by Snellmaninkatu and Oksasenkatu – it is here that the warmhearted and joyful atmosphere of the Karelian way of life is best appreciated.

Lappeen kirkko ⊘ – *On the corner of Valtakatu and Kirkkokatu.* The large wooden church was built in 1794 by master Juhana Salonen. It is unique because of its double-cruciform shape. The Ascension (1887) altar painting is by Aleksandra Såltin, one of the most productive altarpiece painters of the turn of the last century. The belfry stands at some distance from the church.

Satama – Boats leave the harbour daily for excursions on Lake Saimaa and the Saimaa canal.

EXCURSIONS

★ **Saimaan kanava** ⊘ – *6km east.* Several attempts were made over the centuries – the earliest in the 15C – to connect Lake Saimaa to the Gulf of Finland. A reminder of the 17C project, known as the Ditch of Pontus, can be seen by the Muukontie road in Pontus village, next to the main road. The Emperors' Canal was opened in 1856 and with its 28 locks and a total length of 57km it provided an outlet to the sea. The third canal was inaugurated in 1968 and 23km out of the total 43km and three out of eight locks are on the Finnish side. Cargo is shipped from inland towns via the canal to some 20 European ports. Tourist traffic is also important in the summer; canal cruises leave from Lappeenranta. The best viewing points are at Mustola and at Mälkiä locks, the latter situated beside the 19C Emperors' Canal.

★ **Lauritsalan kirkko** ⊘ – *In the centre of Lauritsala, in Keskuskatu.* This astonishing modern church, The Light of Heaven, by Toivo Korhonen and Jaakko Laapotti was dedicated in 1969. Its floor plan is a right-angled triangle and the sloping concrete roof rises to the impressive height of 47m.

Ylämaa – *35km south.* The gemstone spectrolite belongs to the labradorites and is said to be the most beautiful of them all. Spectrolite shines with a range of iridescences from golden brown to darkest blue. The mineral was first found locally by a soldier in 1940. The **Ylämaan Jalokivikylä** ⊘ spectrolite village, with goldsmiths' workshops and a gemstone exhibition, stands close to the quarries where spectrolite has been quarried since the early 1970s.

LAPPI ★★★

FINNISH LAPLAND

Population 200 000

Michelin map 985 BG 20-26 or Atlas Europe pp 105 and 109

Local map see LAPPLAND in the Swedish section

The very word Lapland captivates the imagination and the wild tundra expanses of Finnish Lapland, inextricably associated with the Sami and their culture, are no exception. This mighty wilderness with its great rounded fells, unending marshes and meadows, silent lakes and great glittering rivers has a growing appeal and increasing success with Europe's city dwellers.

Today around 75 000 Sami live on the northern fringes of the Scandinavian peninsula and their homeland territory (Sápmi) extends from the western shores of Norway northwards and eastwards to Sweden, Finland and Russia. Some 4 000 live in northern Finland and a further 1 500 in the south.

Origins – From time immemorial the Sami have occupied these northerly lands, their ancestral homelands. The Roman historian Tacitus spoke of a people here but it is also possible that their ancestors were the prehistoric people of the Komsa culture (6 000 BC).

Sami herder with reindeer

The land: a hostile and harsh environment – Finnish Lapland lies almost entirely within the Arctic Circle (Napapiiri) and the climate is a harsh one where snow covers the ground for over two thirds of the year (October to May). Average annual temperatures vary from -14°C in January to +14°C in July with the absolutes well in excess of these figures. Summers are short but warm for the latitude with approximately 72 days of Midnight Sun from 17 May to 27 July. Winters are long with no daylight from 25 November to 15 January.

Summer arrives in a matter of days at the end of May or the beginning of June, and the incredible power of the sun – shining day and night – awakes the vegetation into rapid growth.

In winter, the velvet dark sky is lit by the moon and milliards of stars, and occasionally by the enhancing northern lights, the aurora borealis.

Livelihood – For more than 2 000 years the Sami of the north have lived from reindeer farming. Traditionally the Sami have always been and still are reindeer herders although some also fish and hunt. The nomads of the mountains and the semi-nomads of the forests practised transhumance and followed, with all their goods, the migrations of the reindeer from the winter grazing grounds to their summer pastures.

Today many of the herders have exchanged their sledge for a snow-scooter, their tent for a house, their reindeer skins for an anorak and practice modern reindeer management with helicopters and walkie talkies.

Many other Sami are employed in the service industries, notably tourism, and also in forestry.

Organisation – The Sami Nordic Council is a unifying organisation which promotes and coordinates cooperation between the Sami of the different countries. In 1973 a Sami Parliament was created with 20 members elected

The Sami flag was officially adopted in 1986 and its colours reproduce the bright hues of the Sami costumes. The circle represents the sun (red), the moon (blue) and the magic drum (see map under Swedish Lappland).

for a four-year term and the principal aim of safeguarding the rights of the Sami. The 6 February is their national day and commemorates the first ever Sami meeting at Trondheim in Norway in 1917.

Sami Language – Lappish is a member of the Finno-Ugric group of the Uralic language family. There are seven Sami dialects but north Sami is spoken by 70-80% of all Sami speaking people.

Costumes – These highly colourful garments vary from group to group. The models, colours and decorative designs on the ribbons identify the group to which they belong.

Handicrafts – Lapp craftwork is noted for an abundant ornamentation and uses traditional materials (wood, bone, horn and leather).

The attractions of Finnish Lapland have been organised around two itineraries, the Arctic Road and the Road of the Four Winds and all the sights are located on the local map under Swedish Lapland. Norwegian and Swedish Laplands are described under Finnmark and Lappland respectively.

JÄÄMERENTIE – THE ARCTIC ROAD

The Arctic Road starts at Rovaniemi and having crossed the Arctic Circle then follows the International E 75 northwards to Inari where shortly afterwards the road divides: one section continues along E 75 to Utsjoki (450km) and the border with Norway. Once over the River Teno the route follows E 6 to the Arctic Ocean. The north-eastern fork (road 971) of the Arctic Road leads to the fjord, Varangerfjord, after having crossed the Norwegian border at Näätämö (Njaydam) 480km from Rovaniemi.

★★ **Rovaniemi** – *See ROVANIEMI.*

Sodankylä – The village grew around the charming old Sami church, **Vanha kirkko** ⊘, built in 1689 of bare pinewood, now beautifully patinated with the centuries. Beside the church, Sodankylä House, houses the tiny **Alariesto Gallery** ⊘ displaying an interesting collection of naive works on Sami folklore by the self-taught Sami painter Andreas Alariesto (1900-89).

★★ **Urho Kekkosen kansallispuisto** – The **Visitor Centre** ⊘ at Tankavaara provides information on hiking and other activities in this large (2 530km2) wilderness area of this national park which extends to the Russian border. A quick view of the wilderness may be obtained by taking one of the shorter nature trails (1, 3 or 6km).

Tankavaara: Kultakylä ⊘ (Gold Village) – This tourist spot comprises a Gold Museum on the history of gold panning and an exhibition of precious stones and minerals in a Gold Rush village where the visitor may also try his hand at gold panning. The bedrock and rivers of Lapland have enough gold to keep the tradition alive.

Gold panning at Tankavaara

A. Koening/EXPLORER

Saariselkä ⊘ – The tourist service centre and holiday village of Saariselkä provides possibilities for all kinds of recreation. The astonishingly densely built area comprises hotels, log cabins, supermarkets and tourist facilities. Saariselkä is the largest winter sports centre in Finland. In summer there is a wide choice of day trips for hikers or mountain bike enthusiasts. Fishing and rapids shooting excursions are arranged by local tour operators, as well as visits to a reindeer farm or to the nearby gold fields *(see Practical information)*.

Ivalo – This village is the administrative and commercial centre of the Inari commune, and with its 3 500 inhabitants, is the largest township in northern Lapland.

★★**Inarijärvi** – This immense lake (1 153km²) is the world's second largest lake beyond the Arctic Circle. The surrounding fells and the rocky pine and birch covered islands – 3 000 in all – reflect in the dark, clear waters, which are only free of their heavy ice cover after mid-June. A folk song says the lake is " as deep as it is long " and is proof of the profound respect that the Sami always have felt towards this lake, rich in fish. In fact, the deepest measured point is 96m whereas the length is 115km. There are **boat trips** ⊙ from Inari to **Ukonkivi★**, an ancient sacrificial island.

★**Inari** – The church village by Inarijärvi is the centre of Sami culture and seat of the Finnish Sami Parliament. The history and destiny of this small minority population can be felt especially in the Sami Church, **Saamelaiskirkko** ⊙, from 1951. The altarpiece by Väinö Saikko, *The Revelation of Christ to Sami People*, was painted in 1938 and saved from the fire that destroyed the earlier church during the war. **Siida** ★★⊙, a new building inaugurated in 1998, houses the Inari Sami Museum and Northern Lapland Nature Centre as well as an auditorium and restaurant. The joint exhibitions of the museum and nature centre show how the Sami together with Lapland's fauna and flora have adapted to the extreme climatic conditions of the region. Sami culture is furthermore illustrated in the 7ha open-air museum area next to Siida where visitors can see Sami dwellings and other traditional buildings and utensils of the Sami people. The oldest items date from the 17C-18C and were collected after the Second World War from the more remote areas, which were often spared the devastation of war. In addition, the Northern Lapland Nature Centre provides information about the Finnish Forest and Park Service, rents out cabins and sells hunting and fishing permits. It also informs visitors about mountain biking, fishing, hunting and natural sights.

The Finnish writer, Arto Paasilinna, author of *The Year of the Hare* gives a good description of the region in his novel *The Forest of the Hung Foxes*. The old lady, Naska Mosnikoff, who fled with her cat Jermakki in mid-winter from well-meaning Sevettijärvi authorities, was a resettled Skolt from Petsamo. She passes an unexpected moment of comfort and luxury with the two main characters of the book, who are holed up in a cabin in the heart of the Finnish wilderness.

Inari is the scene of the reindeer race Inari Kuninkuusajot in March.

★**Pielpajärven erämaakirkko** ⊙ – *If visit-ing in winter remember to bring a torch.* The modest but attractive wilderness church built in 1752-60, in the middle of the forest, can only be visited on foot or by snow-mobile in winter, a fact which largely contributes to the charm of the visit.

★★★**Lemmenjoen kansallispuisto** ⊙ – This beautiful national park covers 2 855km² and it is thus the largest national park in Europe. The holiday village and information cabin at Njurgalahti can be reached by car and form an excellent base for trips along the marked trails. The Lemmenjoki river valley, the Leämmi, is the heart of the area. The beautiful River Ravadas with its thundering **Ravadasköngäs falls★★** makes a good day excursion as does the gold panning district of Kultala, where the river has rewarded many patient gold panners since the 19C.

The E 75-4 branch is 450km long

★**Utsjoki** – The village at the confluence of the River Utsjoki and River Teno is the centre of Finland's northernmost commune and the only one with a Sami majority (52% of a total population of 1 500). The tiny church huts, **Kirkkotuvat★**, by the riverside date from the 18C-19C and were built as overnight accommodation by Sami families from outlying regions and were used on their frequent visits to church.

★★**Teno** – Follow the 360km long river, famous for its delicious salmon, southwest along the border between Finland and Norway. The river valley offers some of the most beautiful **views★★** in Lapland, notably at Pahtavaara where a resting place overlooks the river to the snow-covered fells of Norway.

Reindeer-sledging

The road 971 branch is 480km long

Sevettijärvi – A modest little village is on the north-eastern fork of the Arctic Road. It was established to resettle the Skolt Sami population after they had lost their native land in Petsamo (Pečengal) to the Soviet Union as a result of the Peace Treaty of 1947.

NELJÄN TUULEN TIE – THE FOUR WINDS ROAD
Road E 8 – 460km from Tornio to Kilpisjärvi

This road, E 8, starts in the valley of the River Tornio and runs north-west along the Finnish-Swedish border. It is the main channel for traffic to the north-western fell area and beyond to the fjords of the Tromsø area in Norway. The first part of the route is characterised by the mild greenery of the river valley. The first hill is Aavasaksa (242m) not far from the Arctic Circle at Juoksenki. Gradually the vegetation becomes sparser, more typically coniferous, and the hills higher. At Kaaresuvanto the conifers disappear and the tundra begins. Here the dominant plant is the tiny fell birch. Finland's only fells over 1 000m are in this region, and at Kilpisjärvi the scenery offers superb views over the rounded tops covered by eternal snow.

Tornio – The town was founded in 1621 at the northern end of the Gulf of Bothnia (Perämeri) where the powerful River Tornio meets the sea. When Finland was separated from Sweden, the town lost much of its importance. A sister town, Haparanda, was founded on the Swedish side in 1821. Nowadays the two cities are practically one again, as the daily coming and going belies the existence of a border. Tornio has a charming wooden Baroque **kirkko★★** dating from 1686 and named after Queen Hedvig Eleonora.

★★**Kukkolankoski** – *800m left.* The largest rapids on the River Tornio rush over a total length of 3.5km and provide a picturesque setting for the red-ochre chalets of the fishermen who traditionally scoop out whitefish with a haaf net and prepare them on an open fire. Visitors can be lucky enough to witness the catch and even luckier to taste the delicious result.

Aavasaksa – A village has grown by a hill of the same name, a popular Midsummer Eve celebration site since the 19C. On the top (242m), a pretty wooden chalet built for the visit of Czar Alexander II in 1882 now serves as a cafeteria.

Napapiiri (Arctic Circle) – *80km north of Tornio at Juoksenki.* A signpost indicates the exact location of the Arctic Circle.

Pello – It was here that the Frenchman Pierre Louis Moreau de Maupertuis made his triangulation measurements in 1736-37 which proved that the earth was slightly flat at the poles. A small monument was erected in 1936 on a mound by the roadside.

Kolari – This locality is sometimes called the gateway to Lapland as the fell area spreads away to the north. One of the most popular winter sports and hiking centres, the **Ylläs** area offers magnificent **views★★** of the seven fells of the region.

Särestöniemi has an exhibition of the impressive and colourful paintings of the Sami painter **Reidar Särestöniemi** (1925-81) in a splendid log gallery next to the artist's home and workshop. These were designed by Raili and Reima Pietilä in the 1970s. The 200-year-old house of the artist overlooks the same courtyard.

★ **Muonio** – This is the gateway to the marvellous hiking areas and fells of the national parks, **Pallas -ja Ounastunturin kansallipuisto★★**. The lovely Lake **Jerisjärvi★★** lies 10km to the south-east, whereas the **Information Centre** of Pallastunturi is 20km to the north-east. The 55km-long Hetta-Pallas long-distance footpath ends here.

★ **Enontekiö: Hetta** – Hetta is the church village of the Enontekiö commune. There is a beautiful view from the village away towards Pyhäkero, one of the highest (711m) fells of the Pallas and Ounastunturi National Park.

★★ **Kilpisjärvi** – Kilpisjärvi is near the meeting point of the three borders. The little village nestles at the foot of the **Saana★★**, an ancient sacred fell of the Sami. A 4km path leads to the top (1 029m). The **Information Centre** provides advice on the numerous long-distance paths and nature trails (4 to 550km) of this rugged but magnificent region. One of the most popular though somewhat demanding shorter trails (13km) leads to the Cairn of Three Countries and offers splendid **panoramas★★**. The site can also be reached by boat in summer.

Sami collections and events in the Nordic countries

National Museum, Helsinki: Finno-Ugric Collection
Seurasaari Open-Air Museum, Helsinki
Inari: open-air museum presenting different Sami villages
Hetta: lasso contest where men compete with women
Skansen, Stockholm: Sami camp.

LOHJA

Etelä-Suomi
Population 15 000
Michelin map 985 L 21 or Atlas Europe p 120

Lohja stands on the eastern bank of southern Finland's largest lake, Lohjanjärvi. Visible on the far side is the Lohjanharju ridge which is part of a chain of terminal moraines deposited during the last Ice Age.

Lohja originated as a trading centre and today it is a prosperous community depending mainly on the service sector and flourishing timber and cement industries. The area is popular for summer homes.

★★ **Pyhän Laurin kirkko** ☉ – *Laurinkatu*. This great triple-naved church dates from the 15C. Its walls and vaulting are covered with **frescoes★★** depicting biblical scenes from the Garden of Eden to the Last Judgement. The influence of the Swedish artist Albertus Pictor from Uppland is clearly visible. The frescoes were painted between 1512 and 1522 and then covered with a layer of whitewash in the 19C. They were only rediscovered during restoration work in 1950.

LOVIISA/LOVISA

Etelä-Suomi
Population 8 200
Michelin map 985 L 23 or Atlas Europe p 121

Loviisa was founded in 1745 as a border town two years after the end of the Great Northern War and the westward extension of the Russian border as far as the River Kymi. The town has remained a pleasant provincial centre with some attractive neo-Gothic buildings.

SIGHTS

The centre – The town plan was originally laid out by EB Lohrmann (1803-70) and the Turku city architect Georg Theodor Chiewitz (1815-62) designed the beautiful **town hall** ★⊙ (1862) and a marvellous red-brick church, **Loviisan kirkko** ⊙ (1865) in a neo-Gothic style, both on the market square.

Old Town – *Between Sepänkuja and Mestarinkuja*. The oldest building, **Degerby Gille** *(Sepänkuja 4, now a restaurant)*, dates back to the 17C. The town grew around it but in 1855 a fire destroyed all but this section of wooden houses.

Sibelius-house – *Sibeliuksenkatu 10*. As a young boy Jean Sibelius used to spend the summer here with his grandmother and it was here that he composed one of his first works, the *Kullervo symphony* in 1891. The lovely wooden building is used for small art exhibitions and concerts.

EXCURSIONS

★**Ruotsinpyhtään ruukkialue** ⊙ – *16km east*. The charming 18C **foundry village★** has been remarkably well preserved. The buildings include a small but interesting **Forge Museum** and several craft workshops and exhibitions. The octagonal foundry church from 1770 has Helene Schjerfbeck's only altar painting, *The Resurrection* (1898).

Pyhtään kirkko ⊙ – *20km east in the village of Pyhtää*. Built in c 1460 the three-naved church has rare Gothic-style lancet windows and beautiful star-vaulting. The most impressive of the murals is the huge St Christopher, bearing Christ as a child on his shoulder. The altar comprises several 16C wood sculptures and in the south corner of the chancel is the oldest one, a 14C St Henry of Finnish origin.

NAANTALI/NÅDENDAL ★★

Länsi-Suomi
Population 11 000
Michelin map 985 L 18-19 or Atlas Europe p 120

This splendid summer resort is appropriately surrounded by sea on three sides and enlivened by the visits of hundreds of boats and yachts – and their crews – to its large marina in front of the old town. As early as 1723 Naantali had a reputation with the Russians as a spa town. This tradition has been revived with the opening of a large new spa establishment in Kalevanniemi not far from the town centre. The island of Kailo, beyond the marina, is home to the popular Moomin family. Naantali is the venue of a major international music festival in June.

SIGHTS

★★**Luostarikirkko** ⊙ – The church is the only building remaining from the Brigittine convent founded in 1443. The Swedish name Nådendal is a translation of the convent's name Valley of Grace (Vallis Gratiae) and it was adapted to Finnish as Naantali. The construction of the convent was started under the supervision of Master Johannes Kyle from Vadstena, an important monastic town in Sweden. The church and convent were completed in 1462. Following the Reformation the convent was dissolved in the 16C but the church has served as a Lutheran place of worship ever since.

The painted hands of the church clock used to show 11.30am and the story had it that when the Naantali clock shows noon it will be the end of the world.

The light and spacious **interior★★** is the setting for several very valuable objects, of which the smallest and perhaps the most precious is the sculpture of *Christ with a Crown of Thorns* below the triptych of the altar. The **triptych★★** is from Sweden and the carvings represent the crowning of the Virgin as Queen of Heaven, with on the right St Birgitta and on the left her daughter Catherine. In

Moomin with friends

the centre of the north wall hangs RW Ekman's splendid work, **The Sinful Woman in the House of the Pharisee**★★ (1868). At the entrance to the nave, on the left is a Gothic **pyx**★ dating from 1369, a relic of Catholic times. To the right is a Finnish wooden *Pietà* from the 1460s. The *Pietà* painting was donated to the convent in the mid-16C by Queen Catharina Jagellonica. The beautiful Renaissance **pulpit**★★ was donated in 1622 by Henrik Fleming but its exact origins are unknown.

Old town – Naantali grew up around the walls of the convent and following a fire in 1628 it was rebuilt to the layout of the medieval burgh. Most of the attractive timber buildings date, however, from the 18C and 19C.

OULU/ULEÅBORG

Oulu
Population 114 000
Michelin map 985 G22 or Atlas Europe p 114

Oulu, at the mouth of the Oulujoki, spreads over numerous islands on the Gulf of Bothnia. Today Oulu is a centre for high technology with a local university. King Charles IX founded the town in 1605 and it rapidly developed into a major seaport based on the exportation of tar in the 18C and 19C. The town suffered greatly during fires in 1822 and 1901 and again during the Second World War (1944).

★ **Tuomiokirkko** ⊘ – *In Franzéninpuisto by Kirkkokatu*. The handsome neo-Classical church is another of CL Engel's works, built over the ruins of the previous one. RW Ekman's altarpiece (1859) depicts the Glorification of Christ. The famous 17C historian **Johannes Messenius** (1571-1636) is buried here. Messenius was condemned in 1616 for his Catholic sympathies and for intriguing against the Court. During his imprisonment in Kajaani Castle and then in Oulu he wrote a history of Sweden, *Scandia Illustrata (Scandinavia Illustrated)*.
The main shopping street **Rotuaari**, now a pedestrian precinct, is known for its lively atmosphere and frequent summer concerts, carnivals and street markets. The only wooden houses (Rantakatu) to have survived the 1944 bombings stand near the market square and the market hall. The Civic and Cultural Centre, on the seafront, includes the formalist Municipal Theatre (1972) and the Provincial and City Library (1981) by Marjatta and Matti Jaatinen.

Pohjois-Pohjanmaan museo ⊘ – *Ainolan puisto*. The county museum of northern Ostrobothnia is devoted to the cultural history of the area with sections on the tar industry and local personalities.

Taidemuseo ⊘ – *Kasarmintie 7*. The collections consist essentially of works by 20C artists from northern Finland and of the Heinänen collection of naive art. The gallery is a converted glue factory.

EXCURSIONS

Cruises – *Departures from Kurkelanranta, Kasarmentie 17-19.* Day cruises to the village of Muhos and the open-air museum on Turkansaari *(see below)*.

★ **Turkansaaren ulkomuseo** ⊙ – *14km to the south-east by road 22.* The midstream island of Turkansaari was frequented by tar traders in the 17C-19C as a resting and trading site. The open-air museum illustrates village life in the 17C-18C and includes a tar pit.

PIELINEN ★★
Itä-Suomi
Michelin map 985 I 26 or Atlas Europe p 115

Finnish artists seeking their roots at the turn of the last century came to Karelia where they were enchanted by the rugged landscapes and the fascinating and lively Karelian customs. With a surface area of 868km² this north Karelian lake is Finland's sixth largest. Sandy beaches or high rocky escarpments line its shores whereas the open expanses of the lake are often crisscrossed by sailing boats or windsurfers. There is a wide selection of **cruises**★★ on the lake to choose from.

Lieksa – With its 17 300 inhabitants this town is a busy commercial and tourist centre on the eastern shore of Pielinen. The major attractions are the fine collection of old buildings in the open-air museum, **Pielisen museo** ★⊙, and across the bridge, the modern **kirkko** ★⊙ (1982) by Raili and Reima Pietilä with wood sculptures by Eva Ryynänen *(see below)*. There is a daily car ferry to Koli hill on the opposite shore of Lake Pielinen.

★ **Ruunaankosket** – *25km north-east of Lieksa.* The Ruunaa rapids are in the heart of unspoilt wilderness country. Hiking, canoeing and rapids shooting expeditions are the best way to discover these wild expanses.

★ **Eva Ryynäsen ateljee** ⊙ – *In Paateri, part of the rural village of Vuonisjärvi, 30km south of Lieksa; signposted from road 73.* Take the time to stop and admire the works of the sculptress and woodcarver Eva Ryynänen; her sculptures in wood show a perfect feeling for the material and the **Wilderness Chapel**★ is her masterpiece.

★★★ **Panorama from Koli Hill** – *347m.* At the turn of the last century painters, writers and composers made pilgrimages to the top of Koli hill which dominates the western shore of Lake Pielinen. Sibelius is even said to have dragged a grand piano to the top to celebrate his honeymoon.

View from Koli

F. Jourdan/EXPLORER

A breathtaking **panorama★★★** reveals a peaceful landscape of rolling hills to the north then scattered islands on the lake; it is little wonder that poets, artists and musicians of the National Romantic period were inspired by the scene and to many this is Finland's national scenery. A road now leads to a car park at a height of 200m. Footpaths lead to the summit.

Nurmes – The Karelian town of 11 000 inhabitants, at the northern end of Pielinen, is known for its avenues of birch trees and the Puu-Nurmes area of timber-built houses on a ridge between Lake Pielinen and the smaller Lake Nurmesjärvi. The main tourist attraction is **Bomban talo ★**⊘ in the Karelian Village, approximately 2km from the town centre. The house is an example of traditional Karelian wooden architecture and it illustrates the way of life of a large farming family. The restaurant serves Karelian specialities.

PORI/BJÖRNEBORG ★
Länsi-Suomi
Population 77 000
Michelin map 985 K 18 or Atlas Europe p 120

Pori is known internationally for its **Jazz Festival★★** when, for four days in mid-July, the town works, sleeps and plays to the strains of jazz. The main outdoor concerts are held in the parkland setting of Kirjurinluoto Island and as far away as **Yyteri beach★** *(in Meri-Pori 20km north-west)* known for its windsurfing and good sandy beach.

Duke Johan founded this seaside town in 1558 as a trading centre to replace the nearby town of Ulvila which had become a ghost town in 1550 when King Gustav Vasa ordered the inhabitants to settle the recently founded capital of Helsinki. Duke Johan called his new town Björneborg and with its good site at the mouth of the River Kokemäenjoki it soon prospered and became a major port. With the passing of time the land rose and Pori and its harbour were separated by 10km. Today Pori is a major seaport – despite its harbour being 20km away at Kokemäenjoki – and has important wood processing and chemical industries.

★★Juseliuksen mausoleumi ⊘ – *Käppärä cemetery*. A wealthy business man FA Juselius had this mausoleum built to his daughter Sigrid who died aged 11 in 1898. He commissioned A Gallen-Kallela to decorate the interior with frescoes between 1901 and 1903; however the humidity and then fire almost totally destroyed Gallen-Kallela's masterpiece. It was the artist's son Jorma who spent six years (1933-39) restoring his father's work and today these marvellous frescoes can still be admired. The six large works in the central hall depict, on the right, *Spring, Building* and *The River of Death* and on the left, *Winter, Autumn* and *Destruction*.

Satakunnan museo ⊘ – This regional museum displays local archaeological finds, agricultural tools, hunting and fishing items as well as several period interiors (in the basement) and a local history section.

EXCURSION

Köyliö – *60km to the south-east. Take road 2 to Peipohja and from there road 214 in the direction of the village of Köyliö.* Legend has it that the peasant Lalli killed Finland's first bishop Henry on the frozen Lake Köyliö in the winter of 1156 *(see TURKU: Excursions – Nousiainen)*. The village has a **statue** of **Lalli** by Aimo Tukiainen to commemorate the legend. The Catholic congregation of Finland gathers on Midsummer's Eve near the memorial to Bishop Henry in the nearby village of Korvenkylä.

PORVOO/BORGÅ ★★

Etelä-Suomi
Population 21 000
Michelin map 985 L 22 or Atlas Europe p 121

Porvoo was an important trading centre and second only to Turku until the 18C. The settlement on the banks of the River Porvoo flourished under the protection of a mighty fortress and by 1346 it had been granted a charter by the Swedish king Magnus Eriksson. The medieval town is separated from the empire-style part, planned in the 1830s by Carl Ludvig Engel, by the present town centre.

★★ VANHA PORVOO/GAMLA BORGÅ (AX)

The historic part of Porvoo with its narrow winding streets clusters around the cathedral on its hill; it was the hub of town life until the 19C. In 1760 the town was almost totally destroyed by fire and most of the attractive **wooden houses**★★ date from the late 18C early 19C. The whole quarter is carefully preserved and the visitor has a real feeling of the past as he wanders through the cobbled, winding lanes to admire the trim and often gaily painted houses and carefully tended gardens.

Start from the cathedral square and follow Koulukuja/Skolgränden to the Devil's Steps / Pirunportaat which leads into Itäinen Pitkäkatu / Östra Långgatan the former working-class district and then into Kulmakuja / Hörngränd and back to the cathedral square. Take Kirkontörmä / Kyrkobrinken downhill to Vanha Raatihuoneentori / Gamla Rådhustorget or the old town hall square and finally Jokikatu / Ågatan north to the bridge which offers the most characteristic **view**★★ of Porvoo with the red-ochre warehouses lining the riverside and the old town spreading up the hillside to the white walled cathedral.

★★ **Tuomiokirkko / Domkyrkan** ⊘ **(AX)** – *Kirkkotori / Kyrkotorget.* The grey granite church with red-brick gable decorations and shingle roof dates from the 14C to 16C. Following battles, sieges, fires and even bombing in 1941, the church has been restored (1970s).

The most momentous day in the church's history was 29 March 1809 when Czar Alexander I of Russia gave his solemn oath to respect the laws and freedom of religion of the Finnish people on the creation of an autonomous Grand Duchy. The **statue**★ of the **Czar** (1909) by Walter Runeberg commemorates the 100th anniversary of the declaration of Finnish autonomy. Alongside is a copy of the Czar's oath. The pulpit, pews and galleries are as they were after the 18C rebuilding. The 18C **paintings of the Apostles**★ on the columns were the work of the local artist Adam Lindström and the wooden **hatchments**★ around the walls depict the arms of local nobility and also date from the 18C. The remains of frescoes on the walls and vaulting are 15C likewise the unicorn on one of the pillars.

★★ **Historiallinen museo / Historiska museet** ⊘ **(AX M¹)** – *Vanha Raatihuoneentori.* The museum is housed in the old town hall which dates from 1764. The collections are mainly 18C and 19C. The ground floor assembles harnesses, sleighs, carriages

Porvoo

399

PORVOO / BORGÅ

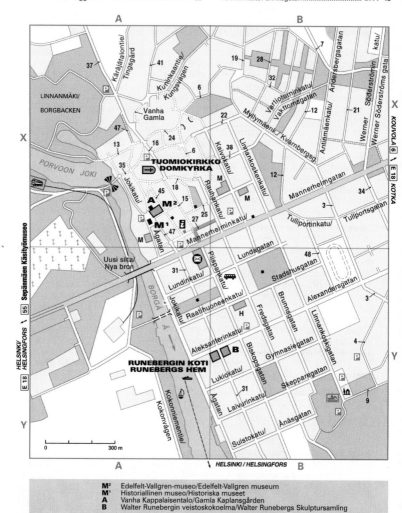

M² Edelfelt-Vallgren-museo/Edelfelt-Vallgren museum
M¹ Historiallinen museo/Historiska museet
A Vanha Kappalaisentalo/Gamla Kaplansgården
B Walter Runebergin veistoskokoelma/Walter Runebergs Skulptursamling

and a lock collection. The first-floor rooms are devoted to life in the manors of the area and the lifestyle of the townspeople. Local history and 19C costumes and textiles are displayed on the second floor.

★★ Edelfelt-Vallgren-museo/Edelfelt-Vallgren museum ⊘ **(AX M²)** – *Välikatu/Mellangatan 11.* Two of Porvoo's and Finland's best-known artists are commemorated in this museum: the artist **Albert Edelfelt** (1854-1905) and the sculptor **Ville Vallgren** (1855-1940). Amid Edelfelt's local scenes and Vallgren's various sculptures look for two examples of their friendship, *Ville Vallgren after a merry breakfast* (1886) and the bust of Edelfelt. Works by other artists include the town and village scenes by Johan Knutson (1816-99) and the portraits of Nils Schillmark (1745-1804). Also of particular interest are the Iris furniture and ceramics, produced between 1897 and 1902, in a local workshop of the same name. The founder and creator of the furniture **Louis Sparre** (1863-1964) engaged Alfred William Finch (1854-1930) as a designer in the ceramic department. The pottery and furniture are in the spirit of Art Nouveau.

The late-18C building **Vanha Kappalaisentalo** ⊘ **(AX A)** next door at no 13 *(Vanha Kappalaisentalo / Gamla Kaplansgården)* was originally intended for the pastor and is now used for temporary art exhibitions.

FINLAND

★★THE EMPIRE TOWN (ABY)

★★**Runebergin koti / Runebergs hem** ⊙ (AY) – *Aleksanterinkatu / Alexandersgatan 3*. The home of Finland's national poet **Johan Ludvig Runeberg** (1804-77) is one of the best-preserved buildings in the Empire town. The interior is as it was during the latter years of the poet's life. In the drawing room note Walter Runeberg's bust of his father (1860) and KE Jansson's work *A Coin in the Collection Box*, a great favourite with the poet. Runeberg's Room is where he spent the last 13 years of his life confined to bed after a stroke.

Walter Runebergin veistoskokoelma / Walter Runebergs Skulptursamling ⊙ (BY B) – *Aleksanterinkatu / Alexandersgatan 5*. The blue house across the road contains a collection of more than 150 sculptures by **Walter Runeberg** (1838-1929), the poet's third son. Two of his most famous works are the statues in Helsinki of Czar Alexander II in Senate Square and one of his father in Esplanadi Park.

EXCURSIONS

Boat trips to Helsinki – *Boats leave from Joikatu / Ågatan* (AY).

Savilinna ⊙ – *In Suomenkyläntie, 32km north-west of Porvoo*. Handicraft centre and showcase for Finnish arts, crafts and design *(goods are for sale)*.

★★**Sepänmäen käsityömuseo** ⊙ – *In Hirvihaara 40km north-west of Porvoo; leave to the west to take road 55 to Mäntsälä where it becomes road 53 and once in Hirvihaara follow the signs.*
This historic village with its 20 houses and 14 craftsmen's workshops is a live museum of traditions, which presents an authentic view of life in the 18C and 19C with various craft demonstrations.
There are several fine manor houses in the area of Mäntsälä; one of them is **Alikartano-Frugård** ⊙, located in the village of Numminen just south of Mäntsälä. The estate dates from the early 17C, but the present manor house was built in 1805. It was the childhood home of the famous explorer, Adolf Erik Nordenskiöld (1832-1901), who discovered the Northeast Passage. Alikartano became State property in 1964 and was turned into a museum in 1983. Note the unusual two-storey drawing room.

RAUMA ★★
Länsi-Suomi
Population 30 000
Michelin map 985 K 18 or Atlas Europe p 120

Finland's third oldest town grew up at the intersection of trade routes on the Gulf of Bothnia and naturally enough its main activities were seafaring and trading. It received its town charter in 1442. In 1550 King Gustav Vasa decreed that the citizens of Rauma were to settle the new town of Helsinki. This royal decree did little to halt the growth of the city as most of the settlers eventually found their way back to Rauma. Present-day Rauma is still a major seaport with some important industrial activities. Rauma is also known for its bobbin lace, probably introduced by seafarers, and its dialect which is unique to the area and quite incomprehensible to outsiders.

★★★**Vanha Rauma** – *Signposted, in the town centre*. The charming old town with its wooden houses dating from the 17C and 18C is without doubt one of the best-preserved historic towns in the Nordic countries and is listed as a UNESCO World Heritage Site. The historic area is best visited on foot starting from the 15C Franciscan church of the Holy Cross, **Pyhän Ristin kirkko** ★⊙, beside the stream Raumanjoki. Once over the bridge follow Isokirkkokatu to the market place, **Kauppatori★**, bordered by the attractive little old town hall (C Schröder 1776) now home to the local museum, **Rauman museo** ★⊙. The exhibitions illustrate Rauma's maritime past with the exception of one section devoted to specimens of local bobbin lace. Continue along Kauppakatu and across to Isopoikkikatu to **Marela** ★★⊙, the richly decorated home of a wealthy shipowner with its 19C furnishings. At the next corner turn left onto the narrow Kitukränn and continue to the bridge. The street ends in the courtyard of a mustard-yellow house **Kirsti**, a sailor's home from the turn of the last century. Pohjankatu returns to the church.

ROVANIEMI ★★

Lappi
Population 35 000
Michelin map 985 F 22 or Atlas Europe p 109

The capital of Finnish Lapland lies just below the Arctic Circle, at the junction of the River Ounasjoki and River Kemijoki, the longest (500km) river in Finland. It is a busy provincial centre all year round and yet at a stone's throw from the very centre, unfolds a magnificent wilderness with the rounded-top fells appearing bluish as far as the eye can see. Already in the Middle Ages furs and salmon were dispatched from here to the royal courts of Europe but the town only started to grow in the 19C with the development of forestry and the sawmill industry.

The Second World War was disastrous; the town was practically burnt to the ground. Alvar Aalto designed the new town plan in the form of reindeer antlers and also undertook several of the buildings, including the remarkable administrative and cultural centre.

SIGHTS

★★★**Arktikum** ⊘ – *Pohjoisranta 4 by E 75 going north.* This ingenious underground construction (Birch-Bonderup-Thorup and Waade, 1992) with a longitudinal glass cupola resembling an ice tunnel on the surface houses two extremely interesting exhibitions illustrating living conditions in the Arctic. The **Arctic Centre★★★** displays the special features of the Arctic flora and fauna and tells about the life and traditions of the indigenous people of the Arctic. The **Provincial Museum of Lapland★★** has a basic exhibition called The Survivors, illustrating life in Lapland from prehistoric times to the present. The building also includes an information centre on Lapland and the arctic regions, a restaurant and a museum shop selling Sami handicraft.

Snow sculpture

★★**Administrative and Cultural Centre** – *Hallituskatu.* This light and elegant complex of three buildings is among the most appreciated works of the world-famous architect Alvar Aalto (1898-1976). **Lappia-talo★★** (1975) at Hallituskatu 11 houses the municipal theatre, concert hall and congress centre. Its form is inspired by the surrounding fells. The first building of the complex to be raised was however the library, **Kirjasto★★**, at Hallituskatu 9, completed in 1965. Finally the town hall, **Kaupungintalo★★**, was completed in 1988 to plans dating from the early 1970s: the consistent modernity of Aalto's works is one of the unique characteristics of his work.

Kirkko ⊘ – *800m south of the commercial centre at Kirkkotie 1.* Built in 1950 near the site of the one destroyed in the war, this church is known for its altarpiece entitled *The Fountain of Life* (Lennart Segerstråle, 1950).

★**Lapin metsämuseo (Forestry Museum of Lapland)** ⊘ – *4km south of the town centre by road 78, then left to Metsämuseontie 7.* This open-air museum presents the life and work of lumberjacks from around the turn of the 20C century to the present.

★**Ounasvaara** – *3km from the town centre to the top.* This 204m-high mountain offers an excellent viewpoint of the city and for admiring the midnight sun. It is the nearest winter sports centre with a variety of ski runs and jumps.

EXCURSIONS

Rovaniemi offers an excellent base for exploring the Lappish wilderness. Some of the local tour operators have programmes for individual travellers as well, and exciting tours vary in length from hours to several days. The wilderness does not reveal its nature unless the visitor leaves the main roads.

Santapark ⊙ – *5km north-east*. This new theme park brought Santa Claus and Christmas to Rovaniemi all the year round. Its location inside a deep cave adds to the magic. A small train brings visitors from the Santa Claus village 2km away. Inside the cave, a world of fantasy and fun awaits them: climbing adventures, sleigh ride, Christmas carrousel, multimedia theatre, cafeteria and shop. The Santa train stops at the reindeer park for visitors to enjoy a reindeer ride.

★ **Napapiiri ja Joulupukin pajakylä** – *8km north*. The exact coordinates here are 66°33'07" north of the Equator and 25°50'51" east of Greenwich. The certificate testifying to the crossing of the Arctic Circle can be obtained from the information desk in the Santa Claus Village, which is essentially a shopping centre for visitors. Santa Claus meets children in his workshop all year round.

★★ **Ranuan eläinpuisto** – *81km south-east; half-day trip*. The world's northernmost wildlife park has some 60 arctic species of predator ; including the polar bear and birds. The animals live in their natural surroundings in vast enclosures.

★★ **Kemijärvi** – *85km east*. The small town lies in a charming site by a curve in the River Kemijoki where it spreads out to quiet waters surrounding the town. The river itself was for a century the most important log-floating waterway of the country, and thus was decisive for the prosperity of the little locality, but ground transportation definitely took over in 1992. Kemijärvi has now become an important excursion centre for tourists and hikers. The impressive wilderness areas of Salla *(65km east)* and Savukoski *(95km north)* stretch up towards the north-eastern fells and bogs where pine and spruce alternate with marshes. The national park, **Pyhätunturin kansallispuisto★**, in the Salla region consists mainly of a chain of rocky fells hiding ancient sacred places of the Sami people. Suomutunturi or Suomu Fell *(53 km south-east)* on the Arctic Circle rises to a height of 408m and is one of the most important mountain ski centres.

SAVONLINNA ★★

Itä-Suomi – Population 29 000
Michelin map 985 25K or Atlas Europe p 121

This charming town is beautifully situated on a group of islands between Lake Haapavesi and Lake Pihlajavesi which are both part of the Saimaa lake system. The town developed in the shadow of the island castle of Olavinlinna and often suffered in the ensuing skirmishes for possession of the strategically important fortress. When you approach the town from the east there is a marvellous **view★★** of the island fortress from the bridge across Kyrönsalmi strait.

Savonlinna is synonymous with the excellent **Savonlinna Opera Festival★★★** held annually in July. The castle's sheltered inner courtyard makes the perfect setting for the month-long opera festival.

Savonlinna Opera Festival

The **market place★★** down by the waterfront has an almost Mediterranean atmosphere as locals and visitors mingle amid the bustle of the stalls and the jaunty steamers and passenger ferries await their quota of holidaymakers. Savonlinna is a major excursion centre for lake **cruises★★** on the Saimaa lake system.

Olavinlinna

SIGHTS

★★★Olavinlinna ⊘ – *Take the bridge at the eastern end of Linnankatu.* The fortress was founded in 1475 to defend the eastern marches of the Finno-Swedish territory by Governor Erik Axelsson Tott (statue on the island on the way to the castle). The castle is triangular in shape with three towers along one side. Extensions and two additional towers were built in the 16C and 17C but when the castle fell to the Russians in the 18C two of the towers were razed.

From the top of the 30m-tall towers an unforgettable landscape of lakes and islands unfolds. Complete the visit of the castle with the small **Castle Museum★** to the left of the entrance. On the right is a splendid little **Orthodox Museum★★** displaying valuable church plate and vestments.

★Maakuntamuseo ⊘ – *On Riihisaari Island next to the castle.* On the ground floor of this provincial museum the main history exhibition includes a particularly interesting **model★** of log floating, an important activity locally. The first floor is given over to temporary exhibitions. The same ticket includes a visit to the museum ships (berthed behind the museum building) that used to carry cargo and passengers from lake to lake.

Sallinen and Savonlinna Opera Festival

The 1995 festival saw the world première of Aulis Sallinen's fifth opera *The Palace.* Sallinen has been largely responsible for making Finland the powerhouse of contemporary opera for the past two decades. His works are exciting and innovative as well as popular. Satirical comedy has replaced the sombre brooding Finn of his previous operas. Veijo Varpio played the king at the centre of his court, cut off from the reality of the outside world. Jaana Mäntynen plays the disillusioned queen discontented with her marriage and role as queen.

EXCURSIONS

★Rauhalinna ⊘ – *At Lehtiniemi, 16km north by road 471/470.* This amazing wooden villa was offered by Lieutenant General Nils Weckman of the Czar's Army to his wife Alma as a silver wedding present in 1900. The building has been refurbished as a summer hotel-restaurant.

★★Retretti taidekeskus ⊘ – *26km south-east by road 14.* Every summer Retretti Arts Centre offers art exhibitions in its unique premises which include a large grotto.

★Kerimäki: kirkko ⊘ – *23km north-east by road 71.* This rural village is dwarfed by the world's largest wooden church with a seating capacity of 3 300 and a cupola rising to a height of 27m. The original plans were drawn up by the architect AF Granstedt (1800-49) but the local builder, master Axel Tolpo, preferred to comply with the grand ideas of the parishioners and today it makes an excellent concert venue during the Savonlinna Opera Festival.

Harjualue – *East of the village of Punkaharju.* The 7km-long and in places, 30m-high **Punkaharju ridge★★** is in fact a terminal moraine deposited during the Ice Age. The ridge winds between Lake Pihlajavesi and Lake Puruvesi and is in places no broader than the old road running along the top. Take the chance to admire **views★★** of glistening lakes and tranquil forests from the various roadside viewing places. One of the best viewing points has a monument to the poet JL Runeberg, and it is claimed that it was here that he wrote his poem *The Fifth Day of July* in 1838. The ridge area was made a conservation area as early as 1843.

E. Baret

SUOMUSSALMI
Oulu
Population 12 500
Michelin map 985 H 26 or Atlas Europe p 115

The commune extends to the wide forests around the Russian border, where the silent beauty of the wilderness has a particular charm. On the morning of 30 November 1939 this silence was brutally broken when the Soviet army attacked; the Winter War had begun. The war caused great devastation and a new township was built on the western shore of Kiantajärvi at Kianta, 10km from the old village, and given the name Ämmänsaari *(see opposite)*.

Suomussalmi Village – In the village, which has regained some of its importance, the **kirkko** ⊘ (O Ermala, 1950) was built with financial help from the United States. At Karhulanvaara, 2.4km from the village, there is Alvar Aalto's Winter War Memorial **The Flame★**.

EXCURSIONS FROM ÄMMÄNSAARI

Lake Kianta Cruise ⊘ – *Departures from the platform (LAIVALAITURI); by road 5 allow 2hr.* The cruise consists of a boat-trip to Turjanlinna, site of the wilderness writer **Ilmari Kianto**'s (1874-1970) residence, where only a curious little lodge and a sauna-cottage were saved from the fire. Kianto wrote novels and poems inspired by the folk tradition and the surrounding wilderness.

Raatteen portti ⊘ – The Raate Museum Road starts at Raate Gate, Raatteen Portti, 24km east and goes 20km further east to the frontier post. A **Winter War Exhibition** at Raatteen Portti is set up in an army-grey painted log construction imitating a dugout. The road proceeds through the wilderness where some of the hardest battles, but also a decisive victory over the Soviets, took place during the Winter War 1939-40. At the border, the tiny old frontier guard building is now a museum furnished as it was when war broke out.

★★ **Hossa** – *100km north-east.* The fisherman's paradise is ideal hiking country with nearly 100km of marked trails and excellent possibilities for fishing in the 130 lakes and ponds or rivers of the area.
Rare **primeval forests★** and one of the world's northernmost **rock paintings★** from c 2500-1500 BC are part of the impressive natural surroundings, which were inhabited by a Sami population for centuries until the Finnish settlers pushed them northwards at the beginning of the 18C. Only few signs of the Sami culture remain, such as deer hunting pits.
Julma Ölkky★ some 10km north of Hossa is a canyon-lake formed during the Ice Age. The austere scenery of the rocky walls of the lake can be admired on a 30min cruise.

TAMPERE ★

Länsi-Suomi
Population 190 000
Michelin map 985 K 20 or Atlas Europe p 120 – Local map see JÄRVI-SUOMI

Finland's third largest city, and the largest inland town of the Nordic countries, stands on an isthmus between two large lakes, **Näsijärvi** (**AY**) to the north and **Pyhäjärvi** (**AZ**) to the south. The lakes are linked by a stretch of rapids, Tammerkoski (**BY**), which rush through the heart of the city. Tampere is a pleasant city with its open layout and many parks framed by the blue waters of the lakes.

Although there had been settlement in the Pirkkala area (**CZ**) to the south-west since the Middle Ages the town was officially founded in 1779 by King Gustav III of Sweden. The first paper mill was built in 1785, but it was not until the 19C that the town acquired its true industrial character.

Tampere has also played a major role in Finnish political history: during the Civil War of 1918 the town became the theatre of bitter fighting between the reds and the whites, and the capture of the city on 6 April 1918 was a decisive factor in securing independence for the country.

Tampere

Finland's Manchester – Tampere has often been described thus on account of its industrial activity. Papermaking was the original industry, but in 1828 **James Finlayson**, a Scotsman who had previously worked in St Petersburg, founded the town's first textile mill. The Scotsman sold his mill in 1836 and under the ownership and direction of the Nottbeck family, the company prospered and grew into a town within a town with its own church, hospital, school, police force and fire brigade (according to the principles of the English social reformer Robert Owen).

The 19C saw the establishment of several other textile mills as well as wood processing and the paper industry. Mechanical engineering and shoemaking were other important activities, and since the mid-20C the town has acquired a reputation for its expertise in high technology based on the presence of a university of technology, two technology parks and research institutes. In addition a second university specialising in social and political sciences as well as a large teaching hospital both contribute to the town's renown as a centre for higher education.

Culture-loving city – Although the city has a variety of museums and art galleries its lively theatrical tradition makes it Finland's leading theatre city. At least 12 professional companies and numerous amateur groups offer a wide repertoire of theatrical productions with the high point in the year being the **International Theatre Festival** *(see below)* which welcomes many foreign companies. The Tampere Philharmonic Orchestra is an important asset to the city's musical life but a number of festivals bring variety to the musical calendar.

EAST OF TAMMERKOSKI

★★**Tuomiokirkko** ⊘ (**CY**) – The red-roofed and grey-granite cathedral is a pure product of Finnish National Romanticism; it was built between 1902 and 1907 by Lars Sonck. A medieval Gothic influence can be seen in the towering spires and the massive piers supporting the vaulting. The interior decoration is one of Finland's finest ensembles of Art Nouveau. The fresco behind the high altar is the **Resurrection** by

Magnus Enckell (1870-1925) who also designed the cross-shaped window in the choir. The huge murals **The Garland Bearers** are by Finland's most important Symbolist **Hugo Simberg** (1873-1917), as are **The Wounded Angel** and **The Garden of Death**. The stained-glass windows by Simberg portray biblical themes in the Symbolist manner: the Dove of the Holy Spirit, The Tree of Life (also interpreted as the burning bush), The Pelican feeding her young with her own blood and the Horsemen of the Apocalypse.

★ **Tampere-talo** ⊘ (**CZ**) – *Yliopistonkatu 55*. Finland's largest conference and concert centre (1990) is striking for its bold, modern design by **Sakari Aartelo** and **Esa Piiroinen**. It provides flexible facilities for conferences, congresses and exhibitions as well as concerts, operas and ballets. The hall is home to Tampere Philharmonic Orchestra.

★ **Kalevan kirkko** ⊘ – *East end of Itsenäisyydenkatu* (**CZ**). This controversial concrete church (known locally as the silo of souls) is another dramatic creation by the architects **Reima** and **Raili Pietilä**; it dates from 1966. The column-free interior achieves an amazing impression of soaring height (30m) and works well as there is nothing to obstruct the view or impede the sound. Eighteen floor-to-ceiling windows reveal the surrounding greenery. Reima Pietilä created a work of art in which his designs for the detail of the ornamentation and the furnishings were an essential contribution to the whole.

Hämeensilta (**BZ 10**) – The bridge's four statues by **Wäinö Aaltonen** (1894-1966) depict characters from the legends of ancient Pirkanmaa: The Merchant, The Hunter, The Tax Collector and The Maid of Finland.

Ortodoksinen kirkko ⊘ (**CZ**) – *Vuolteenkatu by Sorinaukio square*. This Orthodox church was built in 1899 during the last decades of Russian rule in the purest neo-Byzantine style. The seven cupolas symbolise the Seven Sacraments.

Museokeskus Vapriikki ⊘ (**ABY**) – *Veturiaukio 4*. The new Vapriikki Museum Centre is housed in the former Tampella engineering works dating back to the 1880s. The centre forms part of a major renovation project concerning the old Tammerkoski industrial district. Changing themed exhibitions illustrate the history of Tampere and the surrounding Pirkanmaa region from prehistoric times to the present day. Subjects ranging from archaeology to modern art, manual skills, technology and nature form the basis of a series of exhibitions planned for the next few years. The centre also has various cultural and educational facilities, a museum shop and a café with a terrace overlooking Tammerkoski.

WEST OF TAMMERKOSKI

Kirjasto ⊘ (**AZ**) – *Pirkankatu 2 by the corner of Hämeenpuisto*. The exceptional architecture of this modern library created by the husband and wife team, Raili and Reima Pietilä in 1986 takes its inspiration from nature. The contours of the roof arch like the wings of a great bird – thus the name of the building; *Metso* means capercaille. The ground floor includes two exhibitions: the Gemstone and Mineral Museum and the Moomin Valley Museum devoted to the Moomin family of hippo-like characters invented by the Finnish authoress Tove Jansson. Her books on the adventures of the Moomins have been adapted as a cartoon for television by the Japanese. The exhibition consists mainly of the author's original drawings for her books and a miniature Moomin House *(see NAANTALI)*.

Särkänniemi (**AY**) – The high ground of this headland jutting out into Lake Näsijärvi is the location for a recreation park (Huvipuisto), a planetarium, a dolphinarium and the **Näsinneula observation tower** ⊘ which at 168m is the highest in Finland and offers a superb **panorama★★**.

★★ **Sara Hildénin taidemuseo** ⊘ (**AY**) – *Särkänniemi*. The modern building designed by Pekka Ilveskoski and associates in 1979 on the hill by Lake Näsijärvi is a work of art in its own right. The museum houses the Sara Hildén Foundation collection, which amounts to over 3 000 works of Finnish and international modern art (Léger, Picasso, Giacometti, Miró, Klee and Delvaux). The museum also organises temporary exhibitions on modern and contemporary art. The museum's cafeteria, Café Sara, offers a beautiful view of Lake Näsijärvi.

Amurin työläismuseo ⊘ (**AZ M¹**) – *Makasiininkatu 12*. A block of wooden houses (Amuri Workers' Museum) which illustrate the evolution in living conditions of workers in Tampere. Shared kitchens and public saunas were typical of this working class area called Amuri.

Lenin museo ⊘ (**AZ M²**) – *Hämeenpuisto 28, 3rd floor*. This small museum is located in the Tampere Workers' Hall, where the first meeting between Lenin and Stalin took place in 1905 during a secret conference of the Russian revolutionaries. The museum illustrates Lenin's life and work as well as his underground visits to Finland.

TAMPERE

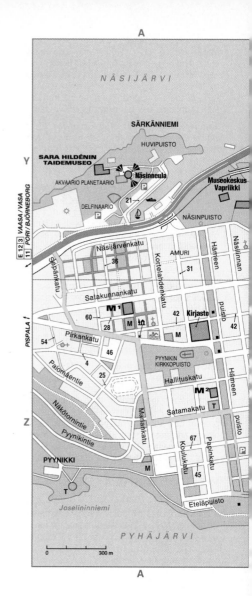

* **Pispala** – *Leave to the west by Satakunnankatu* (**AZ**). This picturesque area of wooden houses on Pyynikki ridge between the two lakes developed in the early 20C when working-class families built small houses on every available space on the ridge. There is a striking **panorama** from the top of the ridge.
The Pyynikki summer theatre has a revolving auditorium.

EXCURSIONS

Hatanpää – *Leave Tampere by Hatanpään valtatie* (**CZ**) *or by water bus from Laukontori* (**BZ**). The late-19C neo-Renaissance manor stands on the site of an old manor where King Gustav III of Sweden made a visit in 1775 which resulted four years later in the founding of Tampere. The beautifully situated lakeside manor makes an ideal setting for the doll and costume collection, **Haiharan nukke– ja puku-museo** ★⊙.

** **Lake cruises** ⊙ – The choice of cruises includes the regular Silverline sailings (*Laukontori embarkation* **BZ**) to Hämeenlinna in the south, one of the most popular lake routes in Finland; the white boats navigate through a kind of labyrinth of waterways where glittering open expanses alternate with narrow winding sounds. There are other sailings to the northern parts of the province around Lake Näsijärvi, with the **Poets' Way** cruise (*embarkation* **AY**) to Ruovesi and Virrat.

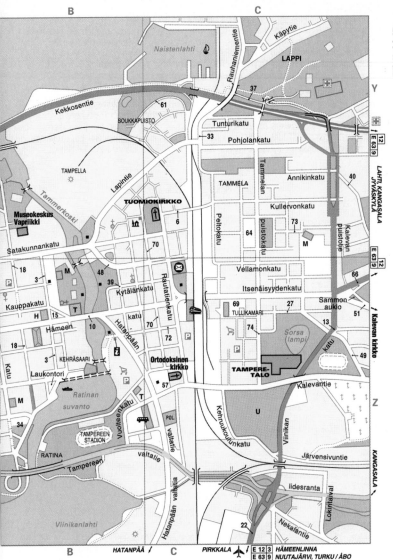

The silent countryside in the vicinity of the lake was a great source of inspiration to the national painter **Akseli Gallen-Kallela** (1865-1931) who claimed that these landscapes were part of a Finn's inner soul. He built a wilderness studio, **Kalela**, in a secluded spot on the lake shore in 1894. It was here that he created many of his *Kalevala* inspired works.

The national poet, **Johan Ludvig Runeberg** (1804-77) spent a short period as tutor to the family in Ritoniemi manor. During his stay at the manor he met many veterans of the 1808-09 war, whose tales inspired him to write many of his heroic poems.

Cultural events	
March	Tampere International Short Film Festival.
April	Tampere Biennal, a festival of modern music every two years (2002, 2004).
June	Tampere International Choir Festival (2001, 2003).
July	Pispalan Sottiisi, a folk dance festival (2002, 2004).
August	Tampere International Theatre Festival; Flower Festival.
Oct / Nov	Tampere Jazz Happening.

★**Kangasala** – *19km to the east* (**CZ**). The locality is surrounded by three lakes – Vesijärvi, Längelmävesi and Roine – and is known for its beautiful setting which inspired **Zacharias Topelius** (1818-98) to write his poem *Summer Day at Kangasala* in 1853. A memorial stone to the poet has been erected on **Haralanharju** ridge. **Mobilia** ⊘ is an interesting automobile and road museum.

Nuutajärvi ⊘ – *60km to the south* (**CZ**). They have been making glass in Nuutajärvi since 1793 when a Dutch-born retired naval officer, Jacob Wilhelm de Pont (1755-1809) founded the glass factory. The site includes the workshops where visitors can watch the glass blowers at work, the museum where they can admire masterpieces of Finnish design, past and present, and the factory shop where they will be tempted by designer pieces by Oiva Toikka, Heikki Orvola or Markku Salo.

TURKU/ÅBO ★★

Länsi-Suomi
Population 170 000
Michelin map 985 L 19 or Atlas Europe p 120

Turku (old Finnish for market place) developed around a trading post at the mouth of the River Aurajoki. For centuries Turku was the national capital and the cradle of civilization. This reputation is continued today by a lively cultural and intellectual life with three universities: a Finnish-speaking one, a Swedish-speaking one and a School of Economics and Business Administration.

Today Turku is the provincial capital of south-western Finland, with important commercial and industrial activities; it is also the second gateway to the country, after Helsinki, with frequent ferries from Sweden and other Baltic ports. The city is divided into two almost equal parts by the River Aurajoki / Aura Å which flows into the sea only 2.5km from the city centre. Turku's seven hills provide a variety of panoramas.

HISTORICAL NOTES

Capital City – Although no records have survived of its foundation, Turku is Finland's oldest town dating from 1229, when the seat of the episcopal see of Finland was transferred to Turku. Both the cathedral and the castle were built in the 13C and the town went from strength to strength in the Middle Ages with the growth of seafaring and trading during the Hanseatic League. In addition to being the centre of secular (Swedish Governor) and ecclesiastical power (See of the bishopric) Turku rapidly became the centre of intellectual life with the founding of the university in 1640 by Per Brahe. The city continued to benefit from its close connections with Stockholm and Central Europe.

Turku / Åbo

A century of change – The 19C brought many changes to the town; when Finland was annexed to the Russian Empire as a Grand Duchy in 1809, Turku was considered by Czar Alexander I to be too close to Stockholm both politically and geographically. When Helsinki was proclaimed the capital in 1812 political and administrative affairs were transferred to the new capital and cultural activity soon followed suit. A second and even more disastrous blow befell the city in 1827 when almost the entire town (2 500 houses) was destroyed by a fire, which has remained in history as the biggest conflagration ever to have ravaged a Nordic town. After the fire the university was transferred to Helsinki.

The architect CL Engel – creator of Helsinki's new administrative centre – drew up a new city plan laid out on the grid system and rebuilding started quickly. Gradually Turku recovered from its misfortunes and soon after the turn of the last century, thanks partly to a number of generous patrons motivated by a strong sense of nationalism, Turku won back its position as an important educational and cultural centre with the founding of Turku University (Finnish) in 1916 and Åbo Akademi (Swedish) two years later.

A resolutely modern town – Apart from its historical and cultural sights Turku has some outstanding examples of 20C architecture: the Resurrection Chapel, **Ylösnousemuskappeli** (1838), by Erik Bryggman in the beautiful Turku cemetery *(on the south-eastern outskirts of the city by road E 18)*, the **Konserttitalo** (Konserthuset) (BX) by RV Luukkonen (1952), the Finnish University Buildings, Turun Yliopisto (CX) (1954), by Aarne Ervi, the **Kaupunginteatteri** (Stadsteatern) (BY **A**) (1955) by Luukkonen and Stenros and next to the busy market place one of the most recent projects which combines old and traditional with modern functionalism the Hansa Shopping Centre **Hansakortteli / Hansakvarteret** (BY) (1989) by Benito Casagrande.

CATHEDRAL AND OTHER SOUTH BANK SIGHTS

★★★**Tuomiokirkko / Domkyrkan** ⊘ (CX **B**) – This imposing Gothic cathedral, the mother church of the Lutheran Church of Finland, has stood on the banks of the Aura since the end of the 13C. The seat of the episcopal see was transferred from nearby Koroinen to the thriving trading centre of Turku in the 13C and by the end of the century a stone church had been built to replace the former wooden structure on Unikankare Mound. Throughout the Middle Ages extensions and alterations were made to the cathedral: a new choir was added in the 14C, side chapels to the nave in the 15C and the height of the vaulting was raised to 24m. The tower and the interior date from the restoration work which was done after the great fire of 1827. CL Engel designed the new tower in a neo-Classical style.

The great brick church is impressive with its massive west tower rising to a height of 102m.

Interior – In Catholic times the side chapels contained altars dedicated to various saints but they have since been converted into funeral vaults and now house the tombs and memorials of many famous Finns. The **Kankainen Chapel** (nearest the chancel on the north side) has one of the most touching memorials in the form of a black marble sarcophagus to Queen Karin Månsdotter (Kaarina Maununtytär), the Finnish-born wife of King Erik XIV. She died in 1613. The beautiful stained-glass windows by the Russian, Wladimir Swertschkoff, show the queen with her two sons. The small **Chapel of St George** *(next door)* is the resting place of the 17C pioneers of popular education in Finland, Bishops Johannes Gezelius, father and son. The chapel also houses the canopied tomb of Bishop Hemming (d 1366) and a church-shaped reliquary.

The octagonal piers of the chancel still show traces of the 1827 fire. The rest of the decoration dates from the 1830s restoration. The **altarpiece** (1834) is the work of the Swedish Court Painter F Westin and depicts the Transfiguration of Christ. Of particular note are the frescoes (1850-54) by the father of Finnish painting, **RW Ekman**. The pulpit was designed by CL Engel. The gallery offers the best overall view of the interior.

The valuable collections of the cathedral museum **Tuomiokirkkomuseo**★★ are exhibited in the south gallery. On display are superb medieval wooden sculptures and church plate.

On leaving the cathedral do not miss the **statue**, standing to the left in Cathedral Park, of **Governor General Pehr Brahe** (1602-80) with his proud bearing. Close to the southern wall stands a **statue** of **Mikael Agricola** (1510-57), the leader of the Reformation in Finland and the first to translate the Bible into Finnish.

Sibelius-museo / Sibelius museet ⊘ (CX **M¹**) – Woldemar Baeckman's austere concrete building (1968) is home to the Sibelius Museum with its extensive collection of musical instruments, especially clavichords, upright pianos and organs as well as traditional instruments from all over the world. Do not miss the **kantele** which figures in the Finnish epic poem the *Kalevala*. In the room dedicated to the

TURKU / ÅBO

FINLAND

*Michelin maps and town plans
are oriented
with north at the top of the page*

composer **Jean Sibelius** (1865-1957) is a valuable collection of the musician's manuscripts, concert programmes and other personal items. The building also houses a concert hall reputed for its good acoustics and the Swedish University's School of Music.

Museo Ett Hem / Museet Ett Hem ⊘ (CX M²) – Consul Alfred Jacobsson and his wife Hélène stipulated in their will (1931) that their home, including an impressive collection of essentially Finnish 19C paintings, should be preserved intact as a museum called Ett Hem (a home).
The rooms are decorated in the wealthy burgher's style of the 19C. The paintings include works by some of Finland's most prominent painters: *Summer Night* (1883) by Albert Edelfelt in the drawing room.

Aboa Vetus and Ars Nova ⊘ (BY) – Two contrasting museums were inaugurated in 1995 on a site close to the River Aurajoki, which has been inhabited since the 14C and where the Rettig Palace now stands.

Aboa Vetus – Excavations down to a depth of 7m revealed the presence of an entire medieval district with its streets, vaults, cellars, arches, wells, parts of houses and a number of objects; a museum was built round the archaeological finds so that visitors got a more realistic idea of life in Turku since the Middle Ages, when clergymen, merchants and craftsmen lived in the area. Several multimedia programs help to recreate medieval life in Turku. Meanwhile excavations are going on inside the museum and visitors are welcome to watch the progress of archaeologists.

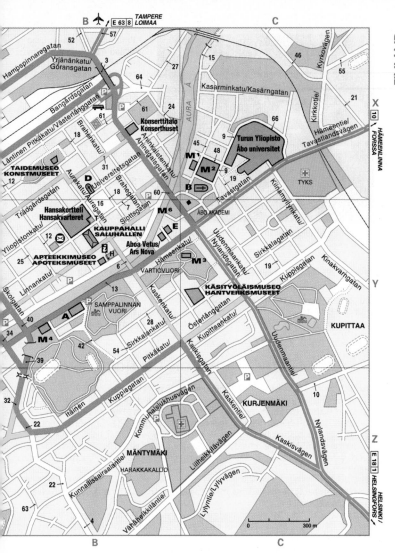

Ars Nova – The new museum of modern and contemporary art is housed in a Classical building known as the Rettig Palace. The museum's collection, normally exhibited upstairs, contains works by Finnish and foreign artists including Karel Appel, Max Ernst and Picasso. The ground floor is devoted to temporary exhibitions of contemporary art.

Merenkulkumuseo / Sjöfartsmuseet ⊘ (CY M³) – The beautiful **Observatory** (1819) on top of Vartiovuori hill was one of CL Engel's earliest Finnish works. Today it houses the collections of the Turku Provincial Museum and the Swedish University of Turku. The main exhibition depicts the development of seafaring and shipping in Turku. The astronomy collection comprises the instruments of the famous Finnish astronomer Yrjö Väisälä.

★★ Käsityöläismuseo / Hantverksmuseet ⊘ (CY) – The Luostarinmäki Open-Air Museum is unique for its authenticity. The area of 18C wooden craftsmen's houses was one of the few parts of Turku to escape the fire of 1827. The museum opened in 1940 and today it comprises 18 sites where the visitor can see a variety of craftsmen at work in premises which date from the second half of the 19C. Part of the charm of Luostarinmäki is that it is a living museum where the visitor intrigued by sounds or smells moves from one workshop to the next, where young craftsmen demonstrate the traditional skills. During the summer months various crafts are represented from goldsmith to furrier, printer to weaver and baker to coppersmith.

FINLAND

Folk musicians in the open-air museum

P. Roy/EXPLORER

*Wäinö Aaltosen museo / Wäinö Aaltonens museum ⊘ **(BY M⁴)** – The modern, light building completed in 1967 was designed by the combined architectural talents of the sculptor's son and daughter-in-law. The custom-built museum has a representative collection of paintings and sculptures by this leading figurative Finnish artist.

Suomen Joutsen ⊘ **(AY)** – *The Swan of Finland*, the Finnish Navy's training ship for some 30 years, was built in the shipyards of St-Nazaire, France in 1912. The ship has been berthed in the River Aura since 1960, where she served as a school for sailors until 1988. The ship has become one of the symbols of Turku.

Museoalus Sigyn / Museifartyget Sigyn ⊘ **(AY M⁵)** – The cargo vessel *Sigyn* was built in 1887 in Gothenburg, Sweden, and now serves as a museum ship. She is the only wooden ocean-going three-masted clipper to have survived to the present day.

CASTLE AND OTHER SIGHTS ON THE NORTH BANK

***Turun Linna / Åbo slott ⊘ – *To the west by E 18.* This massive and proud greystone castle grew gradually over the centuries around an original fortress built in 1280 on a small island at the mouth of the River Aura. The royal governor ruled the country from here. Repairs and extensions after sieges and fires continued apace until the castle's heyday in the late 16C. When King Gustav Vasa took up residence in 1555-56 he added an additional storey with Renaissance style banqueting halls and royal suites for his son Duke Johan and Duchess Katarina Jagellonica, a Polish princess. Duke Johan then built the new or outer castle *(esilinna)*.

In 1614 fire badly destroyed the main castle and the outer castle was refurbished as royal apartments.

In the mid-17C the castle became the residence of Governor General Pehr Brahe, and once again it knew a period of brief glory. But soon it lost both its military and administrative significance and it was left to deteriorate.

During the 19C the castle served as a prison and then in 1941 it was damaged by bombing. The first extensive restoration took place between 1946 and 1961 and today some of the historic banqueting halls are used by the city of Turku for municipal functions.

Main Castle – Tickets are on sale in the entrance hall. The **Porter's Lodge** has the country's first secular **murals*** dating from c 1530, possibly on the occasion of Gustav Vasa's first visit. The room known as the **Sture Church** was appointed as a public place of worship in the 1480s and today houses a good collection of medieval wooden **religious sculptures****. In the **Nun's Chapel**, used as a private chapel by Katarina Jagellonica is the famous 14C Gothic **Virgin*** by the Master of Lieto.

The well-lit and airy Renaissance apartments of Duke Johan are on the top storey. In the **King's Hall** hangs Albert Edelfelt's famous painting **Duke Karl Insulting the Corpse of Klaus Fleming*** (1878), depicting a scene that took place in the Sture Church in 1597. Duke Johan's largest banqueting hall became the **Castle Church** in the 18C; it suffered badly in the bombing of 1941 and the 1757 pulpit is the only original piece of furniture to have survived.

Outer castle – This houses the **Historical Museum of Turku****. The prison of Erik XIV is directly connected with the history of the castle; in his struggle for the crown Duke Johan kept his brother King Erik XIV prisoner in Turku Castle from 1570 to 1571. A remarkable **miniature model***** depicts the whole of the Renaissance floor during its heyday with Duke Johan and his duchess holding court, the children playing and the scribe at work...

The history of the city from the Stone Age to present day archaeological excavations is illustrated in the other rooms which have been decorated in the styles of the 17C to 19C.

FINLAND

★★**Taidemuseo / Konstmuseet** ⊙ (BX) – Second only to the Ateneum in Helsinki the Art Gallery overlooks the city from Puolalanmäki hill. The impressive red-granite building by Gustav Nyström was completed in 1904 and features a harmonious combination of international Art Nouveau and the Finnish National Romantic style of the period.

The beautiful exhibition halls make an ideal setting for the outstanding collection (upper floor) of some 4 000 works of essentially Finnish art from the early 19C to the present day. Pride of place goes to the 30 works by **Akseli Gallen-Kallela** (1865-1931), Finland's national painter. Of particular interest is the famous **Defending the Sampo** (1896), a powerful work inspired by the national epic the *Kalevala*. *The Old Woman with a Cat* (1885) is one of his early Realist paintings done while home on a summer break from Paris. The gallery also has a good selection of works by the Åland islander **Victor Westerholm** (1860-1919) and several fine paintings of the extremely sensitive painter **Helene Schjerfbeck** (1862-1946), notably the *Portrait of the Artist* of 1915. A small corner room is devoted to the charming animal sculptures of Jussi Mäntynen (1886-1967).

In front of the entrance there are two granite **busts** by Wäino Aaltonen representing the father of Finnish painting RW Ekman and his pupil Victor Westerholm.

Ortodoksinen kirkko / Ortodoxa kyrkan (BX D) – The Orthodox church overlooking the market place (Kauppatori) was built in 1846 by CL Engel. It is dedicated to the wife of the Roman Emperor Diocletian, Empress Alexandra, who was martyred in the 4C.

★**Kauppahalli / Saluhallen** (BY) – The late-19C market hall with its many stalls brimming over with fish, meat, vegetables, cheese, pastries etc has conserved the authentic atmosphere of a true indoor market place. Allow time for a pause in the cafeteria to observe the bustle and colour of the trading.

★**Apteekkimuseo / Apoteksmuseet** ⊙ (BY) – Qwensel House is named after a late-17C owner, Judge Qwensel. The Pharmacy Museum is interesting for its collection of 18C and 19C apothecary jars and also for the Gustavian style interiors, typical of a wealthy family in the 18C.

In summer the Musta-Hilu horse cabs leave from in front of the museum for a tour of the city.

Brinkkalan talo / Brinkkala kulturcenter (BY E) – This former hotel became the official residence of the Russian governor of Grand Duchy. The early-19C neo-Classical building houses the Turku Cultural Centre. The building and its balcony are well known as the place from where the Mayor of Turku delivers his Christmas Message of Peace to the country at noon on 24 December.

EXCURSIONS

Medieval Churches and Louhisaari Manor

Round tour of 94km; allow a whole day. Leave Turku to the north-west by road 8 (AX) in the direction of Pori.

Masku – Brick gables were added in the 15C to this single-nave early-14C **kirkko** ⊙. Inside, attractive star vaulting covers the narrow nave and fragments of medieval murals are still visible on the walls. The paintings are 17C (two portraits, one of Peter Henrius Hoffman and his wife).

Once back on road 8 turn right after 3km to take road 201 to Nousiainen.

Nousiainen – The **kirkko** ★★⊙ was built as a memorial to Bishop Henry in the 1280s on the site of an earlier wooden church. The importance of the church is reflected in the abundant use of decorative brickwork.

This important historic monument enshrines one of Finland's most precious medieval relics, the shrine of Bishop Henry. The evangelising bishop founded Finland's first episcopal see in Nousiainen in the 12C. In the winter of 1156 **Bishop Henry** was killed on the ice of nearby Lake Köyliö by a peasant named Lalli. The bishop was given a martyr's burial in his own church at Nousiainen. The 15C marble **tomb**★★ was donated by Bishop Magnus II Tavast and the brass plate covering the tomb shows Bishop Henry with his feet resting on the peasant Lalli. The kneeling figure before the bishop is the donor. In the north aisle there is a superb **wood-carving**★ of the same subject.

Return to road 8 and continue north.

Mynämäki – This 13C **kirkko** ⊙ is sometimes called the Queen of stone churches because of its size. The spacious hall-church has beautiful vaulting. The church is dedicated to St Laurentius whose martyrdom is illustrated in the **carvings**★ on the altar (1400). The 15C wooden reredos above came from Prussia.

Leave Mynämäki to the south to join road 193.

Askainen – The **kirkko**  was built from 1650 to 1653 in a Late Renaissance style by the Governor-General Herman Claesson Fleming who lived at nearby Louhisaari Manor. The story goes that Admiral Fleming brought the richly carved Baroque pulpit and main doors back as booty from Germany where he served in the Thirty Years War. The church is known as the nobles' church with its galleries destined for the aristocracy.

The small yellow building in the churchyard was built in 1823 to designs by CL Engel and serves as the funerary chapel for the Mannerheim family, who also owned Louhisaari Manor.

Drive 3km west of the church in Askainen.

★★ Louhisaari – The Louhisaari estate had belonged to the Fleming family since the mid-15C and the manor house was built by the same Governor-General Herman Fleming who commissioned the church.

In 1795 the manor was bought by Carl Eric Mannerheim, who was to become Senator of the autonomous Grand Duchy of Finland. In 1867 **Carl Gustaf Mannerheim** was born in the manor; he was one day to become Marshal of independent Finland. The Mannerheim family sold the manor at the beginning of the 20C, but it was not until 1960 that Louhisaari became a museum under the National Board of Antiquities.

Today this well-preserved manor house is a good example of an aristocratic country dwelling from the 17C to the 19C. The house is impressive with its three storeys, its white chalk walls and black roofs and adjoining wings. Austere but harmonious, it forms an attractive Renaissance inspired whole.

Interior – Start on the second floor where the rooms still have their original **painted ceilings★★** with Renaissance decoration. In the large **banquet hall★★** the panels running round the top of the wall show different views of the Louhisaari estate and sea battles in which the Admiral Herman Fleming participated. The portraits show the rulers of the joint kingdom of Sweden-Finland. The small blue bedchamber is said to be where Marshal Mannerheim was born and is furnished with family heirlooms. More furniture of the Mannerheim period and family portraits can be seen in the first-floor rooms.

The ground floor was used for domestic purposes. Today the entrance hall has an exhibition presenting the former owners of the manor and the story of its restoration.

In the garden (parkland) behind the main building is a wooden bathing pavilion (1830s) by Granstedt. Look also under the trees in the north-west side for the charming little playhouse which belonged to the Mannerheim family.

Return to Askainen and take road 193 north to the junction with road 190 then turn right.

Lemu – This **kirkko ★** is set in a beautiful churchyard. The 15C Gothic church has a weapons room *(asehuone – vapenhus)*. On the middle pillar of the north aisle is a rare painted **image★** (17C) of the Father of the Reformation, Martin Luther.

Continue on road 190 then turn right when you come to road 192.

Raisio – This single-nave **kirkko** has a wooden vaulted roof typical of the earliest medieval Finnish church architecture. In many churches this type of ceiling was replaced by star vaulting. The **Triumphal Crucifix★** (c 1330) was the work of the legendary Master of Lieto.

★★ Naantali / Nådendal – See NAANTALI.

Lieto – *12km to the north-east; leave Turku by road 10 in the direction of Hämeenlinna then take road 2223 to the left.*

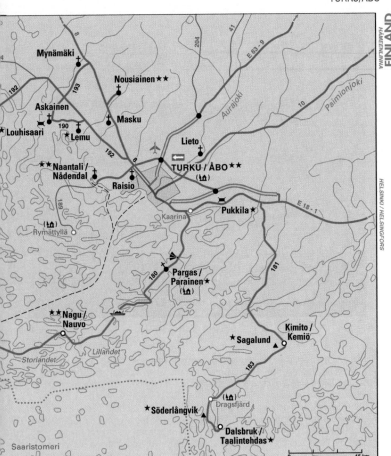

The River Aura flows through the village at the foot of the three-nave church which was built in the 1330s. It was for this **kirkko** ⊘ that the **Master of Lieto** did his superb sculptures in wood. The lovely **Virgin Mary** in the show case beneath the triumphal arch is a replica of the original in the historical museum in Turku Castle. The **altarpiece★** (1908) by Eero Järnefelt, depicting Jesus and the woman who was a sinner, expresses with fine subtility the controversy of the despising crowd and the grace and goodness of Jesus consoling the woman.

★Pukkila ⊘ – *18km by road E 18 in the direction of Helsinki.*
The lovely red-ochre manor house with its mansard roof is a wooden building dating from 1762. The beautifully arranged interior is typical of the lifestyle of high-ranking officials in the 18C and 19C. The styles range from Rococo and Gustavian to Empire. The attic – consisting of three bedrooms, a ladies work room and storeroom – is particularly interesting for the well-preserved timberwork, a good example of craftsmanship of the period.
In the stables behind the manor the **Vehicle Museum** includes sleighs and carriages used by the gentry in the 18C and 19C when roads were few and far between. Some of the sleighs are very finely carved.

★★Turku Archipelago

By boat – *Sightseeing boats leave from the city centre from either Auransilta bridge or Martinsilta bridge* (**AY**). *Several motor boats make trips to the archipelago; these last from a few hours to a whole day. The steamship Ukko-Pekka makes trips both to the archipelago and to Naantali.*

By car – A map of the south-western part of Finland shows a coastline shattered into thousands of islands, which have risen slowly from the sea with the melting of the Scandinavian ice-sheet. The beauty of this Finnish archipelago is comparable to

417

Turku archipelago

that of the Aegean. The archipelago stretches from Kimito / Kemiö in the east to Kustavi overlooking the Gulf of Bothnia in the west. The archipelago's population is mainly Swedish-speaking. The little villages with their attractive wooden houses have changed little since the 19C.

Two main roads reach out into the archipelago and both final destinations are linked by regular ferry services to the Åland islands. The most popular route is road 180, also known as the Archipelago Road, and it hops from one island to the next all the way out to Houtskär / Houtskari. Road 192 on the other hand strikes out north-westwards from Turku to take in the northern islands and end at Kustavi.

From Turku to Houtskär – *86km excluding the ferries. Leave Turku by road E 18-1 (CZ) and in Kaarina take road 180 to the south in the direction of Pargas / Parainen.*

From the suspension bridge high above Kirjala Sound (Kirjalansalmi / Kirjala Sund) there is a splendid **view★★** out over Vapparn towards the open sea.

★**Pargas / Parainen** – The industrial town (limestone quarries) has an idyllic setting where water, rocks, fields and forests alternate. The 14C **kirkko** ★⊙, dedicated to St Simon, has ornate octagonal brick pillars and 15C murals. In the 17C the sacristy was transformed into a chapel (Agricola Chapel) for the Finnish population. A 17C Bible donated to the parish by Pehr Brahe is on display.

★★**Nagu / Nauvo** – This commune comprises the two larger islands of Lillandet and Storlandet as well as a cluster of smaller ones. On Storlandet the village of Nagu with its charming **port★★** has a lovely early-14C **kirkko** ⊙.

★**Korpo / Korppoo** – The 14C stone-built **kirkko** ★⊙ has a western tower which is a feature more typical of the Åland islands. The lovely star vaulting dates from a rebuilding in the 15C.

The ferry for the outermost group of islands leaves from Galtby which lies 4km north of Korpo. 35min ferry trip to Houtskär.

★★**Houtskär / Houtskari** – Only 20 islands are inhabited in the Houtskär group which stretches to the straits of Kihti separating the Turku and the Åland archipelagos. In the centre of the village is a wooden church (1703-4) built to a Greek cross plan and one of the earliest examples of this kind of church. On one of the far western islands is the attractive village of **Hyppeis★** where boat sheds line the waterfront.

From Turku to Kimito / Kemiö – *80km from Turku by E 18-1 (CZ), roads 181 and 183.*

This is the largest of the islands and it includes the parishes of Kimito, Dragsfjärd and Västanfjärd. The vaulting of Kimito's medieval stone-built church was the work of Petrus Murator who was also responsible for the vaulting of Turku Cathedral.

★ **Sagalund Museum** ⊘ – *In the village of Vreta on the western outskirts of Kimito*. This open-air museum, the oldest in Finland, was founded in 1900 by a teacher, Nils Oskar Jansson, and today it regroups 23 buildings including an old schoolhouse, Tjuda Pedagogium, and an 18C courthouse. Of special interest is the founder's own home where he shared the house with the high-spirited and cultivated Adèle Weman. A programme of events is sometimes organised at weekends.

★ **Söderlångvik Museum** ⊘ – *7km south of Dragsfjärd by road 183*. The publisher and art collector **Amos Anderson** (1878-1961) was a native of Kimito and in 1927 he purchased this manor house as a summer residence. It was in these elegant surroundings amid the tranquil beauty of the islands that Anderson entertained artists and personalities of his time. The museum is more of a personal museum to the great art-lover who brought together the collection now on display in the Amos Andersonin Taidemuseo in Helsinki.

★ **Dalsbruk / Taalintehdas** ⊘ – *7.3km south of Dragsfjärd; road 183 then a local road left*. In the centre of this picturesque village an exhibition in the premises of the former ironworks recounts the life and times of the workers and local mining activities in the 18C and 19C.

From Turku to Kustavi – *68km west by road 8* (AX) *and then left for road 192*.

Taivassalo / Tövsala – The medieval stone **kirkko**★ in the centre of the village is richly decorated with colourful frescoes, the oldest of which date from the early 15C. The 14C **Crucifix**★ above the altar is the work of Master of Lieto.

Kustavi – From this flourishing holiday resort there are splendid **views**★★ reaching as far as Vuosnainen / Osnäs the ferry port for the northern route to the Åland islands.

TURKU ARCHIPELAGO ★★

See TURKU / ÅBO: Excursions above

VAASA/VASA ★★

Vaasan Lääni
Population 56 300
Michelin map 985 I 18 or Atlas Europe p 114

This large port on the west coast has the shortest crossing to Sweden. The history of Vaasa goes back to the early 14C, when Swedish seafarers from Norrland settled a forested isle in the Gulf of Bothnia. By the end of the century they had built the castle of Korsholm (Mustasaari in Finnish) as an outer defence for the mainland site.

With the high local rates of isostatic uplift Korsholm *(see Vanha Vaasa below)* slowly gained land and the pioneers were able to extend their settlement area and continued to prosper from their seafaring and trading activities. In 1606 King Charles IX gave Korsholm its town charter and renamed it Vasa in honour of the Swedish royal family.

By 1852, when it was destroyed by the Great Fire, Vaasa/Vasa had become a prosperous seaport and trading centre. Luckily the handsome Court of Appeal was one of the few buildings to survive. The architect Carl Axel Setterberg (1812-71) was commissioned to design a new town plan; he devised an Empire-style ensemble with wide avenues and spacious parks for the new site on the coast which had receded 6km westwards.

> **Isostatic recovery**
>
> The accumulation of glacier ice in Fennoscandia reached a maximum thickness of 2 300m, causing downwarping of the earth's crust. Since the disappearance of the ice sheets 10 000 years ago the Scandinavian peninsula has slowly risen at differential rates: 88 to 100cm per century near the northern end of the Gulf of Bothnia; 40cm near Stockholm.

Present-day Vaasa is an attractive town with a clearly Nordic character: some 30% of the population is Swedish-speaking and the daily ferries to Sundsvall and Umeå reinforce the Swedish connection. Vaasa is an important tourist centre as the gateway to central and northern Finland. The presence of a university and a Swedish School of Economics, as well as other higher educational establishments also contribute to the cosmopolitan atmosphere of the town. The 19C Empire and neo-Renaissance style buildings today fully comply with the 1960s modernism richly present in this native town of one of the most important Finnish architects of the 20C, Viljo Rewell (1910-64).

The suburb of Korsholm (Mustasaari) is known for its **Music Festival**, an international chamber music gathering with highly acclaimed artists.

VAASA / VASA

H Kaupungintalo/Magistraten
M¹ Tikanojan taidekoti/Tikanojas konthem
A Vaasan kirkko/Trefaldighetskyrkan

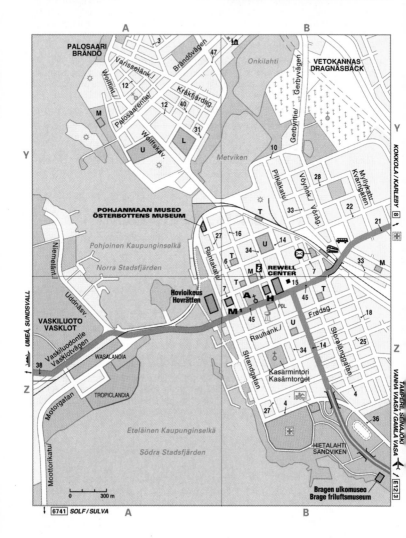

CITY CENTRE

★**Rewell Center** (BYZ) – This complex of commercial buildings, on the western side of the central market square, was built between 1958 and 1962 to plans by Viljo Rewell. It is a good example of the architecture of the period.

★**Kaupungintalo / Magistraten** (BZ **H**) – The neo-Renaissance city hall (1883) by M Isaeus is a beautiful example of late-19C architecture.

Vaasan kirkko / Trefaldighetskyrkan (BZ **A**) – The red-brick neo-Gothic Lutheran church (1862), better known as Kaupunginkirkko, is one of the main works of CA Setterberg, the city planner, who designed the new town plan and many of the public buildings. Inside, the main **altarpiece★★**, *The Kneeling Shepherds*, is a splendid piece by Albert Edelfelt (1854-1905). To the left is Holy Communion (1861) by RW Ekman and to the right, the Entombment of Christ (1897) by Louis Sparre.

FINLAND

★★ Tikanojan taidekoti / Tikanojas konsthem ⊘ (**BZ M'**) – *Hovioikeudenpuistikko 4* – The ground floor of this excellent art gallery comprises collections of foreign art, particularly French paintings from the period 1800 to 1920 including works by Degas, Gauguin, Matisse and Picasso. The first and second floors are devoted to Finnish painting mainly from 1850 to 1940. This extensive collection includes works of many of the finest Finnish artists such as Fanny Churberg, Akseli Gallen-Kallela, Albert Edelfelt, Eero Järnefelt and Tyko Sallinen. An interesting section on works by Ostrobothnian painters comprises pieces by Eemu Myntti (1890-1943), a Romantic colourist who worked in France, and by Professor Arvi Mäenpää (1899-1979), a miniature painter who demonstrated a mischievous sense of humour in his portrayal of local folklore.

Hovioikeus / Hovrätten (**AZ**) – *In the seafront park, Hovioikeuden puisto.* The wide central avenues lead to the handsome red-brick Court of Appeal dating from 1862. The former Court of Appeal in the old town, destroyed by fire, was at the same time being transformed into a church. The new Court of Appeal is the most remarkable of Setterberg's public buildings. An attractive park stretches all along the seafront, facing the island of Vaskiluoto (Vasklot) which is the site of the lively seaport of Vaasa.

ADDITIONAL SIGHTS

★★ Pohjanmaan museo / Österbottens museum ⊘ (**AY**) – *Museokatu 3.* The entrance to the highly interesting museum of Ostrobothnia is through heavy **brass doors★** sculpted in 1929 by Emil Wikström (1864-1942). The scenes portrayed are from local history: the inauguration of the Korsholm Court of Appeal in 1776 and the Great Fire of 1852. There are two main collections: the provincial history section and the Hedman Collections. One of the highlights of the history section is the town's heyday during the tar trade period (16C-18C). The rural **furniture★**, especially the cupboards and long-case clocks, is of particular interest.

The **Hedman Collections★★** were donated by Dr Karl Hedman (1865-1931) and the furnishings of the museum are almost as they were during Karl Hedman's lifetime. The first room is called the Napoleon Room; Hedman was an admirer of the great man. From here on, the rooms contain paintings from different periods and cultures: rooms 2 to 5 are devoted to eminent Finnish painters, notably Fanny Churberg, Helene Schjerfbeck, Hugo Simberg and Tyko Sallinen. Rooms 6 to 8 contain foreign paintings with an emphasis on 15C-17C Italian and Flemish masters.

Bragen ulkomuseo / Brages Friluftsmuseum ⊘ (**BZ**) – This open-air museum comprises an attractive early-19C farmstead from Ostrobothnia. The living room of the main building (1810) is decorated as an Ostrobothnian **wedding room★★** from 1914. This unique decoration is typically Ostrobothnian where a rural wedding was a three-day celebration with a large number of guests.

EXCURSIONS

★ Vanha Vaasa / Gamla Vasa – *6km south-east, leave by road 3* (**BZ**). This is the early site of Korsholm or Old Vaasa, which was burnt to the ground in 1852. Nowadays the area is a pleasant residential suburb. The **Court of Appeal★★** (1776) is the only building to have survived the Great Fire. When the town was rebuilt in its new site this Gustavian masterpiece was refurbished as a Lutheran church and given a belfry in 1863 by Setterberg. An avenue of lime trees leads from the ancient courthouse to the hill where Korsholm Castle once stood.

★ Stundars ⊘ – *In Solf / Sulva village 15km south leave by road 6741* (**AZ**). An open-air museum with typical 19C village houses and handicrafts village in attractive rural surroundings. During July, craftsmen are at work daily using traditional techniques.

★★ Seinäjoki – *77km south-east; leave by road 3* (**BZ**). The road runs through the flat, seemingly never-ending plains of central Ostrobothnia bringing

Reclining chair (1936) by Alvar Aalto

MNAM/CCI, Paris

the traveller right to the heart of one of the 20C architectural achievements: the **Cultural and Administrative Centre★★** of the town of Seinäjoki by Alvar Aalto (1898-1976). The town centre is dominated by the 64m-high belfry of the church (1960) known as the Cross of the Plains with the low building of the Parish Centre (1966) on the left. Next to it stands the ingenious Library building (1965) and behind it, the theatre, built only in 1987, although the drawings were made by Aalto in the early 70s. Opposite the church is the Government Office building (1968) and on the right, the handsome town hall (1962), with its façade clad with dark blue porcelain tiles.

Alvar Aalto architect and furniture designer

As an architect Aalto was noted for his original contribution to the Modern Movement and for his efforts to humanize the machine-based aesthetic of the movement. He also strove to achieve a softer more vernacular approach to modernism, which led him to develop what he called "the world's first soft wooden chair" of bent plywood made from laminated beechwood. The numerous chairs which he designed in this mode also brought him fame as a furniture designer.

ÅLAND/AHVENANMAA ★★

Åland
Population 25 400
Michelin map 985 L 16-17 or Atlas Europe p 120

The Åland islands, now an autonomous province, are strikingly different from the mainland not only for their scenery but also for their culture and folk traditions and its residents are extremely proud of their cultural identity. The archipelago of more than 6 500 islands and skerries straddles the entrance to the Gulf of Bothnia and acts as stepping stones between Finland and Sweden.

The breathtakingly beautiful mosaic of the Åland islands is characterised by the red granite contrasting with an incredibly rich vegetation. Although the highest point of Åland rises only some 130m above sea level, the landscape is often quite undulating.

Historical notes – Excavations have revealed settlements and burial sites dating from the 8C and 9C. For the Vikings on the **Amber Road** from Birka to the Bosporus the islands were the last outpost before the unknown. Some of the oldest stone churches (early 12C) testify to the existence of a sedentary Swedish population prior to the first Swedish Crusade to Finland in 1155-56.

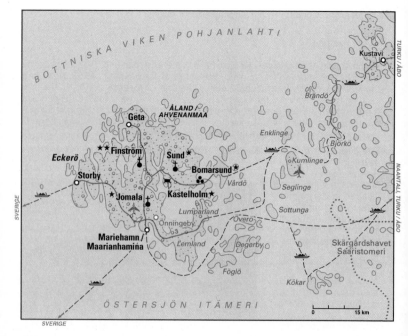

Åland belonged to Sweden until 1809 when the Russians annexed the archipelago along with Finland, making it a province of the Grand Duchy of Finland. When the Russian Empire started to disintegrate in 1917, and Finland proclaimed her independence, Ålanders made it known that they wished to re-establish the union with their old mother country. The matter did not pass without some quarrelling, and finally since the Åland question had an international character, it was submitted to the League of Nations. In June 1921 it was decided that Finland should be accorded sovereignty over the Åland islands and that they should become a demilitarised zone. Finland then agreed to guarantee the Ålanders their Swedish language, culture and customs. The islanders were granted a self-governing status (autonomy act) and today the population of Åland is represented by its own *landsting* or Parliament, which appoints the *landskapsstyrelse*, Åland's government. The islands' interests, on the national level, are safeguarded by its own representative in the national Parliament.

Life on Åland – Ninety percent of the population (24 000) lives on mainland Åland which accounts for more than 70% of the total area. The capital – the only town – Mariehamn has a population of some 10 300. The Ålanders are and always have been 100% Swedish speaking and their cultural ties with Sweden are traditionally very close. Ever since demilitarisation the islanders have been exempt from military service and from national taxation.

The Åland islands are greatly dependent upon the exchange of goods and services with surrounding regions. The Ålanders take great pride in their ancient seafaring tradition – Åland could once boast the world's largest sailing ship fleet – and although a large part of their merchant fleet has been sold, the growing car and passenger ferry operations guarantee excellent communications with the mainland.

Fishing and agriculture occupy 13.5% of the population, but tourism, which has continued to develop since the 1960s, and other service industries are the most important job providers. This miniature land with its landscape full of charm and its valuable historical monuments, including the oldest and maybe the finest medieval stone churches in Finland, attract more than a million visitors every year. The old folk traditions are still cherished and one of the most typical sights in the villages or farmsteads is the Midsummer Pole, decorated with fresh flowers and garlands for the celebration of Midsummer Eve.

Do not leave Åland without tasting the traditional black bread *(svartbröd)*, a slightly sweet farmhouse bread which is delicious with fish, especially with herring.

Island hopping ⊘ – Nowadays many of the islands are linked to one another or the Main Island by bridges or causeways. Car ferries connect Åland with both Finland (Turku / Åbo and Naantali) and Sweden (Stockholm, Norrtälje, Kapellskär and Grisslehamn) and there is an airport in Mariehamn. For the visitor who has plenty of time to spare the best solution is to choose one of the two Turku archipelago itineraries *(see TURKU: Turku Archipelago)* using the small local ferries leaving from Kustavi or Korpo in preference to the larger ferries operating daily out of Turku. The best ways to discover the islands are by boat or as many already do by bicycle.

MARIEHAMN / MAARIANHAMINA Population 10 300

The pleasant capital of Åland was founded in 1861 by Czar Alexander II to meet the needs of merchant navigation. The town spreads over a narrow headland between the east and west harbours and is the economic and political centre of the islands. A quiet place in winter, Mariehamn as a popular summer resort becomes quite hectic in summer.

★★**Sjöfartsmuseet** ⊘ – *Hamngatan, overlooking the west harbour (Västrahamnen)*. This Maritime Museum's superb collection (of some 8 000 items) illustrates Åland's seafaring heritage. The 1920s and 1930s were the heyday of the Åland merchant fleet with its elegant sailing ships. Intrepid sea captains and their barques made passage under sail through the treacherous waters of Cape Horn as they plied the Australian grain trade. The museum, in the form of a ship, has several colourful **figureheads**★ on either side of the entrance. One of the best-known sailing ships was the *Herzogin Cecilie* which was shipwrecked in the English Channel in 1936 on her return from a victorious sailing competition. The Captain's Salon, the Wardroom and the galley were salvaged and their splendour is there for all to admire.

The four-masted steel barque, the **Pommern**, is moored in front of the museum. This museum ship is the only authentic one of her kind to have survived and is a reminder of the wonderful age of sail when these stately ships – already under challenge from the steamers – voyaged between Europe and Australia.

★**Ålands museum and Ålands konstmuseum** ⊘ – *Stadshusparken*. The Åland Museum and Art Gallery are to be found in the same building next to the city's administrative headquarters. The museum's lively and well-presented collection depicts the cultural history of Åland from prehistoric times (4 200 BC) to the present. The art gallery's display includes works by local and other artists, some

FINLAND

well-known, from the early 19C to the present day. Many of the works show local scenes with a strong feeling for nature. The better-known artists are Karl Emanuel Jansson (1846-1887) and Joel Pettersson (1892-1937).

Sankt Görans kyrka ⊘ – *In the centre of town.* Mariehamn's main church, St Göran's Church, was built in 1927 to plans by Åland-born Lars Sonck and is one of the very few non-medieval churches on the island. The symmetrical plan is in keeping with traditional church architecture. The colourful interior decoration is by Bruno Tuukkanen.

Köpmannagården ⊘ – *Parkgatan.* This merchant's dwelling houses a small local history museum depicting the commercial activities and crafts of Åland in the 18C and 19C.

Other sights on the islands

Eckerö – *40km from Mariehamn.* The largest inhabited island to the west of the mainland island of Åland is only a 2hr ferry trip from Sweden. The island was the most important staging post on the postal route from Finland to Sweden for over 350 years. The Post and Customs House, **Post– och tullhuset**, in the village of **Storby** is an imposing, neo-Classical stone building (1828) by CL Engel. At that time no one dreamt that one day the mail would be flown over Eckerö to Stockholm. The local post office is in the side building whereas the main building now serves as a holiday home for postal workers. A very small postal museum, **Postrotemuseet** ★⊘, in a single room next to the post office depicts the incredibly difficult task fulfilled by the postmen especially in the icy winter conditions as they carried the royal mail and other correspondence across the Baltic. Note the model of the ingenious optical telegraph used in the archipelago in the late 18C to transmit urgent messages. (Post Boat Festival every second year between Grisslehamn in Sweden and Eckerö in rowing boats.) Also in Storby is the Labbas Local History and Bank Museum, **Labbas Hembygds– och bankmuseum** ⊘, with displays on village life during the 18C and 19C. The view from the quay of the red-painted boathouses on the waterfront with the grandiose Post House in the background has inspired many an artist including Victor Westerholm and Albert Edelfelt. **Eckerö kyrka** ⊘ was built in the early 13C of Åland red granite. The 13C wooden statues in the north and south window niches represent the Virgin and Child and St Erasmus of Antioch. The altar and pulpit are the work of CL Engel who participated in the 1830s restoration.

Jomala – *10km from Mariehamn.* Åland's oldest church, **Sankt Olofs kyrka** ★⊘, from the early 12C, stands in the centre of the village beside the main road. This remarkably spacious church with a Latin cross plan has interesting **murals★**. Four scenes (13C) on the arch of the tower depict the parable of the Prodigal Son.

Finström – *20km from Mariehamn.* **Sankt Mikaels kyrka** ★★⊘ stands in a lovely isolated setting by the Kyrkoströmmen (church stream). It was built between the 12C and the 15C but the characteristic five-spired Gothic tower is a more recent addition. The splendid **interior★★** comprises well-preserved 15C murals as well as a good collection of wooden sculptures. Two of the statues represent the church's patron saint, St Michael: the one at the back of the south gallery is the older one dating from c 1250 whereas the second one beside the sacristy door is dated 1460. The very handsome votive ship above the entrance was donated in 1688.

Geta – *40km from Mariehamn.* Some of the island's most beautiful scenery is to be found in this northern commune. The **kyrka** ⊘ in the centre of the village dates from the 1460s.
Turn to the right immediately after the church to reach the top of **Getaberget** from where there is a good **panorama** of the archipelago *(cafeteria and restaurant).*

★**Kastelholms slott** ⊘ – This castle stands in a strategic site guarding the Straits of Sund and played an important role in the defense of the country. It was here that the luckless King Erik XIV, who had already been held in other Finnish strongholds, was held prisoner for three months in 1571. The castle is currently undergoing restoration although little remains, other than its solid granite walls, after two great fires in the 18C and 19C. The northern part of the castle houses an exhibition on its history.
Not far from the castle is the open-air museum **Jan Karlsgården** ⊘, one of the many inspired by Skansen in Stockholm. In this particularly authentic milieu it is easy to imagine the life of a wealthy peasant in Åland in the 18C and 19C. In summer there is a regular programme of events and happenings such as the celebration of Midsummer Eve with folk dancing round the maypole.
The small whitewashed building beside the museum entrance served as Åland's only prison for 200 years. It now houses the small **Vita Björns Prison Museum** (White Bear) ⊘ illustrating the evolution of prison life between 1800 and 1950.

Bomarsund – *30km from Mariehamn by road 2.* The ruins of this fort, which extends on both sides of the main road, are a reminder of the strategic role played by the Åland islands in the past. The red-granite fortress was begun in 1800 during the period of Russian sovereignty and was designed to guard the entrance to the Gulf of Bothnia and accommodate 2 500 soldiers and 88 cannon. It was this fort – still in the throes of being built – that the English and the French attacked during the Crimean War *(see above).*

Two years later the peace treaty was signed and building work on this huge fortress was abandoned for good.

Sund – *30km from Mariehamn.* The 13C **Johannes Döparens kyrka** ★⊘ with its 2m-thick walls and its robust tower is famous for the burial cross of Archbishop Wenni of Bremen. Wenni was one of Finland's earliest Christian missionaries and he died here on mission in 936. Legend has it that his head was taken back to Bremen whereas his body was buried in Sund's graveyard. The cross stands in front of the chancel.

Artists colony at Önningeby

Victor Westerholm (1860-1919) began his art studies in Düsseldorf before moving to Paris where he was attracted by Impressionism. Westerholm was essentially an open-air painter and his answer to Karelianism was the Åland islands where he set up an artists colony at Önningeby (6km east of Mariehamn). The Önningeby artists (Westerholm, Hanna Rönnberg, Elin Danielson-Gambogi) experimented with open-air painting.

Rafting on the Klarälven, Sweden

Practical
information

Tourist information

The Scandinavian countries have tourist boards or representatives abroad, and at home in their respective capital cities.

Denmark

Canada: The Danish Tourist Board, PO Box 115, Station " N ", Toronto, Ontario M8V 3S4. b 416-823-9620.

Denmark: Danmarks Turistråd, Vesterbrogade 6D, Postboks 462, DK-1505 København V. ☎ 33 11 14 15, Fax 33 11 14 22.

Finland: Tanskan Matkailutoimisto, PO Box 48, FIN-02701 Kauniainan. ☎ 09 505 0015.

Great Britain: The Danish Tourist Board, 55 Sloane Street, PO Box 2LT, London SW1X 9SY. ☎ (0171) 259 5959.

Norway: Danmarks Turistkontor, Tollbugata 27, Boks 406 Sentrum, N-0103 Oslo. ☎ 22 41 17 76.

Sweden: Danska Turistbyrån, Biblioteksgatan 7, Box 5524, SE-114 85 Stockholm. ☎ 08 11 72 22.

USA: The Danish Tourist Board, 655 Third Avenue, New York, NY 10017. ☎ 212-885 9700.

Norway

Denmark: Norges Turistkontor, Trondhjems Plads 4, DK-2100 København. ☎ 31 38 41 18.

Finland: Norwegian Tourist Board, PO Box 709, FIN-00101 Helsinki.

Canada: *see USA below.*

Great Britain: Norwegian Tourist Board, 5-11 (Lower) Regent Street, London SW1Y 4LR. ☎ 0171 839 6255.

Sweden: Norska Turistbyrån, Mässansgatan 18, PO Box 5023, SE-412 51 Göteborg. ☎ 031 8369 70.

USA: Norwegian Tourist Board, 655 Third Avenue, New York, NY 10017. ☎ 212-949-2333.

Sweden

Denmark: Sveriges Rejse– og Turistråd, Skindergade 38, DK-1159 København K. ☎ 33 30 13 60.

Finland: Oy Routsin Matkailuneuvosto, Sjötullstorget 3A, FIN-00170 Helsinki. ☎ 09 686 462 60.

Great Britain: Swedish Travel and Tourism Council, 11 Montagu Place, London WIH 2AL. ☎ (0171) 724 5868.

Norway: Sveriges reise– og Turistråd, Klingenberggaten 7, 3rd floor (3 etasje), PO Box 1668 Vika, N-0120 Oslo. ☎ 22 11 52 15.

Sweden: Swedish Travel and Tourism Council, Box 3030, SE-103 61 Stockholm. ☎ 08 725 55 00, Fax 08 725 55 31.

USA: Swedish Travel and Tourism Council, PO Box 4649, Grand Central Station, New York, NY 10163-4649. ☎ 212-885 9700.

Finland

Canada: Canadian Representative Office, PO Box 246, Station " Q " Toronto M4T 2M1 Canada. ☎ 416-964-9159.

Denmark: Finlands Turistbureau, Nyhavn 43A, DK-1051 København V. ☎ 33 13 13 62.

Finland: Finnish Tourist Board, Eteläesplanadi 4, FIN-00130 Helsinki. Postal address: PO Box 249, FIN-00131 Helsinki. ☎ 09 4176 9300.

Great Britain: Finnish Tourist Board, 3rd Floor, 30-35 Pall Mall, London SW1Y 5LP. ☎ (0171) 930 5871.

Norway: Finlands Turistkontor, Lille Grensen 7, N-0159 Oslo 1. ☎ 23 10 08 00.

Sweden: Finska Turistbyrån, Snickarbacken 2, SE-11139 Stockholm. ☎ 08 5451 2430.

USA: Finnish Tourist Board, PO Box 4649, Grand Central Station, New York, NY 10163-4649. ☎ 212-885 9700.

Area and local tourist information centres – All the Scandinavian countries have a good network of regional and local tourist offices, located by an ⬛ on the town plans, which provide brochures, maps and lists of hotels, youth hostels and camp sites, often free of charge. The local offices will be able to inform you about festivals, sports events, accommodation in the area and the range of activities provided locally. The addresses and telephone numbers for many of these tourist offices are given in the Admission times and charges section at the end of this guide. Some of the local Tourist Information Centres are open in summer only.

Embassies and consulates

Australia

Denmark: Strandboulevarden 122, DK-2100 København Ø. ☎ 39 29 20 77.

Sweden: Sergels Torg 12, SE-11157 Stockholm. ☎ 08 613 2900.

Canada

Denmark: Kr. Bernikowsgade 1, DK-1105 København K. ☎ 33 48 32 00.

Norway: Wergelandsvn.7, N– 0244 Oslo. ☎ 22 99 53 00.

Sweden: Tegelbacken 4, 7th floor, SE-Stockholm. ☎ 08 453 3000.

Finland: Pohjoisessplanadi 25B, FIN-00100 Helsinki. ☎ 09 171 141.

Great Britain

Denmark: Kastelsvej 40, DK-2100 København Ø. ☎ 35 44 52 00.

Norway: Thomas Heftyesgate 8, N-0244 Oslo. ☎ 23 13 27 00.

Sweden: Skarpögatan 6-8, Box 27819, SE-11593 Stockholm. ☎ 08 671 90 00.

Finland: Itäinen Puistotie 17, FIN-00140 Helsinki. ☎ 09 2286 5100.

Ireland

Denmark: Østbanegade 21, DK-2100 København Ø. ☎ 35 42 32 33.

Norway: Consulate, Halvdan Bjørum Holmenkollvein 120B, N-1390 Oslo. ☎ 22 92 00 80.

Sweden: Östermalmsgatan 97, PO Box 10326, SE-10055 Stockholm. ☎ 08 661 80 05.

Finland: Erottajankatu 7A, FIN-00130 Helsinki. ☎ 09 646 006.

USA

Denmark: Dag Hammerskjölds Allé 24, DK-2100 København. ☎ 31 42 31 44.

Norway: Drammensveien 18, N– 0244 Oslo N. ☎ 22 44 85 50.

Sweden: Strandvägen 101, SE-115 89 Stockholm. ☎ 08 783 53 00.

Finland: Itäinen Puistotie 14A, FIN-00140 Helsinki. ☎ 09 171 931.

Getting to Scandinavia

Documents – Foreigners, including nationals of European Union (EU) countries, should be in possession of a valid identity card or **passport**. This entitles the holder to stay in Denmark, Norway, Sweden and Finland for a total of up to three months.

NB travellers planning a short trip to Russia must have a visa. It is advisable to get this in the country of origin as it may take over a week to obtain a visa in Helsinki.

US citizens should obtain the booklet *Your Trip Abroad (1.25 US$)*, which provides useful information on visa requirements, customs regulations, medical care etc for international travellers. Contact the Superintendent of Documents, PO Box 371954, Pittsburgh, PA 15250-7954, ☎ 202-512-1800.

Drivers must have a valid **national driving licence**, the vehicle's current **log book** (registration document) or a vehicle on hire certificate and a **green card** for insurance. A green card is not always obligatory but it simplifies matters in the event of an accident. All foreign motorists who come from a country which does not belong to the green card system must arrange for border insurance on arrival in one of the four Scandinavian countries. The vehicle must bear a national identification plate.

The minimum age for drivers in Scandinavia is 18 or 20 in Norway depending on the type of vehicle.

By air – There are international services from all major European cities to the four Scandinavian capitals. Airlines with scheduled services to Scandinavia include British Airways (Stavanger, Oslo, København, Stockholm and Helsinki), Finnair (Stockholm and Helsinki), Air UK (Stavanger and Bergen), Braathens SAFE (Oslo, Stavanger/Bergen) and SAS (Bergen, Oslo, Stavanger, København, Stockholm and Göteborg).

Air UK, Stansted House, Stansted Airport, Essex CM24 1QT, ☎ (01279) 680 146, Fax (01279) 680 012.

Braathens SAFE Airtransport, Oksenoeyveien 3, PO Box 55, Oslo Airport, Norway. ☎ 67 58 60 00, Fax 67 12 48 08

British Airways, 156 Regent Street, London W1. ☎ (0171) 434 4700

Finnair 14 Clifford Street, London W1X 1RD. ☎ (0171) 408 1222, Fax (0171) 629 7289.

SAS Scandinavian Airlines, 52-53 Conduit Street, London W1R 0AY. ☎ (0171) 734 4020, Fax (0171) 465 0537.

By ferry and car – Direct services operate from Newcastle (23/24hr) and Harwich (23/24hr) to the Swedish port of Göteborg. Other connections from Newcastle and Harwich are to Esbjerg and Hamburg. After a short overland journey, in both cases, there is a wide choice of regular sailings from the following ports: Frederikshavn, Grenå, Helsingør and København (Denmark), Kiel, Travemünde and Rostock (Germany) to the Scandinavian ferry ports of Oslo, Moss, Göteborg, Varberg, Halmstad, Helsingborg, Malmö, Trelleborg and Helsinki. The high-speed SeaCat offers a rapid service (1hr 45min) between Frederikshavn and Göteborg; it carries cars, caravans and motor-homes. Bookings can be made in the UK through Hoverspeed *(see below)*.

Color Line, International Ferry Terminal, Royal Quays, North Shields NE29 6EE. ☎ (0191) 296 1313, Fax (0191) 296 1540.

P & O European Ferries, Channel House, Channel View Road, Dover CT17 9TJ. ☎ (01304) 203 388.

Hoverspeed, International Hoverport, Marine Parade, Dover, Kent CT17 9TG. ☎ (01304) 240 241.

Scandinavian Seaways, Scandinavia House, Parkeston Quay, Harwich, Essex CO12 4QG. ☎ (01255) 240 240, Fax (01255) 244 382.

Silja Line, for details of schedules and fares apply to Scandinavian Seaways *(see above)*.

Stena Line, Charter House, Park Street, Ashford, Kent TN24 8EX. ☎ (01233) 647 047.

TT-Line, for details of schedules and fares apply to The Swedish Travel and Tourism Council in London. ☎ (0171) 724 5868.

Viking Line, for information on their Baltic services apply to Finman Travel International, 87/89 Church Street, Leigh, Greater Manchester WN7 1AZ. ☎ (01942) 262 662, Fax (01942) 269 898.

To choose the most suitable route between the ferry ports on the coasts of France, Belgium and the Netherlands and the Danish or German ferry ports for Scandinavia, use the Michelin Tourist and Motoring Atlas Europe.

By train – The advent of Eurostar heralds a new golden era for rail travel in Europe but all rail journeys to the Scandinavian countries include one or several ferry trips *(see list of ferry companies and their agents above)*. The **Inter Rail Ticket** entitles persons under 26 who are permanently resident in Europe to unlimited rail travel in over 29 European countries for a period of one month. The **Scanrail Pass** is valid for travel anywhere within Scandinavia for 5 days of travel within 15 days, 10 days within a month or 21 consecutive days. Reductions are available for children and senior citizens. The **Scanrail Pass** also entitles the holder to discounts on certain ferries.

By coach – Eurolines operate daily coach services from London to Göteborg (41hr), and to Stockholm (47hr)

Information from Eurolines, 52 Grosvenor Gardens, London SW1 OAU. ☎ (0171) 730 8235/8111.

Getting around Scandinavia

By air – Airlines operating a comprehensive **domestic service** include SAS (Denmark, Norway and Sweden), Danair (Denmark), Braathens SAFE and Color Air (both Norway), Finnair and Air Bothnia (Finland).

Finnair offers a choice of discounts on tickets purchased in Finland whereas SAS offers special **Airpass** fares, valid for the rest of Scandinavia (except Finland) at an affordable price. Unlike the Finnair discount fares, these special AirPass fares can be bought only in conjunction with an international flight.

In Sweden all domestic flights leave from Arlanda airport, 45km north of Stockholm. Ask your travel agent for further information on various discounts.

By ferry – Ferries are very much a part of the Scandinavian way of life as they bustle their way across the straits, sounds and seas, along the coasts, around the islands and over the inland lakes and waterways. Some of the longer services, and especially the ferries plying the Baltic, are of cruise-liner standard. The Coastal Steamers in Norway are working vessels providing a life line to the northern regions. Ferries run regularly and are an integral part of the road network.

Sailing times:

Frederikshavn to Oslo (9-12hr)   Stockholm to Helsinki (15hr)
Frederikshavn to Göteborg (4hr)   Stockholm to Turku (12hr)
Helsingør to Helsingborg (25min)   Umeå to Vaasa (3hr)
København to Oslo (16hr)

By train – In most Scandinavian countries the rail and ferry systems are well integrated. The Norwegian State Railways (NSB) network is fairly sparse and goes no further north than Bodø. Two of the most scenic routes are the spectacular Raumabanen (Dombås to Åndalsnes) and the Bergensbanen, which crosses the roof of Norway from Oslo to Bergen offering great scenic views. The famous Ofotbanen takes visitors from Narvik on excursions to Sweden.

The Swedish State Railways (SJ) provide an efficient network of train services to the whole of the country including the high-speed train X2000, which takes you to northern Sweden in comfort – with sleepers, family coaches, play areas and cinema coaches. The Wilderness Express (Inlandsbanan) runs through some of Swedish Lapland's most remote and unspoilt areas on its journey from Mora to Gällivare (June to August). Travelling at a leisurely pace visitors discover the beauty of the landscapes from the comfort of the 1930s carriages.

The Finnish rail network connects all important towns and cities and the two main lines go as far north as Kemijärvi and Kolari. Train fares are reputedly quite reasonable. The Finnrail Pass (Finnrailpassi), issued by the Finnish State Railways, is valid for 3, 5 or 10 days during a one month period. Children under 17 are half price. Finnrail Passes can be purchased at booking offices in Finland or from authorised travel agents abroad.

By bus – In Norway as the railway network goes no further north than Bodø, the bus company, Nor-Way Bussekspress, links Bodø to other places in the far north. One of the long-distance bus routes is from Hammerfest south through Sweden to Oslo. Sweden has an excellent express bus service between the larger towns and cities in southern and central Sweden, and between Stockholm and the coastal towns in the north. Finland has a dense bus route network and there is hardly a corner in the country that cannot be reached by bus. For further information about discounts and the advantageous 1 000km card contact Oy Matkahuolto Ab, Lauttasaarentie 8, 00200 Helsinki, ☎ 09 682 701, Fax 09 692 2864.

Motoring in Scandinavia – By European standards the uncluttered roads of Scandinavia are a joy to drive on and in some places you can go for miles without meeting another vehicle. The road network is extensive and well maintained and the motorways are toll-free, with the exception of certain stretches of road in Norway (see below). Vehicles must keep to the right-hand side of the road and generally speaking traffic from the right has precedence.

All roads, except for the minor ones, are numbered. Road numbers prefixed by an E denote an International E-road.

Speed limits

	Motorway	Dual Carriageway	Single Carriageway	Built-up area
Denmark	110kph	80kph	80kph	50kph
Norway	80-90kph	80-90kph	80-90kph	30-50kph
Sweden	90-110kph	70-110kph	70-90kph	30-50kph
Finland	100-120kph		80-100kph	50kph

These speed limits vary when towing with or without a braking device.

Seat belts – In Denmark seat belts are compulsory for drivers and front seat passengers and for those in the back where belts are fitted. In Norway, Sweden and Finland they are compulsory if fitted for the driver and front and rear passengers.

Drink and driving – Scandinavian laws on drink and driving are strictly enforced and heavy fines are imposed on motorists who are under the influence of alcohol. Police make frequent spot checks and foreigners are not exempt.

	Maximum permitted	Penalty incurred
Denmark	0.08%	
Norway	0.05%	Prison sentence; suspension
Sweden	0.02%	Heavy fine levied on the spot
Finland	0.05%	Fine or imprisonment

Lights – Outside buit-up areas all motor vehicles must be driven with headlights on low beam at all hours of the day. On Scandinavian models the lights go on automatically with the starter – most hire cars will have this feature. Remember to have the beam of your headlights adjusted to suit right-hand driving.

Danger zone

Accidents – When involved in a traffic accident drivers should give their name and address to the other party. The emergency number is 112 in all four countries. The local police can advise when a foreigner is involved in an accident, as there are special offices which deal with accidents involving foreign motor vehicles.

Breakdowns – In Norway between late June and the end of August the main roads and mountain passes are patrolled by breakdown vans. In the mountain areas there are roadside emergency telephones. In case of a breakdown in Sweden contact the police or the Larmtjänst organisation which is run by the Swedish insurance companies and operates a 24hr service.

Traffic signs – These largely correspond to those used in the rest of Europe but there are some exceptions. Beware of elk and reindeer as they have little road sense and they have a tendency to cross roads at twilight. A collision with a 600kg elk may have serious consequences. Any accidents with a reindeer or elk should be reported to the local police. Warning signs indicate the danger zones.

Tolls – In Norway certain roads have tolls. The cities of Bergen, Oslo and Trondheim charge a toll for vehicles going into the town centres.

Road conditions in winter – In these northern latitudes roads can be blocked by snow between November and May. Winter tyres can usually be hired and advanced booking is required. In Norway the following number ☎ 22 65 40 40 gives reports in English on road conditions. For driving generally during the same period it is necessary to have special studded tyres or chains.

There are no restrictions for the use of studless winter tyres. In Denmark studded tyres are permitted between 1 October and the 30 April; in Norway from 1 November to the first Monday after Easter – in the far north (Nordland, Troms and Finnmark) from 15 October to 30 April; in Sweden and Finland from 1 November to the first Monday after Easter. When using studded tyres all four must be studded. In Norway, Sweden and Finland the regulation number of studs per tyre is as follows:
13" tyres a maximum of 90 studs per tyre

14-15" tyres a maximum of 110 studs per tyre
>15" tyres a maximum of 150 studs per tyre.

Car hire – Most of the major rental companies (Avis, Hertz, Europcar and Budget) have agencies in the main cities and international airports. Cars can usually be hired at one place and dropped off elsewhere. It is always best to book in advance for an automatic drive. Some airlines propose fly-drive schemes which offer interesting discounts.

Comparative distances and areas

On a world map the areas and distances in northern latitudes are distorted. The adjoining map gives a truer picture of the relative areas of Scandinavian and other European countries and an indication of distances.

The most obvious, yet at the same time, one of the most significant facts about Scandinavia is its size.

The area covers 1 155 056km². From the Arctic Ocean to the Danish frontier with Germany is a distance of nearly 2 700km.

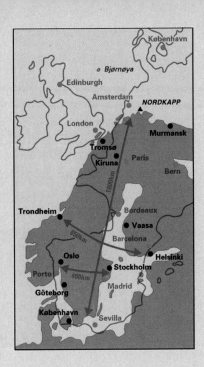

Rallying in Scandinavia

There are two European rallies which take in the great rallying possibilities of Scandinavia. The Cape to Cape Challenge is all about speed and competitors have no time to appreciate the scenery or meet the people, whereas the Paris – North Cape Auto-Photo Rally is on the contrary all about becoming acquainted with the Scandinavian way of life.

Cape to Cape Challenge – This 6 160mi non-stop motoring event goes from Cape Tarifa in Spain to Nordkapp in Norway, the most northerly point on the continent. Drivers determine their own itinerary but must go via certain cities – Madrid, Paris, Brussels, Hamburg, Göteborg and Oslo. Cars must not exceed the national speed limits.

The Paris – North Cape Auto-Photo Rally – This annual rally is not about speed and danger but about taking pictures of Scandinavian landscapes and life. Teams have to return with written and photographic reports of the Scandinavian way of life from their 12 000km journey.

Narvik to...

France 551 600km²;
Spain 504 750km²;
Sweden 450 000km².
Germany 357 000km²;

Finland 338 127km²;
Norway 323 878km², without the Svalbard and Jan Mayen Islands;

Poland 312 677km²;
Greece 131 957km²;
United Kingdom 244 883km².
Denmark 43 077km², without Greenland and the Faroe Islands;
Netherlands 41 863km²;
Switzerland 41 293km²;
Belgium 30 514km².

A few distances *(see the table below)*
København to Oslo 556km; Stockholm 586km; Helsinki 795km

Oslo to København 556km; Stockholm 534km; Helsinki 690km

Stockholm to København 586km; Oslo 534km; Helsinki 165km

Helsinki to København 795km; Oslo 690km; Stockholm 165km

Distances between major towns

Distances are calculated from centres and along the best roads from a motoring point of view, not necessarily the shortest.

Kristiansand–Århus = 204 km

	Bergen	Esbjerg	Göteborg	Kalmar	Kristiansand	København	Lillehammer	Malmö	Norrköping	Odense	Oslo	Stockholm	Uppsala	Ålborg
Esbjerg	811													
Göteborg	790	298												
Kalmar	1110	599	355											
Kristiansand	510	301	71	422										
København	1027	297	241	310	292									
Lillehammer	478	543	497	805	496	734								
Malmö	1072	316	286	290	355	28	779							
Norrköping	931	581	322	250	724	427	568	472						
Odense	856	149	343	457	346	155	589	174	597					
Oslo	472	353	319	639	323	556	191	600	460	399				
Stockholm	1005	739	481	411	798	586	642	631	162	756	534			
Uppsala	987	769	475	476	780	652	624	696	227	822	516	69		
Ålborg	589	219	78	430	79	210	324	222	397	265	134	556	550	
Århus	714	172	146	315	204	108	447	147	412	150	256	571	636	122

Services

Currency – The monetary unit in **Denmark** is the krone, which is divided into 100 øre. The international symbol is DKR but in Denmark it is abbreviated to kr.
The unit of currency in **Norway** is the krone (abbreviated kr or NOK) and it is divided into 100 øre.
In **Sweden** the unit of currency is the krona (plural kronor) (abbreviated Kr, Skr or SEK), divided into 100 öre.
Until December 2001 the official unit of currency in **Finland** is the markka (abbreviated mk or FIM), which is divided into 100 pennis. From January 2002 it will be replaced by the euro (€) divided into 100 cents (1€ = 5.94573FIM).

Bank and Credit cards – Major credit cards (Access, American Express, Diners, Eurocard, Visa and MasterCard) are accepted at hotels, restaurants, car rental offices, department stores and shops across Scandinavia. Remember to take your 24hr hotline numbers in case of loss or theft. You must also report any loss or theft to the local police who will issue you with a certificate (useful proof to show the credit card company). Check with your bank whether your cash card can be used to withdraw money from machines in the Scandinavian countries.

Banks – Banks in **Denmark** are open Mondays to Fridays 9.30am to 4pm (6pm on Thursdays). In **Norway** they are open Mondays to Fridays 8.15am to 3pm (5pm on Thursdays). In **Sweden** banks are open Mondays to Fridays 9.30am to 3pm (6pm on one evening a week). In some of the larger towns banks stay open until 5.30pm. In **Finland** banking hours are Mondays to Fridays 9.15am to 4.15pm.
Travellers cheques are generally accepted.

Time – Denmark, Norway and Sweden follow Central European Time, which is 1hr ahead of Greenwich Mean Time (GMT) whereas Finland follows Eastern European Time, which is 2hr ahead of GMT. Summer time is observed in all four countries from the end of March to the end of October.

Post – In **Denmark** post offices are open Mondays to Fridays 9am to 5pm and Saturdays 9am to noon and post boxes are red. In **Norway** post offices are open Mondays to Fridays from 8am or 8.30am to 4pm or 5pm and Saturdays 8am to 1pm. The Norwegian post boxes are pillar-box red. In **Sweden** post offices are open Mondays to Fridays from 9am to 6pm and Saturdays 10am to 1pm. Post boxes are yellow. In **Finland** post offices are open Mondays to Fridays 9am to 5pm. The main post office in Helsinki is open Saturdays 9am to 6pm and Sundays 11am to 9pm. Letter boxes are yellow and stamps can be bought at post offices, most bookstalls or paper shops. Main post offices usually have *poste restante* facilities; a passport is necessary and remember to give both your first name and surname as it may have been filed under either.

In days gone by

Telephone – In **Denmark** phone calls can be made from all phone booths and post offices, which are open Mondays to Fridays 9am or 10am to 5pm or 6pm and Saturdays 9am to noon. The post office and telephone service are separate in **Norway** and **Sweden** and phone calls can be made from public phone boxes or telegraph offices in the main towns. In Sweden the area codes have 2 to 4 digits and always begin with 0; when calling from another area keep the 0 but when calling from another country drop the 0. In **Finland** post offices are open Mondays to Fridays 9am to 5pm. Pay phones accept cash, prepaid phone cards or credit cards. Note that there are four international prefixes: 00, 990, 994 and 999 depending on the phone company used.

International dialling codes				
From	**Denmark**	**Norway**	**Sweden**	**Finland**
To				
Australia	00 61	00 61	00 61	00 61
Canada	00 1	00 1	00 1	00 1
Denmark	---	00 45	00 45	00 45
Finland	00 358	00 358	00 358	---
Great Britain	00 44	00 44	00 44	00 44
Ireland	00 353	00 353	00 353	00 353
New Zealand	00 64	00 64	00 64	00 64
Norway	00 47	---	00 47	00 47
Sweden	00 46	00 46	---	00 46
United States	00 1	00 1	00 1	00 1

Electricity – The current is generally 220 volts AC throughout the Scandinavian countries with plugs of the two round-pin type. An adaptor will be needed. **Medical treatment** – Visitors from EU countries, where there is an agreement to provide urgent medical care during a temporary stay, will be liable for the same charges as Scandinavian citizens. Before leaving home EU citizens should apply for the Form E 111, which is usually accepted as proof of entitlement to treatment. Nationals of non-EU countries should check with their insurance companies about policy limitations. Reimbursement can then be negotiated with the insurance company according to the policy held. All prescription drugs should be clearly labelled; it is necessary to carry a copy of the prescription. American Express offers a service, "Global Assist", to its cardholders only for any medical, legal or personal emergency.In Finland pharmacies *(apteeki)* sell medicines and chemists *(kemikaalikauppa)* only sell cosmetics. In Denmark, Norway and Sweden an *Apotek* sells medicines. The pharmacies usually follow normal shop hours. In larger towns there is often one open 24hr a day.

Smoking restrictions – Smoking in public places in Denmark is generally allowed, with the exception of public transport; some trains have smoking compartments. Restaurants usually have non-smoking areas. In the other Scandinavian countries smoking restrictions are strictly enforced and smoking is not permitted in public places nor on public transport. Hotels, bars and cafés usually offer smoke-free rooms or areas.

Tourism for the disabled – Some of the sights described in this guide are accessible to handicapped people and are indicated in the Admission times and charges section with the symbol &. The Scandinavian countries are to the fore in this domain and are well equipped with facilities for disabled visitors. Useful booklets or leaflets are available from all four tourist boards.

Denmark: *Access in Denmark – A Travel Guide for the Disabled.* For specific questions contact Dansk Handicap Forbund, Kollektivhuset, Hans Knudsens Plads 1A, DK-62100 København. ☎ 31 29 35 55.

Norway: Norges Handidkapforbund, Folke Bernadottes vei 2, N-0862 Oslo, ☎ 22 17 02 55, Fax 22 17 61 77.

Sweden: De Handikappades Riksförbund, Katrinebergsvägen 6, 117 43 Stockholm. ☎ 08 685 80 00, Fax 08 645 65 41.

Finland: Information and brochure in English available from Rullaten ry, Pajutie 7C, FIN-02 770 Espoo. ☎ 09 805 7393.

School holidays – In Denmark, Sweden and Finland the summer holidays are from early June to mid-August whereas in Norway they are from mid-June to mid-August.

Public holidays	Denmark	Norway	Sweden	Finland
New Year's Day 1 January	◆	◆	◆	◆
Epiphany 6 January			◆	◆
Maundy Thursday	◆	◆		
Good Friday	◆	◆	◆	◆
Easter Sunday	◆	◆	◆	
Easter Monday	◆	◆	◆	◆
May Day or Labour Day 1 May		◆	◆	◆
Common Prayer's Day 4th Friday after Easter	◆			
National Day 17 May		◆		
Ascension Day	◆	◆	◆	◆
Whit Sunday	◆	◆	◆	◆
Whit Monday	◆	◆	◆	
Midsummer's Eve			◆	◆
Midsummer's Day			◆	◆
Constitution Day 5 June	◆			
All Saints Day 1 November			◆	◆
Independence Day 6 December				◆
Christmas Eve 24 December	◆		◆	◆
Christmas Day 25 December	◆	◆	◆	◆
Boxing Day 26 December	◆	◆	◆	◆
New Year's Eve 31 December			◆	◆

Accommodation

Although the Scandinavian countries have a reputation for being expensive there is a wide range of accommodation in all price categories.

Hotels – For those visiting the Scandinavian capitals the **Michelin Red Guide Europe,** which is revised each year, recommends a large selection of establishments together with their type, location, price, amenities and level of comfort.

There is a good selection of hotels with uniformly high standards; many are privately owned but some are operated by groups. Special low rates are sometimes offered in July and early August and for weekend stays throughout the year. Some of the hotel chains offer reduced rates for holders of **hotel cheques.** The cheque is a convenient means of payment and it usually includes accommodation in a double room with private shower/bath and breakfast. Additional payments and other surcharges (eg supplement for single rooms) are payable directly to the hotel. Some chains operate different price categories and the cheques are usually valid from May/June to September. They can usually be purchased and refunded by accredited agents. For information on the discount schemes apply to the national tourist boards or accredited agents for brochures.

In Scandinavia, breakfast, nearly always a copious buffet, is included in the price of a room.

Scandinavia: Best Western Hotel Cheque Scandinavia; Pro Scandinavia; Scandic.

Denmark: Marguerite Hotels, Family Cheque.

Norway: Norway Fjord Pass; Nordic Hotel Cheque.

Sweden: Romantic Hotels; Countryside Hotel Cheque.

Finland: Finncheque; Euro-Guest Cheque; Best Western Finland; Scandic Holiday Cheque.

Farm holidays – For bed and breakfast on a Swedish farm the Stay on a Farm *(Bo på Lantgård)* organisation produces a booklet with a list of all the approved addresses. Finland has a good choice of accommodation in the main farmhouses or converted barns. Bathrooms are usually shared and there is a choice of full board or bed and breakfast. Brochure from the Finnish Tourist Board. Farm holidays are becoming increasingly popular in Norway, contact regional tourist offices.

Self catering – In most of the Scandinavian countries there are many holiday cottages and chalets available for self-catering holidays. In Norway they are mainly on the coast and in the Lofoten and Vesterålen islands the fishing cabins *(rorbu)* are highly popular with visitors.

Finland has many **holiday villages** especially in the lake district *(see Järvi-Suomi)*. The chalets range from simple to luxury but are well equipped and often include a lakeside sauna and boat. The holiday villages offer recreational activities, excursions, trekking, barbecue evenings, minigolf, tennis, water skiing etc. The holiday village often has a café or restaurant.

Youth and family hostels – In the Scandinavian countries youth and family hostels are open to people of all ages and it is not necessary to be a member of the national association, although there are special terms for members and members of affiliated organisations.

No two hostels are alike, some are modern custom-built hostels whereas others occupy older buildings with plenty of character; in both cases accommodation varies from family rooms to dormitories. In winter only a few hostels remain open. In the more popular tourist areas around the coast especially in the archipelagos and near the capitals it is wise to book ahead.

The Finnish summer hostels provide budget accommodation in university halls of residence, which are open to the public from the beginning of June to the end of August. Further information and brochures are available from the national tourist boards or the national youth hostel associations:

Denmark: Danhostel Danmarks Vandrehjem, Vesterbrogade 39, DK-1620 København V. ☎ 33 31 36 12, Fax 33 31 36 26, Internet www.danhostel.dk

Norway: Norske Vandrerhjem (Hostelling International Norway), Dronningensgt. 26, N-0154 Oslo. ☎ 23 13 93 00, Fax 23 13 93 50, Internet www.vandrerhjem.no

Sweden: Svenska Turistföreningen (STF), Stureplan 4C, Box 25, SE-10120 Stockholm. ☎ 08-463 21 00, Fax 08-678 1958, Internet www.meravsverige.nu

Finland: Suomen Retkeilymajajärjestö (SRM) (Finnish Youth Hostel Association), Yrjönkatu 38B, FIN-00100 Helsinki. ☎ 09 694 0377, Fax 09 693 1349, Internet www.srmnet.org

Camping – The Scandinavian countries have a wide variety of camp sites, often in picturesque settings, and as elsewhere prices vary according to the site's classification. Some sites also rent chalets and offer boat, canoe or bicycle hire. Certain sites near the winter sports areas stay open in winter. Holders of an International Camping Card do not require a national camping card. In Norway both propane and butane cylinders are available; in Sweden only propane is available and it should not be used in equipment designed to burn butane; in Finland foreign gas cylinders are not exchanged, so bring your own supply.

Shopping

Opening hours – In **Denmark** the normal opening hours are Mondays to Fridays 9am to 5.30pm or 7pm and Saturdays 9am to 4pm. In **Norway** shops are open Mondays to Fridays 9am to 5pm and Saturdays 9am to 1pm or 3pm. In **Sweden** the shopping hours are Mondays to Fridays 9am to 6pm and Saturdays 9am to 2pm or 4pm. In **Finland** shops are generally open Mondays to Fridays 9am to 5pm or 6pm and Saturdays 9am to 3pm; however, many shops remain open later and open on Sundays in summer.

Tax-free shopping – Anyone resident outside the EU can shop tax-free in Scandinavian countries. Stores will provide customers with a cheque covering the tax refund and this can be cashed on leaving the last EU country visited. There is usually a lower limit for tax-free purchases and the refund does not apply to foodstuffs, confectionery or tobacco products. Norway is the only Scandinavian country where EU visitors can reclaim VAT on their purchases over 308NOK. The private company, Tax-Free Shopping has agents at most customs posts, airports and on ferries leaving Norway; these agents will refund the Norway tax-free cheques.

Souvenirs – Famous **Danish** products include the delicate porcelain (Royal Copenhagen, Bing & Grøndahl and Rosenthal), glassware (Holmegaard), silver and jewellery (Georg Jensen, Hans Hansen), amber products and of course Lego and Duplo bricks. In **Norway** the brightly coloured and delicately patterned knitwear is always a temptation but other products include furs, leatherware, silver jewellery often replicas of Viking pieces, wood and pewterwork, needlework and textiles, not to forget the trolls in all shapes and sizes. **Swedish** glass (Orrefors, Kosta Boda), jewellery and genuine Swedish crafts including the famous Dalarna horse all make ideal gifts. In **Finland** choose from the stylish glassware (Nuutajärvi, Littala and Riihimäki), ceramics and porcelain (Arabia), jewellery (Lapponia and Kalevala Koru), textiles (Marimekko), Ryijy rugs, Raanu wall hangings, furs, leatherware and handicrafts.

Duodje – Sami handicrafts

This label indicates that an article has genuinely been made by a Sami craftsman. Horn, wood, leather and textiles are traditional Sami materials and the resulting handicrafts are usually intricately carved or decorated with Sami symbols and designs. The brightly coloured woven bands used to decorate their costumes use the traditional red, blue, yellow and green colours associated with the Sami.

Buying alcohol – **Denmark** does not have a state monopoly for the sale of alcohol and most alcohols and alcoholic drinks can be bought in grocers shops or supermarkets. In **Norway** the state-run Vinmonopolet hopes to retain its full monopoly. It is however wrangling over the EU's demand for greater internal competition. Recent members to the EU, **Sweden** and **Finland**, agreed to deregulate their state monopolies with the exception of the retail trade. Alcohol shops (*Alko* in Finland, *Systembolaget* in Sweden) will however continue to have full control over sales of alcohol, except low-strength beer. The shops are usually only open on weekdays, the queues can be long and the prices high. A person aged 20 can buy any kind of alcohol and those over 18 can buy mild alcoholic drinks (max 22%).

Sport and recreation

Skiing the Scandinavian way

In Scandinavia, skiing is much more than a sport, it is a way of life which goes back 4 000 years as **rock carvings** clearly show. Prehistoric man used skis to hunt for food or go fishing and, until quite recently, skiing was the only means of transport in winter time since, in remote areas, communities were isolated for several months of the year. Medieval **Icelandic sagas** refer to skiing as a normal way of travelling and it is sufficient to know that there was a god and a goddess of skiing in Norse mythology to understand the importance attached by ancient Scandinavians to this vital activity. It is also interesting to note that the Sami, the native people of Lapland, traditionally used skis when herding reindeer on the high plateaux of Finnmark. Skiing was also a means of fleeing from impending danger as the Norwegian **legend of the Birkebeiners** illustrates: it relates how, in 1296, two warriors carried to safety the two year old prince Håkon Håkonsson across the mountains near Lillehammer, travelling 55km through the night during a blizzard, an endurance test commemorated every year through the popular **Birkebeiner** race which follows the same itinerary. Cross-country skiing was therefore a traditional feature of the Nordic way of life before it became a sport. Today Scandinavians still learn to ski almost before they can walk but it has now become an exciting pastime which they enjoy with family and friends. There are thousands of kilometres of marked ski trails across vast open spaces and through forested areas. And for those who are looking for a challenge, there is the famous Vasaloppet, a 90km race which takes place in the Dalarna region of Sweden and attracts more then 14 000 competitors every year!

Modern skiing as a sport was invented in the 1870s, in the county of **Telemark** (southern Norway) by **Sondre Norheim** who introduced stiff ski bindings, designed new skis and perfected his own technique now known as telemarking: he could turn and twist by keeping one ski ahead of the other, he could also jump and land with his knees bent to absorb the shock, as skiers still do today. And he was so confident about his skiing ability that he skied all the way from Telemark to Oslo in 1867, a distance of some 200km, to enter the first national cross-country ski race.

Modern ski resorts all over Scandinavia have facilities for Alpine skiing as well as for the traditional Nordic cross-country skiing. The season lasts well into May and summer ski centres provide off season skiing. This is becoming more and more popular with young people who often wear bathing suits during the hot summer days and can be seen sunbathing in the snow!

Downhill and cross-country skiing

In the Nordic countries, with the exception of Denmark, skiing is a way of life and few countries offer such a wide range of skiing facilities: Alpine or downhill, Telemark, cross-country or Nordic, ski touring and summer skiing. There is something for everyone from the beginner to the skier looking for adventure. Scandinavian ski resorts are situated at lower altitudes than Alpine resorts, but thanks to the northern latitudes, the snow is of excellent quality, plentiful and early. The visitor can choose between the traditional mountain village or one of the more recent ski resorts, where everything is laid on, and remember that in some areas you can ski all year round. Some of the slopes and ski tracks are illuminated and it is not uncommon to see track patrols with their modern machines to keep tracks in perfect trim.

The map of principal resorts and festivals in the Introduction locates some of Scandinavia's better known ski resorts.

In Norway the Jotunheimen mountain range offers skiers the choice of downhill skiing for all levels, cross-country expeditions on marked tracks or off-piste in the great expanses of loose snow. The **Galdhøpiggrennet Telemark** competition takes place on some of Norway's highest slopes. Summer skiing is particularly popular in Norway especially in the following ski resorts:

Galdhøpiggen Sommarskisenter, 2687 Boverdalen. ☎ 91 38 31 93, Fax 61 21 21 72.

Stryne Sommarskisenter, 6880 Stryn. ☎ 94 55 61 09 or 57 87 23 33.

Folgefonna Sommarskisenter, 5627 Jondal. ☎ and Fax 53 66 80 28.

The main Swedish ski resorts for downhill skiing are from south to north Sälen, Åre Fjällen, Tärnaby and Riksgränsen. Årefjällen and Funäsdalsfjällen are two great cross-country ski centres with tracks for both classic and freestyle skiing. Ski-touring in Swedish Lapland is organised by Camp Abisko, Abisko Östra, PO Box 71, SE-981 07 Abisko, ☎ 0980-40148, Fax 0980-402 10, Internet www.campabisko.com. For further information apply to the Swedish Ski Federation, Svenska Skidförbundet, Smidesvägen 8, Box 20, SE-171 18 Solna, ☎ 08-587 720 00, Fax 08-587 720 88, e-mail info@skidor.com. Since 1922 Sweden has organised the **Vasaloppet** ski race from Sälen to Mora on the first Sunday in March. As many as 14 000 competitors take part in this 90km race; to compete skiers must be over 19 and have filled in an inscription form before the 15 January. More details from Vasaloppets Hus, SE-792 32 Mora, ☎ 0250-392 00, Fax 0250 392 50, Internet www.vasaloppet.se.

Finland's most popular ski resorts include Himos in the south, Tahko in the centre and Iso-Syöte and Ruka in the north of central Finland and Levi and Ylläs in Lapland. The Finnish Ski Federation can provide information on the different resorts Suomen Hiihtoliito, Radiokatu 20, 00240 Helsinki, ☎ 09 158 2366, Fax 09 158 2484, Internet www.hiihtoliitto.fi. Finland is a paradise for cross-country skiing especially in the areas of Saariselkä, Ylläs, Isosyöte, Läuhanvuori, Oulu, Rokua and Ähtäri. Popular cross-country races include the following:

Finlandia Hiihto Ski Race (2 days at the end of February): 75 or 41km (traditional technique then freestyle) from Hameenlinna to Lahti (6 000 competitors). Apply to **Finlandia Hiihto**, Urheilukeskus, 15110 Lahti, ☎ 03 816 813, Fax 03 751 00 79.

Pirkka Ski Race (1 day at the beginning of March): 45km (traditional technique) from Niinisalo to Tampere; 2 000 competitors. Apply to **Pirkan Hiihto**, Aleksanterinkatu 20B, 33100 Tampere, ☎ 03 223 7410, Fax 03 223 4398.

Pogosta Ski Race (2 days in mid-March): 53km (traditional) and 70km (freestyle) in northern Karelia (2 000 competitors). Further information from Ilomantsin Matkailu Oy, Mantsintie 8, 82900 Ilomantsi, ☎ 013 881 707, Fax 013 883 270.

Heli-skiing

The great wilderness areas of Sweden provide ideal country for helicopter skiing and the ski resorts of Riksgränsen and Hemavan/Tärnaby are popular centres. Heli-skiing is banned in Norway and is not common in Finland.

Snowmobile safaris

Only in Lapland can a snowmobile excursion be lived to the full. In the great white wilderness where there are thousands of kilometres of special trails for the snowmobile. Saariselkä, Ounasuvaara near Rovaniami and Ruka are good centres for snowmobile safaris. In Finland contact the tourist office in Salla, 98900 Salla, ☎ 016 832 141, Fax 016 832 147 or Finnair Tour Desk, Lentäjäntie 1, Helsinki-Vantaa Airport, 01053 Finnair, ☎ 09 818 8038, Fax 09 818 8736. Certain Finnish winter sports resorts offer expeditions to Russia.

The main excursion centres in Sweden's Lapland are Kiruna, Nikkåluokta and Abisko all quite near to Kebnekaise, Sweden's highest mountain (2 111m). At some point the trail follows the Kungsleden (Royal Trail), a long-distance footpath crossing Lapland from north to south (Abisko – Hemavan) through outstanding scenery. Contact Camp Abisko, Abisko Östra, Box 71, SE-981 07 Abisko, ☎ 0980 401 48, Fax 0980 402 10, Internet www.campabisko.com. Snowmobiles are banned in Norway. Helmets are a must for snowmobile drivers.

Dog sledging expeditions

Imagine the exhilarating sensation of sliding across the great snowy expanses of the Far North with only the muffled sounds of the Husky paws crunching the crisp snow to break the silence. This is a great sport for nature lovers and those in search of Europe's last wilderness. Lapland is the ideal place for this sport which is not too demanding physically but requires reasonable stamina. From late December to early May there are several ways of discovering dog sledging varying from the 2hr maiden outing to the week-long expedition. Guided expeditions rarely include more than six people. Standing on the sledge's back runners, each member handles his team of four to six dogs, according to the load in tow. The first meeting with the dogs, usually Siberian huskies or Alaskan Malamutes, is a telling moment. Once in harness the dogs dance with impatience and yap continuously, excited by what the French explorer Paul Emile Victor called the "urge to go forward". A hook planted firmly in the snow holds the sledge until the signal to go. Once the musher frees the hook the dog team lurches forward as one. Hold on firmly to the handlebar and brace yourself to enjoy the first magical moments of gliding forward. Excursions cover between 25km and 50km daily as they cover successive stages from hut to hut and take the intrepid through the unspoilt boreal landscapes of frozen lakes, great plains to mountain torrents and the great expanses of low shrubs in the tundra. After the exertion of a day's sledging relax in a real sauna. The dogs look for affection but above all their daily meal, rich in vitamins, before digging a hole in the snow and rolling up into a tight ball for the night. The equipment should not be neglected in these polar latitudes where there are low nighttime temperatures, combined with strong winds.

Thermal underwear, warm suit and boots, waterproof and windproof outer garment (Goretex), special skiing goggles, a bonnet that comes well down over the ears, and mittens are all necessary for this type of expedition. Oil-based sun creams are preferable to water-based ones for skin protection. In Finland the main centres are Kamisak Ky, Törmänen, 99800 Ivalo, ☎ 016 667 736, Fax 016 667 836 or Lahti Blue Lakes

Tours, Aleksanterinkatu 4, 151 10 Lahti, ☎ 03 783 44 00, Fax 03 752 33 85. Numerous excursions are organised at Abisko's national park in Swedish Lapland, contact Camp Abisko, Abisko Östra, Box 71, SE-981 07 Abisko, ☎ 0980-401 48, Fax 0980-402 10, Internet www.campabisko.com or Arjeplog Hundspannsresor, Aspberg, 930 92 Mellanström, ☎ 0961 500 62, Fax 0961 500 62. In Norway you can get information from Jotunheimen Hundsenter, 2680 Vågåmo, ☎ 61 23 98 50.

Reindeer sledging

This sport is almost identical to dog sledging, the only difference is that reindeer are slower than huskies. However, reindeer are highly resistant and can cover very long distances in deep snow where dogs would struggle. The excursions range from short trips of several hours to longer expeditions lasting several days sleeping overnight in a Sami tent.

In Finland you can contact Finnair Tour Desk, Lentäjäntie 1, Helsinki-Vantaa Airport, 01053 Finnair, ☎ 09 818 8038, Fax 09 818 8736. In Norway, Lyngen Adventure, N-9060 Lyngseidet (Troms). In Sweden, Laino Vildmarksturism, Pl 4168, SE-980 10 Vittangi, ☎ 0981-410 25, Fax 0981-410 10, Internet www.laino.com or Tjuonajokks Vildmarkscamp, Box 221, SE-982 22 Gällivare, ☎ 0970-136 30, Fax 0970 136 36.

Long-distance skating

From January to March Scandinavian lakes and archipelagos are transformed into natural skating rinks and they offer skaters great skating. On a sunny winter day there is nothing better than to slide freely over the dark blue ice of a frozen lake or even the Baltic, and discover the attractions of the marvellous landscapes while enjoying a day of sport. Certain safety measures are necessary. All ages can enjoy skating but do not skate on your own. When there is a wind, the cold can seem more intense and always enquire about the state of the ice. If some hardy, well-informed, local skaters do venture out on their own, most Scandinavians skate as a family or with friends. Numerous associations organise weekend outings and inform their members when skating is possible. Warm clothes, wind and waterproofs are necessary. When planning a skating trip try to do the outward journey skating against the wind and the return leg with the wind in your back as you begin to feel tired. The equipment for long distance skating comprises four essentials:

Long distance skates with blades about 50cm long fixed to the underside of the boot;
Boots which according to the type of skates used, can be ski boots, special skating boots or traditional walking boots;
A large stick or a **ski stick** to help keep your balance on the ice. This stick can also be used in an emergency to help pull someone out of the water without going too near the edge of the broken ice;
A safety kit to be fixed around the neck, comprising two small spikes, to be used in the event of falling through the ice; with a spike in each hand it is easier to get a hold on the ice and pull yourself out.

In your backpack you should carry emergency supplies of high-energy food, a thermos with a hot drink, a plastic bag (leave a little air so it will float), containing a change of clothing. In the unlikely event of falling into icy water, always change your wet clothes immediately. For further information apply to the national skating federations:

Denmark: Dansk Skøte Union, Idrættens Hus, 2605 Brondby. ☎ 43 26 22 10, Fax 43 26 22 08;

Norway: Norwegian Skating Association, Sognsveien 75, Ullevål, 0840 Oslo. ☎ 21 02 97 20, Fax 21 02 97 29;

Sweden: Svenska Skridskoförbundet, Idrottens Hus, 123 87 Stockholm. ☎ 08 605 60 00, Fax 08 605 61 87;

Finland: Finnish Speed Skating Association, Radiokatu 20, 00240 Helsinki. ☎ 09 3481 2479, Fax 09 3481 2095.

Land-sailing on ice

Sailing in Scandinavia is not limited to summer, as in winter some land-sail on ice. If you fancy a new sliding sensation over a frozen lake or the frozen Baltic contact Svenska Isseglarförbundet, Slätbaksvägen 21, SE-12051 Årsta. ☎ and Fax 08 556 701 55.

Walking on glaciers

Glacier trips are an exciting adventure but never venture onto one without a guide. A wide range of glacier tours is available with different fitness requirements. For those keen to discover the blue ice, one of the best sites is the Jostedalsbreen, the largest glacier in Europe (490km²) lying between Sognefjord and Nordfjord on the west coast of Norway. This great cap of ice was certainly a means of communication for hundreds of years. Men and their beasts crossed the glaciers at the narrowest point. To climb the glaciers it is necessary to have climbing experience and a good

Walking on the Jostedalsbreen

knowledge of safety techniques and proper equipment. A professional guide is necessary. When you are on your own, follow the warning signs and do not go too near the glacier even if it seems safe. Between June and September professional guides organise daily expeditions onto the glacier for enthusiasts of all levels. The equipment can be hired, but bring your own waterproof and windproof clothes. For these expeditions no previous experience is necessary either of climbing techniques or the glaciers themselves. Anyone in good health and aged over seven can take part. Roped together, no more than 10 per group, you will discover the great blue ice in safety. Apply to Jostedals Nasjonalparksenter, Oppstryn, Rv 15, ☎ 57 87 72 00, Fax 57 87 72 01 or Breheimsenteret, Jostedal Rv 55/604, ☎ 57 68 32 50, Fax 57 68 32 40.

Sailing

Scandinavians have the sea and sailing in their blood, like their illustrious ancestors, the Vikings. In the north the sailing season is limited as the seas and waterways are ice-bound between November and March. Anyone can sail and navigate, neither permit nor certificate are necessary. Yachts and motor boats from other countries must register at the local harbour master's office. The weather is changeable in Scandinavian waters and it is wise to listen to the weather forecast before setting out. Up-to-date nautical charts are necessary. To hire a boat in Denmark contact one of the following agencies:

Danlice Boatcharter, Ronning Bygade 23, Ronninge, 5550 Langeskov. ☎ 65 38 36 36, Fax 65 38 34 28;

Dansk Yacht Charter, Dokvej 4, Marina Nord, 6000 Kolding. ☎ 75 50 79 99, Fax 75 50 79 98;

Maritim Camping Bådferier, PO Box 26, Smedestraede 2, 4040 Jyllinge. ☎ 46 73 28 28, Fax 46 43 28 11;

Nordia Boat Charter ☎ 97 20 99 22, Fax 97 11 88 70.

In Sweden, there is one agency which offers a wide selection of privately owned boats for hire:

RTC Båtkontakten, Bullandö Marina, SE-139 56 Värmdö. ☎ 08-668 33 40, Fax 08-668 33 43.

The thousands of islands in the Stockholm archipelago are an idyllic area for sailing. For sailing lessons apply to ABC Seglarskola, Stallvägen 1, SE-131 50 Saltsjö-Duvnäs, ☎ 08-716 71 40, Fax 08 716 71 11.

In Finland the Åland Islands, Helsinki and Turku archipelagos, are paradise for sailors but there are also the 400km of inland waterways in the Saimaa lake system. For maritime charts and suggested itineraries, and centres hiring boats apply to:

The Finnish Yachting Association (Suomen Purjehtjaliitto), Radiokatu 20, 000 93 SLU Helsinki. ☎ 09 348 121, Fax 09 348 123 69.

To obtain the list of clubs and sailing schools contact the national federations:

Denmark: Dansk Sejlunion, Idraettens Hus, 2605 Brondby. ☎ 43 26 21 88, Fax 43 26 21 91;

Norway: Norges Seilforbund, Serviceboks 1, Ullevål Stadion, 0840 Oslo. ☎ 21 02 90 00, Fax 21 02 90 01;

Sweden: Svenska Seglarförbundet, af Pontins väg 6, SE-115 21 Stockholm. ☎ 08-459 09 90, Fax 08-459 09 99;

Finland: Finnish Boating Association (Suomen Veneilyliitto), Radiokatu 20, 000 93 SLU Helsinki. ☎ 09 3481 25 61, Fax 09 3481 25 72.

Wind surfing

Wind surfing is one of the most popular water sports in these northern countries. Most hotels and camp sites on the coast hire out surf boards. Regattas are organised throughout the summer. Apply to local tourist offices or sailing federations *(see below)*. In Finland: Suomen Purjelautaliitto (Finnish Sailboard Association), c/o mailto:Anne Kärki, Rentukantie 16, 28 660 Pori, ☎ 050 567 10 06, Internet www.kati.fi/~ismo/surf/. In Sweden: Svenska Brädseglarförbundet, af Pontins väg 6, SE-115 21 Stockholm, ☎ 0701 20 20 01, Fax 0707 11 20 28.

Canoeing and kayaking

Considering the Scandinavians enthusiasm for all water sports, it is hardly surprising to find such a great variety of opportunities for canoeing. The canoe is the boat of the Indians with turned-up ends and an open deck and usually used on lakes, whereas the kayak is the Eskimo hunting and sea-going boat. When loading your craft always make sure that the load is evenly distributed. When on a sea-going expedition stay close to the coast to avoid large waves and high winds. The Finnish Tourist Board publishes a comprehensive brochure "Finland on Water" which lists all the possibilities for canoeing in Finland. The best rivers for white-water canoeing are to be found in the north and the east of the country and the best season for canoeing on the lakes is from mid-June to mid-August, when the water has warmed up. In Norway the national canoe and kayak centre (Norges Padleforbund) is in Rud, Hauger Skolevei 1, 1351 Rud, ☎ 67 15 46 00, Fax 67 13 33 35. The River Sjoa, almost an hour's journey north of Lillehammer, has the reputation of being Europe's best rough water for kayaking. For organised canoeing holidays contact Hedmark Tourist Board, Grønnegt. 11, 2300 Hamar, ☎ 62 52 90 06, Fax 62 52 21 49 and Lillehammer-Gudbrandsdal Tourist Board, Storgt. 117, 2600 Lillehammer, ☎ 61 27 99 90, Fax 61 22 20 38. For a weekend, or longer, there are canoeing expeditions in the Stockholm archipelago; contact the Äventyrsresor, Fleminggatan 68, 112 45 Stockholm, ☎ 08-654 11 55, Fax 08-650 41 53. In Finnish and Swedish Lapland the **Arctic Canoe Race** is held annually and is one of, if not the most difficult, canoe races in the world, a real white-knuckle adventure for the participants. During the last week in June and the first week in July, all canoeists looking for an adrenaline-pumping event, descend 150 stretches of rapids (544km). Contestants can choose between being competitors or simply doing the course (the first half of the course or the last part); between the single place canoe or a two-seater. Apply to Jaana and Petri Sutinen, ☎ 016 532 430, Fax 016 532 839, Internet www.tosilappi.fi.

For those interested in a canoeing holiday in a certain area it is best to apply to the different national federations for a list of the best canoeing sites:

Denmark: Dansk Kano og Kayak Forbund, Idrættens Hus, 2605 Brondby, ☎ 43 26 20 94, Fax 43 26 20 95, e-mail dkf@kano-kajak.dk;

Norway: Norges Padleforbund, Serviceboks 1, Ullevål Stadion, 0840 Oslo, ☎ 21 02 90 00;

Sweden: Svenska Kanotförbundet, Idrottens Hus, 123 87 Farsta, ☎ 08-605 60 00, Fax 08-605 65 65, e-mail kanot@rf.se;

Finland: Suomen Kanoottiliitto, Olympiastadion, Eteläkaarre, 00250 Helsinki, ☎ 09 494 965, Fax 09 499 070.

Water-skiing

With several hundreds of thousands of lakes and the unique archipelagos, Scandinavia offers water-skiers some outstanding stretches of water. Since there are a large number of clubs throughout Scandinavia it is probably best to contact one of the four national federations:

Denmark: Dansk Vandski Forbund, Idrættens Hus, 2605 Brondby, ☎ 43 26 23 16, Fax 43 26 23 17;

Norway: Norges Vannskiforbund, Serviceboks 1.U.S., Sognsveien 75, 0840 Oslo, ☎ 21 02 98 70, Fax 21 02 98 71, Internet www.vannski.no;

Sweden: Svenska Vattenskidförbundet, Storforsplan 44, SE-123 87 Farsta. ☎ 08-605 6443, Fax 08-93 80 09, Internet www.svenskidrott.se/vattenskidor/forbundet;

Finland: Finnish Waterski Sports (Pasi Toriseva), Opintie 2, 29200 Harjavalta. ☎ 02 6740 600 and Fax 02 6740 642.

White-water rafting

White-water rafting adventures offer an adrenaline rush but the enjoyment depends, to a large extent, on having a real sense of safety. Make sure the company provides an experienced and qualified guide as well as basic training and safety instructions. Expect to sign a risk release form acknowledging that you are aware of the risks involved and always ask about insurance cover. Rafters must be over 15 and be good swimmers –

White-water rafting

even if it is only to float safely downstream if you fall out of the boat. Check the rating of the rapids (one to six with the latter being unraftable); the international system runs from one to ten. The rafting season is from May to October and various accredited clubs offer rafting on Scandinavian rivers. This action-packed sport provides plenty of high white-knuckle excitement and the chance to work as a team while discovering the beauty of inland Scandinavia. Some of Finland's best-known rafting organisers are:
Holiday Village Lomakouhero, Kouheroisentie 99, 43 480 Pääjärvi. ☎ 014 417 65 00, Fax 014 417 65 55;
Lieksa Tourist Service, Pielisentie 7, 81 700 Lieksa. ☎ 013 520 24 00, Fax 013 526 438;
Six Season Club, Äkäs Hotelli, 95970 Äkäslompolo. ☎ 016 553 000, Fax 016 553 368;
Inari's Youth center, Riutula, 99870 Inari. ☎ 020 564 7960, Fax 020 564 7961.

Of the different Scandinavia countries Norway, without doubt, provides the best rafting. Some of the rivers are classified as protected areas. The Sjoelva, Trysilelva and Driva are among the best rafting rivers. The organiser provides the safety gear (helmet, wetsuit, life-jacket and boots). In addition rafters are advised to take along warm clothes (jumper, socks) in wool or natural fibres but not cotton. In Norway the following clubs are:
Valldal Naturopplevingar, Valldal. ☎ 70 25 77 67, Fax 70 25 70 44;
Dovrefjell Aktivitetssenter, 2660 Dombås. ☎ 61 24 15 55/76, Fax 61 24 15 70;
Flåte-Opplevelser, Sjoa, 2670 Otta. ☎ and Fax 61 23 50 00, mobile 94 64 75 96;
Heidal Rafting, Sjoa Gjestehus, 2670 Otta. ☎ 61 23 60 37, Fax 61 23 60 14;
Sjoa Rafting, 2680 Vågåmo. ☎ 61 23 87 50, Fax 61 23 87 51;
Norwegian Wildlife Rafting, 2254 Lundersaeter. ☎ 62 82 97 94 or 61 23 87 27, Fax 62 82 98 60;
Villmarken Kaller, Postboks 27, Holmenkollen, 0324 Oslo. ☎ and Fax 22 14 40 44.
The Västerdalälven river rapids are the largest in southern Sweden whereas the Indalsälven provides moderately difficult rafting and the River Torneälv exciting stretches on the Kukkola rapids. For those who want to try this sport while visiting Swedish Lapland, contact Kiruna/Lappland, Box 113, 98 122 Kiruna. ☎ 0980 188 80, Fax 0980 182 86.

Deep-sea diving

Scandinavia offers numerous possibilities for those who like to explore the wonders of the underwater world. Choose a recognised diving school or club where they will meet the sport's high standards and provide competent tuition; most clubs organise diving lessons and diving excursions and they can usually provide all the necessary equipment. To refill your own air cylinder make sure you have your certificate of conformity and take your diving proficiency certificate along as it may be requested. The list of the different clubs can be obtained from:

Denmark: Dansk Sportsdykker Forbund Idrættens Hus, 2605 Brondby. ☎ 43 26 25 60, Fax 43 26 25 61;

Norway: Norges Dykkerforbund, Serviceboks 1, Ullevål Stadion, 0840 Oslo. ☎ 21 02 97 40, Fax 21 02 97 41;

Sweden: Padi nordic, Gullbergs Strandgata 36 D, 411 04 Göteborg. ☎ 031-80 88 40, Fax 031-15 32 00, Internet www.padi.com;

Finland: Suomen Urheilusukeltajain Liitto, Radiokatu 20, 00 240 Helsinki. ☎ 09 3481 2258, Fax 09 3481 2516, Internet www.susl.fi.

Canyoning and potholing

These sports are not for the uninitiated. Norway, with its mountains and numerous waterfalls, is ideal country for these sports. Canyoning is for the fearless who can enjoy the beauty of the landscapes on their way to the site and for the more experienced as they swim and negotiate the mountain torrents or explore the mysterious underground world of caves and galleries. Caving and potholing provide a special sensation where time stands still; in the dim light of a headlamp, to a background of eerie noises produced by the underground streams, these excursions stimulate the imagination. The underground caves of Dummedals at Boverdalen and Kåsehole at Rondande provide experiences not to be missed.

Whale safaris

Relive the magic of an encounter with Moby Dick in the Arctic waters of Norway. Expeditions are organised from the Vesterålen Islands at a latitude 70° north, in the open sea off Nyksund or Andenes. Until the magic moment when you finally spy a whale, you will be on the lookout, searching the horizon and wondering. Then suddenly, there is spouting on the port side and she surfaces, just as imposing as in Herman Melville's novel, 60t and 20m long, but friendly, curious, and majestic. It is often said that the book is better than the film. In this case real life surpasses fiction and it is up to you to play the leading role with Moby Dick as co-star.

Whale sighting excursions are scheduled daily from the end of May to mid-September, but can be cancelled due to bad weather. It is always wise to plan a stay of two or three days on the spot and reserve at least two days in advance. The excursion lasts 5hr and a light snack is served on board as well as sea-sickness tablets. To see a whale in its natural environment is an unforgettable experience! Two organisations propose educational and fascinating trips into the Polar waters. Hvalsafari AS, N-8480 Andenes, ☎ 76 11 56 00, Fax 76 11 56 10, Internet www.whalesafari.no and Whale Tours AS, Nyksund, PO Box 336, N-8439 Myre, ☎ 76 13 11 66, Fax 76 13 14 08, Internet www.whaletours.com.

Gold panning

Scandinavia is one of the few places in Europe where the adventurous can try their hand at gold-panning in the gold rich rivers of Lapland. In 1988 the European gold-panning championship was held in Dalsjöfors on the River Lannavaara. The Finnish village of Tankavaara, with its Gold Village, gives the future gold prospector a feel of a gold town and in addition to its museum it runs summer courses in gold panning. Contact Tankavaaran Kultakylä, 99695 Tankavaara, Fax 016 626 261. The village is also the site of a highly colourful event, the **Gold-panning Finnish Open** in the first week of August. The village of Kiilopään, slightly further north, is the starting point for gold prospecting expeditions, Kiilopään Tunturikeskus, 99800 Ivalo, Fax 016 667 121. If you want to try your luck in Swedish Lapland contact, Lannavaara Turism, Box 60, 980 13 Lannavaara, ☎ 0981-310 60 and Lappeasuando Turistbyrån, Lappeasuando 3, 982 99 Gällivare, ☎ 0970-501 70, Fax 0970-503 50.

Fishing through the ice

Fishing

Scandinavia is a paradise for anglers where they have the choice of sea, fjord, river or lake fishing and an even wider choice of catch. Fishing permits (daily, weekly or yearly) can usually be had from local sports shops, Tourist Information Centres, hotels or camp sites. Boats and fishing tackle can usually be hired locally.

In Denmark fishermen between the ages of 18 and 67 must have a fishing permit (daily, weekly or annual), which is sold in Tourist Information Centres and post offices. For further information on fishing possibilities in Denmark, apply to Danmarks Sportsfisker Forbund, Worsøesgade 1, 7100 Vejle, ☎ 75 82 06 99, Fax 75 82 02 09.

Norway has some of Europe's best salmon (Gaula, Orkla, Stordalselva, Tana and Namsen) and trout fishing rivers and the booklet Angling in Norway lists some of the best beats and also the local fishing associations. The season for freshwater fishing is from early April to the end of September and the permit can be purchased from local Tourist Information Centres, post offices and sports or fishing tackle shops. Visitors can go sea fishing all the year round, but cod fishing is best in spring and autumn. The season for salmon and sea trout fishing is from June to mid-September and a tax has to be paid. The Lofoten islands off the west coast of Norway, are a paradise for anglers. The **World Championship for Cod Fishing** is held on the last weekend in March, usually at Svolvær. For more information apply to Destination Lofoten, PO Box 210, N-8301 Svolvær, ☎ 76 07 30 00, Fax 76 07 30 01, Internet www.lofoten-tourist.no.

In Sweden the Bohuslän coast provides good sea fishing, the rivers Ätran near Falkenberg, Lagan and Ljusnan are good salmon runs. North of Haparanda on the River Torneälv they fish for whitebait with long shafted nets (haaf fishing).

Finland gained its angling colours in 1989 when it organised the World Fly Fishing Championships. However in Finland even beginners can enjoy a good day's sport on one of the three main rivers of Kuusamo, in eastern Lapland or the country's many lakes. Tourist Information Centres and some automatic distributors deliver the permit. For those who would like to take part in a fishing competition apply to the Suomen Kalamiesten keskuslitto, Svinhufvudintie II, FIN-00570 Helsinki, ☎ 09 228 91 30, Fax 09 684 9904, Internet www.kalamieslehti.fi.

Fishing through the ice is a typically Scandinavian activity and in Finland contact Lappland Guiding Rune Leskinen, FIN-99400 Enontekiö, ☎ 016 521 230, Fax 016 521 403 or in Sweden contact Camp Abisko, Abisko Östra, Box 71, SE-981 07 Abisko, ☎ 0980-401 48, Fax 0980-402 10, Internet www.campabisko.com for fishing trips in the Abisko national park.

Cycling

Cycling is a pleasant way to discover the Scandinavian countries, where many of the towns are well provided with special cycling lanes. The **Danish** Authority publishes an annual brochure entitled Cykelsemester i Danmark which gives a series of circuits throughout Denmark designed for those visiting by bicycle or contact the Dansk Cyklist Forbund, Rømersgade 7, DK-1362 København K, ☎ 33 32 31 21, Fax 33 32 76 83.

Although it is not absolutely necessary to be an athlete, it is best to have a bike with numerous gears if you plan to visit the fjord region in **Norway**. For those cyclists interested in joining an organised cycling holiday apply to Syklistenes Landsforening, Box 8883 Youngstorget, 0028 Oslo, ☎ 22 47 30 30, Fax 22 47 30 31, Internet www.slf.no. It is usually possible to hire a bicycle from local tourist offices. For those who like to take their bicycle on longer distances most buses and trains allow bicycles on board, at an extra charge. In Norway the ferries of the Coastal Express (Hurtigruten) transport bicycles free of charge. For those ambitious enough to take on the mountain passes make sure you check when they are free of snow.

In **Sweden** you can travel from Trelleborg in the south right up to Nordkapp following special cycling paths signposted Sverigeleden. This cycling path also has branches in Norway and Finland and of course the Baltic ferries will take you down to Denmark the ultimate cycling country. Maps and useful cycling information can be obtained from Svenska Cykelsällskapet, Box 6006, SE-164 06 Kista, ☎ 08-751 62 04, Fax 08 751 19 35, Internet www.svenska-cykelsallskapet.se. The isle of Gotland, known as the Pearl of the Baltic, is a paradise for cyclists (Bornholm also) and is good for all ages and levels. Many hire their bicycles on the spot. When cycling never take more than the strict minimum as any excess kilos weigh heavily when climbing uphill. Divide the baggage evenly between the front and the back of the bike and always take a recent, detailed map. Avoid tunnels − some are prohibited for bicycles − and International E-roads with heavy traffic. Otherwise cycling is the ideal − and economic way − to enjoy the peace and beauty of the Nordic landscapes.

In **Finland** the Åland Islands, the Turku archipelago and the areas of Lake Päijänne, Saimaa and Oulujärvi areas propose special routes for cyclists. For mountain bike fans the wilder regions of Lapland offer a series of old Sami trading routes. Contact the Finnish Cycling Federation, Suomen Pyöräilyunioni, Radiokatu 20, FIN-00240 Helsinki, ☎ 09 278 6575, Fax 09 278 6585.

Golf

Golf is a rapidly growing sport in the Scandinavian countries and although the playing season (May to September) is shorter than in the rest of Europe, in summer you can play round the clock. In **Denmark** ask for the brochure Danemarks Golfbanor which lists the 114 Danish golf courses or contact Dansk Golf Union, Idrættens Hus, 2605 Brondby, ☎ 43 26 27 00, Fax 43 26 27 01.

In **Norway** where the sport is growing rapidly there are 63 courses; apply to Norges Golfforbund, Postbox 163, Lilleaker, 0216 Oslo, ☎ 22 73 66 20, Fax 22 73 66 21.

The youngest of Europe's family of golf nations, **Sweden**, has in the last 10 years produced a great many quality golfers. Many of the country's golf clubs welcome visitors; in summer the coastal courses can be busy at the weekend. Ving Golf organises golfing holidays throughout Sweden including lessons and competitions. Contact Ving Stockholm ☎ 08-789 89 80, Fax 08-411 89 45. The most northerly golf course is at Björkliden near the magnificent Abisko National Park in Swedish Lapland. Apply to Svenska Golfförbundet, Kevinge Strand 20, Box 84, SE-182 11 Danderyd, ☎ 08-622 15 00, Fax 08 755 84 39, e-mail info@sgf.golf.se.

In **Finland** golf is inexpensive and it is growing rapidly in popularity and there are now more than 50 courses with either 18, 27 or 36 holes. Apply to the Suomen Golfliitto, Radiokatu 20, 00240 Helsinki, ☎ 09 3481 2244, Fax 09 147 145, www.golf.fi.

When playing north of the Arctic Circle orange balls are recommended and players are allowed to brush away lumps of snow on the greens. The Tornio course at the head of the Gulf of Bothnia provides the unusual experience of teeing off in Finland and putting the eighteenth in Sweden – there are no customs formalities! During this game golfers will also lose or gain an hour. For anyone who wants to try his hand at playing on ice the **Santa Claus Arctic Golf Tournament** in Rovaniemi is played on the frozen River Kenijoki.

Riding

There are riding centres throughout the Scandinavian countries. Most of these clubs offer riding lessons on an hourly or daily basis. Some of the centres specialise in pony trekking offering daily outings or longer expeditions. For those looking for a more leisurely holiday why not try a horse-drawn caravan to discover the Danish countryside, contact Frostrup Ridecenter, Tommerbyvej 8, 7741 Frostrup, ☎ 97 99 15 45; Enggårdens Ridecenter, Hellebjergvej 27, 3120 Dronningmolle, ☎ 49 70 46 60, Fax 49 70 46 67; Bornholms Praerievogns Ridehesteferie, Lantagevej 23, 3730 Nexo, ☎ 56 49 30 37, Fax 56 48 81 26 or Destination Langeland Fyn Ærø, DK-5935 Bagenkop, ☎ 62 56 14 93, Fax 62 56 19 59.

In Norway the riding centres Steinseth Ridesenter in Asker and Kjells Rideskole in Gol are equipped to welcome handicapped riders. In Sweden you can discover Swedish Lapland by horse, contact Djurgården in Kiruna, SE-981 34 Kiruna, ☎ 0980-189 12. To get a complete listing of the riding centres contact the national organisations:

Denmark: Dansk Ride Forbund, Hestesportens Hus, Traverbanevej 10, 2920 Charlottenlund. ☎ 39 96 20 70;

Norway: Norsk Rytterforbund, Serviceboks 1.U.S., Sognsveien 75, 0840 Oslo. ☎ 21 02 96 50, Fax 21 02 96 51;

Sweden: Svenska Ridsportförbundet, Herrskogsvägen 2 Strömsholm, 73040 Kolbäck. ☎ 02-20 456 00, Fax 02-20 456 70;

Finland: Suomen Ratsastajainliitto (The Equestrian Federation of Finland), Radiokatu 20, 00093 SLU Helsinki. ☎ 09 229 45 10, Fax 09 149 6864.

Trotting

In Norway trotting is a tradition which maintains the horse at the heart of Norwegian culture. Trotting-racing in Norway stems from the American standard-bred trotters developed in the United States in the 19C. The main racecourses *(travbane)* are in Bjerke to the north of Oslo, Forus near Stavanger, Åsan in Bergen and Leangen in Trondheim. Trotters harness-racing is a popular sport in Finland with almost 700 races organised annually. One of Europe's largest racecourses is Vermo near Helsinki where over 80 races are run annually, including the **Finnish Derby** for harness racing in August and the **Finlandia Race** in April, an event in the European trotting championships. For further information apply to the Finnish racing organisation Suomen Hippos, Tulkinkuja 3, FIN-02600 Espoo, ☎ 09 511 00 201, Fax 09 511 00 291.

Sauna

The sauna is known the world over as one of the best forms of relaxation and in Scandinavia the sauna has become an institution, especially in Finland where it is very much part of everyday life. Today saunas number over 1.5 million for a population of 5 million and Finland is generally recognised as the home of the sauna.

Origins – Perspiration baths were common in ancient India, Greece, Rome and Islamic countries and even in Europe during the Middle Ages but the tradition died out as many believed the sauna spread disease.

The earliest form of sauna was a pit in the ground (the Sami word for sauna *saun* means a hole in the ground). In some of the poorer areas of Finland where building materials were scarce, some of the saunas were still built underground as late as the early 20C. In other regions turf was used. The early log saunas had no windows, but the air circulated between the logs. The stove was often in an adjoining vestibule or *kota*. In some regions the sauna was a multipurpose building used for drying grain and flax, curing meat and other household chores – it was not uncommon for babies to be born in the sauna – as it was the cleanest room. Saunas were taken only once a week in winter and twice in summer. There were three different types of sauna.

The Torrbastu or dry / smoke sauna – a dry heat bath where the humidity is low but the temperature can reach 100°C.

The Våtbastu or wet sauna – a humid heat bath where the temperature reaches 75°C but there is a much higher degree of humidity due to the water poured over the stones.

The ångbastu or steam sauna – a steam bath where the temperature is rarely over 60°C but the humidity can reach 100%. This is not typically Scandinavian but is associated more with Turkish baths as the room has no stove and the heat is introduced by jets of steam, into a room tiled to retain the humidity.

The essential features of a sauna – The log-built or wood lined hot room (3 to 25m² in size) of a sauna usually has wooden benches or platforms at different levels and a special stove with a pile of stones on top. Water is poured on the stones from time to time to maintain the humidity level. Good ventilation is important as the air in the sauna should be changed regularly – at least six times per hour. The temperature on the upper platform should be between 75°C and 95°C.

When to take a sauna – Many Scandinavians take a sauna once a week – often at the weekend to relax after a week's hard work. It is wise not to drink or eat heavily before having a sauna. The sauna is usually a place of silence and meditation.

How to take a sauna – Undress in the changing room and take a towel if it is a mixed sauna. Choose your platform, the higher up the hotter it will be. After about 5 to 10min you will begin to sweat and once you have had enough, take a cold shower or a dip in the sea or lake. In winter the hardy will take a dip in the sea through a hole in the ice. This process can be repeated once or twice but it should be a pleasure and not an endurance test.

Where to take a sauna – There are saunas at most swimming pools, hotels, motels, youth hostels, holiday villages, camp sites, apartment blocks and even in some places of work. Some of the mountain huts, belonging to the STF (Svenska Turist Föreningen), in Swedish Lapland have saunas – but you must chop the firewood and carry the water before enjoying an authentic sauna.

Why do people take a sauna? – In brief the pores of the skin dilate with the heat and the toxins liberated with the sweat are eliminated during the cold shower or dip in the sea. The sauna relieves muscular tension and gives a feeling of well-being and relaxation and provides an ideal cure for stress in today's hectic world.

The great outdoors

The vast sparsely populated areas in the north of the Scandinavian peninsula include the last remaining wilderness areas in Europe. With their great love of nature the Scandinavians have shown a dogged determination to preserve what they cherish above everything else. Their environmental awareness has led to a mixture of strict conservation laws and individual responsibility.

The unwritten code of practice – **Everyman's right** – has evolved over the centuries and governs what you can and cannot do in the countryside. In principle, you can roam freely in the Scandinavian countries – on land and on water – as long as you don't intrude on people's privacy, cause a nuisance or damage, or leave litter.

Access to open country – The countryside is there for you to enjoy – on foot, by bike, on skis, by boat – the choice is yours. Remember, though, not to harm plants and animals, not to deface trees, not to damage property, and not to cause disturbance. Everyman's right does not entitle you to enter the yard, garden or grounds of a person's home.

Everyman's right does not always mean the same in summer and winter. Thus for instance, walkers may not cross fields with growing crops in summer, but should keep to the edges, skiers in winter are free to cross fields at will. Fields in fact make good terrain for cross-country skiing.

If you have to cross someone's land, make sure you don't go so near the house that you intrude on the family's privacy. Take a slightly longer route.

Movement is often restricted in protected areas, in which case the restrictions will be clearly displayed.

Take care not to disturb the wildlife. Do not touch nests or disturb young birds or other young animals. Do not remove eggs from their nests. Remember to keep your dog on a lead from 1 March to 19 August, when young are being reared. Hunting dogs can be free during the appropriate season.

You may not venture onto private land with a vehicle without permission from the landowner. The wheels cause rutting and even permanent damage. In winter, no matter how tempting the expanses of snow look, snowmobile drivers must keep to the designated routes; public roads are strictly out of bounds.

Access to water courses – With the exception of military areas, you have free access to most water courses, also when they are frozen in winter. Rowing, canoeing and sailing are rarely restricted. The same is not true for motor boats, however, which are not permitted on some lakes of special ecological value – above all, those frequented by birds – or in protected breeding areas. There are also restrictions in harbours and narrow stretches of water. The same regulations apply to water skis and scooters.

In summer you can anchor for a short stay in a spot that takes your fancy as long as you don't cause inconvenience. Even so, make sure you aren't too near houses on the shore. If you're sailing in a motor boat, remember it is both fast and noisy, and take great care not to disturb the wildlife – or your fellow men.

There are special waste disposal facilities at visitors' marinas and service stations. Human waste contaminates waters, so never empty it into a lake, the water in a harbour, a bay of the sea or any other narrow stretch of water.

Getting about – Everyman's right allows you to rest, swim or sunbathe within reason. You can pitch your tent on private land or even in the wilderness if you like, but not on a beach or in a public place. The Scandinavian countries are well supplied with a network of first-rate camping grounds, which should ideally be your first choice. Your prime consideration should always be not to cause a disturbance or intrude on other people's privacy. Also, you may find that in some towns you are not allowed to spend the night in your own vehicle.

Berries, mushrooms, plants and trees – You can pick wild berries and mushrooms almost freely, with the exception of cloudberries in parts of Lapland. Restrictions are tighter, though, for plants. There are a large number of protected plant species, so to be on the safe side, it is best to leave wild flowers alone. Picking plants, berries and mushrooms is also restricted in protected areas.

Everyman's right does not entitle you to chop down or damage trees in any way, even for firewood. Nor does it permit you to gather moss or pick shrubs.

You can take any water you need for your own use from lakes and rivers, and you can also swim where you like, remembering the same considerations for other people's privacy.

Lighting fires – You may not light a fire outdoors unless you have permission from the landowner on whose land you are. Even then, you should be extremely careful; remember, some areas of Scandinavia have dense forests, and it doesn't take much to start a forest fire. Choose a spot that is sheltered from the wind and has a good supply of water nearby. Make especially sure that you put your fire out. In a dry summer there is often a total ban on fires outdoors, so check first. Notices are displayed in prominent places. Fires may also not be lit on rocks, as the heat may scar the rock and cause it to fracture.

You may not cut growing wood to light a fire. You can, however, collect dead twigs, fallen branches and cones which are plentiful in Scandinavian forests.

The safest place of all to light a fire is at a camp site or in an outdoor recreation area, as these usually have special facilities for outdoor cooking. You don't need permission to use a camp stove.

Litter – Remember the maxim: take back what you take out, and never leave litter in the countryside, whether on public or private land. There are specially designated places for both liquid and solid rubbish. Never leave rubbish bags beside a full bin as wild animals can tear them open and pull out the rubbish. Bottles, cans, bottle tops and plastic bags can cause extreme suffering to animals. Everyman's right requires you to clean up after you and not to leave traces of your stay behind. In a nutshell, leave your surroundings as you would like to find them.

Fishing and hunting – A permit is needed for all hunting. You can fish though without a permit as long as you use a hook and line and not a reel. Ask the nearest tourist office for advice.

Protected areas – You may not immediately spot the signs marking a protected area, so you should make an effort to find out where they are before you start your holiday. Boaters should take particular care, as there are many rocks and islands where birds are protected. If in doubt, don't land.

You are allowed to pitch your tent for a day or two on land which is not used for farming and which is not close to a dwelling. The closer to houses you wish to camp, the more likely you are to cause a disturbance, and the more important it is to ask the landowner for permission. How long you can pitch your tent in the same place depends on the circumstances. It would not be very wise or considerate, for instance, to pitch your tent even for only one night in the immediate vicinity of a private plot of land.

Safeguarding the natural environment

The Scandinavian countries were quick to create national parks and nature reserves to protect areas of natural beauty and ecosystems which are particularly interesting and vulnerable and where no human interference can be tolerated. Some of these parks have been put on UNESCO's list of protected areas.

The system of national parks ensures the preservation of beauty and ecological qualities and the promotion of public access and enjoyment in these wilderness areas.

In Scandinavia's many national parks (Norway 21, Sweden 20 and Finland 30), as in the rest of Europe, these protected areas are open to the public and there is a considerable growth in the provision of leisure activities and facilities: marked trails, camp sites, wilderness cabins (book ahead) and other accommodation. The largest parks often have a visitor centre with an exhibition, café and ranger services. The national parks are indicated on the Michelin map 985.

In Norway Jostedalsbreen covers the glacier of the same name, Jotunheimen the mountain range; Femundsmarka a wild and uninhabited region of pine forests and lakes.

In Sweden, Töfsingdalen in Dalarna covers a genuine wilderness area of rugged boulder fields and ancient forests; the Abisko park, east of Riksgränsen, has a richly varied mountain flora; the Muddas park covers marshlands rich in bird life; the Padjelanta park is a valuable botanical area; the Sarek park is again a park of wild undisturbed mountain landscape; the Ångsö park is an island in the Stockholm archipelago where the flowers, meadow and bird life are protected.

Two Finnish national parks covering large wilderness areas are Lemmenjoki (1956) and Urho Kekkonen (1983) and they offer the unusual activities of gold panning *(see Tankavaara, Urho Kekkonen)* and the reindeer round-up site at Sallivaara, Lemmenjoki. The Oulanka park is known for the Bear's ring hiking trail (Karhunkierros); Koli National Park takes in the typical Karelian landscapes of rocky ridges, eskers, islands and lakes; whereas others take in the mosaic of rocky islands and skerries in Finland's archipelagos.

Nature reserves – These areas are designated to protect a special feature (landscape, wildlife or plant species) or are used for research and hence access is often restricted.

Hiking areas – The seven Finnish national hiking areas are specifically designated for outdoor recreation. They offer a network of hiking trails, rest spots, wilderness huts, maintained ski trails, camping and caravan sites, as well as opportunities for fishing, canoeing and boating.

Books and films

GENERAL HISTORY

A History of Scandinavia by TK Derry (University of Minnesota Press, 1979)
Northern Europe in the Early Modern Period, The Baltic World 1492-1772 by D Kirby (Longman, 1990)
Denmark, A Modern History by WG Jones (Croom Helm)
The Story of Denmark by S Oakley (Faber and Faber, 1972)
A History of Modern Norway 1814-1972 by TK Derry (Oxford University Press, 1973)
Norway: A History from the Vikings to Our Own Times by R Danielsen translated by M Drake (Scandinavian University Press 1991)
The Early Vasas, A History of Sweden 1523-1611 by Michael Roberts (Cambridge, 1968)
Sweden as a Great Power 1611-1697 by M Roberts (London 1968)
Sweden. The Nation's History by F Scott (Minneapolis, 1978)
A History of Finland by E Jutikkala (revised translated edition 1974)
A Short History of Finland by F Singleton (Cambridge University Press)
Scandinavia Past and Present by E Henriksen (Copenhagen, 1958)

THE VIKING AGE

Runes and their Origin: Denmark and Elsewhere by Erik Moltke (Århus University Press)
Saga and Society: An Introduction to Old Norse Literature by Preben Meulengracht Sørensen (Odense University Press)
The Vikings and their Origins by David M Wilson (Thames and Hudson, 1989)
The Vikings by Johannes Brønsted (Pelican, 1965)
The Vikings by Mikael Esping Piccolo (1982)
A History of the Vikings by Gwyn Jones
The Viking World by J Graham-Campbell
The Viking Achievement by PG Foote and DM Wilson (London 1970)
The Gods and Myths of Northern Europe by HR Ellis Davidson (Penguin, 1964)
The Norse Myths and Gods of the Vikings by Kevin Crossley-Holland (Deutsch, 1980)
The Lost Beliefs of Northern Europe by HR Ellis Davidson (Routledge, 1993)
Myths of the Norsemen by RL Green (Puffin, 1970)
Scandinavian Mythology by HR Ellis Davidson (Hamlyn, 1982)
Norse Myths by Raymond I Page (1990)
An Introduction to Viking Mythology by John Grant (The Apple Press, 1990)
Kings and Vikings Scandinavia and Europe AD 700-1100 (Methuen, 1981)
The Viking Road to Byzantium by HR Ellis Davidson (Allen and Unwin, 1976)
The Vikings Lords of the Seas (New Horizons – Gallimard)
The Varangians of Byzantium by S Blöndal (Cambridge 1978)
The Bog People by PV Glob (Faber)

PEOPLE

The Compleat Naturalist: A Life of Linnaeus by Wilfrid Blunt (paperback edition London 1984)
The Prince of Botanists, Carl Linneus by N Gourlie (London, 1953)
The Lapps by Arthur Spencer (David and Charles 1978)
The Magic Lantern, Ingmar Bergman An Autobiography translated by Joan Tate (Hamish Hamilton).
Strindberg and Genre by Michael Robinson (Norvik Press Ltd)
The Fairy Tale of my Life, Hans Christian Andersen's autobiography translated by W Glyn Jones
Charles XII of Sweden by RM Hatton (London, 1968)
Knut Hamsun: Selected Letters (Norvik Press)
Alfred Nobel by Erik Bergenren (Thomas Nelson and Sons Ltd, Edinburgh, 1962)
Nobel, the Man and His Prizes (American Elsevier Publishing Company, New York)
The Legacy of Alfred Nobel by Ragnar Sohlman (The Bodley Head, London 1983)

ART

Viking Art by David M Wilson and Ole Klindt-Jensen (1966)
Scandinavian Painted Decor by Jocusta Innes (Cassell)
Edvard Munch by JP Hodin (Thames and Hudson)
Edvard Munch The Frieze of Life edited by MH Wood (National Gallery Publications 1992)
The Triumph of Light and Nature: Nordic Art 1740-1940 by Neil Kent (Thames and Hudson)
The Northern World edited by David Wilson (1980)

Scandinavian Architecture: Buildings and Society in Denmark, Finland, Norway, Sweden by Thomas Paullsson (London, 1958)
Modern Norwegian Architecture by C Norberg-Schulz (Scandinavian University Press 1986)
Monuments and Sites Norway A Cultural Heritage
Modern Architecture in Finland by Asko Salokorpi (Weidenfeld and Nicholson, 1966)
Modern Finnish Painting by J Boulton-Smith (Weidenfeld and Nicholson, 1970)
The Golden Age of Finnish Art (Otava Publishing Company, Helsinki 1976)

GENERAL

Tale of the Forest Folk by Hannu Hautala (Otava Publishing Company, Helsinki 1984) – photographic essay on Finland's unique natural environment.
Skiing Throughout History by Olav Bø translated by WR Richmond (Det Norske Samlaged)
Kalevala by Elias Lönnrot translated by WF Kirby (Athlone Press)

NOVELS

The Emigrants by Vilhelm Moberg – a Swedish family emigrates to America
The Löwensköld Ring by Selma Lagerlöf – historical novel about the dawning of the railway age in the rural north of Sweden
Naboth's Stone by Sara Lidman translated by Joan Tate
Out of Africa, Letters from Africa, Seven Gothic Tales and *Babette's Feast* all by Karen Blixen (Isak Dinesen)
Hunger, The Wanderer, Mysteries, The Women at the Pump, Wayfarers, Growth of the Soil and *Pan* all by Knut Hamsun
Kristin Lavransdatter and Olav Audunssøn by Sigrid Undset – historical novels set in medieval Norway which won the Nobel Prize
The Story of Gösta Berling by Selma Lagerlöf
The Son of a Servant, The Red Room, The People of Hemsö and *By the Open Sea* all by August Strindberg
Unknown Soldier by Väinö Linna

SOME SCANDINAVIAN BESTSELLERS

The History of Danish Dreams by Peter Høeg translated by Barbara Haveland
Borderliners by Peter Høeg
Miss Smilla's Feeling for Snow by Peter Høeg translated by F David (1994)
The Year of the Hare by Arto Paasilinna translated by Herbert Lomas (Peter Owen)
Sophie's World by Jostein Gaardner translated by Paulette Möller (Farrar, Straus & Giroux, NY).

Norvik Press, EUR, University of East Anglia, Norwich NR4 7TJ, specialises in the best of classical and modern Scandinavian writing in English translation and studies of Scandinavian writers. Scandinavian University Press is a publisher of scholarly books and journals in English and they have an office in Oslo, Kolstadgt 1, P O Box 29 58 Tøyen, N– 0608 Oslo, ☎ 22 57 54 00; fax 22 57 53 53.

CHILDREN'S FAVOURITES FROM SCANDINAVIA

Moomin books by Tove Jansson (Penguin and Heinemann)
The Fairy Tales of Hans Christian Andersen
Pippi Longstocking and other stories by Astrid Lindgren
The Wonderful Adventures of Nils by Selma Lagerlöf

NORDIC FILM FESTIVALS

Scandinavian feature films, short films and documentaries are featured by the German city of Lübeck during its annual Nordic Film Days **(Nordische Filmtage Lübeck)** in early November. The French city of Rouen hosts a Nordic Film Festival **(Festival du Cinéma Nordique)** in March.

DANISH FILMS

Hunger (1966) by Henning Carlsen based on Knut Hamsun's work
Babette's Feast (1987) after the novel by Karen Blixen (Isak Dinesen) by Gabriel Axel – A French refugee in 19C Norway wins the lottery and spends it all on a banquet
Pelle the Conqueror (1987) by director Bille August, based on Martin Andersen Nexø's novel – the son of a Swedish immigrant endures hardship on a Danish farm

My Childhood by director Erik Clausen, an adaptation of Carl Nielsen's romantic auto-biography

Good Will by Bille August, based on Ingmar Bergman's childhood and youth

The Great Day on the Beach (1991) by Stellan Olsson

The Boys from Saint Petri (1992) by S Kragh-Jacobsen – public school boys fight in the wartime resistance

NORWEGIAN FILMS

The Ice Palace (1987) by Per Blom based on Tarjei Vesaas' novel – about the friendship of two girls

For the Days are Evil (1991) by Eldar Einarsen based on the novel by Anne-Karin Elstad

SWEDISH FILMS

Queen Kristina Greta Garbo in the 1934 Hollywood version

Raven's End (1951) by Bo Widerberg

The Emigrants (1970) by Jan Troell, an adaptation of Moberg's novel

The New Land (1995) also by Jan Troell – a sequel to *The Emigrants*

Katinka (1988) by Max Von Sydow based on Herman Bang's novel – the first film by Scandinavia's best-known actor

The Guardian Angel (1990) by Suzanne Osten – a mixture of political thriller and social comedy

Good Evening Mr Wallenberg (1990) by Kjell Grede – the film retraces the last three weeks of Wallenberg's life prior to his arrest

Blackjack (1990) by Colin Nutley – about dance bands

Sofie (1992) by Liv Ullman – her first film as a director is the saga of a Jewish family in København at the end of last century

House of Angels (1992) by Englishman Colin Nutley – the foibles and frailties of the Swedes as they do not see themselves

FINNISH FILMS

The Brothers by Kaurismäki

The White Reindeer (1952) by Erik Blomberg – this classic of the Finnish cinema is a stirring Sami saga

Blue Week (1954) by Matti Kassila – a story of summer love against a Nordic background

The Unknown Soldier (1955) by Edvin Laine based on Väino Linna's novel – about young men struggling to survive the long war against the Soviet Union in the 1940s

The Year of the Hare (1977) by Risto Jarva based on Paasilinna's bestseller

Hamlet goes Business (1977) by Aki Kaurismäki – a humouristic look at Hamlet in a modern setting

Plainlands (1988) by Pekka Parikka based on Antti Tuuri's novel

Splendour and Misery (1988) by Matti Kassila based on FE Sillanpää's Nobel Prize-winning novel

Leningrad Cowboys go America (1989) by Aki Kaurismäki – the adventures of a very mediocre pop group who seek their fortune across the Atlantic

The Love Story of the Century adaptation of the novel *Manrape* by Finnish novelist Märta Tikkanen

Take Care of Your Scarf Tatjana (1994) by Aki Kaurismäki – two dour Finns tangle with two garrulous Russian women hitchhikers

---

Ingmar Bergman – Figurehead of the Seventh Art

Bergman the film maker is world famous for his trademark of anguished appraisal of the human situation; but he was also a theatre, television and opera director. His films portray his personal vision of marriage, or as he described it "hell together", in *Smiles of a Summer Night* (1955) and *Summer with Monika* (1953); the worlds of good and evil in the trilogy of films, *Through a Glass Darkly* (1961), *Winter Light* (1962) and *The Silence* (1963) as well as the *Seventh Seal* (1956); the artist and his world in *The Naked Light* (1953), *Persona* (1966) and *Fanny and Alexander* (1982). His classics include:

1953 *The Naked Light*	1963 *The Silence*
1957 *The Seventh Seal*	1966 *Persona*
1957 *Wild Strawberries*	1982 *Fanny and Alexander*

The photograph on p 61 shows Bergman, Liv Ullman and Bibi Andersson in Björkman's documentary *Bergman on Bergman*.

Useful words and phrases

English	Danish	Norwegian	Swedish	Finnish

SIGHTS

English	Danish	Norwegian	Swedish	Finnish
bridge	bro	bru	bro	silta
castle	slot	slott	slott	linna
cathedral	domkirke	domkirke	domkyrka	tuomiokirkko
church	kirke	kirke	kyrka	kirkko
garden, park	have	hage	park, trädgård	puisto
monastery	kloster	kloster	kloster	luostari
museum	museum	museum	museum, museet	museo
road	vej	vei	väg	tie
square	torv, plads	torg	torg	kauppatori
street	gade	gate	gata	katu
tower	tårn	tårn	torn	torni
town hall	rådhus	rådhus	rådhus	kaupungintalo
university	universitet	universitet	universitet	yliopisto

NATURAL SITES

English	Danish	Norwegian	Swedish	Finnish
beach	strand	strand	strand	ranta
island	ø	øy	ö	saari
forest	skov	skog	skog	metsä
lake	sø	vatn	sjö	järvi
mountain	bjerg, fjeld	berg, fjell	berg, fjäll	vuori
river	å	elv	å, älv	joki
sea	hav	hav	hav	meri
valley	dal	dal	dal	laakso
waterfall	vandfald, foss	foss	vattenfall, fors	köngäs, koski

ON THE ROAD

English	Danish	Norwegian	Swedish	Finnish
driving licence	fører-bevis	førerkort	körkort	ajokortti
garage for repairs	autoværksted	bilverksted	bilverkstad	autokorjaamo
motorway	motorvej	motorvei	motorväg	moottoritie
petrol/gas	benzin	bensin	bensin	bensiini
petrol/gas station	benzin-station	bensin-stasjon	bensin-station, mack	benssiinia-sema
tyre	dæk	ring, dekk	däck	renkaat, rengas
caution	pas på	pas på	se upp	varokaa
no entry	ingen indkørsel	gjennom-kjørning forbudt	infart förbjuden	läpikulku kielletty
one-way street	ensrettet	envegs-kjøring	enkelriktad	yksisuuntainen liikenne
road works	vejarbejde	veiarbeid	vägarbete	tietyö
stop	stop	stopp	stopp	stopp, seis

TIME

English	Danish	Norwegian	Swedish	Finnish
today	i dag	i dag	idag	tänään
tomorrow	i morgen	i morgen	imorgon	huomenna
yesterday	i går	i går	igår	eilen
Monday	mandag	mandag	måndag	maanantai
Tuesday	tirsdag	tirsdag	tisdag	tiistai
Wednesday	onsdag	onsdag	onsdag	keskiviikko
Thursday	torsdag	torsdag	torsdag	torstai
Friday	fredag	fredag	fredag	perjantai
Saturday	lørdag	lørdag	lördag	lauantai
Sunday	søndag	søndag	söndag	sunnuntai

NUMBERS

English	Danish	Norwegian	Swedish	Finnish
0	nul	null	noll	nolla
1	en	en, et	en, ett	yksi
2	to	to	två	kaksi
3	tre	tre	tre	kolme

4	fire	fire	fyra	neljä
5	fem	fem	fem	viisi
6	seks	seks	sex	kuusi
7	syv	sju	sju	seitsemän
8	otte	åtte	åtta	kahdeksen (sän)
9	ni	ni	nio	oyhdeksän
10	ti	ti	tio	okymmenen
100	hundrede	hundre	ett hundra	sata
1000	tusind	tusen	ett tusen	tuhat

USEFUL WORDS

hello	hallo	goddag	hej, goddag	hei, päivää
goodbye	farvel	farvel,	adjö,	hyvästi,
		adjø, ha det	hej då	näkemiin
please	vær så	vær så god	var så god	oikaa hyvä
	venlig			
thank you	tak	takk	tack	kiitos
yes	ja	ja, jo	ja	niin, kyllä, joo
no	nej	nei	nej	en, ei
excuse me	undskyld	unnskyld	ursäkta	pyydän
			mig	anteeksi
open	åben	åpen,	öppen,	avoinna
		åpet	öppet	
closed	lukket	stengt	stängt	suljettu
entrance	indgang	inngang	ingång	sisään
exit	udgang	utgang	utgång	ulos
right	højre	høyre	höger	oikealle
left	venstre	venstre	vänster	vasemmalle
bank	bank	bank	bank	pankki
chemist	apotek	apotek	apotek	apteekki
dentist	tandlæge	tannlege	tandläkare	hammaslääkäri
doctor	læge	lege	läkare,	lääkäri
			doktor	
hospital	sygehus	sykehus	sjukhus	sairaala
hotel	hotel	hotell	hotell	hotelli
police	politi	politi	polis	poliisi
post office	posthus	posthus,	post-	posti-
		postkontor	kontor	konttori
room	stue	værelse	rum	huone
stamp	frimærke	frimerke	frimärke	postmerkki
telephone	telefon	telefon	telefon	puhelin

Calendar of events

Naantali Finland .... Festival of Chamber Music

Sweden .... Especially in the villages around Lake Siljan – maypole raising, folk dancing and music

Harstad Norway .... North Norway Festival – Arts Festival
Frederikssund Denmark ..... Viking Festival
Skagen Denmark .... Folk Music Festival
Haparanda and Torneå
Finland .... Kalottjazz and Blues Festival

Korsholm (Vaasa) Finland.. Music Festival
Kuopio Finland .... Dance Festival and International Wine Festival
Rättvik and Leksand
Sweden .... Music at Lake Siljan – jazz, folk and classical music
Roskilde Denmark .... 4-day Rock Festival
Arjeplog Sweden .... Lappland's Festival of Chamber Music
Mikkeli Finland .... Music Festival
Tromsø Norway .... Midnight Sun International Choir Festival
Hälsingland Sweden .... Hälsinge Hambo Dance Festival

Rebild Denmark .... 4 July Celebrations
Savonlinna Finland .... Opera Festival
Kristiansand Norway .... Music Festival

Århus Denmark .... International Jazz Festival

Finland .... Day of Democracy commemorating the enactment of the Finnish constitution

København Denmark .... Jazz Festival – international 10-day event
Nurmes Finland .... Bomba Festival – Karelian Folklore Event

Pori Finland .... Jazz Festival
Mustion Linna Finland .... Inter Nordic Antiques Fair

Molde Norway .... Molde International Jazz Festival
Iisalmi, Pielavesi Finland .... Pradznik Festivals – traditional Orthodox church and folk festivals
Jyväaskyläa Finland .... Arts Festival

Kuhmo Finland .... Kuhmo Chamber Music Festival

Rättvik Sweden .... Rättvik Folklore Festival

Stiklestad Norway .... St Olav Play Pageant

Nakskov Denmark .... Femø Jazz

Sweden .... Opening of the crayfish season
Helsinki Finland .... Helsinki City Marathon
Oslo Norway .... Jazz Festival
Rättvik Sweden .... Dalhalla Opera Festival
Vinstra-Gålå Norway .... Peer Gynt (Folk) Festival
Bergen Norway .... Fish Festival

Odense Denmark .... Film Festival

Early August

Växjö Sweden...................... Minnesota Day

2nd week in August

Tampere Finland .... International Theatre Festival
Turku Finland...................... Music Festival
Stavanger Norway.............. International Chamber Music Festival
Mandal Norway.................. Shellfish Festival
Visby (Gotland) Sweden .... Medieval Festival Week

3rd week in August

Stockholm Sweden .... Water Festival
Göteborg Sweden............... Jazz Festival

Late August to early September

Helsinki Finland .... Helsinki Festival

September

Århus Denmark.................. Festival of mixed cultural events
København-Malmö region
Denmark-Sweden................ Kulturbro 2000 – Cultural Biennial
København Denmark.......... Golden Days Festival – Biennial of Danish Golden-Age Art

October

Umeå Sweden .... Jazz Festival

December

København Denmark.......... Christmas Fair in Tivoli Gardens
Helsinki Finland .... Christmas Market, Esplanade Park

6 December

Finland .... Independence Day (1922)

10 December

Oslo Norway....................... Nobel Peace Prize Award Ceremony
Stockholm Sweden .... Nobel Prize Ceremony

13 December

Sweden............................. The Santa Lucia Festival with processions of attendants

Office suédois du Tourisme

The Santa Lucia Festival

The Santa Lucia Festival on the 13 December is celebrated to light up the darkest days of winter and is an important part of the festivities leading up to Christmas. Originally the festival was dedicated to St Lucia of Syracuse in Italy. The chosen Lucia, dressed in a white gown with a crown of candles, leads a procession of attendants, gingerbread men and elves. After carols a traditional breakfast of *glögg* (sweet, spiced, mulled red wine), saffron rolls and sweet ginger biscuits is served.

Admission times and charges

Every sight for which there are times and charges is indicated by the symbol K in the main part of the guide. As times and charges for admission are liable to alteration, the information below is given for guidance only. The information was, as far as possible, correct at the time of going to press; information shown in italics indicates that current details were not available.

Order: The information is listed in the same order as the entries in the alphabetical section of the guide.

Dates: Dates given are inclusive.

Last admission: Ticket offices usually shut 30min before closing time; exceptions only are mentioned below.

Charge: The charge is for an individual adult; the charge for a child is given where appropriate.
Concessionary rates may be available for students and old-age pensioners. Large parties should apply in advance.

Disabled tourists: Sights which have facilities for disabled tourists are indicated by the symbol &. below.

Guided tours: Some of the larger or more frequented sights may offer guided tours in other languages. In some cases the term "guided tours" may cover group visiting with a recorded commentary. Enquire at the ticket office or bookstall. Other aids commonly available for foreign tourists are notes, pamphlets or audio-guides.

Tourist information centres: The addresses and telephone numbers are given under ⓘ below for the local tourist information centres, which provide information on market days, early closing days etc. and also on guided tours of towns or parts of the region of particular interest, which are organised in season.

Denmark

B

BILLUND   ⓘ Legolandparken, P.O. Box 46 – 7190 – ☎ 75-33 19 26

Legoland Park – &. Open 17 June to 27 August, daily 10am to 9pm; April to 16 June and 28 August to 29 October, daily 10am to 8pm. Closed 29 October. ☎ 75 33 13 33.

E

EGESKOV SLOT

Egeskov Slot – Open May to mid-October, daily 10am to 5pm; July, daily 10am to 7pm; closed mid-October to April. 106DKR, children 53DKR (park and museum included). ☎ 62 27 10 16.

Museum and park – &. Open 29 April to May, daily 10am to 7pm; June and August, daily 10am to 6pm; September and October, daily 10am to 8pm; July, daily 10am to 8pm. Closed 29 April to 1 October. 60DKR, children 30DKR. ☎ 62 27 10 16.

F

FALSTER   ⓘ 4800 – ☎ 54-85 13 03

Falsters Museum – Open May to 16 September, Tuesdays to Fridays, 11am to 5pm, Saturdays, 11am to 3pm, Sundays, 2pm to 4pm; 16 September to April, Tuesdays to Fridays, 2pm to 4pm, Saturdays, 11am to 3pm, Sundays, 2pm to 4pm. 20DKR, children 5DKR. For guided tours (1hr 30min) apply two weeks in advance. ☎ 54 85 26 71.

Middelaldercentret – ♿ Open May to September, daily 10am to 4pm. Closed October to April. 60DKR, children 30DKR. Guided tours in English. ☎ 54 86 19 34.

Sommerland Falster – ♿ Open first fortnight in June, daily 10am to 6pm; mid-June to first week in August, daily 10am to 7pm, last three weeks in August, daily 10am to 6pm. Closed September to May. 85DKR, children (0-3) free. ☎ 54 13 68 86.

FYRKAT   ❶ 9500 – ☎ 98-52 56 66

Hobro Museum – Open 29 April to 1 October, daily 11am to 5pm; 20 to 24 April and 2 to 31 October, Saturdays and Sundays, 11am to 5pm. 25DKR, children 10DKR. Guided tours (1hr) in English. ☎ 98 51 05 55.

Vikingecenter – Open Easter to late October, daily 10am to 5pm. ☎ 98 51 19 27.

FÅBORG   ❶ 5600 – ☎ 62-61 07 07

Den Gamle Gård: Kulturhistoriske Museet – Open mid-May to mid-September, daily 10.30am to 4.30pm. Closed 16 September to 14 May. 25DKR, children (0-13) free. Guided tours (45min) in English. ☎ 62 61 33 38.

Fåborg Museum for Fynsk Malerkunst – ♿ Open June to August, daily 10am to 5pm; November to March, daily 11am to 3pm; April, May to September and October, daily 10am to 4pm. Closed November to March, 23 to 26 and 31 December, 1 January. 30DKR, children (0-14) free. Guided tours in English. ☎ 62 61 06 45.

H

HADERSLEV   ❶ Honnørkajen 1 – 6100 – ☎ 74-52 55 50

Domkirke – Open May to October, daily 10am to 5pm; October to May, daily 10am to 3pm. ☎ 74 52 51 31.

Ehlers Samlingen – Open June to August, Tuesdays to Fridays, 10am to 5pm, Saturdays and Sundays, 2pm to 5pm, closed Mondays; September to May, Tuesdays and Thursdays, 10am to 5pm, Saturdays, Sundays and public holidays, 2pm to 5pm, closed Mondays, Wednesdays and Fridays. 20DKR, children (0-13) free. Guided tours (1hr) in English. ☎ 74 53 08 58.

Slesvigske Vognsamling – Closed; due to reopen in new premises 2001.

Haderslev Museum – ♿ Open June to August, Tuesdays to Sundays, 10am to 4pm; September to May, Tuesdays to Sundays, 1pm to 4pm. Closed Mondays. Guided tours (1hr) in English. 15DKR, children free. ☎ 74 52 75 66.

HELSINGØR   ❶ Havnepladsen 3 – 3000 – ☎ 49-21 13 33

Kronborg Slot – Open daily May to September, 10.30am to 5pm; November to March, Tuesdays to Sundays, 11am to 3pm; October and April, Tuesdays to Sundays, 11am to 4pm. 30DKR, children 10DKR. Guided tours (45min) in English. ☎ 49 21 30 78.

Sankt Olai Kirke – Open May to August, Mondays to Saturdays, 10am to 4pm; September to April, daily 10am to 2pm. ☎ 49 21 04 43.

Karmeliterklostret – ♿ Open 16 May to 15 September, Mondays to Saturdays, 10am to 5pm; 16 September to 15 May, Mondays to Saturdays, 10am to 2pm. 10DKR, children 5DKR. Guided tours (1hr) in English. ☎ 49 21 17 74.

Sancta Maria Kirke – Open 16 May to 15 September, daily noon to 2pm. ☎ 49 21 17 74.

Marienlyst Slot – Open daily noon to 5pm. Guided tours (1hr) on request. 20DKR, children free. ☎ 49 28 37 91.

Danmarks Tekniske Museum – ♿ Open daily Tuesdays to Sundays, 10am to 5pm. Guided tours (1hr) in English on request. Closed Mondays. 25DKR, children 13DKR. ☎ 49 22 26 11.

HILLERØD   ❶ 3400 – ☎ 42-26 28 52

Frederiksborg Slot – ♿ Open April to October, daily 10am to 5pm; November to March, daily 11am to 3pm. 45DKR, children (6-14) 10DKR. Guided tours in English. ☎ 48 26 04 39.
Park open May to August, daily 10am to 9pm; September and April, daily 10am to 7pm; October and March, daily 10am to 5pm; November to February, 10am to 4pm. Admission free. Guided tours on request. ☎ 33 92 65 85.

Detail of pediment, Frederiksborg, Denmark

Excursion

Fredensborg – Open July only, daily 1pm to 5pm. Guided tours (1hr) in English. 25DKR, children 10DKR. ☎ 48 48 21 00.

HOLBÆK   🚉 Jerbaneplads 3 – 4300 – ☎ 59-43 11 31

Holbæk Museum – Open Tuesdays to Sundays, 10am to 4pm. Closed Mondays. Guided tours in English. 30DKR, children 10DKR.

Excursion

Tveje Merløse Kirke – Open daily 10am to 4pm. ☎ 59 43 24 53.

J

JELLING   🚉 7100 – ☎ 75-82 19 55

Excursion

Givskud: Løveparken – ♿ Open mid-June to mid-August, daily 10am to 8pm; May to mid-June and mid-August to mid-September, 10am to 6pm; mid-September to late-October, 10am to 5pm. Closed late October to late April. Guided tours (1hr) in English. 75DKR, children (4-11) 40DKR. ☎ 75 73 02 22.

K

KALUNDBORG   🚉 Volden 12 – 4400 – ☎ 53-51 09 15

Vor Frue Kirke – Open August to 30 September and October to March, daily 9am to 5pm.

Lindegård – Open May to August, Tuesdays to Sundays, 11am to 4pm; September to April, Saturdays and Sundays, 11am to 4pm. Closed 24-31 December and 1 January. 20DKR, children free. ☎ 59 51 21 41.

Excursions

Ubby, Bregninge, Viskinge Kirke – Open Mondays to Saturdays, 8am to 4pm.

KERTEMINDE

Favergården: Kerteminde Museum – Open March to October, daily 10am to 4pm. Closed November to February. 15DKR, children free. Guided tours (45min) in English. ☎ 65 32 37 27.

Johannes Larsen Museet – ♿ Open all the year round, daily 10am to 4pm (Saturdays until 5pm). Closed Mondays from September until May. 40DKR, children free. Guided tours (1hr) in English. b 65 32 37 27.

Excursion

Ladby: museum – ♿ Open June to August, daily 10am to 5pm; October to 18 February, Wednesdays to Sundays, 11am to 3pm; March to May and September to October, Tuesdays to Sundays, 10am to 4pm. 25DKR, children (0-15) free. Guided tours (1hr) in English on request. ☎ 65 32 16 67.

KOLDING

Koldinghus – Open daily 10am to 5pm. Closed 1 January, 24-25 and 31 December. 45DKR, children (0-15) free. Guided tours in English. ☎ 76 33 81 00.

Geografiske Have – ♿ Open May to September, daily, 10am to 6pm; October to April, Mondays to Fridays, 9am to 2.30pm, Saturdays, 9am to 5pm, Sundays, 9am to 5pm. 40DKR, children 15DKR. ☎ 75 50 38 80.

Kunstmuseet Trapholt – ♿ Open daily 10am to 5pm. Closed 1 January, 24-25 and 31 December. 40DKR, children (0-15) free. Guided tours (30min) on request. ☎ 76 30 05 30.

KØBENHAVN

Christiansborg – May to October, 9.30am to 3.30pm. 40DKR, children 10DKR. ☎ 33 92 64 92.

Royal Library: Christians Brygge – Open Mondays to Saturdays, 10am to 5pm, free.

Thorvaldsens Museum – Open Tuesdays to Sundays, 10am to 5pm. Closed Mondays. 20DKK, children (0-14) free. Wednesdays free admission. ☎ 33 32 15 32.

Vor Frue Kirke – April to August, 11am to 4.30pm; September to March 3.30pm. ☎ 33 14 41 28.

Rundetårn – Open June to August, 10am to 8pm, ; September to May, 10am to 5pm.

Musikhistorisk Museum – Open May to September, Mondays to Wednesdays and Fridays to Sundays, 1pm to 3.50pm, closed Thursdays; October to April, Mondays, Wednesdays, Saturdays and Sundays, 1pm to 3.50pm, closed Tuesdays, Thursdays and Fridays. Closed 1 May. 30DKR, children 10DKR. ☎ 33 11 27 26.

Post and Tele Museum – Open Tuesdays to Sundays, 10am to 5pm (Wednesdays until 8pm). 30DKR, children admission free. ☎ 33 41 09 00.

Rådhuset – Guided tours Mondays to Fridays, 3pm, Saturdays, 10am and 11am. Closed Sundays. 30DKR. Tower tours, June to September, Mondays to Fridays, 10am, noon and 2pm, Saturdays, noon; October to May, Mondays to Saturdays, noon. Closed Sundays. 20DKR. ☎ 33 66 25 82.

Tivoli – ♿ Open in summer, Mondays to Thursdays, 11am to midnight, Fridays and Saturdays, 11am to 1am, the rest of the year, daily 11am to 9pm or 11pm. 45-50DKR, children (0-12) 20-25DKR. ☎ 33 15 10 01.

Nationalmuseet – Open Tuesdays to Sundays, 10am to 5pm. 40DKR, children free; admission free Wednesdays. ☎ 33 13 44 11.

Ny Carlsberg Glyptotek – ♿ Open Tuesdays to Sundays, 10am to 4pm. Closed Mondays, closed 5 June, 24 to 25 December and 1 January. 30DKR, children free; Wednesdays and Sundays free admission. ☎ 33 41 81 41.

Statens Museum for Kunst – Open Tuesdays to Sundays, 10am to 5pm, Wednesdays, 10am to 8pm. 40DKR. ☎ 33 74 84 94.

Rosenborg Slot – Open July to September, daily 10am to 5pm; October, daily 11am to 3pm; November to April, Tuesdays to Sundays, 11am to 2pm; May to June, daily 10am to 4pm. 50DKR, children 10DKR. ☎ 33 15 32 86.

Botanisk Have – Open summer, daily 8.30am to 6pm; winter, 8.30am to 4pm. Palmhouse open daily, 10am to 3pm. Closed Mondays October to May. Admission free. ☎ 35 32 22 40.

Den Hirschsprungske Samling – Open Mondays and Thursdays to Sundays, 11am to 4pm, Wednesdays, 11am to 9pm. Closed Tuesdays. 25DKR, Wednesdays free admission. ☎ 35 42 03 36.

Davids Samling – Open Tuesdays to Sundays, 1pm to 4pm. Closed 5 June and 23, 24-25, 31 December. ☎ 33 73 49 49.

Amalienborg Palace – Open May to October, daily 10am to 4pm; November to April, Tuesdays to Sundays, 11am to 4pm. 40DKR, children (5-15) 5DKR. ☎ 33 12 21 86.

Marmorkirken – Open daily Mondays, Tuesdays and Thursdays 10am to 17pm; Wednesdays 10.30am to 6pm; Saturdays and Sundays noon to 5pm. 20DKR, children 10DKR. ☎ 33 15 01 44.

Det Danske Kunstindustrimuseum – Open Tuesdays to Fridays, 10am to 4pm, Saturdays and Sundays, noon to 4pm. Closed Mondays. 35DKR, children (0-16) free. ☎ 33 14 94 52.

Frihedsmuseet – Open May to mid-September, 10am to 4pm, Sundays, 10am to 5pm; mid-September to April, 11am to 3pm, Sundays, 11am to 4pm. Closed Mondays. Admission free. ☎ 33 13 77 14.

Kongelige Porcelænsfabrik – All year guided tours, at 9am, 10am, 11am, 1pm and 2pm May to September. Closed public holidays, Christmas to New Year. 25DKR. ☎ 38 14 92 97.

Carlsberg A/S – Open all the year round, Mondays to Fridays, 10am to 4pm. Admission free.

Carlsberg Museum – Open Mondays to Fridays, 10am to 3pm, closed 23 December to 2 January, admission free. ☎ 33 27 12 74.

Experimentarium – Open Mondays, Wednesdays to Fridays, 9am to 5pm; Tuesdays 9am to 9pm; Saturdays, Sundays and public holidays 11am to 5pm. 79DKR, children 57DKR.

Dragør Museum – Open May to September, Tuesdays to Fridays, 2pm to 5pm, Saturdays and Sundays, noon to 6pm. Closed Mondays. 20DKR, children 10DKR. ☎ 32 53 41 06.

Ordrupgård – Open all year round, Tuesdays to Sundays, 1pm to 5pm. 25DKR, children (0-15) free. ☎ 39 64 11 83.

Lyngby: **Bredemuseet** – ♿ Open mid-April to end September, Tuesdays to Sundays, 10am to 5pm; October to autumn school holidays, Tuesdays to Sundays, 10am to 4pm. Closed autumn school holidays to Easter. 40DKR, children (0-16) free; Wednesdays free admission. ☎ 45 33 13 44 11.

Lyngby: **Frilandsmuseet** – ♿
Open mid-May to end September, Tuesdays to Sundays, 10am to 5pm; October to autumn school holidays, Tuesdays to Sundays, 10am to 4pm. Closed Mondays and winter. Guided tours in English. 40DKR, children (0-15) free; Wednesdays free admission. ☎ 45 85 02 92.

Arken – Open Tuesdays to Sundays 10am to 5pm (Wednesdays until 9pm). Closed Mondays. 40DKR, children 15DKR. ☎ 43 54 02 22. www.schultz.dk/arken

Excursions

Rungstedlund: **Karen Blixen Museum** – Open May to September, daily 10am to 5pm; October to April, Wednesdays to Fridays, 1pm to 4pm, Saturdays and Sundays, 11am to 4pm. Closed Mondays and Tuesdays. 30DKR. ☎ 425 57 10 57. Internet: www.karen-blixen.dk

Bicycles for hire, København, Denmark

F. Gohier/EXPLORER

DENMARK

Nivågård – &. Open all year round, Tuesdays to Fridays, noon to 4pm, Saturdays and Sundays 11am to 5pm. Closed Mondays, 24-25 and 31 December. Guided tours in English on request at least a week before. 35DKR, children (0-15) free. ☎ 49 14 10 17.

Louisiana – &. Open daily 10am to 5pm (Wednesdays until 10pm). Closed 24-25 and 31 December. Guided tours in English. 55-65DKR, children 15DKR. ☎ 49 19 07 19 and 49 19 07 91. E-mail: press@louisiana. dk

KØGE
🛈 Vestergade 1 – 4600 – ☎ 53-65 58 00

Køge Museum – Open Mondays to Fridays, 1pm to 5.30pm, Saturdays and Sundays, 11am to 5pm. Closed Mondays. 20DKR, children (10-16) 10DKR. ☎ 56 63 42 42.

Sankt Nicolai Kirke – Open June to August, Mondays to Fridays, 10am to 4pm; September to June, Mondays to Fridays, 10am to noon. Open other times on request. 5DKR. ☎ 56 65 58 00, 56 65 13 59.

L

LANGELAND
🛈 Turistbureauet i Rudkøbing – 5900 – ☎ 62-51 35 05

Rudkøbing Kirke – Open daily 8am to 5pm (or sunset).

Langelands Museum – Open Mondays to Fridays, 10am to 4pm. Closed Thursdays, Saturdays and Sundays. 20DKR, children free. ☎ 63 51 10 10.

LOLLAND
🛈 4930 – ☎ 53-88 04 96

Maribo Cathedral – Open daily 9am to 5pm. ☎ 53 88 04 96.

Kunst-og Stiftsmuseet – Open Tuesdays to Sundays, noon to 4pm (1st Wednesday of the month also 7pm to 9pm). Closed Mondays. 20DKR, children free. ☎ 53 88 11 01.

Frilandsmuseet – Open May to September, daily 10am to 5pm. 20DKR, children (0-16) free. ☎ 53 88 11 01.

Lolland-Falsters Kunstmuseum – Open June to August, daily, 10am to 5pm; September to May, 2pm to 4pm, Sundays and holidays 10am to 5pm. Closed Mondays.

Knuthenborg Park – &. Open end April to end September, daily 9am to 5pm; end September to mid-October, Saturdays and Sundays, 9am to 5pm; mid-October to end October, daily 9am to 5pm. Guided tours in English on request. 76DKR, children 38DKR. ☎ 53 88 80 88.

Aalholm Automobil Museum – &. Open June to August, daily 10am to 5pm; April to May and September to end October, Saturdays and Sundays, 10am to 4pm. Closed last week in October to early April. 60DKR, children 40DKR. ☎ 53 87 19 11.

M

MØN
🛈 Turistbureauet 🛈 Stege, Storegade 2 – 4780 – ☎ 55-81 44 11

Keldby Kirke – Open daily. ☎ 55 81 44 11.

Elmelunde Kirke – Open daily. ☎ 55 81 44 11.

Møns Klint – Open daily. 25DKR per car. ☎ 55 81 44 11.

Fanefjord Kirke – Open daily. ☎ 55 81 44 11.

N

NYBORG
🛈 5800 – ☎ 65-31 02 80

Nyborg Slot – Open June to August, daily 10am to 4pm; September to October and March to May, Tuesdays to Sundays, 10am to 3pm. Closed November to February. 25DKR, children 10DKR. ☎ 65 31 02 07.

Vor Frue Kirke – Open March to October, daily 9am to 6pm; November to February, daily 9am to 4pm. ☎ 65 31 16 08.

Excursion

Storebælt Udstillningscenter – &. Open daily 9am to 9pm. Guided tours in English. 35DKR, children 15DKR. ☎ 58 35 01 00.

Sankt Peders Kirke – Open June to August, Tuesdays to Fridays, 10am to noon and 2pm to 4pm; September to May, Tuesdays to Fridays, 10am to noon. ☎ 55 72 31 90.

Sankt Mortens Kirke – Open mid-June to mid-September, Mondays to Fridays, 9am to 11am and 2pm to 5pm; the rest of the year, Mondays to Fridays, 9am to 11am. ☎ 55 72 31 03.

Excursion

Gavnø Slot – Open end April to early June, daily 10am to 5pm; early June to August, daily 10am to 4pm. Guided tours in English. 50-60DKR, children free. ☎ 55 70 02 00.

O

H. C. Andersens Hus – ♿ Open mid-June to August, daily 9am to 7pm; September to mid-June, Tuesdays to Sundays, 10am to 4pm; closed 24-25, 31 December and 1 January. Guided tours in English on request. 25DKR, children 10DKR. ☎ 66 14 88 14.

Fyrtøjet – Open mid-June to early August, daily 9.30am to 6pm; early August to end August, daily 10am to 4pm; September to mid-June, Tuesdays to Fridays, 2pm to 4pm, Saturdays and Sundays, 11am to 4pm. Closed Mondays, Christmas and New Year. 35DKR; combined ticket with access to Andersen's House: 60DKR, children 45DKR.

Carl Nielsen Museet – Open all year round 10am to 4pm. Closed 1 January, 24-25 and 31 December. 15DKR, children 5DKR. ☎ 66-13 13 72/46 71.

Møntergården – Open Tuesdays to Sundays, 10am to 4pm. Closed Mondays, 24-25 and 31 December. Guided tours in English. 15DKR, children 5DKR. ☎ 66 14 88 14.

Sankt Knuds Kirke – Open April to end October, Mondays to Saturdays, 9am to 5pm, Sundays, noon to 3pm; end October to march, Mondays to Saturdays, 10am to 4pm, Sundays, noon to 3pm. Closed between Christmas and New Year's Eve. ☎ 66 12 61 23.

H. C. Andersens Barndomshjem – Open mid-June to August, daily 10am to 4pm; September to mid-June, Tuesdays to Sundays, 11am to 3pm. Closed 24-25, 31 December and 1 January. Guided tours in English. 10DKR, children 5DKR. ☎ 66 14 88 14.

Sankt Hans Kirke – Open Mondays to Saturdays, 10am to 4pm; June to August, also Sundays, 10am to 4pm.

Fyns Kunstmuseum – Open Tuesdays to Sundays, 10am to 4pm. Closed Mondays and 24-25 and 31 December. 25DKR, children 10DKR. ☎ 66 14 88 14.

Danmarks Grafiske museum/Dansk Pressemuseum – ♿ Open daily 10am to 5pm (closed Mondays from September to June). Closed 24-25, 31 December and 1 January. 25DKR, children 10DKR. ☎ 66 12 10 20.

Den Fynske Landsby – Open mid-June to mid-August, daily 9.30am to 7pm; April to mid-June and mid-August to end October, Tuesdays to Sundays, 10am to 5pm; November to March, Sundays and public holidays only, 11am to 3pm. Guided tours. 30DKR, children 10DKR. ☎ 66 14 88 14.

R

Ribe Domkirke – Open May to September, daily 10am to 5pm, Sundays and public holidays, noon to 5pm; April and October, daily 11am to 4pm, Sundays and public holidays, noon to 4pm; November to March, daily, 11am to 5pm, Sundays and public holidays, noon to 5pm. Guided tours (1hr) in English. 7DKR, children (4-14) 3DKR. ☎ 75 42 06 19.

Det Gamle Rådhus – Open June to August, daily 1pm to 3pm; May and September, Mondays to Fridays, 1pm to 3pm. Guided tours in English. 15DKR, children (7-15) 5DKR. ☎ 76 88 11 22.

Skt Catharinæ Kirke – Open May to September, daily 10am to 5pm, Sundays and public holidays, noon to 5pm; April and October, daily 11am to 4pm, Sundays and public holidays, noon to 4pm; November to March, daily 11am to 5pm, Sundays and public holidays, noon to 5pm. Guided tours (1hr) in English. Church: admission free; Abbey: 3DKR, children (0-13) 1DKR. ☎ 75 42 05 34.

Quedens Gaard: Museum – Open June to August, daily 10am to 5pm; March to May and September to October, Tuesdays to Sundays, 11am to 3pm; November to February, Tuesdays to Sundays, 11am to 1pm. Guided tours. 20DKR, children (7-15) 5DKR. ☎ 76 88 11 22.

Ribes Vikinger – Open July to August, 10am to 6pm; April to June, September and October, daily 10am to 4pm; November to March, Tuesdays to Sundays, 10am to 4pm. 45DKR, children (7-15) 15DKR. ☎ 76 88 11 22.

RINGKØBING FJORD
🛈 Torvet – 6950 – ☎ 97-32 00 31

Aal Kirke – Open daily 8am to 5pm. ☎ 75-27 18 00.

Ringkøbing Kirke – Open May to October, Mondays to Saturdays, 9am to 5pm. ☎ 97 32 00 31.

Ringkøbing museum – Open July to August, daily 11am to 5pm; September to June, Mondays to Thursdays, 11am to 4pm, Saturdays and Sundays, 1pm to 4pm. Closed Fridays. Guided tours (1hr) in English. 25DKR, children (8-16) 10DKR. ☎ 97 32 16 15.

Sommerland West – ♿ Open mid-May to third week in June, daily 10am to 5pm; last week in June to early August, daily 10am to 6pm; early August to mid-September, daily 10am to 5pm. Closed mid-September to mid-May. 85DKR (mid-June to mid-August, 100DKR), children (0-3) free. ☎ 97 33 54 11.

RINGSTED
🛈 Turistbureauet i Sorø – 4180 – ☎ 057-82 10 12

Sankt Bendts Kirke – Open May to mid-September, daily 10am to noon and 1pm to 5pm; mid-September to April, 1pm to 3pm. ☎ 57 61 34 00.

ROSKILDE
🛈 Gullandsstraede 15 – 4000 – ☎ 42-35 27 00

Domkirke – Open April to September, Mondays to Fridays, 9am to 4.45pm, Saturdays, 9am to noon, Sundays, 12.30pm to 4.45pm; October to March, Tuesdays to Fridays, 10am to 3.45pm, Saturdays, 11.30am to 3.45pm, Sundays 12.30pm to 3.45pm. Closed Mondays. ☎ 46 35 27 00.

Vikingeskibshallen – Open May to September, daily 9am to 5pm; October to April, daily 10am to 4pm. Closed 24-25, and 31 December. Guided tours (1hr) in English. 42DKR (50DKR in summer), children 26DKR (28DKR in summer). ☎ 46 30 02 00.

Skt Jørgensbjerg Kirke – Open July, Mondays to Fridays, 10am to noon.

Excursions

Lejre: Forsøgscenter – ♿ Open May to 16 June, Tuesdays to Sundays, 10am to 5pm; 17 June to 11 August, daily 10am to 5pm; 12 August to 15 September, Tuesdays to Sundays, 10am to 5pm; Mondays and Autumn holidays, daily 10am to 5pm. 60DKR, children 30DKR. ☎ 46 48 08 78.

Ledreborg Slot – Open mid-June to August, daily 11am to 5pm; May to mid-June and September, Sundays only, 11am to 5pm. Guided tours (1hr) in English. 45DKR, children 25DKR. ☎ 46 48 00 38.

ROSKILDE FJORD
🛈 Frederikssund Initiativråd – 3600 – ☎ 47-31 06 85

Skibby Kirke – Open daily in summer 7am to 5pm; in winter 8am to 4pm. ☎ 47 52 82 32.

Selsø Slot – Open mid-June to mid-August, daily 11am to 4.30pm; mid-April to mid-June and mid-August to September, Saturdays, Sundays and public holidays only, noon to 3.30pm. Guided tours in English. 35DKR, children 12DKR. ☎ 42-32 01 71.

Jægerpris Slot – Guided tours only, May to September, Tuesdays to Sundays, 10am to 4.30pm. Closed Mondays and October to April. Guided tours in English. 30DKR, children 10DKR. ☎ 47 53 10 04.

Frederikssund: JF Willumsen Museum – Open daily 10am to 4pm. Guided tours (1hr) in English. 20DKR, children 10DKR. ☎ 47 31 07 73.

RØMØ
🛈 Havnebyvej 30 – 6792 – ☎ 74-75 51 30

Kommandørgården – Open May to September, daily 10am to 6pm; October, daily 10am to 3pm. Closed Mondays and November to April. Guided tours in English are available on request a few days in advance. 40DKR, children (under 16) free. ☎ 74-75 52 76.

Skt Clemens Kirke – Open Mondays to Fridays, 10am to 4pm, on request.

S

SALLING

🄸 Turistbureauet i Skive – 7800 – ☎ 97-52 32 66

Sevel Kirke – Open daily. ☎ 97-44 80 59.

Hjerl Hede frilandsmuseum – ♿ Open late June to mid-August, daily 9am to 6pm, 60DKR, children, 25DKR; April to late June and mid-August to October, daily 9am to 5pm 35DKR, children, 15DKR. ☎ 97 44 80 60.

Sahl Kirke – Open daily. ☎ 97 44 32 21.

Ejsing Kirke – Open daily. Guided tours in english on request. ☎ 97 44 60 07.

Spøttrup Borg – Open May to August, daily 10am to 6pm; April, Tuesdays, Wednesdays and Sundays, 11am to 5pm; September, daily 10am to 5pm; October, daily 10am to 4pm; November, Wednesdays, 11am to 3pm. Guided tours in English on request in advance. 20DKR, children (5-12) 5DKR. ☎ 97 52 32 66.

SILKEBORG

🄸 8600 – ☎ 86-82 19 11

Kunstmuseum – ♿ Open April to October, Tuesdays to Sundays, 10am to 5pm; November to March, Tuesdays to Fridays, noon to 4pm, Saturdays and Sundays, 10am to 5pm. Closed Mondays. Guided tours (1hr) in English. 30DKR, children (0-16) free. ☎ 86 82 53 88.

Silkeborg Museum – ♿ Open May to mid-October, daily 10am to 5pm; mid-October to April, Wednesdays, Saturdays and Sundays, noon to 4pm. Guided tours (1hr) in English. 20DKR, children 5DKR. ☎ 86 82 14 99.

Excursion

Elmuseet – ♿ Open Easter to October, daily 10am to 5pm. Closed 1 November to Easter. Guided tours (1-2hr) in English. 45DKR, children 20DKR. ☎ 86 68 42 11.

SKAGEN

🄸 Sct. Laurentii Vej 22 – 9990 – ☎ 98-44 13 77

Skagens Museum – Open June to August, daily 10am to 6pm; May and September, daily 10am to 5pm; April and October, Tuesdays to Sundays, 11am to 4pm; November to March, Wednesdays to Fridays, 1pm to 4pm, Saturdays, 11am to 4pm, Sundays, 11am to 3pm; during Easter and autumn school holidays, daily 10am to 5pm. Guided tours (45min) in English on request. 40DKR, children (0-15) free. ☎ 98 44 64 44.

Michael & Anna Anchers Hus – ♿ Open 21 June to mid-August, daily 10am to 6pm; May to 20 June and mid-August to September, daily 10am to 5pm; April and October, daily 11am to 3pm; November to March, Saturdays and Sundays, 11am to 3pm. 30DKR, children (6-15) 10DKR. ☎ 98 44 30 09.

Drachmanns Hus – Open July, daily 10am to 5pm; June, August and early September to mid-September, daily 11am to 3pm; May and mid-September to mid-October, Saturdays and Sundays, 11am to 3pm. Guided tours (30min) in English. 20DKR, children free. ☎ 98 44 51 88.

Skagen By– og Egnsmuseum – ♿ Open May to September, daily 10am to 5pm; March to April and October to November, Mondays to Fridays, 10am to 4pm. Closed Saturdays and Sundays, and December to February. Guided tours (1hr) in English on request. 30DKR, children 5DKR. ☎ 98 44 47 60.

St Laurentii Kirke: Den Tilsandede Kirke – Open June to August, daily 10am to 5pm. 7DKR, children 3DKR. ☎ 98 44 43 71.

Excursion

Ørnereservatet – Show times, April, Wednesdays at 10am, Sundays at 3pm; May, Wednesdays and Thursdays at 10am, Saturdays and Sundays at 3pm; June, Wednesdays and Thursdays, at 10am, Saturdays and Sundays at 5pm; July, Tuesdays to Fridays at 10am and 5pm, Saturdays and Sundays at 5pm; August, Tuesdays and Fridays, to Sundays at 5pm, Wednesdays at 10am and 5pm, Thursdays at 10am; September, Wednesdays and Thursdays at 10am, Saturdays at 3pm; October, Sundays at 3pm; during autumn school holidays, Tuesdays to Sundays at 3pm. Admission to Eagle World 1hr before each show. 65DKR, children 35DEK. ☎ 98 93 20 31. www.eagleworld.dk

SORØ

🄸 Storgade 15 – 4180 – ☎ 57-82 10 12

Sorø Klosterkirke – Open April to mid-September, daily 10am to 4pm. Guided tours on request. ☎ 57 82 10 12.

Excursions

Vester Broby Kirke – Open daily 7am to 5pm. ☎ 57 82 10 12.

Fjenneslev Kirke – Open daily 7am to 5pm. ☎ 57 82 10 12.

Bjernede Kirke – Open daily 8.30am to 4.30pm. ☎ 57 82 10 12.

DENMARK

Vor Frue Kirke – Open daily 8am to 4pm. ☎ 62 21 11 61.

Anne Hvides Gård – Open first fortnight in June, daily 10am to 4pm; mid-June to late October, daily 10am to 5pm. Guided tours in English. 20DKR, children free. ☎ 62 21 76 15.

Viebæltegård – Open May to October, daily 10am to 5pm; November to April, daily 10am to 4pm. Closed 31 December and 1 January. Guided tours in English. 25DKR, children free. ☎ 62 21 02 61.

Sankt Nicolai Kirke – Open summer, Tuesdays to Fridays, 9am to noon, Mondays closed; winter, Mondays to Thursdays, Saturdays and Sundays, 9am to noon, Fridays closed. ☎ 62 21 28 54.

Legetøjsmuseet – Open June to August, daily 10am to 5pm; mid-September to May, Mondays to Fridays, 11am to 5pm, Saturdays, 10am to 1pm. Closed Sundays, 1st fortnight in February and 1st fortnight in September. Guided tours in English. 40DKR, children 20DKR. ☎ 62 20 10 18.

Excursions

Ferries – Ferry from Svendborg to Ærøskøbing, 6 times a day, journey time: 70min ☎ 45 62 52 40 00.

Tourist Office – Vestergade 1B, DK-5970 Ærøskøbing, ☎ 45 62 52 13 00.

Flaskeskibssamlingen – Open May to September, daily 10am to 5pm; October to December and March to April, Tuesdays to Thursdays, 1pm to 3pm, Sundays, 10am to 3pm. 25DKR, children 10DKR. ☎ 45 62 52 29 51.

Rent a Bike – ☎ 45 62 52 11 10.

Sæby Kirke – Open summer, Mondays to Saturdays 8am to 6pm, Sundays, 9am to 4pm; winter, Mondays to Saturdays, 8am to 4pm, Sundays, 9am to noon.

Sønderborg Slot – ♿ Open May to September, daily 10am to 5pm; November to March, daily 1pm to 4pm; April and October, daily 10am to 4pm. Closed 24-25, 31 December and 1 January. Guided tours in English. 25DKR, children 10DKR. ☎ 74 42 25 39.

Excursion

Dybbøl Mill – Open April to October, daily 10am to 5pm. Closed the rest of the year. 25DKR, children 5DKR. Guided tours (1hr) in English. ☎ 74 48 69 91.

Historisk Center Dybbøl Banke – ♿ Open mid-April to September, 10am to 5pm. 45DKR, children 15DKR. Guided tours (1hr) in English. ☎ 74 48 90 00.

T

Christ Kirke – Open Mondays to Saturdays, 10am to 4pm. ☎ 74 72 20 80.

Tønder Museum – ♿ Open June to August, daily 10am to 5pm; September to May, Tuesdays to Sundays, 10am to 5pm. Closed Mondays. Guided tours in English on request. 15DKR, children (0-14) free. ☎ 74 72 26 57.

South Jutland Danish Art Museum – ♿ Open June to August, daily 10am to 5pm; September to May, Tuesdays to Sundays, 10am to 5pm. Closed Mondays. Guided tours in English on request. 15DKR, children (0-14) free. ☎ 74 72 26 57.

Excursion

Højer Mølle – Open April to October, daily 10am to 4pm. Closed November to May. Guided tours in English. 15DKR, children (0-15) free. ☎ 74 78 29 11.

Valdemars Slot – Open May to September, daily 10am to 5pm; last three weeks in April and first fortnight in October, Saturdays, Sundays and public holidays, 10am to 5pm. Closed 24-25 August and mid-October to December. Guided tours in English. 55DKR, children 30DKR. ☎ 62-22 61 06.

V

VIBORG

🏛 Nytorv 9 – 8800 – ☎ 86-61 16 66

Domkirken – Open June to August, Mondays to Saturdays, 10am to 5pm, Sundays, noon to 5pm; April to May and September, Mondays to Saturdays, 11am to 4pm, Sundays, noon to 4pm; October to March, Mondays to Saturdays, 11am to 3pm, Sundays, noon to 3pm. ☎ 87 25 52 50.

Skovgaard Museet – ♿ Open daily, in summer 10.30am to 12.30pm and 1.30pm to 5pm; in winter only 1.30pm to 5pm. Closed 24 to 25 and 31 December and 1 January. Guided tours in English. 10DKR, children (0-18) free. ☎ 86 62 39 75.

Søndre Sogn Kirke – Open Mondays to Fridays on request. ☎ 86 62 49 56.

Excursion

Danmarks Cykelmuseum – Open April to September, daily 10am to 5pm. Guided tours in English. 30DKR, children 10DKR. ☎ 98 64 19 60.

VOERGÅRD SLOT

Voergård Slot – Open mid-June to mid-August, daily 10am to 5pm; mid-April to mid-June and mid-August to mid-October, Saturdays, 2pm to 5pm, Sundays, 10am to 5pm; other times on request for groups. 45DKR, children 15DKR. ☎ 98 46 90 72.

Å

ÅLBORG

🏛 Østerå 8, P.O. Box 1862 – 9100 – ☎ 98-12 60 22

Budolfi Domkirke – Open in summer, Mondays to Fridays, 9am to 4pm, Saturdays, 9am to 1pm; in winter Mondays to Fridays, 9am to 3pm, Saturdays, 9am to noon; Sundays only for church services. ☎ 98-12 46 70/13 49 28.

Ålborgs Historiske Museum – Open Tuesdays to Sundays 10am to 5pm. Closed Mondays, 24 to 26, 31 December and 1 January. 10DKR, children 5DKR; Tuesdays admission free. Guided tours (1hr) in English. ☎ 98 12 45 22.

Helligåndsklostret – Open mid-June to mid-August, Mondays to Fridays, guided tour (1hr) in English 1.30pm; other times on request. 25DKR, children 10DKR. ☎ 98 12 60 22.

Rådhuset – Admission only on official occasions.

Nordjyllands Kunstmuseum – ♿ Open daily 10am to 5pm. Closed Mondays (except in July and August), 24-25 and 31 December. Guided tours (1hr) in English. 30DKR, children free. ☎ 98 13 80 88.

Ålborgtårnet – Open mid-June to mid-August daily, 10am to 7pm; May to mid-June and mid-August to mid-September, 10am to 5pm; first fortnight in October, 10am to 5pm. 15DKR, children 10DKR.

Tivoliland – ♿ Open May, daily 10am or noon to 8 or 10pm; June, daily 10am or noon to 9 or 10pm; July, daily 10am to 10pm; August, daily 10am or 1pm to 7 or 10pm; first week in September, 1pm to 7 or 9pm; open certain weekends only in April. Check exact opening and closing times. Closed September to late April. 40DKR, children 20DKR. Fun card available for rides; 160DKR. ☎ 98 12 33 15.

Excursions

Lindholm Høje Museet – ♿ Open April to mid-October, daily 10am to 5pm; the rest of the year, Tuesdays to Sundays, 10am to 4pm. Closed Mondays, 24-26 December and 1 to 2 January. Guided tours (1hr) in English on request. 20DKR, children 10DKR. ☎ 98 17 55 22.

Lincoln Blokhuset – Open June to August, daily 10.30am to 5pm; September, Saturdays and Sundays, noon to 5pm; Easter and Whitsun, noon to 5pm. Closed October to April. Guided tours in English. 15DKR, children (0-12) free. ☎ 98 39 14 40.

ÅRHUS

🏛 Rådhuset – 8000 – ☎ 89 40 67 00

Vikingemuseet – Open Mondays to Fridays, 10am to 4pm. Guided tours are available through the Tourist Information Centre. Free of charge. ☎ 89-42 11 00.

Århus Domkirke – Open May to September, daily 9.30am to 4pm; October to April, daily 10am to 3pm. ☎ 86 12 38 45.

Vor Frue Kirke – Open Mondays to Fridays, 10am to 2pm, Saturdays 10am to noon.

Rådhuset – Guided tours only; book through the Tourist Information Centre. Visits to the tower, mid-June to August, Mondays to Fridays, 11am, noon and 2pm. 5DKR. ☎ 89 40 67 00.

Musikhuset – ♿ Open daily 11am to 9pm. Closed Easter, Christmas and 1 January. Guided tours (1hr) in English on request. Free concerts in the lobby at weekends. Prices depending on the performance. Tickets ☎ 89 31 82 10, Administration 98 31 82 00.

Den Gamle By – Open June to August, daily 9am to 6pm; April to May and September to October, daily 10am to 5pm; November to December, daily 10am to 4pm; January to March, daily 11am to 3pm. 40-55DKR, children 12-15DKR. ☎ 86 12 31 88.

Århus Kunstmuseum – Open Tuesdays to Sundays, 10am to 5pm (Wednesdays until 8pm). Closed Mondays, 24-25, 31 December and 1 January. Guided tours (1hr) in English. 40DKR, children free. ☎ 86 13 52 55.

Moesgård museum – ♿ Open April to September, daily 10am to 5pm; October to March, Tuesdays to Sundays, 10am to 4pm. Closed 24-25, 31 December and 1 January. Guided tours (1hr) in English. 35DKR, children (0-14) free. ☎ 89 42 11 00. e-mail: farkalh@moes. hum. aau. dk

Excursions

Rosenholm Slot – Guided tours only (1hr) mid-June to end August, daily 10am to 5pm; May, June and September, Saturdays and Sundays only. Guided tours in English. 50DKR, children (6-16) 20DKR. ☎ 86 99 40 10.

Thorsager Rundkirke – Open summer, daily 8am to 5pm; winter, daily 8am to 4pm. ☎ 86 37 90 29.

Ebeltoft Museum – Open June to August, daily 10am to 5pm; September to mid-October, April and May, Tuesdays to Sundays, 11am to 3pm; mid-October to December, Saturdays and Sundays, 11am to 3pm. Closed January to March. 20DKR, children 5DKR. ☎ 86 34 55 99, 86 34 13 82.

Missers Dukke– og Legetøjsmuseum – ♿ Open mid-May to September, daily 10am to noon and 2pm to 4pm. 20DKR, children 10DKR. ☎ 86 34 21 40.

Jyllands Herregårdsmuseum – Open April to October, daily 10am to 5pm; November to March, Tuesdays to Sundays, 11am to 3pm. Guided tours (1hr) in English. Common ticket with the Agricultural Museum. 60DKR, children (0-14) free. ☎ 86 48 30 01.

Dansk Landbrugsmuseum – Open April to October, daily 10am to 5pm; November to March, Tuesdays to Sundays, 10am to 4pm. Guided tours in English on request the day before the visit. 60DKR, children free. ☎ 86 48 30 01.

Clausholm Slot – Open June and August, Saturdays and Sundays, 11am to 4pm; July, daily 11am to 4pm. Guided tours (1hr) in English, on request. 60DKR, children (0-13) free. ☎ 86 49 16 55. www. clausholm.dk

Baker's window in Århus, Denmark

Norway

A

ALTA
🏠 Postboks 1223 – 9501 – ☎ 78-43 54 44

Alta Museum – ♿ Open mid-June to mid-August, daily 8am to 11pm; first fortnight in June and last fortnight in August, daily 8am to 8pm; May and September, daily 9am to 6pm; October to April, Mondays to Fridays, 9am to 3pm, Saturdays and Sundays, 11am to 4pm. Closed public holidays. Guided tours (45min) in English. 40NOK (October to April 30NOK), children (0-15) free. ☎ 78 45 63 30.

B

BERGEN
🏠 Slottsgate 1 – 5023 – ☎ 55-32 14 80

Det Hanseatiske Museum – Open June to August, daily 9am to 5pm; September to May, daily 11am to 2pm. Closed 17 May and 24 December to 1 January. 35NOK (May to September), 20NOK (October to April), children (0-14) free. Guided tours (45min) in English (May to September). ☎ 55 31 41 89.

Schøtstuene – Open June to August, daily 10am to 5pm; May and September, daily 11am to 2pm; October to April, Sundays, 11am to 2pm. Closed between Christmas and New Year's Eve and 17 May. Combined ticket with the Hanseatiske Museum. ☎ 55 31 60 20.

Bryggens Museum – ♿ Open May to August, daily 10am to 5pm; September to April, Mondays to Fridays, 11am to 3pm, Saturdays, noon to 3pm, Sundays, noon to 4pm. Closed 1 and 17 May, 24-25 and 31 December. 30NOK. Guided tours (1hr 30min) in English, June to August, daily 11am and 1pm, 60NOK. ☎ 55 58 80 10.

Mariakirken – Open 19 May to 10 September, Mondays to Fridays, 11am to 4pm; 14 September to 18 May, Tuesday to Friday, noon to 1.30pm. 10NOK, children free. Guided tours on request. ☎ 55 31 63 51.

Rosenkrantztårnet – Open mid-May to August, daily 10am to 4pm; September to mid-May, Sundays only, noon to 3pm. 15NOK, children 5NOK. Guided tours (30min) in English. ☎ 55 58 80 10.

Håkonshallen – Open mid-May to August, daily 10am to 4pm; September to mid-May, noon to 3pm, Thursdays, 3pm to 6pm. Closed during the Bergen International Festival in May and when other events are being arranged in the Hall. 15NOK, children 5NOK. Guided tours (30min) in English. ☎ 55 31 60 67. www.hd.uib.no/haakon

Fløyen – ♿ Funicular operates all year round, Mondays to Fridays, 7.30am to 11pm (midnight in summer), Saturdays, 8am to 11pm (midnight in summer), Sundays, 9am to 11pm (midnight in summer). Return 40NOK, children 20NOK. ☎ 55 31 48 00. www.floibanen.no

Rasmus Meyers Samlinger – ♿ Open all year round. Closed Mondays, 16 September to 14 May. 35NOK, children free. Guided tours (45min) in English. ☎ 55 56 80 00.

Stenersens Samling – ♿ Same opening times as Rasmus Meyers Samlinger. ☎ 55 56 80 00.

Gamle Bergen – Open mid-May to end August, daily 10am to 5pm. Guided tours (45min) in English. 40NOK, children 20NOK. ☎ 55 25 78 50.

Excursions

Fantoft Stavkirke – Open mid-May to mid-September, daily 10.30am to 6pm (closed lunchtime 2pm to 2.30pm). ☎ 55 60 40 00.

Troldhaugen – ♿ Open April to September, daily 9am to 6pm; October to March, Mondays to Fridays, 10am to 2pm; Saturdays, noon to 4pm; Sundays, 10am to 4pm. Closed 22 December to 4 January. 50NOK, children free. Guided tours (1hr) in English. ☎ 55 91 07 10.

Damsgård – Open May to September, Tuesdays to Sundays, 11am to 5pm. Closed Mondays. Guided tours (45min) in English. 30NOK, children 10NOK. ☎ 55 94 08 70.

F

FINNMARK

🅱 Top of Europe, – 9001 Tromsø – ☎ 77 60 35 80

Karasjok: Sápmi – Open mid-June to early August, Mondays to Saturdays, 9am to 6pm, Sundays, 10am to 6pm; early August to mid-June, Mondays to Fridays, 9am to 4pm, Saturdays, 10am to 2pm. Closed Sundays and public holidays. Guided tours in English are available but must be booked 24 hours in advance. ☎ 78 46 69 00.

De Samiske Samlinger – ♿ Open second week in June to second week in August, Mondays to Saturdays, 9am to 6pm, Sundays, 10am to 6pm; second fortnight in August to October, Mondays to Fridays, 9am to 3pm, Saturdays and Sundays, 10am to 3pm; November to first week in June, Mondays to Fridays, 9am to 3pm, Saturdays and Sundays, noon to 3pm. Guided tours in English. 25NOK, children (7-15) 5NOK. ☎ 78 46 99 50.

Kautokeino: Museum – ♿ Open mid-June to mid-August, Mondays to Saturdays, 10am to 6pm, Sundays, noon to 7pm; the rest of the year, 9am to 3pm. Closed Saturdays and Sundays in winter. 20NOK, children free. Guided tours (15min). ☎ 78 48 58 00.

FLEKKEFJORD

🅱 Elvegaten 2, Boks 216 – 4401 – ☎ 038-32 12 61

Rådhuset – ♿ Open summer, Mondays to Fridays, 8am to 3pm; winter, Mondays to Fridays, 8am to 3.30pm. Admission free. ☎ 38 32 43 00.

Flekkefjord Museum – ♿ Open June to August, Mondays to Fridays, 11am to 5pm, Saturdays and Sundays, noon to 3pm. Closed the rest of the year. Guided tours in English. 25NOK, children 10NOK. ☎ 38 32 26 59.

G

GEIRANGER

🅱 6200 – ☎ 0702-607 14

Geiranger Kyrkje – Open June to August, daily 10am to 9pm.

H

HARDANGERFJORD

🅱 Kinsarvik – 5780 – ☎ 053-66 31 12

Hardanger Folk Museum – Open all year round, Mondays to Fridays, 10am to 3pm (Thursdays until 6pm); May to September, weekdays, 10am to 4pm (Thurdays until 6pm), Sundays, noon to 4pm; July, daily 10am to 6pm. Guided tours every hour. 30NOK, children 20NOK. ☎ 47 53 66 69 00.

Tyssedal power station – Open June to August, daily 10am to 4pm (6pm in July); the rest of the year, Tuesdays to Fridays, 10am to 3pm. 50NOK. ☎ 45 53 65 00 50.

Ullensvang Kirke – Open mid-May to mid-September, daily 9am to 7pm.

Kinsarvik Kirke – Open mid-May to mid-September, daily 10am to 7pm.

HEDDAL

🅱 Kongsberg, Storgt. 36 – 3600 – ☎ 03-73 15 26

Heddal Stavkirke – Open 15 May to 19 June, daily 10am to 5pm; 20 June to 20 August, daily 9am to 7pm; 21 August to 15 September, daily 10am to 5pm. Closed 16 September to 14 May and 17 May; open other times on request. 25NOK, children (0-15) free. Guided tours in English. ☎ 35 02 04 00.

K

KONGSBERG

🅱 Storgt. 36 – 3600

Kongsberg Kirke – Open 18 May to August, Mondays to Fridays, 10am to 5pm; September to 17 May, Tuesdays to Fridays, 10am to noon. 20NOK, children 10NOK. Guided tours. ☎ 32 73 50 00.

Norsk Bergverksmuseum – ♿ Open 18 May to 30 September daily; in winter, open Sundays; the rest of the year, on request. 50NOK, children 10NOK. Guided tours in English on request. ☎ 32 73 32 00.

Den Kongelige Mynts museum – Same opening times as Norsk Bergverksmuseum above.

Kongsberg Skimuseum – Same opening times as Norsk Bergverksmuseum above.

Kongsberg Arms Factory Museum – Same opening times as Norsk Bergverksmuseum above.

Lågdalsmuseet – ♿ Open 23 June to 15 August, daily 11am to 5pm; 1 September to 16 May, Mondays to Fridays, 11am to 3pm; 17 May to 23 June and 16 to 31 August, 11am to 3pm (5pm Saturdays, Sundays and public holidays). Closed Easter and Christmas. 25NOK, children 10NOK. Guided tours in English in summer. ☎ 32 73 34 68.

Excursion

Kongsberg Sølvgruver – Open 5 to 31 August, Mondays to Saturdays; September, Sundays only; in winter, on request. 55NOK, children 20NOK. Guided tours (1hr) in English. ☎ 32 73 50 00.

KRISTIANSAND
🛈 Dronningensgt. 2 – 4601 – ☎ 038-02 60 65

Christiansholm Festning – Open mid-May to 29 September, daily 9am to 9pm. Closed 30 September to 14 May. Admission free. Guided tours (30min) in English. ☎ 96 67 20 00.

Vest-Agder Fylkesmuseum – Open mid-June to mid-August, Mondays to Saturdays, 10am to 6pm, Sundays, noon to 6pm; September to May, Sundays only, noon to 5pm. 30NOK, children 10NOK. Guided tours (1hr) in English. ☎ 38 09 02 28.

Agder Naturmuseum og Botaniske hage – Open 20 June to 20 August, Tuesdays to Fridays, 10am to 6pm, Saturdays and Sundays, noon to 6pm; the rest of the year, Tuesdays to Fridays, 10am to 3pm, Sundays, noon to 5pm, Closed Mondays and Saturdays. Guided tours in English. 25NOK, children 5NOK. ☎ 038-09 23 88.

L

LILLEHAMMER
🛈 Postboks 44 – 2601 – ☎ 61-25 92 99

Maihaugen: De Sandvigske Samlinger – ♿ Open last fortnight in May, daily 11am to 4pm; June to mid-August, daily 9am to 6pm; 16 August to 30 September, daily 10am to 5pm; October to mid-May, daily 11am to 4pm. Closed Mondays, 10 October to 16 May. 70NOK, children 30NOK. Guided tours (45min) in English, mid-May to September. ☎ 61 28 89 00.

Lillehammer Kunstmuseum – ♿ Open 26 June to 27 August, daily 10am to 5pm; the rest of the year, Tuesdays to Sundays, 11am to 4pm. Closed Mondays. 40NOK, children (under 12) free. Guided tours in English. ☎ 61 26 94 44.

Norsk Kjøretøyhistorisk Museum – Open mid-June to mid-August, daily 10am to 6pm; the rest of the year, Mondays to Fridays, 11am to 3pm, Saturdays and Sundays, 11am to 4pm. 30NOK, children 15NOK. ☎ 6125 61 65.

Norges Olympiske Museum – ♿ Open in summer, daily 10am to 6pm; in winter, Tuesdays to Sundays, 11am to 4pm. 50NOK, children 25NOK. Guided tours (1hr) in English. ☎ 61 25 21 00. www.ol.museum.no

Excursions

Jernbanemuseet – Open mid-May to August, daily 10am to 4pm (6pm in July). Guided tours in English. 30NOK, children 20NOK. ☎ 62 51 31 60.

Hunderfossen family park – ♿ Open last week in June to first week in August, daily 10am to 8pm; first three weeks in June, second week in August and weekends in August and late May, 10am to 5pm; open other times on request. 145NOK, children 125NOK. ☎ 61 27 72 22.

LOFOTEN
🛈 Destination Lofoten, Svolvær, Postboks 210 – 8301 – ☎ 076-07 30 00

Norsk Fiskeværsmuseum – ♿ Open 20 June to 20 August, daily 10am to 5.30pm; 21 August to 19 June, Mondays to Fridays, 10am to 3.30pm. 40NOK, children 30NOK. Guided tours (1hr) in English. ☎ 76 09 14 88. www. lofoten-info. no/fiskmus. htm.

Dagmars Dukkemuseum – ♿ Open June to August, daily 10am to 8pm; September to October and March to May, Saturdays and Sundays, noon to 5pm. Closed November to February except on request. 35NOK, children (5-15) 20NOK. Guided tours in English on request. ☎ 76 09 21 43. www.lofoten-info.no

Lofotmuseet – Open June to August, daily 9am to 7pm; September to May, Mondays to Fridays, 9am to 3pm. Closed Saturdays and Sundays, Easter and Christmas. 40NOK, children 15NOK. Guided tours in English on request. ☎ 76 07 82 23.

Vesterålen: Museum – Open mid-June to mid-August, daily 11am to 3.30pm. 25NOK, children 10NOK. ☎ 076-15 75 56.

Norsk Fiskeindustrimuseum – Open mid-June to mid-August, Mondays to Fridays, 10am to 5pm, Saturdays and Sundays, 11am to 5pm; rest of the year, Mondays to Fridays, 10am to 2pm. 35NOK. ☎ 45 76 15 98 25.

Hadsel kirke – Open June to August, daily 10am to 6pm; September to May, Sundays, 12.30pm to 1pm; other times on request. ☎ 76 15 00 00.

Hurtigrutemuseet – Open mid-June to mid-August, daily 10am to 6pm; mid-August to mid-September and mid-May to mid-June, daily 12am to 4pm; mid-September to late December and January to mid-May, 2.30pm (12am Saturdays and Sundays) to 4pm. 80NOK, children 30NOK. ☎ 76 11 81 90.

Andenes: Hvalsentret – N-8480 Andenes. ☎ 76 11 56 00, Fax 76 11 56 10

Trondenes Kirke – Open Mondays to Fridays, 9am to 2pm, Sundays, 9am to 11pm. 10NOK, children 5NOK. ☎ 77 06 92 50.

M

MAGERØYA   🚺 Nordkapp Reiseliv i Honningsvåg, Postboks 34 – 9751 – ☎ 78-47 25 99

Nordkappmuseet – Open mid-June to mid-August, Mondays to Saturdays, 9am to 8pm, Sundays, 1pm to 8pm; mid-August to mid-June, Mondays to Fridays, 11am to 4pm. Guided tours (30min) in English. 20NOK, children 5NOK. ☎ 078-47 28 33.

Gjesværstappan Naturreservat – For further information call ☎ 078-47 57 73.

MANDAL   🚺 Brygetgt. – 4500 – ☎ 38-26 08 20

Excursion

Lindesnes Fyr – Open daily 10am to 6pm (10pm in summer). 25NOK, children free. ☎ 97 54 08 15.

N

NARVIK   🚺 Kongensgt. 66, Postboks 318 – 8501

Cable Car – Open mid-June to mid-August, daily noon to 1pm. 70NOK, children 40NOK. ☎ 76 94 16 05.

Krigsminnemuseum – Open 5 June to 25 August, Mondays to Saturdays, 10am to 10pm, Sundays, 11am to 5pm; 26 August to 31 September, Mondays to Saturdays, 10am to 4pm; the rest of the year, on request. 30NOK, children 10NOK. Guided tours (over 15 persons) in English. ☎ 76 94 44 26.

Ofoten Museum – Open Mondays to Fridays, 10.30am to 3.30pm (in July Saturdays and Sundays also, noon to 3pm). 20NOK, children, 5NOK. Guided tours in English. ☎ 76 96 00 50.

NORDFJORD   🚺 Bruggen 5, Postboks 4108 – 5023 – ☎ 055-31 93 00

Norsk Fjordhestsenter – Open daily noon to 8pm. Closed 20 December to 5 January and Easter. 75NOK; horse and carriage ride 80NOK, children 15NOK. ☎ 057 86 02 33.

Nordfjord Folkemuseum – ♿ Main building open in summer, daily 11am to 4pm; in winter, Mondays to Fridays, 9am to 3pm. Closed, 15 September to 1 June, Saturdays and Sundays. 35NOK, children 15NOK. Guided tours in English. ☎ 57 86 61 22.

Olden: gammla kirke – Open daily 10am to 4pm.

Singerheimen – ♿ Open Easter to September, Mondays to Fridays and Sundays, noon to 6pm, Saturdays, 10am to 6pm. Guided tours in English. 20NOK, children 10NOK. ☎ 57 87 31 06.

Stryn Summer Ski Centre – Open daily 9am to 4pm (5pm in summer). ☎ 057-87 23 33. Information on weather and skiing conditions ☎ 94-55 61 09.

NORDKAPP   🚺 Nordkapp Reiseliv AS i Honningsvåg, Postboks 34 – 9750

Nordkapphallen – ♿ Open early April to early October, daily 10am to 2am. Guided tours in English. 175NOK, children (0-12) free, family 350NOK. ☎ 78 48 27 00.

NUMEDAL

🖪 DBC-sentret – 3550 – ☎ 032-07 45 44

Torpo Stavkirke – Open June to August, daily 8.30am to 6pm. 25NOK, children 15NOK. ☎ 32 83 66 93.

Ål: Rolf Nesch Museum – Open mid-June to August, daily noon to 4pm. Closed the rest of the year. A guide is always present. 20NOK, children (under 12) free. ☎ 032-08 17 70.

Uvdal Stavkirke – Open June to August, daily 9am to 6pm. ☎ 032-83 66 93.

Nore Stavkirke – Open daily 20 June to mid-August. ☎ 032-83 66 93.

OPPLAND AND HADMARK

Ringebu Stavkirke – Open 20 May to 7 September, daily 9am to 6pm. ☎ 61 28 43 50.

OSLO

🖪 Vestbaneplassen 1 – 0250 – ☎ 22-83 00 50

Rådhus – ♿ Open daily 9am to 5pm; Sundays, noon to 5pm. 25NOK, children 15NOK, Groups 20NOK. Guided tours in English at 10am, noon and 2pm. ☎ 23 46 16 00.

Akershus Festning – Open May to August, 10am to 6pm, Sundays, 12.30pm to 4pm, Fridays and Saturdays, 10am to 4pm; September to April, 10am to 3pm, Saturdays and Sundays, 11am to 4pm. Closed in Easter holidays, 1 and 17 May, Ascension Day (40 days after Easter) and for Christmas. 30NOK, children 15NOK. ☎ 23 09 39 17.

Norges Hjemmefrontmuseum – Open October to 14 April, Mondays to Fridays, 10am to 3pm, Saturdays and Sundays, 11am to 4pm; mid-June to 31 August, Mondays, Wednesdays, Fridays and Saturdays, 10am to 5pm, Tuesdays and Thursdays, 10am to 6pm. Closed in Easter holidays, Christmas and 31 December. 25NOK, children 10NOK; 8 May free admission. ☎ 23 09 31 38.

Museet for Samtidskunst – ♿ Open Tuesdays and Wednesdays, 10am to 5pm, Thursdays and Fridays, 10am to 8pm, Saturdays, 11am to 4pm, Sundays, 11am to 5pm. Closed Mondays. 40NOK, children free. ☎ 22 33 58 20.

Domkirken – Open daily 10am to 4pm. ☎ 22 86 22 10.

Nasjonalgalleriet – ♿ Open all year round, Mondays, Wednesdays and Fridays, 10am to 6pm, Thursdays, 10am to 8pm, Saturdays, 10am to 4pm, Sundays, 11am to 4pm. Closed Tuesdays, 24-25 December, 1 January, Easter, 1, 17 May and in Whitsun (7th Sunday and Monday after Easter). Guided tours in English must be booked in advance. Admission free. ☎ 22 20 04 04.

Ibsen-museet – ♿ Guided tours noon, 1pm and 2pm. Closed Mondays, Easter, 24-25, 31 December, New Year, 17 May. 40NOK, children 10NOK. ☎ 22 55 20 09.

Norsk Folkemuseum – ♿ Open May to September, daily 10am to 6pm; October to April, 11am to 3pm, Saturdays and Sundays, 11am to 4pm. Closed New Year, 24-26 December. 70NOK, children 20NOK. ☎ 22 12 37 00.

Vikingskipshuset – ♿ Open May to August, daily 9am to 6pm; September, daily 11am to 5pm; October and April, daily 11am to 4pm; November to March, daily 11am to 3pm. Closed Easter, 1 and 17 May, 24-25, 31 December and 1 January. 40NOK, children (7-16) 10NOK. ☎ 22 43 83 79.

Frammuseet – Open mid-June to August, 9am to 6.45 (5.45pm mid-May to mid-June); September to mid-May, 10am to 4.45pm (3.45pm in October); November to February, 11am to 2.45pm (3.45pm Saturdays and Sundays). Closed 1 January, 17 May, 24-26 December. 25NOK, children 15NOK. ☎ 23 28 29 50.

Kon-Tiki museet – ♿ Open June to August, daily 9.30am to 5.45pm; April to May and September, daily 10.30am to 5pm; October to March, daily

Heyerdahl's Kon-Tiki, Norway

W. Louber/VISA

NORWAY

10.30am to 4pm. Closed Good Friday, Easter Day, 17 May, 24-26, 31 December and 1 January. 30NOK, children (over 7) 15NOK. Guided tours (1hr) in English. ☎ 23 08 67 67.

Norsk Sjøfartsmuseum – ♿ Open mid-May to September, daily 10am to 7pm; October to mid-May, Tuesdays and Thursdays, 10.30am to 7pm, Mondays, Wednesdays, Fridays and Saturdays, 10.30am to 4pm, Sundays 10.30am to 5pm. Closed Good Friday, , Easter Day, 17 May, 24-25, 31 December and 1 January. 30NOK, children 20NOK. ☎ 22 43 82 40.

Munch-museet – ♿ Open June to mid-September, daily 10am to 6pm; mid-September to May, Tuesdays to Sundays, 10am to 4pm (Thursdays and Sundays until 6pm). Closed 1, 17 May, 24-25 December. 60NOK, children 20NOK. ☎ 23 24 14 00.

Vigeland-museet – Open May to September, Tuesdays to Saturdays, 10am to 6pm, Sundays, noon to 6pm; October to April, Tuesdays to Sundays, noon to 4pm (7pm Thursdays). Closed Mondays. 30NOK, children 15NOK. ☎ 22 54 25 30.

Skimuseet – ♿ Open July to August, daily 9am to 11pm; June, 9am to 8pm; October to April, daily 10am to 4pm. Closed 24 December and 17 May. 60NOK, children 30NOK. ☎ 22 92 32 00.

Tryvannstårnet – ♿ Open June to August, daily 10am to 6pm; May to September, 10am to 5pm; October to April, daily 10am to 4pm. Closed 24 December and 17 May. 35NOK, children 20NOK. ☎ 22 14 67 11.

Excursions

Henie-Onstad Kunstsenter – ♿ Open all year round, Tuesdays to Thursdays, 10am to 9pm, Fridays to Sundays, 11am to 6pm. 60NOK, children 30NOK. Guided tours (40min) on request in English. ☎ 67 80 49 00.

Asker Museum – Open all year round, Tuesdays to Fridays, 11am to 3pm, Sundays, noon to 4pm. ☎ 47 66 79 00 11.

Eidsvollbygningen Carsten Ankersvei – Open mid-June to mid-August, daily 10am to 5pm; May to mid-June and mid-August to September, daily 10am to 3pm; October to April, daily noon to 2pm. 2NOK, children 1NOK. ☎ 47 63 95 13 0 4.

Byrud Gård – Open April to September, daily 8am to 8pm. 60NOK, children 30NOK. ☎ 47-63 96 86 11.

Fetsund Lenser – Open June to August, Tuesdays to Saturdays, 11am to 4pm, Sundays 11am to 5pm; May and September, Sundays, 11am to 5pm. The Nature Information Centre follows the same opening times as the museum but, in addition, it is open September to April, Saturdays and Sundays, 11am to 5pm. Admission free. ☎ 47 63 88 09 11.

Fjord cruises – Open May to September, Mondays to Fridays, 7.30am to 8pm, Saturdays and Sundays, 8.30am to 8pm; October to April, no cruises. 90NOK, children 45NOK. ☎ 22 20 07 15.

Drøbak: Tregaardens Julehus – Open March to October, Mondays to Fridays, 10am to 3pm; November to December, Mondays to Fridays, 10am to 7pm, Saturdays, 10am to 3pm; June to December, Sundays, noon to 4pm. Closed January and February. ☎ 47 67 93 42 60.

Follo Museum – Open May to September, Tuesdays to Fridays, 11am to 4pm, Saturdays and Sundays, noon to 5pm. 30NOK, children 15NOK. ☎ 47 64 93 26 01.

P

POLARSIRKELEN

Arctic Circle Centre – ♿ Open May, daily 10am to 6pm; 1 to 15 June, daily 9am to 8pm; 16 June to 10 August, daily 8am to 10pm; 11 August to 1 September, daily 9am to 8pm; 1 to 14 September, daily 10am to 6pm. Closed 15 September to April. 45NOK, children 20NOK. ☎ 75 12 96 96.

R

RV 17 🄱 Brønnøysund Turistforening – 8900 – ☎ 075-02 00 44

Sømna Bygdetun – Open mid-June to mid-August, daily noon to 5pm. Guided tours only (45min) in English. 20NOK, children free. ☎ 75 02 92 83.

RØROS

PO Box 123 – 7460 – ☎ 072-41 00 50

Røros Kirke – Open 1 to 20 June, Mondays to Saturdays, noon to 2pm; 21 June to mid-August, Mondays to Saturdays, 10am to 5pm, Sundays, 2pm to 4pm; 16 August to 10 September, Mondays to Satudays, noon to 2pm; 11 September to 31 December, Saturdays, noon to 2pm. 15NOK, children (7-15) 10NOK. Guided tours. ☎ 72 41 11 65.

Smelthytta – Guided tours daily at 10.30am, noon, 1.30pm, 3pm, 4.30pm, 6pm in summer; in winter, Saturdays, 3pm. 45NOK, children 25NOK. ☎ 72 41 00 00.

Pressmuseet – Open only on request. Guided tours only. ☎ 72 41 11 65.

Excursion

Olavsgruva – ♿ Open in summer, Mondays to Fridays, 10.30am to 6pm, Saturdays and Sundays, 10.30am to 4 pm; in winter, Mondays to Fridays, 11am to 3pm, Saturdays and Sundays, 11am to 2pm. 45NOK, children 25NOK. Guided tours in English. ☎ 72 41 00 00.

S

SETESDAL

Setesdal Informasjonssenter AS i Evje – 4660 – ☎ 037-93 14 00

Setesdal Mineralpark – ♿ Only open for groups from April to October on request. Guided tours (1hr) in English, on request. ☎ 38 00 30 70.

SIGDAL

Åmot: Blaafarvevaerket – Open late May to end of September, daily from 10am (Blaafarvevaerket), 11am (Haugfoss), noon (Nyfossum) to 5pm (6pm July to August). 110NOK (admission to art exhibition, technical director's house and mines). ☎ 47 32 78 49 00.

Prestfoss, Sigdal og Eggedal Museum – Open June to August, daily 10am to 5pm. Guided tours. 30NOK, children 15NOK. ☎ 47 32 71 13 00.

Krøderen: Krøderbanen – **Train**: July and August at 10.40am, 2.50pm and 3.45pm. 80NOK (children: 60NOK) or 120NOK (children: 60NOK). **Museum**: June to August, daily 10am to 3pm, admission free. ☎ 32 14 76 03.

Theodor Kittelsens Hjem, Lauvila – Open June to August, daily 11am to 5pm; September, Saturdays and Sundays, groups by appointment. Guided Tours (1h). 40NOK, children 15NOK. ☎ 47 32 71 24 07.

SOGNEFJORD

Postboks 299 – 5801 – ☎ 57-67 23 00

Hopperstad Stavkirke – Open daily from 15 May to 15 September. Guided tours only. ☎ 57 67 88 40.

Norsk Bremuseum – ♿ Open June to August, daily 9am to 7pm; April to May and September to October, daily 10am to 4pm. Closed November to March. 70NOK, children 35NOK. ☎ 57 69 32 88.

Urnes stave church – Open 10 June to 31 August, daily 10.30am to 5.30pm. 40NKR. Guided tours. ☎ 57 67 88 40.

Glacier Centre – ♿ Open May to 20 June and 21 August to 20 September, 10am to 5pm; 21 June to 20 August, 9am to 7pm. Closed in winter. 50NOK, children (over 10) 35NOK. ☎ 57 68 32 50.

STAVANGER

Sølvberget – 4001 – ☎ 51-89 66 00

Domkirken – Open mid-May to mid-September, Mondays and Tuesdays, 11am to 7pm; Wednesdays to Saturdays, 10am to 7pm, Sundays, 1pm to 7pm; the rest of the year, Mondays and Tuesdays, 11am to 2pm, Wednesdays to Saturdays, 10am to 3pm.

Sjöfartsmuseet – ♿ Open mid-June to mid-August, daily 11am to 4pm; 1 to 14 June and 16 to 31 August, Mondays to Tuesdays, 11am to 3pm, Sundays, 11am to 4pm; September to 31 May, Sundays, 11am to 4pm. Closed December. 40NOK, children 10NOK. Guided tours booked in advance. ☎ 51 52 60 35.

Hermetikkmuseet – ♿ Open mid-June to mid-August, daily 11am to 4pm; the rest of the year, Mondays to Thursday, 11am to 3pm, Sundays, 11am to 54pm, closed Saturdays. Closed Fridays, December, 17 May, Easter day and Easter Monday. 40NOK, children 10NOK, price includes four other Stavanger museums. Guided tours in English. ☎ 53 49 89.

NORWAY

Excursions

Olavskirken – Open daily 11am to 6pm. Guided tours every hour in summer. 10NOK, children free. ☎ 52 85 74 18.

Årdal Gamle Kirkje – Open mid-June to mid-August, Mondays to Saturdays, 10am to 4pm, Sundays, 1pm to 5pm. Guided tours available in the summer. ☎ 51 75 71 20.

Jelsa Kirke – Open mid-June to mid-August, noon to 4pm. ☎ 52 79 72 84.

STIKLESTAD
🛈 Stiklestad – 7650 – ☎ 74-07 31 00

Nasjonale Kultursenter – Open June to mid-August, daily 9am to 8pm; the rest of the year, daily 9am to 4pm, Saturdays and Sundays, 11am to 5pm. ☎ 74 04 42 00.

Stiklestad Kirke – Open only on request, call Stiklestad Nasjonale Kultursenter above.

Stiklestad Museum – ♿ Open June to mid-August daily; the rest of the year on request. Guided tours in English, booked in advance out of season. Charge for exhibitions only. ☎ 74 04 42 00.

T

TELEMARK
🛈 Telemark Reiselivsråd i Skien, Postboks 2813 – 3703 – ☎ 035-53 03 00

Norsk Industiarbeidermuseum – ♿ Open May to 14 June, daily 10am to 4pm; mid-June to 14 August, Mondays to Fridays, 10am to 6pm; mid-June to September, Saturdays to Sundays, 10am to 6pm; 14 August to September, Mondays to Fridays, 10am to 4pm. Closed October to March. 55NOK, children 30NOK. Guided tours in English. ☎ 35 09 51 53.

Telemark Museum – ♿ Open mid-May to August, daily 10am to 6pm; the rest of the year by appointment. 40NOK, children (6-16) 10NOK. Guided tours (1hr) in English. ☎ 35 52 35 94.

Eidsborg Stavkirke – Open June to August, daily 11am to 6pm. Guided tours only. 25NOK, children free. ☎ 35 07 73 31.

Lårdal Bygdemuseum – ♿ Open June to August, daily 11am to 6pm; September to May, Mondays to Fridays only, on request. 30NOK, children free. Guided tours in English. ☎ 35 07 73 31.

TROMSØ
🛈 Box 311 – 9001 – ☎ 776-100 00

Domkirken – Open all year round, daily (except Mondays from June to August), noon to 4pm.

Polarmuseet – Open 16 May to mid-June, daily 11am to 5pm; 16 June to mid-August, daily 10am to 7pm; 16 August to mid-September, daily 11am to 5pm; 16 September to mid-May, 11am to 3pm. Closed 1 January, Easter Sunday, 17 May, 24 and 25 December. 30NOK, children, 10NOK. Guided tours in English. ☎ 77 68 43 73.

Nordnorsk Kunstmuseum – Open Tuesdays to Sundays, 11am to 5pm. Admission free. Information: www.museumsnett.no/nordnorsk-kunstmuseum/

Polaria – Open in summer, daily 10am to 7pm; in winter, daily noon to 5pm. 70NOK, children 40NOK. ☎ 47 77 75 01 00.

Ishavskatedralen – Open mid-May to mid-August, daily 10am to 8pm; 14 May, 3pm to 5pm. 20NOK. ☎ 77 63 76 11.

Tromsø Museum – ♿ Open June to August, daily 9am to 8pm; September to May, Mondays to Fridays, 8.30am to 3.30pm, Saturdays, noon to 3pm, Sundays, 11am to 4pm (Wednesdays also 7pm to 10pm). Closed 1 and 17 May, 25 December and 1 January. 20NOK, children 10NOK. ☎ 77 64 50 00.

Nordlysplanitariet – ♿ Shows, June to late August, Mondays to Fridays, 10am to 8pm, Saturdays and Sundays, 10am to 6pm; late August to May, Mondays to Fridays, 3.30pm to 5.30pm, Saturdays and Sundays, 12.30pm to 5.30pm. Closed public holidays. Shows in English. 50NOK, children 25NOK. ☎ 77 67 60 00.

TRONDHEIM
🛈 Munkegt. 19, 2102 – 7001 – ☎ 07-92 93 94

Nidarosdomen – ♿ Open May to 20 June and 20 August to 15 September, Mondays to Fridays, 9am to 3pm, Saturdays, 9am to 2pm, Sundays, 1pm to 4; 21 June to 19 August, Mondays to Fridays, 9am to 6.15pm, Saturdays, 9am to 2pm, Sundays, 1pm to 4pm; 16 September to April, Mondays to Fridays, noon to 2.30pm, Saturdays, 11.30am to 2pm, Sundays, 1pm to 3pm. Guided tours. ☎ 73 89 08 00.

Erkebispegården – ♿ Open 20 June to 20 August, Mondays to Saturdays, 10am to 5pm, Sundays, noon to 5pm; 21 August to 19 June, Tuesdays to Saturdays, 11am to 3pm, Sundays noon to 4pm. Closed Mondays. 25NOK, children 10NOK. Guided tours (1hr) in English. ☎ 73 53 91 60.

Nordenfjeldske Kunstindustrimuseum – ♿ Open 20 June to 20 August, Mondays to Saturdays, 10am to 5pm, Sundays, noon to 4pm; 21 August to 19 June, Tuesdays to Fridays, 10am to 3pm (Thursdays until 5pm), Saturdays, 10am to 3pm, Sundays, noon to 4pm. 40NOK, children 20NOK. Guided tours. ☎ 73 52 13 11.

Ringve Museum – Open 18 May to 17 September, daily; 18 September to 17 December and 6 February to 14 May, Sundays only. 60NOK, children 25NOK. Guided tours in English. ☎ 73 92 24 11.

Å

ÅLESUND   🛈 Rådhuset – 6025 – ☎ 071-21 202

Art nouveau town – Guided tours of the Art nouveau town, mid-June to mid-August, daily at 1pm and 2.30pm. 50NOK. Departure and information from the tourist office, Rådhuset, 6025 Ålesund. ☎ 47 70 15 76 00.

Atlanterhavsparken – Open June to August, daily 10am to 8pm; May-September, daily 10am to 4pm (Sundays until 6pm). 75NOK, children 50NOK. ☎ 47 70 10 70 60.

Excursion

Giske Kirke – Open 1 June to 20 August, Mondays to Saturdays, 11am to 5pm, Sundays, 1pm to 7pm; other times on request. 15NOK. ☎ 70 15 76 00.

Sweden

A

ARVIKA

🛈 Stadsparken – 671 32 – ☎ 0570-135 60

Rackstadmuseet – ♿ Open April to September, Tuesdays to Sundays, 11am to 5pm; October to March, Thursdays, Saturdays and Sundays, 11am to 4pm. 40SEK. ☎ 0570-809 90.

Trefaldighetskyrkan – Open daily 9am to 4pm. ☎ 0570-101 68.

Såguddens Museum – Open in summer on request. 30SEK. ☎ 0570-137 95.

Brunskog – Open last week in July. 60SEK, children (0-14) free. ☎ 0570-522 08.

Excursion

Klässbols Linneväveri – ♿ Open Mondays to Fridays, 8am to 6pm, Saturdays, 10am to 3pm; May to August also Sundays, 10am to 3pm. Guided tours in English for groups. Admission free. ☎ 0570-460 185.

B

BIRKA

Museum – Open May to September, daily 10am to 6pm. Boat trips from Stockholm; 2hr in each direction, 4hr on the island; café on the island, café and restaurant on the boat; information about schedules from Strömma Kanalbolaget, Skeppsbron 22, 111 30 Stockholm. ☎ 08-23 33 75. Boat trips are also organized from other towns on Lake Mälaren (Mariefred, Strängnäs, Södertälje, Västerås); apply to local tourist information office. www.raa.se/birka

BOHUSLÄN

Bohus fästning – Open May to late June, daily 10am to 7pm; late June to early August, 10am to 8pm; rest of August, 10am to 7pm; September, Saturdays and Sundays, 11am to 5pm. Closed Midsummer's Eve. 25SEK, children (6-16) 10SEK. ☎ 0303-156 62.

Kungälvs kyrka – ♿ Open mid-June to mid-August, daily 10am to 5pm; request permission before visiting in winter. Guided tours in English. ☎ 0303-102 10.

Carlstens fästning – Open June to August, daily; spring and autumn, Saturdays and Sundays. 40SEK, children 20SEK. ☎ 0303-602 65.

Skärhamns Sjöfartsmuseum – Open late May to June and first fortnight in August, Saturdays and Sundays, 3pm to 6pm; July, Mondays to Fridays, 5pm to 8pm, Saturdays and Sundays, 3pm to 6pm.

Gullholmen: Skepparhuset – Open 25 June to mid-August, 4pm to 7.30pm. English-speaking guide available.

Lysekil: Havets Hus – ♿ Open Midsummer to early August, daily 10am to 8pm; early June to Midsummer and first three weeks in August, daily 10am to 6pm; last week in August to November and early February to early June, daily 10am to 4pm. 50SEK, children (5-15) 25SEK. ☎ 0523-165 33. www.havetshus.lysekil.se

Lysekil: Vikarvet – Open mid-June to mid-August, Tuesdays to Sundays, 3pm to 5pm; mid-August to mid-June, Sundays, 2pm to 4pm; other times on request. ☎ 0523-137 20 and 0523-61 10 68.

Nordens Ark – Open June to August, daily 10am to 6pm; September to May, daily 10am to 4pm. 90SEK, children 35SEK, family 240SEK. ☎ 0523-522 15.

Smögen Fiskmarknaden – Open Tuesdays to Fridays, 7am.

Svenneby Kyrka – Open mid-May to mid-September, daily 9am to 6pm. ☎ 0525-350 04.

Vitlycke Museum – ♿ Open April to September, daily 10am to 6pm; October to December, Thursdays to Sundays, 11am to 5pm; January to March, Saturdays and Sundays, 11am to 5pm. Guided tours for groups. 45SEK, children (7-16) 25SEK. ☎ 0525-209 50 and 0522-65 65 00.

Skee Kyrka – Open Mondays to Fridays, 8am to 3pm. ☎ 052 621 428.

Strömstad: Koster Islands – For information, timetables, prices and family reductions, contact Kosterbåtarna ☎ 0526-201 10, TidPunkten Kampenhof ☎ 0522-140 30 or Strömstad Tourist Office ☎ 0526– 623 30.

D

DALARNA

Orsa: Grönklitts Björnpark – ♿ Open Midsummer to first week in August, daily 10am to 5pm; mid-May to Midsummer and second week in August to mid-September, daily 10am to 3pm. Guided tours (1hr) in English for groups. 70SEK, children (6-15) 40SEK, family 190SEK. ☎ 0250-462 00.

Porfyrmuseet – Open June to August, 11am to 5pm; September to May, Tuesdays to Fridays, 10am to 3pm. 30SEK, children (0-11) free. ☎ 0251-410 35.

Hagströmsamlingen – Opening times and charges not available at time of going to press.

Särna: Gammelkyrka – Open daily 8am to 8pm. ☎ 0253-102 05.

DROTTNINGHOLM

Drottningholms Slott – Open May to August, daily 10am to 4.30pm; September, daily noon to 3.30pm; October to April, Saturdays to Sundays, noon to 3.30pm. 50SEK. ☎ 08-402 62 80. www.royalcourt.se

Theatre Museum – Open May, daily noon to 5pm; June to August and September, daily 11am to 5pm. ☎ 08-759 04 06. www.drottningholmsteatern.dtm.se

Kina Slott – Open April and October, daily 1pm to 3.30pm; May to August, daily 11am to 4.30pm; September, daily noon to 3.30pm, Saturdays and Sundays, noon to 3.30pm. 50SEK. ☎ 08-402 62 70. www.royalcourt.se

E

ESKILSTUNA
🛈 Hamngatan 19 – 632 20 – ☎ 016-10 70 00

Rademachersmedjorna – Open June to August, daily 10am to 4pm; September to December and March to May, Tuesdays to Fridays, 10am to 4pm, Saturdays and Sundays, noon to 3pm. Closed January and February. Admission free. ☎ 016-10 13 71 and 016-10 28 54.

Faktoriholmarna: Faktorimuseet – ♿ Open Tuesdays to Sundays, 11am to 4pm. Admission free.

Vapentekniska Museet – Open June to August, daily 11am to 4pm; September to May, Thursdays, Saturdays and Sundays, 11am to 4pm. Admission free. ☎ 016-10 23 75 and 016-10 28 54.

Excursion
Sigurdristningen – Open daily. ☎ 161-070 00.

F

FALKENBERG
🛈 Stortorget, box 293 – 311 23 – ☎ 0346-174 10

St Laurentii kyrka – ♿ Open daily 8am to 7pm. Guided tours in English in summer. ☎ 0346-55 210.

Törngrens Krukmakeri – ♿ Open Mondays to Fridays, 8am to 4.30pm (closed for lunch, noon to 1pm). ☎ 0346-103 54.

Falkenbergs Museum – Open June to August, Tuesdays to Fridays, 10am to 4pm, Saturdays and Sundays, noon to 4pm; September to May, Tuesdays to Fridays and Sundays, noon to 4pm. ☎ 0346-861 25.

FALUN
🛈 Stora Torget – 791 83 – ☎ 023-640 04

Falu Koppargruva – Open May to August, daily 10am to 4.30pm; September to mid-November, March and April, Saturdays and Sundays, 12.30pm to 4.30pm. 60SEK, children 30SEK; combined ticket with Stora Museet. ☎ 023-158 25.

Stora Museet – Same opening times as Falu Koppargruva above.

Dalarnas Museum – Open Mondays to Thursdays, 10am to 5pm, Fridays to Sundays, noon to 5pm; September to April (Wednesdays until 9pm). 20SEK, children 10SEK. ☎ 023-765 500. www.dalarnasmuseum.se

Falu Kristine kyrka – ♿ Open daily 10am to 6pm. ☎ 023-10 323.

SWEDEN

Excursions

Carl Larsson-gården, Sundborn – Open May to September, daily 10am to 5pm, other times on request. 65SEK, children 20SEK. ☎ 023-600 53.

Carl Larssons Porträttsamling – Open late June to mid-August, Mondays to Saturdays, 10am to 5pm, Sundays, 1pm to 5pm. 20SEK, children (0-7) free.

Sundborns kyrka – Ġ Open May to August, daily 9am to 8pm, September to April, daily 9am to 4pm. ☎ 023-600 15.

Bjursås Museum – Open early June to early August. Admission free.

G

GOTLAND
🚹 Hamngatan 4 – 621 25 – ☎ 0498-24 70 65

Kruttornet – Open mid-June to mid-August, daily 10am to 6pm. 10SEK, children (0-16) free. ☎ 0498-29 27 00. www.gotmus.i.se

Gotlands fornsal – Open May to mid-September, daily 10am to 5pm; mid-September to April, Tuesdays to Sundays, noon to 4pm. 40SEK, children (0-16) free. ☎ 0498-24 70 10. www.gotmus.i.se

Excursions

Krusmyntagården – Ġ Open July, daily 9am to 8pm; June and first three weeks in August, daily 9am to 6pm. 20SEK, children (0-11) free. ☎ 0498-29 69 00. www.krusmynta.se

Lummelundagrottan – Open May to mid-September. 45SEK, children (5-15) 30SEK. ☎ 0498-27 30 90 and 0498-27 30 50.

Bunge Friluftsmuseum – Open mid-June to mid-August, 10am to 6pm; mid-May to mid-June and last fortnight in August, 10am to 4pm. 50SEK, children (0-16) free. ☎ 0498-22 10 18. E-mail: bunge. museet@swipnet. se

Källunge kyrka – Open May to August, daily 9am to 5pm.

Dalhems kyrka – Open May to August, daily 9am to 5pm. ☎ 0498-380 01.

Lau kyrka – Open May to August, daily 9am to 5pm.

Garde kyrka – Open May to August, daily 9am to 5pm. ☎ 0498-49 10 01.

Lye kyrka – Open May to August, daily 9am to 5pm. ☎ 0498-49 10 01.

Stånga kyrka – Open May to August, daily 9am to 5pm.

Kneippbyn Sommar– & Vattenland – Open early May to first week in June and last three weeks in August, daily 11am to 5pm; second week in June to Midsummer, daily 10am to 5pm; Midsummer to first week in August, daily 10am to 6pm. ☎ 0498-29 61 50.

Fröjels kyrka – Open May to September, daily 9am to 8pm. ☎ 0498-24 00 05.

Petes Museigård – Open June to August, daily noon to 6pm. Guided tours in English. 20SEK, children (0-16) free. ☎ 0498-48 70 54.

Öja kyrka – Open daily 8am to 9pm. ☎ 0498-49 70 06.

Bottarvegården – Open June to August, noon to 4pm. ☎ 0498-49 71 90 and 0498-49 74 22. www.gotland.se

GRIPSHOLM SLOTT
🚹 Mariefreds Turistbyrå, Rådhuset – 647 00 – ☎ 0159-297 90

Open May to August, daily 10am to 4pm; September, Tuesdays to Sundays, 10am to 3pm; October to April, Saturdays and Sundays, noon to 3pm. 50SEK. ☎ 0159-101 94. www.royalcourt.se

GÄLLIVARE-MALMBERGET
🚹 Stora Sjöfallet – 982 99 – ☎ 0973-400 70

Lappkyrka – Open June to August, Mondays to Fridays, 8am to 4pm, Saturdays, Sundays and holidays, 10am to 6pm.

Hembygdsmuseet – Ġ Open late June to mid-August, daily 11am to 4.30pm; mid-August to late June, daily 11am to 3.30pm. Guided tours in English. Admission free. ☎ 0970-153 75.

Hembygdsområdet – Open mid-June to mid-August, 10am to 10pm.

SWEDEN

Gruvmuseet – ♿ Open early June to mid-August. Mondays to Fridays, 10am to 5pm; other times on request. Guided tours in English. 30SEK, children free. ☎ 0970-763 37.

Kåkstan – Open mid-June to mid-August. Mondays to Fridays, 11am to 5pm, Saturdays to Sundays, noon to 3pm; guided tours once a day in the summer cost about 30SEK. ☎ 0970-186 96.

GÖTEBORG
🚹 Kungsportsplatsen 2 – 411 10 – ☎ 031-10 07 40

Lisebergslinjen – Runs Saturdays and Sundays in spring and autumn and late June to early August, noon to 6pm every 15 to 20 minutes.

Paddan – Up to four departures per hour (time: 55min) from late April to early October, 10am to 5pm (9pm late June to early August). 75SEK, children (4-15) 50SEK☎ 031-60 96 60.

Ostindefararen Götheborg – Open Mondays to Fridays, 10am to 6pm, Saturdays and Sundays, 11am to 3pm. Guided tours 11am weekly, Saturdays and Sundays noon and 2pm. 25SEK, 50SEK (guided tours). ☎ 031-779 34 50.

Götheborgs-Utkiken – Open mid-May to August, daily 11am to 7pm; September to mid-May, Saturdays and Sundays, 11am to 4pm. 30SEK, children (4-15) 15SEK. ☎ 031-13 13 00.

Göteborgsoperan – ♿ The Box Office is open daily noon to 6pm or until the performance begins; closed Sundays and public holidays. ☎ 031-10 80 00.

Göteborgs Maritima Centrum – Open July, daily 10am to 9am; May to June and August, daily 10am to 6am; March to April and September to November, daily 10am to 4pm. 50SEK, children 25SEK. ☎ 031-10 59 50.

Sjöfartsmuseet – Open Mondays to Fridays, 9am to 4pm, Saturdays, Sundays and public holidays, 10am (11am September to April) to 5pm. Closed Mondays September to April. **Aquarium**: Open at 10am, closed Saturdays and Sundays. 40SEK, children (7-16) 10SEK. ☎ 031-61 00 00.

Göteborgs Fiskauktion – Open Mondays to Thursdays 7am, Fridays, 6.30am. ☎ 031-42 00 85.

Göteborgs Konstmuseum – Open 11am to 4pm, Saturdays and Sundays, 11am to 5pm; September to April, Tuesdays to Fridays, 11am to 5pm (Wednesdays until 9pm). Closed Mondays September to April. 40SEK. ☎ 031-61 27 53 or 031-61 10 00.

Röhsska Konstslöjdmuseet – ♿ Open noon to 4pm, Saturdays and Sundays, noon to 5pm; September to April, noon to 4pm (Tuesdays until 9pm), Saturdays and Sundays, noon to 5pm. Closed Mondays September to April. 40SEK, children (7-16) 10SEK. ☎ 031-61 38 50.

Göteborgs Stadsmuseum – Open daily 11am to 4pm (Wednesdays until 8pm). Closed Mondays September to April, 24-25 and 31 December. 40SEK, children (7-16) 10SEK. ☎ 031-61 27 70.

Naturhistoriska Museet – Open May to August, 11am to 5pm; September to April, Tuesdays to Fridays, 9am to 4pm, Saturdays to Sundays, 11am to 5pm. Closed 24-25 and 31 December. 40SEK, children (7-16) 10SEK. ☎ 031-775 24 00.

Skansen Kronan – Open Tuesdays and Wednesdays, noon to 2pm. Saturdays and Sundays, noon to 3pm. 30SEK, children (7-16) 10SEK. ☎ 031-14 50 00.

Bankmuseum – Open Sundays, noon to 3pm. Closed 24-25 and 31 December. 20SEK. ☎ 031-40 11 05.

Liseberg – Open mid-May to late August, daily; mid-April to mid-May and late August to late September, only Saturdays and Sundays. 45SEK, children (0-7) free. ☎ 031-40 01 00.

Trädgårdsföreningen – Open June to August, 7am to 9pm; rest of the year 7am to 6pm. Entrance free, May to September 10SEK. ☎ 031-61 18 83. **Fjärilshuset:** ♿ Open June to August, daily 10am to 5pm; April and May, daily 10am to 4pm; September to March, daily 10am to 3pm. 35SEK, children (4-16) 10SEK. ☎ 031-61 19 11. **Palmhuset:** Open daily 10am to 4pm. 20SEK, children (0-18) free. ☎ 031-41 57 75.

Botaniska Trädgården – Garden open 9am to sunset. Greenhouses open May to August, Mondays to Fridays, 10am to 5pm, Saturdays, Sundays and holidays, noon to 5pm; September to April, Mondays to Fridays, 10am to 4pm, Saturdays and Sundays, noon to 4pm. Garden voluntary tree, 10SEK; Greenhouses 20SEK, children (0-18) free. ☎ 031-41 81 12.

Slottsskogen – Open daily.

Volvo Museum – ♿ Open June to August, Mondays to Fridays, 10am to 5pm, Saturdays and Sundays, 11am to 4pm; September to May, Tuesdays to Fridays, noon to 5pm, Saturdays, 11am to 4pm. 30SEK, children (6-12) 10SEK. ☎ 031-66 48 14.

Öckerö kyrka – Open daily 8am to 8pm. ☎ 031-96 57 36.

Fiskemuseet – Open mid-May to mid-August, Mondays to Fridays, 10am to 6pm, Saturdays and Sundays, 10am to 6pm. 20SEK. ☎ 031-96 89 94.

Nya Älvsborgs Fästning – Open May to September, daily. Boats leave from "Lilla Bommen"; 30 min 75SEK, children (4-15) 50SEK.

Excursion

Tjolöholms Slott – Open mid-June to mid-August, daily 11am to 4pm; April to September, only Saturdays and Sundays, 11am to 4pm; other times on request. 50SEK, children (4-14) 10SEK. ☎ 0300-54 42 00.

H

HALMSTAD
🛈 Österkans, Box 47 – 301 02 – ☎ 035- 10 93 45

St Nicolai kyrka – Open June to August, daily 8.30am to 6pm; September to May, daily 8.30am to 3pm. ☎ 035-15 19 00.

Najaden – Open June to August, Tuesdays and Thursdays, 5pm to 7pm, Saturdays, 11am to 3pm.

Museet i Halmstad – Open summer, daily 10am to 7pm (Wednesdays until 9pm); the rest of the year Mondays to Fridays, 10am to 4pm (Wednesdays also 7pm to 9pm), Saturdays and Sundays, noon to 4pm. 20SEK. ☎ 035-16 04 00.

Miniland – Open mid-June to mid-August, daily 10am to 7pm; May to mid-June and mid-August to early September, daily 10am to 6pm. 65SEK, children (3-12) 35SEK. ☎ 035-10 84 60.

Excursions

Konstgård – Open early April to early October, Tuesdays to Sundays, 1pm to 5pm; mid-September to late October, Wednesdays, Saturdays and Sundays, 1pm to 5pm; November to mid-December, Saturdays and Sundays, 1pm to 5pm; closed Midsummer's Eve and when changing the displays. 40SEK. ☎ 035-316 19.

Heagård Konst & Hantverk – Open early June to end of August, daily 1pm to 7pm. 20SEK. ☎ 035-347 57 and 035-511 77.

Svedinos Bil– och Flygmuseum – Open first fortnight in June and last fortnight in August, daily 11am to 4pm; mid-June to mid-August, daily 10am to 6pm. 50SEK, children (5-15) 25SEK. ☎ 0346-431 87. www.algonet.se/~svedinos

Laxbutiken – Open daily. ☎ 0346-511 10.

HELSINGBORG
🛈 Box 54 (Knutpunkten) – 252 78 – ☎ 042-12 03 10

Sankta Maria kyrka – Open daily 8am to 4pm. ☎ 042-18 35 00.

Excursions

Sofiero: gardens – Open April to September, daily 10am to 7pm. 50SEK, children (7-16) 10SEK.

Höganäs Museum och Konstgalleri – ♿ Open mid-February to December, Tuesdays to Sundays, 1pm to 5pm (summer, Wednesdays until 7pm). 20SEK, children 10SEK. ☎ 042-34 13 35. Internet: www.hoganas.se/kultur/museum

Höganäs Saltglaserat AB – Open June to August, Mondays to Fridays, 9am to 4pm, Saturdays, 10am to 1pm; September to May, Mondays to Fridays, 9am to 4pm. ☎ 042-338 333.

BodaNova – Höganäs Keramik AB – Open May to August, Mondays to Fridays, 9am to 6pm, Saturdays and Sundays, 9am to 5pm; September to April, Mondays to Fridays, 10am to 6pm, Saturdays, 10am to 4pm, Sundays, 11am to 4pm.

Krapperup – Gardens open all year. Castle open for visitors on pre-booked guided tours. Art gallery and museum open July and August, daily 1pm to 6pm; May, June and September, Wednesdays, 3pm to 7pm, Saturdays and Sundays, 1pm to 6pm. Gardens, admission free; castle, 60SEK; art gallery, 10SEK; museum, admission free.

Brunnby Kyrka – Open summer, daily 9am to 8pm; winter, daily 9am to 4pm. Guided tours in English. Admission free. ☎ 042-34 65 20.

Flickorna Lundgren – ♿ Open late April to early September, daily 10am to 7pm; closed early September to April. Admission free. ☎ 042-34 60 44.

HÄLSINGLAND

Excursions, Outdoor Activities – For further information about tours and hikes, route-planning, accommodation, museum admission times and charges, boat trips, safaris, etc.

Contact one of the following tourist Offices open year round:

Regional Tourist Office: Hälsinge Tur, Resecentrum, SE-82640 Söderhamn, ☎ 46 27 01 60 90. Internet: www.halsingland.nu

Böllnas Turism, Scandic Hotel, Box 254, SE-82123 Böllnas, ☎ 46 27 82 44 50.

Järvsö turist-och reserservice, Stationsgatan 2, SE-82040 Järvsö, ☎ 46 65 14 03 06.

Hudiksvalls turistbyrå, Möljen, SE-82480 Hudiksvall, ☎ 46 65 01 91 00.

Nordanstigs Turistkontor, Södra Vögen 14, Box 56, SE-82070 Bergsjö, ☎ 46 65 23 61 40.

Voxnadalens Turism, Edsbyl, Ovanåkers Kommun, SE-82880 Edsbyn, ☎ 46 27 12 00 22.

HÄRNÖSAND

🛈 Järnvägsgatan 2 – 871 45 – ☎ 0611-881 40

Härnösands Domkyrka – Open daily 10am to 4pm. Guided tours on request. ☎ 0611-245 25.

Murberget – County Museum open daily 11am to 5pm (Thursdays until 9pm). Open air Museum open mid-June to early August, daily 11am to 5pm. Admission free to both museums. ☎ 0611-886 00. e-mail: museet@ylm.se

Excursions

Nordingrå kyrka – Open daily.

Nordingrå: Café Mannaminne – Open the first three weeks of June, daily noon to 6pm; last week of June to first week of August, daily 11am to 9pm; last three weeks of August, daily noon to 6pm; open Saturdays and Sundays all year round. ☎ 0613-202 90, 204 60.

Villa Fraxinus – Open mid-June to early September, 10am to 6pm. 50SEK, children (under 12) 5SEK. ☎ 0613-121 45.

J

JOKKMOKK

🛈 Stortorget 4, Box 124 – 96223 – ☎ 0971-121 40

Ájtte Svenskt Fjäll– och Samemuseum – ♿ Open mid-June to mid-August, daily, 9am to 6pm; mid-September to mid-June, Mondays to Fridays, 10am to 4pm, Saturdays and Sundays, noon to 4pm; closed Saturdays from October to April. 40SEK, children (0-16) free. ☎ 0971-170 70. www.ajtte.com

Edvin "Sarek" Nilsson Naturfoto – Open mid-June to mid-August, 11am to 8pm, Saturdays and Sundays, 11am to 3pm. ☎ 0971-117 65.

Lars Pirak – Open June to August, 11am to 8pm, Saturdays and Sundays, 11am to 3pm. ☎ 0971-106 32.

Excursion

Vuollerim 6000 – ♿ Open June to mid-September, daily 9am to 6pm; mid-September to May, Mondays to Fridays, 9am to 4pm. Guided tours in English. 50SEK (guided tour included), children (0-16) 40SEK. ☎ 0976-101 65.

JULITA

Julita Gård och Museum – Open May and September, daily 11am to 5pm; June and August, daily 10am to 6pm; July, daily 10am to 7pm. ☎ 0150-912 90.

K

KALMAR

Kalmar Slott – Open June to August, daily 10am to 6pm; April, May and September, daily 10am to 4pm; October to March, second weekend of each month, 11am to 4pm. Guided tours (1hr) in English. 60SEK, children (7-16) 20SEK, family 120SEK. ☎ 0480-451 490.

Domkyrkan – ♿ Open June to August, Mondays to Fridays, 7.30am to 7pm, Saturdays and Sundays, 9am to 5pm; September to May, Mondays to Fridays, 7.30am to 15.30pm, Saturdays and Sundays, 9am to 5pm. ☎ 0480-123 00.

SWEDEN

Länsmuseet – ♿ Open summer, daily 10am to 6pm; winter, daily 10am to 4pm. Guided tours in English. 40SEK (50SEK in summer), children (0-20) free. ☎ 0480-451 300 and 0480-451 358.

KARLSHAMN
🛈 Ronnebygatan 1 – 374 81 – ☎ 0454-165 95

Karlshamns Kulturkvarter – Open early June to mid-August, noon to 5pm. Guided tours in English. ☎ 0454-165 95.

Excursions

Mörrum: Laxens Hus – ♿ Open April to September, daily 9am to 5pm; October, daily 9am to 4pm. Guided tours (40 minutes). 50SEK, children (7-18) 25SEK. ☎ 0454-501 23.

Sölvesborg: St Nicolai kyrka – Open daily, 9am to 3pm. ☎ 0456-135 35

Eriksbergs Naturreservat – ♿ Open June and August, noon to 8pm; July noon to 10pm. Guided tours. 75SEK, children (7-13) 35SEK, family 180SEK. ☎ 0454-600 58.

KARLSKRONA
🛈 Stadsbiblioteket, Stortorget 15-17 – 371 31 – ☎ 0455-834 90

Fredrikskyrkan – Open 6 June to 28 August, Mondays to Fridays, 10am to 4pm, Saturdays, 9am to 2pm. ☎ 0455-33 47 00.

Trefaldighetskyrkan – Open 6 June to 28 August, Mondays to Fridays, 10am to 4pm, Saturdays, 9am to 2pm.

Blekinge Läns Museum – Open July, daily 11am to 6pm (Wednesdays until 8pm); August to June, Tuesdays to Sundays, 11am to 5pm (Wednesdays until 7pm). 20SEK, children free. ☎ 0455-801 20. www.rings.se/ltblekinge/kultur/blmuseum

Amiralitetskyrkan – ♿ Open daily 10am to 5pm. Guided tours 15 May to 15 September, other times on request. ☎ 0455-30 34 90 and 0455-30 34 91.

Marinmuseum – Open mid-May to mid-September, daily 10am to 6pm (Thursdays until 9pm); mid-September to mid-May, Tuesdays to Sundays, 11am to 5pm (Thursdays until 9pm), closed Mondays. 40SEK, children (12-16) 20SEK, (price includes visit on HMS Bremön and the other vessels, which are open June to August). b99070011164. Internet: www.marinmuseum.se

Excursions

Ronneby: Kulturcentrum – Open 10am to 5pm. ☎ 0457-176 50.

Heliga Kors kyrka – Open May to August, Mondays to Fridays, 10am to 3pm; September to April Mondays to Fridays, 10am to 11am. ☎ 0457-178 50.

Möllebackagården – Open June to August, Wednesdays to Sundays, noon to 4pm; other times on request. Admission free. ☎ 0457-134 64.

KARLSTAD
🛈 Tage Erlandsgatan 10 – 651 84 – ☎ 054-14 90 55

Värmlands Museum – Open mid-June to late August, daily 10am to 6pm; late August to mid-June, Mondays to Thursdays, 9am to 6pm, Fridays to Sundays, 11am to 5pm (Thursdays until 9pm). 40SEK, children (0-18) free. ☎ 054-21 14 19 and 054-14 31 00. www.wermlandsmuseum.se

Domkyrkan – Open daily 8am to 4pm.

Excursions

Mårbacka – Open Midsummer to early August, guided tours every 30 min from 10am to 5pm; mid-May to Midsummer and early August to early September, guided tours only, every hour from 10am to 4pm. 50SEK, children 25SEK, family 125SEK. ☎ 0565-310 27.

Rottneros Park – ♿ Open Midsummer to first week in August, daily 10am to 6pm; mid-May to early June and second week in August to first week in September, daily, 10am to 5pm. Guided tours in English, daily at 2pm. 80SEK, children 30SEK. ☎ 0565-602 95.

Alsters Herrgård – ♿ Open May to August, daily 11am to 5pm; other times on request. 25SEK, children (0-17) free. ☎ 054-83 40 81 and 054-83 19 82. www.wermlandsmuseum.se

KIRUNA
🛈 Folkets Hus, Lars Janssonsgatan 17 – 98121 – ☎ 0980-188 80

Kiruna kyrka – Open 11am to 5pm.

Kiruna Stadshus – From mid-June to 20 August an English and German speaking guide is present, Mondays to Fridays, 8am to 6pm, Saturdays and Sundays, 10am to 6pm; the rest of the year, 8am to 5pm, no guide. ☎ 0980-704 96.

Hjalmar Lundbohmsgården – Open June to August, guided tours, 10am to 6pm; the rest of the year on request. ☎ 0980-701 10.

Samegården – Museum and exhibition open January to December, 10am to 6pm; the rest of the year, museum only 8am to 5pm. 10SEK. ☎ 0980-188 80.

L

LAPPLAND 📧 Box 4, Torget – 930 90 Arjeplog – ☎ 0961-142 70

Lycksele Zoo – Open all year round. Mid-May to mid-August, 85SEK, children (3-15) 55SEK; the rest of the year, adults 45SEK, children 30 SEK (3-15). ☎ 0950-163 63.

Gammplatsen – Forestry museum open June and August, 10am to 6pm; the rest of the year, Mondays to Fridays, noon to 4pm, Saturdays and Sundays, noon to 4pm.

Storuman: Kåtakyrkan – For futher information call ☎ 0951-203 15.

Storuman: Järnvägshotellet – Open Mondays to Fridays, noon to 4pm.

Stensele kyrka – For futher information call ☎ 0951-203 15.

Tärnaby: Fjällvindens Alpinarium – Open all year round. ☎ 0954-104 25.

Samegården – Open 20 June to mid-August, daily 11am to 5pm. 15SEK, children (10-15) 10SEK. ☎ 0954-104 40.

Hemavan: Tärna Fjällpark – Open 20 June to 20 September and 12 February to 1 May; at other times contact the Tourist Information Centre at Tärnaby. 35SEK. ☎ 0954-304 30.

Ammarnäs: Lappstan – Open mid-June to late August, 10am to 6.30pm; at other times refer to the tourist office. Excursion to Sami settlement and reindeer marking, 350SEK, children (0-12) 175SEK. ☎ 0960-65 10 26 (phone number for booking a tour).

Samegården – Open mid-June to end August.

Hembygdsgården – Open mid-June to end August.

Arvidsjaur: Hembygdsmuseet – Open June to August, Mondays to Fridays, 10am to 6pm, Saturdays and Sundays, noon to 4pm; September to May, 9am to 4pm. ☎ 0960-124 28.

Arjeplog: Silvermuseet – Open in summer, daily 9am to 6pm; the rest of the year Mondays to Fridays, 10am to 4pm, Saturdays, 10am to 2pm. 40SEK. ☎ 0961-112 90.

Skeppsholmen Saamiland – Open all year round, 24 hours a day. ☎ 0961-142 70.

Arjeplogs kyrka – Open daily 9am to 4pm. Guided tours on request. ☎ 0961-142 70.

Jukkasjärvi kyrka – Open daily 9am to 8pm. ☎ 0980-211 25.

Abisko Turiststation – Open June to late September and mid-February to early May; chair lift, early June to late September, late March to early May. Guided tours 15-210SEK, the higher price when transportation is included.

Riksgränsen: Slide Show – Mid-June to mid-September, daily at 3pm; mid-February to mid-June, Tuesdays at 8pm, Wednesdays at 4.30pm, Saturdays and Sundays at 3pm. 50SEK.

Haparanda kyrka – Open 9am to 6pm.

LEKSAND 📧 Norsgatan 1, Box 52 – 793 22 – ☎ 0247-803 00

Leksands Kulturhus – Open mid-June to mid-August, Mondays to Fridays, 11am to 5pm, Saturdays, 11am to 4pm, Sundays, 1pm to 4pm; the rest of the year, Tuesdays to Fridays, 11am to 4pm, Saturdays, 11am to 2pm, closed Sundays. ☎ 0247-802 45.

Leksands kyrka – Open daily 8am to 4pm. ☎ 0247-108 48.

Excursions

Ljusbodarna – Open June to August. ☎ 0247-330 80.

Alfvéngården – Open mid-June to mid-August, Tuesdays to Sundays, noon to 4pm. 30SEK. ☎ 0247-151 09.

Tällberg: Holens gammelgård – Open mid-June to end July, daily noon to 4pm. Guided tours 10SEK. ☎ 0247-802 45.

Jobs Handtryck – Open mid-June to mid-August, Mondays to Fridays, 10am to 6pm, Saturdays and Sundays, 10am to 4pm; guided tours of workshop, Mondays to Fridays at 11am and 2pm. 40SEK. ☎ 0247-122 22.

Siljansnäs Naturum – Open mid-June to July, 11am to 8pm; August, 11am to 6pm; mid-May to mid-June, 11am to 4pm. 30SEK, children 10SEK. ☎ 0247-221 05.

LIDKÖPING 📧 Box 2012 – 531 02 – ☎ 0510-835 00

Rörstrands porslinsfabrik – Open Mondays to Fridays, 10am to 6pm, Saturdays, 10am to 2pm, Sundays, noon to 4pm. ☎ 0510-823 00.

Excursion

Läckö Slott – Open mid-June to mid-August, 10am to 6pm. Guided tours May to September. 40SEK, children 10SEK; mid-June to mid-August, 50SEK, children (0-15) free. ☎ 0510-103 20.

LINKÖPING

Konsistoriegatan 7/Konserthuset – 581 06 – ☎ 013-20 68 35

SWEDEN

Domkyrkan – Open 9am to 6pm.

Östergötlands länsmuseum – Open June to August, Tuesdays to Sundays, noon to 4pm (Thursdays until 9pm); September to May, Tuesdays to Thursdays, noon to 9pm, Fridays to Sundays, noon to 4pm. 20-40SEK. ☎ 013-23 03 52. www.linkoping.se/lansmuseum

Excursions

Gamla Linköping – & Area always open. Boutiques and workshops open Mondays to Fridays, 10am to 5.30pm, Saturdays and Sundays, noon to 4pm; some shops are closed on Mondays. Guided tours on request. Admission free. ☎ 013-12 11 10.

Flygvapenmuseum – Open June to August, daily 10am to 5pm; September to May, noon to 4pm. 30SEK ☎ 013-28 35 67.

LULEÅ

Rådhusgatan 9 – 971 85 – ☎ 0920-935 05

Norrbottens Museum – & Open Mondays to Fridays, 10am to 4pm, Saturdays and Sundays, noon to 4pm (Wednesdays in July until 8pm). Guided tours (30min to 1hr) in English. Admission free. ☎ 0920-24 35 02.

Teknikens Hus – Open mid-June to mid-August, daily, 11am to 5pm. Admission fee during summer. Open mid-August to mid-June, Tuesdays to Fridays, 9am to 4pm (Wednesdays until 8pm), Saturdays and Sundays, 11am to 4pm. Admission free during winter. ☎ 0920-722 00.

Domkyrkan – Open 10am to 3pm.

LUND

Kyrkogatan 11 – 222 22 – ☎ 046-35 50 40

Domkyrkan – Open Mondays to Fridays, 8am to 6pm, Saturdays, 9.30am to 5pm, Sundays, 9.30am to 6pm. ☎ 046-35 88 80.

Historiska Museet – Open Tuesdays to Fridays, 11am to 4pm. 30SEK, children (8-16) 15SEK. ☎ 046-222 79 44.

Domkyrkomuseet – Open Tuesdays to Fridays, 11am to 4pm. 30SEK, children (7-16) 15SEK. ☎ 046-222 79 44.

Kulturen – Open mid-April to end September, daily 11am to 5pm; early October to mid-April, Tuesdays to Sundays, noon to 4pm. Closed 1 January, Good Friday, Easter Saturday, Midsummer's Eve, 24 and 25 December. 50SEK, children (0-18) free. ☎ 046-35 04 00. www.kulturen.org

Skissernas Museum – Open Tuesdays to Saturdays, noon to 4pm (some Wednesdays also 6.30pm to 8.30pm), Sundays, 1pm to 5pm. Closed Mondays. Guided tours on request. 30SEK, children (0-16) free. ☎ 046-222 72 83.

M

MALMÖ

Skeppsbron 2 – 211 20 – ☎ 040-30 30 50

Form/Design Centre – Open Tuesdays to Fridays, 11am to 5pm, Thursdays, 11am to 6pm, Saturdays, 10am to 4pm, Sundays, noon to 4pm. Closed Sundays in July. ☎ 040-10 36 10.

Sankt Petri kyrka – & Open Mondays to Fridays, 8am to 6pm, Saturdays and Sundays, 10am to 6pm. Guided tours (30min) in English. ☎ 040-35 90 56.

Malmö museer – & (partly). Open June to August, daily 10am to 4pm; September to May, daily noon to 4pm. 40SEK, children (7-15) 10SEK; the admission is for all the museums: Stadsmuseet, Konstmuseet, Naturmuseet, Teknik– och Sjöfartsmuseet and Kommendanthuset. ☎ 040-34 44 00 and 040-34 44 37. malmo. com/malmomuseer

Malmö Teknik– & Sjöfartsmuseum – & Same opening times as Malmö museum. ☎ 040-34 44 38.

Rooseum – Open Tuesdays to Sundays, 11am to 5pm (Thursdays until 8pm). 30SEK, children (0-15) free. ☎ 46640 121 716. www. rooseum. se

MORA

Ångbåtskajen – 792 30 – ☎ 0250-265 50

Zorngården – Guided tours mid-May to mid-September, Mondays to Saturdays, 10am to 4pm, Sundays, 11am to 4pm; mid-September to mid-May, Mondays to Saturdays, noon to 3pm, Sundays 1pm to 4pm. 35SEK, children (7-15) 10SEK. ☎ 0250-165 60.

Vasaloppet – Vasagatan 19, SE-792 00 MORA. ☎ 0250 160 00

Zornmuseet – &. Open June to mid-September, Mondays to Saturdays, 9am to 5pm, Sundays, 11am to 5pm; mid-September to May, Mondays to Saturdays, noon to 5pm, Sundays, 1pm to 5pm. 30SEK, children (7-15) 2SEK. ☎ 0250-165 60.

Zorns Gammelgård och Textilkammare – &. Open June to August, daily noon to 5pm. 20SEK, children 2SEK. ☎ 0250-165 60.

Vasaloppsmuseet – &. Open mid-June to mid-August, daily 10am to 5pm; mid-August to mid June, Mondays to Fridays, 10am to 5pm. Guided tours in English. 30SEK, children (7-16) 20SEK. ☎ 0250-392 25. www.vasaloppet.se

Excursions

Sollerön – Open 26 June to July, noon to 6pm. ☎ 0250-225 67.

Nusnäs – Workshop open, summer, Mondays to Fridays, 8am to 6pm, Saturdays and Sundays, 9am to 5pm; winter, Mondays to Fridays, 8am to 5pm, Saturdays, 10am to 2pm. Admission free. ☎ 0250-372 00.

Sivarsbackens Hemgårdsmuseum – Open 26 June to mid-August, Mondays to Saturdays, noon to 6pm, Sundays, 1pm to 6pm. ☎ 0250-452 60.

N

NYKÖPING   🛈 Stora Torget – 611 83 – ☎ 0155-24 82 00

Nyköpingshus – Exhibitions open July, daily noon to 4pm, August to June, Tuesdays to Sundays, noon to 4pm. Closed Mondays. Courtyards and surroundings always open. ☎ 0155-24 57 00.

Södermanlands Museum – Open July, daily noon to 4pm; August to June, Tuesdays to Sundays, noon to 4pm. Closed Mondays. ☎ 0155-24 57 00.

Tovastugan – Open May to August. ☎ 0155-21 17 70.

Excursions

Kolmårdens Djurpark – Zoo open mid-June to mid-August, daily 9am to 6pm; mid-May to mid-June, 9am to 5pm; last fortnight in August, 10am to 5 pm, September and April to mid-May, 10am to 4pm. Safari park open: mid-May to mid-June, daily 10am to 4pm; Mid-June to mid-August, 9am to 5pm; last fortnight in August, 10am to 4pm (entrance every 30min). Dolphinarium show: July at noon, 1pm, 2pm, 3pm and 5pm; first fortnight in August at noon, 2pm and 5pm, last fortnight in August at 1.30pm and 4pm; September and April to mid-May at 1.30pm. Zoo: 195SEK, children 65SEK; safari park: 80SEK, children 30SEK; combined ticket: 235SEK, children 85SEK. ☎ 46 11 24 90 00.

R

ROSLAGEN

Wira Bruk – &. Open Midsummer to mid-August, daily 11am to 4pm; the rest of the year, Saturdays and Sundays, 11am to 4pm. Guided tours in English. Admission free. ☎ 08-543 530 30 (the café), 08-543 531 03 (the smithy). www.grufkontoret.se/val-lonbruken

Norrtälje: Roslagens Museum – Open Mondays to Fridays, 11am to 4pm. 20 SEK. ☎ 0176-576 30, E-mail: ch. k-ohlberger@swipnet. se

Grisslehamn – Studio mid-June to late August, daily noon to 5pm; early May to mid-June and late August to late September, Saturdays and Sundays, noon to 3pm. 30SEK for studio or museum, combined ticket 50SEK. ☎ 0175-308 90.

Edebo kyrka – Open on request only. ☎ 0175-203 34.

Forsmarks bruk – Museum open 25 June to 31 August, 11am to 4pm. ☎ 0295-200 72. www.grufkontoret.se/vallonbruken

Lövstabruk – Mid-June to mid-August, daily noon, 3pm, guided tours of the mansion. 35SEK, children (0-14) free, guided tours in the village, 3.30pm. 35SEK, children (0-14) free. Church open daily in summer. ☎ 0294-310 70. www.grufkontoret.se/val-lonbruken

Österbybruk – The Walloon forge is open May, Saturdays and Sundays, noon to 4pm; June to August, daily 11am to 5pm; September, the two first Saturdays and Sundays, noon to 4pm. Guided tour of the forge 30SEK, without guide 25SEK, children (0-12) free. ☎ 0295-200 72. www.grufkontoret.se/vallonbruken

Liljeforsateljén – ♿ Open May, Saturdays and Sundays, noon to 4pm; June to mid-August, daily noon to 5pm; two last weekends in August, noon to 5pm. 20SEK, children (0-12) free. ☎ 0295-200 72. www.grufkontoret.se/vallonbruken

RÄTTVIK
🛈 Siljan Turism Rättvik, Stationshuset, Box 90 – 795 22 – ☎ 0248-702 00

Dalhalla – Dalhallas Kausli Box 1, SE-79521 Rätvik. ☎ 46 24 81 20 50.

Rättviks kyrka – Open daily 9am to 6pm. ☎ 0248-734 50.

Rättviks Gammelgård – Open mid-June to mid-August, Mondays to Saturdays, 11am to 5pm, Sundays, noon to 5pm. 20SEK. ☎ 0248-114 45.

Vidablick – Open mid-May to end August. 30SEK, family 50SEK (tower). ☎ 0248-302 50.

Excursion

Danielsgården – Open July and August, Tuesdays, Thursdays and Sundays, 2pm to 4pm. Guided tours only. Guided tours in English. 15SEK, children free. ☎ 0246-400 50 and 0248-702 00.

S

SIGTUNA
🛈 Drekegården, Stora Gatan 33 – 193 22 – ☎ 08-592 500 20

Sigtuna Museum – Open June to August, daily noon to 4pm; September to May, Tuesdays to Sundays, noon to 4pm. 20SEK. ☎ 08-592 510 18.

Lundströmska Gården – Open June to August, daily noon to 4pm; May and September, Saturdays and Sundays only. 10SEK. ☎ 08-592 510 18.

Mariakyrkan – Open June to August, daily 9am to 9pm; September to May, daily 9am to 5pm. ☎ 08-592 515 69.

SIMRISHAMN
🛈 Tullgatan 2 – 272 31 – ☎ 0414-160 60

Gösta Werners Museum – Open summer, Tuesdays to Sundays, noon to 5pm. Closed Mondays. 25SEK, children free. ☎ 0414-104 40.

Tannerymuseet – Open mid-June to mid-August, Mondays, Wednesdays, Saturdays and Sundays, 3pm to 5pm. 5SEK. ☎ 0414-104 85.

Hafreborg – Open mid-June to mid-August, Mondays to Fridays 11am to 6pm, Saturdays, 11am to 4pm, Sundays, 1pm to 4pm; 9 April to mid-June and mid-August to 26 September, 1pm to 4pm; 10SEK. ☎ 0414-104 85.

Sankt Nicolai Kyrka – Open in summer, daily 10.30am to 6.30pm; winter on request. ☎ 0414-146 60.

SKELLEFTEÅ
🛈 Mossgatan – 931 40 – ☎ 0910-188 55

Skellefteå landsförsamlings kyrka – Open Mondays to Fridays, 10am to 4pm, other times on request. ☎ 0910-100 84.

Skellefteå Museum – Open Mondays, noon to 7pm, Tuesdays to Thursdays, 10am to 7pm, Fridays to Sundays, noon to 4pm. Admission free. ☎ 0910-73 55 10.

SKOKLOSTER
🛈 Ekholskrogs, E 18 – 753 10 – ☎ 0717-525 62

Skoklosters Slott – Open daily mid-April to October. Guided tours (1hr) in English. 60SEK, children (7-18) 20SEK. ☎ 018-38 60 77.

Skokloster kyrka – May to August, guided tours, Tuesdays to Sundays, noon to 4pm; the rest of the year on request. ☎ 070-641 25 69.

Skoklosters Motormuseum – Open May to September, daily 11am to 5pm; October to April, Saturdays and Sundays. 40SEK, children 10SEK. ☎ 018-38 61 06.

SWEDEN

Boat Servive – Boat service from Stockholm town hall, May to late September, three times a day.

Kungliga Slottet

Royal Apartments and Rikssalen – ♿ Open June to August, daily 10am to 4pm; September to May, Tuesdays to Sundays, noon to 3pm. 50SEK, children (7-18) 25SEK. www.royalcourt.se

Livrustkammaren – ♿ Open daily 11am to 4pm. Closed Mondays September to April. 60SEK, children 15SEK. ☏ 08-666 44 75.

Skattkammaren – Open June to August, daily 10am to 4pm; September to May, Tuesdays to Sundays, noon to 3pm. 50SEK, children (7-18) 25SEK.

Museum Tre Konor – Open June to August, daily 10am to 4pm; September to May, Tuesdays to Sundays, noon to 3pm. 50SEK, children (7-18) 25SEK.

Slottskyrkan – Open June to August, Mondays to Saturdays, 10am to 4pm, Sundays, 12.30pm to 4pm; service every Sunday. Admission free.

Storkyrkan – Open daily 9am to 4pm (May to August until 6pm). 10SEK. ☏ 08-723 30 16.

Tyska kyrkan – Open May to September, daily noon to 4pm; October to April, Saturdays and Sundays, noon to 4pm. ☏ 08-411 11 88.

Riddarhuset – Open Mondays to Fridays, 11.30am to 12.30pm. Closed public holidays. 40SEK. ☏ 08-723 39 90.

Riddarholmskyrkan – Open June to August, daily 11am to 3.30pm; May and September, noon to 1.30pm. ☏ 08-786 40 00.

Vasamuseet – ♿ Open 10 June to 20 August, 9.30am to 7pm; the rest of the year, 10am to 5pm (Wednesdays until 8pm). 60SEK, children (7-15) 10SEK. ☏ 08-519 548 00.

Skansen – Open June to August, 10am to 10pm; May, 10am to 8pm; the rest of the year, 10am to 4pm. Houses open May to August; 11am to 5pm; the rest of the year, 11am to 3pm. 30-60SEK, children 10-20SEK. ☏ 08-442 80 00.

Riksdagshuset – Guided tours (1hr) late June to late August, Mondays to Fridays at 11am (Swedish), 12.30pm (Swedish, English and German), 2pm (Swedish, English and in August French) and 3.30pm (Swedish); the rest of the year, Saturdays and Sundays, noon and 1.30pm. Admission free. ☏ 08-786 40 00.

Medeltidsmuseet – ♿ Open June to August, daily 11am to 4pm (Tuesdays to Thursdays until 6pm); September to June, Tuesdays to Sundays, 11am to 4pm (Wednesdays until 6pm). Closed Mondays. 40SEK. ☏ 08-508 317 90. www.medeltidsmuseet.kif.stockholm.se

Kulturhuset – Open Tuesdays to Thursdays, 11am to 5pm (Fridays until 6pm), Saturdays and Sundays, noon to 4pm. 30SEK, children free. ☏ 08-700 01 00. www.kulturhuset.stockholm.se

Sankta Clara kyrka – Open daily 10am to 5pm. ☏ 08-723 30 31.

Strindbergsmuseet – Open 11am to 4pm (7pm Tuesdays September to May), Saturdays and Sundays, noon to 4pm. Closed Mondays. 35SEK, children (0-15) free. ☏ 08-411 53 54.

Dansmuseet – Open Tuesdays, 11am to 8pm, Wednesdays to Fridays, 11am to 4pm, Saturdays and Sundays, noon to 5pm. Closed Mondays. 50SEK, children 30SEK. ☏ 04-441 76 50.

Hallwylska Museet – In summer guided tours Tuesdays to Sundays, at 1pm; the rest of the year, Sundays only. 60SEK, children 25SEK. ☏ 08-519 555 99

Nationalmuseum – ♿ Open 11am to 5pm; Tuesdays and Thursdays, 11am to 8pm. Closed Mondays. 75SEK. ☏ 08-519 543 00.

Stadshuset – Guided tours June to August, daily at 10am, 11am, noon and 2pm; September at 10am, noon and 2pm; September to May at 10am and noon. 50SEK. The tower is open May to September, 10am to 4.30pm. 15SEK. ☏ 08-508 290 59.

Östasiatiska Museet – ♿ Open noon to 5pm (Tuesdays until 8pm). Closed Mondays. 50SEK. ☏ 08-519 557 50.

Moderna Museet & Arkitekturmuseet – ♿ Open 11am to 8pm, Fridays to Sundays, 11am to 6pm. Closed Mondays. 75SEK. ☏ 08-519 552 00.

Stockholms Stadsmuseum – ♿ Open June to August, Tuesdays to Sundays, 11am to 5pm (Thursdays until 7pm); September to May, Tuesdays to Sundays 11am to 5pm (Thursdays until 9pm). Closed Mondays. 40SEK, children (0-17) free. ☏ 08-508 31 600.

Hovstallet – ♿ In summer guided tours, Mondays to Fridays, at 2pm; winter, Saturdays and Sundays, at 2pm. Closed Easter, mid-December and mi-January. 30SEK, children (0-13) free. ☏ 08-402 61 06.

Musikmuseet – Open Tuesdays to Sundays, 11am to 4pm. 30SEK, children 15SEK. ☏ 08-519 554 90.

SWEDEN

Historiska Museet – ♿ Open Tuesdays to Sundays, 11am to 5pm (Thursdays from mid-September to mid-May until 8pm). Closed Mondays. 60SEK, children (0-12) free. ☎ 08-519 556 00.

Nordiska Museet – ♿ Open Tuesdays to Sundays, 10am to 9pm. Closed Mondays. 60SEK, children 20SEK. ☎ 08-519 560 00 or 08-467 06 60.

Junibacken – Open June to August, daily, 9am to 6pm; September to May, Wednesdays to Sundays, 10am to 5pm. 85SEK. ☎ 08-587 230 00.

Liljevalchs Konsthall – Open Tuesdays to Sundays, 11am to 5pm (Tuesdays and Thursdays until 8pm). Closed Mondays. 50SEK. ☎ 08-508 313 30.

Prins Eugens Waldemarsudde – ♿ Open May to August, Tuesdays to Sundays, 11am to 5pm (Thursdays until 8pm); September to April, Tuesdays to Fridays, 11am to 4pm (Thursdays until 8pm), Saturdays and Sundays, 11am to 5pm. 60SEK. ☎ 08-545 837 07.

Thielska Galleriet – Open Mondays to Saturdays, noon to 4pm, Sundays, 1pm to 4pm. 50SEK. ☎ 08-662 58 84.

Rosendals Slott – Guided tours, May to August, 11am to 3pm. Closed Mondays. 50SEK, children (7-18) 25SEK. ☎ 08-402 61 30.

Kaknästornet – Open May to August, daily 9am to 10pm; September to April, daily 10am to 9pm. 25SEK, children 15SEK

Folkens Museum Etnografiska – ♿ Open Tuesdays to Fridays, 11am to 4pm (Wednesdays until 8pm), Saturdays and Sundays, noon to 5pm. 50SEK. ☎ 08-519 550 00.

Tekniska Museet – ♿ Open Mondays to Fridays, 10am to 4pm, Saturdays and Sundays, 11am to 4pm. 50SEK, children (7-19) 20SEK. ☎ 08-450 56 00.

Sjöhistoriska museet – ♿ Open daily 10am to 5pm (Tuesdays until 8.30pm). 50SEK, children (7-16) 20SEK. ☎ 08-519 549 00.

Gustav III:s Paviljong – Guided tours only (1hr), June to August, Tuesdays to Sundays at noon, 1pm, 2pm, and 3pm; September, Saturdays and Sundays at noon, 1pm, 2pm, 3pm. 40SEK, children (over 7) 25SEK. ☎ 08-402 60 00.
www.royalcourt.se

Millesgården – Open May to September, daily 10am to 5pm; October to April, Tuesdays to Sundays, noon to 4pm. Closed Easter, 24 and 31 December. 70SEK. ☎ 08-446 75 90.

STRÄNGNÄS
🚹 Mälarturism Strängnäs-Mariefred – 645 80 – ☎ 0152-296 94

Domkyrkan – Open May to August, daily 9am to 6pm; September to April, noon to 3pm. ☎ 0152-142 88.

Café Grassagården – Open in summer, 11am to 5pm, also evenings Tuesdays to Thursdays. ☎ 0152-296 98.

STRÖMSHOLM SLOTT
🚹 Hallstahammar Turistbyrå, Box 507 – 734 27 – ☎ 0220-241 86

Open July, daily noon to 5pm; May, June and August, daily noon to 4pm. 30SEK. ☎ 0220-430 35.

SUNDSVALL
🚹 Stora Torget – 852 30 – ☎ 060-61 42 35

Kulturmagasinet – Open Mondays to Thursdays, 10am to 7pm, Fridays, 10am to 6pm, Saturdays and Sundays, 11am to 4pm. ☎ 060-19 18 00.

Excursions

Alnö kyrka – The old church is open mid-June to mid-August, daily 9am to 7pm; a guide will be there to show visitors the baptismal font of the new church; otherwise only on view during services on Saturdays at 11am, Wednesdays at 7pm.

Lidens kyrka – Open June to August, daily 8am to 7pm. ☎ 0692-100 11/102 95.

U

UDDEVALLA
🚹 Kampenhof – 451 81 – ☎ 0522-117 87

Bohusläns Museum – Open June to August, Mondays to Thursdays 10am to 8pm, Fridays to Sundays 10am to 4pm; the rest of the year closed Mondays. ☎ 0522-65 65 00.

ULRIKSDALS SLOTT

Ulriksdals Slott – Open mid-May to August, Tuesdays to Sundays, noon to 4pm; first fortnight in May and September, Saturdays and Sundays, noon to 4pm. Guided tours of the castle every hour. 40SEK, children (7-18) 20SEK, combined ticket for all entries 70SEK. ☎ 08-58 77 10 00 and 08-402 60 00. www.royalcourt.se

Orangerimuseet – Open mid-May to August, Tuesdays to Sundays, noon to 4pm; first fortnight in May and September, Saturdays and Sundays, noon to 4pm; October to April, Sundays, noon to 4pm, guided tours by torch light; guided tours every hour. 40SEK, children (7-18) 20, 70SEK combined entry ticket. ☎ 08-58 77 10 00 and 08-402 60 00. www.royalcourt.se

Kröningsekipaget – Open mid-May to August, Tuesdays to Sundays, noon to 4pm; first fortnight in May and September, Saturdays and Sundays, noon to 4pm. 10SEK, children (7-18) 5SEK, 70SEK combined entry ticket. ☎ 08-58 77 10 00 and 08-402 60 00. www.royalcourt.se

Confidencen – Open May to September, Mondays to Fridays, 10am to 3pm. ☎ 08-85 70 16 (only May to September).

UMEÅ
🚹 Renmarkstorget 15 – 903 26 – ☎ 090-16 16 16

Gammlia Friluftsmuseum – ♿ Open mid-June to mid-August, Mondays to Fridays, 10am to 5pm, Saturdays and Sundays, noon to 5pm. Admission free. ☎ 090-17 18 00.

Västerbottens Museum – ♿ Open mid-June to mid-August, Mondays to Fridays, noon to 4pm, Saturdays and Sundays, noon to 5pm; the rest of the year, Tuesdays to Fridays, 9am to 4pm, Saturdays, noon to 4pm, Sundays, noon to 5pm. Admission free. ☎ 090-171 800.

Umeå kyrka – Open late June to early August, Mondays to Thursdays, 8am to 9pm, Fridays 8am to 7pm. Saturdays and Sundays during the service.

UPPSALA
🚹 Fyris Torg 8 – 753 10 – ☎ 018-27 48 00

Domkyrkan – ♿ Open daily 8am to 6pm. ☎ 018-18 71 77 and 018-18 71 74

Museum – ♿ Open May to August, Mondays to Saturdays, 10am to 4.30pm, Sundays 12.30pm to 4.30pm; September to April, Sundays 12.30pm to 3pm; other times on request. 20SEK, children 10SEK. ☎ 018-18 71 77, 018-18 71 74.

Museum Gustavianum – ♿ Open mid-May to mid-September, daily 11am to 4pm; the rest of the year, Wednesdays to Sundays, 11am to 4pm; 40SEK, children (0-11) free. ☎ 018-471 75 71.

Universitetshuset – ♿ Guided tours mid-June to mid-August at 2pm. 40SEK. ☎ 018-471 75 71.

Walmstedtska Gården – Open only for booked groups. ☎ 018-16 91 00.

Upplandsmuseet – ♿ Open Wednesdays to Sundays, noon to 5pm. 20SEK, children (0-17) free. ☎ 018-16 91 00. www.uppmus.se

Carolina Rediviva – Open mid-June to mid–August, Mondays to Fridays, 9am to 5pm, Saturdays, 10am to 6 pm, Sundays, 11am to 4pm; the rest of the year, Mondays to Fridays, 9am to 8pm, Saturdays, 10am to 4pm. Admission fee (May to September) 10SEK. ☎ 018-471 39 00.

Slottet – Vasa Vignettes: May to late August, daily 11am to 4pm; late August to late September, Saturdays and Sundays, 11am to 4pm. Closed Midsummer's Eve. 35SEK, children 10SEK. ☎ 018-27 48 00.

Botaniska Trädgården – Park: daily, 7am to 7pm; Tropical Greenhouse: Mondays to Thursdays, 9.30am to 3.30pm, May to September, Saturdays, noon to 3pm; March to October, Sundays, noon to 3pm. 20SEK; Orangery, Mondays to Thursdays, 9.30am to 3.30pm, Fridays, 9.30am to 2.30pm. ☎ 018-471 28 38.

Linnéträdgården – ♿ (Garden only). Museum open June to August, Tuesdays to Sundays, noon to 4pm; May and September, some weekends, noon to 4pm. Admission free (garden), 20SEK (museum), children (0-14) free. ☎ 018-10 94 90 (garden) and 018-13 65 40 (museum).

Bror Hjorths Hus – ♿ Open early June to mid-August, Tuesdays to Sundays, noon to 4pm; the rest of the year, Thursdays, Saturdays and Sundays, noon to 4pm. 30SEK, children (0-18) free. ☎ 018-53 57 24.

Excursions

Linnés Hammarby – Museum open May to September, Tuesdays to Sundays, noon to 4pm. Park open May to September, daily 8am to 8pm. 10SEK, children (0-14) free. ☎ 018-32 60 94.

Härkeberga kyrka – ♿ Open May to October, daily 8am to 6pm; November to April, Saturdays and Sundays only. Guided tours in Swedish. ☎ 0171-41 40 21.

V

VADSTENA
𝐁 Rådhustorget – 592 80 – ☎ 0143-151 25

Klosterkyrkan – Open May and September, daily 9am to 5pm; June and August, daily 9am to 7pm; July, daily 9am to 8pm; October to April, Mondays to Saturdays, 9am to 4pm, Sundays, 10am to 1pm (Sundays in March and April, until 4pm). Guided tours on request through Vadstena Tourist Information. ☎ 0143-315 72.

Bjälboättens Palats – Open May to mid-June and first fortnight in September, guided tours only, daily at 2.15pm; last fortnight in June and August, guided tours daily at 10am, 11am, 2pm, 4pm; July, open 11am to 4pm. 30SEK, children (7-15) 10SEK. ☎ 0143-315 30. www.klosterhotel.se

Slottet – Guided tours daily June to August. Information and reservation through Vadstena Tourist Informaion Centre. 50SEK, children (7-15) 10SEK. ☎ 0143-315 70. www.tourist@vadstena.se

VARBERG
𝐁 Brunnsparken, Box 150 – 432 24 – ☎ 0340-887 70

Varberg Fortress – ♿ Open mid-June to August, Mondays to Fridays, 10am to 7pm, Saturdays and Sundays, noon to 4pm; September to mid-June, Mondays to Fridays, 10am to 4pm, Saturdays and Sundays, noon to 4pm. Guided tours (45min) in Swedish. 40SEK(summer), 20SEK(winter), children (6-15) 10SEK. ☎ 0340-185 20.

Kommunikationsmuseet – Open mid-June to mid-August, daily 10am to 6pm; the rest of the year, Sundays, noon to 4pm. Closed Midsummmer's Eve. 20SEK, children 10SEK. ☎ 0340-185 20.

Länsmuseet Varberg – Open mid-June to mid-August, daily 10am to 6pm; the rest of the year, Mondays to Fridays, 10am to 4pm, Saturdays and Sundays, noon to 4pm. Closed Midsummer's Eve. 40SEK, children 10SEK, 30SEK extra for guided tour. ☎ 0340-185 20.

VÄSTERÅS
𝐁 Stora Gatan 40 – 721 87 – ☎ 021-10 37 00

Domkyrkan – Open 15 June to 15 August, Mondays to Fridays, 8am to 7pm, Saturdays, 9.30am to 5pm, Sundays, 9.30am to 9pm; 15 August to 15 June, Mondays to Fridays, 8am to 5pm, Saturdays, 9.30am to 5pm, Sundays, 9.30am to 7pm. ☎ 021-13 13 25.

Västerås Konstmuseum – Open Tuesdays to Fridays, 10am to 5pm, Saturdays, 11am to 4pm, Sundays, noon to 4pm. ☎ 021-16 13 00.

Turbinhuset – Open May to August, 2pm to 3pm. ☎ 021-15 61 00.

Västerås Slott – Open Tuesdays to Sundays, noon to 4pm. ☎ 021-15 61 00.

Västmanlands läns Museum – The same opening times as Västerås Slott.

Excursions

Engsö Slott – Open May to August, Saturdays and Sundays, 1pm to 5pm; July to mid-August, Mondays to Thursdays, 1pm to 5pm. Closed Fridays. 50SEK. ☎ 0171-44 40 12. www.engsoslott.com

Engsö Naturreservat – Open May to August, Saturdays and Sundays, 1pm to 5pm; July to mid-August, Mondays to Thursdays, 1pm to 5pm. Closed Fridays. 50SEK. ☎ 0171-44 40 12, www.engsoslott.com

Vallby: **Friluftsmuseum** – Open daily 7am to 10pm. Guided tours in English. ☎ 021-16 16 70.

Tidö Slott: **Vagnmuseet** – ♿ Open May and September, Saturdays and Sundays, noon to 5pm; June to August, daily noon to 5pm. Guided tours in Swedish, daily at 3pm, during June to August; in English on request. 15SEK, children (7-15) 10SEK (Mansion 40SEK, children 15SEK.). ☎ 021-531 66.

Sala Sivergruva – Open May to August, daily 10am to 5pm. From 50SEK to 250SEK, children from 25 to 125SEK, depending on the tour chosen. ☎ 46 22 41 95 41.

VÄXJÖ
𝐁 Kungsgatan 11, Box 1222 – 35112 – ☎ 0470-414 10

Utvandrarnas Hus – Open June to September, Mondays to Fridays, 9am to 6pm, Saturdays and Sundays, 11am to 4pm; October to May, Mondays to Fridays, 9am to 4pm, Saturdays and Sundays, 11am to 4pm. 40SEK, children 5SEK. ☎ 0470-201 20. www.svenskaemigrantinstitutet.g.se

Smålands museum – ♿ Open June to August, Mondays to Fridays, 10am to 5pm, Saturdays and Sundays, 11am to 5pm; September to May, Tuesdays to Fridays, 10am to 5pm, Saturdays and Sundays, 11am to 5pm. 40SEK. ☎ 0470-451 45.

Domkyrkan – Open daily 9am to 5pm. ☎ 0470-70 48 24.

Orrefors, Åfors, Kosta Boda – ♿ Open Mondays to Fridays, 9am to 6pm, Saturdays, 10am to 4pm, Sundays, 11am to 4pm. Closed 1 January, Good Friday, Midsummer's Eve, 24-25 and 31 December. Guided tours in English from mid-June to mid-August, other times on request. Admission free. ☎ 0481-341 91 (Orrefors), 0478-345 00 (Kosta), 0481-424 09 (Boda), 0471-418 13 (Åfors).

Studioglas Strömbergshyttan – ♿ Open early June to mid-August, Mondays to Fridays, 9am to 6pm, Saturdays, 9am to 4pm, Sundays, 11am to 4pm; mid-August to early June, Mondays to Fridays, 9am to 4pm, Saturdays, 10am to 4pm, Sundays, noon to 4pm. Closed 1 and 6 January, Good Friday, Midsummer's Eve, 24-25 and 31 December; other public holidays phone in advance to check opening times. Friday afternoon to Sunday only shop open. ☎ 0478-310 75.

Y

YSTAD

🚍 St Knuts Torg – 271 42 – ☎ 0411-776 81

Sankta Maria Kyrkan – Open June and August, daily 10am to 6pm; September to May, daily 10am to 4pm. ☎ 0411-692 00.

Ystads Stadsmuseum – Open Mondays to Fridays, noon to 5pm, Saturdays and Sundays, noon to 4pm. 10SEK. ☎ 0411-772 86.

Ystad Konstmuseum – Open Tuesdays to Fridays, noon to 5pm; Saturdays and Sundays, noon to 4pm. 10SEK. ☎ 0411-772 85.

Ö

ÖLAND

🚍 Busstationen, Sandgatan 25 – 387 31 – ☎ 0485-890 12

Träffpunkten Öland – Open May to late June and August, Mondays to Fridays, 9am to 6pm, Saturdays, 10am to 5pm, Sundays, 10am to 4pm; late June and July, Mondays to Saturdays, 9am to 7pm, Sundays, 10am to 6pm; September to April, Mondays to Fridays, 9am to 5pm, Saturdays (in September only) 10am to 4pm. Admission free (except the Exhibitium Historium: 40SEK, children (7-15) 25SEK). ☎ 0485-390 00.

Borgholms Slott – Open May to August, daily 10am to 6pm; July, daily 10am to 9pm; April and September, daily 10am to 4pm. 40SEK, children (0-15) free. ☎ 0485-123 33.

Solliden – Open mid-May to mid-September, 1pm to 6pm; gates close at 5pm. 45SEK, children (under 10) free.

Borgholm – Summer, Mondays to Saturdays, 9am to 7pm, Sundays, 10am to 4pm; winter, Mondays to Fridays, 9am to 3.45pm. ☎ 0485-890 12.

Sandviks kvarn – Open mid-June to mid-August, 10am to 10pm; May to mid-June and mid-August to beginning of September, noon to 8pm. ☎ 0485-261 72, 260 36, Internet: www.sandvikskvarn.com

Källa kyrka – Open mid-May to end August, 10am to 5pm, on request. ☎ 0485-270 17.

Himmelsberga Museum – Open second week in May to mid-September, daily 10am to 6pm. 40SEK, children (0-15) free. ☎ 0485-561 022, 561 11.

Eketorp – Open May to Midsummer, and August to mid-September, daily 10am to 5pm; Midsummer to July, daily 10am to 6pm. Guided tours. 45SEK (Midsummer to July 50SEK), children 20SEK, children (0-14) with parents free. ☎ 0485-66 20 00. e-mail: eketorp@raa.se

SWEDEN

Jamtli – &. Open mid-June to mid-August, daily 11am to 5pm; the rest of the year, Tuesdays to Sundays, 11am to 5pm. Summer: 80SEK, children 25; winter: 50SEK, children (under 18) free. ☎ 063-15 01 00.

Jämtlands Läns Museum – Tuesdays to Sundays, 11am to 5pm; end June to end August, daily 11am to 5pm.

Excursion

Sommarhagen – Open Midsummer's Eve to first week in August, 11am to 6pm; first three weeks in June and second and third week in August, 11am to 3pm. 30SEK, children (0-15) free. ☎ 063-430 41.

Frösö kyrka – Open June to August, daily 8am to 8pm; September to May, daily 8am to 4pm. ☎ 063-16 11 50.

Östbergets utkikstorn – Open 5 June to mid-August, 9am to 9pm; mid-May to 4 June, 10am to 6pm; mid-August to mid-September, noon to 6pm. 8SEK, children (7-14) 3SEK. ☎ 063-11 57 67.

FINLAND

E

EKENÄS
🅑 Rådhustorget – 10601 – ☎ 19-263 2100

Ekenäs Museum – Open mid-May to mid-August, daily 11am to 5pm; mid-August to mid-May, Tuesdays to Thursdays, 6pm to 8pm, Fridays to Sundays, noon to 4pm. 10FIM, children 5FIM. ☎ 019-263 3161.

Ekenäs kyrka – Open daily in summer, 10am to 6pm. ☎ 019-2411 060.

Excursion

Snappertuna: Raasepori – Open May to August, daily 10am to 8pm. 5FIM, children 2FIM. ☎ 019-234 015.

Snappertuna kirkko – Open mid-May to mid-September; the rest of the year open on request. ☎ 019-234 052.

ESPOO

Espoon kirkko – Open summer, daily 10am to 8pm; the rest of the year, daily 10am to 6pm. ☎ 09-8050 202.

Gallen-Kallelan museo – Open mid-May to August, Mondays to Thursdays, 10am to 8pm, Fridays to Sundays, 10am to 5pm; September to 14 May, Tuesdays to Saturdays, 10am to 4pm, Sundays, 10am to 5pm. ☎ 09-541 3388. www.gallen-kallela.fi

H

HAMINA
🅑 Rautatienkatu 8 – 49400 – ☎ 05-749 5251

Hamina Town Hall – Open 17 May to 31 August, Mondays to Fridays, 9am to 6pm, Saturdays, 9am to 6pm, Sundays, 10am to 3pm.

HANKO

Hangon museo – Open May to August, Tuesdays to Sundays, 11am to 4pm (Thursdays also 6pm to 7pm); September to April, Wednesdays, Thursdays, Saturdays and Sundays, 1pm to 3pm (Thursdays also 6pm to 7pm). 10FIM, children 5FIM.

Vesitorni – Open mid-May to mid-June, daily 11am to 3pm; mid-June to mid-August, daily 10am to 6pm; 15 to 31 August, daily 11pm to 3pm. 5FIM, children 2FIM.

Hauensuoli – The waterbus Marina makes one excursion daily from the beginning of June to the end of August. 60FIM, children 30FIM. ☎ 019– 220 3411.

Neljän Tuulen Tupa – Open mid-May to mid-August. ☎ 019-2481 455.

HELSINKI
🅑 Pohjoisesplanadi 19 – 00100 – ☎ 09 169 3757

The Finnish Youth Hostel Association – Suomen Retkeilymajajärjestö– SRM ry, Finnish Youth Hostel Association– SRM, Yrjönkatu 38 B, FIN-00100 Helsinki, ☎ 09-694 0377, fax 09-693 1349.

Finnish Skating Association – Radiokatu 20, 00240 Helsinki, ☎ 09 3481 2479, Fax 09 3481 2095

City Tourist Office – ♿ Open in summer, Mondays to Fridays, 9am to 7pm, Saturdays and Sundays, 9am to 3pm; in winter, Mondays to Fridays, 9am to 5pm, Saturdays, 9am to 3pm. ☎ 09-169 3757.

Tuomiokirkko – Open daily 10am to 4pm. ☎ 09-709 2455.

Sederholmin talo – ♿ Open June to August, daily 11am to 5pm; September to May, Wednesdays to Saturdays, 11am to 5pm. Closed Easter, 1 May, Midsummer, 6, 24-25 December and 1 January. 20FIM, children (0-17) free; Thursdays admission free. Guided tours (45min) in English. ☎ 09-169 3625. www.hel.fi/kaumuseo/

Rutatieasema – ♿ Open Mondays to Fridays, 8am to 7pm, Saturdays, 8am to 4pm, Sundays, 9am to 6pm. Guided tours in English. ☎ 09-707 3519.

Euskuntatalo – Open July to August, Mondays to Fridays, 2pm, Saturdays, 11am to noon. Guided tours in English, Sundays at noon, 1pm. Admission free. ☎ 09-432 2027.

FINLAND

Finlandia-talo – & Guided tours by appointment only. 25FIM, children 15FIM. ☎ 09-402 4246.

Kansallisooppera / Nationaloperan – & Box Office: Mondays to Fridays 9am to 6pm, Saturdays 3pm to 6pm. Closed in July. ☎ 09-403 021.

Temppeliaukion kirkko – Open Mondays, Wednesdays, Thursdays and Fridays, 10am to 7pm; Tuesdays, 10am to 12.45pm and 2.15pm to 7pm; Saturdays, 10am to 6pm; Sundays, noon to 1.45pm and 3.15pm to 5.45pm. Church is closed during ceremonies and concerts. ☎ 09-494 698.

Ateneum,The Museum of Finnish Art – Open Tuesdays to Fridays, 9am to 6pm (Wednesdays and Thursdays until 8pm), Saturdays and Sundays, 11am to 5pm. Closed Mondays. 15FIM, children (0-18) free. ☎ 09-173 361. www.fng.fi.

Amos Andersonin taidemuseo – Open Mondays to Fridays, 10am to 6pm, Saturdays and Sundays, 11am to 5pm. 30FIM, children (0-18) free. ☎ 09-684 4460. www.amosanderson.fi

Kiasma – & Open Tuesdays, 9am to 5pm; Wednesdays to Sundays, 10am to 10pm; 1, 30 April and 31 December, 9am to 5pm. Closed Mondays, 1 January, 2, 4, 5 April, 1 May, 25, 26 June and 6, 24-26 December. 25FIM, children free. Guided tours (1hr) in English. ☎ 09-173 351. www.kiasma.fng.fi

Kansallismuseo – Open Tuesdays to Sundays, 11am to 6pm (Tuesdays and Wednesdays until 8pm). Closed Mondays. ☎ 09-405 01.

Helsingin kaupunginmuseo – Open Mondays to Fridays, 9am to 5pm, Saturdays and Sundays, 11am to 5pm. 20FIM, children (0-17) free; Thursdays admission free. ☎ 09-169 3933. www.hel.fi/kaumuseo/

Kulttuurien museo – Open Tuesdays to Sundays, 10am to 8pm. Closed Mondays. 25FIM. ☎ 358 9 405 09 09.

Helsingin Kaupungin taidemuseo – Open Tuesdays to Sundays, 11am to 8.30pm. Closed Mondays. 15-35FIM. 358 9 31 08 70 00.

Uspenskin katedraali – Open Mondays, Wednesdays, Thursdays and Fridays, 10am to 4pm; Tuesdays, 10am to 6pm; Saturdays, 9am to 4pm; Sundays, noon to 3pm. ☎ 09-634 267.

Cygnaeuksen galleria – Open Wednesdays, 11am to 7pm, Thursdays to Sundays, 11am to 4pm. Closed Mondays and Tuesdays. 15FIM, children (under 18) free. ☎ 09-656 928.

Mannerheim museo – Open Fridays to Sundays, 11am to 4pm. Closed 21 to 23 April, 23 to 25 June and 22 to 24 December. Guided tours only (1hr). 40FIM, children (0-12) free; 6 December admission free. ☎ 09-635 443.

Suomen Urheilumuseo – Open Mondays to Fridays, 11am to 5pm, Saturdays and Sundays, noon to 4pm. 20FIM, children 10FIM. ☎ 09-434 2250.

Taideteollisuusmuseo – Open Tuesdays, Thursdays and Sundays, 11am to 6pm, Wednesdays, 11am to 8pm. 40FIM, children (0-12) free. ☎ 09-622 0540.

Suomen rakennustaiteen museo – Exhibitions and bookshop open, Tuesdays to Sundays, 10am to 4pm (Wednesdays until 7pm); Archives department open Tuesdays to Fridays, 10am to 4pm. 10-20FIM. ☎ 358 9 66 19 18.

Sinebrychoffin taidemuseo – Open Mondays and Wednesdays to Fridays, 9am to 6pm (Wednesdays until 8pm), Saturdays and Sundays, 11am to 5pm. Closed Tuesdays. 10FIM, children (0-17) free. ☎ 09-1733 6460. www.fng.fi/

Ruiskumestarin talo – Open Wednesdays to Sundays, 11am to 5pm. Closed 2 May to 2 October. 15FIM. ☎ 09-135 1065.

Outskirts

Arabian museo – Open Mondays, 10am to 8pm, Tuesdays to Fridays, 10am to 6pm, Saturdays and Sundays, 9am to 3pm; apply in advance for factory tours. 10FIM, children 5FIM. ☎ 09-3939 260.

Seurasaari ulkomuseo – Open June to August, daily 11am to 5pm (Wednesdays until 7pm); last fortnight in May and first fortnight in September, Mondays to Fridays, 9am to 3pm, Saturdays and Sundays, 11am to 5pm. Closed 16 September to 14 May and 23 June. 20FIM, children (0-17) free; 18 May admission free. Guided tours (1hr) in English. ☎ 09-484 712.

Urho Kekkosen museo – Open daily (except Mondays from mid-August to mid-May) 11am to 5pm. Guided tours in English. 20FIM, children (0-17) free. ☎ 09-480 684. www.nba.fi

Suomenlinna – Area open all year round. Apply locally for opening times of the various museums. ☎ 09-169 3757. www.hel.fi/suomenlinna/

Excursions

Hvitträsk – Open June to August, Mondays to Fridays, 10am to 7pm, Saturdays and Sundays, 10am to 6pm; in the winter, Mondays to Fridays, 11am to 6pm, Saturdays and Sundays, 11am to 5pm. 20FIM, children and students 10FIM. ☎ 221 9230.

Mustion Linna – Open 25 April to 1 October, Mondays to Fridays, 11am to midnight, Saturdays, noon to midnight, Sundays, noon to 6pm; 10 January to 24 April and 2 October to 22 December, Mondays to Fridays only, 11am to 9pm. Closed 22 December to the end of the first week in January. 25FIM, children 10FIM. Guided tours (45min) only. ☎ 019-362 31.

Ainola: Sibelius' Home – Open June to August, Tuesdays to Sundays, 11am to 5pm; May and September, Wednesdays to Sundays, 11am to 5pm. Closed October to May. 20FIM, children 5FIM. Guided tours (40 min) in English. ☎ 09-287 322.

Halosenniemi – Open May to August, Tuesdays to Sundays, 11am to 7pm; September to April, Tuesdays to Sundays, 11am to 5pm. Closed 23 June, 24-25 December. 30FIM (25FIM in winter), children 10FIM. Guided tours (1hr) in English. ☎ 09-8718 3461.

Aleksis Kiven kuolinmökki – Open May to August, Tuesdays to Sundays, 11am to 6pm; September to mid-October, Tuesdays to Sundays, 11am to 5pm. Closed Mondays, 11 October to 1 May and 23 to 25 June. 5FIM, children 3FIM. Guided tours (30 min) in English. ☎ 09-8718 3461.

Vantaa: Heureka Tiedekeskus – ♿ Open daily 10am to 6pm. Closed Midsummer's Eve, 24 and 25 December. Guided tours in English. 65FIM, children 40FIM. ☎ 09-873 4142.

HYVINKÄÄ   🛈 Hämeenkatu 3 D – 05800 – ☎ 019-459 1275

Suomen Rautatiemuseo – Open June to 15 August, daily 11am to 5pm; 16 August to May, Tuesdays to Sundays, noon to 3pm. ☎ 019-456 4241.

HÄMEENLINNA   🛈 Sibeliuksenkatu 5 A – 131 00 – ☎ 019-14 26 49

Hämeen Linna – Open May to mid-August, daily 10am to 6pm; mid-August to April, daily 10am to 4pm. Closed Easter, Midsummer, 6 and 24-31 December and 1 January. 20FIM, children 10FIM. ☎ 03-675 6820. E-mail: hlinna@nba. fi

Sibeliuksen syntymäkoti – Open May to August, daily 10am to 4pm; September to April, daily noon to 4pm. Guided tours in English. 15FIM, children 5FIM. ☎ 03-621 27 55.

Taidemuseo – ♿ Open Tuesdays to Sundays, noon to 6pm (Thursdays until 8pm). Closed Mondays. On the eve of public holidays the museum closes at 4pm. 20FIM. Guided tours, 100FIM. ☎ 03-621 2669 and 03-621 3017.

Excursions

Aulanko: Belvedere – Open June to mid-August, daily 11am to 7pm. 6FIM, children 3FIM.

Hattulan kirkko – Open 15 May to 16 August, daily; the rest of the year on request. ☎ 03-637 2477.

Suomen Lasimuseo – Open May to August, daily 10am to 6pm; September to December and February to April, Tuesdays to Sundays, 10am to 6pm. Closed January. 20FIM, children 10FIM. ☎ 019-741 7494. www.riihimaki.fi/lasimus/

Riihimäki: Suomen Metsästysmuseo – Open May to August, daily 10am to 6pm; September to April, Tuesdays to Sundays, 10am to 6pm. Closed January. 20FIM, children 10FIM. ☎ 019-72 22 93. www.kolumbus.fi/metsastysmuseo/. E-mail: metsastysmuseo@kolumbus. fi

Visavuori, Emil Wikströmin museo – ♿ Open May to September, Mondays, 11am to 5pm, Tuesdays to Sundays, 11am to 7pm; October to April, Tuesdays to Sundays, 1pm to 5pm. Closed Mondays, 24-26 December and Good Friday. ☎ 03-543 6528.

I

IISALMI   🛈 Kauppakatu 22 – 741 00 – ☎ 977-150 1223

Evakkokeskus – Open June to August, daily 8pm to 6pm; September to May, daily 8am to 4pm. ☎ 017-816 441.

IMATRA   🛈 Liikekeskus Mansikkapaikka, PO Box 22 – 551 21 – ☎ 954-681 25 00

Imatrankoski – Open 7 June to 8 August, daily 10am to 6pm, Sundays, 10am to 5pm.

Kolmen Ristin kirkko – Open June to August, daily 9am to 8pm; September to May, daily 10am to 3pm. ☎ 05-682 711.

INGÅ

Ingå kyrka – Open May to September, Mondays to Fridays, 8am to 4pm, Saturdays and Sundays, 9am to 6pm; the rest of the year, Mondays to Fridays, 8am to 4pm. ☎ 09-221 2101.

Fagervik Museiväg – Guided tours only. ☎ 09-295 151.

J

JOENSUU
🖃 Koskikatu 1 – 801 00 – ☎ 013-267 53 00

Ortodoksinen Pyhän Nikolaoksen kirkko – Open 12 June to 13 August, Mondays to Fridays, 10am to 4pm. ☎ 013-220 447.

Taidemuseo – Open Tuesdays to Sundays, 11am to 4pm (Wednesdays until 8pm). Closed Mondays. 20FIM, children (5-18) 5FIM. ☎ 013-267 5391. www.jns.fi/taidemuseo

Pohjois-Karjalan museo – Open Mondays to Fridays, 9am to 6pm, Saturdays and Sundays, 10am to 4pm. 25FIM, children (3-15) 10FIM. ☎ 013-267 5384. www.carelicum. fi.

Tori – Open June to August, Mondays to Fridays, 7am to 5pm, Saturdays, 7am to 2pm.

Excursions

Ilomantsi: Runonlaulajan Pirtti – Open June to August, daily 10am to 7pm. 10FIM, children 5FIM, includes guide. ☎ 013-212 48.

Uusi Valamo – Open June to August, daily 10am to 5pm; September to May on request. 15FIM, children (4-14) 5FIM. ☎ 017-570 111. www.valamo.fi

JYVÄSKYLÄ
🖃 Asemakatu 6 – 40100 – ☎ 014-624 903

Alvar Alto museo – Open Tuesdays to Sundays, 11am to 6pm. Closed Mondays. 10FIM. ☎ 014-624 809. wwwalvaraalto. fi

Keski-Suomen museo – Open Tuesdays to Sundays, 11am to 6pm. Closed Mondays. 20FIM, children free; Fridays admission free. ☎ 014-624 930.

Suomen käsityön museo – Open Tuesdays to Sundays, 11am to 6pm. Closed public holidays. Guided tours. 20FIM, children free; Fridays admission free. ☎ 014-624 946. www.jkl.fi/kultuur/craftmus/

Kansallispukukeskus – Open Tuesdays to Sundays, 11am to 6pm. Closed Mondays. 10FIM. ☎ 014-626 840.

Vesilinnan Näkötorni – Open June and July, daily 11am to 8pm; May and August, daily 11am to 6pm. 5FIM, children (0-15) 3FIM. ☎ 014-626 701.

Laajavuori – Open June to mid-August, daily 11am to 7pm. 5FIM. ☎ 014-624 885.

Excursions

Muurame: Sauna Village – Open 5 June to 27 August, daily 10am to 6pm. 20FIM. ☎ 014-373 2070. www.muurame.fi

Kivikauden kylä – Open mid-May to 4 June, Mondays to Fridays, 10am to 4pm; 5 to 19 June, Tuesdays to Sundays, noon to 7pm; 20 June to 30 July, daily noon to 7pm; August, Tuesdays to Sundays, 10am to 4pm.

JÄRVI-SUOMI

Lahti: Näkötorni – Open May to August, daily 10am to 6pm. 10FIM, children 5FIM. ☎ 918-733 0103.

Hiihtomuseo – Open Mondays to Fridays, 10am to 5pm, Saturdays and Sundays 11am to 5pm. 20FIM, children 10FIM. ☎ 03-814 4523.

Ristin kirkko – Open daily 10am to 3pm. Guided tours on request. ☎ 03-891 241.

Hollolan kirkko – Open in summer daily 11am to 6pm.

Verla Mill museum – Open 2 May to 16 September, daily 10am to 6pm. 30FIM, children 12FIM. ☎ 0204 15 21 00.

Hartola: Itä-Hämeen museo – Open mid-May to mid-August, 11am to 6pm. ☎ 918-161 252.

Pyhäniemen Artcastle Hollola – Open 11 June to 13 August, 11am to 6pm. 45FIM, children 20FIM (including coffee). ☎ 03-788 1466. www. festivals. fi/pyhaniemi

Joutsa: Talomuseo – Open June to mid-August, Mondays to Saturdays, 10am to 4pm, Sundays, noon to 6pm. 3FIM, children 1FIM. ☎ 03-714 4199 and 014-882 748.

Mikkeli: **Kivisakasti** – Open June to August, 11am to 5pm.

Naisvuoren näkötorni – Open June to mid-August, daily 10am to 9pm; May and last fort-night in August, Saturdays and Sundays, 10am to 6pm. 6FIM, children (4-12) 3FIM.

Päämajamuseo – Open mid-May to August, daily 10am to 5pm. 10FIM, children (0-18) free. ☎ 015– 194 2427, 194 2424.

Jälkaväkimuseo – Open mid-June to mid-August, 10am to 5pm. 10FIM, children (under 7) 5FIM.

Varkaus kirkko – Open June to August, daily 9am to 6pm; the rest of the year on request. ☎ 017-5785 207.

Mekaanisen musiikin museo – Open July, daily 10am to 6pm; June and August, Tuesdays to Sundays, 11am to 6pm; March to May and September to mid-December, Tuesdays to Saturdays, 11am to 6pm, Sundays, 11am to 5pm. Closed January and February. 50FIM, children (8-15) 25FIM, children (0-7) free. ☎ 017-5580 643.

K

KAJAANI
☒ Pohjolankatu 16, PO Box 133 – 871 01 – ☎ 08-15 58 45

Castle Ruins and Tar Lock – Ruins open all year round. Lock-keeper's hut open sec-ond week in June to first week in August, Tuesdays to Sundays, 11am to 5pm. Admission free. ☎ 08-615 5410(summer) and 08-615 5407(winter).

Luterilainen kirkko – Open 10 June to 13 August, daily 10am to 6pm; the rest of the year, on request 5pm to 7pm. ☎ 08-617 21.

Kainuun museo – Open Mondays to Fridays, noon to 3pm (Wednesdays until 8pm), Sundays, noon to 5pm. Closed Saturdays. 10FIM, children 5FIM.

Excursion

Paltaniemin kirkko – Open 18 May to 13 August, daily 10am to 6pm. ☎ 08-615 5555.

KEMI
☒ Kauppakatu 22 – 941 00 – ☎ 016-19 94 65

Jäänmurtaja Sampo – Open mid-May to mid-August, daily 11am to 8pm. ☎ 016-256 548 and 016-282 001. www.kemi.fi/sampo.htm

Jalokivigalleria – Open daily 10am to 5pm. 25FIM, children (7-15) 10FIM.

KEURUU
☒ Multiantie 5 – 427 01 – ☎ 014-751 7144

Vanha kirkko – Open June to August, daily 10am to 5pm. 5FIM.

Excursions

Pihjaiaveden vanha kirkko – Open June to August, Saturdays and Sundays, noon to 6pm. ☎ 014-753 302.

Gösta Serlachiuksen taidemuseo – Open June to August, Tuesdays to Sundays, 11am to 6pm; September to May, Saturdays and Sundays, noon to 5pm; other times on request. 30FIM, children (4-16) 5FIM. Guided tours on request: 200FIM, surcharge on Sundays. ☎ 03-474 5500.

KOKKOLA

Historiallinen museo – Open Tuesdays to Fridays, noon to 3pm (Thursdays also 6pm to 8pm), Saturdays and Sundays, noon to 5pm. 3.35FIM , students 0.84FIM , chil-dren free.

Kaarlelan kirkko – Open June to August, daily 10am to 6pm. ☎ 06-829 6111 and 06-831 1902.

Excursion

Väinöntalo – Open mid-May to August, daily 11am to 6pm. 15FIM, children 10FIM. ☎ 06-765 3160.

KOTKA
☒ Keskuskatu 7 – 481 00 – ☎ 52-227 4424

St Nicholas Othodox Church – Open June to mid-August, Tuesdays to Sundays, noon to 3pm. Closed Mondays.

Langinkoski Imperial Fishing Lodge – Open May to August, daily 11am to 7pm; September and October, Saturdays to Sundays, 10am to 7pm, Saturdays and Sundays by arangement. Closed in winter. 15FIM, children 5FIM. ☎ 522-810 50.

KRISTINESTAD ⊞ c/o Vasa City Tourist Inf., Hovioikeudenpuistikko 11 – 651 01 – ☎ 961-325 1145

Ulrika Eleonora kyrka – Open in summer, Mondays to Fridays and Sundays, 9am to 4pm. ☎ 016-2211 073.

Excursion

Lappfjärds kyrka – Open mid-May to August, Mondays to Fridays, 9am to 4pm, Saturdays, 9am to 2pm, Sundays, 9am to noon; the rest of the year, guided tours only. ☎ 06-2221 106.

KUHMO
⊞ Kainuuntie 82 – 889 01 – ☎ 986-655 6382

Kuhmon-talo – Open mid-June to mid-August, daily, according to programme of concerts and exhibitions. ☎ 08-655 6750.

Kuhmo kirkko – Open June to mid-August, daily 10am to 6pm.

Kalevala-kylä – Open 5 June to 27 August, daily 9.30am to 5pm; May and September on request for groups. 60FIM, children 30FIM. ☎ 08 655 4500. www.kuhmonet.fi/kalevalakyla

KUOPIO
⊞ Haapaniemenkatu 17 – 701 10 – ☎ 017-182 584

Ortodoksinen kirkkomuseo – Open June to mid-August, Mondays to Fridays, 10am to 4pm, Sundays, noon to 6pm. Closed Mondays.

Tuomiokirkko – Open June to July, daily 10am to 5pm; August to May, daily 10am to 3pm.

Tori – Open mid-April to September, Mondays to Fridays, 7am to 5pm, Saturdays, 7am to 2pm; the rest of the year, daily 7am to 2pm.

Kuopion museo – Open Mondays to Saturdays, 9am to 4pm (Wednesdays until 8pm), Sundays, 11am to 6pm. Closed Saturdays from September to April. 20FIM, children (0-6) free. ☎ 017-182 603.

Kuopion korttelimuseo – Open mid-May to mid-September, daily 10am to 5pm (Wednesdays until 7pm); 2 January to 14 May and 16 September to 31 December, Tuesdays to Sundays, 10am to 3pm. 15FIM, children (0-16) free. ☎ 017-182 625.

JV Snellmanin Kotimuseo – Open mid-May to August, daily 10am to 5pm (Wednesdays also 5pm to 7pm). 10FIM, children (under 16) free. ☎ 017-182 624.

Puijon näkötorni – Open daily 10am to 10pm. 15FIM, children 5FIM. ☎ 017-209 111.

KUUSAMO
⊞ Torangintaival 2 – 936 00 – ☎ 989-850 2910

Karhuntassu Tourist & Nature Centre – Open mid-June to mid-August, daily 9am to 7pm; mid-August to mid-September, Mondays to Fridays, 9am to 5pm, Saturdays, 10am to 4pm; mid-September to mid-June, Mondays to Fridays, 9am to 5pm. ☎ 08-850 2910. E-mail: ktassu@kuusamo.fi

Excursion

Rukatunturi – For further information call the tourist office.

Oulangan Kansallispuisto – Information centre open mid-June to mid-August, daily 10am to 8pm; May to mid-June and mid-August to September, daily 10am to 6pm; October and mid-February to April, daily 10am to 4pm. Closed November to mid-February. ☎ 0205646850.

L

LAPPEENRANTA
⊞ Bus Station, PO Box 113 – 531 01 – ☎ 953-415 68 60

Ratsuväkimuseo – Open June to late August, Mondays to Fridays, 10am to 6pm, Saturdays and Sundays, 11am to 5pm; the rest of the year by appointment only. 20FIM, children, 10FIM. ☎ 05-6162 257.

Majurska – Café open daily 10am to 5pm. ☎ 05-453 0554.

Ortodoksinen kirkko – Open June to mid-August, Tuesdays to Sundays, noon to 4.30pm. ☎ 05-451 55 11.

Etelä-Karjalan museo & Taidemuseo – ⅙ Open June to August, Mondays to Fridays, 10am to 6pm, Saturdays and Sundays, 11am to 5pm; September to May, Tuesdays to Thursdays, 11am to 5pm, Saturdays and Sundays, 11am to 5pm. Closed Mondays and Fridays. June to August: 20FIM, children (7-16) 10FIM; September to May: 15FIM, children (7-16) 7FIM. ☎ 05-616 2255 (Museo) and 05-616 2256 (Taidemuseo).

Tori – Open mid-May to mid-August, Mondays to Fridays, 7am to 7pm, Saturdays, 7am to 2pm; mid-August to mid-May, Mondays to Saturdays, 7am to 2pm.
Market Hall open Mondays to Fridays, 8am to 5pm, Saturdays, 8am to 2pm.

Lappeen kirkko – Open June to August, daily 10am to 7pm.

Excursions

Saimaan kanava – Cruises available mid-May to mid-August; cruises to Vyborg, Russia till mid-September. ☎ 05-66 77 88.

Lauritsalan kirkko – Open in summer, daily 10am to 5pm. ☎ 05-612 6400.

Ylämaan Jalokivikylä – Village open all year round. Museum open in summer, daily noon to 6pm; other times on request. 10FIM, children (0-12) free.

LAPPI

Sodankylä: **Vanha kirkko** – Open June to mid-August, daily 9am to 6pm; last fortnight in August, Fridays to Mondays, 10am to 6pm. ☎ 016-611 018.

Alariesto Gallery – Open summer, Mondays to Saturdays, 10am to 5pm, Sundays, noon to 6pm; winter, Mondays to Fridays, 10am to 5pm, Saturdays, 10am to 4pm, Sundays, noon to 4pm. 20FIM, students 10FIM. ☎ 016-618 643.

Urho Kekkosen kansallispuisto – Open June to September, daily 9am to 6pm; October to April, Mondays to Fridays, 9am to 4pm. ☎ 0205 64 7251. E-mail: ukpuisto@metsa.fi

Tankavaara: Kultakylä – Open June to September, daily 9am to 6pm (mid-August to September until 5pm); October to May, Mondays to Fridays, 9am to 4pm. ☎ 016-626 158.

Saariselkä – ☎ 016-819 01.

Inarijärvi – Cruises June and August, daily at 1pm; July, daily at 1pm and 6pm.

Saamelaiskirkko – Open on request June to mid-August, daily 9am to 9pm, Sundays, only when there is the service. ☎ 040-7328265.

Siida – Open June to September, daily 9am to 8pm; October to May, Tuesdays to Sundays, 10am to 5pm. 40FIM, children 15FIM. Guided tours (1hr) on request. ☎ 016-665 212.

Pielpajärven erämaakirkko – Open mid-June to mid-August, daily.

Lemmenjoen kansallispuisto – Open June to mid-September, daily 9am to 7pm. ☎ 0205-647 793.

LOHJA
🛈 Kalevankatu 4 – 08100 – ☎ 912-201 217

Pyhän Laurin kirkko – Open daily 10am to 3pm. ☎ 369 1309.

LOVIISA
🛈 Mannerheiminkatu 4 – 07900 – ☎ 915-533 212

Town Hall – Open Mondays to Fridays, 8am to 4pm. Closed 2 weeks in July. Guided tours on request. ☎ 019-555 234.

Loviisan kirkko – Open May to August, daily 10am to 7pm; the rest of the year on request. ☎ 019-532 043.

Excursions

Ruotsinpyhtään ruukkialue – ♿ Open June to mid-August, daily 10am to 6pm; mid-August to May, Mondays to Fridays, 8am to 4pm. Closed Saturdays and Sundays. Guided tours in English. 10FIM, children free. ☎ 019-618 474.

Pyhtään kirkko – Open June to mid-August, daily noon to 6pm. ☎ 05-343 1921.

N

NAANTALI
🛈 Kaivotori 2 – 211 00 – ☎ 02-850

Luostarikirkko – Open 2 May to August, daily noon to 8pm. Guided tours on request. ☎ 02-435 0850.

OULU
🛈 Torikatu 10 – 90100 – ☎ 08-314 1295

Tuomiokirkko – Open June to 20 August, daily 11am to 8pm; the rest of the year, daily noon to 1pm. ☎ 08-3161401.

Pohjois-Pohjanmaan museo – Open Mondays to Thursdays, 8am to 4pm, Fridays closed, Saturdays and Sundays, 11am to 5pm. 10FIM, children 3FIM. ☎ 08-550 47150.

Taidemuseo – Open Tuesdays to Sundays, 11am to 6pm (Wednesdays until 8pm). Closed Mondays. 15FIM, children (0-7) free; Fridays admission free. ☎ 08-558 47463. www. ouka. fi/taidemuseo

Turkansaaren ulkomuseo – Open June to August, daily 11am to 8pm, first fortnight in September, 11am to 5pm. 10FIM, children 3FIM. ☎ 08-55867190.

P

PIELINEN
🛈 Lieksa Tourist Service, Pielisentie 7 – 817 00 – ☎ 975-520 2400

Lieksa: Pielisen museo – Open mid-May to mid-September, daily 10am to 6pm; 16 September to 14 May, Tuesdays to Fridays, 10am to 3pm. Closed Saturdays to Mondays, Midsummer's Eve. 20FIM, children 8FIM. Guided tours (1hr). ☎ 013-520 2402.

Kirkko – Open June to mid-August, daily 11am to 7pm. Other times for groups on request. ☎ 013-520 2400.

Eva Ryynäsen ateljee – ♿ Open mid-May to mid-September, daily 10am to 6pm; in winter for groups only, on request. 25FIM, children 15FIM. Guided tours (45min) in English. ☎ 013-520 2400.

Bomban Talo – Open 16 June to August, Mondays to Fridays and Sundays, 8am to 11pm, Saturdays, 8am to 2am; September to 15 June, Mondays to Fridays and Sundays, 11am to 11pm, Saturdays, 11am to 1am. Guided tours (1-2hr) in English. ☎ 013-687 200.

PORI
🛈 Hallituskatu 9A – 281 00 – ☎ 939-35 57 80

Juseliuksen Mausoleumi – Open May to August, daily noon to 3pm; the rest of the year, Sundays only, noon to 2pm. ☎ 02-623 87 46.

Satakunnan museo – Open Tuesdays to Sundays, 11am to 5pm. Closed Mondays. 10FIM, children (7-17) 3FIM. ☎ 02-621 1078. www.pori.fi/smu E-mail: leena. sammallahti@pori. fi

PORVOO
🛈 Rihkamakatu 4 – 06100 – ☎ 019-580 145

Tuomiokirkko – Open May to September, Mondays to Fridays, 10am to 6pm, Saturdays, 10am to 2pm, Sundays and public holidays, 2pm to 5pm; October to April, Tuesdays to Saturdays, 10am to 2pm, Sundays, 2pm to 4pm. ☎ 019-661 11.

Historiallinen museo – Open May to August, daily 11am to 4pm; September to April, Wednesdays to Sundays, noon to 4pm. 20FIM, children (7-16) 5FIM; (combined ticket with Porvoon Museo/ Edelfelt-Vallgren Museo). ☎ 019-574 7500.

Edelfelt-Vallgren museo – Open May to August, daily 11am to 4pm; September to April, Wednesdays to Sundays, noon to 4pm. 20FIM, children (7-16) 5FIM; (same ticket valid for Porvoon Museo/ Historiallinen Museo). ☎ 019-574 75 00.

Vanha Kappalaisentalo – Open Sundays to Thursdays, 10am to 5pm, Fridays and Saturdays, 10am to 4pm. 5FIM. ☎ 019-523 0052.

Runebergin koti – Open May to August, Mondays to Saturdays, 10am to 4pm, Sundays, 11am to 5pm; September to April, Wednesdays to Saturdays, 10am to 4pm, Sundays, 11am to 5pm. 15FIM, children (5-15) 7.50FIM (combined ticket with Runebergin koti and Walter Runebergin veistoskokoelma). ☎ 019-581 330.

Walter Runebergin veistoskokoelma – Open May to August, Mondays to Saturdays, 10am to 4pm, Sundays, 11am to 5pm; September to April, Wednesdays to Sundays, 10am to 3pm. 15FIM, children (5-15) 7.50FIM (combined ticket with Walter Runebergin veistoskokoelma and Runebergin koti). ☎ 019-582 186.

Excursion

Savilinna – Open all year round, Mondays to Fridays, 10am to 5pm, Saturdays, 10am to 1pm. Closed Sundays. Guided tours on request. ☎ 019-58 34 83.

Sepänmäki käsityömuseo – Open mid-May to August, Tuesdays to Sundays, noon to 6pm. 15FIM. ☎ 019-689 0275.

Alikartano-Frugård – Open mid-May to August, daily 11am to 5pm. Guided tours in English available. 15FIM, children 10FIM. ☎ 358 19 68 83 398.

R

RAUMA
Valtakatu 2 – 261 00 – ☎ 02-834 4551

Pyhän Ristin kirkko – Open June to August, daily 10am to 5pm; other times on request.

Rauman museo – Open 15 May to August, daily 10am to 5pm; September to 14 May, Tuesdays to Fridays, 10am to 5pm, Saturdays, 10am to 2pm, Sundays, 10am to 5pm. Closed Mondays and public holidays. Guided tours for groups on request. 10FIM, children (0-18) free. ☎ 02-834 3532.

Marela – Same opening and entry ticket as Rauman museo. ☎ 02-834 3525.

ROVANIEMI
Aallonkatu 1 – 962 00 – ☎ 960-346 270

Arktikum – Open September to April, Tuesdays to Sundays, 10am to 6pm; May to mid-June, daily 10am to 6pm; 16 June to 15 August, daily 9am to 7pm, 16 August to 31 August; daily 10am to 6pm. Guided tours on Saturdays and Sundays, 330FIM. 50FIM, children (7-15) 20FIM. ☎ 317 840. www.arktikum.fi

Rovaniemi kirkko – Open 17 May to 30 September, daily 9am to 9pm. ☎ 016-33 55 11.

Lapin metsämuseo – Open 1 June to 31 August, Tuesdays to Sundays, noon to 6pm. 10FIM, children 5FIM. ☎ 016-3482083.

Excursion

Santapark – Open mid-May to August, daily 11am to 6pm; the rest of the year, opening times vary. 95FIM, children 65FIM. ☎ 358 16 333 00 00.

S

SAVONLINNA
Puistokatu 1 – 571 00 – ☎ 957-27 34 92

Olavinlinna – Open June to mid-August, daily 10am to 5pm; mid-August to May, 10am to 3pm. Closed Good Friday, 11 April, 1 May, 6, 24-25 December and 1 to 6 January. Guided tours in English: June to August every full hour. 20FIM, children (7-17) 15FIM. ☎ 015-531 164.

Maakuntamuseo – Open July, daily 10am to 8pm; August, daily 11am to 6pm; September to June, Tuesdays to Sundays, 11am to 5pm. Closed Mondays. 20FIM, children (0-14) free. ☎ 015-571 4710.

Excursion

Rauhalinna – Open June to August. ☎ 015-52 31 19.

Retretti Taidekeskus – Open June and August, daily 10am to 5pm; July, daily 10am to 6pm. Guided tours in English on request. 75FIM, children (7-16) 30FIM, families 185FIM. ☎ 015-644 253. www. retretti. fi

Kerimäki kirkko – Open first fortnight in June, daily 10am to 5pm, mid-June to first week in August, daily 10am to 6pm, the rest of August, daily 10am to 4pm. ☎ 015-578 9123.

SUOMUSSALMI
in Ämmänsaari, PO Box 110 – 896 01 – ☎ 986-719 1243

Suomussalmi kirkko – Open summer 10am to 6pm daily.

Lake Kianta Cruise – Departure 24 June to 18 August, 11am and 3pm daily (minimum 10 passengers). 40FIM, children 20FIM. ☎ 986-711 052, 7191 243.

Raateen portti – Open June to mid-September, daily 10am to 6pm; May and mid-September to October, Fridays to Sundays 11am to 5pm. 30FIM, children 10FIM. ☎ 08-721 450.

T

TAMPERE
Box 487 – 33101 – ☎ 3 3146 6800

Tuomiokirkko – Open May to August, daily 9am to 6pm; in winter, 11am to 3pm. ☎ 03-2190 705.

Tampere-talo – Guided tours on request, Mondays to Fridays 280FIM, Saturdays and Sundays 320FIM. Ticket prices for concerts, operas and ballets, 50-500FIM/ticket. ☎ 03-243 4111. www.tampere.fi/TampereHall/

Kalevan kirkko – Open summer, daily 9am to 6pm; winter, daily 11am to 3pm. ☎ 03-219 0705.

Ortodoksinen kirkko – Open May to August, Mondays to Fridays, 10am to 4pm; other times on request. Guided tours. ☎ 03-3141 2724.

Museokeskus Vapriikki – Open Tuesdays to Sundays, 10am to 6pm. Guided tours 100FIM. ☎ 03-314 66966. www.tampere.fi/vapri/.

Kirjasto – Open June to August, Mondays to Fridays, 9.30am to 7pm, Saturdays 9.30am to 3pm; September to May, Mondays to Fridays, 9.30am to 8pm, Saturdays, 9.30am to 3pm, Sundays, noon to 6pm. ☎ 03-314 614. www.tampere. fi/kirjasto/

Särkännniemi – Amusement park and zoo open in the summer; Aquarium, Näsinneilla tower, planetarium, dolphinaruim and Sara Hildén's art gallery open all year round.

Sara Hildénin taidemuseo – Open daily 11am to 6pm. 20FIM, children (0-7) free, students 10FIM. Guided tours for groups on request. ☎ 03-214 3134. www. tampere. fi/culture/hilden.

Amurin työläismuseo – Open mid-May to mid-September, Tuesdays to Sundays, 10am to 6pm. Closed Mondays. Guided tours. ☎ 03-3146 6690.

Lenin museo – Open Mondays to Fridays, 9am to 6pm, Saturdays and Sundays, 11am to 4pm. 20FIM, children 10FIM, children (0-6) free. ☎ 03-276 8100. www. tampere. fi/culture/lenin/. E-mail: lenin@sci. fi

Excursions

Haiharan nukke-ja pukumuseo – Open May to August, Tuesdays to Saturdays, 10am to 5pm, Sundays, noon to 5pm; September to April, Wednesdays to Sundays, noon to 5pm; open other times on request. 30FIM, children (7-15) 5FIM, family 50FIM. Guided tours on request. ☎ 03-222 6261. www. sgic. fi/~haihara/

Lake cruises: Finnish Silverline – Open (office hours) 6 June to 20 August, Mondays to Fridays, 8.30am to 5pm, Saturdays, 8.30am to 1pm; the rest of the year, Mondays to Fridays, 9am to 4pm, Saturdays closed. ☎ 03-212 4804.

Mobilia – Reservation through Tampere City Tourist Office. ☎ 931-212 6652.

Nuutajärvi Glass Factory – Museum open summer, daily 10am to 6pm; winter, Saturdays and Sundays only, 10am to 6pm; shop and café open May to August, daily 9am to 8pm; September to April, 10am to 6pm; guided tours. ☎ 37 54 96 501.

TURKU
🛈 Aurakatu 4 – 201 00 – ☎ 358 2 262 7444

Tuomiokirkko – Open 16 September to 15April, daily 9am to 7pm; 16 April to 15 September, daily 9am to 8pm. 10FIM, children (0-15) free. ☎ 02-251 0651.

Sibelius-museo – Open Tuesdays to Sundays, 11am to 3pm (Wednesdays also 6pm to 8pm). Closed Easter, 1 May, Midsummer, 6, 24-26 December and 1 January. 15FIM, children 5FIM. Guided tours (40min) in English. ☎ 02-215 4494.

Museo Ett Hem – Open 1 June to 30 September, Tuesdays to Sundays, noon to 3pm. Closed 1 to October. 15FIM, children 5FIM. Guided tours (1hr) in English are available. ☎ 215 4279.

Aboa Vetus and Ars Nova – Open May to August, daily 10am to 7pm; September to April, Tuesdays to sundays, 11am to 7pm. 35-50FIM, children 30-40FIM. ☎ 358 22 50 05 52.

Merenkulkumuseo – ♿ Open daily 8am to 8pm. Closed Easter, 1 May, 6, 24-25 December and 1 January. 30FIM, children 15FIM. Guided tours (1hr) in English. ☎ 02-282 9511.

Käsityöläismuseo – Open 16 April to 15 September, daily 10am to 6pm; 16 September to mid-April, Tuesdays to Sundays, 10am to 3pm. Closed Good Friday, 1 May, Midsummer, 6, 24 and 25 December. Guided tours (1hr) in English. 20FIM, children 15FIM. ☎ 02-262 0350.

Wäinö Aaltosen museo – ♿ Open Tuesdays to Sundays, 11am to 7pm. Guided tours (45min). 15FIM, children 8FIM; during special exhibitions higher prices. ☎ 02-235 5690. www.wam.fi.

Suomen Joutsen – Open June to August. Guided tours only. ☎ 02-262 0401.

Museoalus Sigyn – Open 10 May to 15 August, 10am to 6pm. Guided tours (45min) in English. ☎ 02-282 9511.

Turun Linna – Open 16 April to 15 September, daily 10am to 6pm; 16 September to 15 April, Mondays, 2pm to 7pm, Tuesdays to Sundays, 10am to 3pm. Closed Good Friday, 1 May, Midsummer, 6, 24 and 25 December. 30FIM, children 20FIM. Guided tours (1hr to 1hr 30min) in English. ☎ 02-262 0300.

Taidemuseo – Open in summer, Mondays, Tuesdays and Fridays, 10am to 4pm (Wednesdays and Thursdays until 7pm), Sundays, 11am to 6pm (in winter, Thursdays until 7pm. Closed Mondays. 30FIM, children (0-7) free. Guided tours (1hr). ☎ 02-274 7570.

Apteekkimuseo – Open 16 April to 15 September, 10am to 6pm; 16 September to 15 April, 10am to 3pm.

Excursions

Masku kirkko – Open June to mid-August on request.

Nousiainen kirkko – Open 1 June to 15 August, noon to 6pm; other times on request. ☎ 921-4318 549.

Mynämäki kirkko – Open 10 June to 20 August, daily 11am to 5pm; other times on request.

Askainen kirkko – Open on request. ☎ 921-4314 709.

Louhisaari – Open mid-May to August, daily 11am to 5pm; September open for groups on request. Closed October to mid-May. 20FIM, children (0-17) free. Guided tours (1hr) in English. ☎ 02-431 2555.

Lemu kirkko – Open on request. ☎ 921-4314 709.

Raisio kirkko – Open 4 June to 13 August, daily 9am to 8pm; other times on request. ☎ 02-436 0300.

Lieto kirkko – Open 1 June to 31 July, 10am to 6pm daily; other times on request. ☎ 921-4894 122.

Pukkila – Open 1 June to 15 August, daily 11am to 5pm; in May, end August and September, groups by appointement. Closed 1 January to April and 1 October to December. 10FIM, children (under 18) free. Guided tours (45min) in English available. ☎ 02-479 5320.

Pargas / Parainen: kirkko – Open only on request. ☎ 921-4544 448.

Nagu / Nauvo: kirkko – Open mid-May to August, 9am to 6pm. ☎ 02-465 1000.

Korpo / Korppoo: kirkko – Open June to mid-August, daily 9am to 6pm; other times on request. ☎ 02-458 5942.

Sagalund museum – Open June to August, Tuesdays to Sundays, noon to 5pm. 20FIM, children free. Guided tours. ☎ 02-421 738.

Söderlångvik museum – Open 15 May to 31 August, daily 11am to 6pm. Closed Midsummer. 20FIM, children free. ☎ 02-424 662.

Dalsbruk – Open June to August, Tuesdays to Sundays, noon to 6pm. 10FIM, children (under 16) free. ☎ 925-622 00.

V

 VAASA　　　🅸 Hovioikeudenpuisikko 11, PO Box 3 – 651 01 – ☎ 06-325 11 45

Tikanojan taidekoti – Open Tuesdays to Saturdays, 11am to 4pm, Sundays, noon to 5pm. 20FIM, children (0-17) free. ☎ 06-325 3916.

Pohjanmaan museo – Open daily 10am to 5pm (Wednesdays until 8pm). 10FIM, children free; Wednesdays admission free. ☎ 06-325 3800.

Bragen ulkomuseo – Open June to August, Tuesdays to Fridays, 1pm to 6pm, Saturdays and Sundays, noon to 4pm. 15FIM, children 5FIM. ☎ 06-317 2271. www.kulturfonden.fi/brage.

Excursion

Stundars – Open mid-May to mid-August, daily noon to 6pm. 20FIM (price includes guided tour). ☎ 06-344 2200.

Island hopping – Car ferries connect Åland with both Finland (Turku / Åbo and Naantali / Nådendal) and Sweden (Stockholm, Norrtälje, Kapellskär and Grisslehamn). For those with more time to spare local Finnish ferries leave from Kustavi and Korpo.

Mariehamn

Sjöfartsmuseet – Open July, daily 9am to 7pm; May, June and August, 10am to 5pm; September to April 10am to 5pm. 30FIM, children (0-10) free. ☎ 018-199 30. www. maritime-museum. aland. fi

Ålands museum / Ålands Konstmuseum – Open daily (except Mondays from September to April) 10am to 4pm (Tuesdays until 8pm). 15FIM, children (8-15) 10FIM. ☎ 018-254 26. www.aland-museum.aland.fi

Sankt Görans kyrka – Open May to August, Mondays to Saturdays, 10am to 3pm; September to April, noon to 2pm. ☎ 018-5360.

Köpmannagården – Open mid-June to mid-August, Mondays to Fridays, 1pm to 3pm; the rest of the year by arrangement. ☎ 019-238 66.

Storby

Postrotemuseet – Open 2 June to 14 August, daily 10am to 4pm; the rest of the year by arrangement. 10FIM.

Labbas Hembygds- och bankmuseum – Open Mondays to Fridays, noon to 4pm. 7FIM, children free. ☎ 02-394 62.

Eckerö kyrka – Open May to August, Mondays to Fridays, 9am to 7pm, Saturdays, 9am to 6pm, Sundays, 11am to 6pm; other times on request. ☎ 018-383 87.

Jomala

Sankt Olofs kyrka – Open June to August, Mondays to Fridays and Sundays, 9am to 4pm. ☎ 018-310 04.

Finström

Sankt Mikaels kyrka – Open 15 May to August, Mondays to Fridays, 10am to 4pm. ☎ 018-423 30.

Geta

Geta kyrka – Open May to August, daily 10am to 4pm. Closed winter; service every Sunday at 10am. 02-495 82.

Sund

Kastelholms slott – Open July to mid-August, daily 10am to 6pm; May to June and mid-August to September, daily 10am to 5pm. 25FIM, children (8-15) 17FIM. ☎ 018-432 190.

Jan Karlsgården – Open 3 May to September, daily 10am to 5pm. Closed October to 2 May. Admission free. Guided tours available. ☎ 018– 432 158.

Vita Björns Prison museum – Open 3 May to September, daily 10am to 5pm. Closed October to May. 6FIM, children 4FIM. ☎ 018-432 158.

Johannes Döparens kyrka – Open June to August, daily 9am to 4pm on request. ☎ 018-439 30.

Index

Stockholm........................ Towns, sights and tourist regions are followed by the abbreviation of the country (DK, N, SE, FIN). Isolated sights are listed under their proper name.

Ibsen, Henrik.................... People, historical events and subject.

In this index the letters Æ, Ø, Å, Ä and Ö are listed at the end of the alphabet after X, Y and Z.

N

O

T

Å (Aa) – Ä – Æ

Ö

Notes

Please write to us !
Your input will help us to improve our guides.

Please send this questionnaire to the following address:
MICHELIN TRAVEL PUBLICATIONS, The Edward Hyde Building
38 Clarendon Road Watford Herts WD1 1SX

1. Is this the first time you have purchased THE GREEN GUIDE? yes ▢   no ▢

2. Which title did you buy?: _____

3. What influenced your decision to purchase this guide?

	Not important at all	Somewhat important	Important	Very important
Cover	▢	▢	▢	▢
Clear, attractive layout	▢	▢	▢	▢
Structure	▢	▢	▢	▢
Cultural information	▢	▢	▢	▢
Practical information	▢	▢	▢	▢
Maps and plans	▢	▢	▢	▢
Michelin quality	▢	▢	▢	▢
Loyalty to THE GREEN GUIDE collection	▢	▢	▢	▢

Your comments : _____

_____

_____

_____

_____

4. How would you rate the following aspects of THE GREEN GUIDE?

	Poor	Average	Good	Excellent
Maps at the beginning of the guide	▢	▢	▢	▢
Maps and plans throughout the guide	▢	▢	▢	▢
Description of the sites (style, detail...)	▢	▢	▢	▢
Depth of cultural information	▢	▢	▢	▢
Amount of practical information	▢	▢	▢	▢
Format	▢	▢	▢	▢

Please comment if you have responded poor or average on any of the above: _____

_____

_____

_____

_____

5. On a scale of 1-20, please rate THE GREEN GUIDE (1 being the lowest, 20 being the highest):

How would you suggest we improve these guides?

1. Maps and Plans:

2. Sights:

3. Establishments:

4. Practical Information:

5. Other:

Demographic information: (optional)

Male Female Age

Name:

Address:

Data collected may be used by Michelin Travel Publications for internal purposes only and not for resale.